A2 Chemistry
for AQA

Peter Harwood

Series Editor: Janice Perkins

William Collins's dream of knowledge for all began with the publication of his first book in 1819. A self-educated mill worker, he not only enriched millions of lives, but also founded a flourishing publishing house. Today, staying true to this spirit, Collins books are packed with inspiration, innovation and practical expertise. They place you at the centre of a world of possibility and give you exactly what you need to explore it.

Collins. Freedom to teach.

Published by Collins
An imprint of HarperCollinsPublishers
77-85 Fulham Palace Road
Hammersmith
London
W6 8JB

Browse the complete Collins catalogue at
www.collinseducation.com

ISBN-13 978-0-00-726824-5

British Library Cataloguing in Publication Data. A Catalogue record for this publication is available from the British Library.

Commissioned by Penny Fowler
Project management by Laura Deacon
Edited by Geoff Amor and Susan Watt
Proof read by Karen Sawyer and Gudrun Kaiser
Indexing by Laurence Errington
Design by Bookcraft Ltd
Cover design by Angela English
Production by Leonie Kellman
Printed and bound in Hong Kong by Printing Express

Contents

Acknowledgments

Text and diagrams reproduced by kind permission of:
www.celsius.com, NASA, Pacific Science Association, World Resources Institute.

Every effort has been made to contact the holders of copyright material, but if any have been inadvertently overlooked the publishers will be pleased to make the necessary arrangements at the first opportunity.

The publishers would like to thank the following for permission to reproduce photographs
(T = Top, B = Bottom, C = Centre, L = Left, R= Right):

Biology @ Davidson 131TR
Biopol 140
Cephas 80L, 80C
Corbis 204TL
Cyber Chemist 263
Department for Transport 83BR
Encylopedia Britannica 99
Flickr Creative Commons: adactio 189BL; airosan 230BL; Anirudh Koul 131BL; archie4oz 230TL; Beppie K 58BR; Bourne Leisure 58BL; Cyberchemist 263; Daquella manera 135TL; DogwalkerBrasil 6CR; eek the cat 135TC; fotologic 279; G Xianfu 36TR; Gaetan Lee 160; ground.zero 138R; hfb 112; jsmjr 177; jurvetson 96; Luckytom 6TL; makelessnoise 24R; Milosz1 190TR; MitzaBot goes BOOM 89; nyki_m 144; Paraflyer 111; Peanut Gallery 58TR; Puamelia 41; rick 210; Roger H Goun 36TL; salimfadhley 108; sophiem2401 91; Storeyland 204TL; thomasrdotorg 138L; tiloe BC; travelinknu 301
hopkinsmedicine.org 36BR
Hutchison Picture Library 103L
Hydrocarbons technology.com 251T
ICCE/Boulton 166L
ICI 82
John Feltwell 81
Koolpak 214T, 214B
NASA 6TR, 22, 248
Oberlin Filtering Inc 158
Phototake NYC/B Masini 134BL
Picasa/Paddy 168
Quadrant Picture Library/Auto Express 166R
Ardea London/Reg Morrison 35
Robert Harding Picture Library 88, 190BR
Royal Society 146R
Science Photo Library 10BL, 12, 17BL, 17BC, 25, 38, 44TL, 44CL, 48, 85C, 85R, 103R, 122, 132TL, 132CL, 132CR, 132BR, 134TL, 148, 149T, 149CL, 149CR, 149B, 150, 152, 190BL, 191, 200, 204B, 222L, 222R, 223TL, 223TC, 223C, 223TR, 223CL, 224L, 224R, 232, 237, 260, 261L, 261R, 265L, 265R, 266, 267, 275, 281, 282, 286T, 286B, 293, 216, 278, 234L, 234R, 251B, 252
Still Pictures/M Edwards 258T
The Craft Council 250C
Geophotos/Tony Waltham 102
Topham Picturepoint 83BL
Wikimedia Commons 6L, 24C, 24L, 31BR, 31R, 63TL, 64, 78, 118, 131TL, 137, 141L, 141R, 146L, 159, 172, 188L, 189TL, 243, 245BL, 245TR, 258R, 280, 300
WorldTransportPictures.com 83TR

Cover photograph © istockphoto.com kvv515kvv

To the student

This book aims to make your study of advanced science successful and interesting. Science is constantly evolving and, wherever possible, modern issues and problems have been used to make your study stimulating and to encourage you to continue studying science after you complete your current course.

Using the book

Don't try to achieve too much in one reading session. Science is complex and some demanding ideas need to be supported with a lot of facts. Trying to take in too much at one time can make you lose sight of the most important ideas – all you see is a mass of information.

Each chapter starts by showing how the science you will learn is applied somewhere in the world. At other points in the chapter you will find the *How Science Works* boxes. These will help you to pose scientific questions and analyse, interpret and evaluate evidence and data. Using these boxes and the *How Science Works* assignments at the end of each chapter will help you to tackle questions in your final examination with a *How Science Works* element. Please note that chapters 6 and 7 are introductory chapters so there are no how science works assignments at the end of the chapter though there are many *How Science Works* tasks through these two chapters.

The numbered questions in the main text allow you to check that you have understood what is being explained. These are all short and straightforward in style – there are no trick questions. Don't be tempted to pass over these questions, they will give you new insights into the work. Answers are given in the back of the book.

Stretch and Challenge really test your knowledge of chemistry allowing you to go beyond the specification and achieve the maximum grade.

This book covers the content needed for AQA Chemistry at A2-level. The Key Facts for each section summarise the information you will need in your examination. However, the examination will test your ability to apply these facts rather than simply to remember them. The *How Science Works* boxes will help you to develop this skill.

Words written in bold type appear in the glossary at the end of the book. If you don't know the meaning of one of these words, check it out immediately – don't persevere, hoping all will become clear.

Past paper questions are included at the end of each chapter. These will help you to test yourself against the sorts of questions that will come up in your examination. You can find the answers to these questions on the website **www.collinseducation.com/advancedscienceaqa**.

The website also provides sample student answers to these questions – a stronger and a weaker answer for each question – to help you to improve your own answers. On this website you will also find mathematical and examination technique guidance to help you to prepare for your examinations, and PSA (Practical Skills Assessment) and ISA (Investigative Skills Assignment) guidance to help you achieve your best in your practical work.

1 Kinetics

Mario Molina at the Senate of Mexico.

The ozone hole over Antarctica, in September 2006. Being relatively unreactive at ground level, CFCs find their way to the stratosphere and cause ozone depletion there.

Sunblock keeps out all the Sun's rays.

By 2010 the **ozone hole** in the stratosphere over the southern hemisphere will have extended as far as the southern parts of Africa, South America and Australia. Ozone, normally present in the upper atmosphere, absorbs harmful high-energy **ultraviolet-B** (UV-B) rays from the Sun. Without ozone, this radiation reaches the Earth's surface and can be the cause of skin cancers and eye cataracts. This is why schoolchildren in Australia must now wear hats outdoors, and research in Chile has shown a recent 50% increase in skin cancers, a phenomenon not reported prior to the 1970s.

On 28 June 1974, chemists Sherry Rowland and Mario Molina, at the University of California, published the first scientific paper warning that human-generated **chlorofluorocarbons** (CFCs) could cause serious harm to Earth's protective ozone layer. They calculated that, if CFC production continued to increase, CFCs would cause a global 30%–50% loss of ozone by 2050.

The first evidence of ozone depletion was detected by ground-based instruments operated by the British Antarctic Survey at Halley Bay on the Antarctic coast in 1982, but Joe Farman and his team delayed publication till 1985 in order to be

sure of their data. Subsequent analysis of the data revealed that the hole began to appear in 1977. In 1995, Molina and Rowland were awarded the Nobel Prize in Chemistry for their discovery of the link between CFCs and ozone depletion.

Because CFCs are so unreactive at ground level, and therefore safe to health, and because they are easily liquefied under pressure and at moderately low temperatures, they were judged ideal for use as refrigerants and as propellants in aerosols. But the energy in UV light in the stratosphere breaks them down, producing chlorine **free radicals**. These particles react with ozone, O_3, which is broken down to oxygen, O_2, a gas that does not shield the Earth from UV-B. It is the slow rate at which CFCs themselves react that is the problem. If they were reactive, they would break down before reaching the upper atmosphere.

Ozone forms when the intense radiation in the upper atmosphere causes oxygen molecules to split into atoms:

$$O_2 \xrightarrow{h\nu} O + O$$
$$O + O_2 \rightarrow O_3$$

The intense radiation can also catalyse the break-up of CFCs into Cl·, and each Cl· that is formed can result in the destruction of 100 000 ozone molecules. Ozone depletion reactions in the upper atmosphere are very complex, and this is one possible sequence:

$$CCl_2F_2 \xrightarrow{h\nu} CCl\cdot F_2 + Cl\cdot$$
$$Cl\cdot + O_3 \rightarrow OCl\cdot + O_2$$
$$OCl\cdot + O \rightarrow Cl\cdot O_2$$

and so on.

Other reactions are possible, and the sequence of reactions will vary depending on the ozone concentration, the free radicals present and the intensity of the sunlight.

Satellites such as the Nimbus-7 spacecraft monitor ozone levels measured in **Dobson units**. To calculate a Dobson unit, imagine all the ozone in a column of air covering a 10×5 degree area of the Earth's surface compressed to standard temperature and pressure (stp). One Dobson unit (1 DU) is defined to be 0.01 mm thickness of ozone at stp. Usually, ozone concentration is about 300–400 DU.

In 1987, the Montreal Protocol was signed and many countries agreed to reduce the use of CFCs. These reductions are starting to take effect: levels of CFCs in the lower atmosphere are beginning to decline, and so fewer of the CFCs will make their way to the upper atmosphere. Some scientists expect the ozone hole to start shrinking within 10 years, and that it might even vanish by 2050.

1.1 Reaction kinetics

Reaction kinetics is the study of the rate of chemical reactions, and in this chapter we look at the kinetics of reactions whose rates are measurable.

The rate of a chemical reaction is the change in molar concentration of a substance in unit time.

In the laboratory, we calculate the **rate** of a reaction by measuring the change in concentration over time, for example, either as a decrease in concentration of reactant per unit time, or as an increase in concentration of product per unit time. The rate is often measured as change in moles per cubic decimetre per second, mol dm^{-3} s^{-1}, but slower reactions may be measured in moles per cubic decimetre per minute or per hour.

Chemists who design industrial processes need to know the rate of reactions to answer questions such as: Will the reaction give a good yield of product per hour at normal temperatures? What conditions will give optimum reaction rate? Questions like these are answered by studying reaction kinetics. The answers can be found only by experiment, and cannot be predicted merely by looking at an equation for the reaction, as we shall see later.

Following Chapter 8 in *AS Chemistry*, this section examines further aspects of reaction kinetics. We will be looking at how reaction rates change, why they change, and what this tells us about how the species are reacting.

Collision theory

In any gas, liquid or solution, the particles are constantly moving and colliding with each other. At each collision, energy is transferred between the particles, so the particles are continually changing their energies. The distribution of energies between particles in a system is called the **Maxwell–Boltzmann distribution** of energies. The curve in Fig. 1 shows the numbers of particles at each energy value at temperature T_1. The area under the curve represents the total number of particles, so the number, and therefore the area below the curve, does not change when the temperature changes.

Fig. 1 A Maxwell–Boltzmann curve for the distribution of energies for a sample of particles

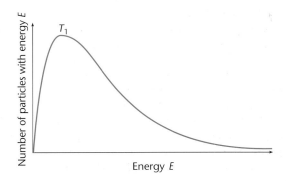

Increasing the temperature adds energy to the system and changes the distribution of energies of the particles. At a higher temperature (T_2 in Fig. 2), more particles have higher energies.

Fig. 2   Maxwell–Boltzmann distribution curves for a sample of particles at two temperatures

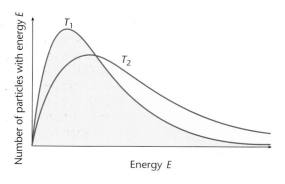

Collision theory tells us that chemical reactions occur when particles have enough energy from these collisions to break existing chemical bonds and form new ones. The amount of energy needed is called the **activation energy**, E_A (see Fig. 3).

Fig. 3   A Maxwell–Boltzmann distribution curve showing E_A

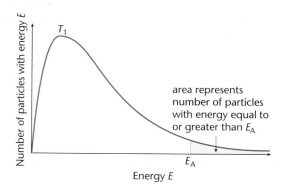

area represents number of particles with energy equal to or greater than E_A

Any factor that affects the *number* of collisions or the *energy* of the collisions will affect the rate of reaction, because it changes the number of collisions possessing the activation energy. Such factors are described in detail in *AS Chemistry*, pages 145–149, and are summarised below.

1 Look at the Maxwell–Boltzmann distribution curves.

a What does the peak of each curve tell you?

b The curves start at the origin. What does this tell us about the energies of the particles?

c Would the curves ever touch the energy axis? Explain your reasoning.

The effect of temperature

Increasing the temperature increases the average kinetic energy of the particles; they move faster and hence there are more collisions. But far more significant in predicting the number of reacting particles is *the number of collisions between particles that possess energies equal to or greater than the activation energy*. As a rough guide, a 10 K rise in temperature will double the number of collisions having energies equal to or greater than the activation energy, so twice as many particles can react at any one time.

You may be wondering: since higher temperatures cause particles to move faster, giving more collisions, doesn't the increased overall number of collisions have a large effect on the reaction rate as well as particle energies? The answer is that, over a 10 K rise, there are only about 3%–4% more collisions, so this effect is quite small.

Consider a set of particles at 300 K. If we heat the particles to 310 K, then twice as many particles will have energies equal to or greater than the activation energy, so twice as many particles can react at any instant. Hence the rate at the higher temperature will be approximately twice that at the lower temperature:

An increase in temperature of 10 K approximately doubles the reaction rate.

Most reactions follow this simple rule, so the Maxwell–Boltzmann curve is a similar shape for their particles. Fig. 4 shows that increasing the temperature by 10 K doubles the number of particles possessing the activation energy.

The higher temperature gives a greater spread of energies of particles, taking the maximum to a higher energy value, so the peak

Fig. 4   The effect on energy distribution of raising the temperature by 10 K

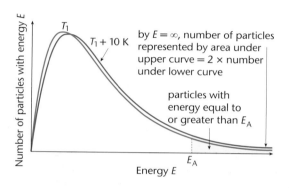

of the curve moves lower and to the right. Remember: the area under the curve stays the same, while the area of the curve beyond the activation energy value is greater – it is twice the area for 300 K.

The effect of surface area
When we increase the surface area of a solid, such as by grinding it to a powder, it reacts faster than if it were still in one solid lump. This is because collisions occur only at the surface of a solid, and if a greater surface area is exposed, there are more locations for collisions to occur, and therefore the reaction happens faster. For example, a 1-cm cube has an area of 6 cm², but if this is ground to a powder of 10^{-7} cm particles, then the surface area is about the same as 30 tennis courts.

The effect of concentration
As the concentration of a reactant increases, there are more particles in a given volume, so there will be a greater number of particles with energies equal to or greater than the activation energy. This produces a greater number of collisions that result in a reaction. The same applies to a gas when pressure is increased.

In the next section, we look at the effect of concentration in more detail.

2

a   If you want to make a jelly by dissolving jelly cubes in water, how much quicker will it dissolve if you slice each of the 2-cm cubes into eight 1-cm cubes?

b   If we increase the temperature, what effect does this have on the rate of dissolving? Explain your answer in terms of collisions that result in a reaction.

---

key facts

- The number of collisions with energies equal to or greater than the activation energy determines the rate of reaction.

- Increasing the temperature of a reaction by 10 K approximately doubles the rate of reaction.

- Increasing the surface area of a solid increases the rate of reaction.

- Increasing the concentration of a solution increases the rate of reaction.

UV danger and protection

Ultraviolet (UV) radiation is split into three different categories, UV-A, UV-B and UV-C. UV-A is the weakest form of UV radiation, while UV-C is the strongest. Fortunately, all UV-C radiation is blocked by the ozone layer. However, some UV-B and most UV-A can pass through the ozone layer and reach the Earth's surface. UV-B radiation reaching the surface can cause sunburn, which may one day lead to skin cancer. If we damage the ozone layer, we will let in more UV radiation, which will be harmful not just to people, but to other forms of wildlife as well.

Sunglasses and hats can protect against UV radiation.

How to protect yourself

- Sunglasses that protect eyes from dangerous UV rays will help to reduce the risk of cataracts and other eye damage. Check the label when buying sunglasses.
- Hats with wide brims will protect eyes and the skin on the head and neck from the Sun's rays, which can lead to skin cancers.
- Clothes provide protection against the risk of skin cancers.
- Sunscreen with a high sun protection factor (SPF) of at least 15 blocks out most harmful rays.
- Limit the time spent in the Sun and try to avoid it between 10 a.m. and 4 p.m. when the rays are strongest.

Choose two of the protection methods above and explain scientifically how the methods work. As well as the ideas contained in this chapter, you can use other ideas, perhaps found by doing an Internet search.

1.2 Deriving the rate equation

The students are measuring a rate of reaction using a colorimeter. They are monitoring the reaction of a haloalkane. As it reacts it releases bromide ions which form a silver bromide precipitate with silver nitrate solution. The students measure the rate at which the solution goes cloudy. This allows them to calculate the concentrations of products and hence the concentrations of the reactants.

Chemists define the **rate** of a reaction as the rate at which a reactant is used up, or the rate at which a product is formed. We state the amount of reactant or product in terms of its concentration, and this is measured as mol dm^{-3}. By measuring concentrations at time intervals, *at a fixed temperature*, we can measure the rate of change of concentration.

In Figs 5 and 6, the line is a curve because the reactant is being used up and its concentration is decreasing more slowly with each successive time interval. This is because, as the reaction proceeds, fewer reactant particles per unit volume are available for collisions, so the time taken for a given number of particles to react increases. The rate of reaction is decreasing and eventually it stops.

At a fixed temperature, increasing the concentration of the reactants usually increases

Fig. 5 Rate at which a reactant is used up in a reaction

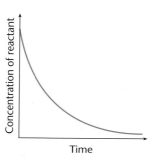

Fig. 6 Rate at which a product is formed in a reaction

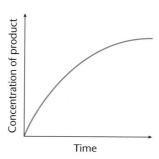

the rate of reaction. In some, but by no means all reactions, doubling the concentration of a reactant (call it A) doubles the number of particles of A with energies equal to or greater than the activation energy, and the reaction rate doubles. When you halve the concentration, the number of particles of A with the activation energy will halve, and the rate will be halved. In other words, the rate of reaction is proportional to the concentration of A, given by the expression:

rate $\propto$ concentration of A

By including a **rate constant**, **k**, we can replace the proportional sign by an equals sign, to give the **rate equation**:

rate $= k \times$ concentration of A

Using the symbol [A] for concentration of A gives:

rate $= k[A]$

In this example, the rate of reaction is determined by the concentration of A, which is $[A]^1$. In other reactions, the concentrations of two reactants may affect the rate in a similar way:

rate $= k[A]^1[B]^1$

The powers in the equation are usually small numbers, or zero, and are called the **orders of reaction**.

So, in this example the rate is first order with respect to A and first order with respect to B, and overall the reaction is second order: the powers are added to give the overall order.

A general rate equation for two reactants is given as:

rate $= k[A]^m[B]^n$

Orders of reaction are found from experimental data and cannot be assumed from the **stoichiometric equation**.

A task sheet and practice questions on the Practical Skills Assessment 'Carry out a kinetic study to determine the order of a reaction' can be found at www.collinseducation.co.uk/advancedscienceaqa

3

a At what stage in a reaction is the reactant used up fastest?

b At what stage is the formation of the product fastest?

Zero-order reactions

There are reactions whose rate does not change when the concentration of a reactant changes. If this applies to reactant A whose rate equation is:

rate $= k[A]^x$

then the expression for $[A]^x$ must always equal 1. This is achieved by using the power zero, hence the reaction is a **zero-order reaction**:

rate $= k[A]^0$ which gives   rate $= k$

An example of a reaction that is zero order is the decomposition of ammonia to nitrogen on a hot tungsten wire:

$$2NH_3 \rightarrow N_2 + 3H_2$$

For a zero-order reaction, the reaction rate is always constant and always equal to the rate constant k, over the concentration range of A being considered. Fig. 7 shows graphs of rate against time and concentration against time for such a zero-order reaction.

Fig. 7   Graphs for a zero-order reaction: (a) rate plotted against time, and (b) concentration plotted against time

(a)

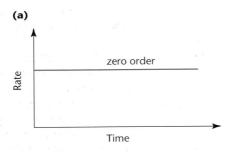

(b)

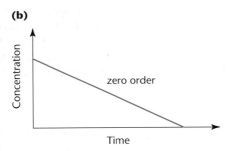

First-order reactions

We have seen that the rate of a reaction may be directly proportional to the concentration of one species, and that, taking this species to be A, the rate equation for reactant A is given as:

rate $= k[A]^1$ or   rate $= k[A]$

Any such reaction is called a **first-order reaction** with respect to A, and the figure for [A] inserted into the rate equation is the value for the concentration of A. If the concentration doubles, the rate of the reaction will also double.

A reaction that behaves in this way is the hydrolysis of the ester methyl ethanoate:

$$CH_3COOCH_3 + H_2O \rightarrow CH_3COOH + CH_3OH$$

The order for the reaction of the ester is calculated by finding its concentration at different stages in the reaction. An easy way is to determine how much has been converted to the acid, and then to calculate the concentration of ester left in the mixture. You do this by titrating a *small*, measured volume of the reaction mixture with alkali. This tells you how much acid has been produced, and so you can calculate the concentration of ester remaining in the reaction mixture. The results from a typical reaction are shown in Table 1.

Table 1   Results for the hydrolysis reaction of methyl ethanoate

Time (min.)	Ester concn. (mol dm⁻³)
0	0.200
5	0.134 = A
10	0.095
15	0.068 = B
20	0.046
25	0.034 = C

The students are titrating the reaction mixture. The small sample they use is mixed with some ice to stop the reaction while they do the titration.

Fig. 8   Concentration of ester remaining in the mixture, plotted against time for the first-order reaction of the hydrolysis of methyl ethanoate

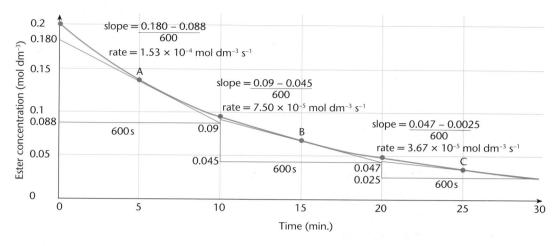

These results are plotted on the graph of Fig. 8, which shows the typical declining curve for a first-order reaction. You can find the rate of reaction at a particular time by drawing a tangent to the curve. The rate is the slope of the curve at the tangent:

$$\text{rate} = \frac{\text{change in concentration}}{\text{time taken}} = \text{slope of curve}$$

The rates of ester hydrolysis in mol dm^{-3} s^{-1} at points A, B and C respectively are 0.000 153, 0.000 075 0 and 0.000 036 7.

Plotting the rates against the concentrations shown in Table 1 gives a straight line (Fig. 9). The graph shows that for this reaction:

rate of hydrolysis ∝ concentration
of ester   of ester

and: rate = $k[CH_3COOCH_3]$

The rate of the reaction is proportional to the concentration of the reagent to the power one, namely rate = $k[CH_3COOCH_3]^1$, so the reaction is first order.

In some reactions it may not be easy to find the reactant concentration, or there may be a more convenient way of following the rate of reaction. For example, the decomposition of hydrogen peroxide in aqueous solution can be easily followed by measuring the volume of oxygen gas evolved (Fig. 10). A catalyst such as powdered metal or manganese(IV) oxide is required to speed up the reaction and is introduced into the flask in a small test-tube. The reaction starts when the catalyst is submerged in the hydrogen peroxide solution. The oxygen evolved is monitored using the gas syringe.

Fig. 9   Rate plotted against concentration of reactant

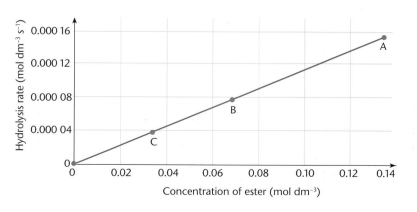

Fig. 10   Monitoring the decomposition of hydrogen peroxide

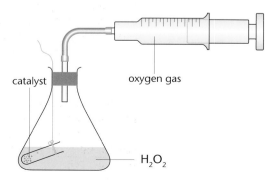

Fig. 11   Graphs of oxygen evolved at concentrations A, B and C

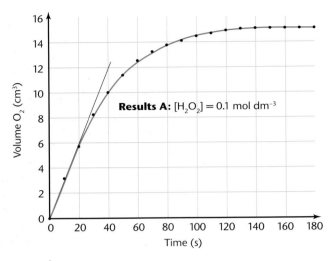

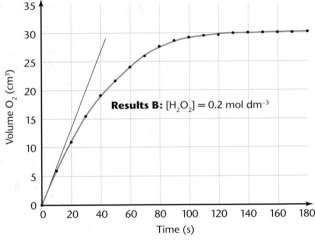

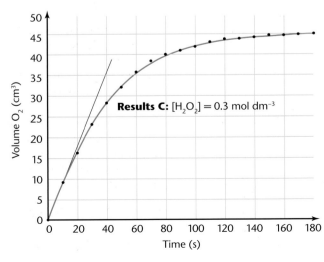

You cannot take samples in this type of reaction, but you know the concentration at the start of the reaction. Plotting a graph of the volume of oxygen evolved against time will allow a tangent to be drawn at time $t = 0$, giving the *initial* rate of reaction when we did know the concentration of the hydrogen peroxide.

Table 2 shows a set of results for the decomposition of hydrogen peroxide using different initial concentrations. The total volume of O_2 produced is given at 10-second intervals. The graphs of the results and the initial rate tangents are shown in Figs 11A–C. By drawing a tangent to each curve at 0 seconds, the initial rates can be calculated as volume of oxygen gas given off per second. The rates are given in Table 3.

Using these results and plotting initial rate against initial concentration gives Fig. 12.

Table 2   Volumes of oxygen produced in the decomposition of hydrogen peroxide

Initial concentration of H_2O_2:
A: 0.1 mol dm^{-3}
B: 0.2 mol dm^{-3}
C: 0.3 mol dm^{-3}

Time (s)	Volume of O_2 (cm^3)		
	A	**B**	**C**
0	0.0	0.0	0.0
10	3.0	6.0	9.0
20	6.0	11.0	17.0
30	8.0	16.0	23.0
40	10.0	19.0	28.0
50	11.0	22.0	32.0
60	12.0	24.0	36.0
70	13.0	26.0	38.0
80	14.0	27.0	40.0
90	14.0	28.0	41.5
100	14.0	29.0	42.0
110	15.0	29.0	43.0
120	15.0	30.0	43.5
130	15.0	30.0	43.5
140	15.0	30.0	44.0

Table 3   Calculated rates

	Initial concn. H_2O_2 (mol dm^{-3})	Rate O_2 prodn. (cm^3 s^{-1})
A	0.1	0.3
B	0.2	0.6
C	0.3	0.9

Fig. 12   Graph of initial rate of O_2 produced plotted against initial concentration of H_2O_2(aq)

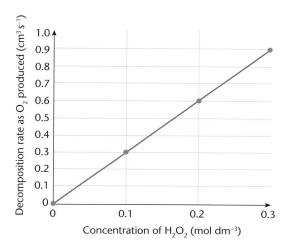

You can see from the graph that:

rate ∝ concentration

so: rate of decomposition of hydrogen peroxide = $k[H_2O_2]^1$

Hence, the reaction for oxygen produced from hydrogen peroxide solution is also first order.

Table 4   Results for six experiments

Expt	$[H_2PO_2^-]$	$[OH^-]$	Initial rate (mol dm^{-3} s^{-1})
1	0.1	6.0	14.4
2	0.2	6.0	28.8
3	0.3	6.0	43.2
4	0.6	1.0	2.4
5	0.6	2.0	9.6
6	0.6	3.0	21.5

The reaction between the phosphinate ion and the hydroxide ion produces hydrogen gas:

$$H_2PO_2^- + OH^- \rightarrow HPO_3^- + H_2$$

You can find the overall order of this reaction by looking at the effect of changing the initial concentration of each reactant in turn. Table 4 gives data for a series of experiments in which phosphinate reacts with hydroxide ions.

If the hydroxide ion concentration is kept constant and the phosphinate ion concentration is doubled from 0.1 to 0.2 mol dm^{-3}, the initial reaction rate also doubles (from 14.4 in Expt 1 to 28.8 in Expt 2). Trebling the phosphinate concentration causes a threefold increase in rate (Expts 1 and 3). In other words, the rate is proportional to the concentration of phosphinate, and we say that the reaction is first order with respect to phosphinate.

Second- and third-order reactions

If in the above reaction we then keep the concentration of phosphinate constant and double the concentration of hydroxide (from 1.0 to 2.0 mol dm^{-3}), the rate increases by a factor of 4 (from 2.4 in Expt 4 to 9.6 in Expt 5). Trebling the hydroxide concentration causes the rate to increase by a factor of 9 (Expts 4 and 6).

Consider Expts 4 and 5 where $[H_2PO_2^-]$ remains constant and $[OH^-]$ doubles. We can write the following equation and cancel:

$$\frac{\text{rate } 5}{\text{rate } 4} = \frac{9.6}{2.4} = \frac{k[2.0]^m \cancel{[0.6]^+}}{k[1.0]^m \cancel{[0.6]^+}} = 4$$

to give: $\dfrac{2.0^m}{1.0^m} = 4$

One to any power is 1, so $2.0^m = 4$ or 2^2. Hence, the small, whole-number value of m that satisfies this expression is 2, and the rate of the reaction is proportional to $[OH^-]^2$. We describe this as a **second-order reaction** with respect to hydroxide ions.

We have therefore found that the reaction is first order with respect to phosphinate, and second order with respect to hydroxide, so that the overall rate equation for the reaction is given by the equation:

rate = $k[H_2PO_2^-]^1[OH^-]^2$

or

rate = $k[H_2PO_2^-][OH^-]^2$

We now refer again to the general rate equation (page 11):

$$\text{rate} = k[A]^m[B]^n$$

and define the order for the whole reaction:

The overall order of a reaction is the sum of the powers of the concentration in terms of the rate equation.

In the rate equation for the phosphinate plus hydroxide reaction, $m = 1$ and $n = 2$, the sum of the powers is $1 + 2 = 3$, so the overall order of reaction is three. This makes the reaction between phosphinate and hydroxide ions a **third-order reaction**.

If a particular reagent is present in large excess, its concentration will change negligibly as the reaction proceeds and will not appear to affect the rate. The hydrolysis of an ester (page 12) is an example of this: the whole reaction is carried out in water, so the amount of water used up is negligible.

Summarising orders of reaction

The graphs of Fig. 13(a) show how the concentration of reactant A changes with time for reactions of orders 0, 1 and 2, and the graphs of Fig. 13(b) show how the reaction rate varies with concentration for reactions of orders 0, 1 and 2.

Units for rate constant k for different orders of reaction

We have seen that rate = (change in concentration)/(time taken), and that rate is measured as $\text{mol dm}^{-3}\ \text{s}^{-1}$. We have also seen that for a first-order reaction:

$$\text{rate} = k \times \text{concentration}$$

For a *zero-order reaction*, where rate $= k[A]^0$, and $[A]^0 = 1$, rate constant: $k = \text{rate}/1$. So the units for a zero-order reaction are those for rate, namely $\text{mol dm}^{-3}\ \text{s}^{-1}$.

For a *first-order reaction*, in which rate $= k[A]$, we can write:

$$k = \frac{\text{rate}}{[A]} \quad \text{or} \quad k = \frac{\text{rate}}{\text{concentration}}$$

We can insert the units of rate and concentration and cancel:

$$\frac{\cancel{\text{mol dm}^{-3}}\ \text{s}^{-1}}{\cancel{\text{mol dm}^{-3}}} = \text{s}^{-1}$$

Therefore, for a first-order reaction, the units for k are s^{-1}.

For a *second-order reaction*, we can write:

$$\text{rate} = k[A]^2 \quad \text{giving} \quad k = \frac{\text{rate}}{[A]^2}$$

Alternatively, the rate can be $k[A][B]$, giving:

$$k = \frac{\text{rate}}{[A][B]}$$

In both cases, we can say that:

$$k = \frac{\text{rate}}{[\text{concentration}]^2}$$

Inserting units and cancelling:

$$\frac{\cancel{\text{mol dm}^{-3}}\ \text{s}^{-1}}{(\cancel{\text{mol dm}^{-3}})(\text{mol dm}^{-3})} = \frac{\text{s}^{-1}}{(\text{mol dm}^{-3})}$$

$$= \text{mol}^{-1}\ \text{dm}^3\ \text{s}^{-1}$$

Therefore, for a second-order reaction, the units for k are $\text{mol}^{-1}\ \text{dm}^3\ \text{s}^{-1}$.

Similar rules apply for higher-order reactions: the rate constant k does not always have the same units since these depend on the order of reaction (see Table 5).

Fig. 13 (a) Concentration of reactant plotted against time. (b) Rate of reaction plotted against reactant concentration

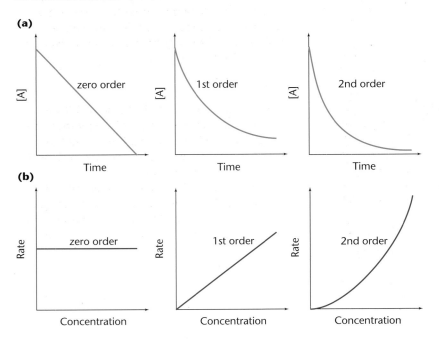

(a)

zero order · 1st order · 2nd order

(b)

zero order · 1st order · 2nd order

Table 5   Summary of units for rate constants

Order of reaction = $n + m$	Rate equation rate = $k \times$ [reactants]$^{n+m}$	Units of the rate constant
0	rate = $k \times$ concn.^{0}	mol dm^{-3} s^{-1}
1	rate = $k \times$ concn.^{1}	s^{-1}
2	rate = $k \times$ concn.^{2}	mol^{-1} dm^3 s^{-1}
3	rate = $k \times$ concn.^{3}	mol^{-2} dm^6 s^{-1}
4	rate = $k \times$ concn.^{4}	mol^{-3} dm^9 s^{-1}

Effect of temperature on the rate constant

When carrying out kinetics investigations and reporting your data to others, you must make a note of the conditions. If you are monitoring the volume of a gas produced, then the atmospheric pressure can affect the volume, so this should be quoted. You should also quote the temperature at which you carried out your experiments, because temperature will affect the rate of reaction and hence the value for the rate constant.

4 For the reaction $2NO + Cl_2 \rightarrow 2NOCl$, the rate equation is: rate = $k[NO]^2[Cl_2]$.

a Give the order of this reaction with respect to the reagent NO.

b Give the order of this reaction with respect to the reagent Cl_2.

c Give the overall order of reaction.

d Work out the units for k in the rate equation.

When acid is added to a solution containing thiosulfate ions, free sulfur is gradually formed, and this turns the solution a cloudy yellow. For the same volumes and concentrations of reactants, the time at different temperatures can be measured for a cross to be obscured.

We have seen that the rate depends upon temperature, since increasing the temperature increases the number of molecules having energies equal to or greater than the activation energy. The rate equation:

$$\text{rate} = k[A]^x$$

shows what happens to the value of k if we increase the rate of reaction. If the temperature is increased without altering the concentration of A, k must increase because the rate increases when the temperature increases.

Remember, a 10 K rise in temperature will approximately double the rate of some simple reactions, so the equation shows it must double the rate constant.

stretch and challenge

Effect of temperature on rate of reaction

If you find the rate constant at different temperatures, you can calculate the activation energy for a reaction, using the Arrhenius equation:

$$k = Ae^{-E_A/RT}$$

where:

k = rate constant
A = Arrhenius/frequency factor
e = exponential term
E_A = activation energy
R = gas constant
T = absolute temperature

It is useful if you convert it to the logarithmic form:

$$\ln k = \ln A - \frac{E_A}{RT}$$

A plot of $\log_{10} k$ versus $1/T$ gives a slope $-2.303\,E_A/R$, then you can calculate E_A.

5 An investigation that you might have done in the laboratory is on the reaction between thiosulfate ions and hydrochloric acid. The reaction gives sulfur as a product: the solution goes cloudy and you can measure the time taken to obscure a cross at the bottom of the flask, as shown on the previous page. Some results for this reaction are:

Temperature (°C)	20	30	40	50	60
Time to obscure cross(es)	140	71	34	17	8

a Which graph in Fig. 14 represents the results of time plotted against temperature?

b Which graph in Fig. 14 represents the results of rate plotted against temperature?

c State the relationship between the temperature in this reaction and the rate constant.

Fig. 14

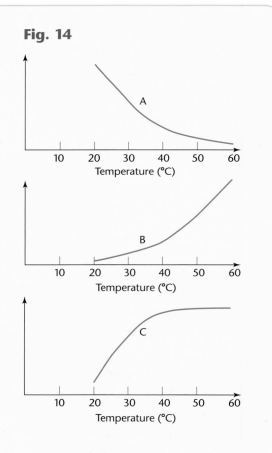

Rate-determining step

This idea is important because, if a reaction involves several steps and they all occur at different speeds, some steps will be faster and one step in particular will be the slowest. The reaction cannot go any faster than the slowest stage. We call the slowest step the **rate-determining step**.

Ozone depletion reactions in the atmosphere are very complex. They are catalysed by **free radicals** and CFCs can be a source of these. Each Cl· that is formed can result in the destruction of 100 000 ozone molecules. This is one possible sequence (as stated earlier in this chapter):

$$CCl_2F_2 \overset{h\nu}{\rightarrow} CCl\cdot F_2 + Cl\cdot$$
$$Cl\cdot + O_3 \rightarrow OCl\cdot + O_2$$
$$OCl\cdot + O \rightarrow Cl\cdot O_2$$

and so on.

The sequence of reactions, and the rate-determining step, will vary depending on the ozone concentration, the free radicals present and the intensity of the sunlight.

The involvement of halogens in the depletion of the ozone layer can be quite complex, but scientists attempt to model these reactions in the laboratory. The hydrolysis of **haloalkanes** can be followed more easily and illustrates how chemists can find out the rate-determining step:

$$RBr + OH^- \rightarrow ROH + Br^-$$

In a reaction for a haloalkane, we have said that there might be two possible ways in which the molecule could react. We can find out more information by using the order of reaction.

If the rate-determining step only involves the RBr, then changing the concentration of this will affect the rate-determining step and therefore the overall rate of reaction:

$$RBr \rightarrow R^+ + Br^- \rightarrow ROH$$

Also, if altering the concentration of OH^- does not affect the rate-determining step, it is not involved at this stage. If it does not affect the rate-determining step, it will not affect the overall rate (provided there are enough OH^- ions to form the final product). A rate equation for this proposal would be:

$$rate = k[RBr]$$

This is a **first-order reaction**. If this rate equation applies, then doubling [RBr] will double the rate of reaction but doubling $[OH^-]$ will have no effect on the rate. If we carry out rate experiments we can find out whether this applies.

If the reaction sequence is:

$$RBr + OH^- \rightarrow HO\text{---}R\text{---}Br \rightarrow ROH$$

(note that ---R--- refers to partial bonds), the rate-determining step involves both RBr and OH^-. Changing the concentrations of both reagents has an effect on the rate of reaction:

$$rate = k[RBr][OH^-]$$

This is a **second-order reaction**. So by determining the order of reaction with respect to both [RBr] and $[OH^-]$, we can gain some insight into the rate-determining step for the reaction.

If the rate of reaction depends only on [RBr], then only this is involved in the rate-determining step, so $RBr \rightarrow R^+$ is the likely mechanism. If the rate of reaction depends on both [RBr] and $[OH^-]$, the reaction is second order, so $RBr + OH^- \rightarrow HO\text{---}R\text{---}Br$ is the likely mechanism.

key facts

- Different stages can have different rates.

- Steps with a lower activation energy can occur more quickly.

- A catalyst speeds up a reaction by having a step with a lower activation energy.

- Any reaction can only proceed at the speed of the slowest stage, called the rate-determining step.

1

a The initial rate of the reaction between compounds **X** and **Y** was measured in a series of experiments at a fixed temperature. The following rate equation was deduced:

$$\text{rate} = k[\mathbf{X}]^2[\mathbf{Y}]^0$$

i Complete the table of data below for the reaction between **X** and **Y**.

Experiment	Initial [X] (mol dm⁻³)	Initial [Y] (mol dm⁻³)	Initial rate (mol dm⁻³)
1	1.20×10^{-3}	3.30×10^{-3}	2.68×10^{-4}
2	1.20×10^{-3}	6.60×10^{-3}	
3	2.40×10^{-3}	6.60×10^{-3}	
4		9.90×10^{-3}	8.04×10^{-4}

ii Using the data for Experiment 1, calculate a value for the rate constant, k, and deduce its units.   (6)

b Sketch a graph to show how the value of the rate constant, k, varies with temperature.   (1)

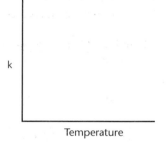

Total 7

AQA, January 2008, Unit 4, Question 6

2

a The rate equation for the reaction between compounds **C** and **D** is:

$$\text{rate} = k[\mathbf{C}][\mathbf{D}]^2$$

i In an experiment where the initial concentration of **C** is 0.15 mol dm⁻³ and the initial concentration of **D** is 0.24 mol dm⁻³, the initial rate of reaction is 0.65 mol dm⁻³ s⁻¹ at a given temperature. Calculate a value for the rate constant, k, at this temperature and deduce its units.

ii The reaction between **C** and **D** is repeated in a second experiment at the same temperature, but the concentrations of both **C** and **D** are half of those in part **a i**. Calculate the initial rate of reaction in this second experiment.   (4)

b The following data were obtained in a series of experiments on the rate of the reaction between compounds **E** and **F** at a constant temperature.

Experiment	Initial concentration of E (mol dm⁻³)	Initial concentration of F (mol dm⁻³)	Initial rate (mol dm⁻³)
1	0.24	0.64	0.80×10^{-2}
2	0.36	0.64	1.80×10^{-2}
3	0.48	0.32	3.20×10^{-2}

i Deduce the order of reaction with respect to **E**.
ii Deduce the order of reaction with respect to **F**.   (2)

Total 6

AQA, June 2007, Unit 4, Question 4

3

a The following data were obtained by studying the reaction between compounds **A**, **B** and **C** at a constant temperature.

Experiment	Initial concentration of A (mol dm⁻³)	Initial concentration of B (mol dm⁻³)	Initial concentration of C (mol dm⁻³)	Initial rate (mol dm⁻³ s⁻¹)
1	0.20	0.10	0.40	0.80×10^{-3}
2	0.20	0.40	0.40	3.20×10^{-3}
3	0.10	0.80	0.40	1.60×10^{-3}
4	0.10	0.30	0.20	0.60×10^{-3}

i Deduce the order of reaction with respect to **A**.
ii Deduce the order of reaction with respect to **B**.
iii Deduce the order of reaction with respect to **C**.   (3)

b The rate equation for the reaction between compounds **D** and **E** at a given temperature is:

$$\text{rate} = k[\mathbf{D}]^2[\mathbf{E}]$$

The initial rate of reaction is 8.36×10^{-4} mol dm⁻³ s⁻¹ when the initial concentration of **D** is 0.84 mol dm⁻³ and the initial concentration of **E** is 1.16 mol dm⁻³. Calculate a value for the rate constant, k, at this temperature and deduce its units.   (3)

Total 6

AQA, January 2007, Unit 4, Question 1

4

The hydrolysis of methyl propanoate was studied in acidic conditions at 25 °C and the rate equation was found to be:

$$\text{rate} = k[CH_3CH_2COOCH_3][H^+]$$

a Use the data below to calculate the value of the rate constant, k, at this temperature. Deduce its units.   (3)

b The reaction in part **a** was repeated at the same temperature, but water was added so that the volume of the reaction mixture was doubled. Calculate the initial rate of reaction under these conditions.   (1)

Initial rate of reaction (mol dm⁻³ s⁻¹)	Initial concentration of methyl propanoate (mol dm⁻³)	Initial concentration of hydrochloric acid (mol dm⁻³)
1.15×10^{-4}	0.150	0.555

c   A third experiment was carried out at a different temperature, with data as shown in the table below.

Initial rate of reaction (mol dm⁻³ s⁻¹)	Value of rate constant at this different temperature	Initial concentration of methylpropanoate (mol dm⁻³)
4.56×10^{-5}	8.94×10^{-4}	0.123

Calculate the initial pH of the reaction mixture. Give your answer to two decimal places.   (3)

Total 7

AQA, June 2006, Unit 4, Question 5

5 The initial rate of the reaction between the gases NO and H_2 was measured in a series of experiments at a constant temperature and the following rate equation was determined:

$$\text{rate} = k[NO]^2[H_2]$$

a   Complete the table of data below for the reaction between NO and H_2 (3)

Experiment	Initial [NO] (mol dm⁻³)	Initial [H₂] (mol dm⁻³)	Initial rate (mol dm⁻³s⁻¹)
1	3.0×10^{-3}	1.0×10^{-3}	1.8×10^{-5}
2	3.0×10^{-3}		7.2×10^{-5}
3	1.5×10^{-3}	1.0×10^{-3}	
4		0.50×10^{-3}	8.1×10^{-5}

b   Using the data from Experiment 1, calculate a value for the rate constant, k, and state its units.   (3)

Total 6

AQA, January 2006, Unit 4, Question 1

6

a   Compound **A**, $HCOOCH_2CH_2CH_3$, is an ester. Name this ester and write an equation for its reaction with aqueous sodium hydroxide.   (2)

b   The initial rate of reaction between ester **A** and aqueous sodium hydroxide was measured in a series of experiments at a constant temperature, with data as shown below. Use the data in the table to deduce the order of reaction with respect to **A** and the order of reaction with respect to NaOH. Hence calculate the initial rate of reaction in Experiment 4.   (3)

Experiment	Initial concentration of NaOH (mol dm⁻³)	Initial concentration of A (mol dm⁻³)	Initial rate (mol dm⁻³s⁻¹)
1	0.040	0.030	4.0×10^{-4}
2	0.040	0.045	6.0×10^{-4}
3	0.060	0.045	9.0×10^{-4}
4	0.120	0.060	to be calculated

c   In a further experiment at a different temperature, the initial rate of reaction was found to be:

9.0×10^{-3} mol dm⁻³ s⁻¹

when the initial concentration of **A** was 0.020 mol dm⁻³ and the initial concentration of NaOH was 2.00 mol dm⁻³. Under these new conditions with the much higher concentration of sodium hydroxide, the reaction is first order with respect to **A** and appears to be zero order with respect to sodium hydroxide.

i   Write a rate equation for the reaction under these new conditions.

ii   Calculate a value for the rate constant under these new conditions and state its units.

iii   Suggest why the order of reaction with respect to sodium hydroxide appears to be zero under these new conditions.   (6)

Total 11

AQA, June 2005, Unit 4, Question 1 (a–c)

7

a   The following table shows the results of three experiments carried out at the same temperature to investigate the rate of the reaction between compounds **P** and **Q**.

	Experiment 1	Experiment 2	Experiment 3
Initial concentration of **P** (mol dm⁻³)	0.50	0.25	0.25
Initial concentration of **Q** (mol dm⁻³)	0.36	0.36	0.72
Initial rate (mol dm⁻³ s⁻¹)	7.6×10^{-3}	1.9×10^{-3}	3.8×10^{-3}

Use the data in the table to deduce the order with respect to **P** and the order with respect to **Q**.   (2)

b   In a reaction between **R** and **S**, the order of reaction with respect to **R** is one, the order of reaction with respect to **S** is two and the rate constant at temperature T_1 has a value of 4.2×10^{-4} mol⁻² dm⁶ s⁻¹.

i   Write a rate equation for the reaction. Calculate a value for the initial rate of reaction when the initial concentration of **R** is 0.16 mol dm⁻³ and that of **S** is 0.84 mol dm⁻³.

ii   In a second experiment performed at a different temperature, T_2, the initial rate of reaction is 8.1×10^{-5} mol dm⁻³ s⁻¹ when the initial concentration of **R** is 0.76 mol dm⁻³ and that of **S** is 0.98 mol dm⁻³. Calculate the value of the rate constant at temperature T_2.

iii   Deduce which of T_1 and T_2 is the higher temperature.   (6)

Total 8

AQA, January 2005, Unit 4, Question 4

how science works **assignment**

Ozone depletion

Farman and his Antarctic-based team reported ozone depletion in 1985. They had delayed publication because the results were so improbable. The Nimbus-7 spacecraft had not found the hole because the analysis was programmed to reject very low concentrations of ozone as impossible. Once corrected, the satellite data clearly confirmed the existence of the hole.

An artist's rendering of the Nimbus-7 satellite.

> **A1**   Why would scientists want to restrict the data in this way?

The Montreal Protocol was the crucial first step in limiting further damage to the ozone layer in the stratosphere. It was signed in 1987 by many countries in order to greatly reduce the production and use of CFCs, which had been shown to be responsible for damage to the ozone layer. Owing to its widespread implementation, it has been hailed as an example of exceptional international cooperation, with Kofi Annan quoted as saying it is 'perhaps the single most successful international agreement to date ...'.

The critics and sceptics, primarily industry spokespeople and scientists from conservative think tanks, immediately attacked the proposals, despite the fact that Molina and Rowland's theory had wide support in the scientific community. A handful of sceptics, helped by the public relations machines of powerful corporations and politicians sympathetic to them, succeeded in delaying controls on CFCs for many years. At the time, the CFC industry was worth about $8 billion in the USA, and employed over 600 000 people directly and 1.4 million people indirectly.

> **A2**   Explain why pressure groups might want to prevent treaties such as the Montreal Protocol.

Fig. 15   Average size of the ozone hole

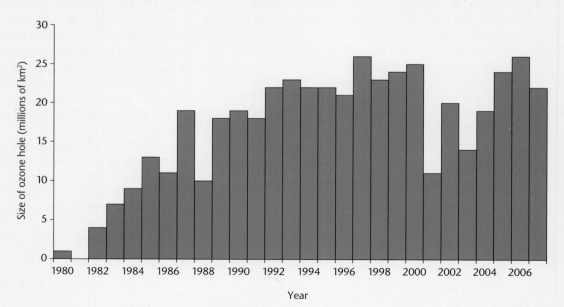

The severity of the ozone hole varies somewhat from year to year. These fluctuations are superimposed on a trend extending over the last three decades. Fig. 15 shows these variations.

> **A3**   Explain why we need international treaties such as the Montreal Protocol.

Leading scientists in the USA hope the ozone hole may 'heal' fully over the next 60 years.

> **A4**   Is there evidence from Fig. 15 that the Montreal Protocol is having an effect?
>
> **A5**   Will you need more evidence to support the 'healing' idea? Explain why.

Articles published in traditional scientific journals undergo a process essential to good science, called peer review.

Scientists use different models and compare them with observations to help our understanding of the processes responsible for ozone depletion.

Box models consider just a single point in the atmosphere. Such models are comparatively cheap to develop and run on a PC or workstation. The advantage of such models is that very complex chemical reactions can be included since only the chemistry at a single point is simulated. This is very useful for comparing model simulations with measurements in idealised cases.

Trajectory models are 'box models that move'. A trajectory of a point (or points) of air is calculated from known wind fields. The chemistry is then calculated for all points along the path that the parcel of air took.

Three-dimensional models simulate the atmospheric system as three dimensions. Such models have a realistic representation of the movement or meteorology of air as well as other processes such as clouds, solar radiation and so on. As many points are being represented, it becomes impossible to use the complex chemistry schemes found in box models as this would place too great a demand on computing power. As it is, these 3D chemical models of the atmosphere require the most powerful supercomputers.

> **A6**   Explain what peer review is and why it is important with issues such as ozone depletion.
>
> **A7**   What factors do you think could affect the size of the ozone hole? Describe the chemistry linked to your choices.
>
> **A8**   Give an advantage and a disadvantage of each model.

2 Equilibria

We require oxygen to break down glucose and provide energy to our body tissues, especially our muscles when we exercise. Carbon dioxide is produced as a waste product. The haemoglobin in our blood can reversibly bind either to oxygen or to carbon dioxide, depending on the concentration of these gases in the tissue and blood fluids.

The concentration of blood oxygen is high in the arteries from our lungs. There, haemoglobin bonds preferentially to oxygen and carries this gas to our cells. If the cells are metabolising, they are using up oxygen, so blood and tissue oxygen concentration is low, and oxygen dissociates from haemoglobin.

When the concentration of carbon dioxide is high, as it is in blood leaving active muscles, haemoglobin bonds to this gas and carries it back to our lungs where, with blood at a lower carbon dioxide level, the gas dissociates, diffuses into the lungs, and we breathe it out.

$$Hb + O_2 \underset{\text{in tissues}}{\overset{\text{in lungs}}{\rightleftharpoons}} HbO_2 \qquad Hb + CO_2 \underset{\text{in lungs}}{\overset{\text{in tissues}}{\rightleftharpoons}} HbCO_2$$

The oxygen needs releasing in the tissues, not in the arteries. How effectively oxygen is transported and released depends upon the strength of the bond between the haemoglobin and the oxygen molecule. Scientists have found that the release of oxygen is triggered by the presence of the HCO_3^- ion in the cells. When each molecule of haemoglobin binds to the hydrogencarbonate ions, its grip on its four oxygen molecules is loosened.

These are **dynamic equilibrium** reactions, and the position of equilibrium shifts to respond to our bodies' needs.

If we hold our breath while swimming under water, the level of carbon dioxide in our blood increases, and this stimulates the need to breathe. An inexperienced diver is very sensitive to carbon dioxide levels and a high concentration of carbon dioxide in the lungs will trigger that 'burning' sensation you feel when you hold your breath.

Free divers have trained their bodies so that they can hold their breath for long periods – up to two minutes. The human body is capable of other remarkable adaptations to the underwater environment. Trained divers can lower their heart rate to an incredible 20 beats per minute under the vastly increased pressure. The lungs' capacity drops, and blood vessels in the skin contract under conditions of low oxygen in order to leave more blood available for important organs, namely the heart, brain and muscles. Changes in blood chemistry allow the body to carry and use oxygen more efficiently. These changes, in effect, squeeze the last molecule of available oxygen from non-essential organs.

Adaptations also occur at high altitudes. Adults normally have about five litres of blood. People who live at high altitudes, where the air contains less oxygen, may have up to 1.9 litres more. Many athletes train at high altitude so that their bodies adapt to a lower oxygen concentration by producing the extra blood. When they run at lower altitudes they have a greater supply of oxygen. Damaged cells also need a supply of oxygen for repair, so the body needs to maintain its flow of oxygen to all parts of the body. In the case of a serious accident or indeed an operation, there may be considerable blood loss and tissues can die. In these cases a blood transfusion may be necessary.

The reversible gas reactions are vital for our bodies' needs, but reversible reactions are also extremely important in economic terms, as explained in this chapter.

Free divers train their bodies to adapt to low blood oxygen levels.

This Andean man's body is adapted to living at high altitude.

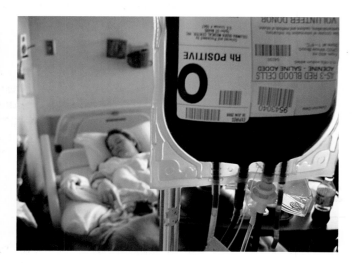

A blood transfusion could be a life saver.

We have seen in Chapter 9 of *AS Chemistry* that some reactions go more or less to completion. Other reactions do not: when the reaction seems to have stopped there are still significant amounts of reactants as well as products in the reaction mixture. Such reactions are **reversible**, and when the reaction appears to have stopped, it is in fact at **dynamic equilibrium**. As an analogy, imagine a runner on a treadmill at the sports centre: to an observer, the runner isn't moving in any direction, yet he or she is going forwards at the same rate as the treadmill is moving backwards.

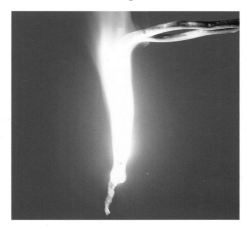

The reaction between magnesium and oxygen is not reversible to any significant extent.

The reaction between hydrogen and iodine is an example of a reversible reaction. At room temperature, hydrogen is a gas and iodine is a solid, but at temperatures over 457 K and at 101 kPa pressure (1 atm), iodine is a gas.

If equimolar quantities of the reactants are heated to 600 K and the two gases are sealed in a container, they combine and form hydrogen iodide:

$$H_2(g) + I_2(g) \rightarrow 2HI(g)$$

However, no matter how long you keep the temperature at 600 K, there is always some hydrogen and iodine present in the container – the reaction does not go to completion. Under these conditions the final reaction mixture contains the three substances in the proportions of 0.2 moles of hydrogen and iodine to 1.6 moles of hydrogen iodide (see Fig. 1).

As the product HI(g) is formed in the reaction, it decomposes to form gaseous hydrogen and gaseous iodine again, so the forward and reverse reactions are happening at the same time. At **equilibrium** the concentrations of reactants and products do not change because the rates of the forward and reverse reactions are equal: this is referred to as a **dynamic equilibrium**:

$$H_2(g) + I_2(g) \rightleftharpoons 2HI(g)$$

Fig. 1   Results for the reversible reaction of HI

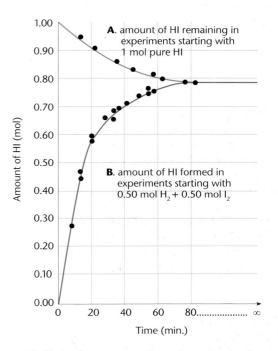

If all the reactants and products are in the same phase, the reaction is called **homogeneous**; if there is a mixture of phases, then the reaction is **heterogeneous**. In this example, the reactants and products are all gases at 600 K, and as they are all in the same phase, we refer to the reaction as homogeneous.

2.1   Equilibrium constant K_c

In *AS Chemistry* we looked at the equilibrium constant only qualitatively. At equilibrium the ratio of the concentrations stays constant and, knowing the concentrations of the various substances, it is easy to calculate the value of the constant. This is very useful since you can predict how a reaction will behave when the concentrations are changed. We call the ratio of the concentrations of the products and reactants the **equilibrium constant**, K_c (where the c stands for molar concentration). Its value is constant only so long as the temperature is constant, and changes if the temperature changes.

For the reaction:

$$H_2(g) + I_2(g) \rightleftharpoons 2HI(g)$$

the equilibrium constant is written as:

$$K_c = \frac{[HI]^2}{[H_2][I_2]}$$

Expressions for product concentrations are above the line, while those for reactants are below the division line. Note also that the concentration terms for a reaction are raised to the power that is stated in the stoichiometric equation. For example, in the reaction above, 2 moles of HI in the reaction equation gives $[HI]^2$ in the equilibrium constant equation.

In the reaction between ethanol, C_2H_5OH, and ethanoic acid, CH_3COOH, the ester ethyl ethanoate, $CH_3COOC_2H_5$, is formed. The equation for this esterification reaction is:

$$C_2H_5OH(l) + CH_3COOH(l)$$
$$\rightleftharpoons CH_3COOC_2H_5(l) + H_2O(l)$$

and the equilibrium constant for this reaction, K_c, is expressed as:

$$K_c = \frac{[CH_3COOC_2H_5][H_2O]}{[C_2H_5OH][CH_3COOH]}$$

We can write a general equation for any homogeneous reaction at equilibrium:

$$aA + bB \rightleftharpoons cC + dD$$

where a, b, c and d are the numbers of moles of substances A, B, C and D in the balanced chemical equation for the equilibrium. The equilibrium constant, K_c, is then expressed as:

$$K_c = \frac{[C]^c[D]^d}{[A]^a[B]^b}$$

Fig. 2   Changes in concentration with time for the reversible reaction of $H_2(g) + I_2(g) \rightleftharpoons 2HI(g)$

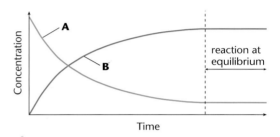

1

a   In Fig. 2, which line, A or B, represents the H_2/I_2 concentration, and which line represents the HI concentration? Explain your answer.

b   What will be the effect on the rates of these two reactions of increasing the temperature?

2.2 Units of K_c

The units of K_c depend upon the number of moles in the chemical equation. For any equilibrium the units of K_c can be calculated by substituting the units of concentration ($mol\ dm^{-3}$) into the equation for K_c.

For the final reaction in the industrial synthesis of ammonia:

$$N_2(g) + 3H_2(g) \rightleftharpoons 2NH_3(g)$$

we have:

$$K_c = \frac{[NH_3]^2}{[N_2][H_2]^3}$$

$$K_c = \frac{(\text{mol dm}^{-3})^2}{(\text{mol dm}^{-3})\ (\text{mol dm}^{-3})^3}$$

and after cancelling the units are:

$$\frac{1}{(\text{mol dm}^{-3})^2} \quad \text{i.e. } mol^{-2}\ dm^6$$

Similarly for the oxidation of sulfur dioxide:

$$2SO_2(g) + O_2(g) \rightleftharpoons 2SO_3(g)$$

we have:

$$K_c = \frac{[SO_3]^2}{[O_2][SO_2]^2}$$

$$K_c = \frac{\cancel{(mol\ dm^{-3})^2}}{(mol\ dm^{-3})\ \cancel{(mol\ dm^{-3})^2}}$$

and the units are:

$$\frac{1}{(mol\ dm^{-3})} \quad \text{i.e. } mol^{-1}\ dm^3$$

For the esterification equilibrium above, the units for K_c are given by:

$$K_c = \frac{[CH_3COOC_2H_5][H_2O]}{[C_2H_5OH][CH_3COOH]}$$

$$= \frac{\cancel{(mol\ dm^{-3})}\cancel{(mol\ dm^{-3})}}{\cancel{(mol\ dm^{-3})}\cancel{(mol\ dm^{-3})}}$$

and in this case cancelling gives no units.

> **2** Write an expression for K_c for the reactions and calculate the units of K_c:
>
> **a** $CO_2(g) + NO(g) \rightleftharpoons CO(g) + NO_2(g)$
>
> **b** $C_2H_6(g) \rightleftharpoons C_2H_4(g) + H_2(g)$
>
> **c** $2NO(g) + O_2(g) \rightleftharpoons 2NO_2(g)$.

2.3 Calculating equilibrium constants

For the esterification reaction, let us look at how we calculate the value of the equilibrium constant at a given temperature. Table 1 gives the concentrations in mol dm^{-3} of the substances present at equilibrium.

The equilibrium constant is:

$$K_c = \frac{[CH_3COOC_2H_5][H_2O]}{[C_2H_5OH][CH_3COOH]}$$

$$K_c = \frac{0.67 \times 0.67}{0.33 \times 0.33} = 4.12$$

We have seen that there are no units for this value because all the concentration terms cancel.

In general, if the **equilibrium position** of a reaction lies well over to the product side, then the equilibrium constant will be relatively large. A small equilibrium constant indicates that the equilibrium position lies well over to the side of the reactants and that not much conversion takes place. For example, the NH_3 equilibrium constant at 600 K is 3.0×10^{-2} mol^{-2} dm^6. This indicates a low equilibrium yield of NH_3: the gas that comes out of the converter is mostly nitrogen and hydrogen, which is why the unconverted gases are recycled in the Haber process.

Table 1

Reagent	Concentration at the start (mol dm^{-2})	Concentration at equilibrium (mol dm^{-2})
C_2H_5OH	1.0	0.33
CH_3COOH	1.0	0.33
$CH_3COOC_2H_5$	0.0	0.67
H_2O	0.0	0.67

 A task sheet and practice questions on the Practical Skills Assessment 'Determine an equilibrium constant' can be found at www.collinseducation.co.uk/advancedscienceaqa

- The general expression for an equilibrium constant in terms of concentrations is given by:

$$K_c = \frac{[C]^c[D]^d}{[A]^a[B]^b}$$

where a, b, c and d are the numbers of moles of each substance A, B, C and D in the balanced chemical equation:

$$aA + bB \rightleftharpoons cC + dD$$

- The units for K_c depend upon the particular equilibrium.

- A high value for K_c indicates a high equilibrium yield of product(s).

- The value of the equilibrium constant for a reaction is constant at a fixed temperature.

2.4   Factors that affect equilibrium

The effect of making changes to the conditions of a reaction at equilibrium can be predicted by using **Le Chatelier's principle**, which states that:

The position of the equilibrium of a system changes to minimise the effect of any imposed change in conditions.

The changes imposed can be changes of concentration, pressure or temperature.

Changing concentration

Consider the esterification reaction again. Le Chatelier's principle predicts that, if the amount of the reactant ethanol is increased, the position of equilibrium shifts to minimise the change. The reaction moves to the right to remove ethanol, which happens when ethanol reacts with more of the ethanoic acid to produce more ethyl ethanoate and water. At the same time the proportion of the reaction mixture that is ethanoic acid is reduced.

3   Dioximes are compounds that can be used to recover copper ions from water because the two substances form strong complexes together. The equilibrium can be represented by a simplified equation, where H_2A is the dioxime:

$$Cu^{2+}(aq) + H_2A(aq) \rightleftharpoons CuA(aq) + 2H^+(aq)$$

A solution containing 0.005 mol dm^{-3} of copper ions was mixed with a solution containing 0.005 mol dm^{-3} of dioxime and at equilibrium the mixture contained 0.0049 mol dm^{-3} of complex CuA(aq).

a   Write an expression for the equilibrium constant for the reaction.

b   Would you expect K_c to be small or large?

c   Calculate the concentrations of copper ions, dioxime molecules and hydrogen ions at equilibrium.

d   Calculate the value for the equilibrium constant and quote the units (if any).

e   What will happen to the position of equilibrium if acid is added to the solution?

f   What will happen to the value for the equilibrium constant if acid is added to the solution?

4   Why might there be a renewed interest in the recovery of low concentrations of copper from water?

So, if we know the value of the equilibrium constant for a reaction in the first place, we can use it to calculate the effect of changing any of the concentrations:

When different proportions of reactants in a reversible reaction are mixed at a fixed temperature, the concentrations of the reactants and products will adjust until the value of the equilibrium constant is achieved.

Consider the following data for the reaction of ethanol with ethanoic acid at 25 °C:

$$C_2H_5OH(l) + CH_3COOH(l) \rightleftharpoons CH_3COOC_2H_5(l) + H_2O(l)$$
initial concentrations:
$$\frac{a}{V} \qquad \frac{b}{V} \qquad 0 \qquad 0$$

where V is the total volume of the reaction mixture.

The concentrations in the equilibrium mixture can be measured by analysing each of the reaction mixtures. If the original amounts in moles of reactants are a and b, and at equilibrium the amount of ester and water are both x, then the amounts of ethanol and acid remaining at equilibrium are $(a - x)$ and $(b - x)$ respectively (i.e. the initial amount minus the amount reacted).

$$C_2H_5OH(l) + CH_3COOH(l) \rightleftharpoons$$
$$CH_3COOC_2H_5(l) + H_2O(l)$$
concentrations at equilibrium:
$$\frac{(a - x)}{V} \qquad \frac{(b - x)}{V} \qquad \frac{x}{V} \qquad \frac{x}{V}$$

So we have:

$$K_c = \frac{[CH_3COOC_2H_5][H_2O]}{[C_2H_5OH][CH_3COOH]}$$

$$K_c = \frac{\left(\dfrac{x}{V}\right)\left(\dfrac{x}{V}\right)}{\left(\dfrac{a - x}{V}\right)\left(\dfrac{b - x}{V}\right)}$$

$$= \frac{x^2}{(a - x)(b - x)}$$

Table 2 gives data for different initial concentrations of ethanol and the resulting equilibrium concentrations. Note that the equilibrium remains constant (given variations in concentration measurements) even though the initial concentrations of ethanol were changed.

Table 2 shows that, when the concentration of ethanol increases, the number of moles of ethyl ethanoate at equilibrium also increases. This is predicted from Le Chatelier's principle – the imposed change is to increase the concentration of ethanol and the system minimises that effect by removing ethanol. In so doing, the concentration of ethyl ethanoate increases and the concentrations of ethanol and ethanoic acid decrease. The value of the equilibrium constant does not change.

Table 2   Data for the esterification reaction at 298 K

Initial moles of ethanol (a)	Initial moles of ethanoic acid (b)	Equilibrium moles of ethanol ($a - x$)	Equilibrium moles of ethanoic acid ($b - x$)	Equilibrium moles of ethyl ethanoate (x)	Equilibrium constant
0.500	1.000	0.075	0.575	0.425	4.188
1.000	1.000	0.330	0.330	0.670	4.122
2.000	1.000	1.153	0.153	0.847	4.067
4.000	1.000	3.067	0.067	0.933	4.236

Effect of temperature

Changing the temperature of the equilibrium changes the equilibrium position and the value of the equilibrium constant, K_c.

Position of equilibrium

Le Chatelier's principle predicts that, if the temperature is changed, the reaction will try to minimise the effect of the change. If the temperature is increased, the reaction will try to remove heat from the system, so it will move in the endothermic direction:

$$N_2(g) + 3H_2(g) \rightleftharpoons 2NH_3(g)$$
$$\Delta H^{\ominus} = -92 \text{ kJ mol}^{-1} \text{ (exothermic)}$$

The production of ammonia is an exothermic process, so increasing the temperature will drive the equilibrium to the left – the endothermic direction – thus decreasing the yield of ammonia:

$$K = \frac{[NH_3]^2}{[N_2][H_2]^3}$$

Fig. 3 shows the effect of pressure and temperature on the percentage of ammonia produced at equilibrium in the Haber process. Note that the percentage yield reduces with higher temperatures and increases with higher pressures.

The reaction now used to produce the hydrogen required for ammonia synthesis is:

$$CH_4(g) + H_2O(g) \rightleftharpoons CO(g) + 3H_2(g)$$
$$\Delta H^{\ominus} = +206 \text{ kJ mol}^{-1} \text{ (endothermic)}$$

The production of hydrogen is an endothermic process, so raising the temperature will drive the equilibrium to the right – the endothermic direction – thus increasing the equilibrium yield of hydrogen. The effects of temperature change are summarised in Table 3.

Fig. 3   Effect of pressure and temperature on ammonia synthesis

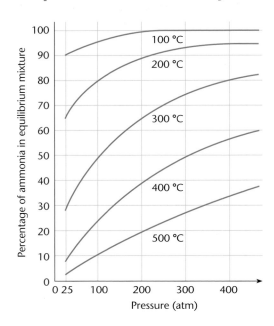

Fig. 3 shows that there is a much higher percentage of ammonia in the equilibrium mixture at 100 °C than at 500 °C. Increasing the pressure has very little effect at 100 °C but has considerable effect at higher temperatures. The rate of reaction at 100 °C is very low, so ammonia is manufactured at 450 °C and 200 atm, and a catalyst is used to increase the rate.

Table 3   Effect of changing temperature on equilibrium

Reaction	Change in temperature	Equilibrium constant	Shift in eqm. position	Eqm. yield of product
exothermic	increase	decreased	left	decreased
exothermic	decrease	increased	right	increased
endothermic	increase	increased	right	increased
endothermic	decrease	decreased	left	decreased

5

a   How does the graph in Fig. 3 show the difference in effect of changing the pressure at 100 °C and 500 °C?

b   Explain how a catalyst increases the rate of a reaction.

c   What are the economic and chemical considerations a manufacturer will have to bear in mind, when deciding on the manufacturing conditions of 450 °C, 200 atm with a suitable catalyst?

Atmospheric pollution

In the reaction:

$$N_2(g) + O_2(g) \rightleftharpoons 2NO(g)$$

$K_c = 4 \times 10^{-31}$ at 20 °C (293 K) but at combustion temperature inside a car engine, typically 800 °C (approx. 1 100 K), $K_c = 8 \times 10^{-9}$.

6 Is this reaction likely to happen at normal room temperature? Explain your reasoning.

7 The temperature of the spark that ignites the fuel/air mixture is about 2 500 K. At this temperature, how does the value of K_c change? How will this affect the yield of NO(g)?

8 Is the reaction endothermic or exothermic? Explain your answer using the change in the value of the equilibrium constant.

9 Explain in detail the shape of the graph for the production of NO and NO$_2$ in Fig. 4.

10 Many EU countries have or are introducing Low Emission Zones (LEZ) for some diesel and petrol vehicles. Give your opinion about these moves, supporting your arguments by sound scientific, financial or libertarian evidence.

Nitrogen oxide from petrol combustion reacts with atmospheric oxygen to give nitrogen dioxide. This gas forms the brown haze seen over polluted towns and cities, such as São Paulo, shown on the right. Nitrogen dioxide causes respiratory problems and acid rain.

Fig. 4 Levels of NO and NO$_2$ in the atmosphere during the day

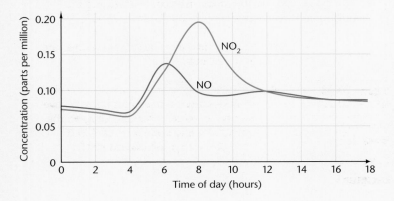

A London 'Low Emission Zone' sign.

Catalysis

As described above, for exothermic reactions, chemists have to balance the reduced yield produced by higher temperatures against the increased rate of reaction.

The production of ethanol from ethene provides a good example:

$$C_2H_4(g) + H_2O(g) \rightleftharpoons C_2H_5OH(g)$$
$$\Delta H = -25 \text{ kJ mol}^{-1}$$

The reaction is slightly exothermic, so the reaction mixture will naturally heat up as ethanol is formed. This has the effect of reducing the yield since, in accordance with Le Chatelier's principle, the system tries to counter the rise in temperature by absorbing heat and shifting the equilibrium to the left. Chemical engineers can cool the reaction mixture, but this slows down the *rate* at which the reaction proceeds.

The problem is helped by using a **catalyst** to speed up the reaction and achieve a reasonable rate of ethanol production. The catalyst speeds up both the forward and reverse reactions equally, so it does not affect the *position* of equilibrium, but it ensures that equilibrium is reached faster.

Computers are used to model the data and show the combined effects of changes in temperature and pressure on ethanol production. Computers can also calculate the likely effect on energy costs, raw material costs and plant costs, and predict the most economical, yet productive, conditions for ethanol manufacture.

The actual conditions used are a temperature of 540 K and a pressure of 6000 kPa. Ethene and steam are passed over a heated catalyst. This is phosphoric acid supported on a very porous powder to give a large surface area. (The powder is the fossilised remains of microscopic sea creatures!) The resulting ratio of ethene to steam is 0.6 moles to 1.0 mole. The higher concentration of steam in the mixture shifts the position of equilibrium towards the product, ethanol, and using steam in excess ensures that it is the concentration of the more expensive ethene that is lowered.

11

a The temperature used in ethanol production is relatively high. How will this affect the ethanol yield?

b How is this factor balanced to increase ethanol yield?

key facts

- For exothermic reactions, increasing the temperature decreases the equilibrium constant.
- For endothermic reactions, increasing the temperature increases the equilibrium constant.
- A higher equilibrium constant indicates a greater yield of product(s).
- A catalyst speeds up the rate at which equilibrium is reached.

examination questions

1 Under suitable conditions the equilibrium represented as follows was established:

$$2CH_4(g) \rightleftharpoons 3H_2(g) + C_2H_2(g) \quad \Delta H^\circ = +377 \text{ kJ mol}^{-1}$$

a Write an expression for the equilibrium constant, K_c, for this reaction. (1)

b At a given temperature and pressure, the equilibrium mixture contained 0.44 mol of methane, 0.28 mol of hydrogen and 0.12 mol of ethyne (C_2H_2) in a container of volume 0.25 dm³.
Calculate the value of K_c under these conditions and deduce its units. (4)

c State the effect of an increase in temperature on the position of this equilibrium and on the value of K_c for this reaction. (2)

d State the effect of an increase in pressure on the position of this equilibrium and on the value of K_c for this reaction. (2)

Total 9

AQA, January 2008, Unit 4, Question 3 (a–d)

2

a The diagram below shows the effect of temperature and pressure on the equilibrium yield of the product in a gaseous equilibrium.

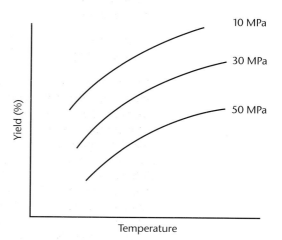

i Use the diagram to deduce whether the forward reaction involves an increase or a decrease in the number of moles of gas. Explain your answer.

ii Use the diagram to deduce whether the forward reaction is exothermic or endothermic. Explain your answer. (6)

b When a 0.218 mol sample of hydrogen iodide was heated in a flask of volume V dm³, the following equilibrium was established at 700 K.

$$H_2(g) + I_2(g) \rightleftharpoons 2HI(g)$$

The equilibrium mixture was found to contain 0.023 mol of hydrogen.

i Calculate the number of moles of iodine and the number of moles of hydrogen iodide in the equilibrium mixture.

ii Write an expression for K_c for the equilibrium.

iii State why the volume of the flask need not be known when calculating a value for K_c.

iv Calculate the value of K_c at 700 K.

v Calculate the value of K_c at 700 K for the equilibrium

$$H_2(g) + I_2(g) \rightleftharpoons 2HI(g)$$ (7)

Total 13

AQA, June 2006, Unit 4, Question 3

3

a The expression for an equilibrium constant, K_c, for a homogeneous equilibrium reaction is as follows:

$$K_c = \frac{[A]^2[B]}{[C][D]^3}$$

i Write an equation for the forward reaction.
ii Deduce the units of K_c
iii State what can be deduced from the fact that the value of K_c is larger when the equilibrium is established at a lower temperature. (3)

b A 36.8 g sample of N_2O_4 was heated in a closed flask of volume 16.0 dm³. An equilibrium was established at a constant temperature according to the following equation:

$$N_2O_4(g) \rightleftharpoons 2NO_2(g)$$

The equilibrium mixture was found to contain 0.180 mol of N_2O_4

i Calculate the number of moles of N_2O_4 in the 36.8 g sample.
ii Calculate the number of moles of NO_2 in the equilibrium mixture.
iii Write an expression for K_c and calculate its value under these conditions.
iv Another 36.8 g sample of N_2O_4 was heated to the same temperature as in the original experiment, but in a larger flask. State the effect, if any, of this change on the position of equilibrium and on the value of K_c compared with the original experiment. (9)

Total 12

AQA, January 2006, Unit 4, Question 3

4

Tetrafluoroethene, C_2F_4, is obtained from chlorodifluoromethane, $CHClF_2$, according to the equation:

$$2CHClF_2(g) \rightleftharpoons C_2F_4(g) + 2HCl(g) \quad \Delta H^\circ = +128 \text{ KJ mol}^{-1}$$

a A 1.0 mol sample of $CHClF_2$ is placed in a container of volume 18.5 dm³ and heated. When equilibrium is reached, the mixture contains 0.20 mol of $CHClF_2$

i Calculate the number of moles of C_2F_4 and the number of moles of HCl present at equilibrium.
ii Write an expression for K_c for the equilibrium.
iii Calculate a value for K_c and give its units. (6)

b i State how the temperature should be changed at constant pressure to increase the equilibrium yield of C_2F_4
ii State how the total pressure should be changed at constant temperature to increase the equilibrium yield of C_2F_4 (2)

Total 8

AQA, January 2005, Unit 4, Question 5 (a–b)

5

At high temperatures, PCl_5 dissociates according to the following equation.

$$PCl_5(g) \rightleftharpoons PCl_3(g) + Cl_2(g) \quad \Delta H^\circ = +93 \text{ kJ mol}^{-1}$$

A 2.60 mol sample of PCl_5 is placed in a sealed container and heated to a fixed temperature. At equilibrium, 1.40 mol of PCl_5 remain unreacted. The total pressure in the container is 125 kPa.

a Calculate the number of moles of Cl_2 and the total number of moles of gas present in the equilibrium mixture. (2)
b Calculate the mole fraction of PCl_5 and the mole fraction of Cl_2 in the equilibrium mixture. (2)
c i Write a general expression for the partial pressure of a gas, in a mixture of gases.
ii Calculate the partial pressure of PCl_5 and the partial pressure of Cl_2 in the equilibrium mixture. (3)
d Write an expression for the equilibrium constant, K_p, for this reaction. (1)
e i State the effect, if any, on the value of K_p of adding more PCl_5 at a constant temperature.
ii State the effect, if any, on the value of K_p of increasing the temperature of the container. (2)
f In a further experiment, a second sample of PCl_5 is heated to a different temperature. In the equilibrium mixture produced at this temperature, the partial pressure of PCl_5 is 36.9 kPa and the partial pressure of Cl_2 is 42.6 kPa. Calculate a value for the equilibrium constant, K_p, for this reaction at this temperature and give its units. (3)

Total 13

AQA, January 2007, Unit 4, Question 2

how science works **assignment**

There is no substitute ... or is there?

William Harvey, in 1628, proposed a theory of blood circulation which contrasted sharply with the accepted beliefs of the time. These were based on the 1 400-year-old teachings of Galen and denied the presence of circulation. Harvey's theory relied on experimentation, comparative anatomy and calculation. Many opposed the circulation theory. They questioned the usefulness of experimentation and the lack of proof that capillaries exist. Other opponents were motivated by personal resentments and professional 'territorialism'.

Since the Middle Ages doctors and scientists have been fascinated by the idea of treating blood loss by injecting blood from one person into another, but for reasons unknown at the time, some patients died. Karl Landsteiner's discovery of the ABO blood typing system in 1900 changed all this, setting the scene for blood transfusion to become a routine and safe medical practice which has saved millions of lives.

The structure of the haemoglobin in a crocodile allows it to retain oxygen to stay underwater for up to an hour while it drowns its prey. The value of K_c for this system depends upon a high concentration of HCO_3^- ions.

A1   How does this sequence of discoveries illustrate the importance of scientific explanations being based on evidence? You can do further research on Harvey, Galen and Landsteiner to support your ideas.

A2   How have scientists used previous ideas to challenge and develop their own theories?

---

a shelf life of between one and three years, compared to 42 days for donated blood, which needs to be kept refrigerated. Dr Nagai foresees the day when it will be possible to freeze-dry synthetic haemoglobin, then simply rehydrate it when and where it is needed. Ideally, it could be given to anyone without triggering rejection, so accident victims could be given transfusions immediately without testing to see what blood group they are. However, Dr Nagai needs an oxygen release mechanism from haemoglobin with an equilibrium constant so that it releases the oxygen in the presence of bicarbonate, i.e. in the capillaries, not in the arteries.

However, the advent of AIDS in the early 1980s and concerns about hepatitis B and prion-transmitted diseases, such as Mad Cow and Creutzfeldt–Jakob disease, has created widespread concerns over the risks of acquiring transmittable diseases through blood transfusion. Although all blood is now carefully screened in the developed world, in the developing nations, where blood supplies and financial resources are limited, a disease-free source of blood substitutes would be incredibly beneficial.

Dr Nagai and his team at Cambridge University are researching ways of creating an artificial form of haemoglobin that could be used successfully as a blood substitute. He has used genetic engineering to create a haemoglobin molecule similar to that in humans, but modified at key sites to give the beneficial oxygen retention features of crocodile haemoglobin, and then introduced this into *E. coli* cells. The bacteria containing the altered genes were fermented to produce large quantities of haemoglobin.

Blood substitutes can be stored for much longer than transfused blood, and can be kept at room temperature. Most haemoglobin-based oxygen carriers in trials today carry

---

A3   What do you think are the benefits and possible objections to Dr Nagai's research?

A4   Artificial blood is being tested using current randomised controlled non-blinded trial. What do these terms mean?

A5   Could our red blood cells be genetically altered so that they permanently carry the modified haemoglobin? And what kind of special abilities would the recipient have?

A6   Is it ethical for athletes to allow their own blood-producing cells to be genetically modified, so they are more efficient at transferring oxygen?

---

3 Acids and bases

Diabetes doesn't have to be a debilitating disease. Diabetics can monitor things like their blood sugar level (before and after exercise), and their diet, to live healthily.

Lactic acid (a weak acid) can reach high levels of concentration in some diabetic patients. The acid can also reach high levels in healthy people, especially after strenuous exercise, giving rise to painful cramps.

Diabetes affects about one person in 20 in the UK. If not controlled, the disease can reduce the pH of the blood, making it more acidic, which can result in a coma, or even death.

The most common cause of diabetes in young people is a deficiency of the hormone insulin. Medical staff in hospitals have an understanding of the chemistry of the metabolic reactions involved, in order to treat the disease effectively.

Lack of insulin means that glucose, which is needed for energy, is not transferred to the muscles. Fat has to be used as an alternative energy source, and its metabolism causes the muscles to tire. When fat is broken down, metabolites can form, including keto acids, e.g. ethanoic acid. When acids are formed they can dissociate, forming H^+ ions. If the hydrogen ion concentration is increased, the pH is decreased.

$$CH_3COOH(aq) \rightleftharpoons CH_3COO^-(aq) + H^+(aq)$$

The keto acid 3-oxobutanoic acid is much more dissociated. The equilibrium lies further to the right, so it releases more $H^+(aq)$ and therefore it is a much stronger acid than ethanoic acid.

Long-term diabetic treatment is based on the body's natural defences against acidity. A solution that can resist, or counteract, a change in pH is called a **buffer**. Every living cell within our body creates acidic waste products, but, in normal circumstances, the body will use buffers, mainly haemoglobin, hydrogencarbonate or phosphate, to control the pH of the

blood. During vigorous exercise, muscles anaerobically produce lactic acid, but again this is controlled by the buffer action of the blood. Keto acids are much stronger than the normal acids in human blood (they are mainly carbonic, citric and lactic acids). The pH of normal blood is 7.4, but if excess keto acids form, the pH can drop to 7.0, and it is when the body cannot control this change in pH that a life-threatening condition can result.

The symptoms of diabetic ketoacidosis include nausea, vomiting, thirst, increased heart rate and decreased blood pressure.

Fig. 1   Ketone body formation

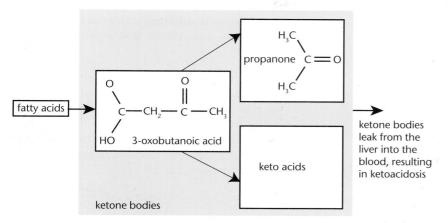

ketone bodies

Medical staff treating diabetes measure the acidity of patients' blood and compare the values with normal blood acidity. This information is required for the correct amount of medication to be prescribed for the patient.

The treatment for diabetes is improving all the time, and now insulin pumps with a slow release mechanism are being used more widely. These have advantages over injections, which give periodic boosts to the insulin levels. Also the way insulin is produced is different and advances in genetic engineering have meant that the complications from using bovine or porcine insulin have been removed.

3.1 Acids and bases

In this chapter you will learn how to describe and calculate the strengths of acids. In addition, you will learn about titrations between acids and bases, how to select an indicator and how buffers can control pH changes.

You will already be familiar with the concept of **acids** and **bases** and of an alkali as a base that is soluble in water. In 1884, the Swedish chemist Arrhenius described an acid as a substance that contains hydrogen and releases hydrogen ions when it dissolves in water:

$$HCl \rightleftharpoons H^+ + Cl^-$$
$$CH_3COOH \rightleftharpoons CH_3COO^- + H^+$$

He also described acids such as HCl, which dissociate fully, as strong acids, and those such as ethanoic acid, CH_3COOH, which only partially dissociate, as weak acids.

For all acid dissociation reactions, an equilibrium is set up between the species involved. The HCl molecule dissociates into hydrogen ions, H^+, which are protons, and chloride ions, Cl^-. For HCl, the equilibrium lies well over to the right: the HCl is virtually completely ionised, and for this reason it is described as a strong acid. In contrast, only 0.1% of ethanoic acid dissociates: the equilibrium lies well over to the left, and therefore ethanoic acid is a weak acid (a value of 50% dissociation is commonly used to differentiate between strong and weak acids).

Be careful not to confuse 'strong' with 'concentrated'. Strong relates to the *proportion of molecules* that have dissociated at equilibrium, and concentrated relates to the *amount of acid* in solution. However, depending on the acid, both can lead to high concentrations of hydrogen ions.

Arrhenius's theory also states that a base is a substance that reacts with H^+ to form water. Here is an example of an insoluble base:

$$MgO(s) + 2H^+(aq) \rightleftharpoons Mg^{2+}(aq) + H_2O(l)$$

and a soluble base:

$$Na^+(aq) + OH^-(aq) + H^+(aq) \rightleftharpoons Na^+(aq) + H_2O(l)$$

A proton, H^+, has no electrons, and chemists realised that this could not exist independently in aqueous solution. (A proton, H^+, can only exist independently under special conditions in the gaseous phase.) H^+ associates with water molecules and forms the hydroxonium ion according to the equation:

$$H^+ \quad + \quad H_2O \quad \rightarrow \quad H_3O^+$$
hydrogen ion   hydroxonium ion
(proton)

H_3O^+ represents a water molecule and a proton attached to the lone pair on the water molecule (Fig. 2). However, when writing reactions, the less precise H^+ is often used for simplicity. Instead of

Fig. 2   Dissociation of HCl and formation of a hydroxonium ion (H_3O^+)

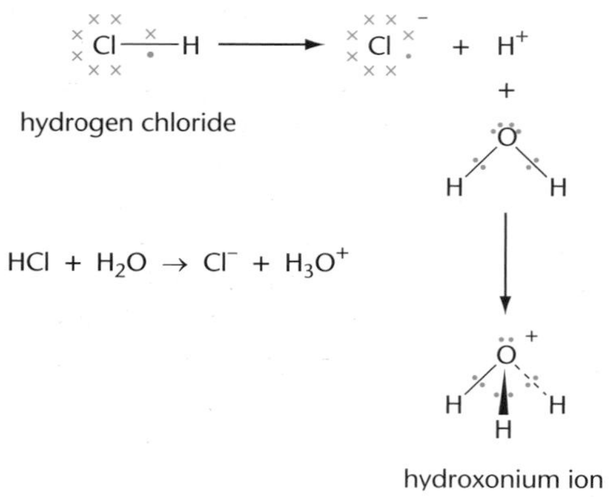

hydrogen chloride

$$HCl + H_2O \rightarrow Cl^- + H_3O^+$$

hydroxonium ion

representing the dissociation of these acids as on the previous page, they are therefore more accurately represented as:

$$HCl(aq) + H_2O(l) \rightleftharpoons H_3O^+(aq) + Cl^-(aq)$$

$$CH_3COOH(aq) + H_2O(l) \rightleftharpoons H_3O^+(aq) + CH_3COO^-(aq)$$

These refinements recognise the important role of water as the solvent. HCl in water behaves as an acid. But if HCl is dissolved in solvents that will not accept H^+, such as methylbenzene, it will not show any acidic properties.

Brønsted–Lowry acids and bases

In 1923 the Danish scientist Johannes Brønsted and the British chemist Thomas Lowry adapted the theory of acid–base behaviour to give a more useful definition which described the behaviour of acids and bases in both aqueous and non-aqueous reactions. They defined an **acid** as follows:

> **An acid is a substance that *donates protons* in a reaction; it is a *proton donor*.**

Brønsted and Lowry also said that, when an acid donates protons, a substance must accept the protons, namely a base, and that this

Fig. 3   The Brønsted–Lowry acid–base reaction of ammonia and hydrochloric acid

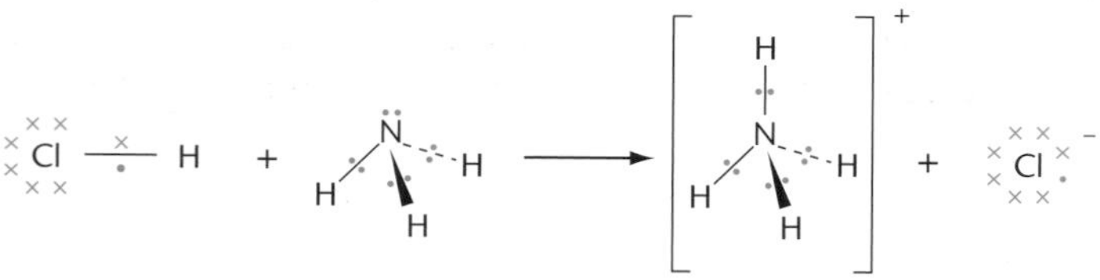

$$HCl + NH_3 \rightarrow NH_4^+ + Cl^-$$

substance behaves oppositely to an acid. They defined a **base** as follows:

> **A base is a substance that *accepts protons* in a reaction; it is a *proton acceptor*.**

Brønsted–Lowry definitions therefore apply to a wide range of reactions of acids and bases, not just those that take place in aqueous solutions.

The reaction between hydrochloric acid and ammonia (Fig. 3) is an acid–base reaction which can occur in aqueous solution, in the gas phase or in non-polar solvents:

$$HCl(aq) + NH_3(aq) \rightleftharpoons NH_4^+(aq) + Cl^-(aq)$$
$$HCl(g) + NH_3(g) \rightleftharpoons NH_4^+Cl^-(s)$$

In these reactions, HCl has donated H^+ and NH_3 has accepted H^+:

$$NH_3 + H^+ \rightarrow NH_4^+$$

The aqueous and gaseous reactions are both Brønsted–Lowry acid–base reactions, but only the aqueous reaction is an Arrhenius acid–base reaction. The Brønsted–Lowry definition clearly covers a wider range of applications.

Now, consider what happens when concentrated HNO_3 and concentrated H_2SO_4 are mixed. We would normally think of both of these substances as acids, but the equation for the reaction that takes place is as follows:

$$\underset{\text{base}}{HNO_3} + \underset{\text{acid}}{H_2SO_4} \rightleftharpoons H_2NO_3^+ + HSO_4^-$$

When the stoppers from hydrochloric acid and ammonia bottles are held near each other, fumes are formed which contain ammonium chloride particles.

Here, H_2SO_4 donates a proton, and therefore acts as the acid, and HNO_3 accepts this proton, and is therefore the base in this reaction.

There are other similar systems that do not include water as the solvent. For example, concentrated ethanoic acid exists as a liquid at room temperature. In the non-aqueous reaction:

$$HNO_3 + CH_3COOH \rightleftharpoons NO_3^- + CH_3COOH_2^+$$

the HNO_3 acts as the acid and the CH_3COOH as the base.

These reactions are showing us that in each system there is a proton donor and a proton acceptor, i.e. an acid *and* a base.

Also, because the reactions are reversible, the proton can be donated back again, so the donor on the right-hand side of the equation must also be considered as an acid, and the acceptor as a base:

$$\underset{\text{acid}}{HCl(aq)} + \underset{\text{base}}{H_2O(l)} \rightleftharpoons \underset{\text{acid}}{H_3O^+(aq)} + \underset{\text{base}}{Cl^-(aq)}$$

$$\underset{\text{acid}}{CH_3COOH(aq)} + \underset{\text{base}}{H_2O(l)} \rightleftharpoons \underset{\text{acid}}{H_3O^+(aq)} + \underset{\text{base}}{CH_3COO^-(aq)}$$

$$\underset{\text{acid}}{H_2SO_4} + \underset{\text{base}}{HNO_3} \rightleftharpoons \underset{\text{acid}}{H_2NO_3^+} + \underset{\text{base}}{HSO_4^-}$$

An acid dissociates to form two ions, namely a proton and a negative ion, and establishes an equilibrium. The negative ion acts as a base because it recombines with the proton and re-forms the acid molecule. The negative ion is referred to as the **conjugate base** of the acid. Also, when a base such as $NH_3(g)$ reacts with H^+ to form NH_4^+, this positive ion is referred to as the **conjugate acid**.

In the shaded box below are some examples. Note that in the last example, the right-hand side shows that the same species can act both as an acid and as a base. Pure water will always contain some hydrogen ions and hydroxide ions: it is **amphoteric**, and can be described as **self-protonating**:

$$2H_2O \rightleftharpoons H_3O^+ + OH^-$$

In water, any species providing H_3O^+ is an acid, and any species providing OH^- is a base.

Other solvents such as liquid ammonia also exhibit this behaviour:

$$2NH_3 \rightleftharpoons NH_4^+ + NH_2^-$$

In liquid ammonia, any species providing NH_4^+ is an acid, and any species providing NH_2^- is a base.

$CH_3COOH(l)$ ethanoic acid	+	$OH^-(aq)$ base	$\rightleftharpoons$	$CH_3COO^-(aq)$ ethanoate ion: conjugate base	+	$H_2O(l)$ conjugate acid
donates proton		accepts proton		accepts proton		donates proton
$HCl(g)$ acid	+	$NH_3(g)$ base	$\rightleftharpoons$	NH_4^+ conjugate acid	+	$Cl^-(s)$ conjugate base
donates proton		accepts proton		donates proton		accepts proton
$HCl(g)$ acid	+	$H_2O(l)$ base	$\rightleftharpoons$	$H_3O^+(aq)$ conjugate acid	+	$Cl^-(aq)$ conjugate base
donates proton		accepts proton		donates proton		accepts proton
$H_3O^+(aq)$ acid	+	$CO_3^{2-}(aq)$ base	$\rightleftharpoons$	$HCO_3^-(aq)$ conjugate acid	+	$H_2O(l)$ conjugate base
donates proton		accepts proton		donates proton		accepts proton
$H_3O^+(aq)$ acid	+	$NH_3(aq)$ base	$\rightleftharpoons$	$NH_4^+(aq)$ conjugate acid	+	$H_2O(l)$ conjugate base
donates proton		accepts proton		donates proton		accepts proton
$H_3O^+(aq)$ acid	+	$OH^-(aq)$ base	$\rightleftharpoons$	$H_2O(l)$ conjugate acid	+	$H_2O(l)$ conjugate base
donates proton		accepts proton		donates proton		accepts proton

3.2 Ionic equations

In aqueous solution, an acid and a base react to form a salt and water only. This is a **neutralisation reaction**. The base accepts one or more protons from the acid:

$$HCl(aq) + NaOH(aq) \rightarrow NaCl(aq) + H_2O(l)$$

This equation does not show what happens to the ions in the solution. When we rewrite it showing all the ions present, some ions appear on both sides of the equation. The above is a reaction of a strong acid with a strong base, so all the reactant species are fully dissociated.

$$H^+(aq) + Cl^-(aq) + Na^+(aq) + OH^-(aq) \rightleftharpoons Na^+(aq) + Cl^-(aq) + H_2O(l)$$

Because sodium ions and chloride ions appear on both sides of the equation, we can say that the sodium ions and chloride ions do not take part in the reaction. They are **spectator ions**. Omitting them allows us to write a simplified equation, the **ionic equation**, for the neutralisation reaction:

$$H^+(aq) + OH^-(aq) \rightleftharpoons H_2O(l)$$

Other strong acids and strong bases (Table 1) react similarly and they can all be represented by the ionic equation for water.

Table 1   Some common strong acids and strong bases

Strong acids	Strong bases
hydrochloric acid HCl	sodium hydroxide NaOH
sulfuric acid H_2SO_4	potassium hydroxide KOH
nitric acid HNO_3	
phosphoric acid H_3PO_4	

The solvent liquid ammonia can be considered in the same way:

$$NH_4^+ + NH_2^- \rightleftharpoons 2NH_3$$

Any species containing NH_4^+ is an acid, any species containing NH_2^- is a base and neutralisations will produce $NH_3(l)$.

1 Write full equations and ionic equations for the reactions between:

a hydrochloric acid and potassium hydroxide solution

b sulfuric acid and sodium hydroxide solution.

2

a Explain why methane does not act as a proton donor, but methanoic acid (HCOOH) does.

b Write an equation to show how methanoic acid ionises in water.

3 Identify the acids and bases in the following reactions:

a $CuO(s) + H_2SO_4(aq)$
  $\rightleftharpoons CuSO_4(aq) + H_2O(l)$

b $NH_4^+(aq) + OH^-(aq) \rightleftharpoons NH_3(aq) + H_2O(l)$

c $CH_3COO^-(aq) + H_3O^+(aq)$
  $\rightleftharpoons CH_3COOH(aq) + H_2O(l).$

key facts

● Acids are proton donors.

● Bases are proton acceptors.

● Acid–base reactions involve the transfer of protons.

● Water can act as an acid or as a base.

3.3 Acid dissociation constants

The vinegar commonly put on chips is a dilute aqueous solution of ethanoic acid with colouring added to it.

Most acids are weak acids. When these dissociate and an equilibrium is set up, significant amounts of all the molecules and ions are present:

$$CH_3COOH(aq) + H_2O(l) \rightleftharpoons CH_3COO^-(aq) + H_3O^+(aq)$$

ethanoic acid   ethanoate ion

The strength of the acid is determined by the position of equilibrium. If the equilibrium lies to the left, the acid is weak (less dissociated); the further to the right the equilibrium lies, the stronger the acid (more dissociated). Strong acids such as hydrochloric acid and sulfuric acid have an equilibrium that lies well over to the right. They are more or less fully dissociated.

The same principle applies to bases:

$$NH_3(aq) + H_2O(l) \rightleftharpoons NH_4^+(aq) + OH^-(aq)$$

When ammonia is dissolved in water, only a small proportion of ammonia molecules dissociate. Ammonia is therefore a weak base, with the equilibrium well over to the left.

When sodium hydroxide dissolves in water, it dissociates completely, releasing sodium ions and hydroxide ions, so it is a strong base, with the equilibrium very much over to the right:

$$Na^+OH^-(s) \rightleftharpoons Na^+(aq) + OH^-(aq)$$

Acid dissociation constants

As with other equilibria (including reaction equilibria, see Chapter 2) acid–base equilibria can be described using equilibrium constants. These are called **acid dissociation constants** and can be used to define the strength of the acid. For acids, they are a measure of how readily hydrogen ions are released. Dissociation constants are calculated in a similar way to equilibrium constants for reversible reactions, with products (right-hand side of equation) divided by reactants (left-hand side).

Consider this equilibrium between the undissociated acid and the ethanoate ions in aqueous solution:

$$CH_3COOH(aq) + H_2O(l)$$
$$\rightleftharpoons CH_3COO^-(aq) + H_3O^+(aq)$$
ethanoic acid   ethanoate ion

The extent of dissociation is given by the **equilibrium constant, K_c,** for the process:

$$K_c = \frac{[CH_3COO^-(aq)]\,[H_3O^+(aq)]}{[CH_3COOH(aq)]\,[H_2O(l)]}$$

The units for concentrations cancel out, so K_c has no units.

Because it is assumed that the water molecules are in vast excess and because they ionise only very slightly, the concentration of the water molecules hardly changes. We can simplify the expression and rewrite the equilibrium using K_a as the acid dissociation constant:

$$K_a = \frac{[CH_3COO^-(aq)]\,[H_3O^+(aq)]}{[CH_3COOH(aq)]}$$

For ethanoic acid, a weak acid, K_a is 1.7×10^{-5} mol dm^{-3}.

For the units for K_a, we insert the units for the terms in the expression for the dissociation constant. Where the acid releases one hydrogen ion only, the units are:

$$\frac{\text{mol dm}^{-3} \times \text{mol dm}^{-3}}{\text{mol dm}^{-3}} \quad \text{i.e. mol dm}^{-3}$$

We can now give a general expression for the dissociation constant K_a of any weak acid, of general formula HA, as:

$$K_a = \frac{[\text{H}^+]\,[\text{A}^-]}{[\text{HA}]}$$

where all concentrations are those at equilibrium and the units are mol dm^{-3}.

The less an acid dissociates, the smaller the value, while the stronger the acid, the higher is the value of its dissociation constant (Table 2).

Table 2   Dissociation constants of some common acids

Acid	K_a (mol dm^{-3})
HCl	1.0×10^7
HNO$_3$	4.0×10^1
HF	5.6×10^{-4}
HNO$_2$	4.7×10^{-4}
HCOOH	1.6×10^{-4}
C$_6$H$_5$COOH	6.5×10^{-5}
CH$_3$COOH	1.7×10^{-5}
C$_2$H$_5$COOH	1.3×10^{-5}
HClO	3.7×10^{-8}
HCN	4.9×10^{-10}

4 Write an expression for the acid dissociation constant of butanoic acid, CH$_3$(CH$_2$)$_2$COOH.

Writing expressions for K_a

Ethanoic acid dissociates only slightly (approximately 0.1% of the molecules dissociate, roughly one in a thousand) so the equilibrium lies well over to the left. We can use this fact to simplify the calculation of K_a.

The weak dissociation of ethanoic acid means that the concentration [CH$_3$COOH] hardly changes because so few molecules dissociate to form CH$_3$COO$^-$ and H$^+$ ions. The equilibrium concentration of CH$_3$COOH can therefore be taken as equal to its initial concentration (this is only valid when a weak acid alone is in aqueous solution). This concentration term can be written as: [CH$_3$COOH]$_{\text{initial}}$

Also for every H$^+$ released a CH$_3$COO$^-$ is released, so their concentrations are equal:

$$[\text{CH}_3\text{COO}^-] = [\text{H}^+]$$

We can then rewrite the expression for K_a as:

$$K_a = \frac{[\text{H}^+]^2}{[\text{CH}_3\text{COOH}]_{\text{initial}}} \quad \text{(neglecting H}^+ \text{ from water)}$$

The keto acid 3-oxobutanoic acid can form in the liver of diabetics (see page 37). It dissociates weakly according to the equation:

CH$_3$COCH$_2$COOH(aq)
$$\rightleftharpoons \text{CH}_3\text{COCH}_2\text{COO}^-\text{(aq)} + \text{H}^+\text{(aq)}$$

The equation for the dissociation constant of this equilibrium is:

$$K_a = \frac{[\text{CH}_3\text{COCH}_2\text{COO}^-]\,[\text{H}^+]}{[\text{CH}_3\text{COCH}_2\text{COOH}]_{\text{initial}}}$$

which according to the above approximation is:

$$K_a = \frac{[\text{H}^+]^2}{[\text{CH}_3\text{COCH}_2\text{COOH}]_{\text{initial}}}$$

If 0.010 mol dm^{-3} solution of the acid contains 1.62×10^{-3} mol dm^{-3} of hydrogen ions, then the value for K_a can be calculated from the expression above:

$$K_a = \frac{[\text{H}^+]^2}{[\text{CH}_3\text{COCH}_2\text{COOH}]_{\text{initial}}}$$

$$= \frac{(1.62 \times 10^{-3})^2}{0.010}$$

$$= 2.62 \times 10^{-4} \text{ dm}^{-3}$$

In these examples we have only considered the release of a single H$^+$ ion. Acids such as CH$_3$COOH that have only one H$^+$ to donate are called monoprotic acids. Many acids can release more than one H$^+$ ion. For example, sulfuric(IV) acid, H_2SO_3, is a weak acid. Two equilibria are involved and there is an equilibrium constant for each of these:

acid → hydrogensulfite ion:

$$H_2SO_3(aq) + H_2O(l) \rightleftharpoons HSO_3^-(aq) + H_3O^+(aq)$$
$$K_a = 1.5 \times 10^{-2} \text{ mol dm}^{-3}$$

hydrogensulfite ion → sulfite ion:

$$HSO_3^-(aq) + H_2O(l) \rightleftharpoons SO_3^{2-}(aq) + H_3O^+(aq)$$
$$K_a = 6.2 \times 10^{-8} \text{ mol dm}^{-3}$$

5 For the two equilibria for sulfuric(IV) acid in water, which reaction indicates the stronger acid? Explain how you used the values of K_a to decide upon your choice.

Fig. 4 General expression for the dissociation constant of a weak acid

A weak acid can be represented by the formula HA and dissociates according to the equilibrium:

$$HA(aq) \rightleftharpoons H^+(aq) + A^-(aq)$$

The expression for its dissociation constant can be written as follows:

$$K_a \approx \frac{[H^+][A^-]}{[HA]}$$

If HA is a weak acid the concentration of HA will not change significantly at equilibrium *relative to* $[A^-]$ and $[H^+]$, so for $[HA]$ we can use the *initial* concentration of the acid. Also $[A^-]$ will be equal to $[H^+]$, so that we can substitute $[H^+]$ for $[A^-]$:

$$K_a \approx \frac{[H^+]^2}{[HA]_{initial}}$$

key facts

- The strength of an acid is defined in terms of its acid dissociation constant.
- A weak acid dissociates only slightly in water, and has a small dissociation constant.
- A strong acid dissociates fully in water, and has a large dissociation constant.

- The dissociation constant, K_a, for a weak acid, HA, can be calculated using:

$$K_a = \frac{[H^+][A^-]}{[HA]_{eqm}}$$

and this can be approximated as:

$$K_a = \frac{[H^+]^2}{[HA]_{initial}}$$

3.4 pH

We could use hydrogen ion concentration as a measure of acidity, but where the values of $[H^+]$ are very small (see Table 2 for examples), the numbers can be cumbersome to work with, so using a log scale makes them easier to handle. This is the pH scale.

The pH of a solution is $-\log_{10}$ of the molar hydrogen ion concentration in that solution.

The H refers to the hydrogen ion concentration, $[H^+]$, and the symbol p is related to the power to which 10 is raised in the expression $-\log_{10}$ to give that concentration.

pH = $-\log_{10}$ [H$^+$]

Because pH values are logarithms, they have no units.

Calculating pH of *strong* acids from concentrations

We can apply the definition above to calculate the pH of a solution of hydrochloric acid containing 0.100 mol dm^{-3}.

Hydrochloric acid is a strong acid. All the hydrogen chloride molecules become fully dissociated into hydrogen ions and chloride ions. So in 1 dm³ of 0.100 mol dm^{-3} hydrochloric acid there are 0.100 moles of H$^+$

The changing colour of chemical indicators gives a rough measure of the pH of a solution. A more accurate and precise measure is given by a pH meter.

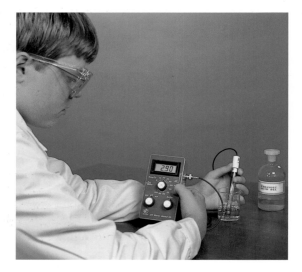

ions and 0.100 moles of Cl^- ions. Writing 0.100 is the same as writing 1×10^{-1} or 10^{-1}; in other words, $[H^+] = 10^{-1}$. Therefore, since $pH = -\log_{10}[H^+]$:

$$pH = -\log_{10} 10^{-1}$$
$$= -(-1)$$

Therefore, the pH of hydrochloric acid of concentration 0.100 mol dm^{-3} is 1.

It is a lot easier to talk about 'a pH of 1' than to say 'a hydrogen ion concentration of 0.100 mol dm^{-3}' or '10^{-1} mol dm^{-3}'. The pH of 0.010 (i.e. 10^{-2}) mol dm^{-3} hydrochloric acid would be $-\log_{10} 10^{-2} = -(-2) = 2$, a lower $[H^+]$, so a higher pH value.

Moving up or down the pH scale by 1 unit means that the hydrogen ion concentration changes by a factor of 10 ($= 10^1$).

The calculation above also indicates that it is possible to have pH values outside the often quoted range of 1–14. A strong acid of concentration 1.000 mol dm^{-3} would have a pH of $-\log_{10} 1 = 0$, so the pH would be 0. Any strong acid with a concentration of greater than

1 mol dm^{-3} will have a pH of less than 0, and therefore a minus value. At the other end of the pH range, for solutions with very low concentrations of hydrogen ions, for example, $[H^+] = 1 \times 10^{-15}$ mol dm^{-3}, the pH would be 15.

Such calculations can be performed quickly using the expression:

$$[H^+] = 10^{-pH}$$

Remember: pH is the power to which 10 is raised to give the $[H^+]$, and the sign is changed (Table 3).

Table 3   Comparison of [H⁺] values with corresponding pH values

$[H^+]$ (mol dm^{-3})	pH
10^{-4}	4
10^{-5}	5
10^{-6}	6
10^{-7}	7
10^{-8}	8
10^{-9}	9

6   Calculate the pH of:

a   0.2 mol dm^{-3} nitric acid (a strong acid, i.e. fully ionised)

b $[H^+] = 1.2 \times 10^{-2}$ mol dm^{-3}

c $[H^+] = 6.7 \times 10^{-5}$ mol dm^{-3}.

7   What is the pH of a 2.00 mol dm^{-3} solution of hydrochloric acid?

Calculating concentration from pH

Given a pH, we can work the other way and calculate the hydrogen ion concentration in the solution. What is the hydrogen ion concentration in a solution of pH 2.61?

$$\text{Since } pH = -\log_{10}[H^+]$$
$$[H^+] = 10^{-pH}$$
$$[H^+] = 10^{-2.61}$$

Therefore: $[H^+] = 0.00245$
$$= 2.45 \times 10^{-3} \text{ mol dm}^{-3}$$

8

a A solution has a pH of 5.49. What is the value of $[H^+]$?

b What is the hydrogen ion concentration in a solution of pH 2.75?

c What is the hydrogen ion concentration in a solution of pH −0.50?

Calculating pH from K_a values for *weak acids*

We can calculate the pH of a solution of a weak acid if we are given the following information:

- the concentration of the weak acid
- the value for its dissociation constant
- the expression: $K_a = \dfrac{[H^+]\,[A^-]}{[HA]}$

This is illustrated in the following example.

Lactic acid forms in muscle cells if insufficient oxygen reaches the muscles during exercise:

$$CH_3CH(OH)COOH(aq) \rightleftharpoons H^+(aq) + CH_3CH(OH)COO^-(aq)$$
lactic acid

The lactic acid concentration is typically 0.01 mol dm^{-3}, and its dissociation constant is $K_a = 1.287 \times 10^{-4}$ mol dm^{-3}.

$$K_a = \frac{[H^+(aq)][CH_3CH(OH)COO^-(aq)]}{[CH_3CH(OH)COOH(aq)]}$$

$$K_a = \frac{[H^+]^2}{[CH_3CH(OH)COOH(aq)]}$$

Rearranging this equation gives:

$$[H^+]^2 = [CH_3CH(OH)COOH(aq)] \times K_a$$

Substituting the values given above:

$$
\begin{aligned}
[H^+]^2 &= 0.01 \times 1.287 \times 10^{-4} \\
&= 1.287 \times 10^{-6} \text{ mol}^2 \text{ dm}^{-6}
\end{aligned}
$$

$$
\begin{aligned}
[H^+] &= \sqrt{1.287 \times 10^{-6}} \\
&= 1.135 \times 10^{-3} \text{ mol dm}^{-3}
\end{aligned}
$$

The pH of the solution can be found using:

$$
\begin{aligned}
\text{pH} &= -\log_{10}[H^+] \\
&= -\log_{10} 1.135 \times 10^{-3} \\
&= 2.95
\end{aligned}
$$

Increasing the concentration of a weak acid increases the hydrogen ion concentration, which decreases the pH of the solution. A higher value of K_a indicates a stronger acid and therefore a lower pH.

9 Calculate the pH of a 0.01 mol dm^{-3} solution of propanoic acid which has a dissociation constant of 1.34×10^{-5} mol dm^{-3}.

3.5 pH of water

We have seen that water can act as an acid and as a base. It acts as a proton acceptor (base) when hydrogen chloride dissolves in it:

$$HCl(g) + H_2O(l) \rightarrow H_3O^+(aq) + Cl^-(aq)$$

It acts as a proton donor (acid) when ammonia dissolves in it:

$$NH_3(g) + H_2O(l) \rightleftharpoons NH_4^+(aq) + OH^-(aq)$$

Pure water itself is very weakly ionised:

$$H_2O(l) \rightleftharpoons H^+(aq) + OH^-(aq)$$

The equilibrium constant for this process is:

$$K_c = \frac{[H^+][OH^-]}{[H_2O]}$$

The concentration of water molecules in the equilibrium is very high. Because of the low degree of ionisation of water, we can consider $[H_2O]$ constant. This gives us a useful expression for the value of the **ionic product of water, K_w**:

$$K_w = [H^+][OH^-]$$

At 298 K, K_w is 10^{-14} mol^2 dm^{-6}.

We can calculate the pH of pure water, using the fact that it contains equal numbers of hydrogen ions and hydroxide ions:

$$[H^+] = [OH^-]$$

At 298 K, from K_w:

$$K_w = [H^+][OH^-] = [H^+]^2 = 10^{-14} \text{ mol}^2 \text{ dm}^{-6}$$

$$[H^+] = 10^{-7} \text{ mol dm}^{-6}$$

(To get the square root of a power, divide by 2.)

$$pH = -\log_{10}[H^+]$$
$$= -\log_{10} 10^{-7}$$
$$= 7$$

The pH of pure water is 7 at 298 K. The pH at other temperatures is listed in Table 4.

10 What is the concentration of hydroxide ions in pure water at 298 K?

Table 4   The pH of pure water at different temperatures

Temperature (°C)	$-\log_{10} K_w$	K_w (mol dm^{-3})	[H$^+$]	pH
0	14.94	1.15×10^{-15}	3.39×10^{-8}	7.47
20	14.17	6.76×10^{-15}	8.22×10^{-8}	7.09
25	14.00	1.00×10^{-14}	1.00×10^{-7}	7.00
30	13.83	1.48×10^{-14}	1.22×10^{-7}	6.91
40	13.54	2.88×10^{-14}	1.70×10^{-7}	6.77
50	13.26	5.50×10^{-14}	2.35×10^{-7}	6.63
60	13.02	9.55×10^{-14}	3.09×10^{-7}	6.51

Bases and pH

When bases dissolve in water they produce hydroxide ions, $[H^+] < [OH^-]$, and the hydroxide ions shift the dissociation of water equilibrium to the left (Fig. 5). But the ionic product of water remains constant at 1×10^{-14}.

$$H_2O(l) \rightleftharpoons H^+(aq) + OH^-(aq)$$
$$K_w = 1 \times 10^{-14} \text{ at 298 K}$$

Fig. 5   Effect on [H⁺] of adding OH⁻(aq)

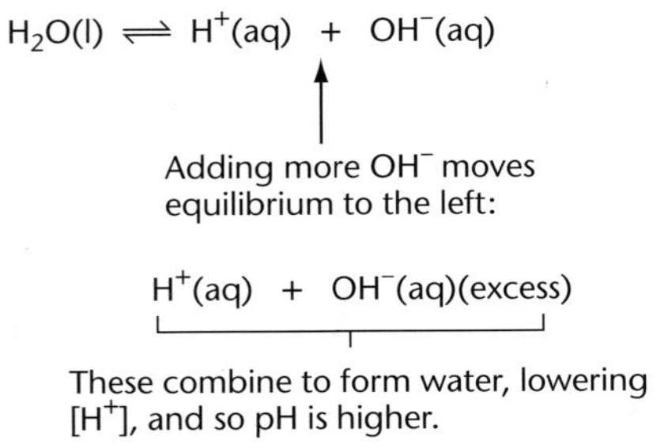

$$H_2O(l) \rightleftharpoons H^+(aq) + OH^-(aq)$$

Adding more OH⁻ moves equilibrium to the left:

$$H^+(aq) + OH^-(aq)(excess)$$

These combine to form water, lowering [H⁺], and so pH is higher.

We can calculate the pH of a strong alkali. It is a little more complex than calculating the pH of a strong acid.

Sodium hydroxide ionises fully in solution:

$$NaOH(aq) \rightarrow Na^+(aq) + OH^-(aq)$$

So in 1 dm^3 of 0.100 mol dm^{-3} sodium hydroxide solution, there are 0.100 moles of hydroxide ions. We use the ionic product of water to calculate the hydrogen ion concentration.

Stage 1

Calculate [H$^+$] from $K_w = [H^+][OH^-]$:

$$[OH^-] = 0.100 \text{ and, at 298 K,}$$
$$K_w \text{ is } 10^{-14} \text{ mol}^2 \text{ dm}^{-6}$$

$$[H^+] = \frac{K_w}{[OH^-]} = \frac{10^{-14}}{0.100}$$

$$= 10^{-13} \text{ mol dm}^{-3}$$

Stage 2
Calculate pH from $[H^+]$:

$$pH = -\log_{10}[H^+] = -\log_{10}10^{-13} = -(-13)$$
$$= 13$$

The pH of a 0.100 mol dm^{-3} solution of sodium hydroxide at 298 K is 13. Try repeating this calculation for a higher concentration of hydroxide ions. You will see that the pH increases.

11 Calculate the pH of:

a 0.01 mol dm^{-3} sodium hydroxide solution,

b 0.3 mol dm^{-3} potassium hydroxide solution.

key facts

- The pH of a solution is the negative of the log to the base 10 of the hydrogen ion concentration in the solution: $pH = -\log_{10}[H^+]$ mol dm^{-3}.

- Water is weakly ionised in an equilibrium reaction.

- The ionic product of water is the product of the concentrations of hydrogen ions and hydroxide ions in pure water: $K_w = [H^+(aq)][OH^-(aq)]$.

- At 298 K, $K_w = 1 \times 10^{-14}$ mol^2 dm^{-6}.

- K_w changes when temperature changes.

3.6 pK_a values

Values of K_a, the acid dissociation constant, can be very small, so again it would be more convenient to deal with them in the same way that we deal with hydrogen ion concentrations. To make $[H^+]$ values more manageable, the numbers are converted to pH, and in a similar manner K_a values can be converted to pK_a values:

$$\mathbf{pK_a = -\log_{10} K_a}$$

K_a for ethanoic acid is 1.754×10^{-5} mol dm^{-3} at 298 K, so

$$pK_a = -\log_{10} K_a$$
$$= -\log_{10}(1.754 \times 10^{-5})$$
$$= 4.76 \text{ (again, there are no units for } pK_a$$
$$\text{values, because they are logarithms)}$$

12

a Calculate K_a for a 0.01 mol dm^{-3} solution of benzoic acid if:
$[H^+] = 7.94 \times 10^{-4}$ mol dm^{-3}.
$C_6H_5COOH(aq)$
$\rightleftharpoons C_6H_5COO^-(aq) + H^+(aq)$

b Use your answer to **a** to decide whether benzoic acid is a strong or a weak acid.

c Calculate the pK_a value for benzoic acid.

13 Citric acid has a pK_a value of 3.075 (for the first ionisation). For a 0.01 mol dm^{-3} solution of the acid and for this ionisation, calculate:

a K_a

b $[H^+]$

c pH.

14 Which will have the higher pK_a value: a weak acid or a strong acid?

Table 5   pK_a values for some common acids

Acid	K_a (mol dm^{-3})	pK_a	Acid	K_a (mol dm^{-3})	pK_a
HCl	1.0×10^7	−7.00	C_6H_5COOH	6.5×10^{-5}	4.19
HNO_3	4.0×10^1	−1.60	CH_3COOH	1.7×10^{-5}	4.77
HF	5.6×10^{-4}	3.25	C_2H_5COOH	1.3×10^{-5}	4.89
HNO_2	4.7×10^{-4}	3.33	HClO	3.7×10^{-8}	7.43
HCOOH	1.6×10^{-4}	3.80	HCN	4.9×10^{-10}	9.31

- pK_a values are a convenient way of dealing with strengths of weak acids.

- The expression for the pK_a of a weak acid is:

  $$pK_a = -\log_{10} K_a$$

- pK_a values do not have units.

- The acid dissociation constant of a weak acid HA is given by the expression:

  $$K_a = \frac{[A^-(aq)]\,[H^+(aq)]}{[HA(aq)]}$$

- The pH of a weak acid can be calculated from its dissociation constant and its concentration in mol dm^{-3}, using the approximation:

  $$K_a = \frac{[H^+]^2}{[HA]}$$

  and

  $$pH = -\log_{10} [H^+]$$

3.7 pH curves

In a typical titration, an alkaline solution is gradually added to an acid solution (or an acid to an alkali) of known volume or concentration, and containing an indicator. Its change in colour shows when the alkali and acid reach stoichiometric equivalence.

During a laboratory titration, the pH changes as one solution is added to the other. A change in indicator colour signals the **equivalence point** of the titration (also called end-point, but see page 53): this corresponds to the mixing of stoichiometrically equivalent amounts of acid and base. Changes in pH at points before and after equivalence can be measured using a pH meter.

If a base is added to an acid, the pH rises as the acid is neutralised. However, the pH change is not directly proportional to the amount of alkali added. This is seen clearly when a graph of measured pH against quantity of solution added is plotted. It produces a plot known as a **pH curve**.

Shapes of pH curves

Strong acid–strong base

Strong acid–strong base curves look like the ones in Figs 6 and 7. They are simply mirror images of each other, depending upon whether the solution in the flask is an acid or a base. Strong acid–strong base curves are typical of reactions such as:

$$HCl(aq) + NaOH(aq) \rightarrow NaCl(aq) + H_2O(l)$$

Both the acid and the base are fully dissociated, existing as individual aqueous ions. When a small volume of base is added to the acid at the start of the titration, the *proportion* of hydrogen ions removed by that base is quite small

Fig. 6 Strong acid with strong base

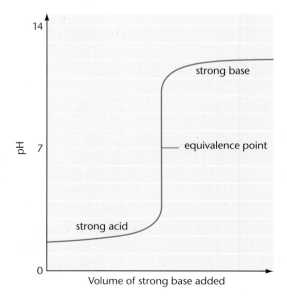

Fig. 7   Strong base with strong acid

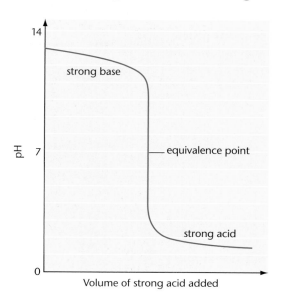

15

a Sketch a pH curve for the titration of a strong base with a weak acid.

b What is the pH at the equivalence point in your diagram?

Fig. 8   Weak acid with strong base

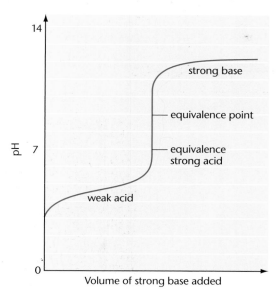

compared to the total amount present. This produces a very small increase in pH. As more base is added, the proportion of hydrogen ions being removed each time (relative to the total number) increases, so there is a larger change in pH. This change is greatest near the equivalence point, where the curve is steepest. The equivalence point for this curve is pH 7, which is the pH of pure water. This is because the salt ions $Na^+(aq)$ and $Cl^-(aq)$ have no acid/base properties and so do not affect the $H^+(aq)$ + $OH^-(aq) \rightleftharpoons H_2O(l)$ equilibrium.

To find the equivalence point on a pH curve, extrapolate the lines at the beginning and end of the curves where the pH is not changing as steeply, then find the midpoint on this vertical section of the graph. The equivalence point for a strong acid with a strong base lies midway between 2 and 12, namely at 7. For a weak acid with a strong base it lies midway between pH 5.8 and 12, namely at 8.9.

All the diagrams for Figs 6 to 10 apply to titrations involving a monobasic acid with a monoacidic base in which one proton only is donated. The first solution in each figure caption is of known concentration and is in the flask, and the second, of unknown concentration, is added from the burette.

Weak acid–strong base

The pH curve for the titration of a weak acid with a strong base (Fig. 8) differs from the curve in Fig. 6.

Consider ethanoic acid reacting with sodium hydroxide:

$$CH_3COOH(aq) + NaOH(aq)$$
$$\rightarrow Na^+(aq) + CH_3COO^-(aq) + H_2O(l)$$

The pH curve starts at a higher pH value, since the weak acid is only slightly dissociated, producing a low $[H^+]$ at equilibrium. The ethanoate ion acts as a weak conjugate base and recombines with $H^+(aq)$ to form $CH_3COOH(aq)$, and the greater the $[CH_3COO^-(aq)]$, the greater is the tendency to do this. This resistance to change in $[H^+]$, despite increasing acid concentration, is called **buffering action** and will be discussed later.

In the titration of strong or weak monobasic acids, where the number of moles of acid is the same, the total number of hydrogen ions that react will be the same because, despite partial dissociation, all the available hydrogens are eventually released to react with a stoichiometric equivalent amount of base. Therefore, strong and weak acids give the same quantities in a calculation, but the pH of the *equivalence point* for weak acid–strong base titrations will have a higher value than for strong acid–strong base titrations: it is greater than 7. After the equivalence point, the curve follows the pattern for a strong acid–strong base titration.

The pH curve for the titration of a strong base with a weak acid is the mirror image and the pH of equivalence is still greater than 7.

Strong acid–weak base

For a strong acid–weak base titration, the curve (Fig. 9) follows the pattern for strong acid initially, but the equivalence point is at a pH of less than 7. The reaction between HCl(aq) and NH_3(aq) shows this:

$$HCl(aq) + NH_3(aq) \rightarrow NH_4^+(aq) + Cl^-(aq) + H_2O(l)$$

Fig. 9   Strong acid with weak base

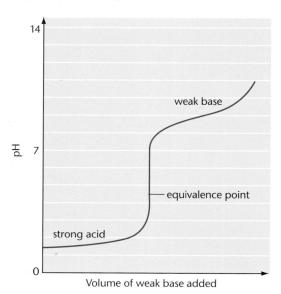

An equilibrium will be set up between the weak base NH_3(aq) and its conjugate acid NH_4^+(aq):

$$H^+(aq) + NH_3(aq) \rightleftharpoons NH_4^+(aq)$$

This increases the concentration of H^+(aq) and lowers the pH compared to that for a strong base solution.

pH curves can be plotted for all the combinations of strong and weak acids with strong and weak bases. For the titration of a weak base with a strong acid (Fig. 10) the curve will start at a high pH but will have an equivalence point with a pH less than that for the titration of a strong base with a strong acid, i.e. less than 7.

Fig. 10   Weak base with strong acid

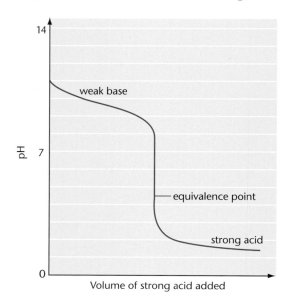

Weak base–weak acid

When a weak base is titrated with a weak acid, the variation in pH with volume of titre is more gradual, and it is not possible to detect an accurate equivalence point (Fig. 11).

Fig 11   Weak base with weak acid

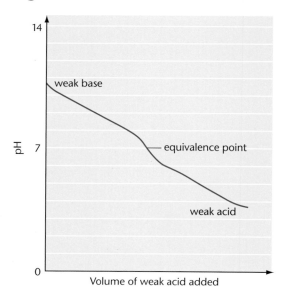

A task sheet and practice questions on the Practical Skills Assessment 'Investigate how pH changes when a weak acid reacts with a strong base or when a strong acid reacts with a weak base' can be found at www.collseducation.co.uk/advancedscienceaqa

● The pH change in an acid–base titration is not directly proportional to the amount of acid or base added.

● The shape of the pH curve for a titration depends on the relative strengths of the acid and base.

● The equivalence point in the titration of an acid with a base (or vice versa) varies according to the relative strengths of the solutions.

Calculating amounts

When the volume of added solution to produce the equivalence point is determined, its concentration can be calculated.

Example: Calculation for strong acid–strong base with a 1 : 1 stoichiometry

Calculate the concentration of sodium hydroxide if 25.0 cm³ of the NaOH solution just neutralises 20.0 cm³ of 0.100 mol dm⁻³ hydrochloric acid solution.

a Calculate the number of moles of the solution of known concentration, HCl(aq): The number of moles of a reacting substance can be calculated using the expression:

$$\begin{array}{c}\text{number of moles}\\\text{in solution}\\\text{(mol)}\end{array} = \begin{array}{c}\text{concentration}\\\text{of solution}\\\text{(mol dm}^{-3}\text{)}\end{array} \times \begin{array}{c}\text{volume of}\\\text{solution}\\\text{(dm}^3\text{)}\end{array}$$

(or $m = C \times V/1\,000$ for volumes in cm³)

$$\begin{array}{c}\text{number of moles}\\\text{of HCl(aq)}\\\text{(mol)}\end{array} = \begin{array}{c}\text{concentration}\\\text{of HCl(aq)}\\\text{(mol dm}^{-3}\text{)}\end{array} \times \begin{array}{c}\text{vol. in cm}^3\text{ of HCl(aq)}\\\hline 1\,000\\\text{(dm}^3\text{)}\end{array}$$

$$= 0.100 \times 20.0/1\,000$$
$$= 0.002 \text{ mol}$$

b Write the equation to find the stoichiometry:

$$\text{HCl(aq)} + \text{NaOH(aq)} \rightarrow \text{NaCl(aq)} + \text{H}_2\text{O(l)}$$

Therefore, 1 mole of HCl(aq) needs 1 mole of NaOH(aq) for neutralisation (stoichiometry is 1 : 1):

$$\text{number of moles of NaOH(aq)} = \text{number of moles of HCl(aq)}$$
$$= 0.002 \text{ mol}$$

c Calculate the concentration of NaOH(aq):

$$\text{concentration of NaOH(aq)} = \frac{\text{number of moles of NaOH(aq)}}{\text{vol. in cm}^3 \text{ NaOH(aq)}/1\,000}$$

$$= \frac{0.002}{0.025}$$

$$= 0.080 \text{ mol dm}^{-3}$$

Example: Calculation for a reaction of strong acid–strong base of 1 : 2 stoichiometry

If 34.0 cm³ of 0.125 mol dm⁻³ sodium hydroxide just neutralises 25.0 cm³ of sulfuric acid, calculate the concentration of the acid.

a Calculate the number of moles of alkali:

$$\text{number of moles} = \text{concentration} \times \text{volume in cm}^3/1\,000$$

$$= 0.125 \times 34.0/1\,000$$
$$= 4.25 \times 10^{-3} \text{ mol}$$

b Use the balanced equation to find the stoichiometry of the reaction:

$$2\text{NaOH(aq)} + \text{H}_2\text{SO}_4\text{(aq)} \rightarrow \text{Na}_2\text{SO}_4\text{(aq)} + \text{H}_2\text{O(l)}$$
ratio $2\text{NaOH(aq)} : 1\text{H}_2\text{SO}_4\text{(aq)}$

c Calculate the number of moles of acid required to neutralise 1 mole of base:

$$\begin{array}{c}\text{number of moles}\\\text{of acid}\end{array} = \begin{array}{c}0.5 \times \text{number of moles}\\\text{of alkali}\end{array}$$

$$= 0.5 \times 4.25 \times 10^{-3} \text{ mol}$$
$$= 2.125 \times 10^{-3} \text{ mol}$$

d Calculate the concentration of the acid:

$$\text{number of moles} = \text{concentration} \times \text{volume in cm}^3/1\,000$$

$$\text{concentration} = \frac{\text{number of moles}}{\text{vol. in cm}^3/1\,000}$$
$$= 2.125 \times 10^{-3}/0.025$$

concentration of the sulfuric acid =
$$0.085 \text{ mol dm}^{-3}$$

pH calculations

Strong acid–strong base titrations

When calculating the pH of a solution at a point during a titration *which is not the equivalence point*, use the equations in the worked examples above. The procedure is as follows:

• Find the number of moles of H⁺ and OH⁻ present from both solutions in the mixture.

- Decide which one is in excess.
- Calculate the total volume of solution present.
- Calculate the concentration of the component in excess.
- Calculate the $[H^+]$ (if OH^- is in excess use $K_w = [H^+] [OH^-] = 10^{-14}$).
- Calculate the pH.

Example: Calculating pH for strong acid–strong base

Calculate the pH in the titration of 20.0 cm^3 of 0.15 mol dm^{-3} HCl(aq) at the point when 10.0 cm^3 of 0.20 mol dm^{-3} of NaOH(aq) have been added.

Calculate the number of moles of H^+ present in the original solution:

$$\text{number of moles} = 0.15 \times 20.0/1\,000$$
$$= 0.003 \text{ mol}$$

Calculate the number of moles of OH^- added to the original solution:

$$\text{number of moles} = 0.20 \times 10.0/1\,000$$
$$= 0.002 \text{ mol}$$

Calculate the number of moles in excess:

$$\text{number of moles} = 0.003 - 0.002$$
$$= 0.001 \text{ mol } (H^+ \text{ is in excess here})$$

The total volume of solution is:
20.0 + 10.0 = 30.0 cm^3.

Calculate the concentration of the H^+ in excess:

$$[H^+] = 0.001/0.030$$
$$= 0.033 \text{ mol dm}^{-3}$$
$$pH = -\log_{10}[H^+] = -\log_{10} 0.033$$
$$= 1.48$$

Example: Calculating pH for strong diprotic acid–strong base

Calculate the pH in the titration of 25.0 cm^3 of 0.150 mol dm^{-3} of NaOH(aq) at the point when 10.5 cm^3 of 0.12 mol dm^{-3} ethanedioic acid $H_2C_2O_4$(aq) (a diprotic acid) have been added.

Calculate the number of moles of OH^- present in the original solution:

$$\text{number of moles} = 0.15 \times 25.0/1\,000$$
$$= 0.003\,75 \text{ mol}$$

Calculate the number of moles of H^+ added to the original solution (remember: there are two H^+ per molecule of acid):

$$\text{number of moles} = 2 \times 0.120 \times 10.5/1\,000$$
$$= 0.002\,52 \text{ mol}$$

Calculate the number of moles in excess:

$$\text{number of moles} = 0.003\,75 - 0.002\,52$$
$$= 0.001\,23 \text{ mol } (OH^- \text{ is in excess here})$$

The total volume of solution is
25.0 + 10.5 = 35.5 cm^3.

Calculate the concentration of the OH^- in excess:

$$[OH^-] = 0.001\,23/0.035\,5$$
$$= 0.034\,7 \text{ mol dm}^{-3}$$
$$[H^+] = 10^{-14}/[OH^-] = 10^{-14}/0.034\,7$$
$$= 2.882 \times 10^{-13}$$
$$pH = -\log_{10} [H^+] = -\log_{10} 2.882 \times 10^{-13}$$
$$= 12.54$$

Weak acid–strong base titrations

The calculations for these examples are similar but will depend on how far the titration has progressed.

- If the weak acid is in excess, the relative proportions of HA and A^- have to be determined using K_a.
- If the strong base is in excess, the calculation is similar to that in strong acid–strong base titrations (see above).

Example: Calculating pH for weak acid–strong base

Calculate the pH in the titration when 10.0 cm^3 of 0.20 mol dm^{-3} NaOH(aq) have been added to 30.0 cm^3 of 0.15 mol dm^{-3} CH$_3$COOH(aq). $K_a = 1.76 \times 10^{-5}$ mol dm^{-3}.

Calculate the number of moles of CH$_3$COOH present in the original solution:

$$\text{number of moles} = 0.15 \times 30.0/1\,000$$
$$= 0.004\,5 \text{ mol}$$

Calculate the number of moles of OH^- added to the original solution:

$$\text{number of moles} = 0.20 \times 10.0/1\,000$$
$$= 0.002 \text{ mol (this is also the number of moles of CH}_3\text{COO}^- \text{ formed)}$$

Calculate the number of moles in excess:

number of moles $=$ 0.004 5 – 0.002
$=$ 0.002 5 mol
($CH_3COOH(aq)$ is in excess here)

Since both CH_3COOH remaining and the CH_3COO^- formed are in the same total volume of solution, then:

concentration ratio $=$ mole ratio (there is no need to calculate the total volume)

$$[H^+] = \frac{K_a \times [CH_3COOH]}{[CH_3COO^-]}$$

$$= \frac{1.76 \times 10^{-5} \times 0.002\,5}{0.002}$$

$$= 2.200 \times 10^{-5} \text{ mol dm}^{-3}$$

$$pH = -\log_{10}[H^+] = -\log_{10} 2.200 \times 10^{-5}$$
$$= 4.66$$

Example: Calculating pH for weak acid–strong base

Calculate the pH in the titration of 25.0 cm³ of 0.150 mol dm⁻³ $NaOH(aq)$ at the point when 10.5 cm³ of 0.12 mol dm⁻³ CH_3COOH have been added.

Calculate the number of moles of OH^- present in the original solution:

number of moles $=$ 0.15 × 25.0/1 000
$=$ 0.003 75 mol

Calculate the number of moles of CH_3COOH added to the original solution:

number of moles $=$ 0.120 × 10.5/1 000
$=$ 0.001 26 mol

Calculate the number of moles in excess:

number of moles $=$ 0.003 75 – 0.001 26
$=$ 0.002 49 mol (OH^- in excess)

Since the strong base is in excess, the calculation is just the same as for strong acid–strong base. The total volume of solution is 25.0 + 10.5 = 35.5 cm³.

Calculate the concentration of the OH^- in excess:

$$[OH^-] = 0.002\,49/0.035\,5$$
$$= 0.070\,1 \text{ mol dm}^{-3}$$

$$[H^+] = 10^{-14}/[OH^-] = 10^{-14}/0.070\,1$$
$$= 1.427 \times 10^{-13} \text{ mol dm}^{-3}$$

$$pH = -\log_{10}[H^+] = -\log_{10} 1.427 \times 10^{-13}$$
$$= 12.85$$

Indicators

Acid–base indicators are solutions that show a colour change at a particular range of $[H^+]$ changes.

Indicators are weak acids (usually written HIn) where the dissociated form (In⁻) and undissociated forms (HIn) have different colours. There is an equilibrium for this reaction:

$$HIn \rightleftharpoons H^+ + In^-$$

If acid is added or neutralised during a titration, then $[H^+]$ changes and this will affect the indicator equilibrium. The indicator should change colour over a narrow pH range. The most significant change in $[H^+]$ in a titration is at the equivalence point, so you need the indicator to change from almost completely one colour to the other when there is this large change in pH. The colour of at least one form of the indicator needs to be quite intense, so that only a small amount (2–3 drops) needs to be used to give a clearly visible change without significantly affecting the $[H^+]$ itself.

When the concentrations of the acid and base forms of the indicator are equal, then this is referred to as the **end-point** of the titration. The **equivalence point** is not necessarily the same, but the indicator will give the most precise result for the titration when the two (end-point and equivalence point) coincide.

Choosing indicators for titrations

Different indicators change colour at different pH values (Table 6). This property can be used to select a suitable indicator for a particular titration. A suitable indicator must change colour in the pH range that corresponds to the steep part of the pH curve. Here there is a marked change in the pH, so that the indicator will change colour completely. The best way to do this is to look at the pH curve for the particular titration and choose one where the pH range of activity for the indicator matches the equivalence point for the titration (see Figs 10 and 11).

Table 6   Colour changes for some indicators

Indicator	Colour in acid (HIn)	Colour in alkali (In⁻)	pH range for colour change
methyl orange	red	yellow	2.9–4.0
methyl red	red	yellow	4.2–6.3
litmus	red	blue	5.0–8.0
bromothymol blue	yellow	blue	6.0–7.6
phenol red	yellow	red	6.6–8.0
thymol blue	yellow	blue	9.1–9.6
phenolphthalein	colourless	purple	8.2–10.0
alizarin yellow	yellow	red	10.1–12.0

For the titration of a strong acid with a strong base, any of the indicators in Table 6 would be suitable, because the steep part of the pH curve runs from pH 2 to pH 12 and all the indicators fall in this range.

For a weak acid being titrated with a strong base, the pH at equivalence is 8.8. This applies for solutions of 0.1 mol dm⁻³ ethanoic acid with 0.1 mol dm⁻³ sodium hydroxide. An indicator such as methyl orange changes colour in the pH range 2.9–4.0 and would not be suitable since it would change colour

Fig. 12   Titration curves for a strong acid and a weak acid with strong base

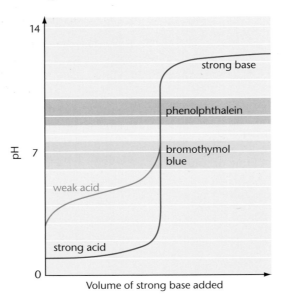

Fig. 13   Titration curves for a strong base and a weak base with a strong acid

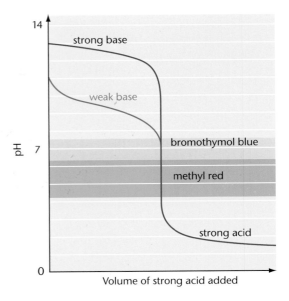

before equivalence is reached. The most suitable indicator in the list would be phenolphthalein, which changes colour between pH 8.2 and 10.0.

The pH equivalence for a strong base with a strong acid is 7, so again any indicator would be suitable. For a weak base with a strong acid, for example 0.1 mol dm⁻³ aqueous ammonia acid with 0.1 mol dm⁻³ hydrochloric acid, the pH at equivalence is 5.2, so methyl red (pH range 4.2–6.3) would be the most suitable.

16 a Choose a suitable indicator for the following titrations (use Tables 6 and 7 to help you):

   i   adding ammonia (weak base) to nitric acid (strong acid)

   ii   adding potassium hydroxide (strong base) to ethanoic acid (weak acid)

   iii   adding ammonia to ethanoic acid.

b   Sketch the pH curve for each titration.

Table 7 shows the pH at equivalence for a range of titrations using 1 mol dm⁻³ solutions. The curve in Fig. 11 shows that during the titration of a weak acid with a weak base the change in pH is so gradual that this reaction cannot be used in the quantitative estimation of concentration.

Table 7   pH range at equivalence

Acid	Base	pH range at equivalence	Suitable indicators
HCl (strong)	NaOH (strong)	3–11	any: the pH change is over a very wide range
CH₃COOH (weak)	NaOH (strong)	7–11	any from phenol red downwards
HCl (strong)	NH₃ (weak)	3–7	methyl orange and methyl red
CH₃COOH (weak)	NH₃ (weak)	no sharp change	no suitable indicator, as there is no sharp change; even a pH meter will be of no use
HCl (strong)	Na₂CO₃ (dibasic)	2.5–5.5	methyl orange or methyl red
		6.5–9.5	phenol red or phenolphthalein
H₂C₂O₄ (diprotic acid)	NaOH (strong)	1.5–3.5	methyl orange, but only just in range; a pH meter is better
		5–11	any from bromothymol blue downwards

● An indicator can be used to determine the equivalence point in a titration.

● The end-point of a titration is where [HIn] = [In⁻].

● Different indicators change colour over different pH ranges.

● Indicators change colour over a narrow pH range.

● pH curves must be used to select a suitable indicator for a particular titration.

● The equation:

$$\text{number of moles in a solution (mol)} = \text{conc. of solution (mol dm}^{-3}) \times \text{volume of solution (dm}^{3})$$

can be used to calculate concentrations and volumes in titrations.

● Some bases can accept more than one hydrogen ion, to act consecutively as multiple Brønsted–Lowry bases, e.g. sodium carbonate; the titration of such a base with a monoprotic acid produces a pH curve with more than one equivalence point.

● Diprotic acids have two hydrogen ion donating groups in each molecule, so they act consecutively as two Brønsted–Lowry acids; the titration of such an acid with a monoprotic base produces a pH curve with two equivalence points.

3.8 Buffer solutions

A solution that can resist a change in pH when small amounts of acid or base are added is called a **buffer**.

Even though there are many different buffers, they all work according to the same principle. Generally, buffers contain either:

- weak acid and a large amount of a strong base salt of the acid (an acid buffer), e.g. ethanoic acid with sodium ethanoate; or
- weak base and a large amount of a strong acid salt of the base (an alkaline buffer), e.g. ammonia with ammonium chloride.

The buffering action works because the weak acid or base maintains a store of associated ions (e.g. ethanoate or ammonium) which are released to stabilise pH.

A mixture of ethanoic acid (CH_3COOH) and ethanoate (CH_3COO^-) has a buffering action. Ethanoic acid, written here as HAc, is a weak acid ('Ac' = 'acetate' from the old name for the acid), while sodium ethanoate dissociates completely in aqueous solution:

$$HAc(aq) + H_2O(l) \rightleftharpoons Ac^-(aq) + H_3O^+(aq)$$
$$NaAc(aq) \rightarrow Na^+(aq) + Ac^-(aq)$$

An acid buffer normally contains relatively high concentrations of both undissociated acid and acid anions (conjugate base).

We can write the acid dissociation constant:

$$K_a = \frac{[Ac^-(aq)]\,[H_3O^+(aq)]}{[HAc(aq)]}$$

Note that $[H_2O]$ is incorporated in K_a.

The presence of ethanoate ions pushes the ethanoic acid equilibrium towards undissociated acid:

$$HAc(aq) + H_2O(l) \rightleftharpoons Ac^-(aq) + H_3O^+(aq)$$

$Ac^-(aq)$ present in large amounts from the salt drives the equilibrium to the left.

If acid is added to the buffer, the equilibrium adjusts, as H_3O^+ combines with some of the large amount of Ac^- to give more undissociated acid:

$$HAc(aq) + H_2O(l) \rightleftharpoons Ac^-(aq) + H_3O^+(aq)$$
$$\leftarrow \text{equilibrium moves to the left}$$

If alkali is added to the buffer, the equilibrium adjusts, as $OH^-(aq)$ reacts with $H_3O^+(aq)$, neutralising it, while some of the large amount of HAc present dissociates to give more H_3O^+:

$$HAc(aq) + H_2O(l) \rightleftharpoons Ac^-(aq) + H_3O^+(aq)$$
$$\text{equilibrium moves to the right} \rightarrow$$

The buffer maintains the equilibrium reaction and the pH remains steady, except in the presence of large quantities of acid or alkali. K_a remains constant throughout.

K_a can be used to show that $[H^+]$ remains fairly constant.

$$K_a = \frac{[Ac^-(aq)]\,[H_3O^+(aq)]}{[HAc(aq)]}$$

$$[H_3O^+(aq)] = \frac{K_a \times [HAc(aq)]}{[Ac^-(aq)]}$$

If both $[Ac^-(aq)]$ and $[HAc(aq)]$ are large, then small changes in their concentrations will not affect the overall ratio significantly, so $[H_3O^+(aq)]$ remains fairly constant.

If equal amounts of salt and acid are present (half-neutralisation) in the buffer, then $[Ac^-(aq)] = [HAc(aq)]$ and:

$$K_a = \frac{\cancel{[Ac^-(aq)]}\,[H_3O^+(aq)]}{\cancel{[HAc(aq)]}} = [H_3O^+(aq)]$$

so:

$$pK_a \text{ (of the acid)} = pH \text{ (of the buffer)}.$$

Calculating buffer pH

The pH of a buffer mixture containing 0.2 mol dm^{-3} of ethanoate ions and 0.25 mol dm^{-3} ethanoic acid, $K_a = 1.76 \times 10^{-5}$, can be calculated as follows:

$$K_a = \frac{[Ac^-(aq)]\,[H_3O^+(aq)]}{[HAc(aq)]}$$

$$[H_3O^+(aq)] = \frac{1.76 \times 10^{-5} \times 0.25}{0.2}$$

$$= 2.20 \times 10^{-5}$$

$$pH = 4.66$$

Example: Calculating buffer pH

Calculate the pH of a buffer made by mixing 35.0 cm^3 of 2.0 mol dm^{-3} ethanoic acid, $K_a = 1.76 \times 10^{-5}$, with 30.0 cm^3 of 1.5 mol dm^{-3} sodium ethanoate.

$$\text{number of moles of HAc} = 2.0 \times 35.0/1\,000$$
$$= 0.070 \text{ mol}$$

$$\text{number of moles of Ac}^- = 1.5 \times 30.0/1\,000$$
$$= 0.045 \text{ mol}$$

Using the expression above:

$$[H_3O^+(aq)] = \frac{K_a \times [HAc(aq)]}{[Ac^-(aq)]}$$

$$= \frac{1.76 \times 10^{-5} \times 0.070}{0.045}$$

$$= 2.738 \times 10^{-5}$$

$$pH = -\log_{10}[H^+]$$
$$= -\log_{10} 2.738 \times 10^{-5}$$
$$= 4.56$$

17

a Explain how an NH$_3$/NH$_4$Cl buffer works.

b Calculate the pH of a propanoic acid/propanoate buffer containing 0.2 mol dm^{-3} salt and 0.05 mol dm^{-3} acid, $K_a = 1.3 \times 10^{-5}$.

18 Calculate the pH of a buffer made by mixing 25.0 cm^3 of 2.0 mol dm^{-3} propanoic acid, $K_a = 1.34 \times 10^{-5}$, with 20.0 cm^3 of 1.5 mol dm^{-3} sodium propanoate.

key facts

● A buffer solution is a mixture that is resistant to changes in pH. Buffers do this by accepting or releasing hydrogen ions.

● Low-pH buffers contain a weak acid and the strong base salt of a weak acid.

● High-pH buffers contain a weak base and the strong acid salt of a weak base.

3.9 Applications of buffers

A common use for buffers in school laboratories is to standardise a pH meter. This is done to make sure the pH meter is giving you an accurate result. The pH meter is often standardised using an acidic buffer and a basic buffer. Strictly speaking you should use a buffer whose pH is either side of the pH of the test solution. pH meters can often read to 0.01 pH units, so they are much more precise than indicators.

As well as being used to calibrate pH meters, buffers are used in hair colouring products. A buffer is used to maintain the high pH of the solution that will modify the hair's structure.

Many biological processes such as fermentation use buffers to maintain optimum conditions, so that the enzymes can operate as efficiently as possible. Buffer solutions are also used in a range of medical treatments where the buffer is set at a pH to make the cell walls more permeable, which then allows particular chemicals into the cell to modify the biological processes taking place.

The pH of this solution is quite high so it uses an ammonia–ammonium salt buffer.

A pH meter must be standardised using buffer solutions before it is used to measure the pH of this swimming pool.

If you wear contact lenses then the cleaning solution may have a buffer solution in it to maintain a constant pH of approximately 7.2 on the surface of your eye.

1 Give all values of pH to two decimal places.

a The dissociation of water can be represented by the following equilibrium:

$$H_2O(l) \rightleftharpoons H^+(aq) + OH^-(aq)$$

   i Write an expression for the ionic product of water, K_w

   ii The pH of a sample of pure water is 6.63 at 50 °C. Calculate the concentration in mol dm^{-3} of H$^+$ ions in this sample of pure water.

   iii Deduce the concentration in mol dm^{-3} of OH$^-$ ions in this sample of pure water.

   iv Calculate the value of K_w at this temperature.   (4)

b At 25 °C the value of K_w is 1.00×10^{-14} mol^2 dm^{-6}. Calculate the pH of a 0.136 mol dm^{-3} solution of KOH at 25 °C.   (2)

Total 6

AQA, January 2008, Unit 4, Question 1

2 Give all values of pH to two decimal places.
The acid dissociation constant, K_a, for propanoic acid has the value 1.35×10^{-5} mol dm^{-3} at 25 °C:

$$K_a = \frac{[H^+] \, [CH_3CH_2COO^-]}{[CH_3CH_2COOH]}$$

a Calculate the pH of a 0.169 mol dm^{-3} solution of propanoic acid.   (3)

b A buffer solution contains 0.250 mol of propanoic acid and 0.190 mol of sodium propanoate in 1 000 cm^3 of solution. A 0.015 mol sample of solid sodium hydroxide is then added to this buffer solution.

   i Write an equation for the reaction of propanoic acid with sodium hydroxide.

   ii Calculate the number of moles of propanoic acid and of propanoate ions present in the buffer solution after the addition of the sodium hydroxide.

   iii Hence, calculate the pH of the buffer solution after the addition of the sodium hydroxide.   (6)

Total 9

AQA, January 2008, Unit 4, Question 2

3 When answering this question, assume that the temperature is 298 K and give all pH values to two decimal places. The acid dissociation constant, K_a, of propanoic acid, CH_3CH_2COOH has the value 1.35×10^{-5} mol dm^{-3}:

$$K_a = \frac{[H^+] \, [CH_3CH_2COO^-]}{[CH_3CH_2COOH]}$$

a Calculate the pH of a 0.550 mol dm^{-3} solution of propanoic acid.   (3)

b A buffer solution is formed when 10.0 cm^3 of 0.230 mol dm^{-3} aqueous sodium hydroxide is added to 30.0 cm^3 of 0.550 mol dm^{-3} aqueous propanoic acid.

   i Calculate the number of moles of propanoic acid originally present.

   ii Calculate the number of moles of sodium hydroxide added.

   iii Hence, calculate the number of moles of propanoic acid present in the buffer solution.

   iv Hence, calculate the pH of the buffer solution.   (6)

Total 9

AQA, June 2007, Unit 4, Question 3

4 In this question, give all pH and pK_a values to two decimal places.

a Hydrochloric acid is described as a strong Brønsted-Lowry acid.

   i State what is meant by the term *Brønsted-Lowry acid*.

   ii State why hydrochloric acid is described as *strong*.   (2)

b A sample of hydrochloric acid contains 7.05×10^{-3} mol of hydrogen chloride in 50 cm^3 of solution.

   i Calculate the concentration, in mol dm^{-3}, of this hydrochloric acid.

   ii Write an expression for the term *pH*.

   iii Calculate the pH of this hydrochloric acid.

   iv When water is added to this 50 cm^3 sample of acid the pH increases. Calculate the total volume of the solution when the pH becomes exactly 1.00.   (6)

c The value of the acid dissociation constant, K_a, for the weak acid HX is 6.10×10^{-5} mol dm^{-3} at 25 °C.

   i Write an expression for the acid dissociation constant, K_a, for the acid HX.

   ii Calculate the pH of a 0.255 mol dm^{-3} solution of HX at 25 °C.   (4)

d A given volume of a buffer solution contains 6.85×10^{-3} mol of the weak acid HY and 2.98×10^{-3} mol of the salt NaY. The pH of the buffer solution is 3.78.

   i Calculate the value of pK_a for the acid HY at this temperature.

   ii State and explain the effect on the pH of the buffer solution when a small amount of hydrochloric acid is added.   (7)

Total 19

AQA, January 2007, Unit 4, Question 3

5

a A sample of hydrochloric acid has a pH of 2.34. Write an expression for pH and calculate the concentration of this acid.   (2)

b A 0.150 mol dm^{-3} solution of a weak acid, HX, also has a pH of 2.34.

i   Write an expression for the acid dissociation constant, K_a, for the acid HX.

ii   Calculate the value of K_a for this acid and state its units.

iii   Calculate the value of pK_a for the acid HX. Give your answer to two decimal places.   (5)

c   A 30.0 cm³ sample of a 0.480 mol dm⁻³ solution of potassium hydroxide was partially neutralised by the addition of 18.0 cm³ of a 0.350 mol dm⁻³ solution of sulfuric acid.

i   Calculate the initial number of moles of potassium hydroxide.

ii   Calculate the number of moles of sulfuric acid added.

iii   Calculate the number of moles of potassium hydroxide remaining in excess in the solution formed.

iv   Calculate the concentration of hydroxide ions in the solution formed.

v   Hence calculate the pH of the solution formed. Give your answer to two decimal places.   (6)

Total 13

AQA, June 2006, Unit 4, Question 3

6 Give all pH values to two decimal places.

a   i   Write expressions for the ionic product of water, K_w, and for pH.

ii   At 318 K, the value of K_w is 4.02×10^{-14} mol² dm⁻⁶ and hence the pH of pure water is 6.70.
State why pure water is not acidic at 318 K.

iii   Calculate the number of moles of sodium hydroxide in 2.00 cm³ of 0.500 mol dm⁻³ aqueous sodium hydroxide.

iv   Use the value of K_w given above and your answer to part **a iii** to calculate the pH of the solution formed when 2.00 cm³ of 0.500 mol dm⁻³ aqueous sodium hydroxide are added to 998 cm³ of pure water at 318 K.   (6)

b   At 298 K, the acid dissociation constant, K_a, for propanoic acid, CH_3CH_2COOH, has the value 1.35×10^{-5} mol dm⁻³.

i   Write an expression for K_a for propanoic acid.

ii   Calculate the pH of 0.125 mol dm⁻³ aqueous propanoic acid at 298 K.   (4)

c   Sodium hydroxide reacts with propanoic acid as shown in the following equation:

$$NaOH + CH_3CH_2COOH \rightarrow CH_3CH_2COONa + H_2O$$

A buffer solution is formed when sodium hydroxide is added to an excess of aqueous propanoic acid.

i   Calculate the number of moles of propanoic acid in 50.0 cm³ of 0.125 mol dm⁻³ aqueous propanoic acid.

ii   Use your answers to part **a iii** and part **c i** to calculate the number of moles of propanoic acid in the buffer solution formed when 2.00 cm³ of 0.500 mol dm⁻³ aqueous sodium hydroxide are added to 50.0 cm³ of 0.125 mol dm⁻³ aqueous propanoic acid.

iii   Hence calculate the pH of this buffer solution at 298 K.   (6)

Total 16

AQA, January 2006, Unit 4, Question 2

7

a   Titration curves labelled A, B, C and D for combinations of different acids and bases are shown below. All solutions have a concentration of 0.1 mol dm⁻³.

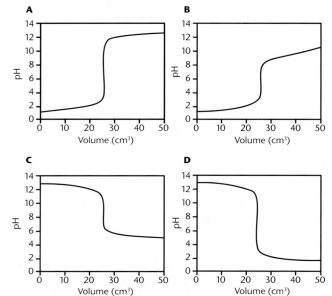

i   From **A**, **B**, **C** and **D**, select the curve produced by the addition of:
  • ammonia to 25 cm³ of hydrochloric acid
  • ethanoic acid to 25 cm³ of sodium hydroxide
  • sodium hydroxide to 25 cm³ of hydrochloric acid.

ii   A table of acid–base indicators and the pH ranges over which they change colour is shown below.

Indicator	pH range
thymol blue	1.2–2.8
bromophenol blue	3.0–4.6
methyl red	4.2–6.3
cresolphthalein	8.2–9.8
thymolphthalein	9.3–10.5

From the table, select an indicator which could be used in the titration which produces curve **A** but not in the titration which produces curve **B**.   (4)

b i Write an expression for the term *pH*.

ii A solution of potassium hydroxide has a pH of 11.90 at 25 °C. Calculate the concentration of potassium hydroxide in the solution. (4)

c The acid dissociation constant, K_a, for propanoic acid has the value of 1.35×10^{-5} mol dm^{-3} at 25 °C:

$$K_a = \frac{[H^+]\,[CH_3CH_2COO^-]}{[CH_3CH_2COOH]}$$

In each of the calculations below, give your answer to two decimal places.

i Calculate the pH of a 0.117 mol dm^{-3} aqueous solution of propanoic acid.

ii Calculate the pH of a mixture formed by adding 25 cm^3 of 0.117 mol dm^{-3} aqueous solution of sodium propanoate to 25 cm^3 of a 0.117 mol dm^{-3} aqueous solution of propanoic acid. (5)

Total 13

AQA, June 2005, Unit 4, Question 2

8 This question concerns the weak acid, ethanoic acid, for which the acid dissociation constant, K_a, has a value of 1.74×10^{-5} mol dm^{-3} at 25 °C:

$$K_a = \frac{[H^+]\,[CH_3COO^-]}{[CH_3COOH]}$$

In each of the calculations below, give your answer to two decimal places.

a Calculate the pH of a 0.150 mol dm^{-3} solution of ethanoic acid. (4)

b A buffer solution is prepared by mixing a solution of ethanoic acid with a solution of sodium ethanoate.

i Explain what is meant by the term *buffer solution*.

ii Write an equation for the reaction which occurs when a small amount of hydrochloric acid is added to this buffer solution. (3)

c In a buffer solution, the concentration of ethanoic acid is 0.150 mol dm^{-3} and the concentration of sodium ethanoate is 0.100 mol dm^{-3}.

i Calculate the pH of this buffer solution.

ii A 10.0 cm^3 portion of 1.00 mol dm^{-3} hydrochloric acid is added to 1 000 cm^3 of this buffer solution. Calculate the number of moles of ethanoic acid and the number of moles of sodium ethanoate in the solution after addition of the hydrochloric acid. Hence, find the pH of this new solution. (8)

Total 15

AQA, January 2005, Unit 4, Question 8

9 The pH curve shown below was obtained when a 0.150 mol dm^{-3} solution of sodium hydroxide was added to 25.0 cm^3 of aqueous solution of weak monoprotic acid, HA.

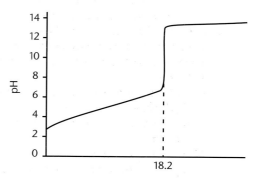

Volume of 0.150 mol dm^{-3}
NaOH added (cm^3)

a Use the information given to calculate the concentration of the acid. (2)

b i Write an expression for the acid dissociation constant, K_a, for HA.

ii Write an expression for pK_a.

iii Using your answers to parts **b i** and **b ii**, show that when sufficient sodium hydroxide has been added to neutralise half of the acid:

pH of the solution = pK_a for the acid HA. (4)

c Explain why dilution with a small volume of water does not affect the pH of a buffer solution. (2)

Total 8

AQA, June 2005, Unit 5, Question 2 (a–c)

10 Chromium(III) ions are weakly acidic in aqueous solution as shown by the following equation:

$$[Cr(H_2O)_6]^{3+}(aq) \rightleftharpoons [Cr(H_2O)_5(OH)]^{2+}(aq) + H^+(aq)$$

The value of K_a for this reaction is 1.15×10^{-4} mol dm^{-3}. Calculate the pH of a 0.500 mol dm^{-3} solution of $[Cr(H_2O)_6]^{3+}(aq)$. (5)

Total 5

AQA, June 2007, Unit 5, Question 3 (c)

how science works **assignment**

Storing carbon dioxide

Much of the carbon dioxide we release into the atmosphere from the combustion of fuels is absorbed by dissolving in the oceans. It is thought that as much as 35%–50% is absorbed in this way. As the amount of CO_2 in the atmosphere rises, more of the gas reacts with seawater to produce hydrogencarbonate and hydrogen ions, increasing the acidity of the surface layer of water.

An equilibrium is set up (see Fig. 14). If CO_2 in the atmosphere increases, more will dissolve:

$$CO_2(g) \rightleftharpoons CO_2(aq)$$

Some CO_2 reacts with water and is removed from the equilibrium. More dissolves to maintain the equilibrium.

The oceans are effective at controlling the pH, as they act as a giant buffer solution. They will release or absorb $H^+(aq)$ as the conditions change. We can regard dissolved carbon dioxide as carbonic acid – a weak acid:

$$CO_2(aq) + H_2O(l) \rightleftharpoons H_2CO_3(aq) \rightleftharpoons H^+(aq) + HCO_3^-(aq)$$

A high concentration of H_2CO_3 is available. HCO_3^- is available in almost limitless supply. Therefore, this reaction acts as a buffer:

$$HCO_3^-(aq) \rightleftharpoons H^+(aq) + CO_3^{2-}(aq)$$

Any removal of H^+ or CO_3^{2-} ions from solution will cause more CO_2 to dissolve (the equilibria are shifted to the right). As a result, through time, many marine organisms have evolved to build protective shells of insoluble calcium

carbonate. Hence shells provide another way of mopping up carbon dioxide and keeping the composition of the atmosphere constant:

$$Ca^{2+} + CO_3^{2-} \rightleftharpoons CaCO_3(s)$$

The atmospheric level of carbon dioxide has risen from about 280 ppm in pre-industrial times to about 380 ppm today, and it is still rising. If CO_2 emissions continue as at present, then the pH of the oceans is predicted to drop by approximately 0.5 units by 2100, giving a three-fold increase in H^+ ions since pre-industrial times. Average pH has dropped from 8.3 to 8.1. Climate change may be veering out of control before we understand the consequences, say scientists studying the world's oceans.

Atmospheric CO_2 has risen well above 2 000 ppm several times in the past 300 million years. Ken Caldeira says this never pushed ocean pH below 7.5 because carbonate rocks on the seafloor act as a natural buffer, limiting seawater's acidity. That process takes 10 000 years or so but there is not enough time to deal with the more rapid changes caused by human activity.

Lowering the pH of seawater ultimately results in a decrease in the concentration of CO_3^{2-}. It is not clear yet what such a dramatic change in acidity would do to ocean life. But acidity tends to dissolve carbonate, so the most vulnerable creatures will be those with calcium carbonate shells or exoskeletons, such as corals, molluscs and some algae. Meanwhile, satellite measurements of chlorophyll

Fig. 14

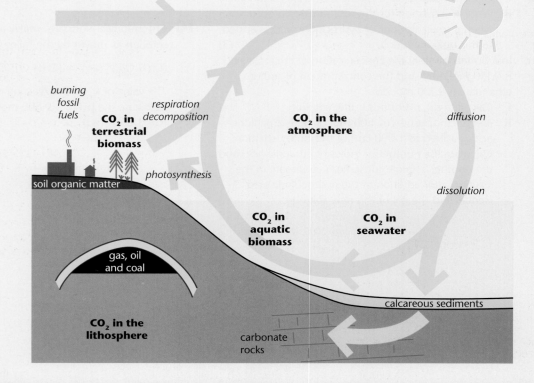

levels in the open ocean show that primary productivity – the amount of new biomass being produced from carbon dioxide by photosynthesis – has dropped sharply in the past couple of decades. As increasingly large amounts of CO_2 become absorbed in the oceans, then their ability to act as a buffer is lessened.

Change in the acidity of the oceans will affect sea life.

'We are changing the chemistry of the ocean and we don't know what it's going to do' says Ken Caldeira, a climate specialist at Lawrence Livermore National Laboratory in California.

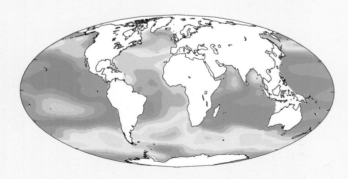

Δ sea–surface pH [–]

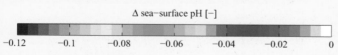

-0.12   -0.1   -0.08   -0.06   -0.04   -0.02   0

Change in sea–surface pH caused by anthropogenic CO_2 between the 1700s and the 1990s.

Summary

Increased emissions of carbon dioxide (CO_2) are causing the oceans to become more acidic.

To date, the oceans have absorbed approximately half of the carbon emitted into the environment by human activity.

The ability of the oceans to continue to absorb carbon dioxide is not well understood.

Increasing carbon acidity could have a significant impact on many marine organisms, specifically calcifying organisms and larger aquatic animals. The effects of ocean acidification on these and other organisms is not completely known.

There are other indirect effects. In the oceans, metals can be in either complexed or free dissolved forms and the equilibrium is pH dependent. Decreasing the pH of the oceans is anticipated to result in an increase in the concentration of free metals, which are considered to be toxic. Predicting the impact of this change is highly problematic though, with the role of trace elements in aquatic biochemical processes still an area of ongoing research.

Clearly much more research is needed and key questions that may need to be addressed include:

- How will CO_2 absorption by the oceans be affected in the future by current absorption and by increased global temperatures?

- Do climate change models need to be addressed with regards to changes in rates of CO_2 absorption?

- What research needs to be done to identify the effects on marine life?

A1

s&c

Prepare a report for a committee, an article or podcast for a science magazine or a PowerPoint presentation for a meeting, summarising the issues about the possible effects of climate change on the oceans.

You can use the article plus your own research to present your arguments.

You should explain the underlying chemistry involved.

You should present any arguments for change and further research, and highlight areas of scientific uncertainty.

4 Naming organic compounds and isomerism

Fig. 1 IUPAC rules enable chemists to name any organic compound

2,6-dimethyl-4,4-diethylcyclohexanone: I'd recognise this anywhere.

What's in a name

You are unique, as described by your fingerprints or your DNA code. However, your name, individual physical characteristics and individual personality traits are not unique. Other people will have the same name; other people will also, for example, have blue eyes and a friendly personality.

Compounds used to be given trivial names, which would often have their roots in the common language or from alchemy. Originally the same substance might have as many as 12 different names. Very old nomenclature was characterised by names such as powder of algaroth, oil of tartar, salt of alembroth, and many others, which often bore little or no relation to the substance's chemical constitution. Lavoisier and his fellow chemists devised the nomenclature that introduced names such as hydrogen and oxygen, which are still in use today. This was to present a systematic view of chemistry and to propose a more rational system of naming chemical compounds.

With the massive expansion of organic chemistry in the mid 19th century and the greater understanding of the structure of organic compounds, the need for an even more systematic nomenclature was felt just as the theoretical tools became available to make this possible.

In the 20th century the task passed to the newly formed International Union of Pure and Applied Chemistry (IUPAC), which first appointed commissions for organic, inorganic and biochemical nomenclature in 1921; continuing to do so to this day.

Many chemicals are so much a part of our lives that we know them by their familiar names, just like our other friends. A given substance may have several trivial names. Ordinary cane sugar, for example, is more formally known as 'sucrose', but asking:

'Please pass the α-D-glucopyranosyl-(1,2)-β-D-fructofuranoside!'

would be excessive. However, 'sucrose' would be quite appropriate if you needed to distinguish this particular sugar from the hundreds of other named sugars.

Chemical substances have been a part of the fabric of civilisation and culture for thousands of years, and present-day chemistry retains a lot of these ancient hidden cultural and historic connections.

Different organic molecules are not quite so numerous as people, but each has its own unique characteristics, determined by its structure. For people, cases of mistaken identity occasionally have serious consequences, but it could be even more serious as far as organic molecules are concerned. One type of thalidomide molecule is a very effective pain reliever but its mirror image caused many serious birth defects in the 1960s. Consequently, it is essential to have a method of naming molecules that describes their structures and allows for even very subtle differences in these structures to be distinguished.

Antoine Lavoisier revolutionised chemistry. He introduced a much more systematic nomenclature for compounds.

4.1 Introduction

Carbon atoms have the unique ability to bond together to make chains, branched chains and rings, which form the skeleton of compounds that contain many carbon atoms. Hydrogen atoms are often bonded to these carbon skeletons, and other atoms (especially oxygen, nitrogen and halogens) can also attach in a variety of positions and combinations. This variety gives us millions of organic molecules, derived from just a few different types of atom.

We name organic compounds according to a set of rules devised by the International Union of Pure and Applied Chemistry (IUPAC). These rules give us a name for each and every molecule that describes the structure of the molecule unambiguously (Fig. 1). The complete set of IUPAC rules fills several books. Naming rules are given in *AS Chemistry*, page 98. Here, you will consider enough of the rules to allow you to name any molecule you may encounter in your study of A level organic chemistry, and many more!

The system easily distinguishes **isomers**, which are molecules with the same **molecular** formula but different **structural formulae**. These may be **structural isomers** (including **chain**, **positional** and **functional group isomers**) or **stereoisomers** (including *E/Z* **isomers** and **optical isomers**), which are all discussed in detail later in this chapter. Fig. 2 shows a simple example of the importance of the IUPAC naming system; ethanol is drinkable, methoxymethane is not!

Fig. 2 Isomers of C_2H_6O

For the molecular formula C_2H_6O, the structural formula could be:

CH_3CH_2OH or CH_3OCH_3

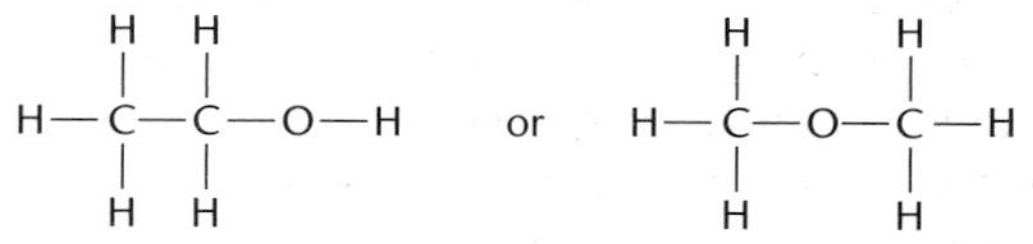

Using the IUPAC naming system, these are **ethanol** and **methoxymethane**.
They are *functional group isomers* of C_2H_6O.

4.2 Rules for naming organic compounds

The IUPAC system begins by considering three basic features common to all organic molecules. These features are each given names, which we then combine to give the overall name. The features are:

- the size and shape of the carbon skeleton
- the presence in the molecule of groups of atoms called **functional groups**
- the position of these functional groups in the molecule.

Size and shape of the carbon skeleton

Table 1 shows the structures of methane, ethane, propane, butane, pentane and hexane, which are the first six members of the hydrocarbon family called the alkanes. We use these names to describe similar chains of carbon atoms in other molecules: a chain provides a name for the 'backbone' around which the rest of the molecule is constructed.

The carbon skeleton in ethanol is C–C (see Fig. 2 and Table 1). The name contains 'eth', which tells you there are two carbon atoms bonded together as in ethane. However, in methoxymethane there are two separate carbon chains that each contain only one carbon atom. Each chain is named by 'meth' as in methane.

During most chemical reactions the carbon backbone remains unchanged and the same naming system occurs in both the name of the reactant and the product.

Each of the three general hydrocarbon groups, **alkanes**, **cycloalkanes** and **arenes**, has a particular type of carbon skeleton.

Table 1   Structures and names of simple alkanes

Structure of alkane	Name	IUPAC code
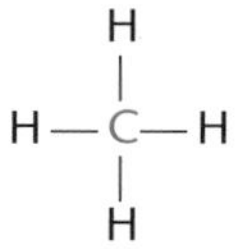 $H-\overset{\overset{H}{\|}}{\underset{\underset{H}{\|}}{C}}-H$ or CH_4	methane	meth = 1 C in chain
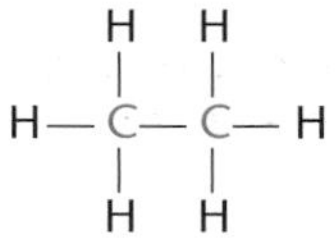 $H-\overset{\overset{H}{\|}}{\underset{\underset{H}{\|}}{C}}-\overset{\overset{H}{\|}}{\underset{\underset{H}{\|}}{C}}-H$ or CH_3CH_3	ethane	eth = 2 C in chain
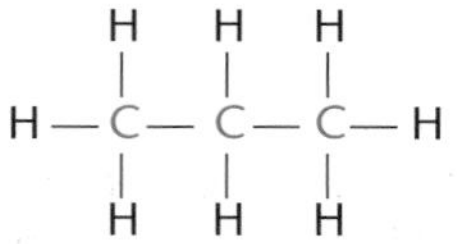 $H-\overset{\overset{H}{\|}}{\underset{\underset{H}{\|}}{C}}-\overset{\overset{H}{\|}}{\underset{\underset{H}{\|}}{C}}-\overset{\overset{H}{\|}}{\underset{\underset{H}{\|}}{C}}-H$ or $CH_3CH_2CH_3$	propane	prop = 3 C in chain
$CH_3CH_2CH_2CH_3$	butane	but = 4 C in chain
$CH_3CH_2CH_2CH_2CH_3$	pentane	pent = 5 C in chain
$CH_3CH_2CH_2CH_2CH_2CH_3$	hexane	hex = 6 C in chain

Alkanes

In alkanes the carbon atoms are bonded in continuous chains, though these may have branches. Table 1 shows how the number of carbon atoms in any chain is named.

Fig. 3   Naming alkanes

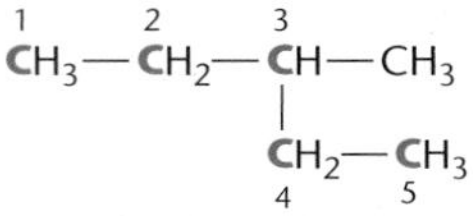

3-methylpentane

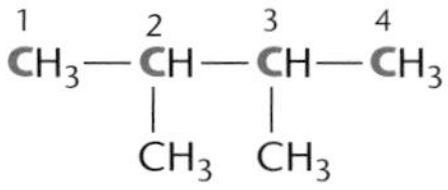

2,3-dimethylbutane

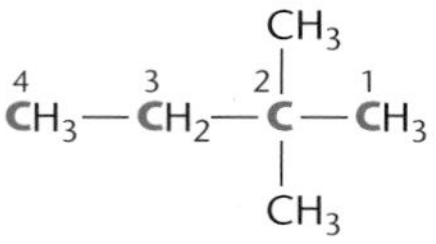

2,2-dimethylbutane

To name a molecule, first identify the longest chain, since the name of the chain structural isomer is based on the name for the longest continuous chain. This name comes at the end of the name for the whole molecule, as in the examples in Fig. 3. If the molecule contains branches to this chain, we name each branch using the relevant prefix from 'methyl-', 'ethyl-', 'propyl-', etc., depending on the number of carbon atoms in the branch. Repetitions of the same side-chain are shown using 'di-', 'tri-', 'tetra-', etc., as shown in the second and third examples in Fig. 3. To identify the positions of branches on the chain, we number the carbon atoms in the main chain, and indicate the carbon atom to which the side-chain is bonded. Hence, **positional isomers** are distinguished by this naming system.

---

1 Predict the IUPAC names for unbranched C_7H_{16}, C_8H_{18} and $C_{10}H_{22}$.

2 Using structural formulae showing *all* bonds, show the structures of:

a pentane

b hexane.

3 Give the name for $CH_3CH(CH_3)CH_3$.

4 Draw the structure of 2,4-dimethylpentane.

5 Name the straight-chain alkane that has 3-methylpentane (see Fig. 3) as chain structural isomer.

6 Draw and name a positional isomer and a chain structural isomer of 3-methylpentane (see Fig. 3).

Cycloalkanes

Carbon atoms can bond together via single bonds to form rings, and we call such compounds **cycloalkanes**. The number of carbon atoms in the ring gives the name, using the same sequence that we used for alkanes (see Table 1), and the ring arrangement itself is indicated by the prefix 'cyclo-'. Two examples can be seen in Table 2.

Table 2   Cycloalkanes

Structure	Abbreviation	Name
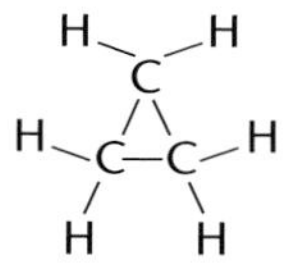		cyclopropane
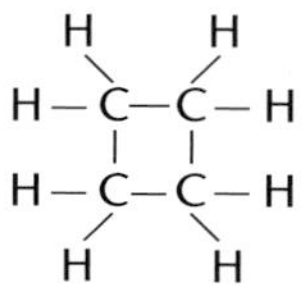		cyclobutane

> **7** Other cycloalkanes are abbreviated by similar regular polygons. How would cyclopentane and cyclohexane be abbreviated?

Arenes

Arenes (also called *aromatics*) are compounds based on the structure of benzene, C_6H_6. The representation of the so-called 'delocalised' structure of benzene is shown in Fig. 4 (see also Chapter 6).

Fig. 4   Benzene

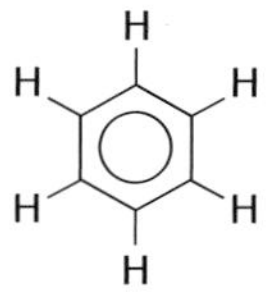

is abbreviated to:

The circle inside the hexagon represents six delocalised electrons which are *not* associated with any particular atom – see Chapter 6.

Many arene compounds exist and we can name these according to the different groups attached to the ring (see Fig. 5).

Fig. 5   Alkylbenzenes

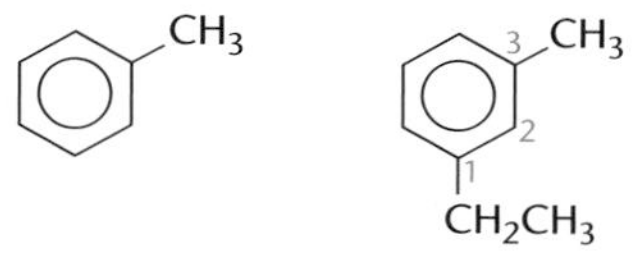

methylbenzene   (3-methyl)ethylbenzene

> **8** Draw the structures of 1-propylbenzene and 2(1-methyl)ethylbenzene.

Functional groups

The groups of atoms that are responsible for the characteristic chemical reactions of a molecule are called **functional groups**. Each different functional group is represented by a unique IUPAC name in the overall name for the molecule.

In Fig. 2, C–O–H is the functional group in ethanol and the '-ol' indicates that this group is present. In methoxymethane C–O–C is the functional group and compounds of this type have '-oxy-' in their name.

Each different functional group has its own IUPAC name (see Table 3), which is added to the name for the carbon skeleton (represented by * in the table). If the carbon atoms in the functional group are part of the longest chain, we must include these to get the correct name.

The functional group name is usually shown at the end of the overall name, but alternative prefix versions are sometimes available when more than one group needs to be identified. This enables us to distinguish **functional group isomers** where the molecules have the same molecular formula but contain different functional groups (e.g. butanal and butanone or ethanoic acid and methyl methanoate).

Positional isomers, such as 1-chloropropane and 2-chloropropane, are indicated by prefixing the functional group's name by the number of the carbon atom in the main chain or ring to which it is bonded. If the functional group is bonded to other atoms such as nitrogen or oxygen, we indicate this by italicising the atomic symbol (e.g. *N* or *O*). When naming positional isomers we use the lowest possible numbers in the sequence. For example, 1,2-dichloropropane is used, rather than 2,3-dichloropropane. Table 3 gives a number of examples of these isomers and you should study it carefully.

9 Write the structures of:

a bromoethane
b propanoic acid
c propanal
d butan-2-one
e methylethanoate
f 2-chloropropane
g 4-methylnitrobenzene
h pent-2-ene
i methanoic acid
j methylpropene
k butan-1-ol
l 2-methylpropan-2-ol
m but-1,3-diene
n 2-amino-2-phenylethanoic acid
o *N*-methylaminomethane
p methanoic ethanoic anhydride
q butanoyl chloride
r ethyl methanoate.

10 Name each of the following molecules. Draw the *full* structure before attempting to name the molecule.

a CH_3Br
b C_6H_5Cl
c $CH_3CH_2CH(OH)CH_3$
d CH_3COOH
e $CH_3CH_2CH_2CH_2CH_2CHO$
f $CH_3CH_2NH_2$
g CH_3COCH_3
h CH_2BrCH_2Br
i CH_3CHBr_2
j $CH_3CH_2CH{=}CH_2$
k C_6H_5COOH
l $CH_3CH_2COOCH_2CH_3$
m $CH_3CH_2CH_2COCl$
n $(CH_3CH_2CH_2CO)_2O$
o $CH_3COOCH_2CH_2CH_2CH_3$
p $CH_3CH_2CH_2COCH_2CH_3$
q $CH_3CH_2CH{=}CHCH(CH_3)CH_3$
r CH_3CH_2CN
s $CH_3CH_2CH(CN)OH$.

key facts

When naming an organic molecule:

- Each different carbon skeleton has a unique IUPAC name.
- Each functional group has a unique IUPAC name.
- Positions of side-chains and functional groups are shown by numbering the carbon atoms of the carbon skeleton.

Table 3 Code for functional groups

Name	Structure	Suffix code	Prefix code	Example	IUPAC name
carboxylic acid		(*)-oic acid	–	$CH_3CH_2CH_2-C$ (=O)(O-H)	butanoic acid
acyl chloride		(*)-oyl chloride	–	CH_3CH_2-C (=O)(Cl)	propanoyl chloride
ester		(*)-oate	–	CH_3-C (=O)(OCH_3)	methyl ethanoate
amide		(*)-amide	–	CH_3-C (=O)(NH_2)	ethanamide
acid anhydride	–C–O–C– (with =O, =O)	(*)-oic anhydride	–	$CH_3-C-O-C-CH_3$ (=O, =O)	ethanoic methanoic anhydride
alcohol	–O–H	(*)-ol	hydroxy-(*)	$CH_3-CH-CH_2OH$ | CH_3	2-methylpropan-1-ol
aldehyde		(*)-al	–	$CH_3CH_2CH_2-C$ (=O)(H)	butanal
ketone	>C=O	(*)-one	oxo-	$CH_3CH_2CH_2-C-CH_3$ (=O)	pentan-2-one
alkene	>C=C<	(*)-ene	–	$CH_3CH_2-CH=CH_2$	but-1-ene
nitro	$-NO_2$	–	nitro-(*)	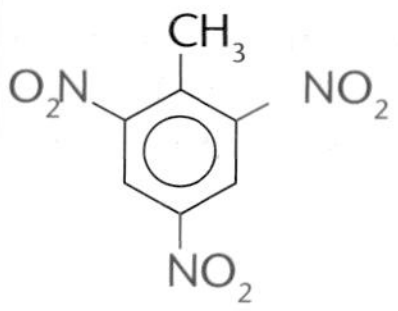 CH_3 / O_2N / NO_2 / NO_2 (benzene ring)	methyl-2,4,6-trinitrobenzene
phenyl	(benzene ring)	–	phenyl-(*)	$CH_3-CH-CH_3$ | (benzene ring)	2-phenylpropane
primary amine	–N(H)(H)	–	amino-(*)	$CH_3CH_2NH_2$	aminoethane
secondary amine	–N(H)	–	N-(*)-amino-(*)	$(CH_3CH_2)_2NH$	N-ethylaminoethane
tertiary amine	–N<	–	N,N-di(*)-amino-(*)	$(CH_3CH_2)_3N$	N,N-diethylaminoethane

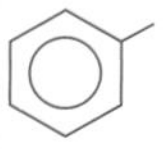

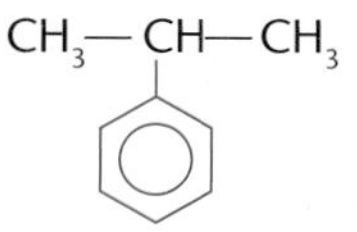

how science works

Diabetes

Diabetics cannot control their blood sugar levels because their pancreases do not produce enough insulin. One of the symptoms of diabetes, called ketosis, occurs when fats stored within the body are broken down to provide the energy that is normally supplied by glucose. This can result in the production of the ketone, propanone, which is detectable as the smell of bad apples on the breath of a sufferer.

Propanone is a problem to people suffering from ketosis but it is also a vital industrial chemical. Now you have experienced many of its structurally related compounds and how they can be clearly differentiated by the IUPAC naming system.

11 Draw the molecular structure of propanone.

12 Draw and name the functional group isomer of propanone.

13 The isomer from question 12 can be oxidised to the corresponding acid and reduced to the corresponding alcohol. Draw and name these molecules.

14 Propanoic acid reacts with ethanol to form the ester, ethyl propanoate, and propan-1-ol reacts with ethanoic acid to form another ester, propyl ethanoate. Draw the structures of these two esters and name the type of isomerism they depict.

15 Propanone can be converted directly or indirectly to each of the other molecules shown in Fig. 6 (a)–(e). Name each of these molecules.

16 How does the IUPAC system help you communicate your ideas to other members of your group?

Fig. 6   Derivatives of propanone

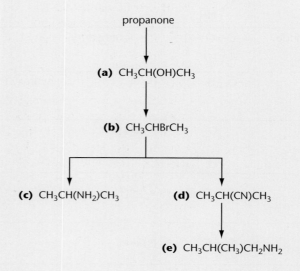

4.3 Isomerism

Isomers are molecules with the same molecular formula but different structures. There are two general types of isomerism: **structural isomerism** and **stereoisomerism**.

Structural isomers

The three types are as follows:

- **Chain isomers** have the same total number of carbon atoms but different patterns of branching, e.g. pentane, methylbutane and dimethylpropane.
- **Positional isomers** have the same carbon skeleton but their functional groups are in different positions, e.g. 1-chloropropane and 2-chloropropane, 1,2-dinitrobenzene and 1,3-dinitrobenzene, and methylpropan-1-ol and methylpropan-2-ol.
- **Functional group isomers** have the same molecular formula but the carbon atoms are bonded differently to form different functional groups (see Table 3), e.g. alkenes and cycloalkanes, alcohols and ethers, carboxylic acids and esters, aldehydes and ketones, and primary, secondary and tertiary amines.

17　Draw and name the chain structural isomers of C_6H_{14}.

18　Draw and name the positional and functional group isomers of:

a　C_4H_8O

b　C_3H_8O

c　$C_4H_8O_2$.

Stereoisomers

These have the same structural formula but have different arrangements of the atoms in space. There are two types of stereoisomerism: **E/Z** and **optical** isomerism.

E/Z isomers

An alkene molecule cannot rotate about the C=C double bond and the four atoms bonded to the C=C bond lie in the same plane. This means that, if two different groups are attached to each end of the C=C double bond, we can draw two different structures, called **E/Z isomers**. One isomer has the groups on the same side of the bond (**Z**, the zusammen (German for 'together') or *cis* isomer), and the other has them on opposite sides of the bond (**E**, the entgegen (German for 'opposite') or *trans* isomer). Fig. 7 shows the structures of **E**- and **Z**-but-2-ene. **E/Z** isomers cannot be formed if the two groups attached to one end of the C=C double bond are the same (Fig. 8).

Fig. 7　*E*- and *Z*-but-2-ene

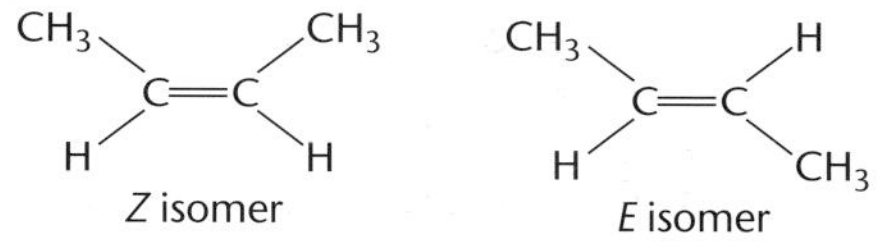

Fig. 8　**Methylbut-2-ene**

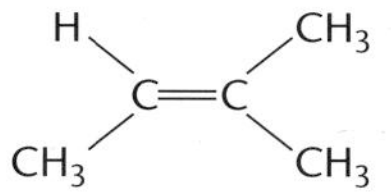

E/Z isomers can also occur in di-substituted cycloalkanes because the ring prevents free rotation of a C–C bond and therefore the two groups may be on the same side (**Z**) or on opposite sides (**E**) of the ring (Fig. 9).

Fig. 9　**The *E/Z* isomers of 1,2-dichlorocyclobutane**

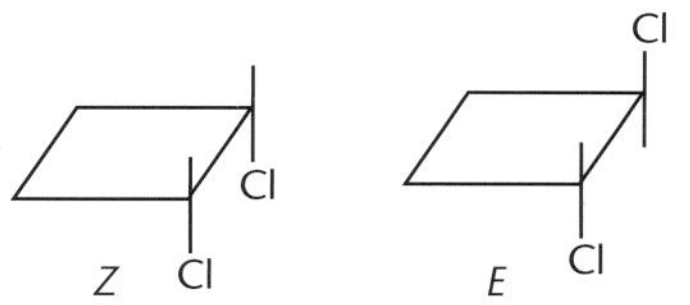

19 For the following compounds, decide which can have *E/Z* isomers; then draw and name them:

a   pent-1-ene

b   pent-2-ene

c   2-methylpent-2-ene

d   cyclohexene

e   cyclohexan-1,4-diol.

Cracking petroleum

The aim of cracking long-chain hydrocarbons is to produce branched structures in preference to straight-chain structures. Branched structures burn more smoothly inside a car's engine. Heptane and 2,2,4-trimethylpentane are typical cracking products.

20 Draw the structures of heptane and 2,2,4-trimethylpentane.

21 Are these molecules isomeric? Explain.

22 Draw and name seven isomers of heptane.

When heptane reacts with bromine, any one of the 16 hydrogen atoms may be replaced (substituted) by a single bromine atom to produce four isomers of bromoheptane.

23 Draw and name all possible positional isomers of bromoheptane.

By removing HBr from 2-bromoheptane, hept-1-ene and hept-2-ene can be formed.

24 Draw the structures of these alkenes.

25 Show the *E/Z* isomers of the alkenes from question 24.

Optical isomers

A carbon atom that is bonded to four different atoms or groups is **asymmetric** (or **chiral**). **Optical isomerism** (also known as **enantiomerism**) occurs when a molecule contains an asymmetric carbon atom. As in Fig. 10, the molecule is without symmetry: like your left and right hands, it is possible to have two different structures that are mirror images of each other. Since the pair of mirror images are not superimposable, they must be isomers and are referred to as **optical isomers** or **enantiomers**. We can only show the difference between a pair of enantiomers properly by three-dimensional drawings.

Fig. 10   Structures of optical isomers

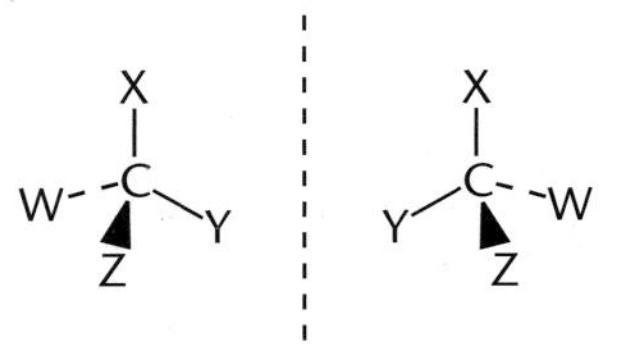

For optical isomers the bonds drawn — represent bonds in the plane of the page, - - - represents bonds going into the page and ◀ represents bonds coming out of the page.

Pairs of enantiomers have identical physical and chemical properties, with two exceptions. They interact differently with other asymmetric molecules, especially enzymes. For example, one enantiomer of the amino acid alanine (see question 26) will be absorbed and converted to protein by the body but the other enantiomer will not.

They also interact differently with plane-polarised light (hence the term *optical* isomers); this is referred to as a difference in **optical activity**.

> **26** Which of the following molecules can exist as optical isomers? For those molecules that can show this property, use three-dimensional structures to show the pair of optical isomers and mark any chiral carbon atoms with an asterisk.
>
> **a** chlorofluoromethane
>
> **b** butan-2-ol
>
> **c** 2-aminopropanoic acid (alanine)
>
> **d** an isomer of heptane, C_7H_{16}

Optical activity

A beam of light consists of waves that vibrate in all possible planes at right angles to the direction in which the beam is travelling. When passed through a **polariser**, all the waves are absorbed except for those vibrating in one particular plane (see Fig. 11). The light is then said to be **plane-polarised**.

Fig. 11   Plane-polarised light

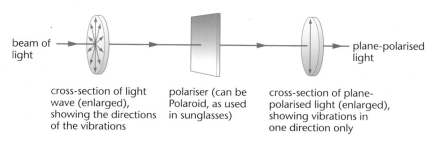

beam of light

cross-section of light wave (enlarged), showing the directions of the vibrations

polariser (can be Polaroid, as used in sunglasses)

cross-section of plane-polarised light (enlarged), showing vibrations in one direction only

plane-polarised light

Optically active molecules rotate the plane of the plane-polarised light. One enantiomer rotates it clockwise and the other enantiomer rotates the plane by the same amount in the anti-clockwise direction. The former is called the **dextrorotatory** or (+) isomer and the latter is called the **laevorotatory** or (−) isomer. We can

Fig. 12   A simple polarimeter

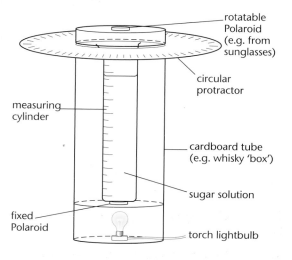

rotatable Polaroid (e.g. from sunglasses)

circular protractor

measuring cylinder

cardboard tube (e.g. whisky 'box')

sugar solution

fixed Polaroid

torch lightbulb

detect and measure this difference experimentally using a **polarimeter** as illustrated in Fig. 12.

If we test a sample and find that it does not produce this rotation effect, then either it is not chiral or it consists of a 50 : 50 mixture of the two enantiomers in which the rotation effects have cancelled each other out. Such a mixture is called a **racemate**. We often obtain racemic mixtures when we do addition reactions on a planar double bond (C=C or C=O), because the reaction can occur with equal probability from either side of the plane. For example (see Fig. 13), ethanal undergoes nucleophilic addition with hydrogen cyanide to form chiral 2-hydroxypropanenitrile. However, this product will be the racemate because there is a 50 : 50 chance of the cyanide nucleophile bonding to either side of the planar molecule. Attack at one side produces one enantiomer, attack at the other side produces the other.

Fig. 13   Racemisation of ethanal

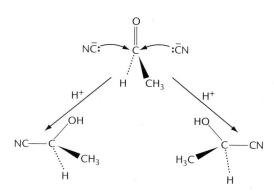

The effect of stereochemistry on the action of drugs

cis-DDP   *trans*-DDP

This sequence shows the differing pharmacological activities of cisplatin and transplatin – note that these drug names have retained their *cis* and *trans* notation and are not using the IUPAC recommended *E/Z* notation. Cisplatin (*cis*-diamminedichloridoplatinum(II)) has long been shown to be significantly more cytotoxic than transplatin.

The two chloride ligands are slowly displaced by water (aqua ligand), which allows cisplatin to coordinate to a basic site in DNA, forming predominantly *intrastrand* cross-links. The

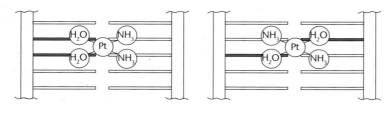

cis forms intrastrand links   *trans* forms interstrand links
with H_2O with H_2O

linking then interferes with cell division, preventing the cancer developing. Transplatin forms predominantly *interstrand* cross-links with little anti-tumour activity, but, beneficially, does not have any toxicity to normal cells at these concentrations.

Bupivacaine is an anaesthetic, but it was found that sometimes cardiac arrest occurred during its use. The drug was modified to a propyl derivative Ropivacaine and this has been produced solely as the laevorotatory enantiomer. This has much less cardiotoxicity than the dextrorotatory isomer.

chiral centres

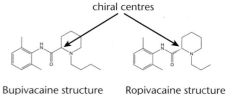

Bupivacaine structure   Ropivacaine structure

27

a Which will be the *E* isomer and which one the *Z* isomer for the platins?

b Explain why cisplatin is effective at interfering with cell formation, but the *trans* form is not.

28

a State one advantage and one disadvantage of Bupivacaine.

b Why was Ropivacaine developed?

If you have studied this chapter thoroughly and worked through the examples, questions, applications and examination questions, you will have a sound foundation on which to base your further study of organic chemistry. The IUPAC system gives you a powerful means of international communication – it is like learning a new language!

examination questions

1 Phenylethanone, $C_6H_5COCH_3$, reacts with HCN according to the equation below:

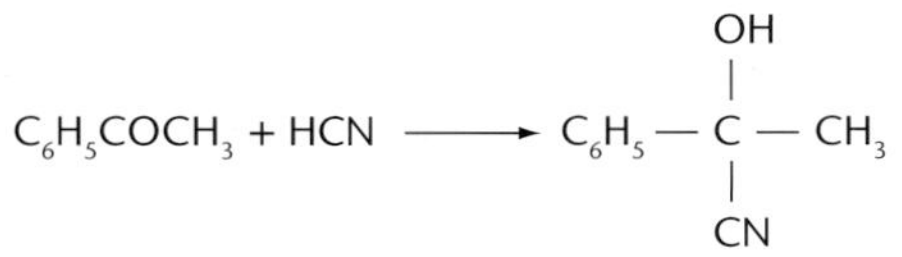

$$C_6H_5COCH_3 + HCN \longrightarrow C_6H_5 - \underset{\underset{CN}{|}}{\overset{\overset{OH}{|}}{C}} - CH_3$$

Name and outline the mechanism of this reaction. The product formed exists as a racemic mixture. State the meaning of the term *racemic mixture* and explain why such a mixture is formed in this reaction.   (8)

Total 8

AQA, January 2007, Unit 4, Question 6(b)

2 Consider the sequence of reactions below.

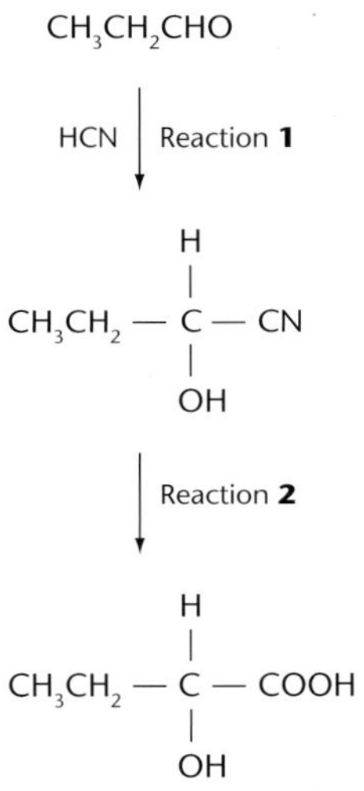

$$CH_3CH_2CHO \qquad \textbf{P}$$

HCN | Reaction **1**

$$CH_3CH_2 - \underset{\underset{OH}{|}}{\overset{\overset{H}{|}}{C}} - CN \qquad \textbf{Q}$$

Reaction **2**

$$CH_3CH_2 - \underset{\underset{OH}{|}}{\overset{\overset{H}{|}}{C}} - COOH \qquad \textbf{R}$$

a Name and outline a mechanism for Reaction **1**.   (5)

b i Name compound **Q**

  ii The molecular formula of **Q** is C_4H_7NO. Draw the structure of the isomer of **Q** which shows geometrical isomerism and is formed by the reaction of ammonia with an acyl chloride.   (3)

c Draw the structure of the main organic product formed in each case when **R** reacts separately with the following substances:

  i methanol in the presence of a few drops of concentrated sulfuric acid

  ii acidified potassium dichromate(VI)

  iii concentrated sulfuric acid in an elimination reaction.   (3)

Total 11

AQA, January 2006, Unit 4, Question 4

3

a Name Compound P.

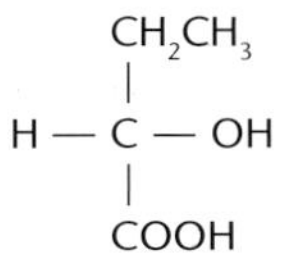

$$H - \underset{\underset{COOH}{|}}{\overset{\overset{CH_2CH_3}{|}}{C}} - OH$$

Compound **P**

b What structural feature in Compound P results in optical isomerism?

c When Compound P is made by the reaction of propanal and hydrogen cyanide, the product is optically inactive. What name is given to such an inactive product, and why is it inactive?   (4)

Total 4

NEAB, June 1997, CH03, Question 4c

4 3-Aminophenylethanone can be obtained from benzene in three steps:

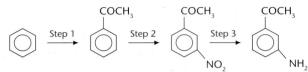

Name the molecules shown in the reaction scheme. (4)

Total 4

5

a The bromoalkane, $CH_3CH_2CHBrCH_3$, can be formed by the reaction of $CH_3CH=CHCH_3$ with HBr. Name $CH_3CH_2CHBrCH_3$. (1)

b $CH_3CH=CHCH_3$ exhibits isomerism.

  i What type of isomerism does this compound exhibit? (1)

  ii Explain why this compound exists as isomers. (1)

  iii Name the two isomers. (2)

Total 5

NEAB, February 1997, CH03 Question 3(a)

6 For the following reaction sequence:

$$CH_3C=CCH_3 \xrightarrow{H_2O/H_2SO_4} CH_3CH(OH)C_2H_5 \xrightarrow{HBr} CH_3CHBrC_2H_5$$
$$\quad\quad A \quad\quad\quad\quad\quad\quad B \quad\quad\quad\quad\quad\quad C$$

a What type of isomerism do each of compounds A, B and C show?

b Draw the two isomers for each compound A, B and C.

c Name the isomers for compound A.

d **i** What special properties are shown by the isomers of B?

  ii The reaction producing compound C gives equal amounts of the isomers. What name is given to this type of mixture? (5)

Total 5

7

a Explain the term *structural isomer*. (1)

b Draw displayed formulae for

  i ethanol and propan-1-ol

  ii propanal and propanone (2)

c Explain why the compounds in **i** are members of an homologous series and those in **ii** are not. (2)

d A compound important in the development of petroleum is isooctane.

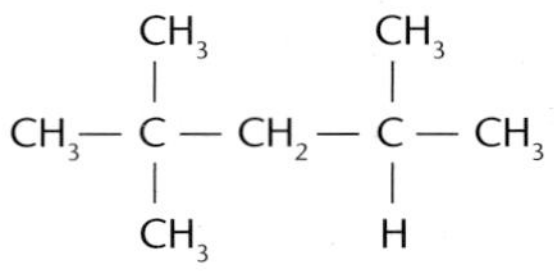

$$CH_3-\overset{\overset{\displaystyle CH_3}{|}}{\underset{\underset{\displaystyle CH_3}{|}}{C}}-CH_2-\overset{\overset{\displaystyle CH_3}{|}}{\underset{\underset{\displaystyle H}{|}}{C}}-CH_3$$

  i Give the IUPAC name for this compound. (1)

There are several isomers of this compound, for example

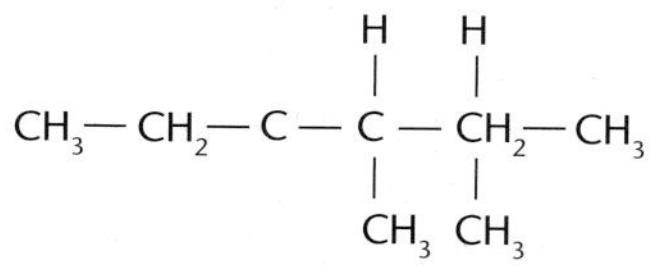

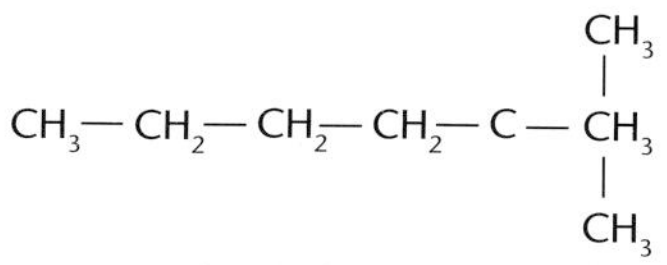

$$CH_3-CH_2-\overset{\overset{\displaystyle H}{|}}{\underset{\underset{\displaystyle CH_3}{|}}{C}}-\overset{\overset{\displaystyle H}{|}}{\underset{\underset{\displaystyle CH_3}{|}}{C}}-CH_2-CH_3$$

$$CH_3-CH_2-CH_2-CH_2-\overset{\overset{\displaystyle CH_3}{|}}{\underset{\underset{\displaystyle CH_3}{|}}{C}}-CH_3$$

ii Give the names for the two isomers above.   (2)

e Draw the displayed formulae for
  i 2,3,4-trimethylpentane
  ii 2,2,3,3-tetramethylbutane.   (2)

Total 10

8 An alcohol has the formula $C_4H_{10}O$.

a Draw the displayed formulae for its four isomers.   (4)

b Only one isomer can be oxidised to a ketone. Draw the alcohol and the corresponding ketone and name both compounds.   (2)

c Two isomers can be oxidised to aldehydes. Draw the alcohols and the corresponding aldehydes and name all the compounds.   (4)

Total 10

9 Different types of isomerism can be demonstrated by these compounds:

1 $CH_3-CH_2-CH_2-CH_3$
2 $CH_3-C=C-CH_3$
3 $CH_3-CH_2-CH(OH)-COOH$

a Allocate a different type of isomerism to each compound.   (3)

b Show the isomers of each compound.   (3)

c Explain the reasons for each type of isomerism.   (3)

d What functional groups are present in the compounds above?   (3)

2-iodobutane is optically active, but dissolved in propanone in the presence of I⁻ ions it racemises.

e Draw the displayed formula of 2-iodobutane and mark the chiral carbon atom with a *.   (1)

f Draw the two structures of 2-iodobutane that will form a racemic mixture.   (2)

g Explain why this mixture will not rotate the plane of plane polarised light.   (1)

Total 16

Thalidomide

Thalidomide first appeared in Germany on 1 October 1957. It was marketed as a sedative with apparently remarkably few side effects. The drug company who developed it believed it was so safe it was suitable for prescribing to pregnant women to help combat morning sickness.

Towards the end of the 1950s, children began to be born with shocking disabilities. It was not immediately obvious what the cause of this was. Probably the most renowned is pharcomelia, the name given to the flipper-like limbs that appeared on the children of women who took thalidomide.

One effect of thalidomide is targeting blood vessels. It is able to block growth and so tends to target parts of the body undergoing growth. Pregnant women taking the drug could feel the benefit of the drug in combating morning sickness, but damage was being done to the rapidly growing foetus. It is possible that so many of the thalidomide babies experienced pharcomelia because morning sickness can appear around the time of foetal limb growth.

Laboratory tests showed that it was the laevorotatory enantiomer that caused problems and the dextrorotatory isomer was an effective sedative. This difference in activity arises because of the complex nature and particular shape of protein molecules in living organisms, which is why cisplatin is an effective anti-tumour drug but transplatin is not. It is now known that, even when only one of the optical isomers of thalidomide is administered, the [H⁺] in the blood can cause racemising, so both enantiomers will be formed in a roughly equal mix in the blood.

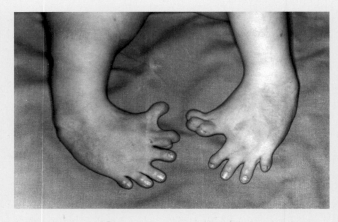

Thalidomide interferes with blood vessels during growth so limbs do not develop properly.

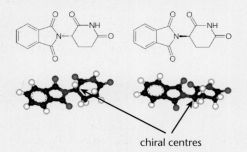

chiral centres

Research is now looking to see whether thalidomide might be effective as a treatment for some types of cancer in some patients. Thalidomide interferes with the growth of new blood vessels. This should reduce the cancer's supply of oxygen and nutrients, which, it is hoped, will cause the tumour to shrink, or at least to stop growing. Because thalidomide has so few side effects, it will help in reducing some of the nasty effects of other treatments, such as night sweats and severe weight loss. Generally, thalidomide is only available in specialist cancer treatment centres where research trials are taking place and specialist doctors have experience in its use.

Part of the research programme for the use of drugs is to perform clinical trials.

A randomised controlled trial is the study design that can provide the most compelling evidence that the study treatment causes the expected effect on human health.

Randomised: Each study subject is randomly assigned to receive either the study treatment or a placebo (fake treatment).

Blind: The subjects involved in the study do not know which treatment they receive.

Double-blind: The researchers also do not know which treatment is being given to any given subject. This 'blinding' is to prevent biases, since if a physician knew which patient was getting the study treatment and which patient was getting the placebo, he/she might be tempted to give the (presumably helpful) study drug to a patient who could more easily benefit from it. In addition, a physician might give extra care to only the patients who receive the placebos to compensate for their ineffectiveness.

Double-dummy: A form of double-blind trial which gives additional insurance against bias or placebo effect. In this kind of study, all patients are given both placebo and active doses in alternating periods of time during the study.

Placebo-controlled: The use of a placebo allows the researchers to isolate the effect of the study treatment.

The Wellcome Trust is an independent charity funding research to improve human and animal health. Established in 1936 and with an endowment of around £15 billion, it is the UK's largest non-governmental source of funds for biomedical research. Recently the Wellcome Trust has invested £91 million in a five-year Seeding Drug Discovery technology transfer initiative, for projects tackling obesity, antibiotic resistance and cancer. Approximately £12 million was committed in the first round of funding.

A1

a Which is an appropriate trial for the use of thalidomide? Explain your choice.

b Choose a different type of trial and select a treatment for which it would be suitable.

c For which patient groups would a thalidomide cancer treatment not be suitable? Explain your choice of groups.

A2

a Why did Lavoisier and his coworkers publish 'Chymical Nomenclature' in 1787?

b Why is the IUPAC system used globally?

c If optical isomers cannot be distinguished chemically, why is there a difference in their pharmacological activity?

A3

a What is peer review?

b What is the purpose of peer review?

c Why do you think peer review did not prevent the problems with thalidomide?

d At what stage of drug development do you think peer review will take place?

A4 Why would a charity support particular areas of drug development?

5 Compounds containing the carbonyl group

Ethanol is familiar as the substance commonly referred to as 'alcohol', found in wine, beer, cider and a wide variety of other alcoholic drinks. As you will know from your studies of AS level chemistry, ethanol is just one example of a large family of compounds to which the general term 'alcohols' is applied.

The world's oldest bottle of wine was unearthed during excavation for building a house in a vineyard near the town of Speyer, Germany. The bottle dates from approximately 325 AD. The ancient liquid has much silty sediment. About two-thirds of the contents are a thicker, hazy mixture. This is most probably olive oil, which the Romans commonly used to 'float' on top of the wine to protect it from oxidation.

The world's oldest bottle of wine.

However careful the tests during fermenting or brewing, carbonyl compounds occasionally form, and make the wine or beer undrinkable.

When the fermentation process for producing beer or wine goes wrong, the beverage tastes vinegary as a result of the ethanol being oxidised by oxygen in the air to the **carboxylic acid** called ethanoic acid.

As a part of the natural fermentation process, **aldehydes**, **ketones** and **esters** may also be produced, which add to, or detract from, the overall flavour of the beverage. They may also add to the hangover effect when over-consumption of alcohol dehydrates the brain. As part of the digestion process, alcohol is broken down in the liver, first to ethanal (acetaldehyde), and then to ethanoic acid. These derivatives of alcohols – aldehydes, ketones, carboxylic acids and esters – all contain a C=O bond and are the central theme of this chapter.

5.1 Aldehydes and ketones

Aldehydes and ketones both contain a **carbonyl group** ($>$**C=O**, often abbreviated to **–CO–**), and so these two groups of compounds are closely related. The carbonyl group is situated at the end of a carbon chain in aldehydes and elsewhere in the carbon chain in ketones. Tables 1 and 2 show the names and structures of some simple aldehydes and ketones.

Aldehydes and ketones are both oxidation products of alcohols. We can make aldehydes by the *partial* oxidation of primary alcohols (which contain a CH_2–OH functional group). If we oxidise a secondary alcohol (which contains a –CH(OH)– group) we get a ketone. (Primary and secondary alcohols are described in *AS Chemistry*, Chapter 16.)

Table 1 Three aldehydes

methanal	HCHO	H—C(=O)H
ethanal	CH_3CHO	H—$C(H_2)$—$C(=O)H$
propanal	C_2H_5CHO	H—$C(H_2)$—$C(H_2)$—$C(=O)H$

Table 2 Three ketones

propanone	CH_3COCH_3	H—$C(H_3)$—$C(=O)$—$C(H_3)$
butanone	$CH_3COCH_2CH_3$	H—$C(H_3)$—$C(=O)$—$C(H_2)$—$C(H_3)$
phenylethanone	$C_6H_5COCH_3$	phenyl—$C(=O)$—CH_3

Oxidation of primary alcohols

A solution of potassium dichromate(VI) acidified with dilute sulfuric acid oxidises primary alcohols (R–CH_2–OH) such as ethanol (where $R = CH_3$). The orange $Cr_2O_7^{2-}$ ion is reduced to the green chromium(III) cation (Cr^{3+}) during the reaction. This colour change indicates that oxidation has occurred. The oxidant [$Cr_2O_7^{2-} + H^+$] is usually represented by [O], as shown in the following equation:

$$R-\underset{\underset{H}{|}}{\overset{\overset{H}{|}}{C}}-O-H \xrightarrow{[O]} H_2O + R-C\underset{H}{\overset{O}{\diagup\!\!\diagdown}} \xrightarrow{[O]} R-C\underset{O-H}{\overset{O}{\diagup\!\!\diagdown}}$$

R represents an alkyl or aryl (aromatic) group.

This equation shows how the aldehyde (e.g. ethanal, $R = CH_3$) can be oxidised further to form a carboxylic acid (e.g. ethanoic acid). Prolonged heating under reflux with excess acidified dichromate completely oxidises an alcohol to a carboxylic acid.

Metaldehyde, a cyclic polymer of four ethanal molecules, is the killer in slug pellets – good for the plants but it poisons the birds that eat the dead slugs and snails.

In order to isolate an aldehyde we have to immediately distil it from the reaction mixture before it can be oxidised further to the acid. Such a distillation is possible because aldehydes have relatively lower boiling points because their molecules are bound by weak dipole–dipole intermolecular forces compared to the stronger hydrogen bonding between both alcohol and acid molecules.

1 Give the structures and names of the oxidation products of:

a methanol

b propan-1-ol.

2 What is the change in the oxidation number of chromium when acidified dichromate is used to oxidise alcohols?

3 Write an equation to show the oxidation of butan-1-ol by potassium dichromate(VI), and name the organic products.

Oxidation of secondary alcohols

Oxidation of secondary alcohols by warm, acidified dichromate(VI) produces ketones. These have the general formula R_1COR_2 where R_1 and R_2 are alkyl or aryl groups. Again, a colour change from orange to green indicates that oxidation has occurred:

secondary alcohol   ketone

e.g.
$$CH_3—CH(OH)—CH_2CH_3 \xrightarrow{[O]} CH_3COCH_2CH_3$$
butan-2-ol   butan-2-one

The ketone propanone is used to make Perspex, a hard, clear plastic used in incubators for premature babies.

4 Give the name and structure of the alcohol that would be oxidised to:

a pentan-2-one

b phenylethanone.

5 Write an equation to show the oxidation (use [O] to represent the oxidant) of cyclohexan-1-ol by acidified potassium dichromate(VI), and name the organic product.

Oxidation of tertiary alcohols

Tertiary alcohols are not easily oxidised. The standard oxidant, acidified dichromate(VI), remains orange when heated with a tertiary alcohol. There is no hydrogen atom to be removed from the carbon to which the –OH group is attached. Hence, the oxidant [O] cannot remove two hydrogen atoms to form water and the carbonyl group. However, a stronger oxidant (e.g. acidified potassium manganate(VII), $KMnO_4$) can break the C–C bonds and oxidise the alcohol. The products are a mixture of compounds, each with shorter carbon chains.

hsw

how science works

Caught by the breathalyser

You're driving down a street when a car suddenly reverses out of a driveway in front of you. You have the choice of braking or swerving around the vehicle. Given that there could be oncoming traffic, the safer option would be to brake, provided there are no vehicles behind you. The time it takes to assess the situation, make a decision and start to take action is your reaction time. Even a small amount of alcohol, e.g. one unit, can affect your reaction time.

Traffic police spend a lot of time trying to catch drivers who have had too much to drink. At one time, police officers had to judge whether drivers were sober or not by deciding if they could talk clearly, or could walk in a straight line.

The first breathalyser, invented in 1960, measured the amount of alcohol in a driver's breath. This chemical breathalyser relied on the reaction between ethanol vapour in the driver's breath and orange crystals of acidified potassium dichromate(VI), the oxidising agent, contained in a glass phial. Ethanol reduces the crystals and they turn green. A police officer would check how much of the orange packing had changed to green. The extent of the change was then related to the amount of ethanol in the driver's breath.

6 Give the full molecular structure of ethanol.

7 Is ethanol a primary, secondary or tertiary alcohol? Explain your answer.

8 Write equations for the oxidations that occur inside the chemical breathalyser and name the organic products formed. You may use [O] to represent the oxidant.

a Give the formulae of the ions responsible for the original orange colour and the final green colour.

b What type of reaction does the chromium species of the oxidant undergo?

If you eat a lot of sweets flavoured with esters, digestive hydrolysis may produce a varied mixture of alcohols and acids, which are detectable on your breath. The mixture might include butan-1-ol, butan-2-ol, 2-methylpropan-2-ol, ethanoic acid and butanoic acid.

9

a   Write the structures of these alcohols and acids.

b   Draw and name the ester responsible for the production of butan-1-ol and butanoic acid.

10   Write an equation for the digestive hydrolysis of the ester from question 9.

The police now prefer to use the modern electronic breathalyser – the 'intoximeter' – which is cheaper than the 'blow in the bag' chemical device and is continually re-usable. Some of these use an infrared cell. This directs infrared rays through the sample and any unabsorbed infrared at the other side is detected (look at Chapter 11 for more detail). The higher the concentration of ethanol, the more infrared absorption occurs. The electronic breathalyser is about the size of a pocket calculator and coloured lights or a digital display indicate clearly the level of ethanol in the breath.

The accuracy depends on the sample of breath being deep lung air. As the driver breathes out, the concentration of ethanol increases, and when the level of ethanol stabilises, the sample of breath is analysed. This ensures accurate alcohol readings and means that the volume of air each person has to blow will depend on how large his or her lungs are.

11   Discuss the relative accuracy and precision of the 'breathalyser' and the 'intoximeter'.

The electronic breathalyser is very convenient and reliable for roadside tests.

'Blow into the bag please!' The original breathalyser of 1960.

5.2 Reactions of aldehydes and ketones

The carbonyl group reacts in similar ways in both aldehydes and ketones, and undergoes **nucleophilic addition**. However, aldehydes are reducing agents but ketones are not.

Nucleophilic addition reactions

Addition of hydrogen cyanide to both aldehydes and ketones is an example of a nucleophilic addition reaction:

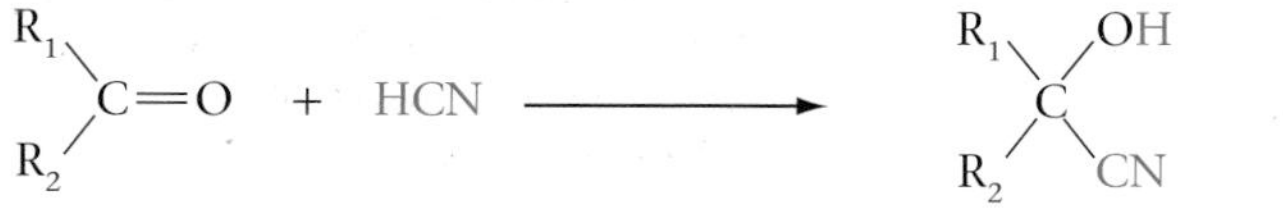

aldehyde: R_1 and/or R_2 = H
ketone: R_1 and R_2 = alkyl groups

a hydroxynitrile

e.g.

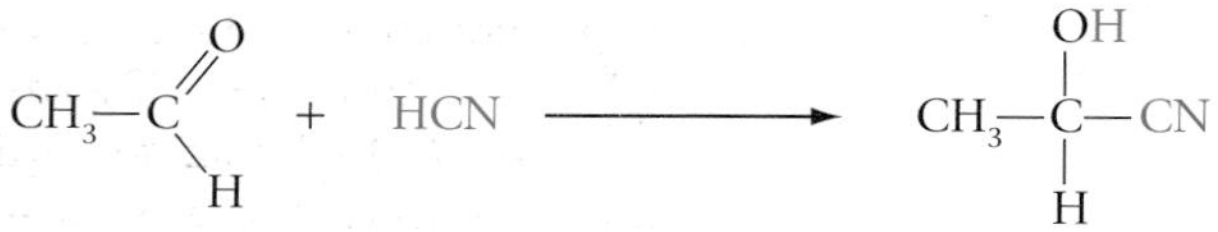

2-hydroxypropanenitrile

2-hydroxy-2-methylpropanenitrile

Figure 1 shows how the high electronegativity of the oxygen atom in the C=O group results in this bond being polar, with the carbon atom electron-deficient. The carbon atom is therefore prone to attack by nucleophiles ('lovers of positive charge'), which have lone pairs of electrons available for bonding. To accommodate this new bond to the carbonyl carbon, the π bond of the C=O bond breaks, and a saturated C–O bond is formed. Hence, an addition reaction results and, overall, the reaction mechanism is called a **nucleophilic addition across the C=O bond**.

Hydrogen cyanide is a very *weak acid*. The degree of ionisation in solution, to produce hydrogen ions (H^+) and nucleophilic cyanide ions (:CN$^-$), is very small. In practice, the cyanide ion is derived from ionic potassium cyanide. This is acidified with sulfuric acid to provide the H^+ ions.

Potassium cyanide is extremely toxic to humans. Hydrogen cyanide, the gas formed from cyanides, is also extremely toxic (100 ppm can quickly cause death) but this gas is also highly flammable, so great care needs to be exercised when using cyanides.

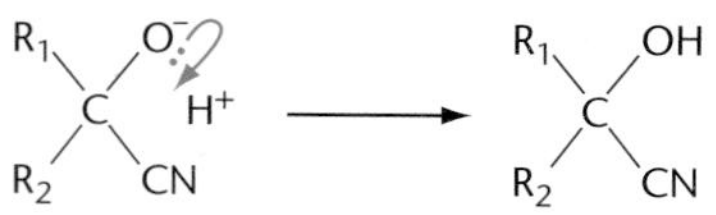

12

a   Write equations to show the reactions with hydrogen cyanide of:

   i   propanal

   ii   butan-2-one.

b   Name the organic products.

13

   Both reactions of question 12 produce racemic products (see Chapter 4). Show the structures of the optical isomers concerned.

Redox reactions

Oxidation reactions

Aldehydes are easily oxidised to form carboxylic acids, but it is difficult to oxidise ketones. Ketones can be oxidised only by very strong oxidising agents, because there is no hydrogen atom attached to the carbon atom of their carbonyl group. This gives us a good way of distinguishing between aldehydes and ketones: we can test an unknown sample with a very

Fig. 1   Nucleophilic addition of cyanide

The reaction happens in stages.

1 The nucleophile (:CN$^-$) attacks the partial positive charge on the carbon atom of the carbonyl group:

2 The reaction intermediate has an oxygen atom carrying a negative charge. An electron pair from this atom is then used to form a covalent bond with a hydrogen ion, forming a hydroxynitrile:

gentle oxidising agent such as **Fehling's solution**. Fehling's solution is blue (see photo) and contains the copper(II) complex ion in alkaline solution. When the solution is warmed with an aldehyde, the aldehyde is oxidised to a carboxylic acid and the blue copper(II) is reduced to a brick-red precipitate of copper(I) oxide:

$$R-\overset{\displaystyle O}{\underset{\displaystyle H}{C}} + 2Cu^{2+}(aq) + 4OH^- \longrightarrow R-\overset{\displaystyle O}{\underset{\displaystyle OH}{C}} + Cu_2O(s) + 2H_2O$$

blue   brick red

Tollens' reagent, a solution made by adding dilute ammonia solution to silver(I) nitrate solution, can be used instead of Fehling's solution. It contains the silver(I) complex ion, diamminesilver(I) ion, $[Ag(NH_3)_2]^+$. When gently warmed with Tollens' reagent, an aldehyde causes the colourless diamminesilver(I) ions to be reduced to metallic Ag(0). This causes a 'silver mirror' to coat the inside of the reaction vessel:

$$R-\overset{\displaystyle O}{\underset{\displaystyle H}{C}} + 2[Ag(NH_3)_2]^+(aq) + 2OH^- \longrightarrow R-\overset{\displaystyle O}{\underset{\displaystyle OH}{C}} + 2Ag(s) + 4NH_3 + H_2O$$

colourless   silver

Table 3 summarises the reactions of alcohols, aldehydes and ketones with the oxidising agents we have discussed above.

> **14** Briefly describe how separate samples of a primary, a secondary and a tertiary alcohol might be distinguished using the redox reactions and Fehling's solution discussed above. (Note that the tests are for aldehydes and ketones, so you need to make them first.)

The copper(II) complex ion gives Fehling's solution its blue colour. After an aldehyde is oxidised, the copper(II) ion is reduced to brick-red Cu_2O.

The silver(I) complex ion in Tollens' reagent is reduced by an aldehyde to metallic silver.

Reduction reactions

The oxidation sequences to make aldehydes and ketones, described in Section 5.1, can be reversed with a strong reducing agent such as lithium tetrahydridoaluminate ($LiAlH_4$, which is used in non-aqueous solvents) or sodium tetrahydridoborate ($NaBH_4$, which can be used in water). These agents (represented as [H] in the equations) reduce aldehydes to primary alcohols and ketones to secondary alcohols. Carboxylic acids can also be reduced to primary alcohols because they are first reduced to aldehydes.

Acids and aldehydes

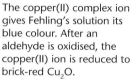

acid   aldehyde   primary alcohol

Ketones

$$R_1-\overset{\displaystyle }{\underset{\displaystyle O}{C}}-R_2 \xrightarrow{2[H]} R_1-\overset{\displaystyle H}{\underset{\displaystyle OH}{C}}-R_2$$

ketone   secondary alcohol

The latter equation shows that such reductions are also nucleophilic addition reactions. $NaBH_4$ provides hydride ions ($:H^-$), which act as the nucleophile. The mechanism for this process is shown in Fig. 2.

Table 3 Oxidation of alcohols, aldehydes and ketones

Oxidising agent	Primary alcohol	Secondary alcohol	Tertiary alcohol	Aldehyde	Ketone
$K_2Cr_2O_7/H^+$	✓	✓	✗	✓	✗
Fehling's reagent	✗	✗	✗	✓	✗
Tollens' reagent	✗	✗	✗	✓	✗

Fig. 2   Nucleophilic addition of hydride

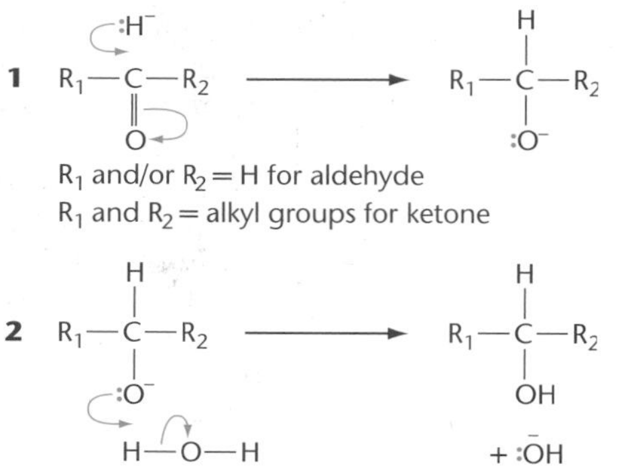

R_1 and/or $R_2 =$ H for aldehyde
R_1 and $R_2 =$ alkyl groups for ketone

15 Naming the organic product, write equations for the reduction of:

a propanal

b pentan-2-one

c butanoic acid

d then using sodium tetrahydridoborate ($NaBH_4$), use [H] to represent the reductant.

key facts

- Primary alcohols can be oxidised first to aldehydes and then to carboxylic acids.
- Secondary alcohols can be oxidised to ketones.
- Tertiary alcohols are not easily oxidised.
- Aldehydes can be reduced to primary alcohols.

- Ketones can be reduced to secondary alcohols.
- Aldehydes and ketones undergo nucleophilic addition reactions.
- Fehling's and Tollens' tests distinguish aldehydes from ketones.

5.3 Carboxylic acids

Table 4   The first four carboxylic acids

methanoic acid	HCOOH	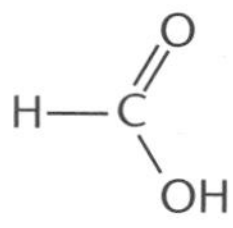
ethanoic acid	CH_3COOH	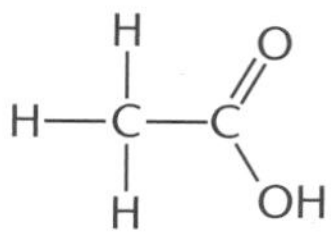
propanoic acid	CH_3CH_2COOH	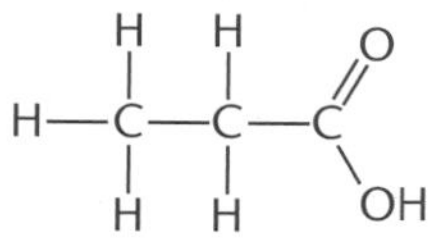
butanoic acid	$CH_3CH_2CH_2COOH$	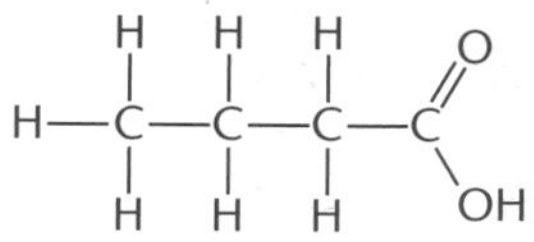

As described earlier, carboxylic acids are produced by the oxidation of primary alcohols or aldehydes. Ethanoic acid is the acid responsible for the vinegary taste of wine that has been oxidised by exposure to air (see the beginning of this chapter). The characteristic functional group of carboxylic acids is:
        –COOH.

Carboxylic acids with fewer than six carbon atoms per molecule are water soluble. In aqueous solution they are only slightly ionised to give low concentrations of hydrogen ions and alkanoate ions:

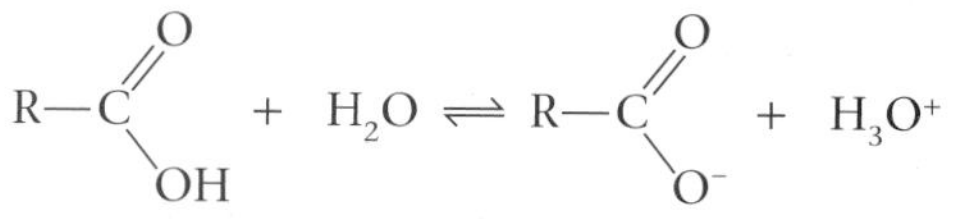

This partial ionisation in solution means that carboxylic acids are *weak acids*.

Nevertheless, the concentration of hydrogen ions is sufficient to displace carbon dioxide gas from an aqueous solution of sodium carbonate. This gaseous product provides a useful test for the possible presence of a carboxylic acid:

$$2RCOOH + Na_2CO_3 \rightarrow 2RCOO^-Na^+ + CO_2 + H_2O$$

16 The values for the acid dissociation constant K_a (see Chapter 3) of some carboxylic acids are:

- ethanoic acid 2×10^{-5} mol dm^{-3}
- benzoic acid 1×10^{-5} mol dm^{-3}
- methanoic acid 1×10^{-4} mol dm^{-3}.

Use these to place 0.1 mol dm^{-3} solutions of these acids in order of increasing pH.

5.4 Esters

An ester is formed when an alcohol and a carboxylic acid react together in the presence of a concentrated, strong acid catalyst (e.g. sulfuric acid or concentrated hydrochloric acid). The general equation for this type of reaction is:

acid   alcohol   ester

Radioactive labelling of the starting materials shows that, in most cases, the C–O bond in the acid breaks rather than the C–O bond in the alcohol. Table 5 gives some examples of ester formation.

structure. Such reactions are vitally important in the production of natural and artificial polymers, as we will see in Chapter 9.

17 Write an equation for the reaction of butanoic acid with propan-1-ol, and name the organic product.

Ester formation reactions are reversible, and produce relatively low yields of esters. Higher yields of esters are obtained by reacting the alcohol with the acid chloride or acid anhydride instead of the carboxylic acid. These reactions are also called **acylations** and will be discussed in detail in Chapter 7.

Esters are the 'smells and flavours' of chemistry. They are responsible for many flower scents and fruit flavours. The artificial fruit flavours (e.g. cherry, banana, pear) used in some confectionery products are made by mixing synthetic esters together. Some of these are shown in Table 6.

We can use the sweet or fruity smell of an ester as a test for the presence of an alcohol or carboxylic acid. If we suspect that the compound

Table 5   Ester formation

Acid	+ methanol gives:	+ ethanol gives:
ethanoic acid CH_3-C (=O) OH	methyl ethanoate $CH_3-C-O-CH_3$ (=O)	ethyl ethanoate $CH_3-C-O-CH_2CH_3$ (=O)
propanoic acid CH_3CH_2-C (=O) OH	methyl propanoate $CH_3CH_2-C-O-CH_3$ (=O)	ethyl propanoate $CH_3CH_2-C-O-CH_2CH_3$ (=O)

This reaction is often referred to as an **esterification**, but it is also known as a **condensation reaction** since a small molecule (e.g. H_2O) is eliminated from two carbon-based molecules that form a larger

Table 6   Ester fragrances

Ester	Essence
ethyl methanoate	raspberry
ethyl butanoate	pineapple
ethyl ethanoate	pear drops
2-pentyl ethanoate	pear

Esters flavour the sweets in this Turkish sweet shop.

we are investigating is an alcohol, we can warm it with a carboxylic acid (e.g. ethanoic acid) in the presence of concentrated sulfuric acid as a catalyst. The excess acid, which has a pungent vinegary smell, is removed by adding warm, aqueous sodium carbonate solution. The sweet smell of an ester confirms the presence of an alcohol. As the ester is immiscible with water, because it cannot form hydrogen bonds to water, the other components of the reaction mixture will dissolve but the ester will float on the surface. The warmth of the solution then causes the ester to evaporate, and the sweet smell is easily detected.

Esters are also used as **plasticisers**, which are additives mixed into polymers to increase the flexibility of the polymer.

Poly(chloroethene), better known as PVC (see Chapter 9), is a strong and rigid polymer suitable for making drainpipes and guttering. However, when treated with up to 18% by mass of an appropriate plasticising ester, it becomes clingfilm, used as a food wrapping material for non-fatty foods.

PVC consists of very long polymer chains. The carbon–chlorine bond is strongly polar and there is considerable intermolecular attraction between the polymer chains (Fig. 3). PVC is therefore a strong and rigid plastic. Plasticiser molecules penetrate between the polymer chains and increase the distance between the chains. The polar effects of the carbon–chlorine bond are weakened and the rigidity of the three-dimensional structure is reduced (Fig. 4). As a result, the polymer chains can slide over each other and the resulting plastic is soft and pliable, as clingfilm must be.

The ester originally used as a plasticiser in clingfilm was di(2-ethylhexyl) adipate (commonly called DEHA). DEHA is an ester of 2-ethylhexan-1-ol and adipic acid (hexanedioic acid). Such placticised PVC is also used to make imitation leather for car seats, shoes, briefcases,

Fig. 3   Intermolecular forces in PVC

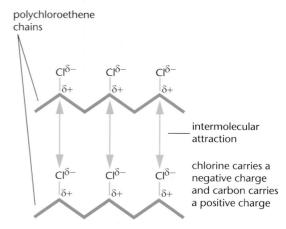

the dipoles in the carbon–chlorine bonds attract adjacent polymer chains

Fig. 4   Plasticiser reduces rigidity

distance too great for intermolecular forces to be effective

etc. Over time the plasticiser evaporates, causing the 'leather' to lose its flexibility and crack.

Unlike the acids and alcohols from which they are derived, esters have no –OH groups with which to form hydrogen bonds. They therefore have lower boiling points than their constituent acids and alcohols. This accounts for their 'smelly' nature: volatile compounds can reach our noses more easily than less volatile ones.

The lack of an –OH group also means that esters are not very soluble in water. The presence of carbon chains, however, makes them fat-soluble. When esters are used as plasticisers in clingfilm, their volatility and solubility in fat poses problems. Clingfilm containing DEHA has caused several health scares

18

a Draw the structural formula of 2-ethylhexan-1-ol.

b Draw the structure of hexanedioic acid.

c Hence, write an equation for the formation of DEHA.

because this ester can dissolve from the film into food. Hence, such clingfilm is not used for foods such as cheese, which has a high fat content. Newer PVC clingfilms have been produced for general use, as well as for use in microwave ovens. The new types of clingfilm contain either a mixture of two plasticisers – a polymeric plasticiser (typically 1%–11%) and DEHA (typically 10%–13%) – or a polymeric plasticiser only. The polymeric plasticiser contains long molecules of polymerised esters, which cannot diffuse from the film to the food very easily, because of their high relative molecular mass.

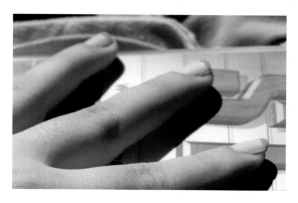

The volatile esters used as solvents in nail varnish quickly evaporate in the air.

Fig. 5 Hydrolysis is the reverse of esterification

$$\text{e.g.} \quad R_1\!-\!\underset{\underset{O}{\|}}{C}\!-\!O\!-\!R_2 + H_2O \;\rightleftharpoons\; R_1\!-\!\underset{\underset{O}{\|}}{C}\!-\!OH + R_2\!-\!OH$$

$$\text{ester} \qquad\qquad\qquad \text{acid} \qquad\quad \text{alcohol}$$

$$\downarrow \text{NaOH}$$

$$R_1\!-\!\underset{\underset{O}{\|}}{C}\!-\!O^-Na^+ + H_2O$$

$$\text{salt}$$

Esters are also commonly used as solvents for organic compounds. Fragrances and nail varnishes, for example, often contain ethyl ethanoate. The ingredients are dissolved in the ester, which evaporates in air and leaves the scent or varnish behind.

Hydrolysis of esters

The reverse of an esterification reaction is called **hydrolysis**. The ester is split ('lysis') by the action of water ('hydro') to re-form the acid and the alcohol (Fig. 5). Such a hydrolysis requires heat and a concentrated sulfuric acid or sodium hydroxide catalyst. If the latter is used, it needs to be present in excess because the carboxylic acid produced from the ester would react to form a salt.

19 Naming the products, write equations for the hydrolysis of:

a ethyl ethanoate by hot concentrated sulfuric acid solution

b methyl propanoate by hot sodium hydroxide solution.

Soaps

Soaps are salts of long-chain carboxylic acids (also called **fatty acids**) produced by ester hydrolysis. The fatty acids are derived from fats and oils which are naturally occurring **tri-esters** of the trihydric (i.e. containing three –OH groups) alcohol propane-1,2,3-triol (also known as 'glycerol'), and three fatty acids. These acids usually have 14, 16, 18 or 20 carbon atoms, one example being octadecanoic acid (stearic acid) as shown in Fig. 7.

Fats and oils are hydrolysed to produce **soaps** by boiling with aqueous sodium hydroxide solution in a process also called **saponification** (Fig. 6). After the boiling is complete, common salt is added to precipitate the soap. Since the hydrolysis is done under alkaline conditions, the product is a mixture of glycerol and the salts of the fatty acids, soaps. Whenever soaps are manufactured, glycerol is a useful by-product that has extensive uses in pharmaceutical and cosmetic preparations.

Soaps are **anionic detergents**. As illustrated in Fig. 8, the negatively charged carboxyl group of a soap is attracted to water: it is hydrophilic.

Fig. 6   Hydrolysis to produce soaps is called saponification

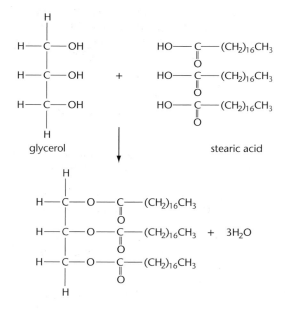

$$H-C-O.CO.R$$

$$\begin{array}{c} H \\ | \\ H-C-O.CO.R \\ | \\ H-C-O.CO.R \\ | \\ H-C-O.CO.R \\ | \\ H \end{array} + 3NaOH \longrightarrow \begin{array}{c} H \\ | \\ H-C-OH \\ | \\ H-C-OH \\ | \\ H-C-OH \\ | \\ H \end{array} + 3R-\underset{\underset{O}{\|}}{C}-O^-Na^+$$

e.g. $R = C_{17}H_{35}$ a soap

e.g. $R = C_{17}H_{35}COONa$, sodium stearate

Conversely, the long hydrocarbon chains are attracted to oil rather than water: they are hydrophobic. When we add soap to an oil–water mixture and agitate the mixture, the oil is broken up into tiny droplets, in a process called emulsification, and dispersed throughout the water.

Fig. 7   Reaction of glycerol and stearic acid

$$\begin{array}{c} H \\ | \\ H-C-OH \\ | \\ H-C-OH \\ | \\ H-C-OH \\ | \\ H \end{array} \quad + \quad \begin{array}{c} HO-\underset{\underset{O}{\|}}{C}-(CH_2)_{16}CH_3 \\ HO-\underset{\underset{O}{\|}}{C}-(CH_2)_{16}CH_3 \\ HO-\underset{\underset{O}{\|}}{C}-(CH_2)_{16}CH_3 \end{array}$$

glycerol   stearic acid

↓

$$\begin{array}{c} H \\ | \\ H-C-O-\underset{\underset{O}{\|}}{C}-(CH_2)_{16}CH_3 \\ | \\ H-C-O-\underset{\underset{O}{\|}}{C}-(CH_2)_{16}CH_3 \\ | \\ H-C-O-\underset{\underset{O}{\|}}{C}-(CH_2)_{16}CH_3 \\ | \\ H \end{array} \quad + \quad 3H_2O$$

Fig. 8   Emulsifying oils

1 Oil covers water in layer a few millimetres thick.

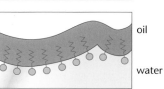

2 Detergent molecules accumulate at interface between oil and water.

$\gtrless$] hydrophobic] hydrocarbon chain

○ polar COO^- group

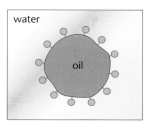

3 Oil breaks up into droplets that can mix with water. The emulsified oil can now be dispersed and broken down much more easily.

The sodium salts (soaps) may be converted to free fatty acids by adding a strong acid such as hydrochloric acid:

$$CH_3-(CH_2)_{16}-\underset{\underset{O^-Na^+}{|}}{\overset{\overset{O}{\|}}{C}} + H^+ \longrightarrow CH_3-(CH_2)_{16}-\underset{\underset{OH}{|}}{\overset{\overset{O}{\|}}{C}} + Na^+$$

sodium stearate   stearic acid

Remember, carboxylic acids are weak acids, so addition of hydrogen ions moves the equilibrium to the right, producing the insoluble fatty acid. This is why it can be a mistake to mix soap-based cosmetics with others based on acidic citric products – slimy fatty acids may precipitate!

key facts

- Esters can be produced by the reaction between an alcohol and a carboxylic acid, an acid chloride or an acid anhydride.
- Esters are commonly used as solvents, flavourings and plasticisers.
- Fats and oils are naturally occurring tri-esters of glycerol with long-chain fatty acids.
- Fats and oils are hydrolysed to soaps by boiling with aqueous sodium hydroxide.

s&c

stretch and challenge

Investigating simple sugars

Simple sugars (monosaccharides) are important biochemical molecules. Glucose (grape sugar) and fructose (fruit sugar) are just two examples (Figs 9 and 10).

Fig. 9   Open-chain structures of glucose and fructose

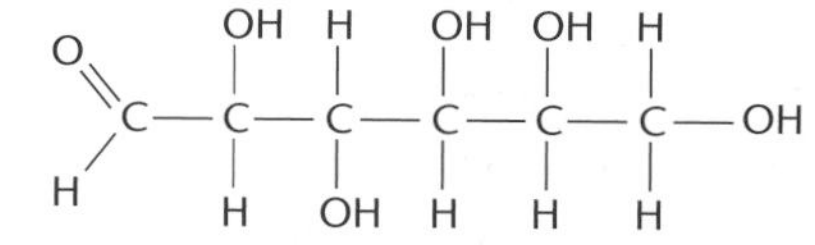

glucose

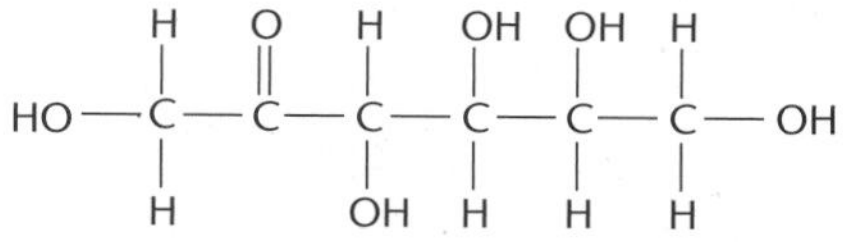

fructose

Fig. 10   Open-chain and ring forms of glucose

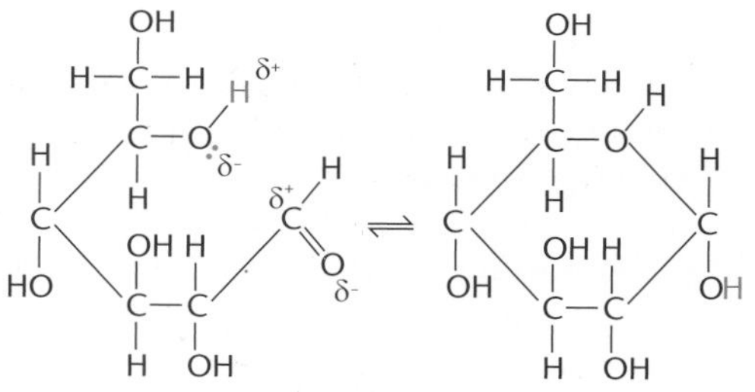

open-chain form   ring form

20 Deduce the molecular formulae of glucose and fructose. What can be concluded from your answers?

DHA is one of the simplest sugars. It interacts with the dead cells located in the upper layer of the epidermis and they change colour to brown. DHA is used as part of sunless skin tanning preparations.

21 DHA stands for dihydroxyacetone. What could be an aldehyde isomer of this compound and what would be its IUPAC name?

22 Redraw the open-chain structures of glucose and fructose in Fig. 9 and mark each of the chiral carbon atoms (see Chapter 4) with an asterisk. Also, in glucose draw circles around any primary alcohol groups, squares around any secondary alcohol groups and triangles around any tertiary alcohol groups.

23 Are these sugars also aldehydes, ketones, acids or esters? Explain.

24 Based on your answers to question 23, describe the procedure and results of a chemical test that should distinguish glucose from fructose. Explain the chemical basis of this test.

This test *does not* produce the expected results! Both glucose and fructose will produce the same visible effects. This is explained by the fact that, in the presence of an acid or alkaline catalyst, fructose will isomerise to glucose.

25 Explain this isomerisation in terms of redox reactions.

26 Draw the structure of the molecule derived from glucose during the test described in question 24.

27 Draw the structure of the molecule produced when fructose reacts with hydrogen cyanide.

28 Name the type of reaction involved in the reaction from the answer to question 27 and show the mechanism.

29 Name the type of mechanism involved in the conversion of open-chain glucose to ring-form glucose.

30 Draw the structure of the first product resulting from the treatment of glucose with hot, acidified potassium dichromate(VI) solution.

31 Draw the structure of one of the products resulting from reacting fructose with ethanoic acid in the presence of concentrated sulfuric acid. What is the purpose of the sulfuric acid?

1 Consider the following reaction sequence:

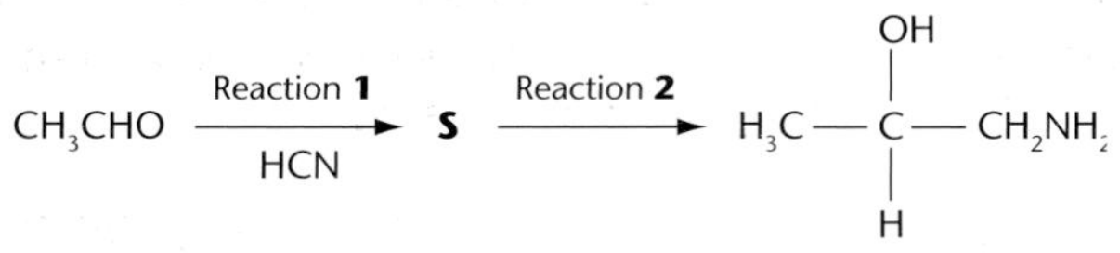

$$CH_3CHO \xrightarrow[HCN]{Reaction\ \mathbf{1}} S \xrightarrow{Reaction\ \mathbf{2}} H_3C - \underset{\underset{H}{|}}{\overset{\overset{OH}{|}}{C}} - CH_2NH_2$$

Name the mechanism for Reaction **1** and deduce the structure of compound **S**.
Give the reagents and name the type of reaction occurring in Reaction **2**. (4)

Total 4

AQA, June 2007, Unit 4, Question 8(b)

2

a Write an equation for the formation of methyl propanoate, $CH_3CH_2COOCH_3$, from methanol and propanoic acid. (1)

b Name and outline a mechanism for the reaction between methanol and propanoyl chloride to form methyl propanoate. (5)

c Propanoic anhydride could be used instead of propanoyl chloride in the preparation of methyl propanoate from methanol. Draw the structure of propanoic anhydride. (1)

d Give **one** advantage of the use of each of the following:

   i propanoyl chloride instead of propanoic acid in the laboratory preparation of methyl propanoate from methanol.

   ii propanoic anhydride instead of propanoyl chloride in the industrial manufacture of methyl propanoate from methanol. (2)

Total 9

AQA, June 2006, Unit 4, Question 1 (a–d)

3 Name and outline a mechanism for the reaction between propanoyl chloride, CH_3CH_2COCl, and methylamine, CH_3NH_2.
Draw the structure of the organic product. (6)

Total 6

AQA, June 2005, Unit 4, Question 7(a)

4 Compound **Z** can be produced by the reaction of compound **X** with compound **Y** as shown in the synthesis outlined below.

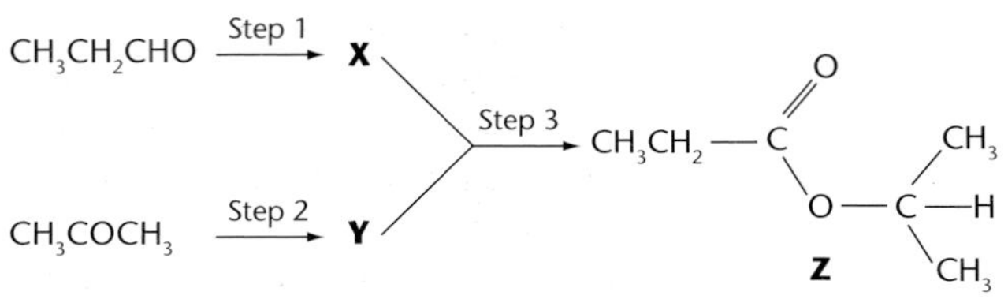

$$CH_3CH_2CHO \xrightarrow{Step\ 1} \mathbf{X}$$
$$CH_3COCH_3 \xrightarrow{Step\ 2} \mathbf{Y}$$
$$\xrightarrow{Step\ 3} CH_3CH_2 - \overset{\overset{O}{\|}}{C} \diagdown \underset{O - \underset{\underset{CH_3}{|}}{\overset{\overset{CH_3}{}}{C}} - H}{}$$

Z

Identify compounds **X** and **Y**.
For each of the three steps in the synthesis, name the type of reaction involved and give reagents and conditions. Equations are **not** required. (10)

Total 10

AQA, January 2005, Unit 4, Question 7(b)

5

a Explain the meaning of the terms *empirical formula* and *molecular formula*. (3)

b Give the three molecular formulas for organic compounds which have the empirical formula CH_2O and relative molecular masses below 100. (3)

In fact, four compounds, **H**, **J**, **K**, and **L** fit this information.

H can be oxidised to a carboxylic acid, **M**, and also reduced to a primary alcohol, **N**.

M and **N** react together, when warmed in the presence of a concentrated sulfuric acid, to form **J**.

L contains a carboxylic acid group and is a structural isomer of **J**.

K contains a carboxylic acid group and shows optical isomerism.

Draw the structures of the six compounds, **H**, **J**, **K**, **L**, **M** and **N**. (6)

Total 12

NEAB, June 1998, CH03, Question 7 (a–b)

6

a **i** Write an equation for the reaction of butan-2-ol with ethanoic acid, showing clearly the structure of the organic product. (2)

   ii Name the type of organic compound formed in part **a i** and suggest a use for this compound. (2)

   iii Give a homogeneous catalyst for the reaction in part **a i** and state the meaning of the term homogeneous. (2)

b Write an equation for the complete combustion of butan-2-ol in an excess of oxygen. (1)

Total 7

AQA, March 1999, CH03, Question 3(a–b)

7

Butan-1-ol can be oxidised by acidified potassium dichromate(VI) using two different methods.

a In the first method, butan-1-ol is added dropwise to acidified potassium dichromate(VI) and the product is distilled off immediately.

   i Using the symbol [O] for the oxidising agent, write an equation for this oxidation of butan-1-ol, showing clearly the structure of the product. State what colour change you would observe. (3)

   ii Butan-1-ol and butan-2-ol give different products on oxidation by this first method. By stating a reagent and the observation with each compound, give a simple test to distinguish between these two oxidation products. (3)

b In a second method, the mixture of butan-1-ol and acidified potassium dichromate(VI) is heated under reflux. Identify the product which is obtained by this reaction. (1)

c Give the structures and names of two branched chain alcohols which are both isomers of butan-1-ol. Only isomer 1 is oxidised when warmed with acidified potassium dichromate(VI) (4)

Total 11

NEAB, February 1997, CH03, Question 4

8

Consider the reaction scheme shown below.

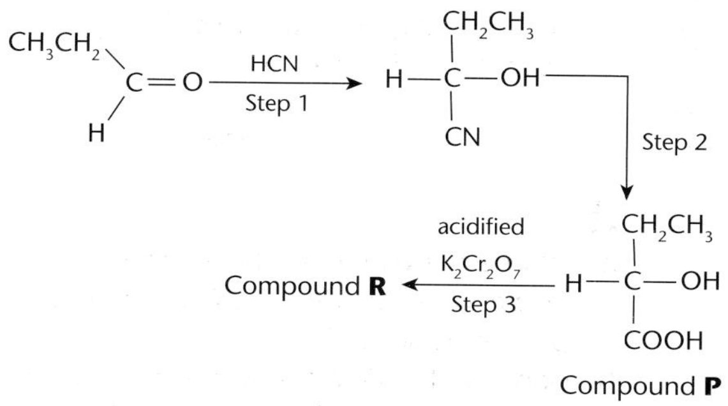

a Name the type of reaction in Step 1 and outline a mechanism for the reaction. (5)

b **i** Name compound **P**.

   ii What structural feature in compound **P** results in optical isomerism?

   iii When compound **P** is made by the above method, the product is optically inactive. What name is given to such an inactive product and why is it inactive? (4)

c Draw the structure of compound **R** formed in Step 3. (1)

Total 10

NEAB, June 1997, CH03, Question 4

how science works **assignment**

Biodiesel and biofuels

Biodiesel, which can be used in normal diesel engines, is made from vegetable oils such as rapeseed oil, sunflower oil or soybean oil, or from animal fat. We therefore refer to biodiesel as a 'green' fuel. The natural oils are converted to esters of methanol, which makes them less viscous. Biodiesel is carbon neutral and is therefore completely sustainable, causing less pollution.

Emission data will vary, depending on the type of biofuel and the engine used, but the following data are typical for using 100% biofuel in a diesel engine.

Type of emission	Change in emissions (%) biofuel replacing mineral diesel
particulates (non-carcinogenic)	−47
carbon monoxide	−48
nitrogen oxides	+10
greenhouse gases	−80
sulfur oxides	−100

A1 What does 'sustainable' mean?

A2 What does 'carbon neutral' mean?

A3 Explain the chemistry associated with the polluting effects of the emissions shown in the table above.

There are also economic advantages of using biofuel: farmers can grow these cash crops on, for example, set-aside land, and the production could lead to increased employment in the agricultural sector.

A4 What are the social disadvantages of farmers worldwide using land for biodiesel production?

Biodiesel, for example, made from rapeseed oil, is produced by a process of transesterification. In this process the triglycerol ester, which gives a thicker oil, is converted to the less viscous methanol-based ester (Rape Methyl Ester, or RME) using a sodium hydroxide catalyst. This esterification is a reversible reaction, so an excess of methanol is used to drive the equilibrium to the right, and under the most appropriate conditions this process can produce a 98% yield.

$$CH_2O-\overset{\overset{O}{\|}}{C}-R$$
$$CH-O-\overset{\overset{O}{\|}}{C}-R + CH_3OH \underset{catalyst}{\overset{OH^-}{\rightleftharpoons}} 3CH_3O-\overset{\overset{O}{\|}}{C}-R + CH-O$$
$$CH_2O-\overset{\overset{O}{\|}}{C}-R \qquad\qquad\qquad\qquad CH_2OH$$

glyceride   alcohol   esters   glycerol

A5 The reaction mix is kept just above the boiling point of the alcohol (75 °C) to speed up the reaction, but the system is totally closed to the atmosphere to prevent loss by evaporation. Which compound would be the most volatile?

A6 What name would be given to the reverse chemical reaction?

There are still issues concerning the growing of oil-rich products or sugar cane, which can be fermented to ethanol, because this method of land use might be in competition with food crops. Oil companies are currently researching technologies whereby the cellulose from non-food plants such as straw can be converted to cellulose ethanol, or wood chip can be converted using an enzyme-based reaction to kerosene (an aeroplane fuel) or diesel.

A7 In the paragraph on the left, the biodiesels can be referred to as first or second generation. Which would you classify as first generation, and which would you classify as second generation?

A8 What are the benefits of 'second generation' biofuels?

6 Aromatic chemistry

Victorian merchants made fortunes sailing to eastern countries for supplies of natural dyes such as blue indigo. This dye was mixed with others to make different coloured shades such as in the purple fabric that was much sought after by royalty and the rich. However, the bottom dropped out of the indigo trade when chemists developed methods for making a much wider variety of equally good, if not better, dyes on a large scale from oil-based materials. Dye molecules are almost always **aromatic compounds**, and the essential feature of most of them is that they contain a benzene ring. This is also true of many pesticides, pharmaceutical drugs, polymers and explosives, which shows the importance of studying the chemistry of benzene specifically and aromatic chemistry in general. Nowadays, the most vivid dyes are synthesised from aromatic compounds and nitrogen compounds.

Modifying the nitro group by reducing the $-NO_2$ functional group to $-NH_2$ produces an amine, which in turn is converted by a process called **diazotisation** to an azo compound. These compounds contain the functional group $-N=N-$ and are the most widely used of all dye compounds. The most important dyestuffs are formed when the azo group ($-N=N-$) is part of a conjugated system (this use of 'conjugated' is not the same as in Chapter 3).

When a molecule contains a series of alternate single and double bonds, this is called **conjugation**. In a conjugated system, the electron charge from the p bonds is spread over more of the molecule – the electrons have become **delocalised**. This spreading of the charge makes the system more stable, reducing the energy of the p → p* transitions. As the transition energies decrease, the absorptions move towards the visible part of the spectrum and give colour.

In 1850, during the era of the Californian Gold Rush, a general trader called Levi Strauss moved to San Francisco and brought with him some canvas material, used for tent making. While working in his store, he realised that the gold miners needed some sturdy hard-wearing trousers that could stand up to all the heavy, rough work of digging and loading the gold-bearing rock. Levi thought he might be able to use the heavy-duty tent material to make some trousers, so he asked a friend of his to make up a few pairs. They were made in a style that was first used for working trousers in Genoa in the 16th century (the French name for Genoa is Genes). The material that Levi used was a type of serge cotton, like that originally made in Nimes in France. So the style became known as jeans (from Genes) and the cloth, which was Serge de Nimes, became known as denim.

White cotton wasn't a very serviceable colour for miners' trousers, so Levi dyed them using the blue dye indigo, which was the one most readily available at that time. From that small beginning, blue denim jeans have become a multi-million-pound industry.

The ancient Britons supposedly covered themselves in indigo (from woad) to make them look fierce.

At the same time Julius Caesar was decked in Tyrian purple. This dye was extracted from molluscs that grew in certain parts of the Mediterranean Sea. It took 9 000 molluscs to produce one gram of purple dye, so it was very expensive and only kings and emperors could afford it. For this reason it was often called 'Royal purple'.

The irony is that the only chemical difference between the two dyes (Fig. 1) is two bromine atoms. Such is the price of vanity – especially if you are a mollusc.

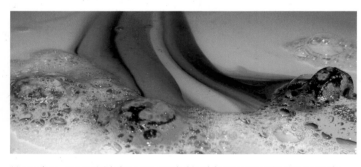

Nowadays, most vivid dyes are synthesised from aromatic compounds and nitrogen compounds.

Fig. 1   Chemical difference between two dyes

indigo

Tyrian purple

6.1 The structure of benzene

hsw

how science works

The word 'benzene' derives historically from 'gum benzoin', an aromatic resin known to European pharmacists and perfumers since the 15th century. In 1825, Michael Faraday extracted a gas. He set it alight and the gas burned; he called it 'bicarburet of hydrogen'. He determined its composition as containing six carbon atoms and six hydrogen atoms. In 1846, A. W. Hoffman isolated the same product, later called benzene, by distilling coal.

The empirical formula for benzene was long known, but its highly polyunsaturated structure was challenging to determine. Archibald Scott Couper in 1858 and Joseph Loschmidt in 1861 suggested possible structures that contained multiple double bonds (Fig. 2) or multiple rings. But the study of aromatic compounds was in its very early years, and too little evidence was then available to help chemists decide on any particular structure.

Although benzene was first isolated in 1825, it was not until 1931 that chemists determined its precise structure. Despite this, as we can see from Fig. 3, a large number of chemicals based on benzene were made and used in the years between: all the products shown in Fig. 3 were developed before the structure of benzene was fully explained! In some cases the eventual main use of a particular chemical was totally different from that originally intended. For example, TNT, a powerful explosive, was initially developed as a yellow dye.

Fig. 2   Early proposed structure of benzene

Until the structure of benzene was fully understood, the development of benzene derivatives and the processes for developing new products were very hit and miss. Nowadays, chemists use detailed structural information and theories to assess whether the production of a new material is feasible before ever trying to produce it in the laboratory. Benzene is one of the first chemicals in history whose unique properties were studied by chemists. The breakthrough came in 1865 when the German chemist, Friedrich August Kekulé, proposed a hexagonal structure with an

Fig. 3   The discovery of important benzene derivatives

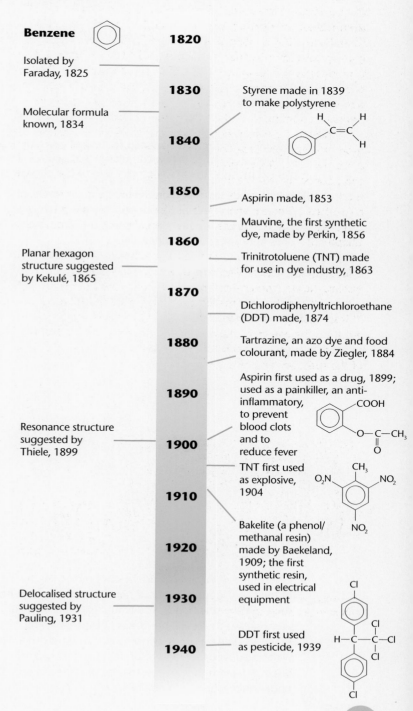

Benzene   1820

Isolated by Faraday, 1825

Molecular formula known, 1834   1830

1840

Styrene made in 1839 to make polystyrene

1850

Aspirin made, 1853

Mauvine, the first synthetic dye, made by Perkin, 1856

1860

Planar hexagon structure suggested by Kekulé, 1865

Trinitrotoluene (TNT) made for use in dye industry, 1863

1870

Dichlorodiphenyltrichloroethane (DDT) made, 1874

1880

Tartrazine, an azo dye and food colourant, made by Ziegler, 1884

1890

Aspirin first used as a drug, 1899; used as a painkiller, an anti-inflammatory, to prevent blood clots and to reduce fever

Resonance structure suggested by Thiele, 1899   1900

TNT first used as explosive, 1904

1910

Bakelite (a phenol/methanal resin) made by Baekeland, 1909; the first synthetic resin, used in electrical equipment

1920

Delocalised structure suggested by Pauling, 1931   1930

DDT first used as pesticide, 1939

1940

atom of carbon and an atom of hydrogen at each corner, with alternate double and single bonds between carbon atoms (Fig. 4). The London Chemical Society proclaimed it to be 'the most brilliant piece of scientific production to be found in the whole of Organic Chemistry', because it served as a new imaginative outlook in chemistry.

Fig. 4   Kekulé structure

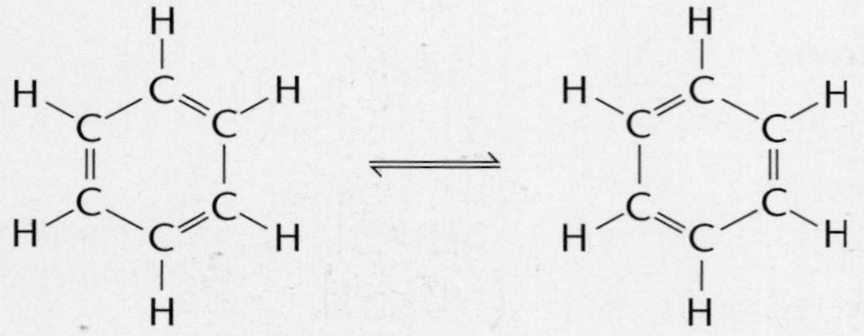

Kekulé's structure was accepted for several years, until experimental evidence was accumulated that could not be explained by his structure. These are four of the anomalies:

1 Kekulé predicted that there would be four isomers of dibromobenzene (Fig. 5), but only three isomers exist: 1,2-, 1,3- and 1,4-dibromobenzene. 1,6-Dibromobenzene does not exist as a separate isomer.

Fig. 5   Kekulé's four isomers of dibromobenzene

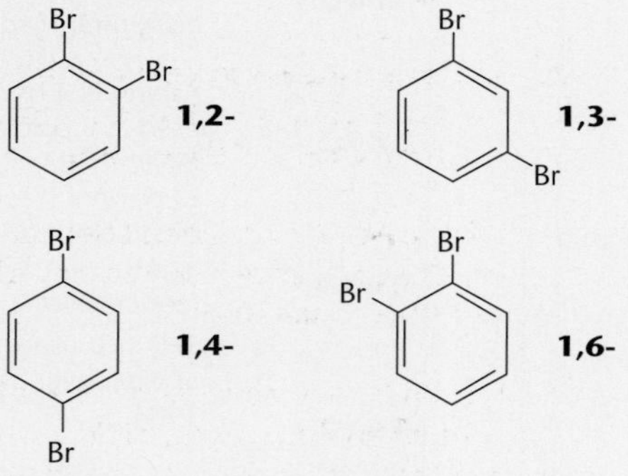

2 Ethene and other alkenes are reactive molecules, because of their C=C double bonds. If benzene contained three such C=C double bonds, you would expect it to be a very reactive molecule, but this is not the case. For example, unlike alkenes, benzene does not react readily with an aqueous solution of bromine. In fact, we will discover later in this chapter that benzene reacts only under quite vigorous conditions.

3 The enthalpy change when a C=C bond is hydrogenated (reacted with hydrogen) is 119 kJ mol^{-1} (see cyclohexene in Fig. 6). Therefore the Kekulé structure suggests that, in complete hydrogenation, $-119 \times 3 = 357$ kJ mol^{-1} should be evolved (Fig. 6). However, the hydrogenation of benzene releases only 208 kJ mol^{-1}. For some reason, benzene is 149 kJ mol^{-1} more stable than the Kekulé structure would suggest.

Fig. 6   The hydrogenation of benzene

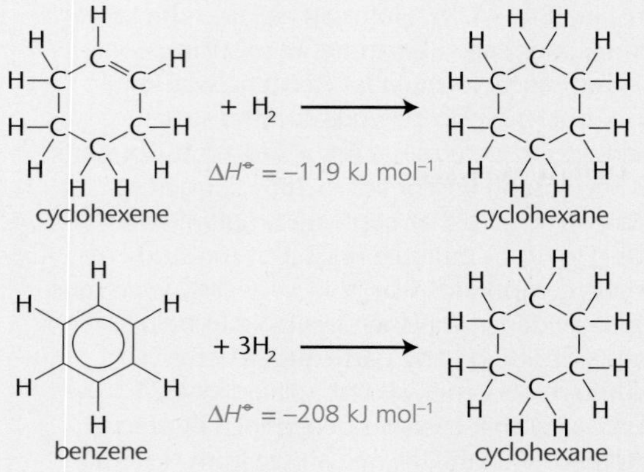

Pauling presented another theory based upon quantum mechanics. Kekulé had proposed that benzene existed in two states and shifted back and forth continually between the two. Pauling believed that the benzene molecule was neither of the two forms that Kekulé presented, but rather a superposition of both Kekulé molecules is the **delocalised structure** (see Fig. 7). Each carbon atom has four bonding, or valence, electrons. Pauling proposed that one electron is used in the bond to the hydrogen atom and two are used in the bonds to the adjacent carbon atoms. The remaining bonding electron from each carbon atom (totalling six) form an electron cloud, which is spread, or **delocalised**, evenly above and below the plane of the hexagon of carbons. This structure for benzene helps to explain the four points that were the problems of Kekulé's structure and explains benzene's non-polarity. Evidence shows that there is an uneven electron distribution located above and below the hexagonal plane. Pauling's discoveries did more than explain the structure of benzene: they established the idea of resonance that chemists still use to explain chemical structures today.

4 The cyclic nature of benzene was finally confirmed by the eminent crystallographer Kathleen Lonsdale in 1931. When the carbon–carbon bond lengths in benzene are measured by X-ray diffraction techniques, they are *all* found to be 0.140 nm. This is intermediate between the lengths of longer C–C (0.154 nm) and shorter C=C (0.134 nm) bonds suggested by Kekulé's structure (Fig. 8).

Fig. 7 The currently accepted structure of benzene

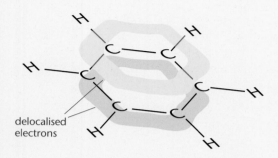

delocalised electrons

Abbreviated to:

Dame Kathleen Lonsdale established that the benzene ring is planar, by doing the complex calculations to analyse the X-ray patterns at home, by hand. She was the first woman to be elected to Fellowship of the Royal Society. (Like Rosalind Franklin, Lonsdale was an outstanding scientist, whose ability was not recognised until later.)

Fig. 8 Bond lengths in benzene

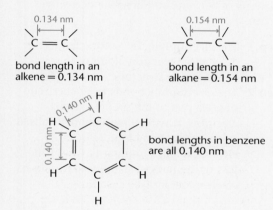

bond length in an alkene = 0.134 nm

bond length in an alkane = 0.154 nm

bond lengths in benzene are all 0.140 nm

We can see that predictions based on Kekulé's structure do not match the actual properties of benzene.

1 The 1,6-dibromobenzene predicted by Kekulé is now identical to the 1,2-isomer.

2 Benzene does not contain C=C double bonds and so does not react in a similar manner to ethene.

3 The delocalised electron structure accounts for the extra stability of the benzene molecule (this has been shown theoretically by Pauling, using quantum mechanics calculations). This extra stability is called the **delocalisation energy**.

4 The delocalisation of electrons accounts for the observed intermediate carbon–carbon bond length. If the six delocalised electrons are 'shared' evenly between the six carbon–carbon bonds, each bond can be thought of (do not take this literally!) as having an extra 'half a bond'.

The structure for benzene currently accepted is that proposed in 1931 by Linus Pauling (Fig. 7).

1 What, according to Kekulé's original structure for benzene, is the difference between the 1,2- and 1,6-isomers of dibromobenzene?

2 Give two examples of reactions you would expect if benzene *did* contain double bonds.

3 How were the bond energies of the carbon–carbon bond used to provide evidence against Kekule's structure?

4 What evidence provided the final structure of benzene and how did the evidence confirm this?

5 Scientists use theories and models to develop and modify scientific explanations. These can form the basis of experimental work. How did the work of Pauling and Lonsdale illustrate this?

6 Scientists had to:
- obtain data to confirm the molecular formula for benzene
- measure and calculate bond energies for C–H and C–C for benzene

For one of these, research and describe briefly how this can be done and describe the scientific representations.

- The benzene molecule (C_6H_6) is a planar regular hexagon.

- The structure of the benzene molecule involves six delocalised electrons.

- Delocalisation of electrons confers stability on the benzene molecule.

6.2 The reactions of benzene

The main reactions of benzene involve the replacement of one or more of the six hydrogen atoms by a functional group. The hydrogen atom is said to be 'substituted' by the reacting functional group. Hence, all such reactions are called **substitution reactions**. Because the delocalised electron system is a region of *high* electron density, such substitution reactions generally involve reaction with electron-deficient (often positively charged) chemical species that have the potential to accept electrons to form new covalent bonds. These are called **electrophiles** ('electron lovers'), so this type of reaction is more fully described as **electrophilic substitution**, as opposed to electrophilic additions, which are the characteristic reactions of alkenes studied in Chapter 15 of *AS Chemistry*.

One general reaction mechanism can be used to describe all the electrophilic substitution reactions of benzene and benzene derivatives (Fig. 9).

Step 1   The electrophile 'E+' is attracted to the delocalised electron cloud of the benzene ring structure.

Step 2   The electrophile bonds to the benzene ring via two of the six delocalised electrons, leaving a partially delocalised system containing four delocalised electrons. This temporarily causes the loss of the natural stability of the six-electron delocalised system.

Fig. 9   The mechanism for electrophilic substitution

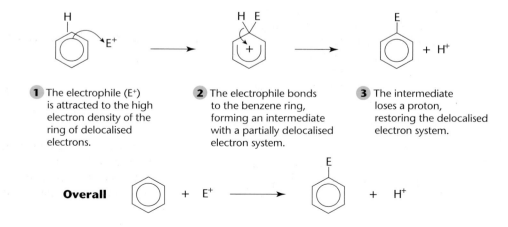

1 The electrophile (E+) is attracted to the high electron density of the ring of delocalised electrons.

2 The electrophile bonds to the benzene ring, forming an intermediate with a partially delocalised electron system.

3 The intermediate loses a proton, restoring the delocalised electron system.

Step 3 A H⁺ ion is lost by breaking the C–H bond. The electrons from this bond re-form the stable delocalised six-electron system.

Several different types of electrophiles (E⁺) react with benzene (Fig. 10). These electrophiles cannot simply be added to benzene to give the required reaction. They have to be produced in the reaction mixture by mixing appropriate reagents. The reaction conditions are generally severe: we have to use heat, concentrated reagents and catalysts to make these reactions take place. This is because of the high stability (low reactivity) of the delocalised benzene structure.

Fig. 10   Products of electrophilic substitution

nitrobenzene

Friedel–Crafts acylation

Friedel–Crafts alkylation

phenylethanone

methylbenzene

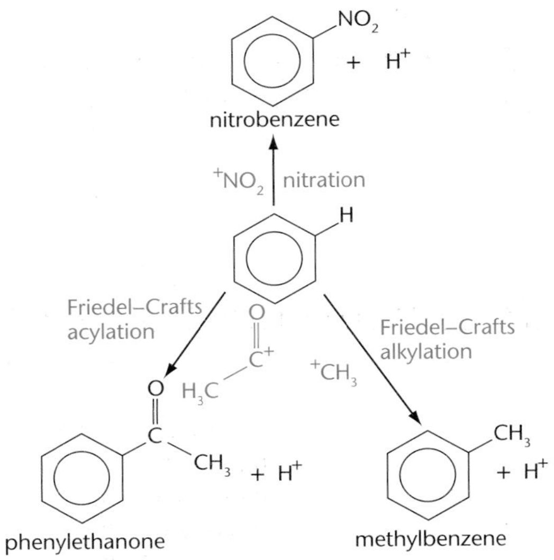

key facts

- Delocalised electrons cause benzene to have a stable structure.

- The delocalised electrons cause benzene to react with electrophiles.

- Benzene usually undergoes substitution reactions.

- Nitration, alkylation and acylation are examples of electrophilic substitutions of benzene.

- Severe reaction conditions and catalysts are required to make these reactions occur.

6.3 Electrophilic substitution – nitration of benzene

When benzene undergoes **nitration,** a nitro group, $-NO_2$, replaces one of the hydrogen atoms. The electrophile is the nitronium ion, NO_2^+, which is generated by mixing concentrated nitric acid and concentrated sulfuric acid, and heating to 50 °C. The overall reaction is represented by the equation in Fig. 11.

The concentrated sulfuric acid donates a proton to nitric acid. This produces an intermediate, $[H_2NO_3]^+$, which decomposes to yield the electrophilic nitronium ion as shown in Fig. 12.

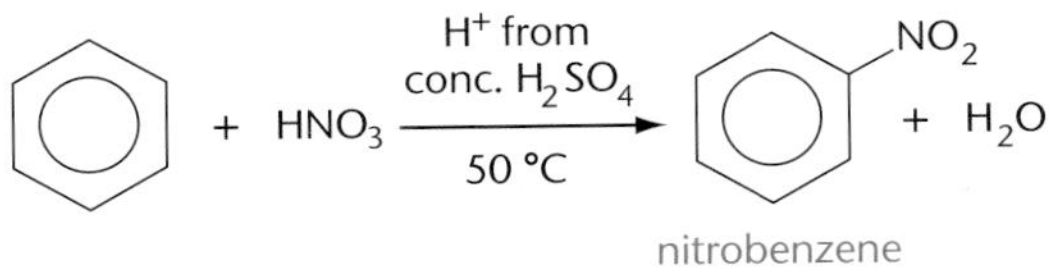

Fig. 12   Production of nitronium ion

$$H_2SO_4 + HNO_3 \rightleftharpoons [H_2NO_3]^+ + HSO_4^-$$

then $[H_2NO_3]^+ \rightleftharpoons NO_2^+ + H_2O$

The concentrated sulfuric acid also acts as a catalyst in the reaction, as it is regenerated when the HSO_4^- ion reacts with the H⁺ ion released in the third step of the reaction mechanism (see Fig. 9).

Fig. 11   Nitration of benzene

nitrobenzene

how science works

Explosives

The well-known explosive TNT was widely used by armed forces, especially during the First World War, and is still used to demolish buildings and bridges and for blasting in mines and quarries.

The full IUPAC name for TNT is 2,4,6-trinitromethylbenzene. TNT is made by nitrating methylbenzene using 'fuming' (very concentrated) nitric and sulfuric acids at a temperature of over 120 °C. The process proceeds via mono- and dinitro-compounds.

7   Name and draw the structures of the three isomers of mononitromethylbenzene.

8   State the type of reaction involved in these nitration processes.

9   Give the reaction mechanism for the mononitration of methylbenzene.

10   The mononitration of methylbenzene occurs more easily than the mononitration of benzene. Does this suggest that the methyl group increases or decreases the electron density in the benzene ring?

11   The second and third nitrations of methylbenzene occur much less easily than the first nitration. Does this suggest that a nitro group increases or decreases the electron density in the benzene ring?

12   What will be the product of reacting 4-nitromethylbenzene with iron and hydrochloric acid? Give its name and structure.

13   What type of substance is produced after diazotisation and coupling of the molecule formed in question 12?

The nitration of benzene and other related compounds is an important industrial reaction. Nitrobenzene is often subsequently converted to phenylamine (aniline or aminobenzene) by reduction of the NO_2 group to an NH_2 group. In industry, iron is used; and in the lab, tin is used with moderately concentrated hydrochloric acid as the reductant. Alternatively, catalytic hydrogenation can be carried out with nickel and hydrogen gas.

14   Write an equation to describe the reduction of nitrobenzene to phenylamine. Use [H] to represent the reductant.

Fig. 13   Making an azo dye

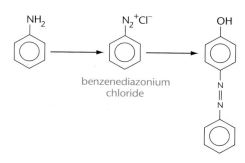

benzenediazonium chloride

4-hydroxyazobenzene an azo dye

Phenylamine is important because it is widely used in the dye industry. As shown in Fig. 13, it can be converted to benzenediazonium chloride

Indigo is a traditional dye derived from plants, which gradually washes out of fabrics; it is still popular for dyeing denim. Synthesised azo dyes are 'faster' dyes, less likely to wash out or fade, and more brightly coloured.

and then to an **azo dye**. These compounds contain two aromatic groups linked by the azo functional group, –N=N–, in a **coupling** reaction. The aromatic groups and the azo group are together called a **chromophore** or **chromophoric group**, and this gives rise to the colour of the dye.

Aromatic nitration is also important in the manufacture of explosives such as 2,4,6-trinitromethylbenzene, better known as 'trinitrotoluene' or TNT. As shown in Fig. 14, this involves substituting three nitro groups on to the benzene ring of methylbenzene (also called toluene).

Fig. 14   Nitro groups in explosives

2,4,6-trinitromethylbenzene
(trinitrotoluene, TNT)

2,4,6-trinitrophenol
(picric acid)

Similarly, 2,4,6-trinitrophenol (also known as picric acid) is an explosive that was widely used during the First World War.

key facts

- Benzene is nitrated by concentrated nitric acid in the presence of concentrated sulfuric acid.

- Nitration of benzene is an electrophilic substitution reaction.

- The electrophile is the nitronium ion (NO_2^+).

- The reduction product of nitrobenzene, phenylamine, is used to make azo dyes.

- Some commercial explosives are made by nitrating aromatic compounds.

6.4 Electrophilic substitutions: Friedel–Crafts reactions

The Friedel–Crafts reactions were developed in 1877 by the French chemist Charles Friedel (1832–1899) and the American chemist James Mason Crafts (1839–1917). They are electrophilic substitution reactions where an acyl group (or an alkyl group) is attached to the ring. An acyl chloride is bonded directly on to a benzene ring using a catalyst such as aluminium chloride or iron(III) chloride. $AlCl_3$ and $FeCl_3$ are Lewis acids and accept a lone pair of electrons from the chloride of the acyl chloride. As we can see from Fig. 15, this process generates acyl carbocations, which are the electrophiles required for reaction with benzene.

Fig. 15   The electrophilic acylation of benzene

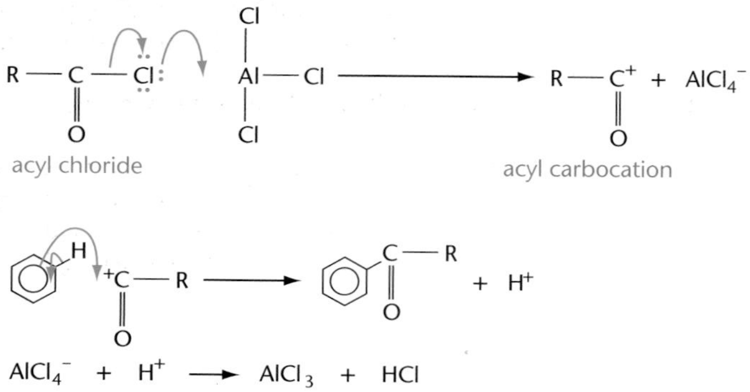

acyl chloride   acyl carbocation

$$AlCl_4^- + H^+ \longrightarrow AlCl_3 + HCl$$

Friedel–Crafts acylation

Ethylbenzene can be prepared using an **acylation** reaction (Fig. 16). When benzene reacts with ethanoyl chloride, the product is

Fig. 16   Friedel–Crafts acylation to produce ethylbenzene

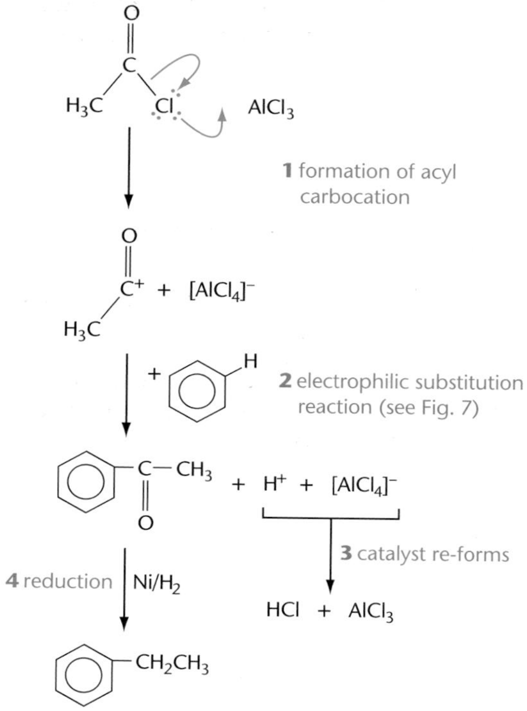

1 formation of acyl carbocation

2 electrophilic substitution reaction (see Fig. 7)

3 catalyst re-forms

4 reduction | Ni/H_2

ethylbenzene

phenylethanone. This ketone is then reduced by hydrogen, using a nickel catalyst, to produce ethylbenzene. As with the other electrophilic substitution reactions studied in this chapter, vigorous conditions are required, in this case, a catalyst and a temperature of about 80 °C. It is also essential to ensure that the reaction mixture is totally free of water because $AlCl_3$ and $FeCl_3$ react vigorously with water.

15 What is a Lewis acid?

16 Draw the structure of the product of the reaction between benzene and butanoyl chloride in the presence of anhydrous aluminium chloride.

17 Describe how ethylbenzene can be made from benzene.

18 Describe the reaction mechanism for the conversion of benzene to ethylbenzene.

19 Ethylbenzene is often converted to phenylethene by heating at about 650 °C in the presence of an iron(III) oxide catalyst.

a Write an equation for this reaction.

b Phenylethene is the precursor for which common polymer?

c Show the general repeat structure of this polymer.

d What are the common uses of this polymer?

Friedel–Crafts alkylation reactions

The alkylation reactions may give polyalkylated products, so the Friedel–Crafts alkylation is a valuable alternative to acylation.

A Friedel–Crafts alkylation reaction is similar to the acylation reaction, but involves a benzene compound, a haloalkane and a catalyst ($AlCl_3$ or $FeCl_3$). When $AlCl_3$ or $FeCl_3$ reacts with a haloalkane, an alkyl carbocation is formed, for example, $C_2H_5^+$, an ethyl carbocation. It is this carbocation that is responsible for the electrophilic substitution reaction. The substituted H^+ subsequently regenerates the catalyst.

Alkylation reactions are used extensively in the petrochemicals industry. For example, the reaction between chloromethane and benzene produces methylbenzene (also known as toluene). This can then be nitrated to give 2,4,6–trinitromethylbenzene (trinitrotoluene or TNT). Very large quantities of ethylbenzene are manufactured for conversion to phenylethene (also known as styrene), which is polymerised to poly(phenylethene), better known as polystyrene. Expanded polystyrene is probably one of the most common packaging and insulating materials in use today.

The alkylation of benzene by propene is known as the cumene process. The product of the reaction is 2-phenylpropane (cumene), which can be oxidised to form phenol and propanone. Propanone is an important solvent used in medical and cosmetic applications; phenol is used as a coupling agent in the dye-making industry.

6.5 Summary

The reactions of benzene and its derivatives form the basis for the manufacture of many everyday materials. A thorough understanding of the structure of the benzene molecule and the nature of its electrophilic substitution reactions allows industry to create, control and develop new applications as the need arises. Many reaction sequences involve combinations of nitration, coupling and acylation reactions, all of which are electrophilic substitution reactions. In this way, a great variety of complex structures containing benzene rings can be constructed.

- The benzene molecule undergoes electrophilic substitution reactions.

- Nitronium ions and acyl carbocations act as electrophiles towards benzene.

- Friedel–Crafts acylations are catalysed by $AlCl_3$ and $FeCl_3$.

- The Friedel–Crafts acylation reactions use acyl halides.

- New carbon–carbon bonds are formed during Friedel–Crafts reactions.

- Ethylbenzene, used in the manufacture of polystyrene, can be made by both Friedel–Crafts acylation and alkylation.

1 Chloroethane (CH_3CH_2Cl) can be used as a reagent in each of the following reactions.

a

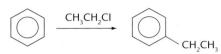

Identify a catalyst for this reaction and show how the catalyst reacts and is regenerated.
Name and outline a mechanism for this reaction.
Name the product shown and identify an important industrial chemical manufactured from it. (9)

b

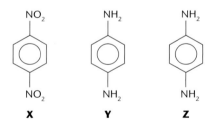

Name and outline a mechanism for this reaction and name the product shown. (6)

Total 15

AQA, January 2008, Unit 4, Question 7

2

a Give reagents and conditions and write equations to show the formation of nitrobenzene from benzene. Name and outline a mechanism for this reaction of benzene. (8)

b Compounds **X**, **Y** and **Z** are shown below:

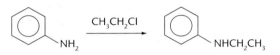

NO$_2$	NH$_2$	NH$_2$
NO$_2$	NH$_2$	NH$_2$
X	**Y**	**Z**

Name **X** and give reagents for the conversion of **X** into **Y**. Write an equation for this reaction using [H] to represent the reductant.
Explain why **Y** is a weaker base than **Z**. (6)

Total 14

AQA, June 2007, Unit 4, Question 7 (a–b)

3 An acylium ion has the structure $R–\overset{+}{C}=O$ where R is any alkyl group.
In the conversion of benzene into phenylethanone, $C_6H_5COCH_3$, an acylium ion $CH_3\overset{+}{C}O$ reacts with a benzene molecule.
Write an equation to show the formation of this acylium ion from ethanoyl chloride and one other substance.
Name and outline the mechanism of the reaction of this acylium ion with benzene. (6)

Total 6

AQA, January 2007, Unit 4, Question 6 (a)

4 i Give the reagents needed for the reduction of nitrobenzene to form phenylamine.
Write an equation for the reaction. Use [H] to represent the reductant.

ii Name the type of mechanism for the reaction between phenylamine and bromomethane. Draw the structure of the product of the reaction of phenylamine with a large excess of bromomethane. (5)

Total 5

AQA, January 2007, Unit 4, Question 7 (b i–ii)

5 A possible synthesis of phenylethene (*styrene*) is outlined below.

a In Reaction **1**, ethanoyl chloride and aluminium chloride are used to form a reactive species which then reacts with benzene.
Write an equation to show the formation of the reactive species.
Name and outline the mechanism by which this reactive species reacts with benzene. (6)

b $NaBH_4$ is a possible reagent for Reaction **2**.
Name and outline the mechanism for the reaction with $NaBH_4$ in Reaction **2**.
Name the product of Reaction **2**. (6)

c Name the type of reaction involved in Reaction **3** and give a reagent for the reaction. (2)

Total 14

AQA, June 2006, Unit 4, Question 6

6 Two reactions of benzene are shown below:

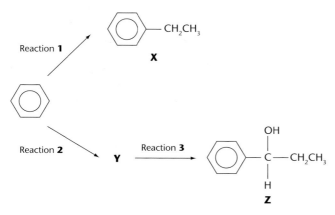

a Name **X** and give the reagent and catalyst required for Reaction **1**.
Write an equation for the formation of the reactive intermediate involved in this reaction.
Name and outline a mechanism for the reaction of this reactive intermediate with benzene to form **X**. (8)

b i Deduce the structure of **Y** and give the organic reagent needed for Reaction **2**.

ii Give the reagent(s) needed for Reaction **3**. (3)

Total 11

AQA, January 2006, Unit 4, Question 7

7 Consider the following reaction sequence:

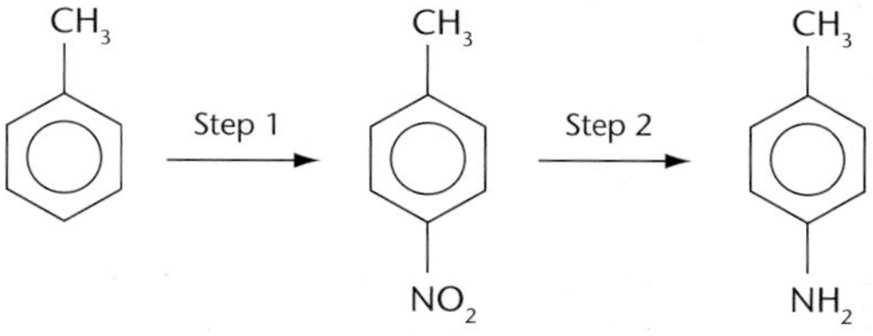

a For Step 1, name the mechanism and give the reagents involved. (3)

b For Step 2, give a reagent or combination of reagents. Write an equation for this reaction using [H] to represent the reductant. (2)

Total 5

AQA, June 2005, Unit 4, Question 5 (a–b)

8 Benzene reacts with propanoyl chloride in the presence of aluminium chloride.
Write equations to show the role of aluminium chloride as a catalyst in this reaction.
Outline a mechanism for this reaction of benzene. (5)

Total 5

AQA, June 2005, Unit 4, Question 7 (b)

7 Amines

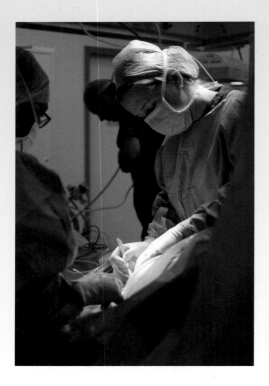

Modern anaesthesia uses a sophisticated range of chemicals and techniques to help the surgeon operate safely.

The main component of curare, tubocurarine (Fig. 1), is both a tertiary amine and a quaternary ammonium compound and is still widely used in medicine. Some nerve gases (Fig. 2) and insecticides are also amines, and the presence of this group is fundamental to their ability to affect nerve action.

Fig. 1   Tubocurarine, a muscle relaxant

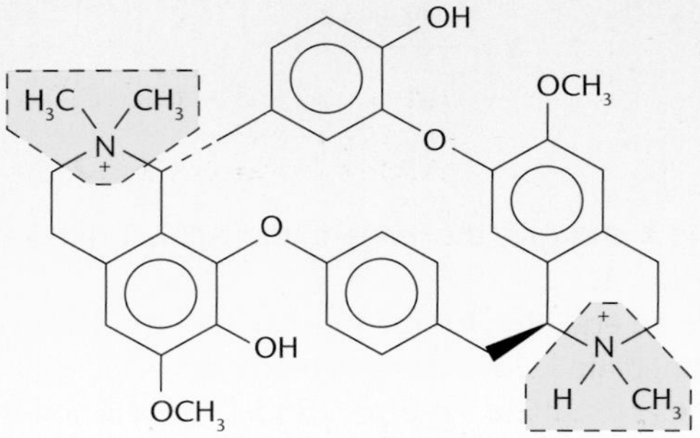

Fig. 2   Tabun, a nerve gas

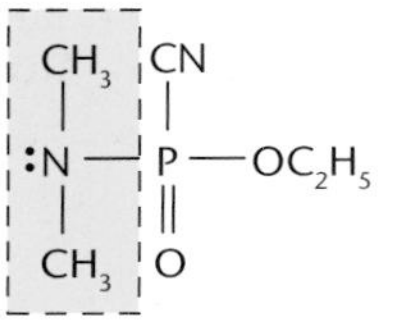

Anaesthetising a patient during surgery involves more than just making the patient unconscious. An important aspect of the process is muscle relaxation, which enables the surgeon to operate more easily and helps the patient to breathe. In the past, large amounts of anaesthetic were used, sometimes not far short of a lethal dose. Nowadays, small amounts of specific muscle-relaxing drugs are used. This has made surgery much safer.

The first muscle relaxant used in surgery was curare. For centuries South American Indians have extracted curare from the bark of a tree and used it when hunting. The extract is applied to the tips of arrows and works by paralysing the prey. Chemists have extracted, purified and determined the structure of the main active compound in curare. They showed it to be derived from organic relatives of ammonia: the amines and quaternary ammonium salts. Tubocurarine, the active chemical isolated from curare, contains two quaternary ammonium groups. Nowadays surgeons understand much more about the chemical structure and the physiological effects of anaesthetics, so use a much safer, synthetic alternative, but still based on the chemical structure found in curare.

Local anaesthetics generally have two features of chemical structure: a fat/lipid-soluble hydrophobic aromatic group and a charged, more water-soluble, amide group. A local anaesthetic will need both of these features to operate effectively. The aromatic ring structure and hydrocarbon chain length determine the lipid solubility of the drug and hence how quickly it can penetrate the cell membrane. The nitrogen-based group interacts with the nerve responses. There are two classes of local anaesthetic drugs defined by the nature of the carbonyl-containing linkage group. The bond between these two groups determines the class of the drug, and it may be amide or ester. Examples of amides include lignocaine (Fig. 3), bupivacaine and prilocaine. Examples of esters include cocaine and amethocaine. Amide drugs are often preferred because they are more stable in solution, heat-stable and very rarely cause allergic phenomena.

All local anaesthetic agents are weak bases, meaning that they exist in two forms: unionised (B) and ionised (BH+). Local anaesthetics are more ionised than unionised. A drug that is more unionised at physiological pH will reach its target site more quickly than a drug that is less so. Most local anaesthetic agents are tertiary amine bases (B) that are administered as water-soluble hydrochlorides (B.HCl). After injection, the tertiary amine base is liberated by the relatively alkaline pH of tissue fluids. The amine group can be primary with one alkyl group attached,

Fig. 3   Lignocaine

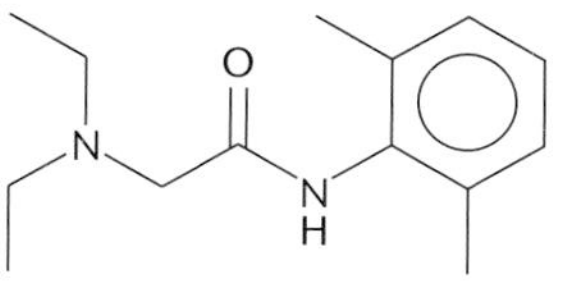

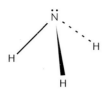

Formal chemical name (IUPAC)
2-(diethylamino)-*N*-(2,6-dimethylphenyl)ethanamide

secondary with two or tertiary with three. The lignocaine molecule contains a secondary and a tertiary amine.

Normally a nerve controlling a muscle releases a compound called acetylcholine into the gap between the nerve and the muscle, which then causes the muscle to contract. Curare and other muscle relaxants stop the acetylcholine from having this effect. Acetylcholine is a quaternary ammonium compound, as are many muscle relaxants.

One such compound is decamethonium (see Fig. 8), which contains two such groups. Decamethonium is used because it mimics acetylcholine but is not broken down by the enzyme that destroys acetylcholine. As a result, decamethonium stays attached to the muscle cell for much longer than acetylcholine and prevents acetylcholine from binding to the muscle cell. The muscle contracts once, relaxes and then cannot contract again even if acetylcholine is released from the nerve cell.

7.1   The structure of ammonia and amines

An ammonia molecule consists of a nitrogen atom bonded to three hydrogen atoms (Fig. 4). In addition to these three covalent bonds, the nitrogen atom also has a lone pair of electrons. This structure is the starting point for the study of the chemistry of ammonia and its derivatives, the amines. The lone pair on the nitrogen atom is responsible for the two main properties of ammonia: its tendency to act as a **nucleophile** and its action as a **Brønsted–Lowry base**.

Fig. 4   Ammonia

Fig. 5   Primary, secondary and tertiary amines

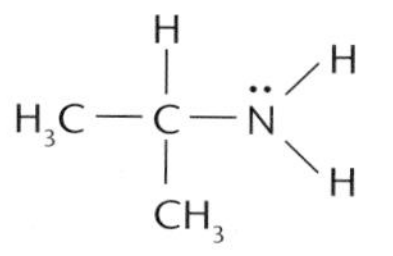

2-Aminopropane (2-propylamine), a primary amine. The nitrogen is bonded to one alkyl group.

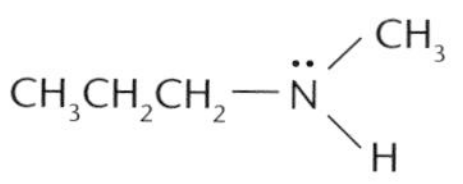

N-Methyl-1-aminopropane (*N*-methylpropylamine), a secondary amine. The nitrogen is bonded to two alkyl groups.

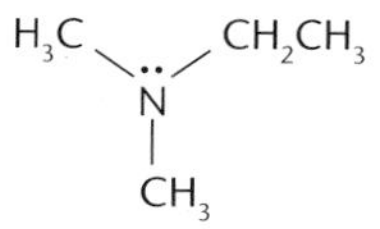

N,*N*-Dimethylaminoethane (*N*,*N*-dimethylethylamine), a tertiary amine. The nitrogen is bonded to three alkyl groups.

There are three types of amines: primary, secondary and tertiary (Fig. 5). These are derived from ammonia when one, two or all three hydrogen atoms are replaced by alkyl or aryl groups. All amines have a lone pair of electrons and so, like ammonia, have nucleophilic and basic properties.

Naming secondary and tertiary amines can be a complicated business (see Chapter 4 for

naming of organic compounds). First we must identify the longest hydrocarbon chain attached to the nitrogen. This, with the ending 'amine' or the prefix 'amino', forms the basis for the name. Then we identify the other smaller hydrocarbon groups attached to the nitrogen and list these at the beginning of the name. The prefix *N*- is used to show that the smaller groups are attached to the main chain via the nitrogen atom.

> **1 a** Draw the structures of:
>
> **i** *N*-ethylbutylamine (or *N*-ethyl-1-aminobutane)
>
> **ii** *N*-ethyl-*N*-methylpropylamine (or *N*-ethyl-*N*-methyl-1-aminopropane).
>
> **b** Classify each as primary, secondary or tertiary.

Many ammonium compounds are used to stimulate or suppress the action of nerves that control our muscles. The primary amine 2-aminopropane (see Fig. 5) is used to manufacture the drug propanolol (Fig. 6), a common heart stimulant used to control irregular heartbeat patterns.

Fig. 6   Propanolol

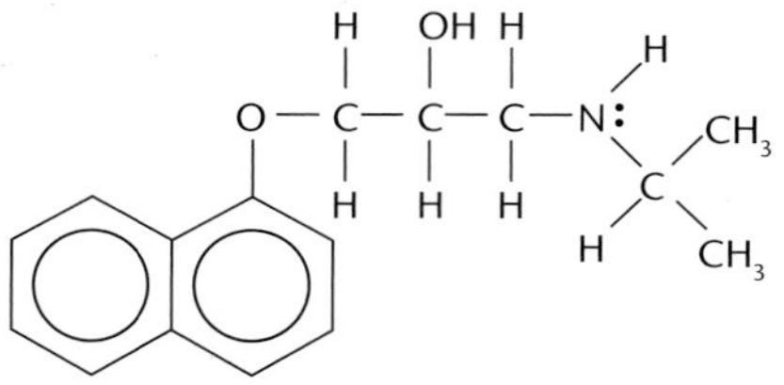

Quaternary ammonium salts (Fig. 7) are produced from tertiary amines when the nitrogen atom's lone pair of electrons forms a dative (coordinate) bond to a fourth hydrocarbon group. Hence, a quaternary ammonium salt is like an ammonium ion (NH_4^+) where alkyl or aryl groups have replaced all four hydrogens. Like ammonium salts, they are crystalline, ionic solids.

Fig. 7   Quaternary ammonium ions

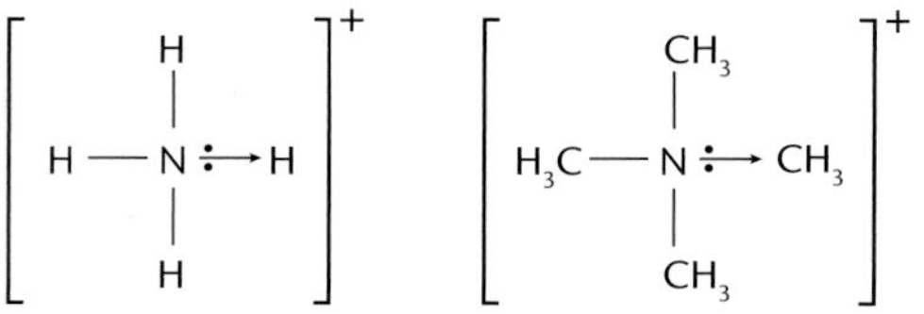

ammonium ion

tetramethylammonium ion, a quaternary ammonium ion

Many compounds that affect the nervous system contain a quaternary ammonium group. Acetylcholine (Fig. 8), which helps in the transmission of nerve signals to muscle cells, contains one such group. Decamethonium (Fig. 8), a drug used as a muscle relaxant, contains two such groups.

Fig. 8   Compounds that act on nerves

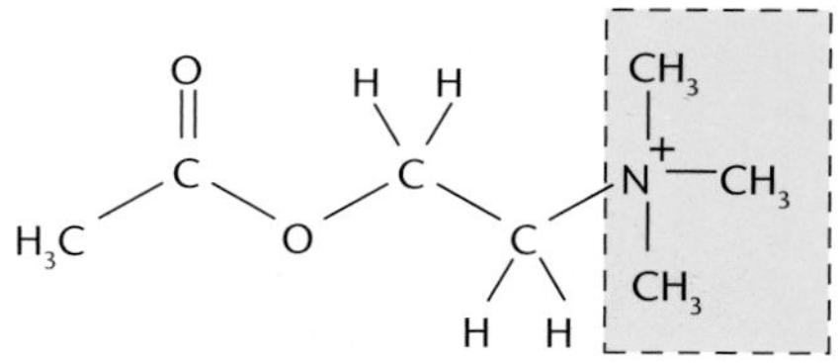

acetylcholine

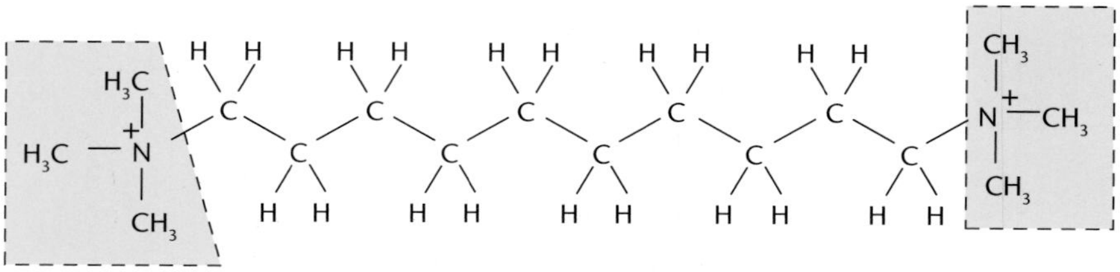

decamethonium

7.2 Nucleophilic properties of amines

Preparing aliphatic amines

Aliphatic primary amines can be made by reacting ammonia with an appropriate haloalkane. This must have the same number of carbon atoms as the amine we are trying to make, and the halogen atom(s) must be positioned on the carbon atoms to which the amino group(s) need to be bonded. Excess ammonia is dissolved in ethanol and heated with the haloalkane in a sealed vessel. Using a sealed vessel leads to an increased pressure, which promotes the reaction.

> **2** Based on the carbon chain of each of the following primary amines, which haloalkane could be used to make:
>
> **a** ethylamine (or aminoethane)?
>
> **b** 1-methylethylamine (or 2-aminopropane)?
>
> **c** hexane-1,6-diamine (or 1,6-diaminohexane), a substance used to make nylon?

Nylon is an extremely versatile material. Because of its high strength, a paraglider can use nylon ropes when climbing a mountain and a nylon parachute when returning to the ground.

The formation of a primary amine from the reaction between a haloalkane and excess ammonia involves three stages (see Fig. 9):

1 The lone pair on the nitrogen atom of the ammonia molecule is attracted to the $\delta+$ charge on the carbon atom of the polar carbon–halogen bond.

2 The lone pair forms a covalent bond between the nitrogen atom and the carbon atom.

3 The amine is released from this salt by the removal of a proton. This can be caused by the excess of ammonia or by adding sodium hydroxide solution.

Fig. 9 Reaction between a haloalkane and ammonia

1 Attraction of ammonia's lone pair to $\delta+$ charge on carbon atom of the polar carbon–halogen bond (R is alkyl group, C_nH_{2n+1}).

2 Covalent bond forms between nitrogen and carbon, with release of bromide ion. An alkylammonium salt is produced.

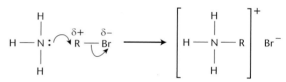

3 Amine released by adding alkali to alkylammonium salt.

The overall reaction is a **nucleophilic substitution** of the halogen atom in the haloalkane by ammonia.

Chloro- and bromoalkanes are preferred as sources of the hydrocarbon groups because they are more readily available than iodoalkanes and are more reactive than fluoroalkanes. For example, 2-phenylethylamine (or 1-amino-2-phenylethane), the primary amine responsible for the common yearning for chocolate, can be made by reacting 1-bromo-2-phenylethane with excess ethanolic ammonia (Fig. 10).

It is not possible to guarantee that only one hydrogen on ammonia will be substituted in an alkylation reaction. Like ammonia, primary,

Fig. 10 The 'chocolate' amine

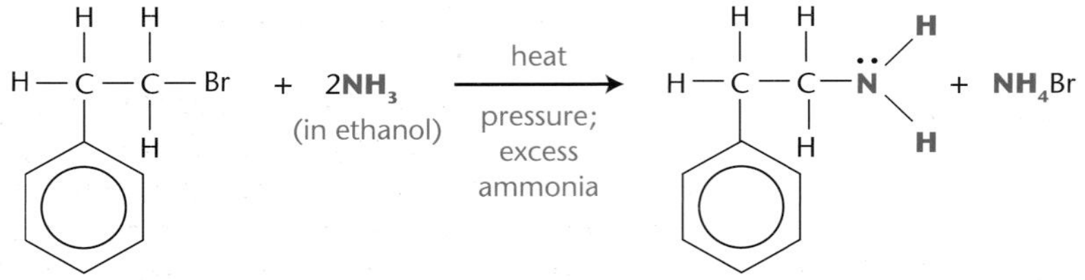

$$H_3C-CH_2-Br + 2NH_3 \xrightarrow[\text{pressure; excess ammonia}]{\text{heat}} H_3C-CH_2-NH_2 + NH_4Br$$

(in ethanol)

2-phenylethylamine
(2-phenylaminoethane)

secondary and tertiary amines have a lone pair of electrons. This allows repeated nucleophilic substitution by the haloalkane. Alkyl groups are electron releasing, and so increase the electron density on the nitrogen they bond to. This in turn means that the product of each alkylation reaction is a better nucleophile than the starting material. As a result, mixtures of primary, secondary and tertiary amines and quaternary ammonium salts will always be produced (Fig. 11).

Fig. 11 Successive substitutions of an amine

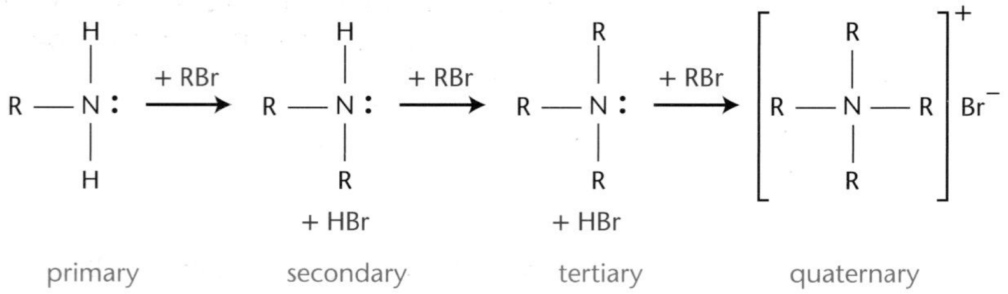

> **3** Give the names and structures of the other amines that could be produced when trying to make ethylamine (or aminoethane) using bromoethane and ammonia.

We can adjust the composition of the initial reaction mixture to favour a particular type of amine. Excess ammonia favours the production of primary amines because it is less likely that a second haloalkane molecule will react with a primary amine when there is a large number of unreacted ammonia molecules available. An excess of the haloalkane, to ensure that each ammonia molecule reacts with four haloalkane molecules, encourages the formation of quaternary ammonium salts.

Quaternary ammonium salts can be manufactured using long-chain (e.g. C_{12}) haloalkanes (Fig. 12). These compounds can be used as **cationic surfactants** because the positive charge on the nitrogen atom of the quaternary ammonium ion is attracted to negatively charged surfaces such as glass, hair, fibres, metals and plastics. This gives rise to applications in fabric conditioners, leather softeners, sewage flocculants (bringing particles to the surface), corrosion inhibitors, hair conditioners, anti-static agents and emulsifiers. Some quaternary ammonium salts with shorter carbon chains are also used in disinfectants where they combine surfactant action with germicidal properties.

Fig. 12 A cationic surfactant

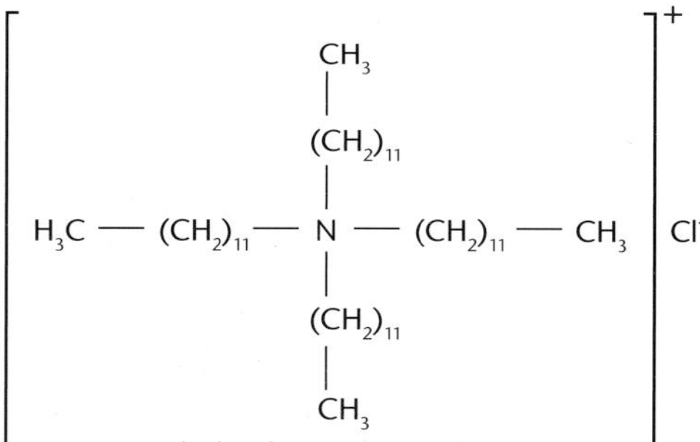

tetradodecylammonium chloride

- Amines and quaternary ammonium salts are derived from ammonia.
- There are three types of amine: primary, secondary and tertiary.
- Amines and quaternary ammonium salts can be produced by reacting ammonia with a haloalkane.

7.3 Preparing primary aliphatic and primary aromatic amines

Preparing primary aliphatic amines

The production of primary amines from haloalkanes is not efficient because mixtures containing secondary and tertiary amines and quaternary ammonium salts are inevitably produced. The way around this problem is to introduce the –NH₂ group indirectly into a molecule.

The first step is to reflux an appropriate haloalkane, such as bromoethane, with a solution of potassium cyanide dissolved in a mixture of water and ethanol. The lone pair of the cyanide ion (:CN⁻) allows nucleophilic substitution of the halogen atom to take place and introduces the cyanide group (–CN) into the organic molecule. Such organic cyanides are called **nitriles**. For example, refluxing bromoethane with potassium cyanide yields propanenitrile (Fig. 13). Note that this procedure allows the carbon chain to be extended by one carbon atom.

Fig. 13 Nucleophilic substitution of bromoethane by cyanide

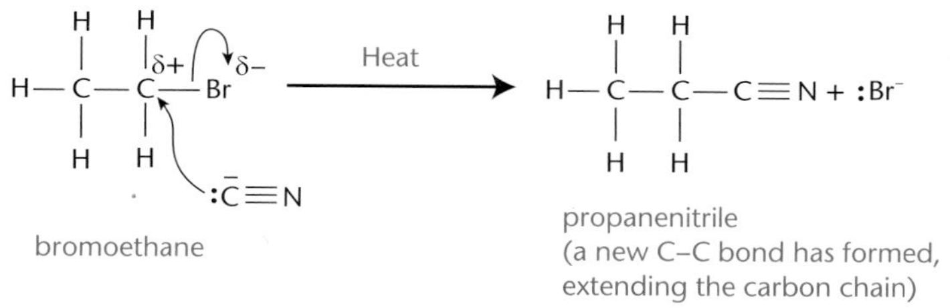

bromoethane

propanenitrile
(a new C–C bond has formed, extending the carbon chain)

The nitrile group contains a carbon–nitrogen triple bond, and it is this bond that forms the basis of the amine group. The triple bond undergoes an addition reaction with two molecules of hydrogen, giving the primary amine. This addition of hydrogen (reduction) can be achieved by using lithium tetrahydridoaluminate (LiAlH₄) dissolved in dry ethoxyethane, followed by aqueous hydrolysis. An alternative reducing agent for this reaction is hydrogen gas with a nickel catalyst. For example, propanenitrile is reduced to propylamine (1-aminopropane) as shown in Fig. 14. Aliphatic primary amines can also be made by reducing nitro compounds and amides.

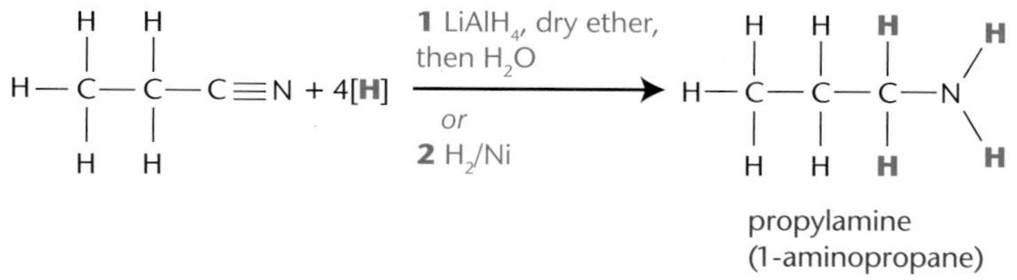

4

a Devise a reaction sequence to prepare 2-methylbutylamine (or 1-amino-2-methylbutane), stating which haloalkane you will use.

b Can 1-methylethylamine (2-aminopropane) be prepared by making and reducing a nitrile? If it can, give the equations. If it can't, explain why not.

Preparing primary aromatic amines

Primary aromatic amines are compounds that contain an –NH₂ functional group directly bonded to the benzene ring. The simplest example of a primary aromatic amine is phenylamine (or aminobenzene) as shown in Fig. 15. The methods we used to make aliphatic amines do not work for aromatic amines. For example, reacting bromobenzene with ethanolic ammonia does not produce a reasonable yield of phenylamine.

Fig. 14 Reduction of propanenitrile to propylamine

propylamine
(1-aminopropane)

Fig. 15 Phenylamine

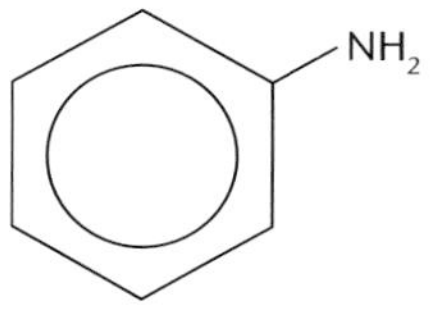

(also called aminobenzene)

There are two reasons why halobenzenes do not react strongly with ammonia:

1. The nitrogen atom in ammonia is nucleophilic, but benzene usually reacts with electrophiles (see Chapter 6) – the high electron density of the delocalised electron cloud of the benzene ring repels electron-rich nucleophiles such as ammonia.

2. The lone pairs of the halogen atom are delocalised towards the benzene ring (Fig. 16).

Fig. 16 The extended delocalisation in chlorobenzene

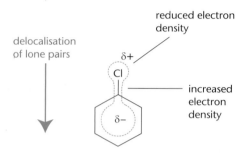

The delocalisation of the halogen lone pairs has the effect of increasing the electron density of the carbon–halogen bond, which, in turn, reduces the polarity of the bond. Consequently, the carbon atom is less attractive to the

nucleophilic lone pair in an ammonia molecule. The increased electron density of the bond also makes it shorter and stronger than the corresponding bond in a haloalkane. This means that the bond is much more reluctant to break and, consequently, the substitution of the halogen by ammonia is much less likely.

As a result of these two factors, preparation of aromatic amines has to take a roundabout route. The nitrogen atom is substituted into an aromatic structure in the form of a nitro ($-NO_2$) group (Fig. 17; see also Chapter 6).

The nitro group is then reduced to a primary amine group using an acid together with a metal (Fig. 18). On an industrial scale, scrap iron and hydrochloric acid are used, but tin and hydrochloric acid is the preferred combination in the laboratory. Since excess acid is present, the product is the protonated form of phenylamine (or aminobenzene), $C_6H_5NH_3^+$. The amine is released from this ion by the addition of a base such as sodium hydroxide; this removes the proton from the $C_6H_5NH_3^+$ ion.

Fig. 18 Reduction of nitrobenzene

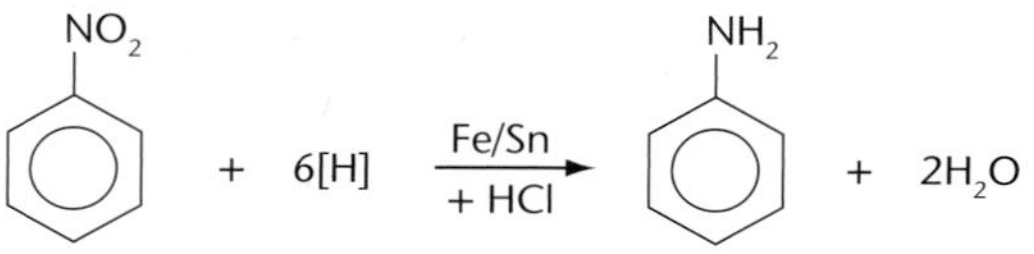

$$\text{NO}_2\text{-ring} + 6[H] \xrightarrow[+ \text{ HCl}]{\text{Fe/Sn}} \text{NH}_2\text{-ring} + 2H_2O$$

The reduction can also be achieved using hydrogen gas and a nickel catalyst:

$$C_6H_5NO_2 + 3H_2 \xrightarrow{\text{Ni catalyst}} C_6H_5NH_2 + 2H_2O$$

The conversion of aromatic nitro groups to aromatic amines is vitally important in the dye industry. It is used to introduce primary amine groups into a wide variety of aromatic molecules used for making dyes or into dye molecules themselves, causing changes in colour and ability to bond to fabrics.

Fig. 17 The nitration of benzene

1. $HNO_3 \text{ (conc.)} + 2H_2SO_4 \text{ (conc.)} \longrightarrow NO_2^+ + 2HSO_4^- + H_3O^+$

2. $\text{benzene-H} + NO_2^+ \xrightarrow{50\,°C} \text{benzene-NO}_2 + H^+$

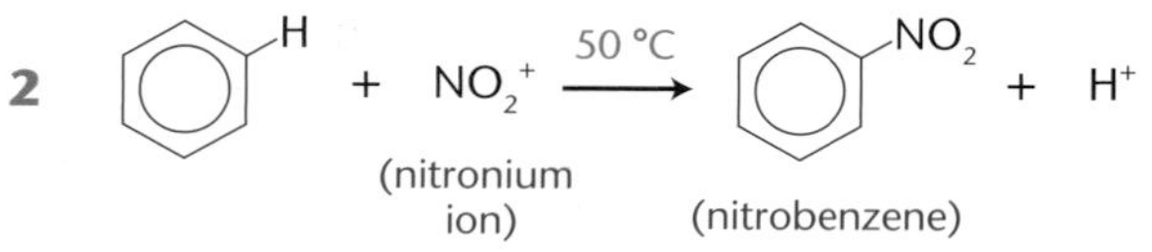

   (nitronium ion)   (nitrobenzene)

3. $H^+ + H_3O^+ + 2HSO_4^- \longrightarrow 2H_2SO_4 + H_2O$

key facts

● Primary aliphatic amines are best produced by the reduction of nitriles.

● Primary aromatic amines are prepared by the reduction of aromatic nitro compounds.

7.4 The base properties of ammonia and amines

Quaternary ammonium compounds such as tubocurarine (the main active component of curare, see Fig. 1) and other muscle relaxants (see Fig. 8) are ionic compounds. Animals killed using curare are safe to eat because the ionic quaternary ammonium salts are not absorbed from the gut into the body. As ammonia and amines are bases, they can accept protons (H^+) from other molecules and also form positively charged ions.

In aqueous solution, ammonia and amine molecules can accept a proton from a water molecule, producing an ammonium ion (NH_4^+) or a substituted ammonium ion ($R-NH_3^+$) respectively, along with a hydroxide (OH^-) ion (Fig. 19). The presence of OH^- ions in the solution means that the solution is alkaline. Ammonia and amine molecules can accept protons because the lone pair of electrons on the nitrogen atom is available to form a dative (coordinate) bond with a proton. However, the reactions are equilibrium reactions (Fig. 19); in other words, ammonia and amines are weak bases.

Fig. 19 Amines as weak bases

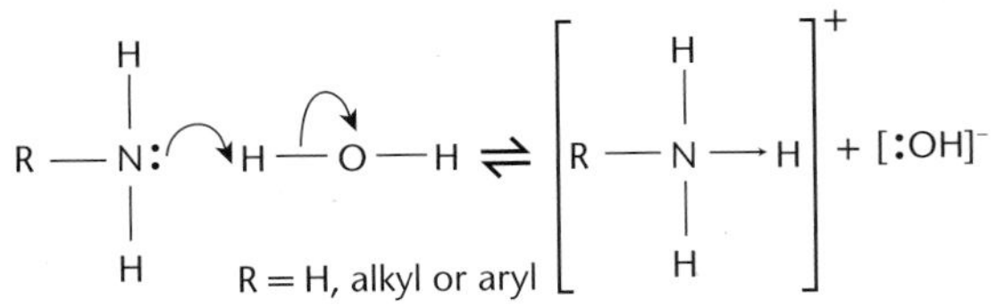

The degree of reaction of ammonia or an amine with water is an indication of the strength of the amine as a base. If we compare the basic properties of equimolar solutions of ammonia, primary aliphatic amines and a primary aromatic amine such as phenylamine (or aminobenzene) (see Table 1), we find that amines are all weak bases: they are not completely converted to ions by reaction with water. Table 1 also shows that an amine's base strength depends on the nature of the group

attached to nitrogen. The base strength of primary amines is increased relative to ammonia by alkyl groups but decreased by aromatic groups. For comparison, Table 1 also contains data on sodium hydroxide, a strong base fully ionised in dilute solution.

Table 1 Comparison of different amines as bases

Substance	pH of 1 mol dm^{-3} solution	% of molecules reacted in solution
ammonia	11.63	0.42
methylamine	12.32	2.08
ethylamine	12.35	2.25
phenylamine	9.32	2.08×10^{-3}
NaOH	14.00	100

In aromatic amines, the nitrogen lone pair is delocalised towards the benzene ring in much the same way as shown in Fig. 16 for chlorobenzene. Overlap occurs between the lone pair and the delocalised electron system of the benzene ring. The electron density on the nitrogen atom is lowered and this reduces the ability of nitrogen to accept a proton.

Alkyl groups, however, are electron releasing and electron density shifts away from the alkyl group towards the amine group. Because of this, the electron density on the nitrogen atom increases, increasing its ability to accept a proton.

This difference in base strength accounts for the need to use dilute acid to dissolve aromatic amines in water. Acid forces the equilibrium shown in Fig. 19 to move to the right (by removing OH^-), causing the amine to dissolve because it is converted to its ionic salt. In contrast, provided the alkyl group is not too large, aliphatic amines are relatively soluble in water alone because there is a stronger natural tendency for the equilibrium (Fig. 19) to move to the right.

- Ammonia and amines act as bases because of the lone pair of electrons on the nitrogen atom.

- Aliphatic primary amines are stronger bases than ammonia.

- Aromatic primary amines are weaker bases than ammonia.

7.5 Acylation of amines and other molecules

Acyl groups (Fig. 20) can be introduced into many molecules by acyl chlorides (also known as acid chlorides) or acid anhydrides, which are known as **acylating agents**.

Fig. 20   Acyl groups

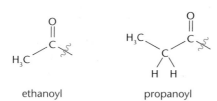

ethanoyl   propanoyl

Acyl chlorides and acid anhydrides (Fig. 21) are derivatives of carboxylic acids. Acyl chlorides are derived from carboxylic acids by substitution of the –OH group by a chlorine atom. Acid anhydrides are derived by substitution of the –OH group by an alkanoate. Hence, the acyl chloride and acid anhydrides of ethanoic acid are ethanoyl chloride and ethanoic anhydride (Fig. 21) respectively.

Fig. 21   Ethanoic acid derivatives

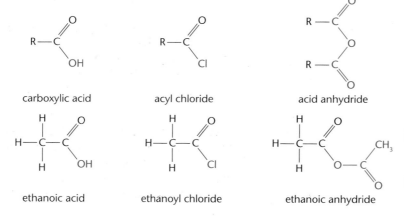

carboxylic acid   acyl chloride   acid anhydride

ethanoic acid   ethanoyl chloride   ethanoic anhydride

5 Draw the structures of benzoyl chloride and benzoic anhydride.

Reactions in which acyl groups are introduced into molecules are called **acylations**. Acylation reactions have many uses, for example, in the pharmaceutical and textile industries. Acylation reactions are used to make drugs such as aspirin and textiles such as cellulose acetate. In general, acid anhydrides make better acylating agents than acyl chlorides. The anhydrides are cheaper to produce and, as they are less reactive, their reactions can be more easily controlled. They are also less corrosive, as acyl chlorides produce hydrogen chloride gas (HCl) when they react. For example, the industrial processes to produce aspirin and cellulose acetate use ethanoic anhydride rather than ethanoyl chloride.

Acyl chlorides and acid anhydrides are both extremely reactive towards nucleophiles. The electronegative oxygen atoms and/or chlorine atoms cause the carbon atom of an acyl group to be electron deficient and therefore open to attack by nucleophiles such as ammonia. This results in an **addition–elimination reaction** as shown in Fig. 22 for the ethanoylation of ammonia. The addition–elimination reaction occurs in four stages:

1 Attraction: the $\delta+$ carbon atom of the polar C=O bond attracts the lone pair of a nucleophile such as ammonia.

2 Addition: the lone pair of the ammonia molecule forms a new bond to the carbon

Fig. 22 Nucleophilic addition–elimination of an acyl compound

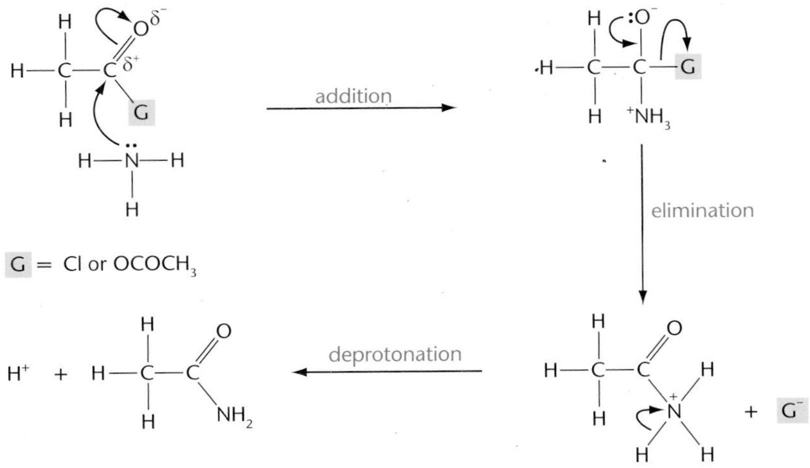

G = Cl or OCOCH₃

atom, producing a saturated ion that has both positive and negative charges.

3 Elimination: the C–Cl of the acyl chloride or the C–O of the anhydride breaks, liberating a chloride ion (Cl⁻) or ethanoate (CH₃COO⁻) as, simultaneously, the C=O bond re-forms.

4 Deprotonation: the new compound is formed by removal of a proton by basic ammonia.

Fig. 23 Nucleophilic acylation reactions

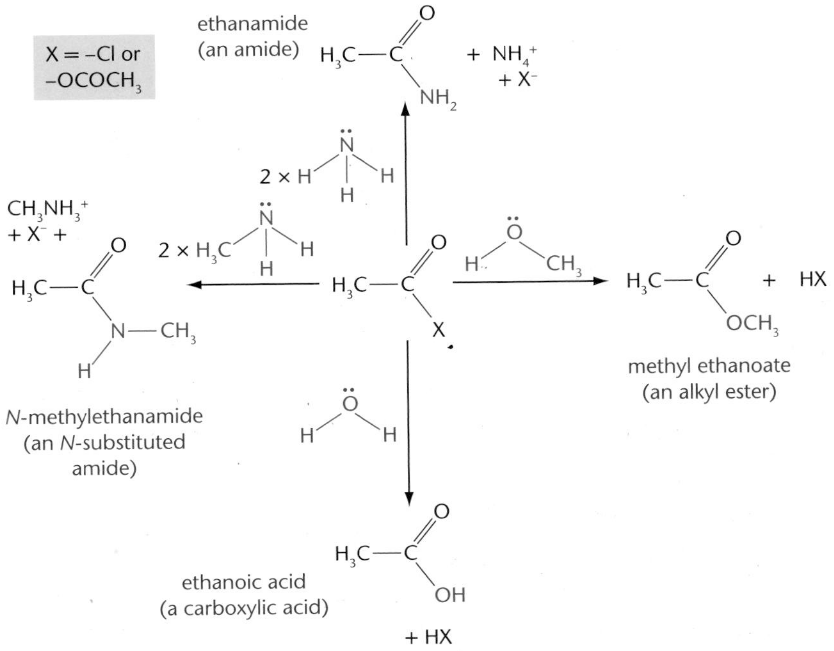

The reaction is a nucleophilic addition–elimination, but overall it looks like a nucleophilic substitution. The nucleophile is said to be acylated, i.e. an acyl group has replaced a hydrogen atom in the nucleophile. Ammonia and primary amines are suitable nucleophiles, as are water and alcohols.

All these nucleophiles have lone pairs, associated with an oxygen atom or a nitrogen atom, *and* a hydrogen atom directly bonded to that oxygen atom or nitrogen atom.

Acylation of ammonia (NH_3) or a primary amine ($R-NH_2$) produces an **amide** ($R-CO-NH_2$). Similarly, acylation of an alcohol ($R'-OH$) produces an **ester** ($R-CO-OR'$). These are shown in Figs 23 and 24.

Fig. 24 Amides and esters

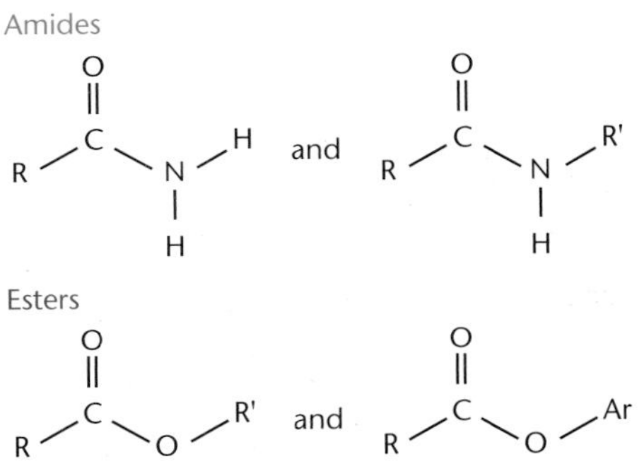

6 Give the name and structure of the principal organic products from each of the following reactions:

a benzoic anhydride with water

b propanoyl chloride with ammonia

c butanoic anhydride with ethylamine (aminoethane).

Write an equation for each reaction.

Extracts from willow bark or leaves were found to relieve pain and lower fever as long ago as 400 BC. The active ingredient in the extract was eventually shown to be 2-hydroxybenzoic acid (salicylic acid, see Fig. 25).

Fig. 25 Synthesis of aspirin

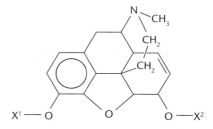

phenol → (CO₂, Kolbe process) → 2-hydroxybenzoic acid (salicylic acid) + ethanoic anhydride → aspirin + ethanoic acid

Another German chemist, August Hofmann (1818–1892), prepared several derivatives of salicylic acid. His aim was to find one with similar pain-relieving properties but no side effects. Acylation of the phenolic –OH group with ethanoic anhydride finally proved to be the answer, producing the compound known as aspirin (Fig. 25). Aspirin was first used as a drug in 1899. Ironically, aspirin had first been made in 1853, but its value as a drug remained hidden for almost 50 years.

> **7** Give three reasons why the manufacture of aspirin uses ethanoic anhydride as the acylating agent, rather than ethanoyl chloride.

Obtaining this directly from the willow tree is not practicable for several reasons: supplies are limited, the concentration of salicylic acid in the woody tissues varies with the season of the year, and any extract is inevitably impure.

The German chemist Adolf Kolbe (1818–1884) discovered that phenol could be converted to salicylic acid by reaction with carbon dioxide. This provided the basis for a relatively easy and cheap manufacturing process, and the Bayer chemical company of Germany was soon producing large quantities of the 'new' drug. However, it soon became evident that salicylic acid caused unacceptable side effects, including severe irritation of the mouth, throat and stomach.

Morphine, a derivative of opium, is a powerful painkiller but it is also highly addictive. As shown in Fig. 26, it contains two –OH groups. If both of these groups are acylated using ethanoic anhydride, heroin is produced. Heroin is even more effective as a painkiller, but unfortunately it is also even more addictive. Codeine has been developed as a compromise; one of the –OH groups is methylated, rather than acylated, resulting in an effective painkiller that doesn't carry the same risk of addiction.

Fig. 26 Derivatives of morphine

Codeine, a valuable painkiller, and heroin, a class A controlled substance, can both be made from opium poppies.

Drug	X¹	X²
morphine	H	H
heroin	CH₃CO	CH₃CO
codeine	CH₃	H

key facts

- Acylation reactions can be carried out using ethanoyl chloride or ethanoic anhydride.

- Industrial acylation reactions are usually carried out using ethanoic anhydride.

- Nucleophilic molecules containing :N–H or :O–H bonds are readily acylated.

- Acylation reactions are used in a wide variety of industrial processes, for example, producing aspirin.

how science works

Making paracetamol

Paracetamol is a well-known analgesic (a pain-relieving medicine), usually sold in tablet form, often mixed with other analgesics. Using the IUPAC naming system, paracetamol is known as 4-hydroxy-(N-ethanoyl-aminobenzene).

> **8** Draw the full structure of paracetamol.

One possible synthetic route for making paracetamol from benzene is summarised in the following flowchart:

benzene → nitrobenzene → aminobenzene → [warm with acidified sodium nitrate(III)] → phenol (or hydroxybenzene) → 4-nitrohydroxybenzene → 4-aminohydroxybenzene → paracetamol

> **9** Including all essential experimental details, write full equations (see Chapter 4) to represent the changes for each of the following steps in this flowchart:
>
> **a** benzene → nitrobenzene
>
> **b** nitrobenzene → aminobenzene.

> **10** Give detailed equations to show the stages of the mechanism for the conversion of benzene to nitrobenzene.

The reaction sequence:

hydroxybenzene → 4-nitrohydroxybenzene → 4-aminohydroxybenzene

can be achieved using the same sort of reactions as in question 9.

> **11** After protecting the OH from reaction, the final stage of the synthesis involves the ethanoylation of 4-amino-hydroxybenzene using ethanoic anhydride. The protecting group then needs to be removed. Ignoring the protecting group:
>
> **a** Write an equation for this reaction.
>
> **b** Describe the mechanism for this reaction.
>
> **c** State two reasons for using ethanoic anhydride rather than ethanoyl chloride as the acylating agent.

Using more efficient methods than described here, thousands of tonnes of paracetamol are manufactured every year and, under controlled use, it has proved a very effective pain-reliever for many minor ailments. This is not to say it has no drawbacks: excessive use of paracetamol can lead to irreversible liver damage.

> **12** Paracetamol is quite cheap to buy. Why do you think some drugs cost so much? Give some reasons for and against drug companies making such large profits.

> **13** Plants in rainforests are a potential source of new drugs. Why is this an important current issue?

1

a Name the compound $(CH_3)_2NH$. (1)

b $(CH_3)_2NH$ can be formed by the reaction of an excess of CH_3NH_2 with CH_3Br. Name and outline a mechanism for this reaction. (5)

c Name the type of compound produced when a large excess of CH_3Br reacts with CH_3NH_2. Give a use for this type of compound. (2)

d Draw the structures of the two compounds formed in the reaction of CH_3NH_2 with ethanoic anhydride. (2)

Total 10

AQA, January 2006, Unit 4, Question 5

2 The following reaction scheme shows the formation of two amines, **K** and **L**, from methylbenzene.

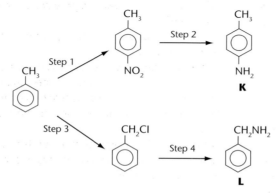

a i Give the reagents needed to carry out Step 1. Write an equation for the formation from these reagents of the inorganic species which reacts with methylbenzene.

ii Name and outline a mechanism for the reaction between this inorganic species and methylbenzene. (7)

b Give a suitable reagent or combination of reagents for Step 2. (1)

c i Give the reagent for Step 4 and state a condition to ensure that the primary amine is the major product.

ii Name and outline a mechanism for Step 4. (7)

d Explain why amine **K** is a weaker base than ammonia. (2)

e Draw the structure of the organic compound formed when a large excess of bromomethane reacts with amine **L**. (1)

f Draw the structure of the organic compound formed when ethanoyl chloride reacts with amine **L** in an addition–elimination reaction. (1)

Total 19

AQA, January 2005, Unit 4, Question 1

3

a Explain how methylamine can act as a Brønsted–Lowry base.

b Explain why phenylamine is a weaker base than ammonia.

c i Name the type of mechanism involved when methylamine is formed from bromomethane and ammonia.

ii Give the structures of three organic compounds other than methylamine which can be obtained from the reaction between an excess of bromomethane and ammonia.

iii Name the type of compound formed in part **c ii** which can be used as a cationic surfactant. (5)

Total 5

AQA, CH06 March 1999, Question 3

4

a Give the structural formulae of the **four** isomers of C_3H_9N.

b Show, by means of an equation, how one of the above isomers can be obtained from the reaction between 1-bromopropane and ammonia.
Name the type of reaction taking place and outline a mechanism.

c Explain why the reduction of propanenitrile is a more suitable method for preparing this isomer than the reaction you have given in part **b**. (6)

Total 6

NEAB, CH06 February 1996, Question 3

5

a Write an equation for the reaction between ethanoyl chloride and dimethylamine. Name and outline the mechanism of this reaction.

b Aspirin is manufactured by the reaction of 2-hydroxybenzenecarboxylic acid with ethanoic anhydride. Write an equation for this reaction and give two reasons why ethanoic anhydride, rather than ethanoyl chloride, is used. (4)

Total 4

NEAB, CH06, March 1998, Question 3

6 The hormone adrenalin is secreted by the adrenal gland and it stimulates the nervous system allowing rapid response to danger or unusual circumstances. Its chemical structure is:

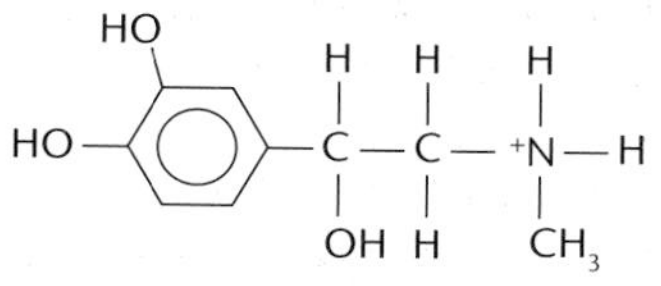

adrenalin

a Ignoring any effects on other functional groups, draw the structure of the amine (amine A) which would be produced by adding sodium hydroxide solution to adrenalin. How would this product be reconverted to adrenalin?

b Explaining your answer, classify amine A as primary, secondary or tertiary.

c Draw the structures of the two different products resulting from the reaction between amine A and chloromethane. How would reaction conditions be adjusted to favour the production of either of these possibilities?

d Using $R–NHCH_3$ as an abbreviation for the amine A, describe the mechanism of the first reaction between it and chloromethane. (8)

Total 8

8 Amino acids

It is said that we are what we eat. This is not strictly true: we are composed of similar materials to those we eat, but the food materials are broken down by digestive processes and then built up again in the way that our bodies require.

Every cell contains protein – our muscles are made up of a high percentage of protein – so it is not surprising that we need a daily balanced intake of protein. The protein molecules are broken down to provide a supply of **amino acids**. Our own characteristic proteins, vital for a healthy life, are then built up from these amino acids and their breakdown products.

Meat, eggs, dairy products, fish, peas and beans are all protein-rich foods.

8.1 Structure of amino acids

As the name suggests, amino acids are molecules that contain both amino ($-NH_2$) and carboxylic acid ($-COOH$) functional groups. Consequently they are sometimes called **bifunctional compounds**. Fig. 1 shows the structure of alanine, an **α-amino acid** where the amino group is bonded to the

Fig. 1   Structures of α- and γ-amino acids

alanine   α-aminopropanoic acid   γ-aminobutanoic acid (GABA)

carbon atom adjacent to the carboxylic acid group. Because this carbon atom is the second from the acid end of the molecule, α-amino acids may also be called 2-amino acids. The methyl group in alanine could be replaced by any other alkyl group, but they would still be

α-amino acids. Other amino acids are referred to as β-, γ-, δ-, etc. (or 3-, 4-, 5-, etc.) amino acids.

Only α-amino acids occur as part of proteins; other amino acids may occur naturally or can be synthesised. For example, γ-aminobutanoic acid (better known as GABA) is a molecule involved in nerve transmission in the brain, and 6-aminohexanoic acid can be a starting material for manufacturing one form of nylon.

1 a Draw a general structure for:

  i a β-amino acid

  ii a 5-amino acid.

b Give the IUPAC name for GABA.

The side chain of the α-amino acids may be represented by R. It may be a simple group such as $-H$ in the amino acid glycine, or $-CH_3$ in alanine (Fig. 1). It can also be a much more complex group such as $-CH_2C_6H_5$ in phenylalanine, or $-CH_2COOH$ in aspartic acid. Table 1 shows the 20 different R groups that give rise to the 20 naturally occurring α-amino acids.

Apart from glycine (R = H), all α-amino acids have optical isomers (enantiomers), meaning that one form (dextrorotatory form) rotates plane-polarised light clockwise, while the second form (laevorotatory form) rotates it anticlockwise. The central carbon atom in these amino acids is bonded to four different groups: we describe the molecule as **chiral** and **asymmetric**. (This form of stereoisomerism is discussed in Chapter 4.) As shown in Fig. 2, the result is that each α-amino acid occurs as either of two non-identical mirror images, which cannot be superimposed. However, only the L-isomers occur naturally in our body proteins.

2 Why does glycine (R = H) not have optical isomers?

Fig. 2 **Enantiomers of an α-amino acid**

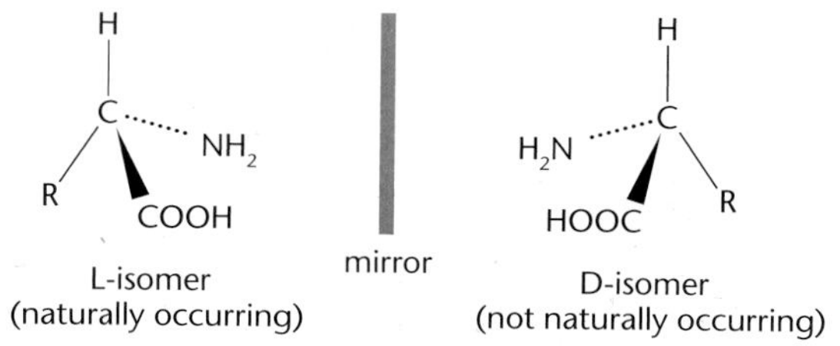

L-isomer
(naturally occurring)

mirror

D-isomer
(not naturally occurring)

Table 1   The naturally occurring α-amino acids

Amino acid	Abbreviation	R group (side chain)
glycine	Gly	$-H$
alanine	Ala	$-CH_3$
valine	Val	$-CH(CH_3)_2$
leucine	Leu	$-CH_2CH(CH_3)_2$
isoleucine	Ile	$-CH(CH_3)CH_2CH_3$
serine	Ser	$-CH_2OH$
threonine	Thr	$-CH(OH)CH_3$
lysine	Lys	$-CH_2CH_2CH_2CH_2NH_2$
arginine	Arg	$-CH_2CH_2CH_2NHC(NH)NH_2$
histidine	His	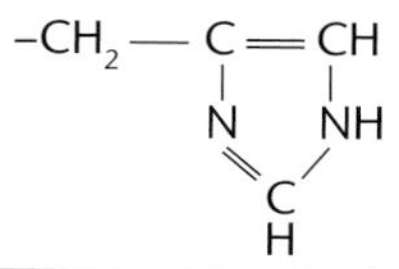
aspartic acid	Asp	$-CH_2COOH$
asparagine	Asn	$-CH_2CONH_2$

Amino acid	Abbreviation	R group (side-chain)
glutamic acid	Glu	$-CH_2CH_2COOH$
glutamine	Gln	$-CH_2CH_2CONH_2$
proline	Pro	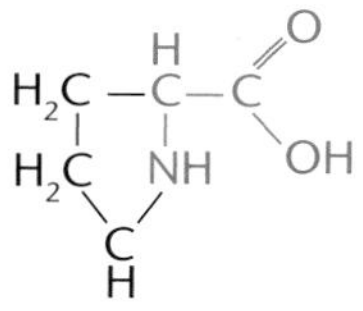
phenylalanine	Phe	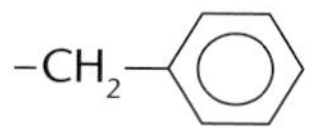
tyrosine	Tyr	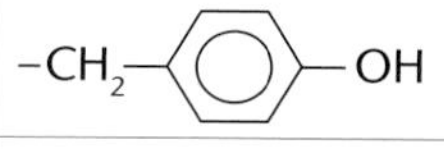
tryptophan	Trp	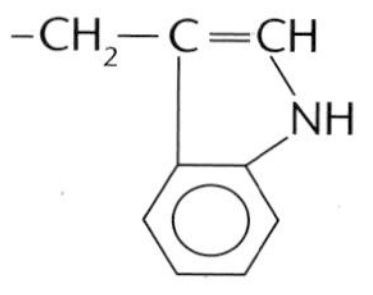
methionine	Met	$-CH_2CH_2SCH_3$
cysteine	Cys	$-CH_2SH$

8.2 Acid–base properties of amino acids

The –COOH group is weakly acidic and tends to donate its proton to water, while the $-NH_2$ group is weakly basic and tends to accept a proton from water via the nitrogen lone pair. These characteristics are discussed in Chapters 5 and 7 respectively.

An α-amino acid therefore has the ability to act as both a weak acid and a weak base. When dissolved in a highly acidic solution, the amino acid is transformed to its corresponding cation (Fig. 3). Similarly, when dissolved in a highly alkaline solution, the amino acid exists as its corresponding anion (Fig. 3). Consequently, at some intermediate pH value, it exists simultaneously as both an anion and a cation. Such an ion is called the **zwitterion** of the α-amino acid.

Fig. 3 pH-dependent equilibria shown by α-amino acids

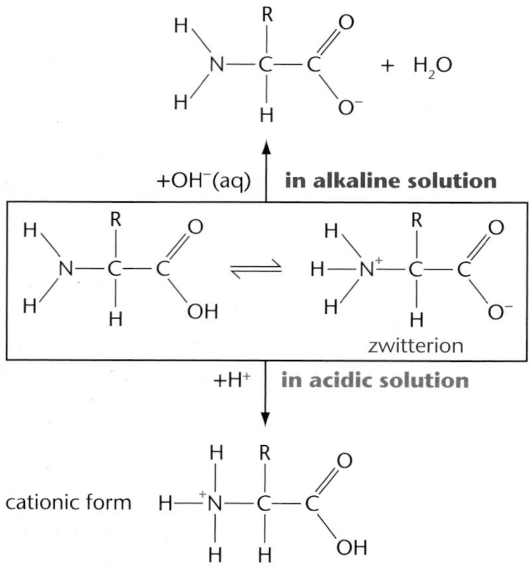

In solution, the zwitterion exists at a unique pH value for each α-amino acid. This value is referred to as the acid's **isoelectric pH**. At the isoelectric pH the ion–dipole forces between the amino acid and the surrounding water molecules are at their weakest, and so this is the pH at which the α-amino acid is most likely to precipitate from solution. The isoelectric pH is not exactly 7 because, even though the proton-donating power of the –COOH group and the proton-accepting power of the $-NH_2$ group are approximately equal

(though opposite), the overall effect is also influenced by the different electron-attracting powers of the different R groups.

Simple paper chromatography can be used to identify amino acids. The completed chromatogram is sprayed with ninhydrin solution in a fume cupboard. This should have the effect of making the dots appear purple.

The R_f values can be used to identify the amino acid composition of the unknown samples:

$$R_f \text{ value} = \frac{\text{distance moved by compound}}{\text{distance moved by solvent}}$$

The technique is often extended to electrophoresis. The ions separate under the influence of an electric field unless they are electrically neutral (zwitterion) and this only happens at a particular pH for each amino acid. At a particular buffered pH, positive ions will migrate to the negative electrode (cathode) and negative ions will migrate to the positive electrode (anode). The zwitterions, being electrically neutral, will not migrate at all. The pH of the solution is adjusted using buffers, in such a way that an optimal separation occurs.

Zwitterions also exist in the crystalline form of the amino acid. The electrostatic attraction between the oppositely charged parts of the ion accounts for the relatively high melting point values of α-amino acids. For example, even the smallest amino acid molecule, glycine, is a crystalline solid at room temperature, whereas the corresponding amine ($CH_3CH_2CH_2NH_2$, m.p. 190 K) or acid (CH_3CH_2COOH, m.p. 252 K) *of similar molecular size* are both liquids.

3 State whether an amino acid ion subjected to an electric field will migrate towards a positive or a negative electrode if first dissolved in:

a dilute hydrochloric acid

b dilute sodium hydroxide.

4 What would happen to a zwitterion under the influence of an electric field?

- Amino acids have the same basic structure: $RCH(NH_2)COOH$. There are 20 alternatives for group R.

- Amino acids have acidic properties due to the $-COOH$ group and basic properties due to the $-NH_2$ group.

8.3 The peptide link

Amino acids are the building units from which proteins are constructed. As shown in Fig. 4, the $-NH_2$ group of one amino acid can undergo a **condensation** reaction with the $-COOH$ group of another amino acid, eliminating a water molecule and forming a **dipeptide**. The $-CONH-$ group that links the two amino acids is called a **peptide link** (green tint on Fig. 4)

and the C–N bond within this group is called the **peptide bond**. In general terms the arrangements of atoms correspond to the arrangement in N-substituted amides.

5 Draw the structures of the two different dipeptides that may be produced by condensing 2-aminoethanoic acid (glycine) with 2-aminopropanoic acid (alanine).

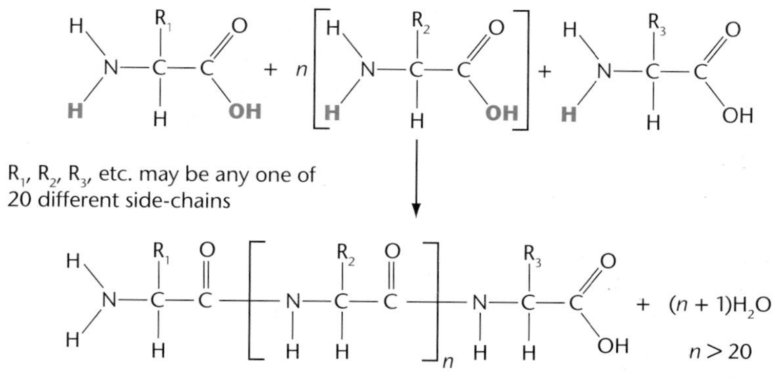

The dipeptide we obtain from this reaction has an amino group at one end of the molecule and a carboxylic acid group at the other. Consequently, under the control of the body's enzyme system and predetermined by the genetic code, condensation reactions with other amino acids can occur repeatedly, as shown in Fig. 5. The result is a **polyamide** or **polypeptide**. Its length ranges from 20 to more than 10 000 amino acids bonded together to form a continuous chain via repeated peptide links. This chain is the amino acid sequence of a protein and is called its **primary structure**.

The polyamide chain has many N–H and C=O groups along its length. Hydrogen bonds form between an N–H group from one acid and a C=O group from another acid further along the chain. As a result, the polyamide chain is coiled to form a helical shape held in place by a regular pattern of hydrogen bonds, as seen in Fig. 6. This helix is the **secondary structure** of the protein.

The helix is then folded into a characteristic three-dimensional shape (see Fig. 7) called its **tertiary structure**.

Fig. 4   The peptide link

peptide bond

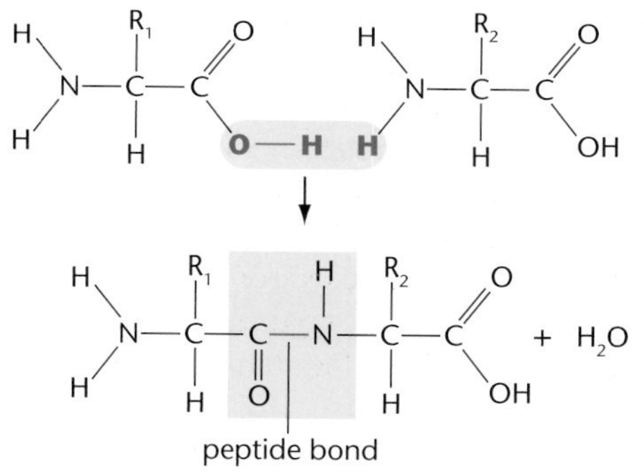

Fig. 5   Polyamide (polypeptide) formation

R_1, R_2, R_3, etc. may be any one of 20 different side-chains

$n > 20$

Fig. 6   3D secondary structure of a protein

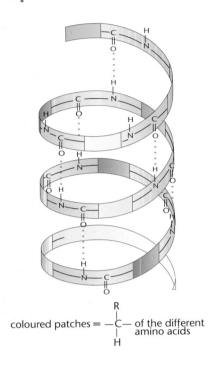

coloured patches = $-\overset{\displaystyle R}{\underset{\displaystyle H}{\overset{|}{\underset{|}{C}}}}-$ of the different amino acids

Fig. 7   Tertiary structure of the muscle protein myoglobin

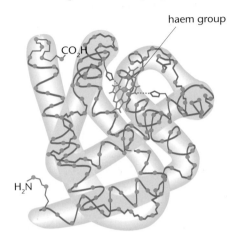

Various electrostatic or covalent bonds between the R side chains of particular amino acids in the polyamide chain determine the pattern of folding. It is only in this form that the structure is capable of its characteristic biochemical functions and can be correctly called a protein.

8.4 Hydrolysis of peptide bonds

The construction of a polyamide chain is a complex biochemical process, but its breakdown to liberate the component amino acids is relatively simple. Whenever we digest protein, our bodies break up these chains. This process can also be achieved by heating a protein with 5 mol dm^{-3} hydrochloric acid for about 24 hours. The secondary and tertiary structures of the protein are rapidly broken down, and this causes the polyamide chain to unravel. The chain is then **hydrolysed** (split by reaction with water) at each of the peptide links and liberates the component amino acids (Fig. 8).

6 What is the other purpose of the 5 mol dm^{-3} hydrochloric acid in this hydrolysis process?

We can use this **hydrolysis** as the first stage in determining the structure of a polyamide because it allows the types of 2-amino acids present in the polyamide chain to be identified and counted. Determining the sequence of the 2-amino acids and the three-dimensional structure of the chain is a much more difficult task and has earned some chemists Nobel Prizes in the past!

Fig. 8   Peptide link hydrolysis

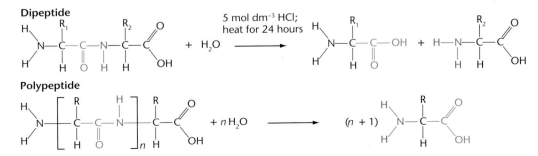

key facts

- Proteins are sequences of amino acids joined during condensation reactions by peptide links.

- When polyamides (polypeptides) are hydrolysed, the peptide links are broken and the constituent amino acids are formed.

- Hydrogen bonding is involved in maintaining the secondary structure of proteins.

- The tertiary structure of proteins is required for biochemical activity.

stretch and challenge

Structure of proteins

The painkiller leucine encephalin

The naturally occurring oligopeptide (a peptide with less than 20 amino acids), known as leucine encephalin, contains five amino acids. This molecule was discovered in the 1970s during an investigation into how morphine's and codeine's pain-killing properties worked. Research showed that these molecules fit into brain receptor sites, in a sense imitating the role of the brain's own pain-suppressing molecules, of which leucine encephalin is just one example.

When hydrolysed using 5 mol dm^{-3} hydrochloric acid for 24 hours, leucine encephalin releases four different amino acids, which were shown to be glycine (Gly), tyrosine (Tyr), phenylalanine (Phe) and leucine (Leu) in the ratio 2 : 1 : 1 : 1. The structures of these amino acids are given earlier in Table 1.

When partially hydrolysed using a shorter reaction time, apart from the individual amino acids, the following dipeptides and tripeptides are identified:

A	HOOC-Tyr-Gly-NH$_2$
B	HOOC-Phe-Leu-NH$_2$
C	HOOC-Gly-Gly-Phe-NH$_2$

7 Which of these are dipeptides and which are tripeptides? Explain.

8 Showing all atoms and all bonds, draw the structures of molecules **A** and **C**.

9 Deduce the order of the five amino acids in the leucine encephalin chain. Explain your reasoning.

10 Which of the amino acids released from leucine encephalin would not be optically active? Explain.

11 Write a balanced equation for the complete hydrolysis of molecule **B**.

Essential and non-essential amino acids

Alanine (2-aminopropanoic acid) and aspartic acid (1-carboxy-2-aminopropanoic acid) are non-essential amino acids. They are called 'non-essential' amino acids because it is not vital that we eat proteins containing them since our bodies can make them from other nutrients, provided we eat a properly balanced diet. However, lysine (2,6-diaminohexanoic acid) is one of the eight amino acids that are *essential*: we cannot synthesise them, so they must be eaten regularly.

12 Use the IUPAC names and the information from Table 1 to draw the full structures of alanine, aspartic acid and lysine.

13 All three of the amino acids mentioned here can exist as optical isomers (enantiomers). Draw three-dimensional diagrams to represent the optical isomers of lysine. Outline the differences in their chemical and physical properties.

14 By comparing their structures, explain why equimolar solutions of lysine, alanine and aspartic acid would produce solutions of decreasing pH.

15 Draw the structures of the molecules or ions that would be present if:

a alanine were placed in a pH 1 buffer solution

b alanine were placed in a pH 11 buffer solution

c alanine were placed in a buffer solution of pH equal to the isoelectric point of alanine.

1

a The structure of the amino acid *alanine* is shown below:

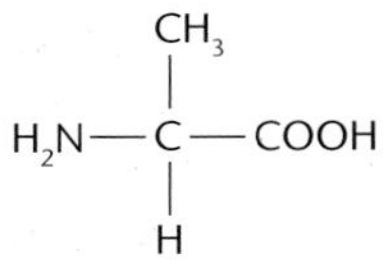

$$H_2N-\underset{\underset{H}{|}}{\overset{\overset{CH_3}{|}}{C}}-COOH$$

i Draw the structure of the zwitterion formed by *alanine*.

ii Draw the structure of the organic product formed in each case from *alanine* when it reacts with:
- CH_3OH in the presence of a small amount of concentrated sulfuric acid
- Na_2CO_3
- CH_3Cl in a 1:1 mole ratio.   (4)

b The amino acid *lysine* is shown below:

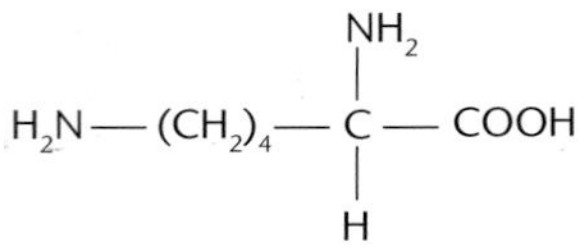

$$H_2N-(CH_2)_4-\underset{\underset{H}{|}}{\overset{\overset{NH_2}{|}}{C}}-COOH$$

Draw the structure of the *lysine* species present in a solution at low pH.   (1)

c The amino acid *proline* is shown below:

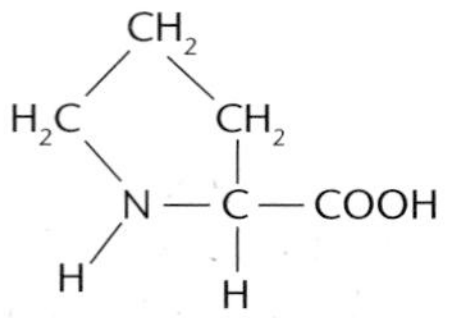

Draw the structure of the dipeptide formed from two *proline* molecules.   (1)

Total 6

AQA, June 2007, Unit 4, Question 5

2 The amino acid *alanine* is shown below:

$$H_2N-\underset{\underset{H}{|}}{\overset{\overset{CH_3}{|}}{C}}-COOH$$

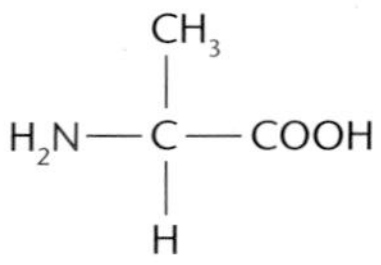

a Give the systematic name for alanine.   (1)

b **i** Draw the structure of the dipeptide formed from two alanine molecules, showing clearly the full structure of the peptide link.

ii Draw the structure of the organic compound formed by the reaction of alanine with propan-2-ol in the presence of a small amount of the catalyst concentrated sulfuric acid.

iii Draw the structure of the *N*–substituted amide formed by the reaction of alanine with ethanoyl chloride. Name the type of mechanism involved.   (4)

Total 5

AQA, January 2007, Unit 4, Question 5 (a–b)

3

a Draw the structure of the species present in solid aminoethanoic acid, H_2NCH_2COOH.   (1)

b Explain why the melting point of aminoethanoic acid is much higher than that of hydroxyethanoic acid, $HOCH_2COOH$.   (2)

Total 3

AQA, January 2006, Unit 4, Question 6 (b–c)

4 The amino acid *alanine* is shown below:

$$H_2N-\underset{\underset{H}{|}}{\overset{\overset{CH_3}{|}}{C}}-COOH$$

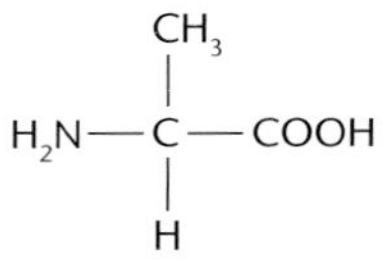

a A sample of alanine is dissolved in water.

i Draw the structure of the main alanine species present in this aqueous solution and give the name of this type of species.

ii Draw the structure of the alanine species formed when an excess of hydrochloric acid is added to the solution.   (3)

b Alanine molecules may be reacted together to form a polypeptide. Give the repeating unit of this polypeptide and name the type of polymerisation involved in its formation.   (2)

Total 5

AQA, January 2005, Unit 4, Question 2 (a–b)

5 The structure of the D-isomer of 2,6-diaminohexanoic acid (lysine) is shown below:

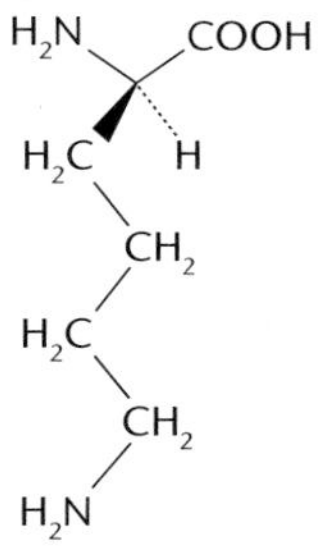

Draw the structure of L-lysine next to that of the D-isomer above.   (1)
Copy and complete the structures below to show the main species of lysine present in aqueous solution at pH 2, pH 7 and pH 11.

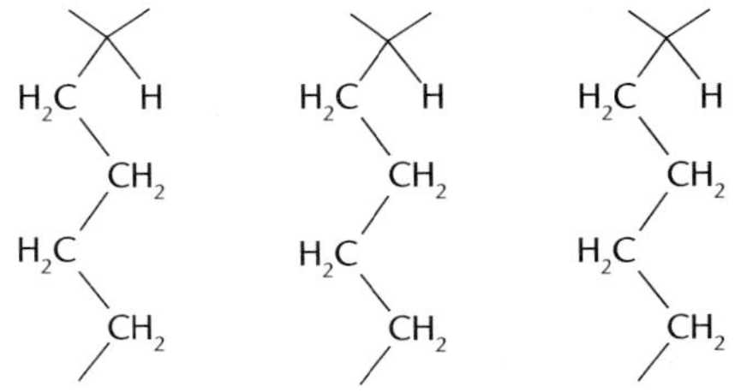

pH 2   pH 7   pH 11   (6)

Total 7

NEAB, June 1998, CH09, Question 4 (a–b)

6 The structural formulae of the three amino acids are shown below:

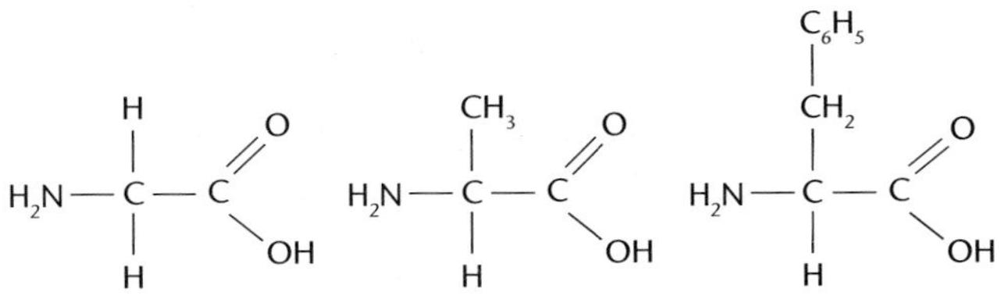

glycine   alanine   phenylalanine

a Explain why alanine and phenylalanine have optical isomers, but glycine does not.   (2)
Amino acids can react both with acids and with bases and are also capable of forming zwitterions.

b Write equations for the reactions between:
  i phenylalanine and hydrochloric acid,
  ii alanine and sodium hydroxide.   (2)
The isoelectric point is described in terms of the pH at which an amino acid forms its zwitterions. The isoelectric point is different for each amino acid.

c **i** The isoelectric point for glycine is at pH = 5.97. Draw the zwitterion formed by glycine at this point.
  ii Draw the ions that would be formed at pH = 5.75 by alanine and phenylalanine.   (2)
Glycine and alanine can react together to form the dipeptide shown below:

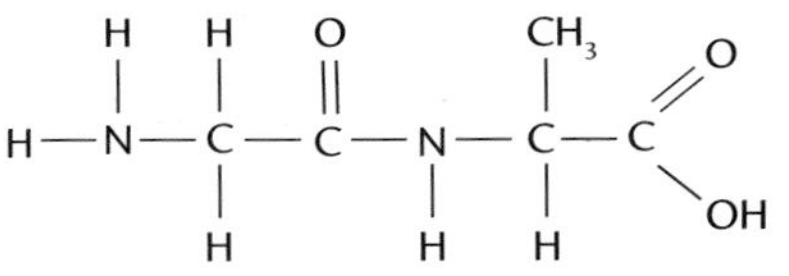

d A different dipeptide can be formed from the reaction between glycine and alanine. Draw its displayed formula.   (1)

Total 7

7 The systematic name for alanine is 2-aminopropanoic acid. Its molecular formula is $CH_3CH(NH_2)COOH$.
a Draw the displayed formula of alanine:
  i In its uncharged form;
  ii when in a solution of pH 1.   (2)
b **i** Write down the name given to an amino acid as a dipolar molecule.
  ii Draw the displayed formula of alanine in this state.   (3)

Total 5

Genetic fingerprinting

Separation of proteins into amino acids using electrophoresis is the basis of genetic fingerprinting. The sample is placed on an agarose gel at a particular pH and a voltage is applied, which separates the ions for each amino acid under the influence of the electric field. The most commonly used technique today is STR (short tandem repeats), where the DNA is 'cut up' by enzymes into sequences of bases (usually four), then these are identified on the sample. The next step is to add radioactive pieces of DNA, called probes, to the separated DNA fragments. These will bind to specific sequences on the DNA, thus marking some of the fragments, and X-ray film placed on top of the gel will become exposed by the radioactivity, giving black bands on the film. Unlike conventional fingerprints, which are often difficult to gather at a crime scene, a DNA fingerprint can be made from a very small sample of blood, skin or semen — or even a single hair!

Although no two unrelated people have been found with the same fingerprint, this cannot be ruled out. Geneticists usually talk about the probability of a certain fingerprint matching a randomly selected person. However, some researchers point out that certain patterns of DNA are more common in some ethnic groups, and a match may be more likely than currently thought. As techniques develop, the probability of a likely match decreases. With some techniques, a match that had a probability of one in five million occurring by chance might lead a lawyer to argue that this meant that in a country of say 60 million people there were 12 people who would match the profile. This can then be translated to a one in 12 chance of the suspect being the guilty one. With more refined techniques, the theoretical risk of a coincidental match is approaching one in 100 billion (100 000 000 000). Proponents of this idea suggest that extensive and expensive population studies must be completed before reliable estimates of probabilities could be introduced into the courtroom, even if this takes a decade or more. In the meantime, how many suspects will go free if the evidence is not allowed? In many countries, all convicted criminals, or sometimes just those convicted of serious offences, have their DNA profile taken and recorded along with their conventional fingerprints.

It has been suggested that carrying out a nationwide survey and keeping a database of the DNA of the entire population could be a very effective deterrent to potential criminals. However, the idea raises many questions about civil liberties, and the fear that it could be abused by corrupt authorities. Like fingerprints, however, the police (who hold such records) are obliged to destroy DNA evidence if a defendant is acquitted. The potential for misuse increases if DNA fingerprint results are kept in a database. What information will be contained in the database? Who will have access to the database? How secure will the database be? Privacy concerns are a major disadvantage to genetic testing programmes and the number of laws addressing the protection of genetic information seem to be few.

There may be other contentious issues with laboratory procedures. Humans interpret the results, so there is always a possibility that mistakes will be made. There may be an imperfection in the agarose gel, and a laboratory worker may conclude that similar — but not precisely identical — band patterns result from identical genetic samples. DNA fingerprinting requires scientists to work with whatever samples have been found at the crime scene. These samples may be degraded or may be mixtures from several sources. Often, a scientist may have only enough of a sample to run one test, so if the test is ambiguous, it cannot be repeated.

There are many non-criminal cases where genetic fingerprinting has potential uses.

- An adopted child attempting to reunify with his or her biological mother, potential hospital mix-ups, and *in vitro* fertilisation, where the laboratory may have implanted an unrelated embryo inside the mother.
- Some have serious reservations about preimplantation genetic diagnosis (PGD) that stems from *in vitro* fertilisation. Here embryos that are due to be implanted are first screened for genetic disorders, which might affect the decision as to whether they would be implanted or not. Identification of abnormal genes for cystic fibrosis or other genetic disorders, such as Huntington's disease or Duchenne muscular dystrophy, that have no cure but are detectable by carrier screening, can help couples. They could use this information to make informed reproductive decisions.
- 'I think that knowing you are likely to develop a serious genetic disorder could cause serious damage to your family and social life and to your career.'
  'I think that knowing what might happen could be a huge relief to some people.'
  These are two opposing views, to which scientists do not have the answer.
- What if testing for cancer predisposition provides information that allows a young person to change their lifestyle, thus reducing their cancer risk?
- As more and more genetic information becomes available, there is a growing concern that insurance companies will screen potential policyholders to exclude those carrying genetic disorders. This would reduce the likelihood of any payments under insurance policies. But it might lead to parents not having their children tested, for fear of them becoming uninsurable, even though testing can lead to therapies in some cases.

These are examples of scenarios where science cannot provide a definitive answer — it can only provide the information. It is up to the person to decide.

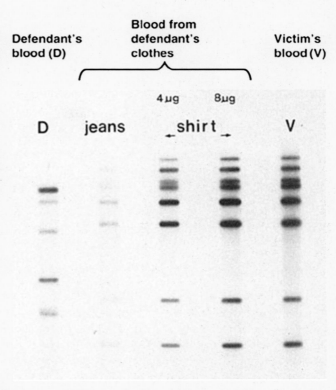

Defendant's blood (D)	Blood from defendant's clothes			Victim's blood (V)
		4 µg	8 µg	
D	jeans	← shirt →		V

A3 'In rape cases, when the semen has been matched with the defendant's and the chance that it came from another person is 33 billion to one, you don't need a jury.' Discuss this lawyer's comments.

A4 How accurate do DNA results have to be before they should be admitted in court?

A5 Give two arguments for and against having a national DNA database.

A6 Do you think there should be a national DNA test? Give your reasons.

A7 Write a paragraph to discuss the benefits and difficulties of knowledge about a genetic disorder. You could include the person's feelings, the views of insurance companies and parents considering preimplantation genetic diagnosis (PGD).

A1 Would identical twins have the same DNA fingerprint? Explain your decision.

A2 What is your interpretation of the genetic fingerprints shown above right. Explain how certain you can be about your conclusions.

9 Polymers

The window frame, sponge, the woman's clothing, including her shoes, and the bucket, are all made of types of plastic.

The discovery and development of polymers revolutionised 20th-century living, and innovative polymers continue to be created. This is because **plastics**, as they are commonly known (because many are easily moulded to any desired shape), have provided materials with a vast variety of uses. Each polymer has its own specific properties that determine its applications. In general, plastics have high strength-to-weight ratios, are easily shaped and are relatively cheap compared to wood, glass and metals. Plastics also degrade slowly.

Polymer science has undoubtedly provided many new and useful materials, but there are concerns about environmental issues. Many polymers are manufactured from chemicals that come from oil. As this precious, non-renewable resource will eventually be used up, chemists are searching for alternative ways to make polymers. One approach is to make use of natural polymers such as starch, cellulose and protein. Research is also aimed at using bacteria to 'grow' new and useful polymers. Another problem is that many polymers are non-biodegradable and are responsible for considerable environmental pollution and danger to wildlife. These problems are now being addressed, and polymers that biodegrade when exposed to water or sunlight are being developed.

Polymers are today as essential a part of our lives as wood and metal were to people 100 years ago. More chemists now work with polymers than with any other type of material, to provide us with the types of materials we demand in the goods we buy, with new polymers continually being created to satisfy particular needs.

The word **polymer** comes from a combination of two Greek words: *poly* meaning 'many' and *meros* meaning 'part'. Polymers are large molecules built by the chemical combination of many small molecules. These building blocks are called **monomers**. For example, as we saw in Chapter 8, polypeptides are polymers derived from amino acid monomers. The number of combined monomer units may vary considerably, but can often be tens of thousands per molecule.

Plastics have many advantages over traditional materials: nylon gears have low friction; the plastic chair seat is rigid and hard wearing as well as being lightweight; the plastic carrier bag is flexible and comfortable to hold; and the Teflon® lining of the frying pan is non-stick.

9.1 Types of polymers

Poly(ethene) – or polythene as it is popularly known – and nylon are two well-known materials that illustrate the two general types of polymers. Poly(ethene) is an example of an **addition polymer** produced by repeated addition reactions in which many alkene monomers add to the end of the carbon chain to form very long chain molecules (see Fig. 1).

Nylon is an example of a **condensation polymer** produced by repeated condensation reactions between appropriately designed monomers to form the condensation polymer *and* one small molecule such as water, methanol or hydrogen chloride for every two bonded monomers (see Fig. 2).

Fig. 1   A general addition polymerisation

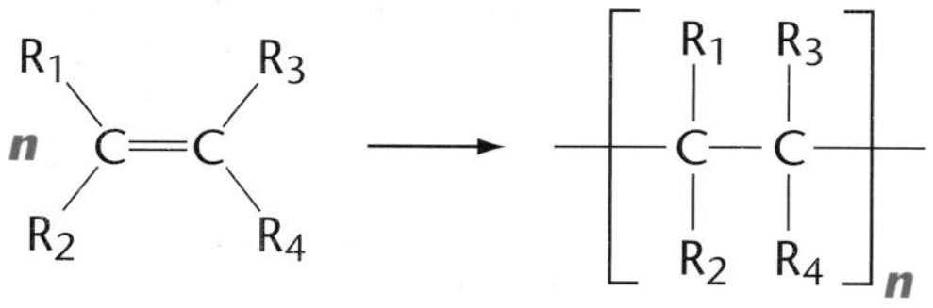

Fig. 2   A general condensation polymerisation

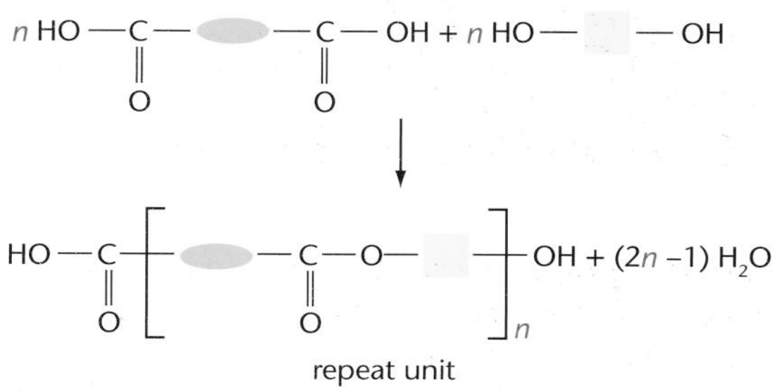

repeat unit

9.2 Addition polymers

Alkenes (see *AS Chemistry*, Chapter 15) are molecules that contain C=C bonds. As we have seen in Chapter 4, alkenes undergo addition reactions. In these reactions the C=C double bond becomes a single bond, with two more single bonds created. Addition polymerisation works on the same general principle, except that the alkene molecules repeatedly add to themselves (see Fig. 3) many thousands of times, rather than just once.

Also, the reaction mechanism may involve free radicals, carbocations or carbanions, depending on the exact nature of the catalyst.

The first useful addition polymer was discovered by accident in 1933 by Eric William Fawcett and Reginald Oswald Gibson. These two British chemists worked for ICI (now part of Alzo Nobel) and were experimenting with ethene under high pressure in an attempt to produce a ketone. However, a flaw in their process produced instead a small amount of white waxy solid that was later shown to be poly(ethene).

Fig. 3   Propene polymerisation

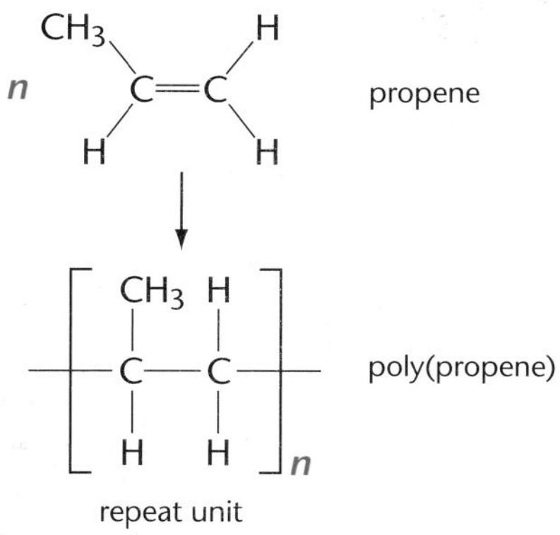

repeat unit

Poly(ethene) is called an addition polymer because many ethene monomer molecules bond together to form poly(ethene) as the *only* product (Fig. 4). Take particular note of the **repeat unit,** which is shown in square brackets.

Fig. 4   Formation of poly(ethene)

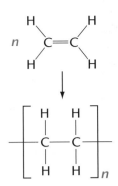

repeat unit of poly(ethene)

The bottle on the left is made from HDPE, and the one on the right is made from LDPE.

Poly(ethene) is manufactured in two forms: low-density poly(ethene) (LDPE) and high-density poly(ethene) (HDPE). LDPE is the more common form and, being softer and more pliable, is widely used for packaging and electrical insulation. Its molecules contain about 50 000 carbon atoms and there is considerable branching of the main chains, which makes the material softer and results in melting points in the low range.

HDPE molecules contain more than 50 000 carbon atoms, with little branching of the main chains, resulting in more rigid materials with a higher range of melting points.

Soluble polymers have many uses (see photographs on opposite page): laundry bags in hospitals, where infection might be a risk, dissolve as linen is washed; dishwasher tablets are made of soluble plastics. The polymer is made by reacting polyethenyl ethanoate with methanol (see Fig. 5).

1   In terms of appropriate intermolecular forces, explain why LDPE melts more easily than HDPE.

Fig. 5   Formation of soluble polymers

Polyethenyl ethanoate reacts with methanol

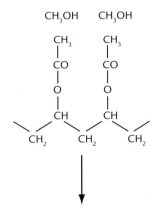

Some ester groups on the side-chains are removed and new ester groups form in methyl ethanoate

Hot, low-density poly(ethene) can be blown to form 'polythene' bags.

2 Explain how the number of OH groups affects the solubility of a polymer in water.

The percentage of OH groups in the polymer determines the solubility in water. However, a high proportion of OH groups can lead to intramolecular hydrogen bonding and reduced linking with water.

The range of addition polymers has been vastly expanded by varying the structure of the alkene monomer. This is shown generally in Fig. 6, where G represents a general group that has been substituted for one of the hydrogen atoms in ethene. Table 1 shows some common addition polymers and their uses.

Table 1   Common addition polymers and their uses

Alkene monomer	Structural formula	Polymer	Structure of polymer (monomer unit)	Uses
ethene	$H_2C=CH_2$	poly(ethene)	$\left[-CH_2-CH_2-\right]_n$	bags, insulation for wires, squeezy bottles
propene	$H_2C=CHCH_3$	poly(propene)	$\left[-CH_2-CH(CH_3)-\right]_n$	bottles, plastic plates, clothing, carpets, crates, ropes and twine
phenylethene	$H_2C=CHC_6H_5$	poly(phenylethene) (polystyrene)	$\left[-CH_2-CH(C_6H_5)-\right]_n$	insulation, packaging, food containers, model kits, flowerpots, housewares
chloroethene	$H_2C=CHCl$	poly(chloroethene) (polyvinyl chloride, PVC)	$\left[-CH_2-CHCl-\right]_n$	synthetic leather, water pipes, floor covering, guttering, window frames, curtain rails, wall cladding
methyl-2-methylpropenoate	$H_2C=C(CH_3)C(O)OCH_3$	poly(methyl-2-methylpropenoate)	$\left[-CH_2-C(CH_3)(C(O)OCH_3)-\right]_n$	light fittings, car lights, tap tops, lenses
tetrafluoroethene	$F_2C=CF_2$	poly(tetrafluoroethene) (Teflon®, PTFE)	$\left[-CF_2-CF_2-\right]_n$	non-stick pans, lubricant-free bearings

Fig. 6 General addition polymers

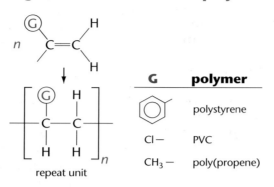

G	polymer
⬡	polystyrene
Cl—	PVC
CH_3—	poly(propene)

Although addition polymers are flammable, in other respects they are generally chemically inert. This lack of reactivity is due to the very strong C–C and C–H bonds and the lack of

polarisation of the bonds within poly(alkenes). Consequently, once formed, it is very difficult to break down materials made from addition polymers. They are **non-biodegradable** and not easily recycled. This causes the environmental problem of how to get rid of worn out or unfashionable items so that they can be replaced by newer, equally non-biodegradable merchandise! Using them as fuels in specially designed power stations is certainly one way forward here.

> **3** Explain why poly(ethene) can be considered to be an alkane.

9.3 Condensation polymers

Manufactured condensation polymers (e.g. **nylon**) are artificial polymers with properties designed to mimic those of natural condensation polymers, such as silk, a polymer of amino acids, starch, which is a polysaccharide, and DNA, a polymer of nucleic acids. These polymers are **biodegradable** and combine structural strength, low density and resistance to some forms of chemical attack.

The name 'condensation' polymer derives from the type of chemical reaction used to link monomers. A condensation reaction links two organic molecules together by formation of an ester or amide group between the molecules with elimination of a small molecule such as water, methanol or hydrogen chloride (see Fig. 7). Natural condensation polymers are all formed by elimination of water; the other possible elimination products are only formed in the synthesis of artificial condensation polymers.

In order to allow repeated condensation reactions, and so build up a polymeric structure, the monomers used for condensation

Fig. 7 Forming esters and amides by condensation reactions

$$R_1 - C \begin{Bmatrix} Cl \\ OH \\ OCH_3 \end{Bmatrix} + HO - R_2$$
$$\parallel$$
$$O$$

$$\downarrow$$

$$R_1 - C - O - R_2 + \begin{Bmatrix} HCl \ \text{or} \\ H_2O \ \text{or} \\ CH_3OH \end{Bmatrix}$$
$$\parallel$$
$$O$$
ester

$$R_1 - C \begin{Bmatrix} Cl \\ OH \end{Bmatrix} + \begin{array}{c} H \\ N - R_2 \\ H \end{array}$$
$$\parallel$$
$$O$$

$$\downarrow$$

$$R_1 - C - N - R_2 + \begin{Bmatrix} HCl \ \text{or} \\ H_2O \end{Bmatrix}$$
$$\parallel \quad \ |$$
$$O \quad H$$
amide

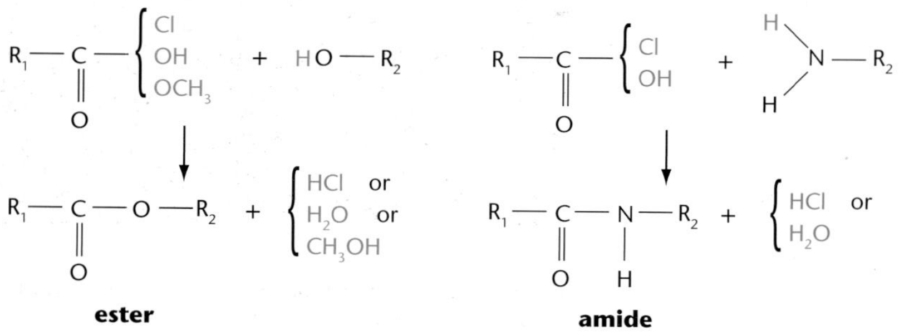

polymers must be **bifunctional**. This means they must contain two functional groups. For example, amino acids (see Chapter 8), which contain both –COOH and –NH₂ functional groups, are the monomers for polyamides. However, for most synthetic polymers, it is more convenient to have two different monomers, one containing two acid (–COOH) functional groups and the other containing two alcohol (–OH) groups to make a **polyester** or two amine (–NH₂) groups to make a **polyamide**. Examples of bifunctional monomers are shown in Fig. 8.

Fig. 8 Monomers with two functional groups

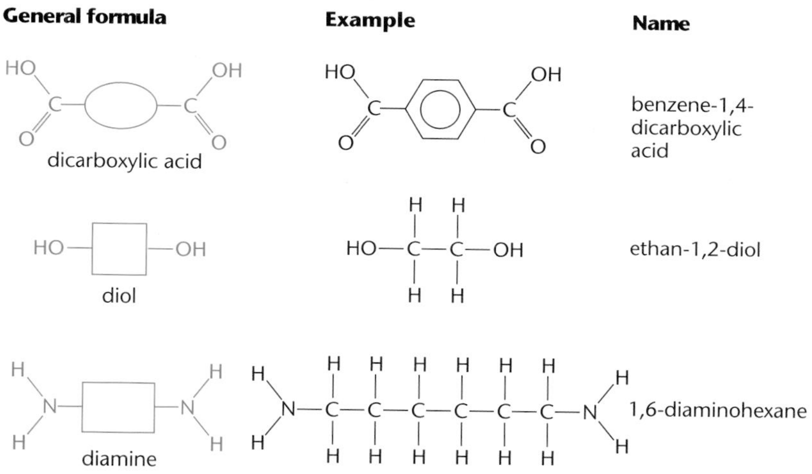

General formula	Example	Name
dicarboxylic acid	benzene-1,4-dicarboxylic acid	benzene-1,4-dicarboxylic acid
diol	ethan-1,2-diol	ethan-1,2-diol
diamine	1,6-diaminohexane	1,6-diaminohexane

Fig. 9 Production of a polyester

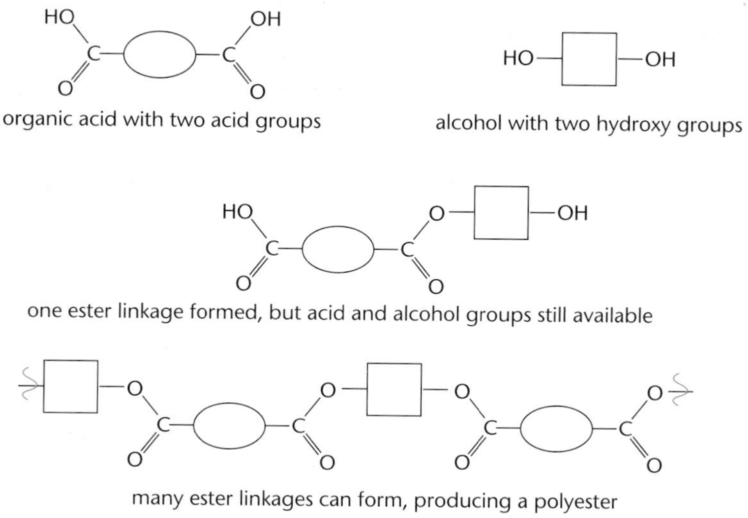

organic acid with two acid groups   alcohol with two hydroxy groups

one ester linkage formed, but acid and alcohol groups still available

many ester linkages can form, producing a polyester

The production of synthetic polyesters

A polyester is a polymer produced by linking together many small molecules (monomers) via ester linkages. When an alcohol with one –OH group reacts with an organic acid with one –COOH group, an ester and water are formed and no further esterification reactions can take place. If the alcohol has two –OH groups and the organic acid has two –COOH groups, then the ester that is formed will still contain an –OH group at one end and a –COOH group at the other. Further esterification reactions are still possible, and, in theory, can continue to be possible indefinitely (Fig. 9). A polyester will have been formed. The chain length is limited because it becomes less likely, as the chain length grows, that further monomers will collide with the end of the growing chain.

The production of PET (Terylene)

Terylene is one of the trade names for the polyester made by linking 1,4-benzenedicarboxylic acid and the alcohol ethane-1,2-diol. Another name, poly(ethylene)terephthalate (or PET), is derived from terephthalic acid, which is the old name for 1,4-benzenedicarboxylic acid. Ethane-1,2-diol plays the part of the alcohol in the production of PET. Repeated condensation reactions occur between the –COOH group of 1,4-benzenedicarboxylic acid molecules and –OH groups of the ethane-1,2-diol molecules (Fig. 10).

PET is an ideal material for carbonated drinks bottles as it is light, tough and won't shatter when dropped.

Fig. 10 Condensation reaction to form poly(ethylene)terephthalate (PET) – a polyester

n HO—C(=O)—⟨benzene ring⟩—C(=O)—OH + n HO—CH$_2$—CH$_2$—OH

benzene-1,4-dicarboxylic acid   ethane-1,2-diol

1 heat and pressure
2 heat and antimony catalyst

HO—[—C(=O)—⟨benzene ring⟩—C(=O)—O—CH$_2$—CH$_2$—O—]$_n$—H + ($2n$–1)H$_2$O

poly(ethane-1,2-diolbenzene-1,4-dicarboxylate) (PET; Terylene)

Molten PET can be forced through a fine mesh (extruded) to form strands. These are water-cooled and chopped into small pellets for convenient storage and transportation. The polyester is thermoplastic, which means it can be repeatedly heated to soften and melt it. A thermosetting plastic has many more cross-links so is much more difficult to soften.

Windsurfer sails are commonly made of Melinex®.

A thermoplastic polymer can be extruded to form fine fibres for use in artificial fabrics, or to be blow moulded into fizzy drink bottles and other containers.

A common process is to cast the molten polymer on a rotating drum to form a film, which is heated and stretched. It is then stretched at right angles to the first direction and 'set' at 220 °C–240 °C. This produces a transparent, tough, dimensionally stable and chemically resistant film (sold by ICI as Melinex®) that contains the polyester molecules partially aligned along both axes.

Melinex® and similar products are used extensively for packaging, especially for food, helping to keep it fresh and free from contamination. Melinex® is also used for making windsurfer sails, flexible printed circuit boards, cable insulation, touch pads (e.g. microwave controls) and, when coated with a thin layer of metal, it can be used for making things such as hot-air balloons.

The production of synthetic polyamides

Types of **nylon** are the best-known examples of artificial polyamides. The brand name 'Nylon' was created in the 1930s by the DuPontTH chemical company in America. It followed the discovery of how to make the polymer by one of their employees, Wallace Carothers. Nylon proved to be a very acceptable, cheap substitute for the silk used to make women's stockings and became a huge commercial success for DuPontTH.

One type of nylon is **nylon-6,6**. The 6,6 refers to the fact that both monomers (a diamine and a dicarboxylic acid – see Fig. 8) contain six carbon atoms. Hence, the diamine is 1,6-diaminohexane and the dicarboxylic acid is 1,6-hexandioic acid and there are six carbon atoms between each of the amide links in the polymer chain.

Since its use as a substitute for silk in stockings, nylon has found many other applications. It is used to make ropes, twines, Velcro®, machinery parts and a wide range of clothing. In clothing and carpets, natural fibres such as cotton or wool are often mixed with nylon to make them last longer.

The reaction between an amine group and a carboxylic acid group to form an amide link is not very efficient. The reaction is slow and the equilibrium established contains a significant proportion of unreacted amine and acid.

Consequently, the dicarboxylic acid is usually first converted (see Fig. 11) to hexane-1,6-dioyl chloride by reaction with thionyl chloride (SOCl$_2$). This diacyl chloride then reacts (see Fig. 12) with the diamine much faster and, because of the evolution of hydrogen chloride, the equilibrium shifts almost entirely towards the polymer product.

Fig. 11 Converting 1,6-hexandioic acid to hexane-1,6-dioyl chloride

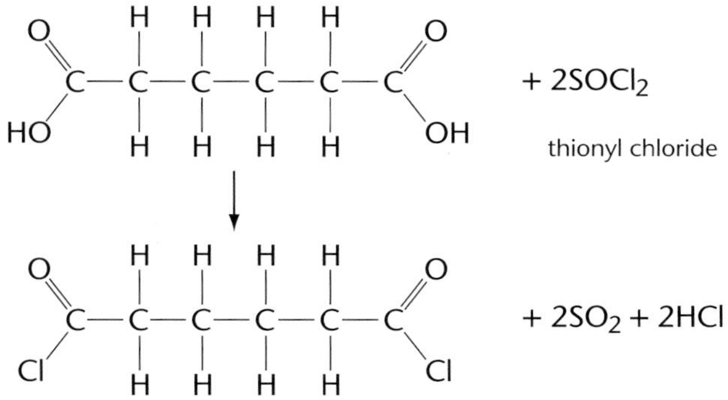

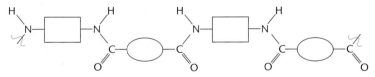

Fig. 12 Production of a polyamide

organic acid with two acid groups

amine with two amino groups

one amide linkage formed, but acid and amino groups still available

many amide linkages can form, producing a polyamide

Unlike addition polymers, condensation polymers such as nylon-6,6 do not form side-chains because the reaction is confined to the ends of the monomer molecules. Consequently the molecules tend to be long, single chains, which allows them to be drawn out at room temperature to form fibres. During this process the linear molecules align and become increasingly linked by hydrogen bonds between adjacent chains. This causes the strength of the fibre to increase during the drawing process.

Biodegradability of polyesters and polyamides

As shown in Fig. 13, unlike the links between alkenes in poly(alkenes), the amide and ester links in polyamides and polyesters are hydrolysable. Under the influence of acid catalysts or bacterial enzymes, polyester and polyamide chains can be broken into smaller and smaller fragments. In other words, unlike poly(alkenes), such materials will biodegrade when placed in landfill sites.

Fig. 13 Biodegradation of polyesters and polyamides

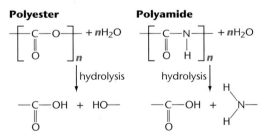

---

4 Nylon-6,10 is also made from 1,6-diaminohexane and a dicarboxylic acid. Give the structure of the dicarboxylic acid used to make this form of nylon and the structure of nylon-6,10 showing the repeat unit.

---

5 Ester and amide bonds react with water in the presence of an acid catalyst.

a Write equations for such reactions for ethyl ethanoate and N-ethylethanamide.

b What type of reaction is involved in both of these reactions?

c Why is this reaction important from the point of view of biodegradability?

key facts

● Condensation polymers include polyesters and polyamides.

● Condensation polymers are biodegradable because the links are hydrolysable.

● Condensation polymers are derived from bifunctional compounds or two monomers.

● Proteins are naturally occurring condensation polymers.

9.4   Conclusion

Both addition and condensation polymers have contributed a lot to the way we live today, and will continue to do so as new polymers are developed and old ones are modified. The main problems facing the use of synthetic polymers in the future are the dwindling supplies of the petroleum oil that is the source of all monomers, and the non-biodegradability of addition polymers.

Future developments may focus on the use of certain bacteria to 'grow' polymers as a natural part of their life-cycles. One example is the polyester Biopol, which was first grown using the bacterium *Alcaligenes eutrophus* in the early 1990s.

These polymers produced by fermentation are fully biodegradable. PHB (polyhydroxybutyrate) is produced by bacteria fermenting glucose. The plastic produced will solidify into a polymer similar to poly(ethene) but the high production costs, e.g. energy, mean its use is limited. However, PHB is produced naturally in the stomach, so would not be rejected, and could be used for slow release of drugs as it degrades.

These polymers will not require any fossil fuels as raw materials, but will require fossil fuels as an energy source for production. Fig. 14 shows the total consumption of fossil fuels for a range of polymers.

Over time, bottles made from Biopol degrade far more quickly than non-biodegradable polymers.

Fig. 14   Energy consumption of biological versus crude oil derived plastics

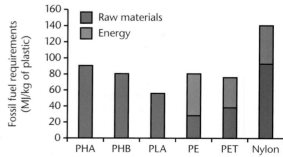

PHA = poly(hydroxyacetate)
PLA = poly(lactic acid)

Aramids

The condensation polymers discussed so far, including Terylene, nylon-6,6 and proteins, are all biodegradable because their ester or amide links are relatively easily hydrolysed. A group of polymers called **aramids** are also polyamides, but they are much tougher molecules to biodegrade. In fact, they are so tough and lightweight they are used to make bulletproof vests, fireproof suits, puncture-resistant bicycle tyres, reinforced concrete and Formula One racing cars.

Being stronger and lighter than steel cable, Kevlar® is used to make sails.

Nomex® (made from 1,3-diaminobenzene and 1,3-benzenedicarboxylic acid) and Kevlar® are the two best-known examples of aramids. This general name derives from the fact that they involve benzene rings (from **ar**enes) linked via **amid**e bonds.

Kevlar® was discovered long before it was put to use. This is because it was so inert that processing proved very difficult. It does not dissolve in any of the usual solvents and it does not melt until 500 °C. It has these properties because the polymer chain is particularly regular in shape and has very strong and numerous intermolecular forces.

Its fire resistance makes Nomex® ideal for firefighters' hoods.

6

a Draw the structures of the Nomex® monomers.

b The monomers link via amide bonds to form chains. Showing the repeat unit, draw the structure of Nomex®.

7

a Kevlar® is made from 1,4-diaminobenzene and 1,4-benzenedicarboxylic acid. Draw the structures of these monomers.

b Again, the monomers link via amide bonds to form chains. Showing the repeat unit, draw the structure of Kevlar®.

8

What type of intermolecular force will occur between Kevlar® polymer chains?

9

Draw a diagram to show this type of intermolecular force.

10

Which will have the higher melting point, Kevlar® or Nomex®? Explain your reasoning.

Having discovered such resilient materials, the chemists researching them set about finding ways of processing them into useful items. However, it was by chance that Stephanie Kwolek added calcium chloride as well as her favoured solvent (*N*-methyl pyrrolinidone). The ions from this salt are attracted to the C=O bonds in the polymer chain, and this breaks the intermolecular forces (see questions 8 and 9). Bingo, the polymer dissolved!

1 Sections of different polymers **P** to **U** are shown below.

P —N—C—C—N—C—C—
with CH$_3$ groups on the carbons and H on the N's, O double-bonded:

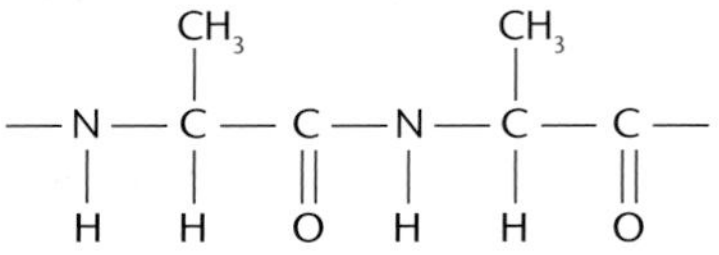

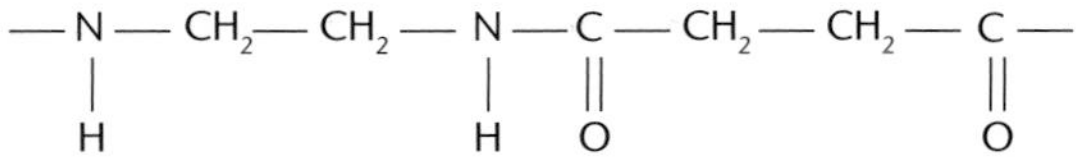

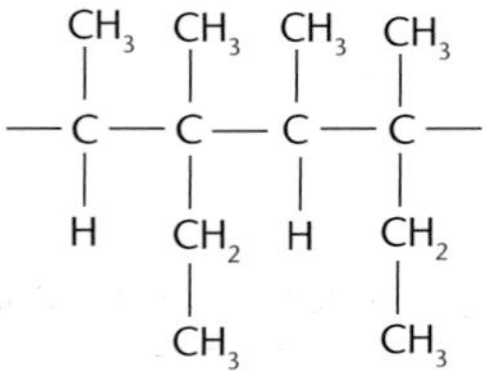

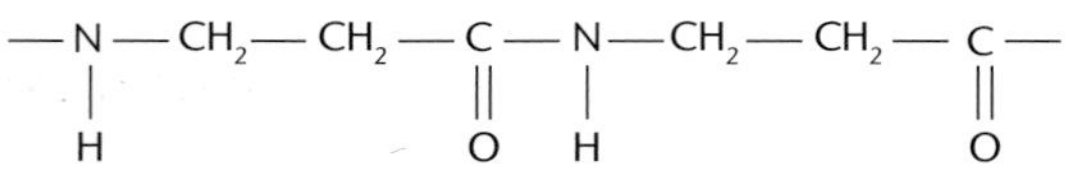

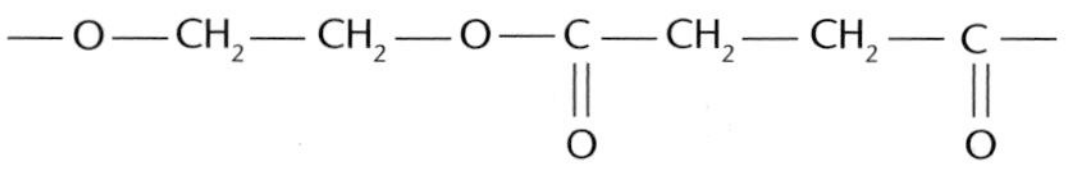

$$\text{P} \quad -\!N\!-\!\underset{H}{\overset{CH_3}{C}}\!-\!\underset{O}{C}\!-\!N\!-\!\underset{H}{\overset{CH_3}{C}}\!-\!\underset{O}{C}\!-$$

$$\text{Q} \quad -\!N\!-\!CH_2\!-\!CH_2\!-\!N\!-\!\underset{O}{C}\!-\!CH_2\!-\!CH_2\!-\!\underset{O}{C}\!-$$
(H on N's)

$$\text{R} \quad -\!\underset{H}{\overset{CH_3}{C}}\!-\!\underset{CH_2}{\overset{CH_3}{C}}\!-\!\underset{H}{\overset{CH_3}{C}}\!-\!\underset{CH_2}{\overset{CH_3}{C}}\!-$$
(with CH$_3$ below the CH$_2$ groups)

$$\text{S} \quad -\!N\!-\!CH_2\!-\!CH_2\!-\!\underset{O}{C}\!-\!N\!-\!CH_2\!-\!CH_2\!-\!\underset{O}{C}\!-$$
(H on N's)

$$\text{T} \quad -\!O\!-\!CH_2\!-\!CH_2\!-\!O\!-\!\underset{O}{C}\!-\!CH_2\!-\!CH_2\!-\!\underset{O}{C}\!-$$

$$\text{U} \quad -\!O\!-\!CH_2\!-\!CH_2\!-\!\underset{O}{C}\!-\!O\!-\!CH_2\!-\!CH_2\!-\!\underset{O}{C}\!-$$

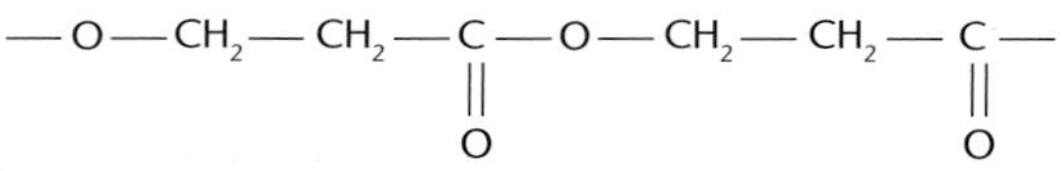

a i Polymer **P** is formed from the single amino acid, 2-aminopropanoic acid.
Draw the structure of the zwitterion of this amino acid.

ii One other polymer represented above is formed from a single amino acid. Give the formula of this amino acid.

iii Name the monomers used in the formation of polymer **Q**. (4)

b Polymer **R** is formed from an alkene monomer.

i Name the type of polymerisation involved in the formation of polymer **R**.

ii Name the alkene monomer. (2)

c Polymers **T** and **U** are polyesters.

i Draw the structures of the monomers used to produce polymer **T**.

ii Draw the structure of the species formed when polymer **U** is hydrolysed by heating with aqueous sodium hydroxide. (3)

d i Name the strongest type of intermolecular force in polymer **R**.

ii Name the strongest type of intermolecular force in polymer **T**. (2)

Total 11

AQA, January 2008, Unit 4, Question 5

2

a The repeating units of two polymers, **P** and **Q**, are shown below.

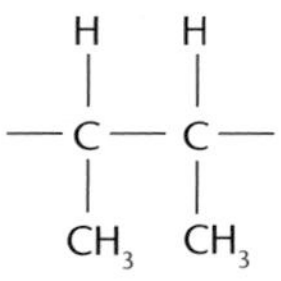

$$\text{P} \quad -\!\underset{CH_3}{\overset{H}{C}}\!-\!\underset{CH_3}{\overset{H}{C}}\!-$$

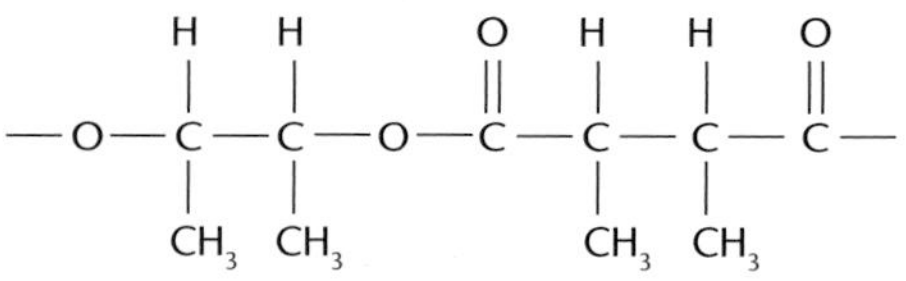

$$\text{Q} \quad -\!O\!-\!\underset{CH_3}{\overset{H}{C}}\!-\!\underset{CH_3}{\overset{H}{C}}\!-\!O\!-\!\underset{O}{\overset{}{C}}\!-\!\underset{CH_3}{\overset{H}{C}}\!-\!\underset{CH_3}{\overset{H}{C}}\!-\!\underset{O}{\overset{}{C}}\!-$$

i Draw the structure of the monomer used to form polymer **P**. Name the type of polymerisation involved.

ii Draw the structures of **two** compounds which react together to form polymer **Q**.
Name these **two** compounds and name the type of polymerisation involved.

iii Identify a compound which, in aqueous solution, will break down polymer **Q** but not polymer **P**. (8)

b Draw the structures of the **two** dipeptides which can form when one of the amino acids shown below reacts with the other.

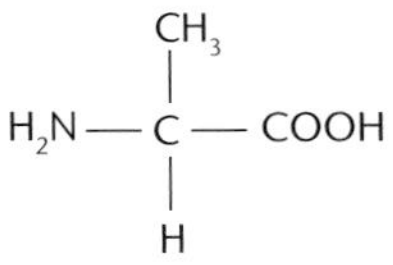

CH$_3$ | CH$_2$OH
H$_2$N — C — COOH   H$_2$N — C — COOH
H | H
Structure 1 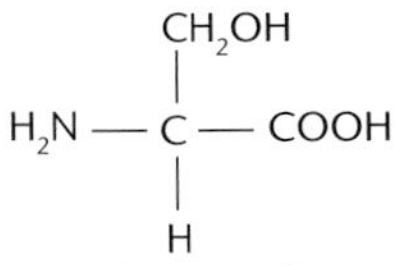   *Structure 2* (2)

c Propylamine, $CH_3CH_2CH_2NH_2$, can be formed either by nucleophilic substitution or by reduction.

i Draw the structure of a compound which can undergo nucleophilic substitution to form propylamine.

ii Draw the structure of the nitrile which can be reduced to form propylamine.

iii State and explain which of the two routes to propylamine, by nucleophilic substitution or by reduction, gives the less pure product. Draw the structure of a compound formed as an impurity. (5)

Total 15

AQA, June 2006, Unit 4, Question 4

3 The structure below shows the repeating unit of a polymer.

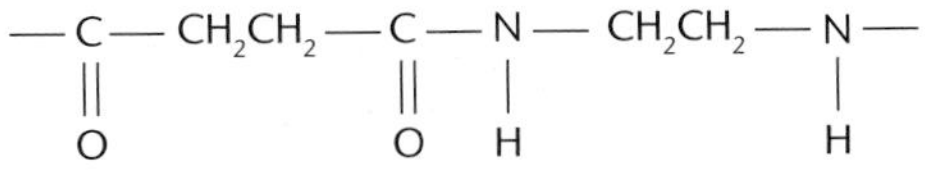

— C — CH$_2$CH$_2$ — C — N — CH$_2$CH$_2$ — N —
‖   ‖ | |
O   O H   H

By considering the functional group formed during polymerisation, name this type of polymer and the type of polymerisation involved in its formation. (2)

Total 2

AQA, January 2006, Unit 4, Question 6a

4 An isomer of **Q** which has the structure shown below is polymerised to form the biodegradeable polymer known as PHB.

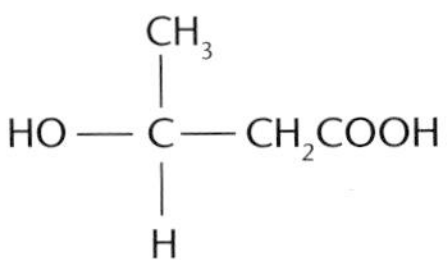

CH$_3$
HO — C — CH$_2$COOH
H

i Draw the repeating unit of the polymer PHB.

ii Suggest a reason why the polymer is biodegradeable. (2)

Total 2

AQA, June 2005, Unit 4, Question 3c

5 The repeating unit of a polyalkene is shown below.

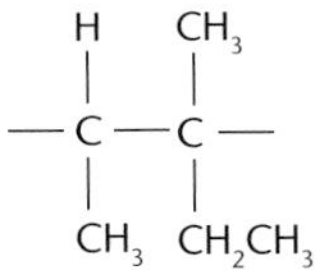

H   CH$_3$
| |
— C — C —
| |
CH$_3$ CH$_2$CH$_3$

Give the name of the alkene which is used to form this polymer. (1)

Total 1

AQA, January 2005, Unit 4, Question 2c

Recycling plastics

Turn over a plastic bottle and you are likely to find one of the symbols in the table below imprinted on the bottom. This is to allow quick and accurate identification of plastics so they can be sorted for recycling.

The different plastic types must be identified and sorted, often by hand, before recycling. Because they cannot be mixed to manufacture new components, a simple identification process is the key to cost-effective plastics recycling. Thermosets are more difficult to recycle but they are biodegradable.

Symbol	Acronym	Full name and uses
01 PET	PET	Poly(ethene) terephthalate – Fizzy drink bottles and frozen ready meal packages
02 PE-HD	HDPE	High-density polyethylene – Milk and washing-up liquid bottles
03 PVC	PVC	Poly(chloroethane) (polyvinyl chloride) – Food trays, clingfilm, bottles for squash, mineral water and shampoo
04 PE-LD	LDPE	Low-density poly(ethene) – Carrier bags and bin liners
05 PP	PP	Poly(propene) – Margarine tubs, microwaveable meal trays
06 PS	PS	Polystyrene – Yoghurt pots, foam meat or fish trays, hamburger containers and egg cartons, vending cups, plastic cutlery, protective packaging for electronic goods and toys
07 O	Other	Any other plastics that do not fall into any of the above categories. For example, melamine, often used to manufacture plastic plates and cups

Difficulties

There are difficulties associated with recycling plastics:

- cost of collection and separation of materials
- unavailability of stream of clean homogeneous material
- unavailability of suitable market for products
- lack of public pressure
- because current manufacturing plants are set up to produce plastics from scratch, they are inefficient when used to recycle plastics
- expensive to collect and sort
- removal of additives like dyes and fillers.

Waste plastics can be burnt in incinerators or sent to landfill. In the year 2000, 80% of post-consumer plastic waste was sent to landfill, 8% was incinerated and only 7% was recycled.

Advantages

Recycling plastic can have several other advantages:

- conservation of non-renewable fossil fuels – plastic production uses 8% of the world's oil production, 4% as feedstock and 4% during manufacture
- reduced consumption of energy
- reduced amounts of solid waste going to landfill
- reduced emissions of carbon dioxide (CO_2), nitrogen oxide (NO) and sulfur dioxide (SO_2).

The amount of plastics recycling has to increase. The UK has set a target of recycling more than 25% of plastics by 2010. Many more uses are being found for waste plastic. They are used as fillers instead of other natural materials or oil-based products. PET from used plastic bottles is used to make fibres for fleeces. At the reprocessing plant, the bottles are chopped up into flakes in water, cleaned and dried. The flakes are then melted and squeezed into filaments of synthetic fibre, then stretched to several times their original length, crimpled to introduce a wave, and cut to length. The final fibres are spun into yarn and the yarn is woven to produce the PCR fleece material.

For every 3 700 bottles recycled, a barrel of oil (42 gallons) is saved and about half a ton of toxic air emissions is avoided. Worldwide, three billion bottles and containers could be recycled annually. The amount of petroleum that could be saved by using PCR bottles instead of virgin materials in the manufacturing process would be enough to power a city the size of Birmingham for a year.

A1   List five ways in which your consumption of plastics materials could be reduced.

A2   A lot of the plastic that is re-used is sent to China to be recycled. How does this raise ethical questions?

A3   Explain the benefits of recycling plastics over landfill and incineration.

10 Organic synthesis and analysis

Chewing the bark or leaves from a willow tree has been known for centuries to give pain relief and reduce fevers. This was probably discovered by accident and the practice spread by word of mouth.

In the early 19th century, the active ingredient in the bark was extracted, analysed and shown to be a substance called salicin, a compound closely related to 2-hydroxybenzoic acid. The tree population of the world could not be expected to supply enough of this material to satisfy the growing demand. As a result, chemists, armed with their recent knowledge of its structure, set about the task of synthesising this or a closely related substance on a large scale.

In 1874, mass production of 2-hydroxybenzoic acid began, following a synthesis developed by the German chemist Adolf Kolbe, using readily available phenol (hydroxybenzene), sodium hydroxide and carbon dioxide. After prolonged use, this acid was shown to cause stomach irritations, and its structure was modified again by esterification of the phenolic –OH group. In 1899, this produced what we know now as aspirin, 2-ethanoyloxybenzoic acid, a drug used worldwide for all sorts of treatments from headache to heart disease. This development is typical of the role played by analytical and synthetic chemists in a wide range of industries.

In 1763, Edward Stone reported that an extract of willow bark (from the willow tree, as shown in the photograph) was a 'Cure of Agues'. Nowadays, its derivative, aspirin, is used to relieve symptoms such as headaches. It also helps to prevent blood clots and so reduces the likelihood of heart attacks and strokes.

[195]

XXXII. *An Account of the Success of the Bark of the Willow in the Cure of Agues. In a Letter to the Right Honourable* George Earl *of* Macclesfield, *President of R. S. from the Rev. Mr.* Edmund Stone, *of* Chipping-Norton *in* Oxfordshire.

My Lord,

Read June 2d, 1763.

Among the many useful discoveries, which this age hath made, there are very few which, better deserve the attention of the public than what I am going to lay before your Lordship.

There is a bark of an English tree, which I have found by experience to be a powerful astringent, and very efficacious in curing aguish and intermitting disorders.

About six years ago, I accidentally tasted it, and was surprised at its extraordinary bitterness; which immediately raised me a suspicion of its having the properties of the Peruvian bark. As this tree delights in a moist or wet soil, where agues chiefly abound, the general maxim, that many natural maladies carry their cures along with them, or that their remedies lie not far from their causes, was so very apposite to this particular case, that I could not help applying it; and that this might be the intention of Providence here, I must own had some little weight with me.

The excessive plenty of this bark furnished me, in my speculative disquisitions upon it, with an

D d 2   argument

A portion of a letter written to the Right Honourable George Earl of Macclesfield, from the Reverend Mr Edmund Stone, about the success of using the bark of the willow tree.

A task sheet and practice questions on the Practical Skills Assessment 'Prepare a solid organic compound' can be found at www.collinseducation.co.uk/advancedscienceaqa.

10.1 Introduction

Previous chapters have given you some insight into the vast variety of organic molecules that can occur both naturally and artificially. In this chapter, you will be considering two problems that face organic chemists in research and industrial laboratories throughout the world: chemical **analysis** and chemical **synthesis**.

Analysis tells us the chemical composition, the structure and the chemical characteristics of a particular compound. Synthesis tells us how to make a particular compound efficiently from available starting materials. To understand both analysis and synthesis, you will need to apply the chemical reactions you have studied in previous chapters.

In analysis, the absence or presence of a particular functional group can be determined from the observations made during chemical reactions. In synthesis, we choose reactions that will convert one material efficiently to the required product or to a material (called an **intermediate**) that can eventually, directly or indirectly, be converted to the required product.

10.2 Organic compound analysis

If you are presented with an organic molecule of unknown composition, you can gain detailed structural information about functional groups, relative molecular mass and distributions of hydrogen atoms by using the techniques of infrared spectroscopy, mass spectrometry and nuclear magnetic resonance spectroscopy (see Chapter 11).

However, before using spectroscopic analysis, if we chemically analyse an organic compound, we can find out a great deal of information about the molecule. This approach cuts down the number of possibilities considerably.

Combustion

Most organic compounds will burn under the right circumstances. But how they burn in air, where the supply of oxygen is limited, often gives us useful general information about the molecule. Smaller molecules, particularly those containing only carbon, hydrogen and oxygen, tend to ignite more easily and burn more rapidly in air.

However, it is the appearance of the flame that gives us clues about the nature of an organic molecule. Saturated molecules tend to burn with colourless, non-smoky flames, whereas molecules containing unsaturated carbon-to-carbon bonds produce sooty flames. This is particularly true for benzene-related molecules, where the percentage of carbon is very high. In these compounds, there is a high degree of incomplete combustion, and large particles of soot (carbon) appear in the smoke.

Testing for alkenes

The electrophilic addition of bromine to an **alkene** (see *AS Chemistry*, pages 247–248) provides a test for the presence of C=C bonds in a molecule. As shown in Fig. 1, dilute, aqueous bromine solution (orange) is rapidly decolourised when reacted with an alkene.

1 Why does the presence of oxygen in the structure enhance the burning properties of an organic molecule?

2 What is the predominant electrophile present in dilute, aqueous bromine solution?

3 Identify the colourless organic product formed when but-1-ene decolourises aqueous bromine solution.

Fig. 1   Alkene test

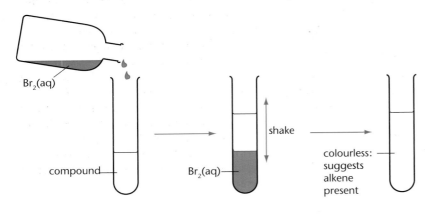

Bromine water before and after shaking with hex-1-ene.

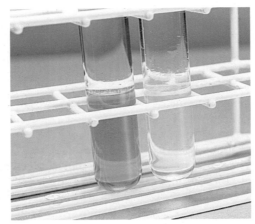

Testing for haloalkanes

The carbon–halogen bond in a **haloalkane** molecule is polar and susceptible to nucleophilic substitution (see *AS Chemistry*, Chapter 14). For example, hydrolysis of a haloalkane by warming it with dilute sodium hydroxide solution causes the covalently bonded halogen to be released in the form of a halide ion.

> **4**   Write an equation for the hydrolysis of a general haloalkane, RX (where X represents a halogen atom), by the hydroxide ion.

Once the excess sodium hydroxide has been neutralised by dilute nitric acid, the halide ion can be identified using silver nitrate solution followed by ammonia solution (see *AS Chemistry*, Chapter 11). As shown in Table 1 and the photo, the visible effects tell you whether a chloro-, bromo- or iodoalkane is present or not and, indeed, which halogen it is. Fluoroalkanes are not detected because silver fluoride is water soluble.

Table 1   Tests for haloalkanes

Procedure	Observation			
	For control, e.g. water	For a chloroalkane	For a bromoalkane	For an iodoalkane
Step 1 Warm with dilute sodium hydroxide solution	no visible effect	aqueous and organic phases more miscible	aqueous and organic phases more miscible	aqueous and organic phases more miscible
Step 2 Add excess dilute nitric acid followed by silver nitrate solution	no visible effect	white precipitate of silver chloride	cream precipitate of silver bromide	pale yellow precipitate of silver iodide
Step 3 Add dilute ammonia solution then concentrated ammonia solution	no visible effect	white precipitate dissolves to form colourless solution when dilute ammonia added	cream precipitate dissolves to form colourless solution only when concentrated ammonia solution added	precipitate insoluble in both dilute and concentrated ammonia solution

Note: Fluoroalkanes are not included in this analytical scheme because Step 1 does not occur readily for fluoroalkanes and Step 2 does not produce a distinctive result because silver fluoride is water soluble.

At Step 2 (see Table 1), a chloroalkane (left) gives a white precipitate, a bromoalkane (centre) gives a cream precipitate and an iodoalkane (right) gives a pale yellow precipitate.

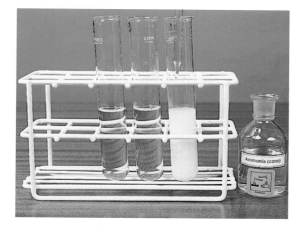

At Step 3, the precipitate from the chloride gives a colourless solution in dilute ammonia (left); the bromide precipitate dissolves only with concentrated ammonia (centre); and the iodide precipitate is not soluble in concentrated ammonia (right).

Testing for compounds containing oxygen

This group of organic compounds is extensive and includes **alcohols, aldehydes, ketones, acids** and **esters**. As seen in Chapter 5 and summarised in Fig. 2, these molecules are closely related.

Fig. 2   Oxidation of alcohols

Primary alcohol	Secondary alcohol	Tertiary alcohol
↓	↓	
aldehyde	ketone	no easy oxidation
↓		
acid		

You could use infrared spectroscopy (see Chapter 11) to find out whether the C–O and C=O bonds that are characteristic of these molecules are present in a compound you are testing.

However, in order to distinguish the different types of compounds, you have to use a combination of chemical tests based on acidity, redox reactions and condensation. It is important to apply these tests in the correct order, so that eliminations can be made as efficiently as possible. This sequence is summarised in Table 2. Some results are illustrated in the photos and text that follow.

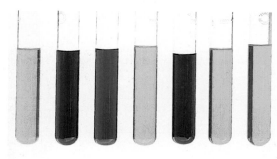

Results at Test 4, after warming with acidified potassium dichromate(VI) solution, are shown for (from left) water, primary alcohol, secondary alcohol, tertiary alcohol, aldehyde, ketone and carboxylic acid.

For Test 8, with Fehling's solution, an aldehyde gives a brick-red precipitate, while a ketone remains blue.

Most of the chemistry involved in these tests is discussed in *AS Chemistry* or earlier chapters in this book. The reactions with sodium metal and Brady's reagent are exceptions, but are included because they easily give specific information.

Table 2 Testing for molecules containing oxygen

Test	1 Add water and test the pH of the solution	2 Add sodium hydrogen-carbonate solution	3 Add sodium metal	4 Warm with acidified potassium dichromate (VI) solution	5 Warm with ethanoic acid and conc. sulfuric acid catalyst	6 Warm with ethanol and conc. sulfuric acid catalyst	7 Reaction with Brady's reagent (2,4-dinitro-phenylhydrazine in acid)	8 Fehling's test (see Chapter 5): warm with alkaline Cu^{2+}	9 Tollens' test (see Chapter 5): warm with ammoniacal Ag^+
primary alcohol	neutral	no effect	colourless H_2 gas evolved quickly	orange to green	sweet-smelling ester produced	no reaction	remains as orange solution	remains blue	remains colourless
secondary alcohol	neutral	no effect	colourless H_2 gas evolved slowly	orange to green	sweet-smelling ester produced	no reaction	remains as orange solution	remains blue	remains colourless
tertiary alcohol	neutral	no effect	colourless H_2 gas evolved very slowly	remains orange	sweet-smelling ester produced	no reaction	remains as orange solution	remains blue	remains colourless
aldehyde	neutral	no effect	no reaction	orange to green	no reaction	no reaction	bright orange-red precipitate	blue solution to brick-red precipitate	colourless solution forms silver mirror
ketone	neutral	no effect	no reaction	remains orange	no reaction	no reaction	bright orange-red precipitate	remains blue	remains colourless
carboxylic acid	red with indicator: pH about 3	colourless CO_2 evolved	colourless H_2 gas evolved quickly	remains orange	no reaction	sweet-smelling ester produced	remains orange	remains blue	remains colourless

Moreover, we can also adapt these tests to characterise an ester, acyl halide or acid anhydride. If we hydrolyse esters, acyl halides or acid anhydrides (see Fig. 3), we produce other compounds that can be identified using the tests described above. Acyl halides and anhydrides react particularly vigorously during the initial hydrolysis.

Fig. 3 How to characterise esters, acyl halides and acid anhydrides

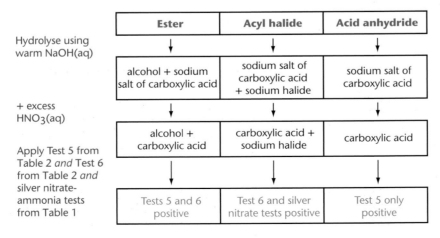

	Ester	**Acyl halide**	**Acid anhydride**
Hydrolyse using warm NaOH(aq)	↓	↓	↓
	alcohol + sodium salt of carboxylic acid	sodium salt of carboxylic acid + sodium halide	sodium salt of carboxylic acid
+ excess HNO_3(aq)	↓	↓	↓
	alcohol + carboxylic acid	carboxylic acid + sodium halide	carboxylic acid
Apply Test 5 from Table 2 *and* Test 6 from Table 2 *and* silver nitrate-ammonia tests from Table 1	↓	↓	↓
	Tests 5 and 6 positive	Test 6 and silver nitrate tests positive	Test 5 only positive

For Test 9, with Tollens' reagent, an aldehyde (left) gives a silver coating, while a ketone (right) remains colourless.

5 Why does the acid in Table 2 give a weakly acidic pH?

6 Which group of atoms is responsible for the production of hydrogen gas when reacted with sodium metal?

7 Why must the sample be absolutely dry before applying the sodium metal test?

8 Identify the species responsible for the green colour in the test with acidified dichromate(VI).

9 Identify the species responsible for the brick-red precipitate in the test with Fehling's solution.

10 Identify the species responsible for the silver mirror in the test using Tollens' reagent.

solution that reacts to form dense, orange-red precipitates called hydrazones when mixed with any carbonyl compound. This is shown in Fig. 4. Hence, we can use this solution to confirm the presence or absence of aldehydes and ketones.

Fig. 4   Brady's test

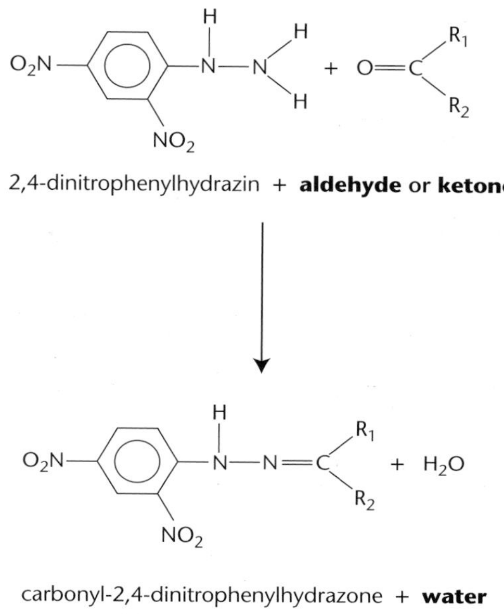

2,4-dinitrophenylhydrazin + **aldehyde** or **ketone**

carbonyl-2,4-dinitrophenylhydrazone + **water**

Testing with sodium metal

As you will know from Module 1 studies, sodium metal reacts vigorously with water to produce sodium hydroxide solution and hydrogen gas:

$$Na + H_2O \rightarrow Na^+(aq) + OH^-(aq) + \tfrac{1}{2}H_2(g)$$

This reaction depends on the reducing properties of sodium. Electrons are donated to the water molecule and this causes one of the O–H bonds to break: molecular hydrogen gas is released and a hydroxide ion is left behind.

Primary alcohols, secondary alcohols, tertiary alcohols and acids all react in a similar fashion because they too contain the necessary O–H bond:

$$Na + ROH \rightarrow Na^+(aq) + RO^-(aq) + \tfrac{1}{2}H_2(g)$$

$$Na + RCOOH \rightarrow$$
$$Na^+(aq) + RCOO^-(aq) + \tfrac{1}{2}H_2(g)$$

The organic products are alkoxides (RO⁻) and alkanoates (RCOO⁻), respectively. Acids react faster because the O–H bond in these molecules is more strongly polarised. Primary, secondary and tertiary alcohols react increasingly slowly because the added hydrocarbon groups 'get in the way' and slow down the reduction process.

Testing with Brady's reagent

For Test 7 in Table 2, **Brady's reagent** is a solution of 2,4-dinitrophenylhydrazine dissolved in sulfuric acid. It is a bright orange

11 If a positive Brady's test is observed, what should be the next step in your analysis?

12 What type of reaction is involved in a positive Brady's test?

Testing for amines and amino acids

These two groups, **amines** and **amino acids**, are both related to ammonia. Ammonia displaces water ligands to form a distinctively dark blue complex when added to aqueous copper(II) ions:

$$[Cu(H_2O)_6]^{2+}(aq) + 4NH_3(aq) \rightarrow$$
$$[Cu(NH_3)_4(H_2O)_2]^{2+}(aq) + 4H_2O(aq)$$
dark blue ammonia complex

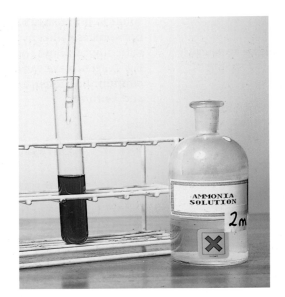

With aqueous copper(II) ions and excess ammonia, amines and amino acids give a dark blue soluble complex.

Amines and amino acids can be detected in a similar manner. It is worth noting that aromatic amines tend to form green, insoluble complexes, so giving further useful information on the identity of an organic compound.

13 Which structural feature common to ammonia, amines and amino acids allows the copper(II) ion test to work?

Once we have eliminated the possibility that the compound is ammonia by testing its combustibility in air, we can then distinguish amines from amino acids by adding Full Range indicator, followed by drops of very dilute sodium hydroxide solution.

The initial pH of an amine is considerably higher than that of an amino acid. If we have an amine, when we add the hydroxide, the indicator colour changes rapidly to the highly alkaline pH region. But this change requires significantly more alkali if the compound is an amino acid.

14 Why do amines and amino acids react differently with sodium hydroxide solution?

15 What chemical tests would you apply to identify the functional group(s) present in each of the following molecules?

a $CH_3CH_2CH_2COOH$

b $CH_3CH_2CH_2OH$

c $C_6H_5CH_2Br$

d $CH_3CH_2CH_2CH_2CHO$

e $CH_3CH(OH)CH_2COOH$

f CH_3COCl

g $CH_3CH=CHCH_2CH_2CH_3$

h $CH_3C(CH_3)(OH)CH_2CH_3$

i $CH_3CH_2NH_2$

16 What chemical tests would you apply to distinguish between the following pairs of molecules?

a $CH_3CH_2CH_2CH_2CH_2OH$ and $CH_3C(CH_3)(OH)CH_2CH_3$

b $CH_3CH_2CH_2CH_2Cl$ and $CH_3CH_2CH_2CH_2Br$

c $CH_3CH_2CH_2CH_3$ and $CH_3CH=CHCH_3$

d $CH_3CH_2COCH_3$ and $CH_3CH_2CH_2CHO$

e $CH_3CH_2CH_2COOCH_3$ and $CH_3CH(OH)CH_2COCH_3$

Conclusion

As part of the analysis of an unknown organic compound, identifying functional groups by chemical testing can be very fruitful. But remember that it is very easy to get misleading results because of contamination and incorrect procedures. Furthermore, negative tests are often more useful than positive tests; negative tests allow us to eliminate the possibility that certain functional groups are present.

10.3 Organic compound synthesis

Designing the synthesis of one organic molecule from another is a true test of your knowledge of organic chemistry. Furthermore, it is a major activity in industrial research laboratories, because it allows new molecules, which may have useful properties, to be made from other, readily available, molecules. Penicillin, quinine, aspirin, vitamins and insect repellents are just a few examples of useful molecules that are not available in adequate quantities in nature and have to be synthesised. Synthesis is also the final stage in the analysis of any new compound. Once a chemist has deduced a structure using chemical testing and spectroscopy, that structure must be confirmed by showing that it can be reproduced identically using synthesis.

You can use just the reactions you have already studied in Chemistry to devise a vast number of different syntheses, both for well-known molecules and, possibly, for totally unknown molecules. When designing such a synthesis, many factors will influence your final choice of pathway. These include the following:

- The availability of a suitable starting material from which the target molecule can be synthesised. The suitable starting material is usually arrived at by working backwards from the target and considering what carbon groups need to be 'joined' and what functional groups need to be created.

- The number of stages needed to convert the starting material to the target molecule. These will include both chemical reactions and subsequent separation and purification processes.
- The percentage yield that can be expected from each of the stages.
- Whether competing reactions can occur at any of the stages of the synthesis, resulting in lower yields and contamination.
- Are there any additional problems involved in scaling the synthesis to manufacturing proportions, particularly relative costs of starting materials, special designs for chemical plant and safety considerations?

17 In a three-stage synthesis, the molar yields of the individual stages are 50%, 40% and 75%. What is the overall molar percentage yield?

The interconnections between the more significant synthetic reactions are shown in Figs 5 and 6. These emphasise the fact that, because of delocalisation effects, functional groups bonded directly to benzene ring structures are likely to behave differently from those bonded to saturated structures. Hence, this is often an important consideration when selecting reactions to achieve a particular synthesis.

Fig. 5   Reaction pathways for alkane derivatives

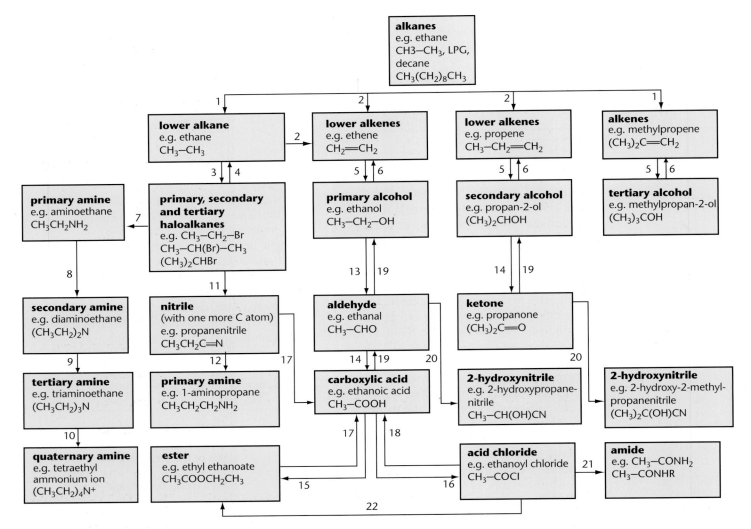

KEY	Reaction Number	Reaction type	Reactants and reaction conditions
	1	catalytic cracking	$Al_2O_3 + SiO_2$ catalyst at 500 °C
	2	steam cracking	steam, 850 °C
	3	free radical substitution	halogen with UV light to initiate
	4	reduction	H_2 with Ni catalyst
	5	electrophilic addition–hydration	$H_2O + H_3PO_4$ catalyst at 330 °C
	6	elimination–dehydration	conc. H_2SO_4 at 170 °C
	7	nucleophilic substitution	excess conc. NH_3 in ethanol solvent; heat
	8	nucleophilic substitution	haloalkane in ethanol solvent; heat
	9	nucleophilic substitution	excess haloalkane in ethanol solvent; heat
	10	nucleophilic substitution	large excess of haloalkane in ethanol solvent; heat
	11	nucleophilic substitution	KCN in ethanol solvent; heat
	12	reduction	$LiAlH_4$ in ethoxyethane solvent
	13	partial oxidation	$K_2Cr_2O_7 + H_2SO_4$; distill
	14	full oxidation	Excess $K_2Cr_2O_7 + H_2SO_4$ catalyst
	15	condensation–esterification	alcohol with concentrated H_2SO_4 catalyst
	16	nucleophilic substitution	PCl_5
	17	hydrolysis	heat with dilute H_2SO_4
	18	nucleophilic substitution–hydrolysis	H_2O
	19	reduction	$LiAlH_4$ in ethoxyethane solvent
	20	nucleophilic addition	concentrated solution of HCN and acidification
	21	acylation	ammonia or amine
	22	esterification–condensation	alcohol

Fig. 6   Reaction pathways for benzene derivatives

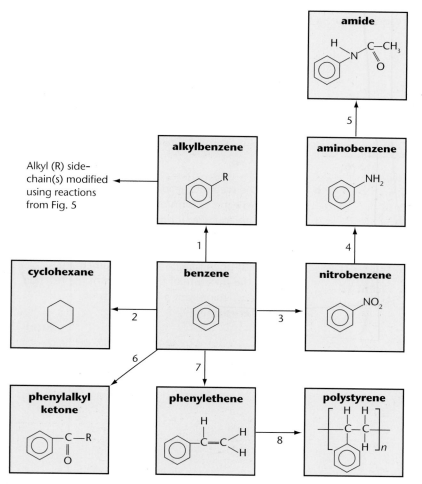

Reaction Number	Reaction type	Reactants and reaction conditions
1	electrophilic substitution (acylation: Friedel–Crafts)	RCl + $AlCl_3$ catalyst at 40 °C
2	reduction	H_2 + Ni catalyst at 150 °C
3	electrophilic substitution (nitration)	conc. H_2SO_4 + conc. HNO_3 at 50 °C
4	reduction	Sn + conc. HCl followed by NaOH
5	acylation	ethanoyl chloride
6	electrophilic substitution (acylation: Friedel–Crafts)	$RCOCl$ + $AlCl_3$ catalyst at 40 °C
7	electrophilic substitution (acylation: Friedel–Crafts)	CH_3CH_2Cl + $AlCl_3$ catalyst followed by catalytic dehydrogenation
8	polymerisation	Ziegler-Natta catalyst

18 State the reagent(s) and conditions needed to achieve each of the following conversions. Write equations for the reactions that occur.

a $CH_3CH_2CH(OH)CH_3$ to $CH_3CH_2COCH_3$

b $CH_3CH_2CH_2OH$ to $CH_3CH_2CH_2OCOCH_3$

c $CH_3CH_2CH_2CH_2OH$ to $CH_3CH_2CH=CH_2$

d $CH_3CH_2CH_2COOH$ to $CH_3CH_2CH_2CH_2OH$

e CH_3CH_2Br to $CH_3CH_2NH_2$

19 Devise reaction schemes for each of the following syntheses:

a ethanoic acid from chloroethane

b propanoic acid from bromoethane

c propanone from propene

d ethyl ethanoate from ethanol

e aminobenzene from benzene.

The pathways described allow you to select possible synthetic routes to your target molecule from different starting materials via different numbers of steps, each with differing yield expectations. However, in industry, only by experimentation and with a thorough costing of the alternative routes is it possible to assess the relative merits of the synthetic processes.

 A task sheet and practice questions on the Practical Skills Assessment 'Purify an organic solid' can be found at www.collinseducation.co.uk/advancedscienceaqa.

 A task sheet and practice questions on the Practical Skills Assessment 'Test the purity of an organic solid' can be found at www.collinseducation.co.uk/advancedscienceaqa.

1

a Chloroethane (CH_3CH_2Cl) can be used as a reagent in each of the following reactions.

(a)

Identify a catalyst for this reaction and show how the catalyst reacts and is regenerated.
Name and outline a mechanism for this reaction.
Name the product shown and identify an important industrial chemical manufactured from it.   (9)

b

(b)

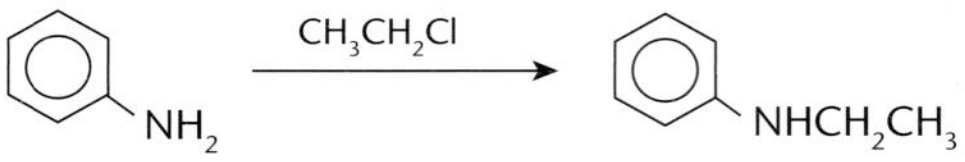

Name and outline a mechanism for this reaction and name the product shown.   (6)

Total 15

AQA, January 2008, Unit 4, Question 7

2

a Describe, by giving reagents and stating observations, how you could distinguish between the compounds in the following pairs using simple test-tube reactions.

(i)

P   **Q**

(ii) CH_3CH_2COCl and CH_3CH_2Cl

R   **S**   (6)

b i Give the reagents needed for the reduction of nitrobenzene to form phenylamine.
Write an equation for the reaction. Use [H] to represent the reductant.

ii Name the type of mechanism for the reaction between phenylamine and bromomethane.
Draw the structure of the product of the reaction of phenylamine with a large excess of bromomethane.   (5)

Total 11

AQA, January 2007, Unit 4, Question 7

3

a Describe how propanal, CH_3CH_2CHO, and propanone, CH_3COCH_3, can be distinguished using
  i a chemical test and
  ii the number of peaks in their proton n.m.r. spectra. (2)

b Compound **Z** can be produced by the reaction of compound **X** with compound **Y** as shown in the synthesis outlined below.

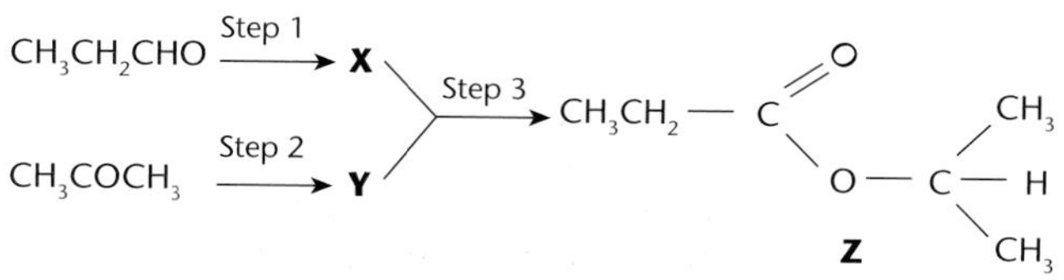

Identify compounds **X** and **Y**.
For each of the three steps in the synthesis, name the type of reaction involved and give reagents and conditions. Equations are **not** required. (10)

Total 12

AQA, January 2005, Unit 5, Question 7

4 Aqueous silver nitrate can be used to distinguish between chloroethanoic acid and ethanoyl chloride.

  i Draw the structure of ethanoyl chloride. Predict what, if anything, you would observe when ethanoyl chloride is added to aqueous silver nitrate.

  ii Draw the structure of chloroethanoic acid. Predict what, if anything, you would observe when chloroethanoic acid is added to aqueous silver nitrate. (4)

Total 4

AQA, June 2005, Unit 5, Question 3c

Synthesising new products in the laboratory

Benzocaine

Benzocaine is chemically related to cocaine. Cocaine is extracted from the leaves of the coca plant, which is grown in South America. Both cocaine and benzocaine have medical uses, particularly as anaesthetics. But cocaine is dangerously addictive and has become a substance of abuse, associated with worldwide crime.

Fig. 7   Benzocaine

The following list gives some additional information about the benzene ring, and making benzocaine from benzene. You will need to use this to answer the first two questions.

- The presence of a nitro group on a benzene ring causes the next substitution to occur preferentially at the 3 position.
- The presence of an alkyl group on a benzene ring causes the next substitution to occur preferentially at the 2 and 4 positions.
- Any alkyl group on a benzene ring can be oxidised to a –COOH group by heating with alkaline potassium manganate(VII). In an equation, this can be represented by [O].

> **A1**   Given the additional information in the list, devise a scheme for making benzocaine from benzene.
>
> **A2**   Explain your choice of reaction sequence, and write a balanced equation for each step of the process.

Synthesising new products in industry

A **batch process** is where the reactants are placed in the reaction vessel and the products are removed after the reaction has stopped or reached equilibrium and the vessel cleaned. This is similar to most laboratory syntheses that you will do, such as the one you devised above to synthesise benzocaine. The method is used in industry where the amounts of products are smaller. Manufacturers

of large-scale chemicals often prefer a **continuous process**, where the reactants are fed in at one end of the plant and the products are drawn off at the other end with the process running continuously. Co-products are compounds the company can usefully sell. By-products will be disposed of by the company.

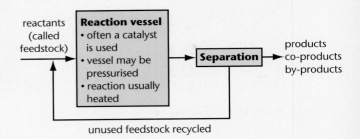

These are high-grade chemicals for a highly specialised use being manufactured using a batch process.

Fig. 8   Schematic diagram of a continuous process

reactants (called feedstock) → **Reaction vessel**
- often a catalyst is used
- vessel may be pressurised
- reaction usually heated

→ **Separation** → products, co-products, by-products

unused feedstock recycled

> **A3**   Where would industry prefer a continuous process over a batch process?
>
> **A4**   Why do you want to keep by-products to a minimum?
>
> **A5**   Explain other ways a company can save costs in a continuous process.
>
> **A6**   Explain how contamination might be a problem with industrial batch processes.

A7 Explain why recycling unreacted material might be environmentally beneficial.

Feedstocks are made from raw materials. For example, oil and gas are major sources of feedstocks for the manufacture of petrochemicals. The oil or gas is often cracked, using steam or a catalyst, or re-formed.

Refining of crude oil gives a wide range of feedstocks.

A8 What is the economic advantage of cracking and re-forming in the petrochemical industry?

A9 In the reaction to produce epoxyethane from ethene, the desired reaction is:

$$2C_2H_4 + O_2 \rightarrow 2(CH_2)_2O$$

But the following reaction may also occur:

$$C_2H_4 + 3O_2 \rightarrow 2CO_2 + 2H_2O$$

Do you think these would be considered co-products or by-products? Justify your choice.

A10 At one time waste products were simply dumped in the nearest convenient place. But this is no longer acceptable. Give two waste products from industrial processes, say why they cannot be dumped and state how the effect on the environment is now minimised.

A11 Explain what particular health and safety issues may be more important in industry than in school or college laboratories.

11 Structure determination

MRI (magnetic resonance imaging) scanners are powerful tools for medical diagnosis. The first commercial MRI scanners were available in 1983, only seven years after the scanner was first developed, and they are now used in major hospitals worldwide. These scanners provide fast and accurate diagnosis of a very wide range of illnesses.

MRI has its origins in a technique called nuclear magnetic resonance (NMR) spectroscopy that chemists have been using regularly since the 1950s. The technique helps chemists to deduce molecular structures by pinpointing and counting the positions of atoms such as ^1H in molecules. This led the way to MRI scanners, because ^1H occurs in all organic and biochemical molecules. It is particularly abundant in the body in water, which makes up about 70% of living tissues. This makes it possible for MRI to investigate living tissues by looking at the different effects caused by their varying water content.

MRI easily shows the distribution of different tissues. Mainly because of their different water contents, bone is easily distinguished from muscle, and muscle from fat, giving clearly defined images. More importantly, diseased tissue is distinguished from healthy tissue!

This technique and others are discussed in this chapter to explain structures.

Scanning by MRI: the patient's body lies along the central axis of a superconducting electronic magnet.

How do chemists know the structure of any particular molecule? By the time you reach this chapter, you will be aware of the vast variety of structures for organic compounds that occur both naturally and artificially. Variations in the numbers of carbon atoms per molecule, the arrangements of those carbon atoms, functional groups and isomers all add to the almost unlimited number of organic structures, each of which is unique. Consequently, structure determination involves some fascinating detective work, where experimental results from a variety of sources are each analysed to provide a piece of the jigsaw, finally arriving at the overall picture.

What experimental sources are used? Apart from chemical analysis, which can give general information such as the empirical formula of the compound and indicate the presence of particular

1 An organic compound is found to contain carbon, hydrogen and oxygen. Also, it is found that 0.44 g of the compound reacts to produce 0.88 g of carbon dioxide and 0.36 g of water. Calculate the empirical formula of the compound.

2 The relative molecular mass of the compound from question 1 is 88. Deduce the molecular formula of the compound.

3 Given that the compound from questions 1 and 2 is weakly acidic, deduce the possible structures for the compound.

functional groups in the compound, spectroscopic methods are the most generally useful sources of evidence for molecular structure.

In general, spectroscopic methods involve making observations of how molecules react when subjected to various physical stimuli such as infrared radiation, microwave radiation, ultraviolet radiation, magnetic fields and radio-frequency radiation. They are all useful for determining particular aspects of molecular structure. Chromatography is a useful addition to the scientist's range of analytical techniques.

11.1 Infrared spectroscopy

What is **infrared spectroscopy**? First, we need to consider what it is that is measured in infrared spectroscopy. Light from the Sun consists of a wide range of electromagnetic radiation of different frequencies (Fig. 1). There is infrared radiation, which is responsible for the warmth we all feel on a summer's day; there is 'visible' light, which we can see as different colours; and there is ultraviolet radiation, which is associated with getting a suntan. These three different types of radiation differ in wavelength and in the amount of energy that they carry. The wavelength λ (cm) of an electromagnetic wave is the distance between adjacent peaks (Fig. 2).

Infrared radiation corresponds approximately to wavelengths between 1.0×10^{-3} and 0.7×10^{-6} m (1 mm and 0.7 μm), as shown in Fig. 1. The different regions of the electromagnetic spectrum can also be described by frequency f (Hz or s^{-1}), energy per mole E (J mol^{-1}) or wavenumber v (cm^{-1}). These are interrelated and each can be calculated from one or more of the others using the following universal constants:

- the speed of light ($c = 3.00 \times 10^8$ m s^{-1})
- Planck's constant ($h = 6.63 \times 10^{-34}$ J s)
- Avogadro's constant ($L = 6.02 \times 10^{23}$ mol^{-1}).

The interrelationships are described by the following equations:

- $f = c/\lambda$ (Hz or s^{-1})
- $E = hf = hc/\lambda$ (J)
- $v = 1/\lambda$ (cm^{-1}).

For historical reasons, wavenumbers are most often used in infrared spectroscopy. The wavenumber equals the number of wavelengths that will fit into 1 cm: $v = 1/\lambda$. Hence, radiations with shorter wavelengths, higher energies and higher frequencies correspond to larger wavenumbers, and vice versa.

The full range of infrared radiation is not used in infrared spectroscopy. Most infrared

Fig. 1 Part of the electromagnetic spectrum

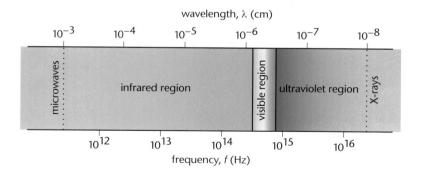

Fig. 2 Wavelength of an electromagnetic wave

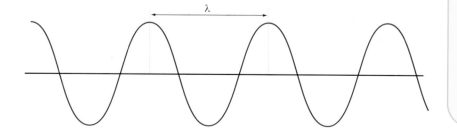

4 Using information overleaf calculate the range of wavelengths (λ) used in infrared spectroscopy.

5 Calculate the range of frequencies (*f*) used in infrared spectroscopy.

6 Calculate the energies (*E*) corresponding to the infrared radiation used in infrared spectroscopy.

spectrophotometers (the instruments used for carrying out infrared spectroscopy) operate at wavenumbers from 600 to 4 000 cm⁻¹. This provides a range of radiation suitable for detecting all types of covalent bonds.

Absorption of infrared radiation

Why does measuring infrared radiation give information about the structure of a molecule? It is the covalent bonds in molecules that are actually responsible for molecules absorbing different parts of the infrared spectrum. The covalent bonds in molecules act like springs in continuous, high-frequency vibration (Fig. 3). The natural vibrational frequencies of covalent bonds are in the same range as the frequencies of infrared radiation, but they vary slightly from bond to bond. They are characteristic of any particular bond and depend on the type of bond (single, double, etc.) and the atoms combined by the bond. For example, a C–Cl bond vibrates at about 2.0×10^{13} s⁻¹, but a C–Br bond vibrates at about 1.7×10^{13} s⁻¹.

When a molecule is exposed to infrared radiation, a vibrating bond will absorb infrared energy when the infrared frequency and the natural vibrational frequency of the bond coincide. This is referred to as a **resonance** effect. Since different bonds have different natural vibrational frequencies, we can identify different bonds by analysing which infrared frequencies are absorbed.

There are several types of bond vibrations. They are generally either 'stretching' vibrations, i.e. along the bond (Fig. 4), or 'bending' vibrations, i.e. across the bond (Fig. 5). Both the stretching and bending vibrations can be 'symmetric' (in step) or 'asymmetric' (out of step), with each having its own characteristic vibrational frequency. These different types of bond vibrations occur simultaneously for any particular group of atoms, making the overall vibrational pattern very complex even for the simplest molecule.

Fig. 4   Bond-stretching vibrations

(a) symmetric type   (b) asymmetric type

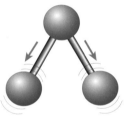
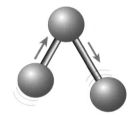

Fig. 3   Bond vibration

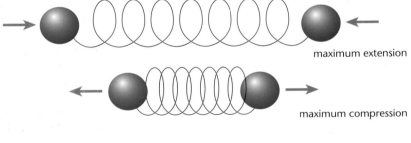

maximum extension

maximum compression

Fig. 5   Bond bending vibrations

(a) symmetric type   (b) asymmetric type

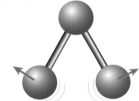
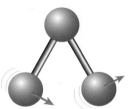

7 Why does the bond in C–Br vibrate more slowly than the bond in C–Cl?

● Covalent bonds are in continuous vibration.

● Different bonds absorb different infrared frequencies.

● Absorption of infrared frequency depends on the frequency of the radiation matching the vibrational frequency of the bond.

Infrared spectra

Almost all molecules contain several different types of bonds. Each bond will have several simultaneous stretching and bending types of vibrations, with each type of vibration having a characteristic vibrational frequency. Consequently, molecules will cause many absorptions (some strong, some weak, some sharp, some broad) in the infrared region. Together, these absorptions are called the 'infrared spectrum' of the molecule.

Recording an infrared spectrum

The infrared absorptions are measured using an infrared spectrophotometer (Fig. 6). The infrared (IR) beam, produced by a heating element, is split into two identical beams – the sample beam and the reference beam. By comparing the frequencies remaining in the sample beam after passing through the sample with those present in the reference beam, the wavenumber of each

absorption and the degree of each absorption can be measured. The use of two beams enables strong, misleading absorptions caused by water vapour and carbon dioxide gas in the air inside the spectrophotometer to be cancelled out because they are common to both beams.

Liquid, dissolved or suspended samples are usually 'sandwiched' as a thin film between polished discs made from sodium chloride (NaCl) or potassium bromide (KBr). These materials are used because they are both transparent to infrared radiation. This 'sandwich' is positioned in the sample beam. Gaseous samples are examined in specially designed sealed cells with a much larger thickness (path length) of sample to allow adequate absorption.

> **8** Can you think of any practical problems that might result from using a sample in 'solution' or 'suspension' form?

Fig. 6   Diagrammatic scheme for an infrared spectrophotometer

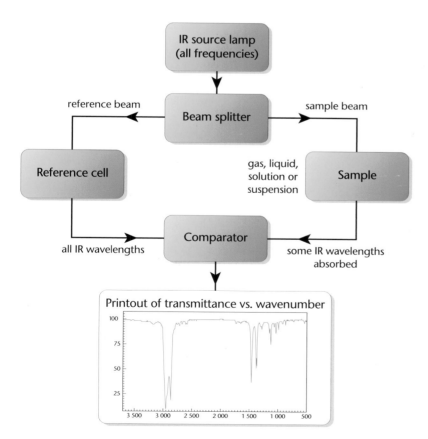

Identifying functional groups

By comparing structures and spectra, absorptions of a particular wavenumber can be associated with a particular covalent bond. This is shown in Fig. 7 for an alkane, an alkene and an alkyne.

The spectrum of 2,3-dimethylbutane (an alkane; Fig. 7(a)) contains two main groups of absorptions. These can be shown to be due to stretching of the C–H bond (the absorptions at $2\,960$ cm^{-1} and $2\,876$ cm^{-1}) and bending of the C–H bond (the absorptions at $1\,464$ cm^{-1} and $1\,380$ cm^{-1}).

The spectrum of 3-methylpent-1-ene (an alkene; Fig. 7(b)) contains two more main absorptions, when compared with the spectrum of the alkane. These two absorptions are due to stretching vibrations of the C–H bonds attached to the C=C double bond (the absorption at $3\,084$ cm^{-1}) and stretching vibrations of the C=C bond (the absorption at $1\,644$ cm^{-1}).

When looking at the spectrum of 3,3-dimethylbut-1-yne (an alkyne; Fig. 7(c)), the C–H stretching and bending absorptions are still present. The extra absorptions are those arising from stretching vibrations of the C–H attached to the C≡C bond ($3\,312$ cm^{-1}) and stretching vibrations of the C≡C bond ($2\,103$ cm^{-1}).

Fig. 7   Infrared spectra of (a) an alkane, (b) an alkene and (c) an alkyne

(a) 2,3-dimethylbutane

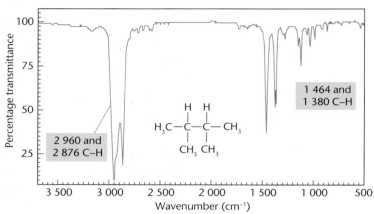

(b) 3-methylpent-1-ene

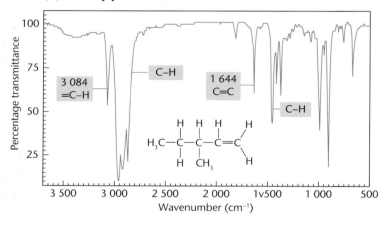

(c) 3,3-dimethylbut-1-yne

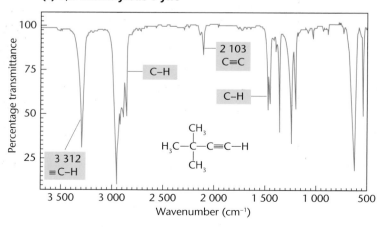

A comparison of the wavenumbers for the C=C and C≡C bonds shows that the shorter, stronger triple bond absorbs at a higher frequency (higher wavenumber).

9 Compare the absorptions caused by the stretching vibrations of the C–H bonds attached to C–C, C=C and C≡C groups. What pattern can you see?

10 Compare the spectra in Fig. 8 (for cyclohexane, cyclohexanol and cyclohexanone) and, as far as possible, associate the absorptions labelled **1–11** with C–H, C–O, O–H or C=O bonds. Explain your deductions.

By comparing the spectra of a large number of molecules of known structure, correlation tables of bond types versus infrared absorption regions can be compiled. Table 1 is such a table, although far more extensive tables are available. However, Table 1 does include all the groups you are likely to encounter during your advanced level studies. Such correlation tables allow particular bonds and groups of atoms (called **functional groups**) in a molecule to be recognised by matching experimental absorptions with data from the table.

The values in Table 1 are for bond-stretching vibrations, except for the bond-bending vibration of the C–H bond. Notice that stretching vibrations require more energy than bending vibrations, so bond stretches occur at higher wavenumbers. Vibrations involving either stronger bonds (e.g. double and triple bonds) or bonds to lighter atoms (e.g. hydrogen) occur at higher wavenumbers. Thus single bonds to hydrogen (C–H, O–H, N–H) absorb between 4 000 and 2 500 cm^{-1}, double bonds absorb between 1 500 and 2 000 cm^{-1} and triple bonds absorb between 2 000 and 2 500 cm^{-1}.

Bonds involved in hydrogen bonding tend to give broad absorptions rather than sharp discrete absorptions. As a result, it is easy to

Fig. 8 **Infrared spectra of (a) cyclohexane, (b) cyclohexanol and (c) cyclohexanone**

(a) Cyclohexane

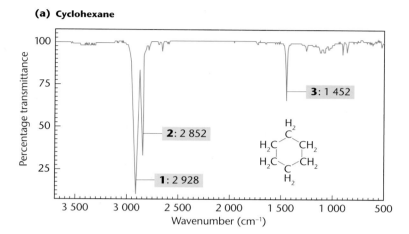

(b) Cyclohexanol

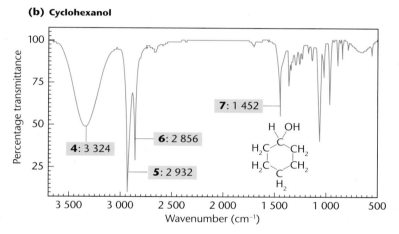

(c) Cyclohexanone

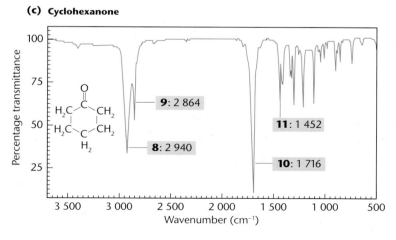

Table 1   An infrared correlation table

Bond	Functional group	Wavenumber (cm⁻¹)
C–H	alkyne	3 250–3 310
C–H	alkene	3 000–3 100
C–H	alkane	2 850–2 975
C–H	arene	3 030–3 080
C–H	aldehyde	2 650–2 880
N–H	amine (non H-bonded)	3 320–3 560
N–H	amide (non H-bonded)	3 320–3 560
N–H	amine (H-bonded)	3 100–3 400
O–H	alcohol (non H-bonded)	3 580–3 670
O–H	alcohol (H-bonded)	3 230–3 550
O–H	phenol	3 100–3 380
O–H	acid (H-bonded)	2 500–3 000
C≡N	nitrile	2 210–2 260
C≡C	alkyne	2 100–2 260
C=C	alkene	1 620–1 690
C=C	arene	1 450–1 600
C=O	acid chloride	1 790–1 815
C=O	ester	1 730–1 750
C=O	acid (alkyl)	1 700–1 725
C=O	acid (aryl)	1 680–1 700
C=O	aldehyde	1 685–1 740
C=O	ketone	1 680–1 725
C=O	amide	1 630–1 700
C–F	fluoro	1 000–1 400
C–Cl	chloro	600–800
C–Br	bromo	500–600
C–I	iodo	about 500
C–C	alkane	720–1 175
C–O	ester	1 180–1 310
C–O	phenol	1 120–1 220
C–O	alcohol	1 050–1 150
C–N	amine	1 030–1 230
C–N	amide	1 590–1 650
C–H bend	arene	700–880
C–H bend	alkane	1 365–1 485

recognise molecules containing –OH and –NH groups, i.e. alcohols, phenols (where OH is bonded directly to a benzene ring), carboxylic acids and amines.

The O–H bonds in water molecules cause hydrogen bonding. As a result, organic compounds that are 'wet' (contain traces of water) can be easily identified. Any residual water will cause a very strong, very broad absorption around 3 500 cm^{-1}. The ratio of the intensity of the water absorption to the intensity of one of the stronger absorptions caused by the pure compound can be used to measure the water content.

key facts

● Using correlation tables, infrared absorptions above 1 500 cm^{-1} can be associated with particular functional groups.

● Using correlation tables, infrared absorptions below 1 500 cm^{-1} can be associated with particular general molecular skeletons.

Using infrared spectroscopy

Infrared spectroscopy has many applications. By focusing on particular bonds with known infrared absorptions, molecules that cause sweetness in ripened fruits can be recognised and measured without having to peel the fruit. Atmospheric pollutants, poisons and illegal drugs can be monitored in a similar fashion by focusing on a particular absorption. The method allows very closely related drugs to be distinguished, identified and measured quickly and accurately.

Because infrared spectroscopy is such a fast process, it can be used to measure the pollution created by individual cars as they pass by an infrared spectrophotometer positioned at the roadside. Such a device uses infrared frequencies corresponding to the carbon–oxygen triple bond of carbon monoxide, the nitrogen–oxygen bonds of the various oxides of nitrogen and the carbon–hydrogen bonds of unburnt hydrocarbons, all of which are common pollutants. This type of system is also used to test the exhaust gases of cars during their annual MOT test.

It is also possible to identify the whole molecule by matching the whole infrared spectrum to known spectra. A computer, using an appropriate database, usually does the storage and matching of spectra. However, it can be done manually using an overlay system where spectra of known compounds are printed on transparent sheets, which can be superimposed on unknown spectra in search of a match. Either way, the spectrum acts as a 'fingerprint' for the molecule. Identifying compounds by this direct matching technique is an everyday routine in forensic science and various chemical industries. Pure compounds, for example, a drug such as aspirin, are identified directly, while the components of complex mixtures such as cigarette smoke can each be identified following separation by chromatography.

Analysing car exhaust gases using IR. For cars fitted with catalytic converters, the maximum allowed level of CO is 0.3% and of hydrocarbons (HC) is 200 ppm (parts per million). For cars without catalytic converters, the levels are 3.5% for CO and 1 200 ppm for HC.

Fig. 9   Aspirin and salicylic acid

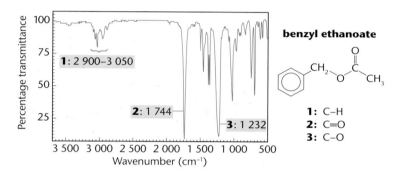

salicylic acid   ethanoic anhydride   aspirin   ethanoic acid
                                                                        (acetic acid)

Fig. 10   Infrared spectra of benzyl ethanoate, prop-2-en-1-ol and 2-methylbutanoic acid

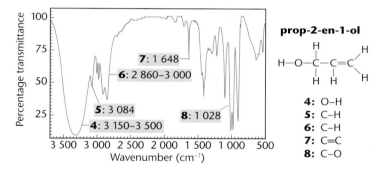

benzyl ethanoate

1: 2 900–3 050
2: 1 744
3: 1 232

1: C–H
2: C=O
3: C–O

prop-2-en-1-ol

7: 1 648
6: 2 860–3 000
5: 3 084
4: 3 150–3 500
8: 1 028

4: O–H
5: C–H
6: C–H
7: C=C
8: C–O

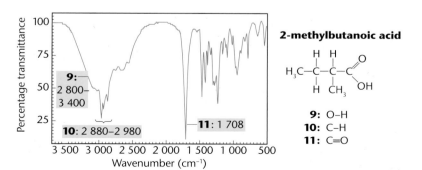

2-methylbutanoic acid

9: 2 800–3 400
10: 2 880–2 980
11: 1 708

9: O–H
10: C–H
11: C=O

Applications of infrared spectra

One important factor to remember when analysing infrared spectra is to avoid trying to account for *every* absorption. The minor absorptions might be caused by impurities, background electronic noise from the spectrophotometer or non-tabulated vibrations. In fact, impurities can be identified and measured by the technique. For example, newly manufactured impure aspirin will contain some unreacted salicylic acid (2-hydroxybenzenecarboxylic acid), which is the main starting material (Fig. 9). This impurity will be detected by an absorption caused by the phenolic O–H group at about 3 250 cm^{-1}. This absorption will disappear as the aspirin undergoes recrystallisation to produce a sample pure enough for safe use as a drug.

All that remains is to try applying the technique for yourself!

- Concentrate on the major absorptions.
- Be aware that one absorption may overshadow or merge with another.
- The *absence* of a particular absorption can tell you a lot. For example, if an infrared spectrum does not show a sharp, strong absorption in the range 1 630–1 815 cm^{-1}, it does not contain a carbonyl group, so it cannot be an aldehyde, ketone, acid or acid derivative.
- Unless a direct comparison with an authentic sample can be made, do not expect to make an absolutely definite identification using infrared spectroscopy. Definite identification usually requires additional information from other analytical techniques such as mass spectrometry (see section 11.2) and nuclear magnetic resonance spectroscopy (see section 11.3).

Worked examples should help. Compare the infrared spectra and structures of benzyl ethanoate, prop-2-en-1-ol and 2-methylbutanoic acid (Fig. 10). Absorptions corresponding to C–H bonds (from alkanes and alkenes), C=O bonds (two different types), C=C bonds, C–O bonds and O–H bonds can be distinguished. It can be seen that the infrared spectra provide a lot of useful information about the structures of these molecules, but in none of the examples is the information sufficient for absolute identification.

11 The infrared spectra in Fig. 11(a) to (d) are of hex-1-ene, ethanenitrile, hexane and 3-methylbutanal, but not necessarily in that order.

a Draw a structure for each of these four molecules.

b For each structure, list the major bonds and groups of atoms present in each molecule. Use Table 1 to list the wavenumber(s) of the absorption(s) associated with each of these groups.

c By comparing these expected absorptions with the main actual absorptions in the spectra, decide which spectrum belongs to which compound.

Infrared spectroscopy has applications in many different areas of science and technology, including pure research, forensic science and environmental science. It is used to help to determine the structure of new molecules and to identify drugs, poisons and many other molecules.

Infrared monitoring and measuring of atmospheric pollutants such as carbon dioxide, oxides of nitrogen, methane and chlorofluoro-carbons are particularly important nowadays because of their involvement in the greenhouse effect and the consequent global warming.

Recordings are made at the Mauna Loa Observatory in Hawaii of the levels of carbon dioxide in the atmosphere. In 1960 the average level was 316 ppm, but by 1990 this had increased to 354 ppm. Carbon dioxide absorbs infrared radiation at 1 700 cm^{-1}.

Fig. 11 Infrared spectra for question 11

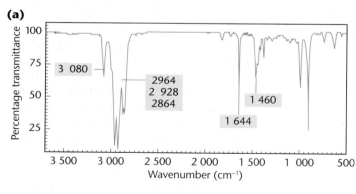

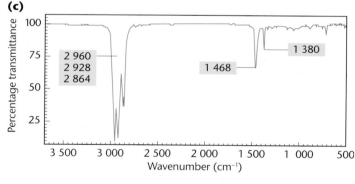

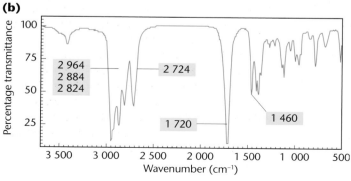

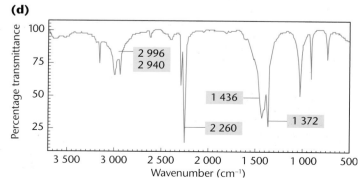

11.2 Mass spectrometry

Mass spectrometry is an important tool in chemical investigations. It has many applications, in both research and general analysis. Its use extends to forensic science, dating of geological and archaeological samples, investigations of foreign materials in food and drink, separation and measurement of isotopes, and deducing reaction mechanisms.

A **mass spectrometer** is a device for detecting the presence of chemical particles, measuring their mass and recording their relative abundance. The particles may be atoms, molecules or molecular fragments. In brief, a mass spectrometer converts the chemical particles into ions (with charge z), and then records the m/z ratio for the particles (where m is the mass of the particle).

The separation and measurement of a sample in a mass spectrometer occurs in six main steps (Fig. 12), as follows:

1 The sample, which may be an element, a compound or a mixture of both, is introduced into the mass spectrometer.
2 The sample is vaporised.
3 The sample is converted to positive ions.
4 The positive ions are accelerated by a fixed, known electric field, and then 'collimated' (focused) to form a narrow beam.
5 The ions are deflected by a variable radial magnetic field at 90° to the beam.
6 The ions are detected and the signal is amplified, measured and recorded.

The pressure inside the mass spectrometer is very low, so that ions from the sample can reach the detector without colliding with 'air' molecules (and to remove other unionised material).

High-energy electrons (Step 3 in Fig. 12) are produced when a current is passed through a coil of wire (C). The wire gets hot, giving off electrons. The electrons are attracted towards a positively charged electrode (A). This accelerates the electrons to high velocity, i.e. high kinetic energy. These electrons pass across the path of the vaporised sample and collide with some of the vaporised atoms or molecules. If an electron has sufficient energy, it will knock an electron off the atom or molecule. This loss of an electron produces a gaseous radical ion, $M^{+\bullet}(g)$, which is a single positive ion with an unpaired electron. A second electron may be knocked off, but this is a rare event. Ionisation of the sample is essential because subsequent stages (acceleration, deflection and detection) would not occur if the particles remained neutral.

Acceleration of the positive ions in an electric field follows ionisation (Step 4 in Fig. 12). A negative electrode causes this. This needs to occur because the next stage is deflection, which depends on the mass-to-charge ratio (m/z) and the ion's velocity.

Fig. 12   The basic principles of mass spectrometry

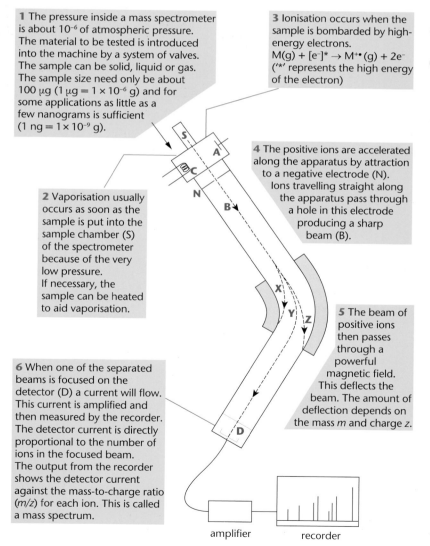

1 The pressure inside a mass spectrometer is about 10^{-6} of atmospheric pressure. The material to be tested is introduced into the machine by a system of valves. The sample can be solid, liquid or gas. The sample size need only be about 100 µg (1 µg = 1×10^{-6} g) and for some applications as little as a few nanograms is sufficient (1 ng = 1×10^{-9} g).

2 Vaporisation usually occurs as soon as the sample is put into the sample chamber (S) of the spectrometer because of the very low pressure. If necessary, the sample can be heated to aid vaporisation.

3 Ionisation occurs when the sample is bombarded by high-energy electrons.
$M(g) + [e^-]^* \rightarrow M^{+\bullet}(g) + 2e^-$
('*' represents the high energy of the electron)

4 The positive ions are accelerated along the apparatus by attraction to a negative electrode (N). Ions travelling straight along the apparatus pass through a hole in this electrode producing a sharp beam (B).

5 The beam of positive ions then passes through a powerful magnetic field. This deflects the beam. The amount of deflection depends on the mass m and charge z.

6 When one of the separated beams is focused on the detector (D) a current will flow. This current is amplified and then measured by the recorder. The detector current is directly proportional to the number of ions in the focused beam. The output from the recorder shows the detector current against the mass-to-charge ratio (m/z) for each ion. This is called a mass spectrum.

amplifier   recorder

During the deflection stage, for a particular magnetic field strength, heavier ions are deflected less than lighter ions. Also, ions with a double positive charge are deflected more than ions with a single positive charge (Step 5 in Fig. 12). Because the probability of a second electron being knocked off an ion is very small, mass spectrometry usually deals with ions with a single positive charge, i.e. $z = 1$. As a result, m/z for an ion is directly related to the mass of the ion.

Different ions experience different magnetic forces, depending on their m/z ratio, causing different degrees of deflection. The original beam is separated into a number of beams (e.g. X, Y and Z), each corresponding to an ion with different m/z (Step 6 in Fig. 12). The strength of the magnetic field is varied until one of the separated beams (e.g. beam Y in Fig. 12) is focused on the detector (D) – a negative plate. The ions take electrons from the detector, resulting in a minute electric current, which can be amplified to aid measurement. The current is proportional to the number of electrons taken and hence to the number of ions with that m/z, giving a measure of the abundance of each ion. The magnetic field is varied, so that each ion beam is successively focused and measured to give the relative abundance of each m/z value in the original sample after ionisation.

Mass spectrometry to distinguish between isotopes

Many of the techniques that use mass spectrometry involve the separation, measurement and comparison of compounds that differ only in the relative amounts of different isotopes of the same element contained within those compounds. For example, the only difference between cane sugar ethanol and grape sugar ethanol is the proportions of ^{12}C and ^{13}C in the ethanol molecule. Carbon compounds usually contain about 1.1% ^{13}C but, because the metabolisms of these two plants (sugar cane and grape vine) are different, the sugars they produce contain slightly different amounts of ^{13}C. These differences are still present when the sugar is converted to ethanol by fermentation. Mass spectrometry is sufficiently sensitive to measure these differences and to allow the source of ethanol to be decided.

> **14** State the difference between the isotopes ^{12}C and ^{13}C.

When a sample of copper is introduced into a mass spectrometer, a **mass spectrum** containing two peaks is produced (Fig. 13). The **relative atomic mass** (A_r) of an element, in this case copper, can be calculated from its mass spectrum (Fig. 14).

> **12** Positive ions are accelerated by attraction to a negative electrode (Step 4 in Fig. 12). Some ions pass through a hole in the electrode. What do you suppose happens to the ions that do not pass through the electrode?
>
> **13** The separation of three ions is shown in Fig. 12. For strontium, which beam (X, Y or Z) could be:
>
> **a** $^{86}Sr^{+\bullet}$
>
> **b** $^{88}Sr^{+\bullet}$
>
> **c** $^{87}Sr^{+\bullet}$

Fig. 13   Mass spectrum of copper

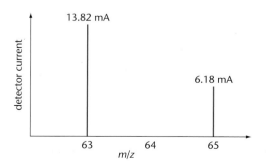

Fig. 14 Calculating the relative atomic mass of copper

1 Record the size of each peak. In this case the amount of each isotope present is proportional to the output of the detector (measured in mA).

$$^{63}Cu \ \ 13.82 \ mA$$
$$^{65}Cu \ \ \ 6.18 \ mA$$

2 Calculate the percentage abundance of each isotope.

$$\% \ ^{63}Cu = \frac{13.82}{13.82 + 6.18} \times 100$$
$$= 69.10\%$$

$$\% \ ^{65}Cu = \frac{6.18}{13.82 + 6.18} \times 100$$
$$= 30.90\%$$

3 Use the percentage abundances to calculate the average atomic mass of copper.

$$A_r(Cu) = \frac{69.10}{100} \times 63 + \frac{30.90}{100} \times 65$$
$$= 63.62 \ (to \ 4 \ s.f.)$$

15 Mass spectrometers can be calibrated to give percentage isotopic abundances directly. Use the isotopic abundances shown in Table 2 to calculate the relative atomic mass of zinc.

Table 2 Isotopic abundance for zinc

Isotope	Abundance (%)
^{64}Zn	48.89
^{66}Zn	27.81
^{67}Zn	4.11
^{68}Zn	18.56
^{70}Zn	0.62

Mass spectrometry of molecular elements and compounds

The examples considered so far have been elements that exist as giant atomic structures made from individual atoms, e.g. metals such as copper and zinc. Many non-metallic elements consist of diatomic molecules. Oxygen (O_2),

chlorine (Cl_2) and nitrogen (N_2) should be familiar examples. What happens to these molecular elements when they are subjected to mass spectrometry?

When chlorine (Cl_2) is analysed by mass spectrometry, the spectrum (Fig. 15) contains peaks produced by the molecular ion $Cl_2^{+\bullet}$ (the superscript $\bullet$ indicates an unpaired electron on a radical ion) and also contains peaks produced by the $Cl^{+\bullet}$ ion. These peaks arise because some of the chlorine molecules have 'broken' in the spectrometer. This breaking up of molecules is called **fragmentation** and occurs for all types of molecules, both elements and compounds. Bombardment by high-energy electrons in the mass spectrometer ionises the chlorine molecules and, since the ions have high energy, breaks some of the covalent bonds.

Fig. 15 Mass spectrum of chlorine

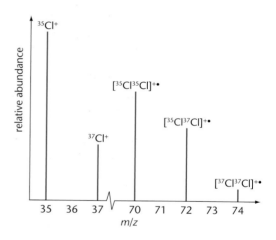

16 The ratio of ^{35}Cl to ^{37}Cl is 3:1. Calculate the ratio of peak heights for:

a $[^{35}Cl^{35}Cl]^{+\bullet}$

b $[^{35}Cl^{37}Cl]^{+\bullet}$

c $[^{37}Cl^{37}Cl]^{+\bullet}$

17 What feature would you expect to see in the mass spectrum of chloroethane?

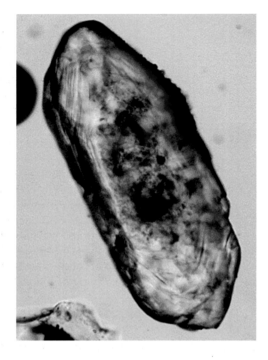

Crystals of zircon contain traces of the radioactive elements uranium and thorium, which both decay to stable isotopes of lead. The amounts of uranium, thorium and lead can be measured by mass spectrometry and used to date the rocks that contain zircon.

evacuated. For example, a molecular radical ion $M^{+\bullet}$ will fragment to produce the ion X^+ and the radical $Y^\bullet$, thus:

$$M^{+\bullet} \rightarrow Y^\bullet + X^+$$

X^+ is detected and measured, but the radical $Y^\bullet$ is not.

Although it is strictly correct to write molecular ions as $M^{+\bullet}$, they are normally written as M^+, and this is the convention that will be followed from now on.

As molecules get larger, the number of different bonds that can break increases, so a greater number of different fragments may result (Fig. 16). The fragment ions have different m/z ratios and, like isotopes, are separated by the mass spectrometer. This produces a mass spectrum (Fig. 17), with each signal corresponding to a different fragment ion from the original molecule. Usually, the signal occurring at the highest value on the m/z ratio axis is caused by the unfragmented ion (the **molecular ion** or **parent ion**), and this gives the **relative molecular mass** of the compound. For pentane, this occurs at a mass-to-charge ratio of 72, which corresponds to the formula of C_5H_{12}.

Using their m/z values, many of the main fragments can be identified. They can then be pieced together, partly or completely, to deduce some or all of the original structure. The **molecular ion peak** in the mass spectrum only gives information about the molecular formula of this ion. For example, three isomers exist for the formula C_5H_{12}, which cannot be completely distinguished by considering only the molecular ion. However, pentane and methylbutane can both produce the fragments shown in Fig. 16 for pentane. The two lower fragments arise when the first C–C bond breaks, whereas cleavage of the second C–C bond produces the two upper fragments.

Molecular compounds, e.g. pentane, $CH_3CH_2CH_2CH_2CH_3$, may be ionised by electron bombardment to form the molecular radical ion $[C_5H_{12}]^{+\bullet}$, thus:

$$CH_3CH_2CH_2CH_2CH_3 + [e^-]^* \rightarrow$$
$$[CH_3CH_2CH_2CH_2CH_3]^{+\bullet} + 2e^-$$

But this is not the end of the story. The molecular ion is unstable. This results in breaking of some of its weaker covalent bonds (e.g. C–C more likely than C–H), just as some of the Cl–Cl bonds broke for chlorine. This produces a range of fragments, some of which are also positively charged. Only the ions are subsequently detected, with the radicals being

Fig. 16   Fragmentation of pentane

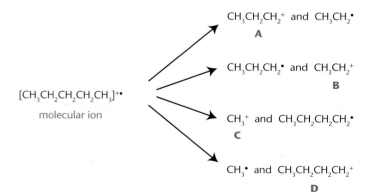

18 Which m/z ratio values would not be observed in the mass spectra of the other isomer of pentane, dimethylpropane?

19 For each major signal at mass-to-charge $m/z = M$, what causes the weak signals (not to scale) at $m/z = (M + 1)$?

Fig. 17 Mass spectrum of pentane

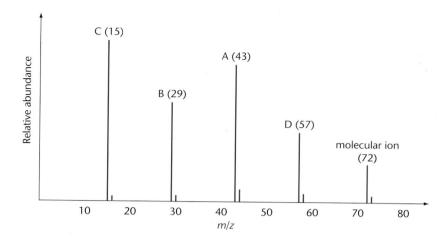

The relative heights of the peaks can also yield useful information because a more intense peak is associated with a more stable ion. Hence, tertiary carbocations will produce higher peaks than secondary carbocations, which, in turn, produce higher peaks than primary carbocations. Hence, a very high peak at $m/z = 57$ is an indication of the tertiary $(CH_3)_3C^+$ carbocation rather than the secondary $(CH_3)_2CH^+$ carbocation or the primary $CH_3CH_2CH_2CH_2^+$ carbocation. Similarly, stable acylium ions (RCO^+) will give high peaks and provide a good indication that the R–CO– group is present in the sample molecule. For example, a relatively weak signal at $m/z = 43$ is more likely to suggest the presence of a $CH_3CH_2CH_2$ group, but a strong signal might suggest a CH_3CO group. Another particularly stable carbocation to look out for is the delocalised carbocation $(C_6H_5^+)$ at $m/z = 77$, which would suggest that the compound is a mono-substituted benzene.

Identifying compounds using mass spectrometry

The overall mass spectrum of a molecule can be used to identify it. Thousands of mass spectra can be stored in an appropriate computer database. Rapid and accurate comparisons can be made, leading to identification of a sample.

When analysing a mass spectrum, there are certain m/z ratios to look out for. Their presence in a spectrum is a good indicator that the molecule contains that fragment. Some of the more common fragments to look for are summarised in Table 3.

Also, remember that the *absence* of a particular fragment can give a lot of information. For example, if the spectrum of a compound with molecular formula C_4H_{10} does *not* have a peak at mass-to-charge ratio $m/z = 29$, it must be methylpropane rather than butane (Fig. 18). This is because methylpropane does not contain a C_2H_5 group (which would have $m/z = 29$).

Table 3 Common fragments found in mass spectra or lost during fragmentation

Mass-to-charge ratio/value	Possible fragments
15	CH_3^+
17	HO^+
19	F^+
26	NC^+
29	$C_2H_5^+$, CHO^+
31	CH_3O^+, CH_2OH^+
35/37 (in a 3:1 ratio)	Cl^+
43	$C_3H_7^+$, CH_3CO^+
44	$CONH_2^+$
45	$COOH^+$
77	$C_6H_5^+$
79/81 (in a 1:1 ratio)	Br^+

Note: mass-to-charge ratio/values often differ by 14. This is usually caused by a difference of CH_2 in the structure.

Fig. 18   The two isomers with molecular formula C_4H_{10}

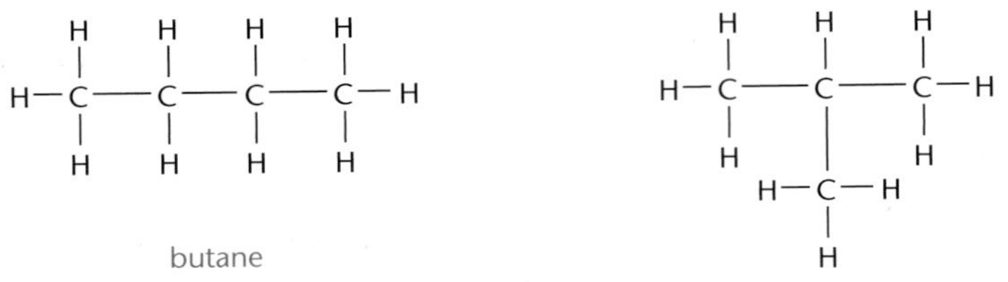

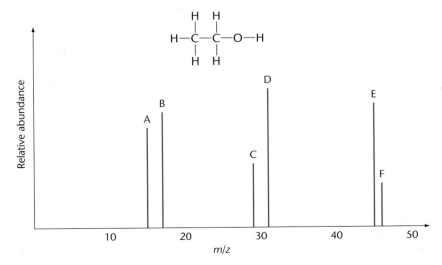

butane

methylpropane

The peaks in the mass spectrum of ethanol C_2H_5OH (Fig. 19) can be accounted for by considering the various fragmentations that can occur. Using the relative atomic masses of carbon, oxygen and hydrogen ($A_r[C] = 12$, $A_r[O] = 16$ and $A_r[H] = 1$), the signals in Fig. 19 can be assigned as follows:

- Signal A ($m/z = 15$) corresponds to a CH_3^+ fragment produced by breaking a C–C bond.
- Signal B ($m/z = 17$) corresponds to an HO^+ fragment produced by breaking a C–O bond.
- Signal C ($m/z = 29$) corresponds to a $C_2H_5^+$ fragment produced by breaking a C–O bond.
- Signal D ($m/z = 31$) corresponds to a CH_2OH^+ fragment produced by breaking a C–C bond.
- Signal E ($m/z = 45$) corresponds to a $C_2H_5O^+$ fragment produced by breaking an O–H bond.
- Signal F ($m/z = 46$) corresponds to the unfragmented molecular ion, which is simply the original ethanol molecule minus one

20 How would the mass spectrum of methoxymethane (CH_3–O–CH_3), an isomer of ethanol, differ from the mass spectrum of ethanol?

electron. This signal (with the highest m/z ratio) gives the relative molecular mass of the compound.

Another powerful approach is to examine the changes in m/z values rather than the actual m/z values. This gives very useful information about undetected free radicals that may be lost during fragmentation. For example, the presence of a methyl group is implied by detection of a fragment [F^+] at ($M - 15$), even though a fragment may not be detected at $m/z = 15$. This is caused by the loss of a methyl free radical from the molecular ion [M^+], as follows:

$$[M^+] \quad \rightarrow \quad [F^+] \quad + \quad CH_3$$
$$m/z \qquad\qquad M \qquad\quad M - 15$$

Similarly, an ethyl group or aldehyde group (CHO) is implied by a peak at ($M - 29$), a C–Cl group by peaks at ($M - 35$) and ($M - 37$), and a phenyl group by a peak at ($M - 77$). Patterns such as these can be looked for using the data from Table 3.

So far we have interpreted mass spectra of compounds where we have known the molecular structure. The next example involves an unknown molecule X, and shows how unknown structures can be deduced. Sample X is known to contain only carbon, hydrogen and oxygen, and it produces the mass spectrum shown in Fig. 20.

The steps in deducing the structure of X from the mass spectrum shown in Fig. 20 are as follows:

1 The signal at 134 corresponds to the molecular ion. The molecular formula of X could well be $C_9H_{10}O$.

21 What other 'sensible' molecular formulae are possible for a compound containing C, H and O, with a molecular mass of 134?

Fig. 19   Mass spectrum of ethanol

Fig. 20 Mass spectrum of unknown molecule X

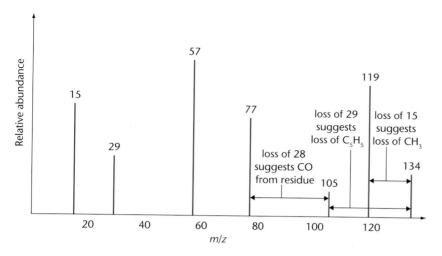

2 The signal at 77 is very important, as it suggests the presence of a phenyl ($C_6H_5^-$) group. Alternatively, the signal at 57 also suggests this group because it represents the ($M - 77$) fragment.

3 If X contains a $C_6H_5^-$ group, the remainder of the molecule is formed from C_3H_5O. If evidence from infrared spectroscopy (see Section 11.1) shows that X contains a C=O group but no C=C bond, this means that X could be any one of three isomers (Fig. 21).

Fig. 21 Three possible structures for X

1   C_6H_5—$\overset{\displaystyle O}{\overset{\|}{C}}$—$CH_2$—$CH_3$

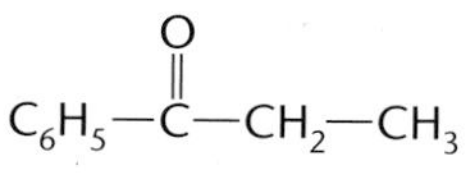

2   C_6H_5—CH_2—$\overset{\displaystyle O}{\overset{\|}{C}}$—$CH_3$

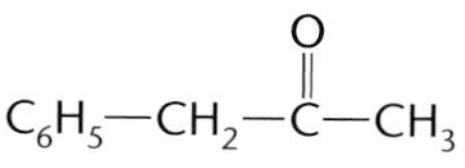

3   C_6H_5—CH_2—CH_2—$\overset{\displaystyle O}{\overset{\|}{C}}$—H

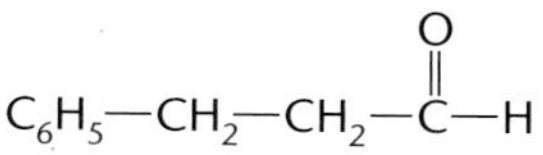

4 Isomers involving disubstituted benzenes are excluded because they do not contain an isolated phenyl group (Fig. 22).

Fig. 22 Three impossible structures for X

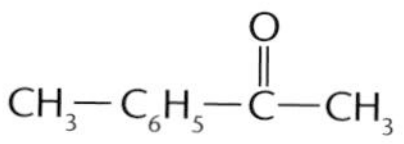

CH_3—C_6H_5—$\overset{\displaystyle O}{\overset{\|}{C}}$—$CH_3$ impossible – no C_6H_5- fragment

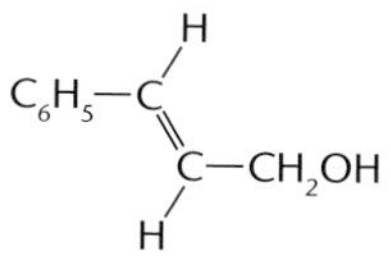

C_6H_5—$C\overset{\displaystyle H}{\underset{\displaystyle H}{\big<}}C$—$CH_2OH$ impossible – no C=O group

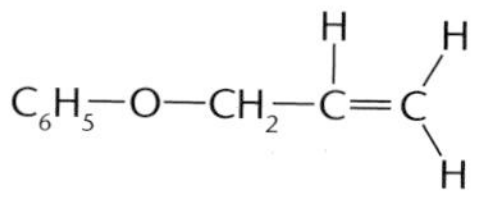

C_6H_5—O—CH_2—C=$C\overset{H}{\underset{H}{\big<}}$ impossible – no C=O group

5 The C–OH (alcohol), C–O–C or C–O–C–C (ether) groups are excluded by the absence of fragments at $M - 17 = 117$, $M - 31 = 103$ and $M - 45 = 89$, respectively.

6 Isomer 3 in Fig. 21 is excluded as a possibility because of the absence of signals at $m/z = 43$ and 91.

7 Isomer 2 in Fig. 21 is excluded as a possibility because of the absence of a signal at $m/z = 43$, which would be expected to be strong for the particularly stable acylium ion, CH_3C^+O.

8 Isomer 1 in Fig. 21 is a particular possibility because of the presence of a very strong signal at $m/z = 57$, which would be expected for the particularly stable acylium ion, $CH_3CH_2C^+O$.

9 If you consider the three possible isomers in turn and predict their possible fragmentation patterns (Table 4), it is possible to identify X as 1-phenylpropan-1-one, isomer 1 in Fig. 21.

10 It is reasonably certain that X is isomer 1 rather than one of the other two possibilities. In practice, other techniques such as infrared spectroscopy (Section 11.1), and particularly nuclear magnetic resonance spectroscopy (Section 11.3), are used to confirm the identification or to sort out any ambiguities.

22 How would the fragmentation patterns of propan-1-ol and propan-2-ol differ?

Table 4   Fragmentation patterns for the three possible isomers of X

Isomer structure	Peaks expected from breaking each bond		
	A	**B**	**C**
1 $C_6H_5\overset{A}{-}\overset{\overset{\displaystyle O}{\|}}{C}\overset{B}{-}CH_2\overset{C}{-}CH_3$	77 and/or 57	105 and/or 29	119 and/or 15
2 $C_6H_5\overset{A}{-}CH_2\overset{B}{-}\overset{\overset{\displaystyle O}{\|}}{C}\overset{C}{-}CH_3$	77 and/or 57	91 and/or 43	119 and/or 15
3 $C_6H_5\overset{A}{-}CH_2\overset{B}{-}CH_2\overset{C}{-}\overset{\overset{\displaystyle O}{\|}}{C}-H$	77 and/or 57	91 and/or 43	105 and/or 29

Table 5   Accurate relative atomic masses

Element	Accurate A_r
carbon	12.000000
hydrogen	1.007825
oxygen	15.994910
nitrogen	14.003070

Suppose a high-resolution mass spectrometer is used and the relative mass is measured to be 60.03235. Using equally accurate relative atomic mass data (see Table 5), the compound can be shown to be urea rather than ethanoic acid or propanol (Table 6).

Mass spectrometry is a powerful analytical method. Chemists have used it to help archaeologists date ancient artefacts very accurately and identify materials used by humans in past ages. It can be used to help distinguish between closely related molecules of importance in many areas of science and technology. For example, one can tell octane from methylheptane in petrochemistry, morphine from heroin in forensic science, and aspirin from paracetamol in pharmaceutical chemistry. The research chemist will often use mass spectrometry to help determine the structure of new molecules. Who knows what other diverse applications for mass spectrometry will arise in the future?

High-resolution mass spectrometry

Mass spectrometry can be used to deduce even more information. With an appropriately accurate and sensitive spectrometer, the mass of the molecular ion can be measured to seven significant figures. This is referred to as **high-resolution mass spectrometry**. By using very accurate relative atomic masses (Table 5), it is then possible to distinguish molecules with very similar molecular mass values. For example, ethanoic acid (CH_3COOH), urea (also known as carbamide or aminomethanamide, NH_2CONH_2) and propanol (C_3H_7OH) would all produce a molecular ion with a mass-to-charge ratio of 60 using a low-resolution mass spectrometer.

Table 6   Calculating molecular mass

For CH_3COOH (ethanoic acid)	For NH_2CONH_2 (urea)	For C_3H_7OH (propanol)
$2 \times 12.00000 = 24.00000$	$1 \times 12.00000 = 12.00000$	$3 \times 12.00000 = 36.00000$
$4 \times 1.007825 = 4.03130$	$4 \times 1.007825 = 4.03130$	$8 \times 1.007825 = 8.06260$
$2 \times 15.99491 = 31.98982$	$1 \times 15.99491 = 15.99491$	$1 \times 15.99491 = 15.99491$
	$2 \times 14.00307 = 28.00614$	
Total = 60.021 12	**Total = 60.032 35**	**Total = 60.057 51**

● Mass spectrometry distinguishes closely related molecules from one another by comparison of their fragmentation patterns.

● Accurate m/z values of parent ions can be used to deduce molecular formulae.

11.3 Nuclear magnetic resonance (NMR) spectroscopy

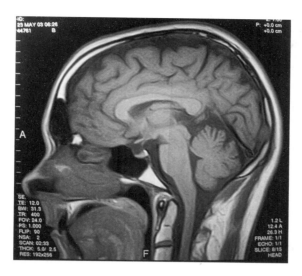

An MRI scan section through a human head. How many structures can you identify?

MRI scanners are powerful diagnostic tools used by doctors. MRI stands for magnetic resonance imaging. It is a technique that was first reported in 1976 and has developed very rapidly since then. The first commercial machines were available in 1983 and are now to be found in most major hospitals worldwide.

However, MRI has its origins in a technique that chemists have been using regularly since the 1950s. This technique is called **nuclear magnetic resonance (NMR) spectroscopy** and, along with information from other spectroscopic methods, it allows molecular structures to be deduced.

Using nuclear magnetic resonance

During NMR spectroscopy, molecules in solution are placed in a strong magnetic field and then irradiated with radio frequency electromagnetic radiation. At certain frequencies, the nuclei of some of the atoms in the molecules absorb the radio wave. These absorptions, called **resonances**, are used to identify the atoms, count them and work out their positions in the molecule relative to other atoms.

How does NMR work?

The nuclei of most atoms have a property known as **nuclear spin**. It is only those atoms with both even atomic number and even mass number (e.g. $^{12}_{6}C$) that do *not* have 'spin'; such atoms are *not* NMR-active. Nuclei that do possess spin have their own **magnetic moment** and **magnetic field**, and can be considered to behave as if they are small bar magnets (Fig. 23). It is this behaviour that leads to the production of NMR spectra.

When nuclei of NMR-active atoms (Table 7) are placed in a strong external magnetic field (Fig. 24), the nuclei align themselves with the

Fig. 23   Nuclear spin and magnetic field

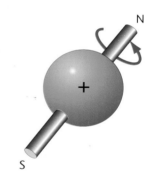

A nucleus with spin can be considered as if it was a small bar magnet and is shown as ⊕.

Table 7 Some NMR-active nuclei

^{1}H
^{13}C
^{14}N
^{15}N
^{19}F
^{31}P

Fig. 24   Schematic diagram for the recording of an NMR spectrum

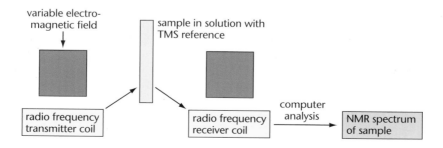

direction of the applied magnetic field (Fig. 25). This is just like the behaviour of compass needles in a magnetic field. The tendency of nuclei to align with a magnetic field is not very useful by itself. However, the spinning nuclei have a second option: they can align themselves in the *opposite* direction to the applied magnetic field. This second spin state is at a slightly higher energy (Fig. 26).

If the magnetised nuclei are subjected to an appropriate radio frequency radiation via a coil surrounding the sample, then **resonance** can occur. Nuclei in the α state are promoted to the higher-energy β state. The excited nuclei can then relax back to the α state, releasing a small amount of energy as electromagnetic radiation. A second coil surrounding the sample can detect this energy (Fig. 24).

Fig. 25   Nuclei: random and aligned

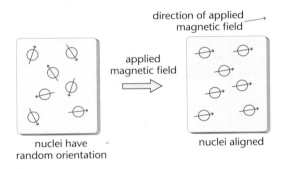

nuclei have random orientation

nuclei aligned

Fig. 26   Two types of alignment

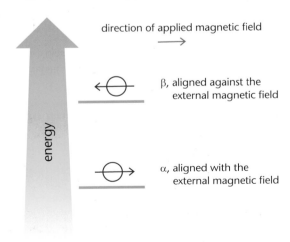

In practice, the radio frequency radiation is kept constant and the external magnetic field strength is gradually increased until, at an appropriate value of the field strength, resonance will occur. The nuclei in the sample will have been detected.

Which atoms are investigated?
The ^{1}H atom is particularly useful for investigation by NMR because of the large number of hydrogen atoms in almost all organic compounds. This is often referred to as proton NMR because the nucleus of this atom is a single proton. The following sections look at proton NMR spectroscopy.

Producing and interpreting a proton NMR spectrum
Not all the ^{1}H nuclei in an organic sample will resonate at the same magnetic field strength for a particular radio frequency. ^{1}H nuclei that have different neighbouring atoms (said to have different **chemical environments**) absorb at slightly different external field strengths. The different environments are said to cause a **chemical shift** of the absorption. For example, the H of an O–H group, the H of a CH_2 group, the H of a CH_3 group and the H of an N–H group all have different chemical shifts.

Chemical shifts are related to the electron density *near* the resonating nucleus. This provides a 'shield' between the resonating nucleus and the applied magnetic field. If the electron density around the resonating nucleus is low as a result of attachment to an electronegative group of atoms or a delocalised system, the nucleus is said to be 'deshielded' and will resonate at a lower applied magnetic field. For example, compare the ^{1}H atoms in C–H and O–H groups. The electronegative oxygen atom in an O–H group attracts electrons and reduces the electron density around the ^{1}H atom. So the electron density around the ^{1}H atom of an O–H group is a lot lower than around the ^{1}H atom of a C–H group. The ^{1}H nucleus in the O–H group is said to be deshielded, and it reaches resonance at a lower external field strength than the ^{1}H nucleus of a C–H group.

All organic molecules – with the exception of 'symmetrical' compounds such as methane – contain ^{1}H atoms in different chemical environments. As the external magnetic field is varied for a fixed radio frequency, ^1H nuclei in different environments will resonate in turn. If the value of the external field is recorded as the different resonances occur, a spectrum, known as an **NMR spectrum**, can be produced. The ^1H atoms of the molecule with any particular chemical environment have been detected separately from each other.

Samples are investigated in dilute solution. This separates the sample molecules from each other, preventing them from interacting with each other and causing very complex absorptions.

The choice of solvent is important. When investigating ^1H atoms, tetrachloromethane (CCl_4) or deuterated trichloromethane ($CDCl_3$) are commonly used because they are very powerful solvents for organic compounds and they do not contain ^1H atoms. This means that they do not resonate and so do not interfere with the ^1H NMR spectrum of the sample.

During the production of an NMR spectrum, **tetramethylsilane (TMS)** (see Fig. 27) is mixed with the sample. This is added to provide

Fig. 27 Tetramethylsilane (TMS)

a reference point to which the NMR spectrometer is tuned. The magnetic field is adjusted until the ^1H nuclei of TMS resonate: this is given a chemical shift value of 0. TMS is used for the following reasons:

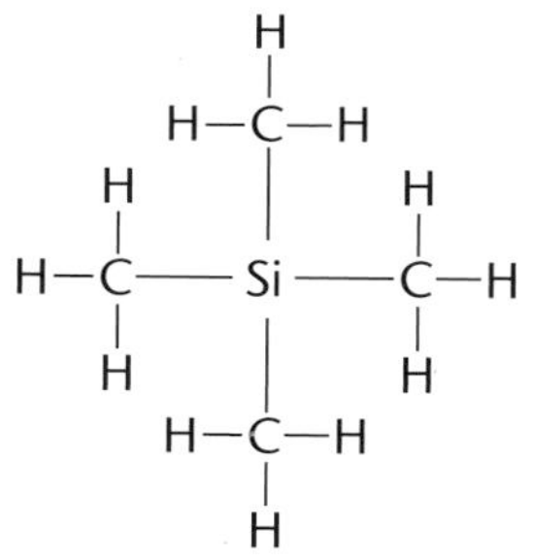

- The hydrogen nuclei in TMS are highly shielded because silicon has a very low electronegativity. As a result, the hydrogen nuclei in TMS resonate at a field strength well above that of any ^1H nuclei in common organic molecules.
- It gives one strong, sharp and easily detected absorption because it is caused by the combined effects of 12 equivalent ^1H atoms

(equivalent atoms are those in identical chemical environments, usually due to symmetry within the molecule).
- TMS is non-toxic and cheap.
- It does not react with the sample.
- TMS is easily separated from the sample molecule because it has a low boiling point.

The chemical shifts of ^1H atoms in a sample molecule are measured and tabulated relative to the TMS reference absorption on the 'δ-scale' using:

$$\delta = \frac{B_{TMS} - B_{sample}}{B_{TMS}} \times 10^6$$

where B_{TMS} and B_{sample} represent the applied external magnetic field strengths at resonance for TMS and the sample, respectively.

The value of the external magnetic field that causes a particular proton to resonate depends on the radio frequency that the NMR spectrometer uses. This means that chemical shifts would vary from machine to machine, making comparisons difficult. The use of a reference compound (TMS) and a scale for chemical shift without units (the δ-scale) avoids this problem. The use of the δ-scale for measuring chemical shifts avoids the need to quote both the magnetic field strength and the radio frequency. The δ-value for a particular resonance is the same for all NMR spectrometers, whether they operate at radio frequencies of 60 MHz, 100 MHz or 250 MHz.

23 Why do you suppose the 10^6 factor is included in the chemical shift calculation?

In general, ^1H atoms bonded to electronegative atoms, e.g. O–H in alcohols and acids or N–H in amines, are said to be deshielded and so absorb at lower field strengths, i.e. have larger chemical shifts, whereas ^1H atoms in alkanes and alkenes are shielded and so absorb at higher field strengths, i.e. have smaller chemical shifts (Fig. 28). A map of some of the more common ^1H absorptions is shown in Fig. 29.

Fig. 28 Explaining chemical shifts

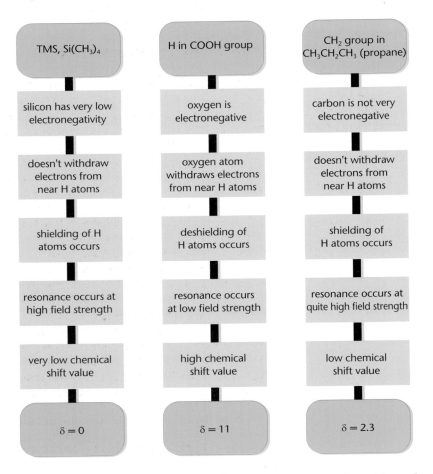

TMS, Si(CH₃)₄	H in COOH group	CH₂ group in CH₃CH₂CH₃ (propane)
silicon has very low electronegativity	oxygen is electronegative	carbon is not very electronegative
doesn't withdraw electrons from near H atoms	oxygen atom withdraws electrons from near H atoms	doesn't withdraw electrons from near H atoms
shielding of H atoms occurs	deshielding of H atoms occurs	shielding of H atoms occurs
resonance occurs at high field strength	resonance occurs at low field strength	resonance occurs at quite high field strength
very low chemical shift value	high chemical shift value	low chemical shift value
$\delta = 0$	$\delta = 11$	$\delta = 2.3$

Low-resolution proton NMR spectra

A low-resolution NMR spectrum of ethanol (Fig. 30) shows three absorptions (A, B and C) because the ethanol molecule contains three sets of ^{1}H atoms. Signal A is produced by the three equivalent ^{1}H atoms in the CH_3 group, signal B by the two equivalent ^{1}H atoms in the CH_2 group and signal C by the single ^{1}H atom in the OH group. Notice that signal C has the largest chemical shift because the ^{1}H atom is directly bonded to an electronegative oxygen atom. Signal B has a larger chemical shift than A because the CH_2 group is nearer to the electronegative oxygen atom than the CH_3 group.

Fig. 30 A low-resolution NMR spectrum of ethanol

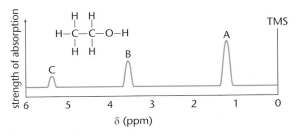

Fig. 29 Chemical shifts of some common functional groups

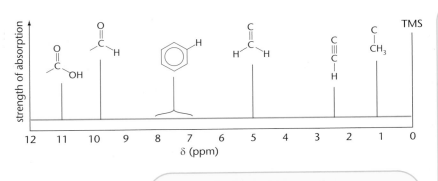

24 Why does the hydrogen atom of an aldehyde group (CHO) absorb at a much higher chemical shift than the hydrogen atom of an alkene group (C=C–H)?

25 Explain why the three hydrogen atoms of the CH_3 group in ethanol are equivalent.

26 Deduce the number of absorptions in the low-resolution NMR spectra of each of the following:

a   benzene

b   propane

c   propanal

d   propanone

e   ethanoic acid.

The strengths of the absorptions are proportional to the number of equivalent ^{1}H atoms causing the absorption. The strengths of the absorptions are measured by the area under each absorption peak. Hence, the areas of absorptions A, B and C in the spectrum of ethanol are in the ratio of 3:2:1. In modern spectrometers these are measured electronically and superimposed digitally or graphically on the main spectrum. This is called the **integrated spectrum**.

The integrated spectrum of ethanol is shown in Fig. 31. The distances between the plateaux in the integrated spectrum represent the areas under the absorption peaks. The ratio of these distances gives the ratio of the number of ^{1}H atoms in each equivalent group.

High-resolution proton NMR spectra

The previous NMR spectrum of ethanol (see Fig. 30) was highly simplified. Nevertheless, it did allow the sets of equivalent ^{1}H atoms to be identified and it did allow the number of protons in each set to be counted. When examined in more detail with a more sensitive spectrometer, some of the basic signals are split into groups of signals (Fig. 32). In the case of CH_3CH_2OH, the CH_3 signal is split into three, producing what is called a **triplet**, while the CH_2 signal is split to form a **quartet**. Strangely, the OH signal is not split – it appears as a **singlet**. This splitting of the absorptions is caused by the influence of ^{1}H atoms bonded to neighbouring atoms, and the influence is called a **coupling effect**.

You should remember that each spinning ^{1}H nucleus generates a slight magnetic field. When a particular ^{1}H nucleus resonates in an applied magnetic field, the actual magnetic field that acts on it is the sum of the applied field and

Fig. 31   The integrated NMR spectrum of ethanol

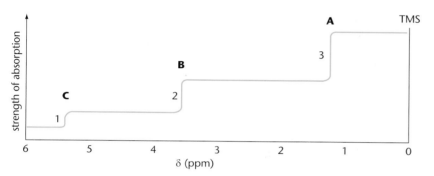

27 Deduce the ratios of the areas under the absorptions for the following compounds:

a   ethanoic acid

b   propane

c   methylbenzene.

Fig. 32   A detailed NMR spectrum of ethanol

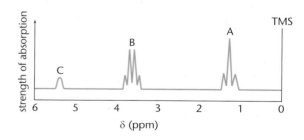

the fields from its neighbours. Thus the ^{1}H atoms are linked through space (**coupled**) by the interactions of their own magnetic fields (Figs 33 and 34).

The magnetic field from a single neighbouring ^{1}H nucleus (Fig. 33) may act with or against the applied magnetic field. There is a 50:50 chance of either. This means that the nucleus will resonate either at a slightly lower applied field or at a slightly higher applied field. The end result is that the original resonance is split into a **doublet** in a ratio of 1:1.

Fig. 33   Coupling to one ^{1}H atom

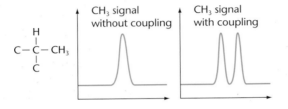

Fig. 34   Coupling to two ^{1}H atoms

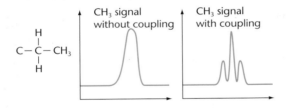

Suppose that there are two equivalent neighbouring ^{1}H atoms (Fig. 34) instead of just one. Their magnetic fields could be both with the applied field, or both against it, or one with while the other is against (Fig. 35). This means that a ^{1}H nucleus is coupled to two neighbours in three different ways. The result is a **triplet**. If the magnetic fields from the two neighbours are both with the applied field, the group will absorb at slightly lower field. Conversely, if the magnetic fields from the two neighbours are both against the applied field, the group will absorb at slightly higher field. Finally, if the magnetic field from one of the neighbours is with the applied field and the field from the other is against, they will cancel each other out, and the group will absorb at its own

Fig. 35   How triplet signals are formed

Direction of applied field	Direction of fields from two neighbours	Proportion	Effect on resonance position
→	← ←	1	higher field
→	← → or → ←	2	no effect
→	→ →	1	lower field

characteristic field strength. The intensity of the triplet will be 1:2:1 (Fig. 35). These are the relative probabilities of the neighbour's fields adding with, cancelling out or adding against the applied field. This is the situation for the CH$_3$ group in ethanol. The absorption associated with these three ^{1}H atoms is split into a triplet because of the coupling effect of the two ^{1}H atoms bonded to the neighbouring carbon atom.

The number of atoms in the group itself has no influence on splitting because all such atoms absorb at the same field strength; they do not couple with each other. Furthermore, because the magnetic fields involved are so weak, coupling with 'next-door-but-one' neighbours is negligible.

Table 8 summarises the pattern of significant couplings, all of which can be summarised by the **$n + 1$ rule**, which states the following:

The NMR absorption of a proton that has n equivalent neighbouring protons will be split into $n + 1$ peaks.

28 Calculate the splitting effect experienced by a ^{1}H atom adjacent to a CH$_3$ group. Check your answer by looking at part of the spectrum of ethanol (Fig. 32).

Table 8   Coupling patterns

Number of equivalent neighbouring (coupled) ^1H atoms	Splitting effect	Resulting signal	Ratio
1	into 2 signals	doublet	1:1
2	into 3 signals	triplet	1:2:1
3	into 4 signals	quartet	1:3:3:1
n	into $n + 1$ signals	$n + 1$ peaks	

Fig. 36   NMR spectrum of propane

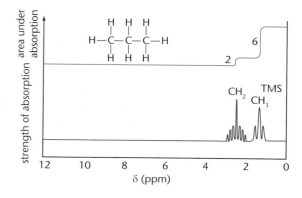

To further understand NMR, it is worthwhile to consider the following two questions.

- Why is the OH signal from ethanol not split into three by coupling with the ^1H atoms of the neighbouring CH_2 group?
- What happens when coupling occurs with neighbours on two sides?

The H of the OH group absorbs at low field because of the high electronegativity of the oxygen atom. The signal is not split for a related reason. The polarity of the O–H bond causes the H atom to be very readily exchanged with other H atoms from neighbouring hydrogen-bonded molecules. The exchanged H atom has a 50:50 chance of having the same spin direction as the one displaced and, since this exchange occurs more rapidly than the actual resonance effect, the coupling with neighbours averages to zero and no splitting can be detected. This rapid exchange can be shown by adding deuterated water (heavy water, D_2O) to the sample. The O–H absorption gets weaker as the H is exchanged for D (D is not sensitive to NMR under the conditions that are used to record ^1H spectra).

The H atoms of C–H bonds do not exchange because carbon and hydrogen have very similar electronegativities. Consequently, the CH_2 signal in ethanol is split into a quartet by the neighbouring CH_3 group but is not split further by its neighbour on the other side as this is the exchanging H of the OH group.

Coupling with neighbours on two sides can happen. With propane, for example, the CH_2 signal is seen as a heptet (Fig. 36) because it has six neighbouring H atoms, three on either side in two equivalent CH_3 groups. This is associated with the symmetry of the propane molecule. The CH_3 groups produce identical triplets by coupling with the CH_2 group.

However, for propanal (Fig. 37), three sets of signals are seen. The ratios (3:2:1) from the integrated spectrum show that these are caused by the ^1H atoms of the CH_3 group, the CH_2 group and the CHO group. The CH_2 signal is split into a quartet by coupling with the CH_3 group, and the H of the CHO group on the other side then splits each part of the quartet into a doublet. This produces a 'quartet of doublets'. The CHO and CH_3 signals are both triplets because of coupling with the central CH_2 group. Thus the spectrum gets much more complicated for non-symmetrical molecules.

This double splitting of the CH_2 signal can also be seen in the ethanol spectrum if conditions are changed to prevent exchange occurring for the OH group. This can be done by cooling the sample to about -70 °C. At such temperatures the exchange process occurs more slowly than the resonance effect, resulting in the coupling between the OH and CH_2 groups becoming detectable. The OH signal is split by the CH_2 group to form a triplet and the CH_2 signal becomes a 'quartet of doublets'.

Although a number of nuclei other than ^1H will give NMR spectra, the most useful is ^{13}C. This isotope has a very low abundance (1.1%), so the probability of two ^{13}C atoms being bonded to each other is very low. For this reason, coupling is not observed, and even if it

29 What sort of splitting will be seen for the CH_2 group of ethanol when its NMR spectrum is measured at -70 °C?

Fig. 37   NMR spectrum of propanal

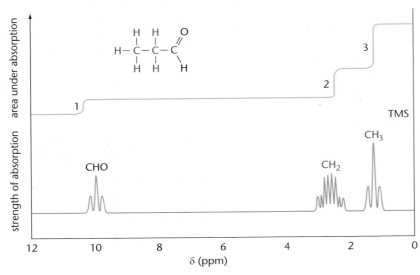

Fig. 38   The ^{13}C spectrum of ethyl ethanoate dissolved in $CDCl_3$

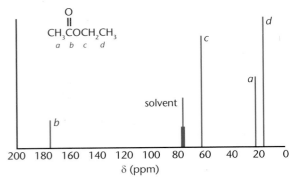

did happen the signal would be so low it would not be detected. There is a possibility of ^{13}C–^1H coupling, which would complicate the spectrum, so spin decoupling is used to simplify the spectrum. This results in the ^{13}C spectrum being very easy to read because it consists of a series of single peaks, with each peak equating to one carbon atom in a different chemical environment. However, you cannot obtain a useful integrated peak with a ^{13}C spectrum because the signal strength depends upon the environment of the carbon atoms, not the number. A typical example, the ^{13}C NMR spectrum of ethyl ethanoate, is shown in Fig. 38.

Conclusions

NMR has been used by chemists for several decades, but they are still developing the technique and applying it to more complex and sophisticated examples.

Three-dimensional structures of large molecules, such as proteins and other natural products, can be determined, because atoms can be identified that are close to each other as a result of the way the molecule is folded.

However, even though NMR gives a lot of information about molecular structures, it does not give all the answers. It needs to be used in conjunction with information acquired by other chemical and spectroscopic methods.

One way of separating mixtures to help analysis is chromatography, which is the topic of the next section.

key facts

- NMR signal intensities are proportional to the number of hydrogen atoms in the group responsible for the signal. These are measured by the integrated NMR spectrum.

- Each NMR signal may be split as a result of coupling with neighbouring atoms.

- If there are n equivalent neighbouring ^1H atoms, this causes an NMR signal to be split into $n + 1$ peaks.

- ^{13}C gives a much simpler spectrum than ^1H.

11.4 Chromatography

Column chromatography

The foundation for all chromatographic techniques was column chromatography. It was developed in the early 1900s by Mikhail Tsvet to separate plant pigments, and his arrangement is still used today. Other chromatographic techniques such as paper chromatography, thin-layer chromatography and gas–liquid chromatography were subsequently devised.

In column chromatography (Fig. 39), an inert, solid **stationary phase** (usually powdered silica gel or alumina) is placed in the column with a liquid solvent phase, called the **mobile phase**. Usually the two are mixed together to form a slurry to remove all the air bubbles, which would cause a non-uniform separation. A wide range of solvents is possible, so that optimum separation is obtained for the particular mixture. The sample mixture, dissolved in the solvent, is introduced at the top of the column, and the column is kept topped up with fresh solvent (eluent) as the sample flows through. The component with the greatest attraction to the stationary phase takes the longest time to flow through the column. If the

Fig. 39 Column chromatography. Analysis uses narrow columns and preparation uses wider columns

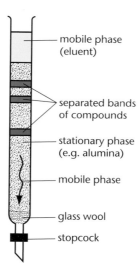

- mobile phase (eluent)
- separated bands of compounds
- stationary phase (e.g. alumina)
- mobile phase
- glass wool
- stopcock

components are coloured, as plant pigments are, then they can be identified by eye or by R_f value (see Chapter 8). If the components are colourless, then other techniques may be used, e.g. fluorescence under UV radiation, to show their position in the column.

Gas–liquid chromatography

Gas–liquid chromatography (GLC) uses a solid phase that is usually diatomaceous earth (the ground-up remains of very small plant skeletons, also known as kieselguhr). This is coated with a non-volatile liquid and placed in a coil in a heated oven (Fig. 40). For GLC the

sample must be either a gas or a volatile liquid in the oven. The sample is injected into the column through a self-sealing disc, and the vapour formed is carried through the stationary phase using an inert carrier gas such as dry

Fig. 40 Schematic diagram of GLC apparatus

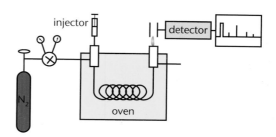

injector

detector

N₂

oven

nitrogen or helium. The temperature gradient of the stationary phase can be varied to optimise the separation of the mixture in the sample. The time taken to pass through the column is called the **retention time**. This will depend upon: the nature of the solute; the volatility of the solute; the nature of the stationary and mobile phases; and the attraction between the solute and the stationary and mobile phases. The components of the mixture will be detected by either thermal conductivity or, more commonly, flame ionisation. In the latter, the outlet gas is mixed with hydrogen and air, and burnt to produce CH* radicals, which are then oxidised to CHO^+ ions. These ions allow a current to be transmitted via a cathode, which is then converted to a signal on a chart recorder. A typical example of a gas–liquid chromatogram is shown in Fig. 41.

Fig. 41 A typical chart recording of a sample that has passed through GLC

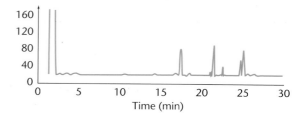

Time (min)

1

a Each part below concerns a different pair of isomers. Draw one possible structure for each of the compounds **A** to **J**.
Use the Infrared wavenumber data at the back of the book if you need to.

  i Compounds **A** and **B** have the molecular formula C_6H_{12}
Both have only one peak in their proton n.m.r. spectra.
A has an absorption at $1\,650\ cm^{-1}$ in its infra-red spectrum but **B** does not.

  ii Compounds **C** and **D** have the molecular formula $C_5H_{10}O$ and both have only two peaks in their proton n.m.r. spectra.
C forms a silver mirror with Tollens' reagent but **D** does not.

  iii Compounds **E** and **F** have the molecular formula $C_3H_6O_2$ and both have only a quartet, a triplet and a singlet peak in their proton n.m.r. spectra.
E gives an effervescence with aqueous sodium hydrogencarbonate but **F** does not.

  iv Compounds **G** and **H** have the molecular formula C_6H_{12}
G shows geometrical isomerism but not optical isomerism.
H shows optical isomerism but not geometrical isomerism.

  v Compounds **I** and **J** have the molecular formula $C_5H_{12}O$
I cannot be oxidised by acidified potassium dichromate(VI) but can be dehydrated to form an alkene.
J can be oxidised by acidified potassium dichromate(VI) but cannot be dehydrated to form an alkene. (10)

b Consider the compound below.

$$\underset{\underset{a}{H_3C}}{}{-}\,\underset{\underset{OH}{|}}{C}\,{-}\,\underset{\underset{O}{\|}}{\overset{CH_3}{\overset{|}{C}}}\,{-}\,CH_2\,{-}\,\underset{b}{CH_2}\,{-}\,\underset{\underset{O}{\|}}{C}\,{-}\,OH$$

  i Predict the number of peaks in its proton n.m.r. spectrum.

  ii The protons labelled *a* and *b* each produce a peak in the proton n.m.r. spectrum.
Name the splitting pattern for each of these peaks. (3)

Total 13

AQA, January 2008, Unit 4, Question 4

2 The ester methyl benzenecarboxylate ($C_6H_5COOCH_3$) can be prepared by the reaction of methanol with benzenecarbonyl chloride, C_6H_5COCl

a Name and outline a mechanism for this reaction. (5)

b The mass spectrum of methyl benzenecarboxylate is shown below.

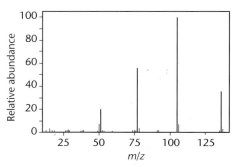

Suggest structures for the fragment ions which produce peaks at $m/z = 105$ and $m/z = 77$ in the mass spectrum above.
Write an equation for the fragmentation of the molecular ion to give the ion which produces the peak at $m/z = 105$. (4)

c Esters **V** and **W** are isomers of methyl benzenecarboxylate and both contain a benzene ring.
V has a major peak at $m/z = 43$ in its mass spectrum. Suggest a structure for the fragment ion which produces this peak and hence suggest a structure for **V**.
W has a major peak at $m/z = 91$ in its mass spectrum. Suggest a structure for the fragment ion which produces this peak and hence suggest a structure for **W**. (4)

d i Infra-red spectroscopy can be used to distinguish between esters and carboxylic acids. Identify an absorption that would enable you to distinguish between methyl benzenecarboxylate and its isomer 4-methylbenzenecarboxylic acid.

  ii State how infra-red spectroscopy can be used to show that an unknown ester is definitely methyl benzenecarboxylate. (2)

Total 15

AQA, January 2008, Unit 4, Question 8

3 Compounds **J**, **K**, **L** and **M** are structural isomers of $C_4H_{10}O_2$
Some of these isomers are ethers. Ethers contain the C–O–C linkage.
Isomers **J**, **K**, **L** and **M** can be distinguished using proton n.m.r. spectroscopy and infra-red spectroscopy.

a The substance TMS is used as a standard in recording proton n.m.r. spectra.
Draw the structure of TMS and give two reasons why it is used as a standard. (3)

b State the number of peaks in the proton n.m.r. spectrum of isomer **J**, $CH_3OCH_2CH_2OCH_3$ (1)

c **i** Isomer **K**, shown below, has five peaks in its proton n.m.r. spectrum. Predict the splitting pattern of the peaks due to the protons labelled *a* and *b*.

$$\begin{array}{cc} a & b \\ \end{array}$$
$CH_3CH_2OCH_2CH_2OH$

 ii Identify the wavenumber of an absorption which would be present in the infrared spectrum of **K** but which would not be present in the infra-red spectrum of **J**. (3)

d Isomer **L**, $HOCH_2CH_2CH_2CH_2OH$, can be used to form polyesters.
 i Give the name of **L**.
 ii Isomer **L** reacts with pentanedioic acid to form a polyester. Name the type of polymerisation involved and draw the repeating unit of the polyester formed. (4)

e The proton n.m.r. spectrum of isomer **M** is shown below. The measured integration trace gives the ratio 0.4 to 2.4 to 1.2 for the peaks at δ 4.6, 3.3 and 1.3, respectively.

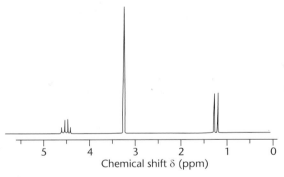

Chemical shift δ (ppm)

 i State what you can deduce from the integration value for the peak at δ 3.3
 ii Use the table at the back of this book (Proton n.m.r. chemical shift data) to help you identify the type of proton leading to the peak at δ 3.3
 iii Draw the part of the structure which can be deduced from the splitting of the peaks at δ 1.3 and δ 4.6 and from their integration values.
 iv Hence, deduce the structure of **M**. (4)

Total 15

AQA, January 2007, Unit 4, Question 4

4 This question concerns four isomers, **W**, **X**, **Y** and **Z**, with the molecular formula $C_5H_{10}O_2$

a The proton n.m.r. spectrum of **W** shows 4 peaks. The table below gives the chemical shifts, δ values, for each of these peaks, together with their splitting patterns and integration values.

δ (ppm)	2.18	2.59	3.33	3.64
Splitting pattern	singlet	triplet	singlet	triplet
Integration value	3	2	3	2

State what can be deduced about the structure of **W** from the presence of the following in its n.m.r. spectrum.
 i The singlet peak at $\delta = 2.18$
 ii The singlet peak at $\delta = 3.33$
 iii Two triplet peaks.
 iv Hence, deduce the structure of **W**. (4)

b The infra-red spectrum of **X** is shown below.

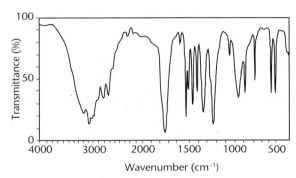

 i What can be deduced from the broad absorption centred on 3 000 cm⁻¹ in the infra-red spectrum of **X**?
 ii Given that the proton n.m.r. spectrum of **X** contains only two peaks with the integration ratio 9:1, deduce the structure of **X**. (2)

c Isomers **Y** and **Z** have the structures shown below.

Identify the two reagents you could use in a simple chemical test to distinguish between **Y** and **Z**. State what you would observe when each of **Y** and **Z** is tested with a mixture of these two reagents. (3)

Total 9

AQA, June 2005, Unit 4, Question 4

Drug testing

The Tour de France: has drug testing reached its limit?

Blood testing for cyclists has become the norm. A test for EPO (erythropoietin) measures the concentration of EPO in blood, as well as four other markers of abnormally high EPO levels, by immunoassay and other cellular measurements. These markers leak out of the bone marrow when red blood cells are overproduced, or they may be involved in iron metabolism, which influences the production of the oxygen-carrying haemoglobin in red blood cells. However, EPO is present in urine for only about 48–72 hours after injection, whereas the effects remain in blood for the life of the red blood cell.

The goal of random testing is to discourage drug use among individuals by not telling anyone when or where testing will take place.

> **A1** Give your reasoned opinion as to whether random testing is justified:
>
> **a** in sport
>
> **b** at work or college.

The Enzyme Multiplied Immunoassay Technique (or EMIT) is a common method for screening urine and blood for drugs, whether legal or illicit. The technique is relatively non-specific compared to some other analysis methods, such as mass spectrometry, but has the advantage of being fast and inexpensive. It has, however, been shown in some cases to be somewhat inaccurate in its findings. It works by looking for antibodies that will attach themselves to the drug, and these are compared to standard solutions. However, the scientists have to know which drug they are testing for, and there are some false positives for the EMIT

test. The most reliable test we have is using a machine that is a combination of gas chromatography and mass spectrometry, the GC/MS test. No laboratory process is completely free from error. The GC/MS test is virtually error-free, but the EMIT is far from accurate.

Ben Johnson was stripped of his gold medal. For a positive test to withstand an athlete's legal challenge, IOC (Institute of Organic Chemistry) chemists must develop highly accurate tests. 'The test must be 100% accurate, because you're destroying an athlete's character' (Craig Kammerer, Chemist at the UCLA Olympic Analytical Laboratory).

> **A2** Outline the main principles of how you think the principles for combined gas chromatography and mass spectrometry could analyse for drugs or their metabolites.
>
> **A3** GC/MS is 100–1 000 times more sensitive than thin-layer chromatography. Explain what is meant by 'sensitivity' in this context.
>
> **A4** What do you think is meant by the term 'false positives', and how might they arise?
>
> **A5** Can any test be 100% accurate?

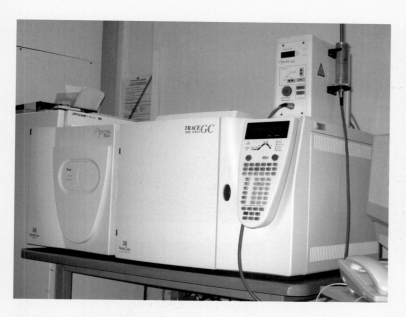

At the Olympics, GC/MS testing is carried out routinely on urine samples from all medal winners.

Poppy seeds, usually on breads, contain traces of morphine. Could they lead to positives for opiates? For instance, you would have to eat 100 poppy seed bagels in a short space of time to score a positive on a drug test. Also, the metabolites have different patterns when viewed with the GC/MS.

The future?

Some drugs and metabolites are quickly lost from blood samples (typically 24 hours) and urine (typically one to three days). But analytical tests of hair samples may offer the best lab-based approach to catching athletes who stop doping themselves in the periods leading up to major

competitions. Drugs circulating in the bloodstream become permanently incorporated into the keratin matrix of the hair shaft (and may be detected for up to 90 days). Even a small fragment of hair serves as a time-resolved record of substance abuse. The technique cannot yet rule out environmental contaminants as the source of the banned substance, but it certainly has this potential. It is not fully recognised by the World AntiDoping Agency (WADA), whose rules govern international sport, including the Olympics. Under existing regulations, no results taken from samples of hair, nails, oral fluid or other biological material can override the findings from urine or blood. A WADA spokesperson has said: 'Hair testing is not considered sufficiently reliable for application in antidoping by the overwhelming majority of the experts we have consulted. Most consider that urine and blood allow more accurate analysis.'

A6 Discuss how society is using the scientific evidence from drug testing to ensure fair competition.

A7 Fig. 42 shows the structure of the pain killing (and perfectly legal) drug ibuprofen and the main peaks in its mass spectrum used for its identification. Identify the fragments produced by drawing their structures. One of the peaks is from the tropyllium ion, a seven-membered aromatic ring.

Fig. 42   The structure of ibuprofen and its mass spectrum

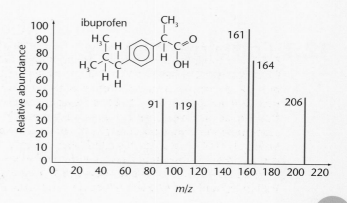

12 Thermodynamics

Many chemical reactions are accompanied by a measurable heat energy change called an **enthalpy change** – symbol ΔH ('enthalpy' comes from the Greek word for 'warm'). Reactions that release energy are called **exothermic**: ΔH is negative. Reactions that absorb energy are called **endothermic**: ΔH is positive. Enthalpy changes occur because of energy changes when bonds break and new bonds form during the chemical reaction.

A good example of an exothermic reaction is combustion – heat is produced. Energy can also be released when some substances, such as concentrated sulfuric acid, are mixed with water.

If you have mixed plaster of Paris, you may have noticed that the mixture becomes warm, but not nearly as hot as sulfuric acid.

Some clays mixed with water also become warm, which makes them useful for 'hot mud' facial packs in applications such as deep cleansing the pores of the skin. When the skin is warm, the pores open. This allows it to sweat, a process that is important for regulating body temperature. A deep-cleansing product that generates heat stimulates blood flow and opens the pores. By mixing cleansing oils with the heating material, grease and dirt deep inside the pores can be removed. Of course, the mixture should be safe for use on the skin and easy to remove.

When methane combines with oxygen (as shown on this cooker plate), a lot of energy is released resulting in flames and heat.

A beauty treatment: deep cleansing of facial skin with a 'hot mud' pack.

When concentrated sulfuric acid is added to water, so much heat is released that the water nearly boils. Always add the acid to water and not the water to acid, and stir.

12.1 Enthalpy changes

Chapter 7 of *AS Chemistry* covered **enthalpy change** for reactions involving covalent compounds. In this chapter we will consider reactions involving electrovalent (ionic) compounds.

The enthalpy change, ΔH, for a system is the heat taken in or given off during a chemical or physical change that takes place at constant pressure.

The reaction of sodium and chlorine is highly exothermic.

The overall enthalpy change in a reaction is often the sum of several endothermic and exothermic processes.

A reaction, such as making sodium chloride from its elements, can be used to show the endothermic and exothermic steps. In the formation of sodium chloride from its elements, several changes are involved:

- Sodium atoms in the solid state separate to form gaseous atoms.
- Gaseous atoms form gaseous positive sodium ions.
- Gaseous chlorine molecules split into gaseous chlorine atoms.
- Gaseous chlorine atoms form gaseous negative chloride ions.
- Gaseous positive and negative ions attract each other and form a solid crystal lattice.

When the element sodium reacts with the element chlorine, a lot of energy is released. The heat from this reaction can be measured, and it is the sum of a number of different enthalpy changes. The overall reaction is exothermic:

$$\Delta H^{\ominus}_{f,298} = -411 \text{ kJ mol}^{-1}$$

Here $\Delta H^{\ominus}_{f,298}$ is called the **standard enthalpy of formation** (Fig. 1). It is the enthalpy change when one mole of sodium chloride is formed from its elements in their standard states under standard conditions:

$$Na(s) + \tfrac{1}{2}Cl_2(g) \rightarrow NaCl(s)$$
$$\Delta H^{\ominus}_{f,298} = -411 \text{ kJ mol}^{-1}$$

Fig. 1 Standard enthalpy of formation

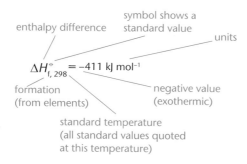

enthalpy difference — symbol shows a standard value — units

$$\Delta H^{\ominus}_{f,\,298} = -411 \text{ kJ mol}^{-1}$$

formation (from elements) — negative value (exothermic)

standard temperature (all standard values quoted at this temperature)

Standard enthalpy changes, $\Delta H^{\ominus}$

The size of any enthalpy change depends on the amount of substance used and on the conditions of measurement. Chemists have agreed **standard amounts** and **standard conditions** so that comparisons can be made between different measurements. The symbols for standard enthalpy changes are always followed by the sign $^{\ominus}$.

Amount of substance

The standard amount used by chemists is the **mole** (see *AS Chemistry*, page 32), and this will be quoted in the units as per mole using the symbol mol^{-1}.

Standard states

The size of an enthalpy change for a given reaction alters if either the pressure or the temperature at which it is measured is altered. In order to make comparisons between different sets of data, it is convenient to quote enthalpy changes measured under agreed **standard conditions**.

- **Standard pressure** – the standard pressure chosen is 100 kPa (1 bar).
- **Standard temperature** – the most common reference temperature used is 298 K.

Once these are specified, the enthalpy change is the **standard enthalpy change**, $\Delta H^{\ominus}_{298}$ (see *AS Chemistry*, page 126).

Standard quantities at temperatures other than 298 K can be quoted if this is more convenient for a particular reaction. So $\Delta H^{\ominus}_{1\,000}$ refers to a standard molar enthalpy change at a temperature of 1 000 K. If no temperature is stated, it is assumed that the reference temperature is 298 K. Thus $\Delta H^{\ominus}$ on its own is the same as $\Delta H^{\ominus}_{298}$.

Forming sodium chloride

The whole process of forming sodium chloride from its elements involves a number of enthalpy changes (some of which may occur simultaneously). We shall use this reaction as an example to look at the various enthalpy changes. These changes are summarised below and later in Fig. 6.

Enthalpy of atomisation

Energy is supplied to solid sodium metal to form gaseous sodium atoms. The energy required to vaporise one mole of solid atoms is called the enthalpy of atomisation ΔH_{at}. For a metallic (or atomic) lattice, this is simply the enthalpy of sublimation ΔH_{sub}. It is an endothermic process (ΔH is positive), because the atoms are attracted to each other and need to be separated:

$$Na(s) \rightarrow Na(g) \quad \Delta H^{\ominus}_{sub} = +107 \text{ kJ mol}^{-1}$$

The enthalpy of atomisation is related to the forces of attraction between atoms. Magnesium has a greater enthalpy of atomisation than sodium (Table 1), because the greater ionic charge attracts the two delocalised electrons in the metallic lattice of magnesium more strongly. More energy must be supplied to overcome these forces.

Table 1 Enthalpies of atomisation

Element	$\Delta H^{\ominus}_{at}$ (kJ mol^{-1})
lithium	+159
sodium	+107
magnesium	+149
aluminium	+326
potassium	+89

Aluminium has an even greater ionic charge than magnesium, so its enthalpy of atomisation is even greater. Potassium is a larger atom than sodium and has more inner electron shells to screen the outer delocalised electrons from the nucleus. Also, because it is a larger atom than sodium, the electrons are further away from the nucleus, so the force of attraction is weaker and the enthalpy of atomisation is less than that for sodium.

The enthalpy of atomisation is the standard enthalpy change that accompanies the formation of one mole of gaseous atoms.

Ionisation

The next stage involves removing the outer electron from each gaseous sodium atom to form a gaseous sodium ion. This change is the first ionisation enthalpy for sodium. It, too, is an endothermic process (ΔH_i is positive).

$$Na(g) \rightarrow Na^+(g) + e^- \quad \Delta H_i^{\ominus} = +496 \text{ kJ mol}^{-1}$$

1 Explain why removing an electron from an atom is an endothermic process.

Many metals lose more than one electron from their outer shell when they form ions, so further ionisation enthalpies may need to be considered. For example, the ionisation enthalpy required to form the Mg^{2+} ion is the sum of the first and second ionisation enthalpies:

$$Mg(g) \rightarrow Mg^+(g) + e^- \quad \Delta H_i^{\ominus} = +738 \text{ kJ mol}^{-1}$$
$$Mg^+(g) \rightarrow Mg^{2+}(g) + e^- \quad \Delta H_i^{\ominus} = +1451 \text{ kJ mol}^{-1}$$

Total enthalpy required for the overall process:

$$Mg(g) \rightarrow Mg^{2+}(g) + 2e^- \quad \Delta H_i^{\ominus} = +2189 \text{ kJ mol}^{-1}$$

It is theoretically possible to remove all the electrons from atoms. These successive ionisation enthalpy values can be used to indicate which group of the Periodic Table the element is in (Table 2 and Fig. 2).

Table 2 Successive molar ionisation enthalpies for magnesium

No. of ionisation	$\Delta H_i^{\ominus}$ (kJ mol^{-1})
1	+738
2	+1451
3	+7733
4	+10541
5	+13629
6	+17995
7	+21704
8	+25657
9	+31644
10	+35463
11	+169996
12	+189371

The energy needed to remove one electron from each atom in one mole of magnesium atoms is 738 kJ mol^{-1}. When an electron is removed from an Mg atom to form an Mg$^+$ ion, the repulsion between the second and third shells is decreased, so the outer shell moves nearer to the nucleus.

Because the remaining outer-shell electron is now closer to the nucleus, the force of attraction between it and the nucleus is greater than in the neutral atom. Therefore, the second ionisation enthalpy (+1451 kJ mol^{-1}) is greater than the first ionisation enthalpy (+738 kJ mol^{-1}).

The third electron must be removed from an inner orbital that is much nearer to the nucleus. Electrons in this level are attracted far more

Fig. 2 Ionisation enthalpies for magnesium: successive removal of (a) the first 10 electrons and (b) all 12 electrons

(a)

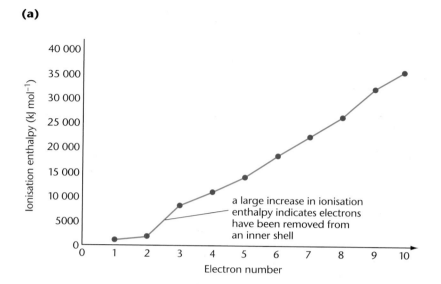

(b)

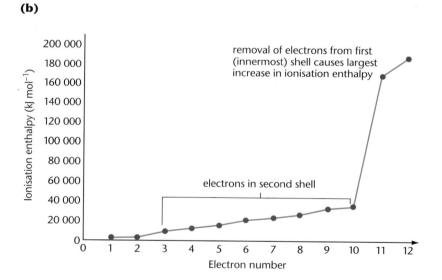

strongly to the nucleus, so far more energy is required to remove them. There is therefore a large increase in ionisation energy between the second and the third values (Fig. 2(a)). This indicates that there are two electrons in the outer shell.

> **The ionisation enthalpy is the standard enthalpy change for the removal of an electron from a species in the gas phase to form a positive ion and an electron, both also in the gas phase.**

> **2** The successive ionisation enthalpies in kJ mol⁻¹ for three different elements are:
>
> **a** 801, 2 427, 3 660, 25 026, 32 828;
>
> **b** 1 086, 2 353, 4 621, 6 223, 37 832, 47 278;
>
> **c** 1 314, 3 388, 5 301, 7 469, 10 989, 13 327, 71 337, 84 080.
>
> Determine which group of the Periodic Table each of the elements is in, stating reasons.

Atomisation of chlorine

Chloride ions are formed in two stages. The first of these involves splitting gaseous chlorine molecules into gaseous atoms. Atomisation of chlorine is another endothermic process.

$$\tfrac{1}{2}Cl_2(g) \rightarrow Cl(g) \qquad \Delta H_{at}^{\ominus} = +121 \text{ kJ mol}^{-1}$$

Here, the molar enthalpy of atomisation is defined as the enthalpy change needed to produce one mole of atoms in their standard states from the element in its standard state. This value is half of the value for the Cl–Cl bond enthalpy.

Sometimes the enthalpy of dissociation is used to describe a change from gaseous molecules to gaseous atoms. For chlorine, it is the enthalpy required to dissociate one mole of $Cl_2(g)$ molecules in their standard state into their constituent atoms.

$$Cl_2(g) \rightarrow 2Cl(g) \qquad \Delta H_{diss}^{\ominus} = +242 \text{ kJ mol}^{-1}$$

> **The bond dissociation enthalpy is the standard enthalpy change that accompanies the breaking of a covalent bond in a gaseous molecule to form two free radicals also in the gaseous phase.**

Table 3 shows a comparison of bond dissociation enthalpy values for different elements. The values for the different halogens are quite similar because they all have single covalent bonds that are being broken. The

> **3** Why is atomisation an endothermic process?

values decrease as the halogen atoms get larger, since the forces holding the atoms together are weaker. The values for O_2 and N_2 are larger than for any of the halogens, because atomising oxygen involves breaking a double bond and for nitrogen a triple bond.

In each of the changes described so far, the particles have gained energy. Other changes can release energy.

Table 3 Bond dissociation enthalpy values for different elements

Molecule	Cl_2	Br_2	I_2	O_2	N_2
$\Delta H_{at}^{\ominus}$ (kJ mol^{-1})	121	112	107	249	472

Electron affinity

A gaseous chlorine atom can form a negative gaseous chloride ion:

$$Cl(g) + e^- \rightarrow Cl^-(g) \quad \Delta H_{ea}^{\ominus} = -349 \text{ kJ mol}^{-1}$$

The enthalpy change for this process is its **electron affinity**. Electron affinities can be exothermic for the atoms to the right-hand side of the Periodic Table (the non-metallic elements). These are atoms with a strong attractive force produced by a relatively high nuclear charge (for that period).

Do not confuse electron affinity with ionisation energy. All ionisation enthalpies are endothermic because there must be an energy input for the electron to move away from the attractive force of the nucleus. If one electron is added to a highly electronegative atom, energy may be released (exothermic). However, if more than one electron is required to complete the outer shell, the second or third electron affinities are endothermic. This is because energy is needed to overcome the increasing amount of repulsion against a further electron going into the shell. Since an ion has a lower nuclear charge than the corresponding atom with the same number of electrons, attraction by an 'ionic' nucleus is less than that for an 'atomic' nucleus. Since the positive nuclear charge in the ionic nucleus cannot fully offset the increased repulsive forces of putting yet another electron into occupied orbitals, the process is endothermic (see Fig. 3).

For the fluorine atom and the singly charged oxygen ion in Fig. 3, the change in electronic structure is the same for each process. Fluorine

Fig. 3 Comparison of $F \rightarrow F^-$ with $O^- \rightarrow O^{2-}$

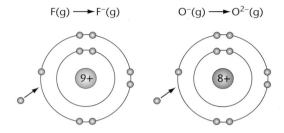

$F(g) \longrightarrow F^-(g)$ $\quad$ $O^-(g) \longrightarrow O^{2-}(g)$

For $O^-(g) \longrightarrow O^{2-}(g)$ there is a weaker attraction from the nucleus because: the nuclear charge in $O^-(g)$ is less than $F(g)$; and $O^-(g)$ is larger than $F(g)$.

has nine protons and oxygen has eight. At the same time, O^- is larger than F, so the force of attraction between the nucleus and the outer electrons is less in the O^- ion.

Electron affinity and electronegativity

Electron affinity occurs only in atoms with relatively high **electronegativity**. The higher the electronegativity, the stronger the force of attraction for electrons. Because a chlorine atom in the gas phase has a strong affinity for an electron, the formation of a chloride ion gives out heat to the surroundings. The electron affinity for this atom is exothermic.

However, electron affinities can be endothermic. Forming a gaseous O^{2-} ion from a gaseous O^- ion is endothermic. The electron affinities of some negative ions are shown in Table 4.

Electron affinity is the standard enthalpy change when an electron is added to an isolated atom in the gas phase.

Lattice enthalpy

The strongly attractive electrostatic forces between chloride ions and sodium ions in the gaseous state pull the ions together to form a close-packed, solid ionic lattice (Fig. 4):

$$Na^+(g) + Cl^-(g) \rightarrow NaCl(s) \quad \Delta H_L^{\ominus} = -786 \text{ kJ mol}^{-1}$$

A considerable amount of energy is released in this process, and the particles move to a much lower energy level. This energy is called the lattice formation enthalpy $\Delta H_L^{\ominus}$.

Table 4 Electron affinities for some negative ions

	$\Delta H_{ea}^{\ominus}$ (kJ mol^{-1}) (1st electron affinity)		$\Delta H_{ea}^{\ominus}$ (kJ mol^{-1}) (2nd electron affinity)
$H(g) \rightarrow H^-(g)$	−72		
$F(g) \rightarrow F^-(g)$	−328		
$Cl(g) \rightarrow Cl^-(g)$	−348		
$Br(g) \rightarrow Br^-(g)$	−324		
$I(g) \rightarrow I^-(g)$	−295		
$N(g) \rightarrow N^-(g)$	0		
$O(g) \rightarrow O^-(g)$	−141	$O^-(g) \rightarrow O^{2-}(g)$	+798
$S(g) \rightarrow S^-(g)$	−200	$S^-(g) \rightarrow S^{2-}(g)$	+640
$P(g) \rightarrow P^-(g)$	−72		

Fig. 4 Lattice formation from gaseous ions

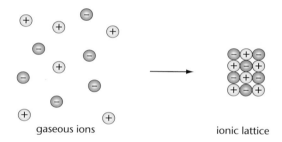

gaseous ions   ionic lattice

The strength of the attraction can be related to several features of the ions, which means that the amount of energy released is related to: the charges on the ions, their size and the type of lattice formed. A larger exothermic lattice enthalpy is favoured by a greater charge on the ions, smaller ions and a closer alignment in the lattice.

Because the sodium ion is much smaller than the original sodium atom, the two newly formed Na$^+$ and Cl$^-$ ions can align much more closely. This produces much stronger forces of attraction, so we talk about positive and negative ions attracting each other.

Note that, in the above example, the lattice enthalpy is stated for the *formation of solid* NaCl from its gaseous ions. The value stated is negative, showing that it is an exothermic process. Lattice enthalpy values can be quoted for the lattice *dissociation* process:

$$NaCl(s) \rightarrow Na^+(g) + Cl^-(g) \quad \Delta H_L^{\ominus} = +786 \text{ kJ mol}^{-1}$$

Here, the lattice enthalpy is positive; energy must be supplied to break up the solid lattice and form gaseous ions.

The enthalpy of lattice dissociation is the standard enthalpy change that accompanies the separation of one mole of a solid ionic lattice into its gaseous ions.

Enthalpy of formation

The energy released during the formation of one mole of sodium chloride from its constituent elements in their standard states under standard conditions is called the standard molar enthalpy of formation (Fig. 5). The first law of thermodynamics tells us that energy cannot be created or destroyed, but it can be stored or transferred. When energy is transferred, it produces an effect. All the energy changes relating to the stages in the formation of NaCl, or in any other chemical reaction, can be linked by a **Born–Haber cycle** (Fig. 6). The sum of all the energy changes is the enthalpy of formation.

Fig. 5 Enthalpy of formation

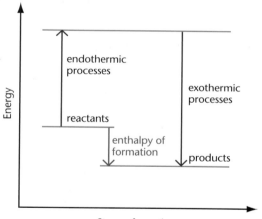

According to **Hess's law** (see *AS Chemistry*, page 131), the overall enthalpy change in a complete cycle must be zero, i.e. the sum of the steps $\Delta H^{\ominus} = 0$. Using Hess's law, the overall energy change is independent of the number of steps (Fig. 7).

$$\Delta H^{\ominus}(\text{single step}) = \Delta H^{\ominus}(\text{five steps})$$
$$\Delta H_f^{\ominus} = \text{steps } 1 \rightarrow 5$$
$$\Delta H_L^{\ominus} = \Delta H_f^{\ominus} - \text{steps } 1 \rightarrow 4$$
$$= -411 - 107 - 496 - 121 - (-349)$$
$$= -786 \text{ kJ mol}^{-1}$$

Fig. 6   Born–Haber cycle for NaCl

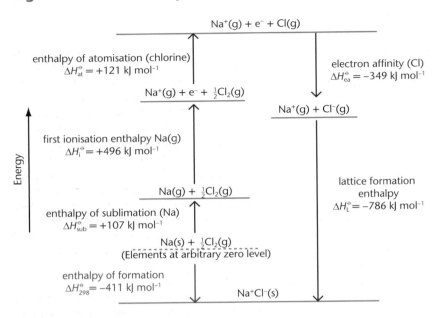

Because the lattice enthalpy value is so high, the enthalpy of formation is strongly exothermic, and so the compound formed is very stable compared with its elements. Energy cycles are a useful way of calculating the overall energy change in a reaction. They can also be used to help us to understand why some compounds exist and others do not.

If we construct a Born–Haber cycle for the hypothetical compound MgCl(s), we can estimate the enthalpy of formation.

$$\Delta H_f^\ominus = Mg(s) \rightarrow Mg(g) \rightarrow Mg^+(g)$$
$$\qquad\qquad +148 \qquad +740$$

$$\tfrac{1}{2}Cl_2(g) \rightarrow Cl(g) \rightarrow Cl^-(g)$$
$$\qquad\quad +121 \qquad -349$$

$$Mg^+(g) + Cl^-(g) \rightarrow MgCl(s)$$
$$\qquad\qquad\qquad -815 \text{ (est)}$$

$$\Delta H_f^\ominus (MgCl(s)) = 148 + 740 + 121 - 349 - 815$$
$$= -170 \text{ kJ mol}^{-1}$$

The enthalpy of formation for $MgCl_2(s)$ is in fact -641 kJ mol^{-1}. This is a much larger negative value than for the hypothetical MgCl(s), so more energy can be released if $MgCl_2(s)$ is formed, making $MgCl_2(s)$ more stable than MgCl(s). This means that $MgCl_2(s)$ is the chloride formed when magnesium reacts with chlorine.

The standard enthalpy of formation is the enthalpy change involved in the production of one mole of a compound from its elements under standard conditions, reactants and products being in their standard states.

Fig. 7   Using Hess's law to calculate lattice formation

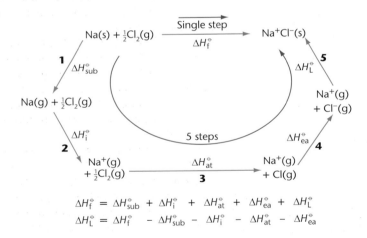

$$\Delta H_f^\ominus = \Delta H_{sub}^\ominus + \Delta H_i^\ominus + \Delta H_{at}^\ominus + \Delta H_{ea}^\ominus + \Delta H_L^\ominus$$
$$\Delta H_L^\ominus = \Delta H_f^\ominus - \Delta H_{sub}^\ominus - \Delta H_i^\ominus - \Delta H_{at}^\ominus - \Delta H_{ea}^\ominus$$

- The formation of compounds involves endothermic and exothermic reactions.

- An endothermic change occurs when forces must be overcome, e.g. atomisation, ionisation or breaking up a lattice.

- An exothermic change occurs when forces of attraction operate, e.g. electron affinity or forming an ionic lattice.

12.2 Heat from solution

The process of dissolving

Water molecules are polar because of electronegativity differences within the molecule (Fig. 8).

Fig. 8   Polarity in water molecules

The polar ends of the water molecules are attracted to the ions in the ionic lattice of a solid. This attraction distorts the charge cloud of the positive and negative ions in the lattice and reduces the forces holding them together (Fig. 9).

Fig. 9   Breaking down an ionic lattice

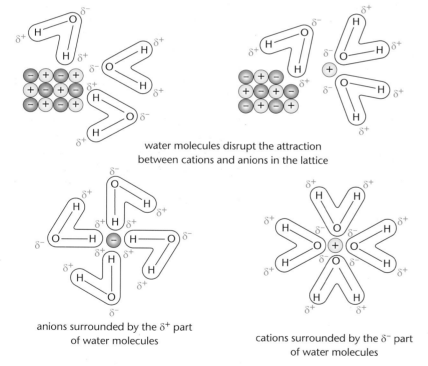

water molecules disrupt the attraction between cations and anions in the lattice

anions surrounded by the δ^+ part of water molecules

cations surrounded by the δ^- part of water molecules

The ions move from the lattice into solution and become surrounded by water molecules – the ions are then said to be **hydrated**. Positive cations are attracted to the negative end of the dipole (the oxygen atom in the water molecule). Similarly, negative anions are attracted to the positive end of the dipole (the hydrogen atoms in the water molecule). The force of attraction between water molecules and the cations and anions means that energy is released.

The arrangement of water molecules around the cations and anions leads to further layers of water molecules being attracted, releasing yet more energy. The hydrated ions tend to have a particular number of water molecules associated with them. When the ions move through the solution, these water molecules move with them, and this is called the hydration sheath. The number of water molecules attached to the ion is called its hydration number (see Table 5).

Enthalpy of hydration

When some compounds are put in water, there can be a measurable enthalpy change. There are two processes that can take place between ions and water: **hydration** of gaseous ions, which is the **enthalpy of hydration**, and dissolving a solid compound to form a solution, which is the **enthalpy of solution**.

Both positive and negative ions of an ionic compound will be hydrated in the presence of water. As discussed some compounds, such as concentrated sulfuric acid, produce a lot of heat when mixed with water. Other compounds, such as anhydrous copper sulfate, produce less heat when added to water.

For ions to dissolve in water, they need to be separated from one another. The ions in an ionic lattice are attracted by strong forces, so separating them is an endothermic process. For any compound to dissolve in water, a large amount of energy is needed to compensate for this endothermic change. Part of the energy is released when the ions become surrounded with water molecules. Ions and water molecules are attracted to each other, so this process releases energy. It is called the enthalpy of hydration ΔH_{hyd}. (For any solvent, the enthalpy released when a solution forms is referred to as the solvation enthalpy.)

The enthalpy of hydration is the standard enthalpy change for the process:

$$X^{+/-}(g) \xrightarrow{\text{water}} X^{+/-}(aq) \quad \Delta H^\ominus = \Delta H^\ominus_{hyd}$$

The enthalpy of hydration, ΔH_{hyd}, is the enthalpy change when one mole of gaseous ions completely dissolves in water, meaning that one mole of gaseous ions is surrounded by water molecules. Ions with strong forces of attraction will release large amounts of energy, while others with weaker forces will not become as warm. Where ionic compounds have hydration energies higher than their lattice energies, dissolving is an exothermic process.

The amount of water used in hydration will affect the amount of energy released. For all the energy to be released, the ion must have all the possible layers of water molecules attached. Water molecules close to the central ion are strongly attracted and a lot of energy is released. The molecules that are further away from the central ion exert weaker forces and lesser amounts of energy are released. The force of attraction is weaker at each layer until the water molecules are far enough away to not be attracted to the ion. This is said to be a state of **infinite dilution** (Fig. 10). Once infinite dilution is reached, no further energy will be released due to hydration.

Fig. 10   Hydration of a cation

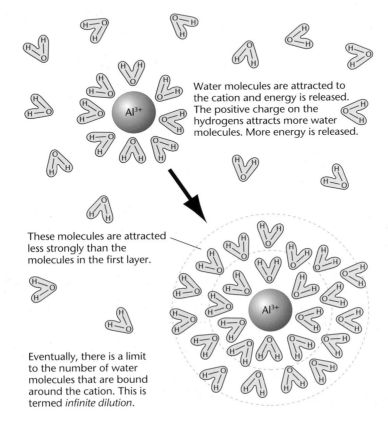

Water molecules are attracted to the cation and energy is released. The positive charge on the hydrogens attracts more water molecules. More energy is released.

These molecules are attracted less strongly than the molecules in the first layer.

Eventually, there is a limit to the number of water molecules that are bound around the cation. This is termed *infinite dilution*.

When anhydrous copper sulfate mixes with water, six water molecules form covalent bonds with the lone pairs on the oxygens. Then this complex ion is hydrated. The hydration enthalpy released is greater than the energy needed to break down the lattice. The energy output is greater than the energy input, so the mixture feels warmer than the original components (Fig. 11). Fig. 12 shows an energy profile for hydration.

Fig. 11   Hydration of a Cu²⁺ ion

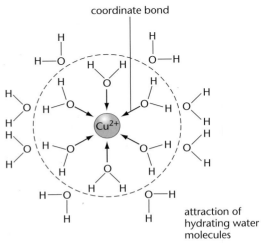

coordinate bond

attraction of hydrating water molecules

Fig. 12   Energy profile for hydration

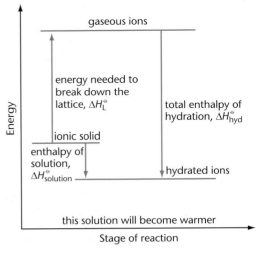

gaseous ions

energy needed to break down the lattice, $\Delta H_L^{\ominus}$

total enthalpy of hydration, $\Delta H_{hyd}^{\ominus}$

ionic solid

enthalpy of solution, $\Delta H_{solution}^{\ominus}$

hydrated ions

Energy

this solution will become warmer

Stage of reaction

Factors affecting enthalpy of hydration

The force of attraction between ions and water molecules depends upon the charge and the size of the ion. Consider the ions Na^+, Mg^{2+} and Al^{3+}.

The cations all have the same electronic structure, but they have different nuclear charges and sizes (Fig. 13).

Fig. 13 Electron structures of cations

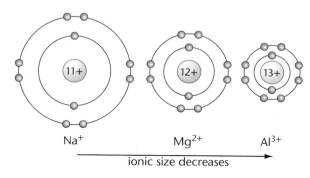

Na⁺   Mg²⁺   Al³⁺

ionic size decreases

The positive nuclear charge increases from Na^+ to Al^{3+}. Therefore, the force of attraction for the negative pole of the water dipole is greater for Al^{3+} than for Na^+. So Al^{3+} attracts water molecules very strongly and has a greater enthalpy of hydration than Na^+ (Fig. 14).

Fig. 14 Hydration of an Al³⁺ ion

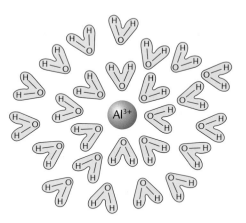

For ions in the same period, the ionic charge increases as you move across from left to right, while the ionic size decreases. Therefore, the enthalpy of hydration increases considerably. For ions in the same group – where ionic charge is constant and ionic size increases down the group – there is a less dramatic change. The enthalpy of hydration decreases down the group (compare the values for Na^+, K^+ and Rb^+ in Table 5). Table 5 shows that 2⁺ and 3⁺ ions have

Table 5 Enthalpies of hydration and hydration numbers for different cations

	Na⁺	Mg²⁺	Al³⁺	K⁺	Rb⁺
Enthalpy of hydration (kJ mol⁻¹)	−390	−1 891	−4 613	−305	−281
Average hydration number	5	15	26	4	4

much larger hydration enthalpies than the 1⁺ ions. Ionic charge is a more significant factor than ionic size for producing larger hydration enthalpies.

Negative ions are also hydrated, but these will attract the positive end of the water dipole (see Fig. 9). The attraction of oppositely charged species will release energy and contribute to the overall value for the enthalpy of solution. Further data on the hydration enthalpies for some anions, and the lattice enthalpies and hydration enthalpies of some chlorides, are listed in Tables 6 and 7.

Table 6 Hydration enthalpies for some negative ions

Ion	$\Delta H_{hyd}^{\ominus}$ (kJ mol⁻¹)
F⁻	−457
Cl⁻	−381
Br⁻	−351
I⁻	−307
OH⁻	−460

Table 7 Lattice enthalpies and hydration enthalpies for various chlorides

	NaCl	KCl	RbCl	MgCl₂	SrCl₂
Enthalpy of lattice (kJ mol⁻¹)	−780	−711	−2 526	−2 258	−2 156
Enthalpy of hydration (kJ mol⁻¹)	−771	−686	−662	−2 653	−2 323

Fig. 15 Energy diagrams of dissolving (a) NaCl and (b) MgCl$_2$

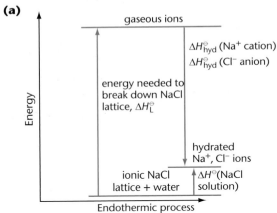

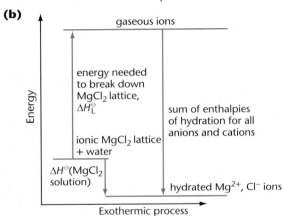

The following are the calculations for the enthalpies of hydration for sodium chloride and magnesium chloride, illustrated in Fig. 15.

(a) NaCl

$$\Delta H^\ominus_{\text{solution}} = \Delta H^\ominus_{\text{hyd(cation)}} + \Delta H^\ominus_{\text{hyd(anion)}} - \Delta H^\ominus_{\text{L}}$$
$$= -390 \quad + (-381) \quad - (-780)$$
$$= +9 \text{ kJ mol}^{-1}$$

(b) MgCl$_2$

$$\Delta H^\ominus_{\text{solution}} = \Delta H^\ominus_{\text{hyd(cation)}} + \Delta H^\ominus_{\text{hyd(anion)}} - \Delta H^\ominus_{\text{L}}$$
$$= -1891 \quad + 2(-381) \quad - (-2526)$$
$$= -127 \text{ kJ mol}^{-1}$$

Enthalpy of solution

The enthalpy of solution, $\Delta H^\ominus_{\text{solution}}$, is the enthalpy change when one mole of solute is dissolved to form a solution of infinite dilution.

The enthalpy of solution is the standard enthalpy change for the process in which one mole of an ionic solid dissolves in an amount of water large enough to ensure that the dissolved ions are well separated and do not interact with one another.

12.3 Calculating enthalpy changes

For some reactions it is difficult to measure the enthalpy change experimentally. Again, we can calculate them from other known data using Hess's law (*AS Chemistry*, page 131).

An example is the reaction of ammonia with hydrogen chloride:

$$\text{NH}_3(\text{g}) + \text{HCl}(\text{g}) \xrightarrow{\Delta H} \text{NH}_4\text{Cl}(\text{s})$$

At one end there is cotton wool soaked in concentrated ammonia solution, and at the other end cotton wool soaked in hydrogen chloride solution. The gases diffuse along the tube to form white ammonium chloride.

We can use ΔH_f° values to calculate the enthalpy change in this reaction (Table 8). The steps are as follows:

Table 8 Enthalpy values for ammonia reacting with hydrogen chloride

Compound	$NH_3(g)$	$HCl(g)$	$NH_4Cl(s)$
$\Delta H_f^\bullet$ (kJ mol^{-1})	−46.1	−92.3	−314.4

1 Look back at Table 4, and work out two ways of producing NH_4Cl from the elements:

(a) $N_2(g)/H_2(g)/Cl_2(g) \rightarrow NH_4Cl(s)$
(one stage directly)

(b) $N_2(g)/H_2(g)/Cl_2(g) \rightarrow HCl(g) + NH_3(g)$
$\rightarrow NH_4Cl(s)$
(two stages indirectly)

2 Draw a Hess's law diagram like the one in Fig. 16. You should have arrows going clockwise and anticlockwise. Check you have used matching quantities for the process. Label each step with:

$\Delta H_1, \Delta H_2, \Delta H_3, \Delta H_4.$

3 Clockwise enthalpy = anticlockwise enthalpy
    changes   changes
(indirect route)   (direct route)

$\Delta H_1 + \Delta H_2 + \Delta H_3 = \Delta H_4$

4 Substitute the values and calculate ΔH_3:

$$\begin{aligned} \Delta H_3 &= \Delta H_4 - \Delta H_1 - \Delta H_2 \\ &= -314.4 - (-46.1) - (-92.3) \\ &= -176.0 \text{ kJ mol}^{-1} \end{aligned}$$

---

4 Calculate the energy change for the reaction:

$$2NaHCO_3(s) \rightarrow Na_2CO_3(s) + CO_2(g) + H_2O(l)$$

using the following data:

$\Delta H_f(CO_2(g)) \quad = -393.5 \text{ kJ mol}^{-1},$
$\Delta H_f(H_2O(l)) \quad = -285.8 \text{ kJ mol}^{-1},$
$\Delta H_f(Na_2CO_3(s)) = -1\,130.7 \text{ kJ mol}^{-1},$
$\Delta H_f(NaHCO_3(s)) = -950.8 \text{ kJ mol}^{-1}.$

Fig. 16 Hess's law diagram for the reaction of ammonia with hydrogen chloride

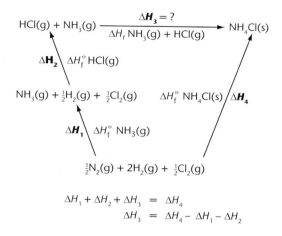

$$\Delta H_1 + \Delta H_2 + \Delta H_3 = \Delta H_4$$
$$\Delta H_3 = \Delta H_4 - \Delta H_1 - \Delta H_2$$

Mean bond enthalpies

A method of calculating enthalpy changes in reactions is to use **mean bond enthalpy** values. This is the enthalpy change when one mole of bonds of a specified type is broken (averaged over several compounds). They are covered in Section 7.7 of Chapter 7 in *AS Chemistry*, where the discussion describes how mean bond enthalpies are normally quoted in data books.

If a molecule of ammonia is dissociated, the bonds are broken successively (Fig. 17). When this happens, one electron from the covalent pair is retained by each atom. These species are free radicals (see *AS Chemistry*, page 228).

The standard molar bond dissociation enthalpy ΔH_{diss}° is the enthalpy change when one mole of bonds of the same type in gaseous molecules under standard conditions is broken, producing free radicals.

The enthalpy change for each stage in Fig. 17 will be different because each stage is in a different environment each time a hydrogen is removed. The mean bond enthalpy is simply one-third of the total dissociation energy change. This is an approximation but provides a useful guide:

$$\tfrac{1}{2}N_2(g) + \tfrac{3}{2}H_2(g) \rightarrow NH_3(g)$$

We can use the data in Table 9 to check if this approximation is acceptable.

Fig. 17 Successive bonds dissociating in ammonia

$NH_3(g) \rightarrow NH_2(g) + H(g)$
one bond broken

$+ \, ^\times H$

$NH_2(g) + H(g) \rightarrow NH(g) + 2H(g)$
two bonds broken

$+ \begin{matrix} ^\times H \\ ^\times H \end{matrix}$

$NH(g) + 2H(g) \rightarrow N(g) + 3H(g)$

$\cdot \ddot{N} \cdot \, + \begin{matrix} ^\times H \\ ^\times H \\ ^\times H \end{matrix}$

three bonds broken

Table 9 Mean bond enthalpies

Bond	Bond enthalpy (kJ mol⁻¹)
N≡N	945.4
H–H	435.9
N–H	391.0
Cl–H	432.0
Cl–Cl	243.4

The enthalpy change for the formation of ammonia can be found as follows.

(a) Breaking the bonds in $N_2(g)$ and $H_2(g)$ to form $N(g) + 3H(g)$:

$\frac{1}{2}N_2(g) = \frac{1}{2} \times 945.4 = +472.7$

$\frac{3}{2}H_2(g) = \frac{3}{2} \times 435.9 = +653.9$

total $= +1\,126.6$ kJ mol⁻¹

(b) Forming the bonds in $NH_3(g)$:
$3N–H = 3 \times -391 = -1\,173$

(c) Total enthalpy change for bond breaking and bond forming:
$= +1\,126.6 + (-1\,173)$
$= -46.4$ kJ mol⁻¹

For comparison, the experimental value for this is $\Delta H_f = -46.1$ kJ mol⁻¹. The calculated value is quite close to the experimental value, so mean

> **5** Use Table 9 to calculate the enthalpy of formation for HCl(g). The value quoted for HCl(g) is −92.3 kJ mol⁻¹. Comment on the two values.

bond enthalpy values are satisfactory here.

Using mean bond enthalpy values can help us to understand the bonding in certain compounds. The bond enthalpy values are considered separately and it is assumed that

there is no interaction between adjacent bonds or atoms. When this is the case, the values agree with experimental data. If the values do not agree, we need to consider how the bonding is affecting the values. These discrepancies can occur with both covalent and ionic compounds.

One famous example is Kekulé's description of the bonding in benzene. He said that the molecule consisted of alternate single and double bonds. Addition of hydrogen to a double bond gives an enthalpy change of −120 kJ mol⁻¹, so hydrogenation of three separate double bonds would give −360 kJ mol⁻¹. The enthalpy change for the hydrogenation of benzene is only −208 kJ mol⁻¹. The molecule is more stable than predicted by 152 kJ mol⁻¹. The extra stability is now explained by delocalisation of the electrons in benzene (Fig. 18).

Fig. 18 Structures of benzene

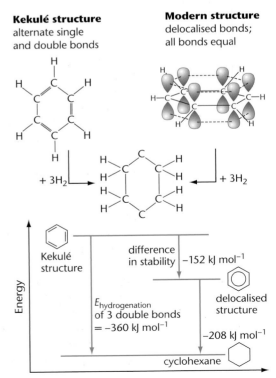

Another example is the ethanoate ion CH_3COO^-, as shown in Fig. 19. Bond enthalpy values and bond lengths indicate two identical C–O bonds, not a single bond and a double bond.

Fig. 19   Ethanoate ion

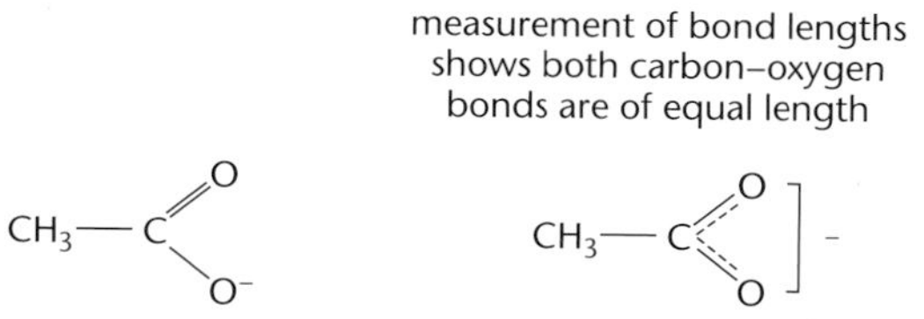

measurement of bond lengths shows both carbon–oxygen bonds are of equal length

Table 10   A selection of lattice enthalpy values

| Lattice | Enthalpy values (kJ mol^{-1}) | | |
	Experimental value	Theoretical value	Difference
NaCl	780	770	−10
MgCl$_2$	2526	2326	−200
CaCl$_2$	2258	2223	−35
SrCl$_2$	2156	2127	−29

For ionic compounds, it is assumed that the ions are completely separate particles. However, many ionic compounds demonstrate some covalent character in the ionic bond. It is possible to calculate a theoretical lattice energy from the attractive and repulsive forces. When the positive and negative ions have a larger difference in electronegativity, there is good agreement between the theoretical and experimental values from Born–Haber cycles (Table 10).

If there is some covalent character in the ionic crystal, there are greater forces of attraction and a greater energy value. Look at Table 10. NaCl gives good agreement (-10 kJ mol^{-1}), but MgCl$_2$ does not (-200 kJ mol^{-1}). Mg^{2+} is a much more polarising ion and has a greater electronegativity than sodium. The larger Group II ions such as calcium and strontium have less polarising power than magnesium, so the values are closer to the theoretical values.

12.4 Entropy

Spontaneous changes

Why do things happen the way they do? Why does ice melt? Why does your tea go cold? If a metal bar is hot at one end and you leave it, the heat will be conducted throughout the bar until all the bar is at the same temperature. These are all examples of spontaneous changes. If you have a metal bar at a uniform temperature, you wouldn't expect it to become hotter at one end and colder at the other.

Spontaneous changes seem to happen without us having to do anything. We don't have to put energy into them to make them happen. There are other spontaneous changes – a gas expands from high pressure to low pressure and not the reverse. For example, a balloon will let all the air out unless you tie a knot in it, but the balloon will not blow itself up. Also, if a smelly gas is in an open container in one corner of a room, the gas will spread out and fill the room. It will not go back into the container spontaneously. Although it might theoretically be possible if all the particles just happened to move in that direction at the same time, it's just very, very unlikely.

Some of these changes can be reversed if there is an energy input. For example, you can blow up a balloon if you expend some energy and use the energy to make the particles move closer together.

Evaporation and condensation are reversible, but there is an enthalpy change if either process occurs. Iron, if left, will rust spontaneously. But iron oxide can be changed back into iron if it is heated to a high temperature with carbon. A rechargeable battery can be changed back to its original state if electricity is passed through it in the reverse direction.

The reaction that occurs when iron rusts (left) is reversed when rust is heated in the absence of oxygen (right).

To understand why these things happen, we need to consider something about probability, because all physical and chemical changes are governed by the laws of probability.

If you buy a lottery ticket, your six numbers have just as much chance of coming up as anyone else's. But it is much more likely that someone else will win rather than you. That is because about 20 million sets of numbers are chosen every week. Your combination is one possibility, but there are another 19 999 999 possibilities, so it is much more likely not to be you.

If you look at the bromine gas in the photo, when you remove the card separating the jars, the gas diffuses through both jars until the jars appear identical. This is simplified in Fig. 20.

Fig. 20   Diffusion

After about an hour, bromine in the lower gas jar has just reached the upper jar. It takes several hours for the gases to reach a uniform distribution.

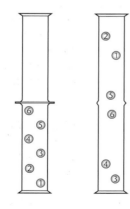

Consider the simple situation shown in Fig. 20, with just six particles. There is only one arrangement with all the particles in the lower jar and none in the upper; and only one arrangement with all the particles in the upper jar and none in the lower. But there are numerous other combinations with particles in both jars.

The total number of possibilities for just six molecules in two jars is:

$$2 \times 2 \times 2 \times 2 \times 2 \times 2 = 2^6 = 64.$$

Therefore, you are very unlikely to see all the particles in the top or bottom jar.

In the photo there are something like 10^{22} molecules, so the number of ways of arranging 10^{22} molecules in two jars would be $(2^{10})^{22}$, a vast number. The chances of all the molecules being in one jar are so remote that all you will ever see is a random arrangement of the molecules between the two jars.

An ordered state, such as all the particles in one jar or the other, has fewer possible arrangements than a disordered state, where they are arranged randomly between both jars, so is less likely to happen. If bricks are tipped out of a lorry, then an ordered state would be a nice, neat brick wall, and a disordered state would be a random pile of bricks. There are few arrangements for a neat brick wall, but millions of arrangements for a pile of bricks, so that's what you will get.

In physical and chemical changes, the processes will always go spontaneously from an ordered state to a disordered state. However, when we are considering physical and chemical processes, we must consider the total order for both the systems: the change taking place, and its surroundings.

The degree of disorder in a system is called its **entropy** (from the Greek word for 'change'). As the disorder increases, so does the entropy value, and an increase in entropy relates to how many ways the particles can be arranged and how many ways the energy can be distributed between the particles. As the temperature increases, the number of energy levels available in the particles increases, so the entropy increases. There will be a sudden change of entropy if there is a change of state (Fig. 21).

Fig. 21   Graph relating entropy variation to temperature and change of state

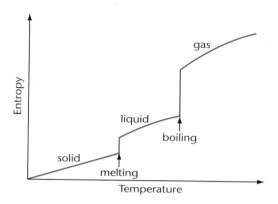

We can examine some of the examples mentioned above and apply the idea of entropy.

If a crystal melts, there is a dramatic change from an ordered state in the crystal to a disordered state in the liquid. If the liquid then changes to a gas, there will be an even larger increase in disorder.

A beaker of hot water has a higher entropy value than a cold one, but if it cools down it warms up the surrounding particles in the room. There are then many more ways of distributing the energy, so if we consider the system and its surroundings, the total entropy will increase and the process will be spontaneous.

If the iron bar is hot at one end, statistics shows that there are fewer arrangements for the distribution of energy than if all the particles in the bar were used, so the energy will distribute itself uniformly along the bar.

When a crystal dissolves in water, it goes from a highly ordered state to a much more disordered state, so the entropy will increase.

Absolute entropies

Since entropy is linked to disorder and decreases with temperature decrease, at 0 K (absolute zero) for a perfectly ordered pure crystal the entropy value should be zero. From this it is possible to calculate absolute standard entropy values $S^\ominus$ and hence calculate standard entropy changes $\Delta S^\ominus$.

You cannot calculate absolute enthalpy values, only relative changes in enthalpy values from one system to another. The units for standard entropy values are $J\ K^{-1}\ mol^{-1}$.

Note that J is used and not kJ as in enthalpy changes. This is because entropy values are quite small when compared to values for enthalpy changes.

Calculating entropy changes $\Delta S^\ominus_{298}$

These are the differences between the total entropies of the products and reactants, and they can be calculated from standard entropy values like the ones in Table 11.

Table 11   Standard entropy values

	$\Delta S^\ominus_{298}$ (J K^{-1} mol^{-1})		
H_2(g)	131	diamond	2.4
O_2(g)	205	graphite	5.7
N_2(g)	192	HCl(g)	187.0
Cl_2(g)	223	HNO_3(l)	156.0
H_2O(g)	189	NO_2(g)	240.0
H_2O(l)	70	NaCl(s)	72.0

For example, consider the example of the reaction between hydrogen and chlorine:

$$H_2(g) + Cl_2(g) \rightarrow 2HCl(g)$$
$$\Delta S^\ominus = \Sigma S^\ominus_{products} - \Sigma S^\ominus_{reactants}\ (\Sigma = \text{sum of})$$
$$\Sigma S^\ominus_{products} = 2 \times 187 = 374$$
$$\Sigma S^\ominus_{reactants} = 131 + 223 = 354$$
$$\Delta S^\ominus = +20\ J\ K^{-1}\ mol^{-1}$$

In the above reaction, all the molecules are gases and individually have quite high entropy values, but there is only a small increase in entropy when they react.

Now consider another example, the decomposition of nitric acid:

$$4HNO_3(l) \rightarrow 4NO_2(g) + O_2(g) + 2H_2O(l)$$
$$\Delta S^\ominus = \Sigma S^\ominus_{products} - \Sigma S^\ominus_{reactants}$$
$$\Sigma S^\ominus_{products} = (4 \times 240) + 205 + (2 \times 70) = 1305$$
$$\Sigma S^\ominus_{reactants} = 4 \times 156 = 624$$
$$\Delta S^\ominus = +681\ J\ K^{-1}$$

For one mole of HNO_3(l) reacting, the entropy change will be +170 J K^{-1} mol^{-1}. There is a considerable increase in disorder in this reaction, and therefore a large entropy change. Nitric acid is a liquid, so has a lower entropy value, and when the reaction occurs gas molecules with high entropy values are formed in the products.

12.5 Free energy change

Look at the values for H_2O in Table 11, and you will see that the entropy for water vapour is $189\ J\ K^{-1}\ mol^{-1}$ and the value for liquid water is $70\ J\ K^{-1}\ mol^{-1}$. If entropy must always increase, can water vapour form liquid water? Yes, it can if we also consider the surroundings. Steam will condense on a cold surface, and when this happens energy transfers from the vapour to the cold surface. This increases the entropy of the surface, so the total entropy of the system and the surroundings increases. The water has decreased in entropy by $119\ J\ K^{-1}\ mol^{-1}$ but the entropy increase in the surroundings is $148\ J\ K^{-1}\ mol^{-1}$ (calculated from the enthalpy transferred, see Fig. 22):

$$\Delta S^\ominus_{total} = \Delta S^\ominus_{system} + \Delta S^\ominus_{surroundings}$$
$$= -119 + 148$$
$$= +29\ J\ K^{-1}\ mol^{-1}$$

So the overall entropy increases.

Fig. 22   Steam condensing on a cold surface

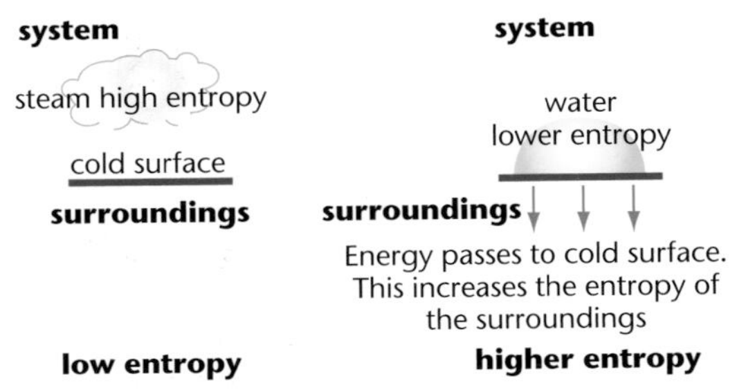

system

steam high entropy

cold surface

surroundings

low entropy

system

water
lower entropy

surroundings

Energy passes to cold surface.
This increases the entropy of
the surroundings

higher entropy

The *total* entropy increase gives rise to the term $-T\Delta S^\ominus_{total}$ and to the standard free energy change $\Delta G^\ominus$, also called the **Gibbs free energy change**, whose units are $kJ\ mol^{-1}$. We can use the changes in enthalpy and entropy values of the system to calculate the total entropy change for the system plus its surroundings, to determine whether the process will be spontaneous.

For a process to be spontaneous, the free energy change must be zero or have a negative value.

Reaction feasibility

We often use the term *feasibility* to mean whether or not a reaction or process can take place spontaneously. Even if a process has a negative $\Delta G^\ominus$ value, the calculation does not give any indication about the rate at which it takes place. For example, diamond is thermodynamically less stable than graphite, so diamond should spontaneously revert to graphite, but the reaction is infinitely slow, so it doesn't happen.

A chemical or physical change is said to be feasible if the value for $\Delta G^\ominus$ is negative or zero, and this feasibility depends upon the relative magnitude of the enthalpy and entropy terms. The standard enthalpy change, $\Delta H^\ominus$, and the standard entropy change, $\Delta S^\ominus$, are linked to $\Delta G^\ominus$ by the expression:

$$\Delta G^\ominus = \Delta H^\ominus - T\Delta S^\ominus$$

The enthalpy change will affect the entropy of the surroundings. If energy is released in a reaction, it will be absorbed by the surroundings, increasing the entropy of the surroundings.

The magnitude of entropy values is much smaller than that for enthalpy values. Enthalpy and free energy are quoted using kJ and entropy using J, so it is important in calculations to use compatible units (usually the entropy term is divided by 1 000 to use kJ throughout).

If the combined enthalpy and entropy terms give a zero or negative value for $\Delta G^\ominus$, the process is feasible. By looking at the equation, you can see that, if $\Delta H^\ominus$ is large and positive, it is not possible under usual conditions to achieve a negative value for $\Delta G^\ominus$, because entropy values are smaller, so these endothermic reactions will not be feasible.

Many reactions release heat. These have negative $\Delta H^{\ominus}$ values, so $\Delta G^{\ominus}$ will probably be negative, and the reaction feasible. Reactions will go spontaneously from a high-energy state to a low-energy state, and when they do this they release energy. You might not expect a reaction to go spontaneously in the opposite direction, i.e. from a low-energy state to a high-energy one. It's a bit like asking water to flow uphill! However, some changes are spontaneous *and* endothermic. The most common of these involve reactions that produce gases, e.g. a hydrogencarbonate with acid, dissolving certain compounds in water, e.g. ammonium nitrate, or changing state, e.g. melting ice. These changes involve a large increase in the disorder of the particles in the system. This increased disorder can enable endothermic reactions to occur.

If $\Delta H^{\ominus}$ is small and positive, the combined $-T\Delta S^{\ominus}$ term can be large enough to compensate, giving a negative $\Delta G^{\ominus}$ value and the process may take place spontaneously. Increasing the temperature will increase the magnitude of this combined term, so often these processes are temperature dependent. However, remember that temperature also affects rate, and this is not the same as feasibility.

We shall now look at, and discuss, a number of examples.

Example 1: Feasibility of reaction $H_2(g) + \frac{1}{2}O_2(g) \rightarrow H_2O(g)$ at 298 K (25°C)

For the reaction:

$$H_2(g) + \tfrac{1}{2}O_2(g) \rightarrow H_2O(g)$$

we have:

$$H_2(g) + O_2(g) \rightarrow H_2O(g)$$
$$\Delta H^{\ominus} = -242 \text{ kJ mol}^{-1}$$
$$\Delta S^{\ominus} = -147 \text{ J K}^{-1} \text{ mol}^{-1}$$
$$T = 298 \text{ K}$$

$$\Delta G^{\ominus} = \Delta H^{\ominus} - T\Delta S^{\ominus}$$

$$= -242 - 298 \left(\frac{-147}{1\,000} \right)$$

$$= -242 + 44$$
$$= -198 \text{ kJ mol}^{-1}$$

There is a decrease in entropy in changing from 1.5 moles of gas molecules to 1.0 moles, but this is quite a small term compared to the negative enthalpy term $\Delta H^{\ominus}$, so, overall, $\Delta G^{\ominus}$ is negative. Even though entropy is decreasing, the reaction is still feasible due to the large negative enthalpy change.

If gases are evolved from solids during a reaction, there will be a considerable increase in entropy, as shown by the following example.

Example 2: Feasibility of neutralising carbonate that evolves carbon dioxide

We need to consider both the overall enthalpy change and the overall entropy change for this reaction:

$$H^+(aq) + HCO_3^-(aq) \rightarrow H_2O(l) + CO_2(g)$$

The enthalpy changes for the reaction are:

$$\Delta H^{\ominus} = \Delta H^{\ominus}_{products} - \Delta H^{\ominus}_{reactants}$$
$$\Delta H^{\ominus}_{products} = -679$$
$$\Delta H^{\ominus}_{reactants} = -692$$
$$\Delta H^{\ominus} = +13 \text{ kJ mol}^{-1}$$

Overall, this results in a positive enthalpy change, so the reaction is endothermic. The system is moving from lower to higher energy, and it takes in heat from the surroundings, which will therefore decrease in entropy.

The entropy changes for the reaction are:

$$\Delta S^{\ominus} = \Delta S^{\ominus}_{products} - \Delta S^{\ominus}_{reactants}$$
$$\Delta S^{\ominus}_{products} = 283 \text{ J K}^{-1} \text{ mol}^{-1}$$
$$\Delta S_{reactants} = 91 \text{ J K}^{-1} \text{ mol}^{-1}$$
$$\Delta S^{\ominus} = +192 \text{ J K}^{-1} \text{ mol}^{-1}$$

Thus overall the entropy of the system (the reaction) is increasing. It is a large entropy increase because a gas is being produced during the reaction.

The feasibility of the reaction is determined by combining these two terms, i.e. finding the Gibbs free energy. The free energy change can be calculated from these values. We have:

$$\Delta H^{\ominus} = +13 \text{ kJ mol}^{-1}$$
$$\Delta S^{\ominus} = +192 \text{ J K}^{-1} \text{ mol}^{-1}$$
$$T = 298 \text{ K}$$

$$\Delta G^{\ominus} = \Delta H^{\ominus} - T\Delta S^{\ominus}$$

$$= +13 - 298 \left(\frac{192}{1\,000} \right)$$

$$= +13 - 57$$
$$= -44 \text{ kJ mol}^{-1}$$

(Note that the entropy term was divided by 1 000 to give units in kJ not J.) This calculation gives a negative value for $\Delta G^{\ominus}$. At room temperature the combined $-T\Delta S^{\ominus}$ term of -57 kJ K^{-1} mol^{-1} is sufficient to enable the endothermic reaction of neutralising hydrogencarbonates to take place.

Whether a compound dissolves or not depends largely upon the difference between the lattice enthalpy and the sum of the hydration enthalpies. Some possible changes are shown in Fig. 23.

When a crystal dissolves, it changes from an ordered state and forms a solution of randomly arranged ions (i.e. less ordered arrangement), so the overall entropy increases (Fig. 24). Increasing ΔS will make the $-T\Delta S$ term more significant and it will be sufficient to produce a negative ΔG value.

Fig. 23   Enthalpy changes in dissolving

(a) sum of hydration enthalpies > lattice enthalpy
In this case, a lot more energy is released during hydration than is needed to break down the lattice; the compound dissolves and the reaction is exothermic.

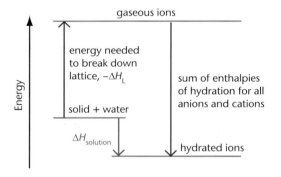

(b) sum of hydration enthalpies < lattice enthalpy
$\Delta H_{solution}$ is large and positive (endothermic) so the reaction does not proceed spontaneously.

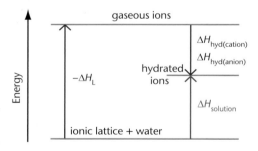

(c) small endothermic enthalpy of solution
However, when $\Delta H_{solution}$ is only slightly positive it is possible for the salt to dissolve even though the process is endothermic.

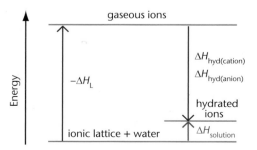

Example 3: Calculating entropy change on dissolving ammonium chloride

Ammonium chloride is a salt with a positive enthalpy of solution (i.e. endothermic), but when it dissolves there is an increase in entropy. The ΔH value for dissolving ammonium chloride is quite low (+14.4 kJ mol^{-1}), so the increase in disorder produced by the regular crystal dissolving to form freely moving hydrated ions enables the change to happen spontaneously – a negative value for ΔG (Table 12).

So from Table 12, we can write down the entropy values for the reaction as:

$$NH_4Cl(s) \rightarrow NH_4^+(aq) + Cl^-(aq)$$
$$94.6 \quad \rightarrow \quad 113.4 \quad + \quad 56.5$$

$$\text{Increase in entropy} = 113.4 + 56.5 - 94.6$$
$$= +75.3 \text{ J}$$

At 298 K the combined entropy term is:

$$-T\Delta S^\ominus = -298 \times 75.3 = -22.4 \text{ kJ}$$
$$\Delta G^\ominus = \Delta H^\ominus - T\Delta S^\ominus$$
$$= 14.4 - 22.4$$
$$= -8.0 \text{ kJ mol}^{-1}$$

$\Delta G^\ominus$ is negative, so at 298 K ammonium chloride will dissolve spontaneously in water.

Table 12   Entropy values for dissolving ammonium chloride

Species	S (J K^{-1} mol^{-1})
NH$_4$Cl(s)	94.6
NH$_4^+$(aq)	113.4
Cl$^-$(aq)	56.5

Temperature has a significant effect on whether the process is spontaneous. At a given temperature T, the $-T\Delta S^\ominus$ term may not be large enough to give a negative value for $\Delta G^\ominus$. In some cases it is possible to raise T to the point where the reaction does become spontaneous. However, you should be aware that, even when a reaction is said to be feasible, it does not necessarily mean that a reaction will proceed. The activation energy may still be very high and therefore the rate very low.

Fig. 24 Dissolving a salt crystal

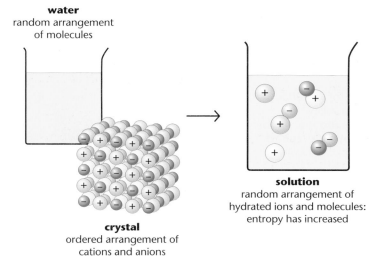

water
random arrangement
of molecules

crystal
ordered arrangement of
cations and anions

solution
random arrangement of
hydrated ions and molecules:
entropy has increased

Example 4: Calculating ΔH, ΔS and ΔG for the thermal decomposition of calcite

Study the data in Table 13, for the thermal decomposition of calcite:

$$CaCO_3(s) \rightarrow CO_2(g) + CaO(s)$$

a Calculate the following:

i the standard enthalpy change
ii the standard entropy change
iii the Gibb's free energy change at 298 K.

b Above what temperature might the reaction proceed spontaneously?

Table 13 Entropy and enthalpy data for the thermal decomposition of calcite

	S (J K^{-1} mol^{-1})	$\Delta H_f^{\ominus}$ (kJ mol^{-1})
CaCO$_3$(s)	92.9	−1 206.9
CO$_2$(g)	213.6	−393.5
CaO(s)	39.7	−635.1

a **i** From the data listed in the table, for the reaction we have:

enthalpy change = −635.1 − 393.5 − (−1 206.9)
= −1 028.6 − (−1 206.9)
= +178.3 kJ mol^{-1}

(Remember, the units for entropy include J (not kJ), i.e. J K^{-1} mol^{-1}.)

ii Then from the data listed we find the entropy change for the reaction:

$$CaCO_3(s) \rightarrow CaO(s) + CO_2(g)$$
$$92.9 \rightarrow 39.7 + 213.6$$

entropy increase = 39.7 + 213.6 − 92.9
= 160.4 J mol^{-1}
= 0.160 4 kJ mol^{-1}

iii At 298 K, the combined entropy term is:

$$-T\Delta S^{\ominus} = -298 \times 0.160\,4$$
$$= -47.8 \text{ kJ mol}^{-1}$$

and so, at 298 K:

$$\Delta G^{\ominus} = \Delta H^{\ominus} - T\Delta S^{\ominus}$$
$$= 178.3 - 47.8$$
$$= +130.5 \text{ kJ mol}^{-1}$$

So, at 298 K, $\Delta G^{\ominus} = \Delta H^{\ominus} - T\Delta S^{\ominus}$ is positive. The reaction is not thermodynamically feasible at this temperature.

b To find the temperature at which feasibility occurs, we note that, when $\Delta G^{\ominus} = 0$, the reaction becomes just feasible. So:
$$\Delta G^{\ominus} = \Delta H^{\ominus} - T\Delta S^{\ominus}$$
$$T\Delta S^{\ominus} = \Delta H^{\ominus} \text{ if } \Delta G^{\ominus} = 0$$
$$T = \Delta H^{\ominus} / \Delta S^{\ominus}$$
$$= 178.3/0.160\,4$$
$$= 1\,111 \text{ K}$$

This means that the calcite must be heated to at least 1 111 K. Note that this is only the temperature at which the reaction becomes feasible, and it gives no indication of the rate.

Entropy and changing state

Ice melts at 0 °C and water freezes at 0 °C, so this is an example of a system at equilibrium. Under these conditions, $\Delta H^{\ominus} = T\Delta S^{\ominus}$ and $\Delta G^{\ominus} = 0$. If the temperature remains constant and a small amount of heat is put into the system, the energy of the system increases (and $\Delta G^{\ominus}$ would be increasingly positive). This can be compensated for by increasing the entropy and therefore the combined $-T\Delta S^{\ominus}$ term. Thus $\Delta G^{\ominus}$ is still zero. If energy goes into the system, the entropy must increase to keep $\Delta G^{\ominus} = 0$. The system can do this by changing from a solid to a liquid, i.e. if energy is put in, the ice melts. Heat must be supplied to break down the order of the crystals, i.e. it is an endothermic process.

6 Calculate the temperature at which the thermal decomposition of sodium hydrogencarbonate becomes feasible.

$$2NaHCO_3(s) \rightarrow Na_2CO_3(s) + H_2O(g) + CO_2(g)$$

The stoichiometry for the equation does not affect the feasibility temperature, since halving the number of moles will affect both $\Delta H^\ominus$ and $\Delta S^\ominus$ equally (Table 14).

Table 14   Entropy and enthalpy data for the thermal decomposition of sodium hydrogencarbonate

	$\Delta S^\ominus$ (J K^{-1} mol^{-1})	$\Delta H_f^\ominus$ (kJ mol^{-1})
NaHCO$_3$(s)	102	−951
Na$_2$CO$_3$(s)	135	−1 131
CO$_2$(g)	214	−394
H$_2$O(g)	189	−242

The value for the enthalpy change for ice melting is 6.01 kJ mol^{-1}, and the entropy increase when ice melts is 22 J K^{-1} mol^{-1}. That is, at 0 °C, the enthalpy term is $\Delta H^\ominus = +6.01$ kJ mol^{-1}, and the entropy change on changing state is $-T\Delta S^\ominus = -273 \times 22.0 = -6.01$ kJ mol^{-1}. So we can see that we get:

$$\Delta G^\ominus = \Delta H^\ominus - T\Delta S^\ominus$$
$$= 0 \text{ kJ mol}^{-1}$$

At 0°C, the arrangement of water molecules is more random. This increases the value of the combined entropy term $T\Delta S$, so that it is equal to or greater than 6.01 kJ mol^{-1}. This gives a zero $\Delta G^\ominus$ value and the ice melts. The endothermic process of ice melting means that there is a cooling effect on the surroundings. Each 18 g (1 mole) of ice at 0 °C takes in 6.01 kJ of energy when it melts.

If energy is removed from water at 0 °C, ice forms, the entropy term decreases (ice is more

ordered than water) and $-T\Delta S^\ominus$ becomes less negative. However, since ΔH is now exothermic, and therefore negative when ice melts, ΔG will be zero. The water is able to freeze to a more ordered structure, with a lower entropy.

Example 5: Calculating the entropy change when water boils

Calculate the entropy change when water boils. The molar enthalpy of vaporisation of water is +44.0 kJ mol^{-1}.

The reaction can be written as:

$$H_2O(l) \rightarrow H_2O(g)$$

At equilibrium:

$$\Delta H^\ominus = T\Delta S^\ominus \text{ and } \Delta G^\ominus = 0$$

So we have:

So $\Delta S_{vap}^\ominus = \Delta H_{vap}^\ominus / T_{vap}$
$\Delta H_{vap}^\ominus = +44$ kJ mol^{-1}
$T_{vap} = 373$ K
$= 44 \times 10^3/373$
$= 118$ J K^{-1} mol^{-1}

The entropy value for changing from liquid to vapour is 118 J K^{-1} mol^{-1}, which is much greater than that for changing from solid to liquid, 22 J K^{-1} mol^{-1}. Both melting and boiling are endothermic, but the enthalpy change for vaporisation is also much greater.

- Above or at 0 °C, $\Delta H^\ominus = +6.01$ kJ mol^{-1}, but $-T\Delta S^\ominus$ is greater than or equal to 6.01 kJ mol^{-1}, so $\Delta G^\ominus$ is zero/negative; ice → water.

- Below or at 0 °C, $\Delta H^\ominus = -6.01$ kJ mol^{-1}, but $-T\Delta S^\ominus$ decreases by less than or equal to $+6.01$ kJ mol^{-1}, so $\Delta G^\ominus$ is zero/negative; water → ice.

- The feasibility of a process is determined by the standard Gibbs free energy, $\Delta G^\ominus = \Delta H^\ominus - T\Delta S^\ominus$.

- If $\Delta G^\ominus$ is negative at temperature T, the process will be spontaneous.

- A system is at equilibrium when $\Delta G^\ominus$ is zero.

1 Consider the incomplete Born–Haber cycle and the table of data below.

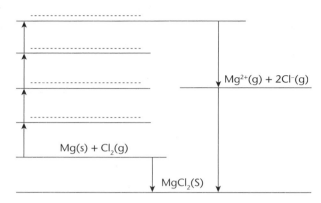

$Mg^{2+}(g) + 2Cl^-(g)$

$Mg(s) + Cl_2(g)$

$MgCl_2(S)$

Name of standard enthalpy change	Substance to which enthalpy change refers	Value of enthalpy change (kJ mol⁻¹)
Enthalpy of atomisation	chlorine	+121
Enthalpy of atomisation	magnesium	+150
Enthalpy of formation	magnesium chloride	−642
First ionisation enthalpy	magnesium	+736
Electron affinity	chlorine	−364
Enthalpy of lattice formation	magnesium chloride	−2493

a Complete the Born-Haber cycle above by writing the appropriate chemical formulae, with state symbols, on the dotted lines. (4)

b Use the cycle and the values given in the table to calculate the second ionisation enthalpy of magnesium. (3)

c The standard enthalpies of hydration of the Mg^{2+} and the Cl^- ions are −1 920 kJ mol⁻¹ and −364 kJ mol⁻¹, respectively. Use this information and data from the table in part **a** to calculate the enthalpy of solution of magnesium chloride. (3)

d The standard enthalpy of solution of ammonium chloride, $NH_4^+Cl^-$, is +15 kJ mol⁻¹.

i Explain why ammonium chloride dissolves spontaneously in water even though this process is endothermic. (2)

ii A 2.0 g sample of ammonium chloride is dissolved in 50 g of water. Both substances are initially at 20 °C. Calculate the temperature change and the final temperature of the solution. Assume that the specific heat capacity of the solution is 4.2 JK⁻¹ g⁻¹. (5)

Total 17

AQA, June 2007, Unit 5, Question 1

2 Data for the following reaction, which represents the reduction of aluminium oxide by carbon, are shown in the table below.

$Al_2O_3(s) + 3C(s) \rightarrow + 2Al(s) + 3CO(g)$

Substance	$\Delta H_f^{\ominus}$ (kJ mol⁻¹)	$S^{\ominus}$ (J K⁻¹ mol⁻¹)
$Al_2O_3(s)$	−1 669	51
C(s)	0	6
Al(s)	0	28
CO(g)	−111	198

a Calculate the values of $\Delta H^{\ominus}$, $\Delta S^{\ominus}$ and $\Delta G^{\ominus}$ for the above reaction at 298 K and suggest why this reaction is not feasible at 298 K. (8)

b Calculate the temperature above which this reaction is feasible.
(If you have been unable to calculate values for $\Delta H^{\ominus}$ and $\Delta S^{\ominus}$ in part **a** you may assume that they are +906 kJ mol⁻¹ and +394 JK⁻¹ mol⁻¹ respectively. These are not the correct values.) (2)

c The reaction between aluminium oxide and carbon to form aluminium and carbon monoxide does not occur to a significant extent until the temperature reaches a value about 1 000 K above that of the answer to part **b**. Give one reason for this. (1)

d State the method used to reduce aluminium oxide on an industrial scale. Give the essential conditions for this industrial process. (3)

Total 14

AQA, June 2007, Unit 5, Question 2

3 The sketch graph below shows how the entropy of a sample of water varies with temperature.

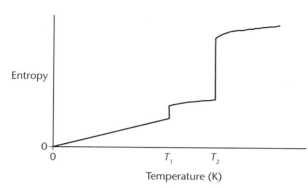

a Suggest why the entropy of water is zero at 0 K.   (1)
b What change of state occurs at temperature T_1?   (1)
c Explain why the entropy change, ΔS, at temperature T_2 is much larger than that at temperature T_1.   (2)
d It requires 3.49 kJ of heat energy to convert 1.53 g of liquid water into steam at 373 K and 100 kPa.
　i Use these data to calculate the enthalpy change, ΔH, when 1.00 mol of liquid water forms 1.00 mol of steam at 373 K and 100 kPa.
　ii Write an expression showing the relationship between free-energy change, ΔG, enthalpy change, ΔH, and entropy change, ΔS.
　iii For the conversion of liquid water into steam at 373 K and 100 kPa, $\Delta G = 0$ kJ mol^{-1}
　Calculate the value of ΔS for the conversion of one mole of water into steam under these conditions. State the units.
　(If you have been unable to complete part **d i** you should assume that $\Delta H = 45.0$ kJ mol^{-1}. This is not the correct answer.)   (6)

Total 10

AQA, June 2006, Unit 5, Question 2

4 A Born–Haber cycle for the formation of calcium sulfide is shown below. The cycle includes enthalpy changes for all Steps except Step **F**. (The cycle is not drawn to scale.)

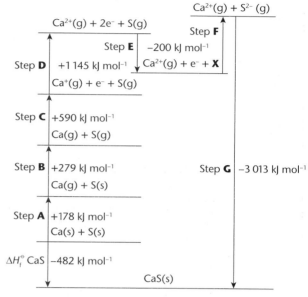

a Give the full electronic arrangement of the ion S^{2-} (1)
b Identify the species **X** formed in Step **E**.   (1)
c Suggest why Step **F** is an endothermic process.   (2)
d Name the enthalpy change for each of the following steps.
　i Step **B**
　ii Step **D**
　iii Step **F**   (3)
e Explain why the enthalpy change for Step **D** is larger than that for Step **C**.   (2)
f Use the data shown in the cycle to calculate a value for the enthalpy change for Step **F**.   (2)

Total 11

AQA, January 2005, Unit 5, Question 2

Limiting sports injury damage

Sports injuries such as muscle strains need to be cooled down to help prevent swelling. In most circumstances, a simple ice pack is enough to do the job, but storing ice in a 'first response box' – a large, portable first aid kit – would be impracticable. What sports coaches and physiotherapists need is a pack that can be stored at room temperature and will cool down when required.

Central Scientific have been asked to design a portable, easily used pack that cools 'on demand'. Dissolving a stable compound seemed the most promising method.

When ionic compounds are formed, a series of endothermic and exothermic processes takes place. These processes involved in making salts can be summarised in a Born–Haber cycle and can be used to calculate the relative stabilities of compounds.

> **A1** From the values in Table 15, construct a Born–Haber cycle for KCl(s) to calculate the standard molar enthalpy of formation. Define all the terms you use, and explain why each one is either exothermic or endothermic.
>
> **A2** Construct a Born–Haber cycle for $KCl_2(s)$ to show why this compound will not be found naturally. Use the data in Table 16.

Table 15   Enthalpy values (kJ mol⁻¹) for KCl(s)

Atomis'n of K	1st ionis'n of K	Atomis'n of Cl	Electron affinity of Cl	Lattice enthalpy
89	+419	122	−348	−711

Whether a compound dissolves or not depends largely upon the difference between the lattice enthalpy and the sum of the hydration enthalpies. Some possible changes were shown in Fig. 23.

In an endothermic reaction, heat is drawn from the surroundings. If a cooling pack is applied to an injury, it will draw heat from that part of the body, so cooling it down. Another compound that would produce a cooling effect

Table 16 Enthalpy values (kJ mol⁻¹) for KCl₂(s)

Atomis'n of K	1st ionis'n of K	2nd ionis'n of K	Atomis'n of Cl	Electron affinity of Cl	Lattice enthalpy est.
89	+419	3 051	122	−348	−2 350

on mixing with water is ammonium nitrate. The researchers' data book gave the enthalpy of solution value for ammonium nitrate as +26.5 kJ mol⁻¹. This more endothermic reaction would produce a greater cooling effect than ammonium chloride.

The development team consulted with medical staff to find out what temperature the pack had to cool down to. They recommended a temperature of 1.5 °C to be maintained for at least 15 minutes. Central Scientific planned to make a pack of approximately 200 g, and this needed to cool down from 18 °C to 1.5 °C. The enthalpy change will be given by the expression:

$$H = mc\Delta T$$

where m = the mass of the pack, c = the specific heat capacity and ΔT = the temperature change.

A3 Dissolving ammonium chloride in water will produce a cooling effect. Draw an enthalpy cycle (see Fig. 12) for the hydration of NH_4Cl. Use the data below to calculate the enthalpy of solution, $\Delta H_{solution}$:

$$\Delta H_L = -676 \text{ kJ mol}^{-1}$$
$$\Delta H_{hyd(cation)} + \Delta H_{hyd(anion)} = -664 \text{ kJ mol}^{-1}$$

A4 Exothermic processes are favoured energetically, yet the above process is endothermic. Explain the idea of entropy and use it to explain why an endothermic process, such as dissolving ammonium chloride, can happen spontaneously.

A5 For a 200 g cooling pack, assuming a specific heat capacity of 4.2 J g⁻¹ K⁻¹, calculate the enthalpy change taking place.

A6 Calculate the number of moles of ammonium nitrate that will produce this amount of cooling.

13 Periodicity

Linus Pauling was a brilliant theoretical and investigative chemist. His contributions to science are held in very high esteem by many. The magazine *New Scientist* included Pauling (and Albert Einstein – the only two scientists from the 20th century) in a list of the 20 greatest scientists of all time. Pauling combined his experimental work with a high level of theoretical interpretation. However, his real talent was in his ability to translate these into simple concepts that are of use to a wide range of scientists. The beginning of modern quantum chemistry was indicative of Pauling's work on chemical bonding. In fact, many of his contributions form part of standard chemistry textbooks, for example, *hybridisation* and *electronegativity*. No other modern-day chemist has worked on such a wide range of research topics as Linus Pauling. He studied crystals by X-ray diffraction, identified the alpha-helix in many proteins, and worked on the structure of metals, the theory of magnetism, Van der Waals forces and human illnesses.

Linus Pauling gained the Nobel Prize in chemistry for his research into the nature of the chemical bond and its application to elucidating the structure of complex substances. He was also later awarded the Nobel Peace Prize, making him one of only a few people to have won two Nobel Prizes.

hsw

how science works

Linus Pauling

Some of Pauling's contributions to chemistry

In writing his book *The Nature of the Chemical Bond*, Pauling developed the concept of hybridisation, and from this, improved our understanding of the structure of benzene. Kekulé had considered benzene as a rapid interconversion of two isomers with alternate single and double bonds. Pauling used quantum mechanics to describe benzene as an intermediate structure of hybridised bonds and not as a molecule containing separate single and double bonds. The term **resonance** was later applied to this phenomenon.

Pauling will also be remembered for his scale of electronegativity, in which he assigned an electronegativity value to each atom, based on the angles and the positions of the atoms in molecules (determined by X-ray analysis), other experimental data and bond energy calculations. The order of the elements in the Pauling scale is exactly reflected in the Periodic Table. In recognition of all his contributions, Pauling was awarded the Nobel Prize in chemistry.

1 The development of scientific theories and ideas is often made because scientists question each other's work. How does the determination of the structure of benzene illustrate this?

Pauling on biological molecules

Pauling suggested a helical structure for deoxyribonucleic acid (DNA), but he made several basic mistakes when building his model. James Watson and Francis Crick, working on the structure of DNA at the Cavendish Laboratory in Cambridge, learned that Pauling was also trying to devise the structure of DNA. In their work, Watson and Crick used some unpublished X-ray diffraction data from Maurice Wilkins and Rosalind Franklin at King's

College, London. This led them to propose the, now accepted, double helix structure for DNA in early 1953. If Pauling had been able to access these superior data and X-ray photographs, he might have developed a correct structure. We will never know. He had planned to come to England and might have seen the data, but his passport was withheld by the authorities on suspicion of Communist sympathies. (He had declined an offer to be part of the Oppenheimer Project to develop atomic weapons.) He was so prominent in campaigning for nuclear disarmament that he was awarded the Nobel Peace Prize in 1962.

Pauling's discovery of sickle-cell anaemia as a 'molecular disease' led the way towards the study of genetic mutations as a cause of disease. This was the first documented example of a molecular disorder. He proposed that sufferers from sickle-cell anaemia produce more than one type of haemoglobin, and the sickle cells do not function properly under reduced oxygen conditions. This discovery opened up new fields in medicine, biochemistry and genetics.

Three quotes attributed to Linus Pauling, and one directed to him, are listed below. Read these, and then answer the question that follows.

Said by Pauling:

- 'A couple of days after my talk, there was a man in my office from the FBI saying, "Who told you how much plutonium there is in an atomic bomb?" And I said, "Nobody told me. I figured it out." '
- 'Your elder, no matter whether he has grey hair or lost his hair, no matter whether he is a Nobel Laureate, may be wrong … So you must always be sceptical – always think for yourself.'
- 'Well, you just have lots of ideas and throw away the bad ones. You aren't going to have good ideas, unless you have lots of ideas and some principle of selection.'

Said to Pauling:

- 'You should recognise, that there is in almost every investigation a lack of complete rigour. You should understand just how reliable the arguments are that you are presenting.'

2 Choose an illustration, from any of the work of Pauling, to show how scientific knowledge can take a leap forward.

3 Choose two quotes from above and explain their importance in scientific thought.

13.1 Electronegativity and periodicity

Linus Pauling defined **electronegativity** as the tendency of an atom involved in a bond to attract the bonding electrons to itself. So, when two different atoms are bonded together, the one with the higher electronegativity takes a larger share of the electron density.

Electronegativity cannot be directly measured and must be calculated from other atomic or molecular properties. There are several methods of calculation, but the most commonly used method is that originally proposed by Pauling.

Pauling calculated the electronegativities from bond dissociation energies, and assigned an electronegativity value (which he originally called 'charge continuity value') to every element. He assigned the value 4.0 to fluorine,

the most electronegative element of all. As only *differences* in electronegativity are defined, it is necessary to choose an arbitrary reference point in order to construct a scale. Hydrogen was chosen as the reference, as it forms covalent bonds with a large variety of elements. Pauling assigned the electronegativity of hydrogen as 2.1, later revised to 2.20.

In 1932, when Pauling first proposed electronegativities, he quoted values to one decimal place, for example, fluorine was F = 4.0. Now, more precise data are available, so we have F = 3.98. A. L. Allred updated Pauling's original values in 1961 to take account of the greater availability of thermodynamic data. It is these 'revised Pauling' values of electronegativity that are most usually used today.

> **4** How did the work of Allred contribute to scientific development?

There are good correlations between electronegativity values and chemical shifts in NMR spectroscopy. The NMR measurements indicate the s-electron density at the nucleus. So measurements indicate that these electronegativity values describe the ability of an atom in a molecule to attract electrons to itself.

The match-up of electronegativity to the Periodic Table can be seen in Table 1, which contains 'revised Pauling' electronegativity values.

The *larger the difference* between the electronegativities of the two bonded atoms, the *more polar* the bond. When one element from the left of the Periodic Table combines with one from the right, an **ionic bond** will be formed. When two elements from the right-hand side of the Periodic Table combine they will form a **covalent bond**. So, in NaCl, an ionic compound, there is a large difference in electronegativity between the two elements in the compound, and therefore a very unequal share of the electrons within the bond. The pull on the electrons is towards the chlorine, which forms Cl^-. The Na forms Na^+ and they are held together by an ionic bond.

Pauling said that other compounds will have bonding types intermediate between these. A compound such as aluminium chloride will have some ionic character and some covalent character. It will have polar bonds. These are indicated by an arrow with the head pointing towards the more negative end of the molecule and a tail to the more positive end, e.g. Al↦Cl. Sometimes polarity is written as $\delta+$ and $\delta-$ (see Chapter 12, Fig. 8).

Table 1   Electronegativities of selected elements

2.20 H																
0.98 Li	1.57 Be											2.04 B	2.55 C	3.04 N	3.44 O	3.98 F
0.93 Na	1.31 Mg											1.61 Al	1.90 Si	2.19 P	2.58 S	3.16 Cl
0.82 K	1.00 Ca	1.36 Sc	1.54 Ti	1.63 V	1.66 Cr	1.55 Mn	1.83 Fe	1.88 Co	1.91 Ni	1.90 Cu	1.65 Zn	1.81 Ga	2.01 Ge	2.18 As	2.55 Se	2.96 Br

13.2 Properties and periodicity

The term **periodicity** relates to how the properties of elements and compounds change in patterns across a **period** and down a **group** in the Periodic Table, and it uses Pauling's ideas to help understand them. Various sections in *AS Chemistry* looked at the changes in chemical properties going down different groups. Section 4.2 in *AS Chemistry* looked at the changes in some physical and chemical properties on going across Period 3. In this chapter we will look more closely at how the properties change for the elements across Period 3 from sodium to chlorine.

For the properties of the elements in the Periodic Table, we discuss trends from the left-hand side (Group 1) to the right-hand side (Group 7). There are only small changes at the atomic level (micro-scale), but these can produce quite startling differences in the chemical and physical properties of compounds or elements (macro-scale).

Look at Table 2 and you will see definite patterns. It is very useful to be familiar with these trends in behaviour, because they will allow you to make sound predictions about how particular elements and compounds will react. The reactions of elements depend upon their electronic structure. So if the electronic structure of their constituents is changing in a pattern, the properties will also change in a pattern. The reactivities and properties of elements depend upon a combination of things: nuclear charge, size of the atom,

Table 2   Changes in atomic properties across Period 3

Group number	1	2	3	4	5	6	7	8/0
Elements in Period 3	Na	Mg	Al	Si	P	S	Cl	Ar
Nuclear charge	11	12	13	14	15	16	17	18
[Ne] electron configuration	[Ne] $3s^1$	[Ne] $3s^2$	[Ne] $3s^23p^1$	[Ne] $3s^23p^2$	[Ne] $3s^23p^3$	[Ne] $3s^23p^4$	[Ne] $3s^23p^5$	[Ne] $3s^23p^6$
Atomic radius (nm)	0.191	0.160	0.143	0.118	0.110	0.102	0.099	0.095
First ionisation energy (kJ mol^{-1})	496	738	578	789	1 012	1 000	1 251	1 521
Electronegativity (revised Pauling values)	0.93	1.31	1.61	1.90	2.19	2.58	3.16	–
Formulae of oxides	Na_2O Na_2O_2	MgO	Al_2O_3	SiO_2	P_4O P_4O_{10}	SO_2 SO_3	Cl_2O Cl_2O_2	
Formulae of chlorides	NaCl	$MgCl_2$	Al_2Cl_6	$SiCl_4$	PCl_3 PCl_5	SCl_2	Cl_2	–

number of outer electrons and number of shielding electrons (Fig. 1). For details on the electronic structure of atoms, see pages 19–23 in *AS Chemistry*. These help us to explain and predict the properties of many compounds.

Linus Pauling used electronegativity to explain trends in the Periodic Table (for electronegativity, see pages 59–60 in *AS Chemistry*). You can see from Table 2 that electronegativity increases across the period from left to right, which means that elements to the right will attract the electrons in a bond more strongly.

In a compound, the ionic or covalent character depends upon the electronegativity difference between the two elements. If there is a large difference in electronegativity, the ions formed stay as separate ions. If the electronegativity difference is smaller, distortion of the charge cloud of the negative ion occurs, and some covalent character in the ionic bond results. This effect is called **polarisation** (Fig. 2). Bond polarity is discussed in Section 3.4 in *As Chemistry*.

The ability of an atom to attract electrons will be the same in different compounds, but the overall polarisation of the covalent bond

Fig. 1   Factors affecting electronegativity

cation   anion

Large difference in electronegativity: there is no polarisation of the anion by the cation, so there is no covalent character.

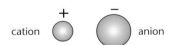

Smaller difference in electronegativity: the cation is polarising the anion, so there is some covalent character in the ionic bond.
The polarising effect is greater in an ion with a higher positive charge and smaller ionic size:

+   2+   3+

increasing polarising power

Fig. 2   Polarisation

The electronegativity value depends on:
- nuclear charge
- size of atom
- shielding electrons.

These factors influence the chemical properties of an element.

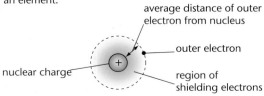

average distance of outer electron from nucleus

outer electron

nuclear charge

region of shielding electrons

will differ, depending on the two elements forming the bond. We now look at three examples:

- **Na–Cl**. Na would have a relatively weak attraction for electrons in a covalent bond, and Cl would have a strong attraction. So the electron charge will be found almost completely on the Cl. This is written as Na^+Cl^-. The bond is ionic.
- **Si–Cl**. Si has a much stronger attraction for the electrons in a covalent bond than Na has, so the electrons in the Si–Cl bond are shared. However, the Cl has a higher electronegativity than Si, so there is some polarity in the bond, resulting in partial ionic character. We describe molecules like these as having polar bonds or possessing dipoles. This is written as $Si^{\delta+}$–$Cl^{\delta-}$ or $Si \mapsto Cl$.
- **Cl–Cl**. Two Cl atoms will have identical electronegativities, so there will be no polarity in the bond. So Cl–Cl forms a completely non-polar (100% covalent) bond.

5 The Cl–Cl bond is completely covalent. Can you have a completely ionic bond? Explain your reasoning.

Fig. 3 shows the changes in the oxidation states of oxides and chlorides as you go across Period 3.

Sodium and magnesium lose all their outer electrons during ionic (electrovalent) bonding, and the oxidation number equals the number of

Fig. 3 Changes in oxidation states in oxides and chlorides

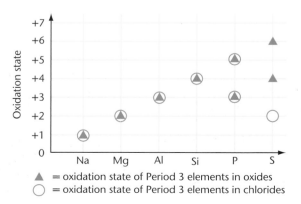

▲ = oxidation state of Period 3 elements in oxides
◯ = oxidation state of Period 3 elements in chlorides

6 Deduce the oxidation state of Cl in PCl_5 and in Cl_2O_7.

7

a Why do atomic radii decrease across Period 3?

b Explain why the melting point of magnesium is greater than that of sodium.

c Explain why the first ionisation energy of sodium is the lowest in Period 3.

electrons lost. Aluminium forms both ionic and covalent compounds in oxidation state +3. The elements silicon, phosphorus and sulfur form mainly covalent compounds, but they can still be considered as having positive oxidation states. Chlorine forms ionic and covalent compounds in oxidation states from −1 to +7.

The difference in the type of bonding that occurs can be explained by electronegativity differences. Ionic bonding occurs between elements with a large difference in electronegativity, and covalent bonding between elements with a small difference in electronegativity. Between these two extremes, the compounds formed have both ionic and covalent characteristics. The formulae of compounds formed often relate to the number of electrons needed to empty or complete the outer electron shells. Other oxidation states can be related to electrons in s, p and d orbitals and follow more complex rules.

As has been shown in Table 1, the ionisation energies of the elements generally increase across Period 3 (Fig. 4). Sodium has the lowest ionisation energy of any of the elements in Period 3, so its attraction for its outer electrons is the weakest. The energy needed to move the electron to a higher level or even remove it completely is the lowest.

In any period, the elements with the lowest ionisation energies are metals and show properties that reflect the weaker forces of attraction for electrons. In a metal, the outer electrons are delocalised, forming a 'sea' of mobile electrons (Fig. 5). This structure gives metals their typical properties of high electrical and thermal conductivities. The mobility of the

Fig. 4 First ionisation energy for Period 3 elements

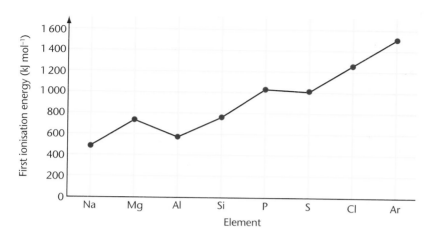

Fig. 5 A model of metallic bonding

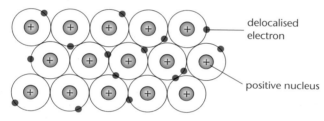

The outer electrons are delocalised. The electrons are free to drift from one metal ion to another through the outer energy levels.

The greater the number of delocalised electrons, the stronger the lattice.

electrons means that they can easily transfer energy throughout the structure. Also, the attraction between the electrons and the central ions holds the structure together. The strength of this attraction will depend upon the size of the ion, ionic charge and number of mobile electrons. A greater attraction will produce a stronger metallic bond, which results in properties such as a higher melting point and greater metal hardness.

The low first ionisation energy of the sodium atom means that it has weaker forces holding the outer electron in place than other atoms in the same period. As a result, a relatively small amount of energy is needed to remove the outer electron completely. For sodium, the relatively lower nuclear charge means that the electron shells are spaced out more and the atomic radius is much larger for sodium (0.191 nm) compared with magnesium (0.160 nm) and aluminium (0.143 nm). This means that sodium has relatively weak forces holding the atoms together in the metal:

- Sodium is soft: the crystal structures in the metal are easily separated.
- It has a low melting point: the atoms can be easily moved from a structured arrangement in a solid to a random arrangement in a liquid.
- It has a low density: the large size of the atom gives a large volume to the structure.

key facts

- Electronegativity is the tendency of an atom involved in a covalent bond to attract the bonding electrons to itself.

- Electronegativity increases across Period 3.
- Electronegativity of an element depends upon nuclear charge, shielding electrons and size of atom.

13.3 Elements in water

When sodium is put into water, it floats (it has a low density), it reacts violently (it loses one outer electron relatively easily) and it liberates hydrogen. The large amount of energy released during the reaction melts the sodium:

$$2Na(s) + 2H_2O(l) \rightarrow 2NaOH(aq) + H_2(g)$$

This reaction is written as an ionic equation:

$$2Na(s) + 2H_2O(l) \rightarrow \\ 2Na^+(aq) + 2OH^-(aq) + H_2(g)$$

Because the NaOH(aq) is completely dissociated and all the OH⁻(aq) ions are released, the resulting solution will be strongly alkaline, with a pH of approximately 13.

Sodium reacts with water to form aqueous sodium hydroxide and hydrogen.

Compared with sodium, magnesium has a smaller atomic radius, a higher ionic charge and two delocalised electrons. This results in stronger forces holding the magnesium lattice together. The two mobile electrons available give a greater electrical conductivity than sodium has. The greater forces of attraction mean that the two outer electrons are more difficult to remove, so it is much less reactive than sodium. The reaction is still very exothermic, but because of the high activation energy the magnesium must be heated strongly to start the reaction, and the water must be heated to form steam, which is passed over the hot magnesium. The products are hydrogen and magnesium oxide:

$$Mg(s) + H_2O(g) \rightarrow MgO(s) + H_2(g)$$

Aluminium continues the trend. It is smaller than magnesium, has a higher electrical conductivity and is less reactive in water.

Formation of oxides

All the elements in Period 3 react with oxygen and usually form an oxide with the highest possible oxidation state (see Table 3). The metals are all highly reactive when you heat them in pure oxygen. They all glow brightly during the reaction. The equations for the reactions of sodium, magnesium and aluminium are:

$$4Na(s) + O_2(g) \rightarrow 2Na_2O(s) \text{ (in limited air)}$$
$$2Mg(s) + O_2(g) \rightarrow 2MgO(s)$$
$$4Al(s) + 3O_2(g) \rightarrow 2Al_2O_3(s)$$

The reaction of magnesium with steam.

Table 3 The properties of oxides in Period 3

Element	Na	Mg	Al	Si	P	S	
Formula of oxide	Na_2O	MgO	Al_2O_3	SiO_2	P_4O_{10}	SO_2	SO_3
State at 25 °C	solid	solid	solid	solid	solid	gas	liquid
Melting point (K)	1 548 (sublimes)	3 125	2 345	1 883	853 > 1atm	200	290
Boiling point (K)	–	3 873	3 253	2503 (sublimes)	573	263	318
Electrical conductivity when molten	good	good	good	none	none	none	none
Structure	giant ionic	giant ionic	giant ionic	giant molecule	simple molecule	simple molecule	simple molecule
Enthalpy of formation 298 K (kJ mol⁻¹) per mole of O atoms	–416	–602	–559	–455	–298	–149	–132
Adding water	reacts and forms hydroxide ions in solution	slightly soluble, dissolved oxide forms a few hydroxide ions in solution	insoluble but amphoteric	insoluble but acidic	acidic; reacts and gives H^+ ions in solution	acidic; reacts and forms weak acid H_2SO_3 with a few H^+ ions in solution	acidic; reacts and forms strong acid H_2SO_4 with H^+ ions in solution
Typical pH of aqueous solution of oxide	13	8	7, i.e. no reaction	7, i.e. no reaction	2	3	1

All the metals produce ionic oxides due to the large differences in electronegativity. Sodium and magnesium oxides are basic, and aluminium oxide is **amphoteric**, illustrating the increasing electronegativity of the metal (Table 2).

Sodium burning in oxygen.

Sodium oxide is a white solid powder.

Magnesium ribbon burning in air.

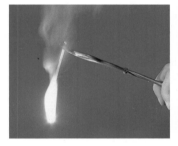

Magnesium oxide is a white solid.

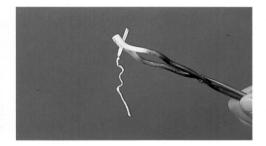

Aluminium burns in oxygen to form aluminium oxide, a white solid powder.

Fig. 6 Structures of silicon, phosphorus and sulfur oxides

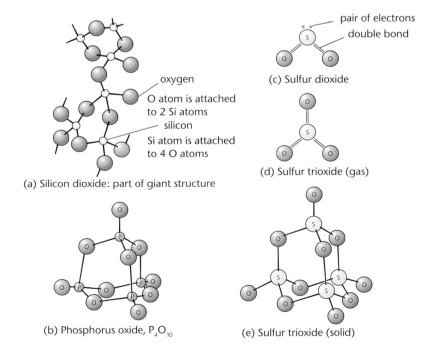

(a) Silicon dioxide: part of giant structure

oxygen
O atom is attached to 2 Si atoms
silicon
Si atom is attached to 4 O atoms

(b) Phosphorus oxide, P_4O_{10}

pair of electrons
double bond

(c) Sulfur dioxide

(d) Sulfur trioxide (gas)

(e) Sulfur trioxide (solid)

Silicon, phosphorus and sulfur all react with oxygen. They are non-metallic elements. There is a small electronegativity difference, so they form covalent oxides (Fig. 6). In the absence of a catalyst, sulfur forms SO_2 and not SO_3 (see the contact process on pages 213 and 214 in *AS Chemistry*), so it does not use its highest possible oxidation state, as the other elements do. The equations for the reactions of silicon, phosphorus and sulfur are:

$$Si(s) + O_2(g) \rightarrow SiO_2(s)$$
$$4P(s) + 5O_2(g) \rightarrow P_4O_{10}(s)$$
$$S(s) + O_2(g) \rightarrow SO_2(g)$$

All these oxides form acidic solutions in water. Fig. 7 summarises the properties of the Period 3 elements.

Fig. 7 Properties of the elements of Period 3

Na	Mg	Al	Si	P	S	Cl

Bonding:

covalent character increases →

← ionic character increases

electronegativity difference between element and oxygen decreases →

Oxide properties related to bonding

The melting points of the oxides are listed in Table 3. Melting points are an indication of the forces of attraction between atoms, ions or molecules. The bonding in these oxides can be grouped into three types:

- Ionic oxides
- Covalent oxide – macromolecular
- Covalent oxides – simple molecules

Ionic oxides
Sodium, magnesium and aluminium. The forces between ions tend to be stronger than the forces between molecules, which are usually weak Van der Waals forces. For ions with higher charges, there will be a greater force of attraction, which leads to a stronger bond. The greater charge on the positive ion, however, gives a greater polarising effect, increased covalency and therefore a lower melting point.

For the ions from Na^+ to Mg^{2+} to Al^{3+}, the increasing ionic charge and the decreasing size of the ions gives increasing electrostatic attractive forces and higher melting points from Na to Mg. However, the greater polarising effect for Al gives a lower melting point than for Mg.

Covalent oxide – macromolecular
Silicon. As the molecule is a giant structure, the forces holding the major particles together are forces between atoms. These are covalent bonds and are extremely strong. This gives high melting points. The high melting point of $SiO_2(s)$ illustrates this.

Covalent oxides – simple molecules
Phosphorus and sulfur. Moving on across Period 3, after $SiO_2(s)$, the melting points decrease significantly because the compounds are simple covalent molecules and so there are weaker forces of attraction between the molecules. Sulfur dioxide SO_2 consists of simple, discrete molecules with weak forces of attraction between them, so the melting and boiling points are low. SO_2 is a gas at room temperature. Sulfur trioxide SO_3 can form groups of molecules (Fig. 6(e)), so it can be solidified by cooling to just below room temperature. Phosphorus(V) oxide P_4O_{10} is a larger molecule than SO_2, so there are stronger Van der Waals forces of attraction and a higher melting point.

> **8** Use electronegativity values to explain the change from ionic to covalent character in the Period 3 oxides.

Electrical conductivity in the molten oxides or in compounds dissolved in water is an indication of ionic character. The molten oxides show good conductivity for sodium, magnesium and aluminium oxides, but poor conductivity for the others. This indicates significant ionic bonding for sodium, magnesium and aluminium oxides, but covalent bonding for oxides from silicon to sulfur.

The electrical conductivities in aqueous solutions are more complex. Sodium oxide dissolves in water and reacts to give sodium hydroxide – the ions produced conduct electricity. Magnesium oxide is only sparingly soluble, and aluminium oxide is insoluble, so there are no mobile ions to provide any

> **9** Suggest why sodium fluoride has a lower melting point (1 266 K) than magnesium fluoride (1 534 K).
>
> **10** Look at Fig. 8 and explain how the bonding in the oxides of silicon and sulfur produces such a difference in their melting points.

Phosphorus burns in air to give phosphorus(V) oxide, P_4O_{10}, a white solid powder.

Sulfur burns in oxygen with a blue flame to give a colourless gas.

conductivity for these two compounds. SiO_2(s) is covalent and insoluble, so will not conduct. P_4O_{10}(s) and SO_2(g) are both covalent, so will not conduct in the molten state. But both P_4O_{10}(s) and SO_2(g) react with water to give acidic solutions, so the hydrogen cations and the anions produced conduct electricity.

Fig. 8   Melting points of Period 3 oxides

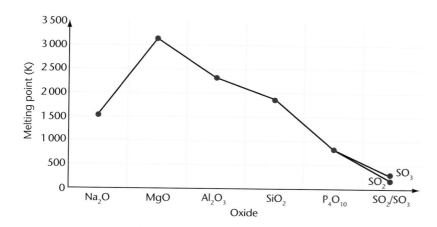

Reactions of Period 3 oxides with water

Table 3 shows the change in pH of the solutions of the oxides across Period 3. There is an evident chemical trend, but it is masked by the change in solubilities. A substance will only change the pH of water if it dissolves. The oxide ion is too highly charged to exist on its own in water. It attracts water molecules and hydrolyses to give OH⁻(aq) ions (Fig. 9):

$$O^{2-}(aq) + H_2O(l) \rightarrow 2OH^-(aq)$$

Fig. 9   Hydrolysis of the oxide ion

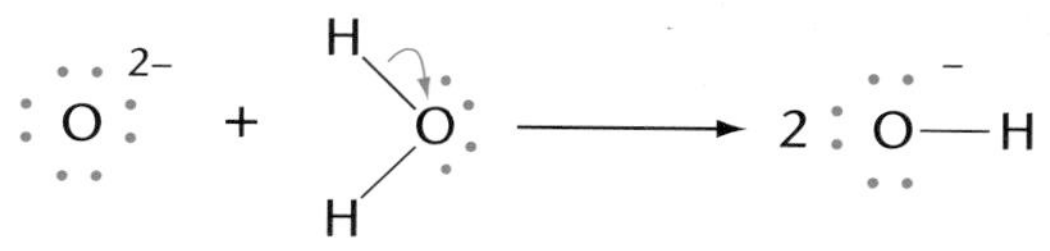

Again, the oxides can be considered in three groups:

- Ionic oxides
- Covalent oxide – macromolecular
- Covalent oxides – simple molecules

Ionic oxides

Sodium. Sodium oxide (Na_2O) is very soluble in water, so many OH⁻(aq) ions will be formed from its reaction with water, as outlined above. This will give an alkaline solution with a very high pH. We can consider the system as one with interactions within the X–O–H system, where X is the Period 3 element. There is equilibrium between the various possible species. There is a large difference in electronegativity between Na and O, so this will be an ionic bond. The O–H bond has a smaller difference in electronegativity and so will be covalent. We have Na^+ ⁻O–H and an alkaline solution.

Magnesium. Magnesium oxide (MgO) is only slightly soluble, which can be related in part to the higher lattice energy from the Mg^{2+} ion (compared with Na^+). If only a small amount of Mg^{2+} dissolves, only a few O^{2-} ions are dissociated. So only a few OH⁻ ions will be formed and the solution will be only slightly alkaline, having a pH of only 8.

Aluminium. Aluminium oxide (Al_2O_3) is insoluble, so no O^{2-} ions will be dissociated, no OH⁻ ions will be formed and the pH will be 7. Although Al_2O_3 does not change the pH of water from 7, it will react with acids and with alkalis such as sodium hydroxide, hence it is amphoteric.

The electronegativity difference between Al and O is less than between Na and O or between Mg and O, so there is more covalent character in the Al–O bond than in Na–O or Mg–O. This allows Al_2O_3 to show some acidic characteristics, as well as it being a metal oxide and therefore showing basic characteristics.

Aluminium oxide will react with compounds that are more basic, such as NaOH(aq), and it will react with compounds that are more acidic, such as H_2SO_4(aq). The equations for the reactions are as follows.

In acid:

$$Al_2O_3(s) + 3H_2SO_4(aq) \rightarrow$$
$$Al_2(SO_4)_3(aq) + 3H_2O(l)$$

or (as an ionic equation):

$$Al_2O_3(s) + 6H^+(aq) \rightarrow$$
$$2[Al(OH)_6]^{3+}(aq) + 3H_2O$$

In alkali:

$$Al_2O_3(s) + 2NaOH(aq) + 3H_2O(l) \rightarrow 2NaAl(OH)_4(aq)$$

or (as an ionic equation):

$$Al_2O_3(s) + 2OH^-(aq) + 3H_2O(l) \rightarrow 2Al(OH)_4^-(aq)$$

Overall:

$$[Al(OH)_4]^- \xleftarrow{\text{with alkali}} Al_2O_3 \xrightarrow{\text{with acid}} [Al(H_2O)_6]^{3+}$$

behaves as an acid   behaves as a base

Covalent oxide – macromolecular

Silicon. Silicon dioxide (SiO_2) is a macromolecule, a stable compound, and it is insoluble in water. Also, there is only a small difference in electronegativity between Si and O, so there is minimal attraction for the water molecule. H^+ and OH^- ions are not formed and the pH will remain neutral.

Covalent oxides – simple molecules

Phosphorus and sulfur. These acidic oxides (P_4O_{10}, SO_2 and SO_3) hydrolyse in water and give the corresponding acids. The mechanism of how the oxides hydrolyse are all different and are laid out in Fig. 10. The equations for the reactions are:

$$P_4O_{10}(s) + 6H_2O(l) \rightarrow 4H_3PO_4(aq)$$
$$SO_2(g) + H_2O(l) \rightarrow H_2SO_3(aq)$$
$$SO_3(g) + H_2O(l) \rightarrow H_2SO_4(aq)$$

As the electronegativity difference decreases across Period 3, the X–O bond is strengthening and the likelihood of it ionising is decreasing, so the likelihood of the O–H bond ionising is increasing. When this happens, the O still retains the electrons and $H^+(aq)$ is formed. This gives an increase in $[H^+]$ and a more acidic solution, so a decrease in pH (see Fig. 11).

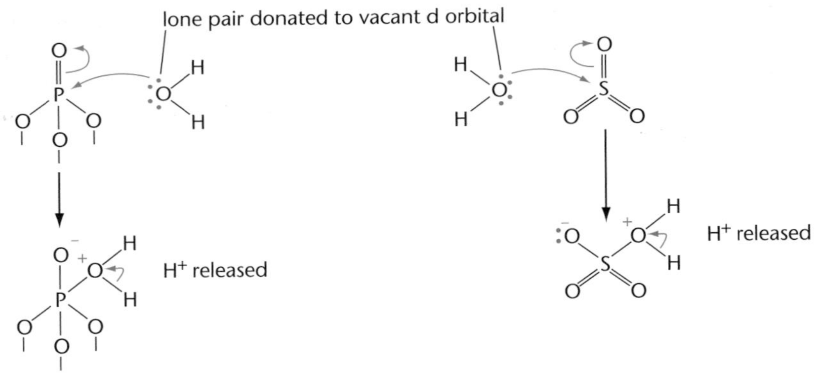

Fig. 11   Summary of alkaline and acidic solutions

Low electronegativity of X gives alkaline solution.

High electronegativity of X gives acidic solution.

$$X^+ \; {}^-O\text{—}H \qquad\qquad X\text{—}O^- \; H^+$$

The degree of acidity is related to the electronegativity difference between the Period 3 element and oxygen.

Fig. 10   Hydrolysis of covalent oxides: phosphorus(V) and sulfur(VI) oxides

lone pair donated to vacant d orbital

H^+ released

H^+ released

> **11** Explain how the pH values of aqueous sodium oxide (Na_2O), magnesium oxide (MgO) and aluminium oxide (Al_2O_3) are related to electronegativity.

key facts

- The decreasing electronegativity differences across Period 3 determine the change in chemical characteristics of the oxides.
- The ionic character of the oxides decreases from left to right across Period 3.
- The basic character of the oxides in water decreases from left to right across Period 3.
- Sodium and magnesium have basic oxides, aluminium oxide is amphoteric, and silicon, phosphorus and sulfur oxides are acidic.

examination questions

1 State what you would observe after addition of the following reagents to separate aqueous solutions containing $[Cr(H_2O)_6]^{3+}$ ions.
In each case give the formula of the chromium-containing product.

  i an excess of NaOH(aq)

  ii Na_2CO_3(aq) (5)

  Total 5

  AQA, June 2007, Unit 5, Question 3d

2

a Give the meaning of the term *electronegativity*. (2)

b State and explain the trend in electronegativity across Period 3 from Na to Cl. (3)

c **i** Name the main type of bonding in each of the oxides MgO and P_4O_{10}

  ii Explain how the type of bonding in P_4O_{10} can be predicted by a consideration of electronegativity. (3)

d Write equations for the reaction of Na_2O and of SO_2 with water. (2)

e Write an equation for the reaction of MgO with dilute hydrochloric acid. (1)

f Write an equation for the reaction of P_4O_{10} with an excess of aqueous sodium hydroxide. (1)

  Total 12

  AQA, June 2007, Unit 5, Question 4

3 State what is observed when separate samples of sodium oxide and phosphorus(V) oxide are added to water. Write equations for the reactions which occur and, in each case, state the approximate pH of the solution formed. (6)

  Total 6

  AQA, June 2005, Unit 5, Question 7b

4 The table below contains electronegativity values for the Period 3 elements, except chlorine.

Element	Na	Mg	Al	Si	P	S	Cl	Ar
Electronegativity	0.9	1.2	1.5	1.8	2.1	2.5		No value

a Explain why electronegativity increases across Period 3. (2)

b Predict values for the electronegativities of chlorine and of lithium. (2)

c State why argon has no electronegativity value. (1)

d State the type of bonding in sodium oxide. (1)

e Write an equation for the reaction of sodium oxide with water and suggest a value for the pH of the resulting solution. (8)

  Total 10

  AQA, March 2000 CH01 Question 5 (b–e, g,h)

5

a Why are the elements sodium to argon placed in Period 3 of the Periodic Table? Describe and explain the trends in electronegativity and atomic radius across Period 3 from sodium to sulfur. (7)

b Describe the trend in pH of the solutions formed when the oxides of the Period 3 elements, sodium to sulfur, are added separately to water. Explain this trend by reference to the structure and bonding in the oxides and by writing equations for the reactions with water. (19)

  Total 26

  AQA, March 1999, CH01, Question 6(a–b)

6

a Explain the meaning of the term *periodic trend* when applied to trends in the Periodic Table. (2)

b Explain why atomic radius decreases across Period 2 from lithium to fluorine. (2)

c The table below shows the melting temperatures, T_m, of the Period 3 elements.

Element	Na	Mg	Al	Si	P	S	Cl	Ar
T_m (K)	371	923	933	1 680	317	392	172	84

Explain the following in terms of structure and bonding.

i Magnesium has a higher melting temperature than sodium.

ii Silicon has a very high melting temperature.

iii Sulfur has a higher melting temperature than phosphorous.

iv Argon has the lowest melting temperature in Period 3. (8)

Total 12

NEAB, June 1998, CH01, Question 6

7

a Explain why the first ionisation energy of aluminium is less than the first ionisation energy of magnesium. (3)

b Explain why the first ionisation energy of aluminium is less than the first ionisation energy of silicon. (2)

c Explain why the second ionisation energy of aluminium is greater than the first ionisation energy of aluminium. (2)

d Write an equation to illustrate the third ionisation energy of aluminium. (1)

e Explain why the third ionisation energy of aluminium is much less than the third ionisation energy of magnesium. (2)

Total 10

NEAB, March 1998, CH01, Question 6

8

a Write equations to show what happens when the following oxides are added to water and predict approximate values for the pH of the resulting solutions.

i sodium oxide

ii sulfur dioxide (4)

b What is the general relationship between bond type in the oxides of the Period 3 elements and the pH of the solutions which result from addition of the oxides to water? (2)

Total 6

NEAB, June 1997, CH01, Question 6

9

a Magnesium oxide and sulfur dioxide are added separately to water. In each case describe what happens. Write equations for any reactions which occur and state the approximate pH of any solution formed. (6)

b Write equations for two reactions which together show the amphoteric character of aluminium hydroxide. (4)

Total 10

AQA, June 2006, Unit 5, Question 7 (c–d)

Davy's observations of the more reactive elements

Many of the elements and compounds mentioned in this chapter were discovered in the early 1800s. Although the scientists of the time could make the compounds and examine their properties, they could not explain them. That was because they did not have the detailed knowledge about atoms (such as ionic and covalent bonding, and electronegativity) that we have today. One of the scientists who did a lot of the work was Humphry Davy. He was a leading scientist of his day and his lectures at the Royal Institution (where the Children's Christmas Lectures are filmed) were very popular. In his work, he used electricity to isolate many of the more reactive elements. He kept notes of his observations in his experiments. Some of them included inhaling gases and tasting solids, which would certainly *not* be recommended today.

The passages in *italics* below are taken from Davy's laboratory notes about metallic sodium and potassium, and the oxides of sodium, magnesium, aluminium, phosphorus and sulfur. Read them, and answer the questions that follow.

Sodium

When thrown upon water it effervesces violently, but does not inflame, swims on the surface, gradually diminishes with great agitation and renders the water a solution of soda.

Potassium

When thrown upon water, it acts with great violence, swims on the surface and burns with a beautiful light, which is white mixed with red and violet; the water in which it burns is found alkaline, and contains a solution of potassa.

Sodium oxide

When a little water is added to it, there is a violent reaction between the two bodies.

Magnesium oxide

It is scarcely soluble in water, but produces heat when the water is mixed with it, and it absorbs a considerable portion of the fluid.

Aluminium oxide

Has no taste or smell, adheres strongly to the tongue, has no action on vegetable colours, is insoluble in water, is soluble with all the mineral acids and in hot solutions of ... alkalis.

The experimental notes from Davy seemed to indicate that he was surprised about the reactions of aluminium oxide. His experimental observation that aluminium oxide 'is soluble with all the mineral acids and hot solutions of ... alkalis' seemed unusual to him. He did not expect it to react with both acids *and* alkalis.

Phosphorus oxide

Has no smell; its taste is intensely, but not disagreeably acid. It dissolves in water, producing great heat; and its saturated solution is the consistence of syrup. It unites with alkalis.

Sulfur oxide

Is obtained when sulfur is burnt in oxygen with a beautiful violet flame. It reddens vegetable blues and gradually destroys most of them. It is absorbed by water; this fluid takes up about 30 times its bulk, and gains a nauseous subacid taste.

A1 Why do both of these alkali metals float on water?

A2 Write equations for the reactions when these metals react with water.

A3 Give two reasons why the reaction between potassium and water seems to be more violent than that for sodium and water.

A4 Why is sodium oxide soluble, but magnesium and aluminium oxides are not?

A5 Write an equation for the violent reaction between sodium oxide and water.

A6 Write equations for the reaction of aluminium oxide with hydrochloric acid (a mineral acid) and with potassium hydroxide (an alkali).

A7 How can we explain these unusual properties of aluminium oxide?

A8 Write equations to explain how both these oxides react with water to give acidic solutions.

A9 Explain why these oxides give acidic behaviour, but sodium and magnesium oxides give basic behaviour.

14 Redox equilibria

Many modern appliances need a portable source of electricity – for example, watches, personal stereos, mobile phones and laptop computers (some of which are shown in the photograph, left). The list is almost endless. Scientists regularly develop newer and better batteries, claiming that they give 'more energy', 'more power', are 'longer lasting' or are 'the best'. What determines how powerful and long lasting they are depends on the use to which they are put, and particularly on their chemical construction.

Chemical changes take place inside batteries. These changes cause electrons to move around a circuit in the same direction. This is what we call the current. A battery, or 'cell', has one component that releases electrons (it is oxidised) and another component that accepts electrons (it is reduced). When we combine one of each component to make a cell, a voltage is produced. The size of the voltage depends on the particular combination of components used.

The AA batteries we buy for use in most of our everyday items, such as stereos and torches, use zinc and carbon. Such a battery produces a voltage of about 1.5 V (V = volts) because of the particular reactivity of zinc and carbon. Watches often use lithium batteries, because lithium is light and can give a high voltage, but they have to be replaced when they wear out. Mobile phones also use lithium-ion batteries, but these can be recharged by passing a current through them in the reverse direction. A car battery supplies only 12 V, which you could obtain from eight AA batteries in series. But a car battery supplies a very large current – enough to give you a nasty shock.

The very first batteries invented were so poor that they hardly worked at all, and were difficult to incorporate into equipment powered by them. But the chemical changes in them were exactly the same as in modern batteries. The chemical reactions determine the voltage. The engineering and design determine how efficiently they work, and how suitable they are for different uses.

The use of electric vehicles has been proposed as a way to reduce pollution. However, wide use of electric transport will depend upon the availability of charging points and modern battery technology, which can provide the vehicle with its range (how far it can go between charges). Nowadays, most manufacturers are favouring the lithium-ion option.

A standard battery has a voltage of 1.5 V.

14.1 Oxidation states

A characteristic of transition elements is their **variable oxidation state**. The transition elements are all metals and they lose electrons when they react. We can represent this in a general equation:

$$M \rightarrow M^{n+} + ne$$

In this reaction, transition metal M is oxidised to M^{n+} by loss of n electrons. Remember the memory aid OIL RIG from *AS Chemistry*:

Oxidation **I**s **L**oss of electrons
Reduction **I**s **G**ain of electrons

When the metal reacts with a non-metallic element, there is a **redox (reduction–oxidation) reaction** and electrons are transferred. In the reaction:

$$X + ne^- \rightarrow X^{n-}$$

X is reduced by gaining electrons. When these equations for loss and gain of electrons are written separately, they are called **half-equations** (see Chapter 10 in *AS Chemistry*).

Assigning oxidation states

The number of electrons lost or gained is called the **oxidation state**. You will have read about oxidation states in *AS Chemistry*, Chapter 10.

A metal forming a positive ion has a positive oxidation state. For example, when calcium metal loses two electrons, $Ca \rightarrow Ca^{2+} + 2e^-$, its oxidation state changes from 0 to +2. Note that the oxidation state and the charge on the ion have the same value, but for the oxidation state the sign is put in front of the numeral. So, in this example, the oxidation state of calcium is +2 and the charge on the calcium ion is 2+.

A non-metal combined with a metal will have a negative oxidation state. In the example, $Cl_2 + 2e^- \rightarrow 2Cl^-$, the oxidation state of chlorine changes from 0 to −1.

If two non-metals are joined to each other, the more *electronegative* element (see Section 13.1 in this book and pages 59–60 in *AS Chemistry*) is assigned the negative oxidation state.

For compounds, this rule applies:

In a neutral compound, the sum of the positive and the negative oxidation states is zero.

So, for copper(II) chloride:

$$CuCl_2 \rightarrow Cu^{2+} + 2Cl^-$$

the oxidation state of Cu is +2, and the oxidation state of Cl is −1:

$$\begin{array}{cc} Cu & Cl_2 \\ +2 & + \quad (2 \times -1) = 0 \end{array}$$

Many of the s and p block elements have just one or perhaps two oxidation states that are common to nearly all their reactions. For example, oxygen is almost always −2, and chlorine is almost always −1.

However, transition metals are special. They have electrons in the d orbital and, because the

energy levels in the d orbital are similar, several oxidation states can exist with similar stabilities. For example, chromium has oxidation states of +2 (e.g. $CrCl_2$), +3 (e.g. $CrCl_3$) and +6 (e.g. CrO_2Cl_2).

Calculating oxidation states

Oxidation states in compounds

To work out the oxidation state of an element X in a compound, we write down the charges of all the other elements and, given that the overall charge of the compound is zero, we can then calculate the charge of X. We will look at a couple of examples.

The oxidation state of iron in Fe_2O_3 can be found as follows. The oxidation state of oxygen is −2, so its charge is 2−. Since Fe_2 is the only other species, and the overall charge of the compound is zero, we know that the charge of each Fe ion must be positive, which we denote by $n+$:

$$\begin{array}{rl} Fe_2O_3: & 2 \times Fe^{n+} = 3 \times O^{2-} \\ & (2 \times [n+]) + (3 \times [2-]) = 0 \\ & 2[n+] + [6-] = 0 \\ & 2[n+] = [6+] \\ & 2n = 6 \\ & n = 3 \end{array}$$

So the charge on each Fe ion is 3+. The oxidation state of iron in Fe_2O_3 is +3.

A more complicated calculation, to find the oxidation state of manganese in $KMnO_4$, follows the same rules:

$$\begin{array}{rl} KMnO_4: & 1 \times K^{1+} \quad 1 \times Mn^{n+} \quad 4 \times O^{2-} \\ & (1 \times [1+]) + (1 \times [n+]) + (4 \times [2-]) = 0 \\ & [1+] + [n+] + 4[2-] = 0 \\ & [(n+1)+] + [8-] = 0 \\ & [(n+1)+] = [8+] \\ & (n+1) = 8 \\ & n = 7 \end{array}$$

So the charge on each Mn ion is 7+. The oxidation state of manganese in $KMnO_4$ is +7.

Oxidation states in ions

Transition elements form complex ions with a wide variety of ligands, groups arranged around the central ion of the transition element. Some complexes are shown in Table 1. For complex ions, this rule applies:

For a complex ion, the sum of the charges inside the bracket must equal the overall charge on the ion.

Table 1   Oxidation states for some complex ions

Complex ion	Charge due to ligands	Charge on complex	Charge on central ion
$[Co(H_2O)_6]^{2+}$	0	2+	2+
$[Cr_2O_7]^{2-}$	$7 \times 2- = 14-$	2–	6+
$[Cu(NH_3)_4(H_2O)_2]^{2+}$	0	2+	2+
$[Ni(CN)_4]^{2-}$	$4 \times 1- = 4-$	2–	2+
$[Co(C_2O_4)_3]^{3-}$	$3 \times 2- = 6-$	3–	3+
$[Co(en)_3]^{3+}$	0	3+	3+

(en = ethane-1,2-diamine)

For the complex ion $[Fe(CN)_6]^{4-}$, the overall charge is 4–. To find out the oxidation state of iron, we need to know that the overall charge of each of the six –CN groups (ligands) is 1– (see $[Ni(CN)_4]^{2-}$ in Table 1). Then the calculation is this:

$$[Fe(CN)_6]^{4-}: \quad 1 \times Fe^{n+} \quad 6 \times (CN)^{1-}$$
$$[n+] \quad + \quad (6 \times [1-] = [4-]$$
$$n = 2+$$

The oxidation state of iron in $[Fe(CN)_6]^{4-} = +2$.

1 Calculate the oxidation states of chromium in each of the following:

a $Cr_2(SO_4)_3$

b $K_2Cr_2O_7$

c CrO_3

d $[Cr(H_2O)_4Cl_2]^-$.

The changing oxidation states of transition metals

It can be relatively easy for the oxidation state of transition elements to be changed chemically, for example, for Fe^{2+} to be changed to Fe^{3+}. In the change from one oxidation state to another, a redox reaction will occur, and often the colour changes as well.

Take, for example, soluble iron(II) ions in water. As iron(II) loses one electron, the iron(II) ions are oxidised to iron(III) ions:

$$Fe^{2+}(aq) \rightarrow Fe^{3+}(aq)$$

In an aqueous solution, iron(II) ions (left) darken to iron(III) ions (right).

An oxidant will accept this electron and become reduced. In this case, oxygen dissolved in the water is reduced (gains electrons) to form hydroxide ions:

$$H_2O(l) + O_2(aq) + 4e^- \rightarrow 4OH^-(aq)$$

Balancing full redox equations

Oxidation of iron(II) to iron(III)
To write a balanced overall equation for the oxidation of iron(II) to iron(III) described above, we carry out the following steps.

Step 1 Calculate the changes in oxidation state for the two ions:

$$Fe^{2+}(aq) \rightarrow Fe^{3+}(aq) + e^-$$

$$O_2(aq) + 4e^- \rightarrow 4OH^-(aq)$$

Step 2 Balance the O and H atoms by adding $H_2O(l)$ or $H^+(aq)$ (if needed) and complete the two half-equations:

$$Fe^{2+}(aq) \rightarrow Fe^{3+}(aq) + e^-$$
(no $H_2O(l)$ or $H^+(aq)$ needed here)

$$2H_2O(l) + O_2(aq) + 4e^- \rightarrow 4OH^-(aq)$$

Step 3 Balance the electron transfer (four electrons) in the two half-equations:

$$4Fe^{2+}(aq) \rightarrow 4Fe^{3+}(aq) + 4e^-$$

$$2H_2O(l) + O_2(aq) + 4e^- \rightarrow 4OH^-(aq)$$

Step 4 Add the two half-reactions:

$$4Fe^{2+}(aq) \rightarrow 4Fe^{3+}(aq) + 4e^-$$
$$2H_2O(l) + O_2(aq) + 4e^- \rightarrow 4OH^-(aq)$$

$$\overline{4Fe^{2+}(aq) + 2H_2O(l) + O_2(aq) \rightarrow 4Fe^{3+}(aq) + 4OH^-(aq)}$$

Step 5 Check that the charges in the equation balance. In this method, H_2O sometimes needs cancelling out as well at a later stage.

Oxidation of sulfur dioxide by potassium chromate(VI)

For this reaction, $H_2O(l)$ and $H^+(aq)$ should be cancelled in the final equation.

Step 1 Calculate the changes in oxidation state for the two ions:

$$SO_2(aq) \rightarrow SO_4^{2-}(aq) + 2e^-$$

$$Cr_2O_7^{2-}(aq) + 6e^- \rightarrow 2Cr^{3+}(aq)$$

Step 2 Balance the O and H atoms by adding $H_2O(l)$ or $H^+(aq)$ (if needed), and complete the two half-equations:

$$SO_2(aq) + 2H_2O(l) \rightarrow SO_4^{2-}(aq) + 2e^- + 4H^+(aq)$$

$$Cr_2O_7^{2-}(aq) + 6e^- + 14H^+(aq) \rightarrow 2Cr^{3+}(aq) + 7H_2O(l)$$

Step 3 Balance the electron transfer in the two half-equations:

$$3SO_2(aq) + 6H_2O(l) \rightarrow 3SO_4^{2-}(aq) + 6e^- + 12H^+(aq)$$

$$Cr_2O_7^{2-}(aq) + 6e^- + 14H^+(aq) \rightarrow 2Cr^{3+}(aq) + 7H_2O(l)$$

Step 4 Add the two half-reactions:

$$3SO_2(aq) + 6H_2O(l) \rightarrow 3SO_4^{2-}(aq) + 6e^- + 12H^+(aq)$$
$$Cr_2O_7^{2-}(aq) + 6e^- + 14H^+(aq) \rightarrow 2Cr^{3+}(aq) + 7H_2O(l)$$

$$\overline{3SO_2(aq) + 6H_2O(l) + Cr_2O_7^{2-}(aq) + 14H^+(aq) \rightarrow 3SO_4^{2-}(aq) + 12H^+(aq) + 2Cr^{3+}(aq) + 7H_2O(l)}$$

Here, some cancelling is needed for $H_2O(l)$ and $H^+(aq)$:

$$\overset{2H^+(aq)}{} \qquad \qquad \overset{H_2O(l)}{}$$
$$3SO_2(aq) + \cancel{6H_2O(l)} + Cr_2O_7^{2-}(aq) + \cancel{14H^+(aq)} \rightarrow 3SO_4^{2-}(aq) + \cancel{12H^+(aq)} + 2Cr^{3+}(aq) + \cancel{7H_2O(l)}$$

The full equation is therefore:

$$3SO_2(aq) + Cr_2O_7^{2-}(aq) + 2H^+(aq) \rightarrow 3SO_4^{2-}(aq) + 2Cr^{3+}(aq) + H_2O(l)$$

Step 5 Check that the totals of all the charges in the equation balance. In the last equation, the totals are 0 to the left and 0 to the right: the equation is balanced.

Oxidation of iron(II) by potassium manganate(VII)

Potassium manganate(VII) can be used to determine the concentration of iron(II) ions in an acidified solution. In the titration, the potassium manganate(VII) is the oxidising agent and is reduced to $Mn^{2+}(aq)$. The Fe^{2+} is the reducing agent and is oxidised to $Fe^{3+}(aq)$.

Step 1 For the change in oxidation states, insert the charges:

$$Mn \quad O_4^- \qquad \rightarrow Mn^{2+}$$
$$[7+] + [8-] = [1-] \rightarrow [2+]$$

The oxidation state of manganese has changed from +7 to +2: Mn has gained five electrons ($5e^-$):

$$MnO_4^- + 5e^- \rightarrow Mn^{2+}$$

For the $Fe^{2+}(aq)$:

$$Fe^{2+}(aq) \rightarrow Fe^{3+}(aq) + e^-$$
$$2+ \quad \rightarrow \quad 3+$$

Step 2 Balance the oxygen and hydrogen atoms by adding $H_2O(l)$ or $H^+(aq)$ (if needed) and complete the two half-equations:

$$MnO_4^-(aq) + 5e^- + 8H^+(aq) \rightarrow Mn^{2+}(aq) + 4H_2O(l)$$

$$Fe^{2+}(aq) \rightarrow Fe^{3+}(aq) + e^-$$

Step 3 Balance the electron transfer in the two half-equations:

$$MnO_4^-(aq) + 5e^- + 8H^+(aq) \rightarrow Mn^{2+}(aq) + 4H_2O(l)$$

$$5Fe^{2+}(aq) \rightarrow 5Fe^{3+}(aq) + 5e^-$$

Step 4 Add the two half-reactions:

$$MnO_4^-(aq) + \cancel{5e^-} + 8H^+(aq) + 5Fe^{2+}(aq) \rightarrow Mn^{2+}(aq) + 4H_2O(l) + 5Fe^{3+}(aq) + \cancel{5e^-}$$

$$[1-] \quad [\cancel{5-}] \quad [8+] \quad 5 \times [2+] \rightarrow \quad [2+] \qquad\qquad 5 \times [3+] \quad [\cancel{5-}]$$

Step 5 Check that the charges balance: 17+ on the left and 17+ on the right. The full equation is:

$$MnO_4^-(aq) + 8H^+(aq) + 5Fe^{2+}(aq) \rightarrow Mn^{2+}(aq) + 4H_2O(l) + 5Fe^{3+}(aq)$$

14.2 Half-reactions

Batteries

When an electrical circuit containing a battery is connected, the transfer of electrons in redox reactions inside the battery produces a flow of electrons in an external circuit. The flow of charge in the system is the current, and so a component in the circuit, such as a bulb or watch mechanism, will be switched on.

Modern batteries are much more advanced than the first, crude, electrochemical cells constructed by Alessandro Volta in 1800, but the chemical principles are the same. Volta used silver and zinc discs separated by pasteboard soaked in salt solution to produce a voltage. Today's batteries use metal/metal-ion solutions separated by an electrolyte.

The batteries of this electric vehicle are being recharged using solar power. This not only cuts out urban pollution, it also eliminates the pollution caused when electricity is generated from non-renewable fuels.

Half-reactions

To understand how chemical reactions produce a voltage, we first look at what happens when a metal strip is dipped in a solution of one of its salts. Some of the metal atoms give up electrons and dissolve to form metal ions, leaving behind electrons on the metal strip (Fig. 1).

For zinc leaving the metal strip, the half-equation is:

$$Zn(s) \rightarrow Zn^{2+}(aq) + 2e^- \qquad \text{(Equation 1)}$$

However, metal ions in the solution are free to recombine with the electrons on the metal

Fig. 1   Zinc rod in zinc salt solution

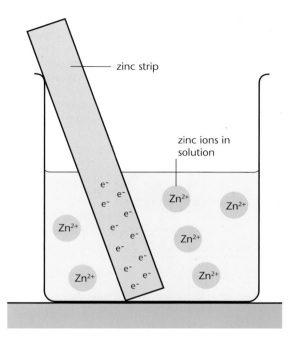

to form metal atoms. The half-equation for this is:

$$Zn^{2+}(aq) + 2e^- \rightarrow Zn(s) \qquad \text{(Equation 2)}$$

The greater the excess of charge on the metal strip, the more likely it is that metal ions will form atoms again. An equilibrium is set up, where the rate of formation of metal *ions* equals the rate of formation of metal *atoms*:

$$\underset{\text{zinc atoms oxidised}}{\overset{\text{zinc ions reduced}}{Zn^{2+}(aq) + 2e^- \rightleftharpoons Zn(s)}}$$

This is an example of a **dynamic equilibrium**. At equilibrium, the negative charge on the metal strip sets up a **potential difference** (voltage) between the metal and the solution. The greater the tendency of the metal to produce ions (and therefore hold a negative charge on the metal), the greater is the potential difference at equilibrium.

Zinc tends to give up electrons and dissolve in a solution of its ions more readily than copper (see Fig. 2). At equilibrium, the potential difference for the zinc/zinc-ion system is greater than for the copper/copper-ion system. For copper and zinc, very few metal ions actually end up in solution, and the equilibrium in each of the half-equations above lies well over to the right in both cases.

In summary, the half-reactions for metal/metal-ion systems are described by half-equations.

Redox equilibria

We have seen that half-reactions are examples of redox reactions. By convention, standard half-reactions are written as reductions. This convention was set by the International Union of Pure and Applied Chemistry (IUPAC). Conventions such as these are important, as they enable information to be communicated consistently by chemists across the world, whether they are researchers working worldwide, or students studying in UK schools or colleges. For example, the half-reaction for the zinc/zinc-ion system is written in the IUPAC convention as follows:

$$Zn^{2+}(aq) + 2e^- \rightleftharpoons Zn(s)$$
reduction of zinc ions to zinc atoms.

Electrochemical cells: Zn/Cu

Half-reactions in a metal/metal-ion system produce an electrode potential. How is this used to generate useful electric current? If two metal/metal-ion systems are linked (Fig. 2), the electrons on the metal strips can move around the new circuit. This set-up is called an **electrochemical cell.** It consists of two electrodes (metal conductors) immersed in electrolytes. The electrolyte can be a solution or a molten salt.

Electrons flow when two different half-reactions, such as Zn/Zn^{2+} with Cu/Cu^{2+}, are connected as part of a complete circuit. The zinc metal (Fig. 2) has a greater build-up of negative charge at its surface than the copper does. This means that the zinc electrode has a more negative **electrode potential**. Relative to the zinc, the copper has a less negative electrode potential, so the copper is said to be the more positive electrode.

The difference in electrode potential, the electromotive force (**e.m.f.**), is a measure of the force that moves the electrons around the circuit. The bigger the difference in electrode potential and the more cells connected in series (see the opening page of this chapter), the greater is the e.m.f.

Batteries have a vast range of uses, and can be made using different combinations of metals and numbers of cells, so they can have different electrode potentials appropriate to their uses.

The two half-reactions for the zinc/copper cell can be combined to give the overall equation. Electrons flow around the circuit from the *more*

235

Fig. 2   Zinc/copper electrochemical cell

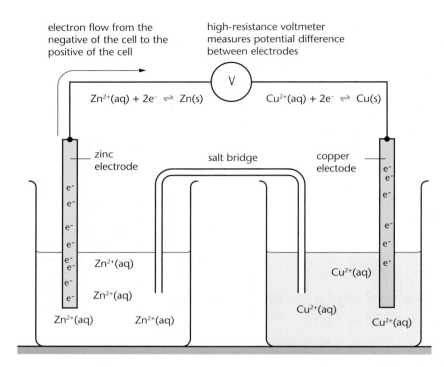

electron flow from the negative of the cell to the positive of the cell

high-resistance voltmeter measures potential difference between electrodes

$Zn^{2+}(aq) + 2e^- \rightleftharpoons Zn(s)$ $Cu^{2+}(aq) + 2e^- \rightleftharpoons Cu(s)$

zinc electrode

salt bridge

copper electode

$Zn^{2+}(aq)$

$Zn^{2+}(aq)$

$Zn^{2+}(aq)$ $Zn^{2+}(aq)$

$Cu^{2+}(aq)$

$Cu^{2+}(aq)$

$Cu^{2+}(aq)$

negative electrode to the *less* negative electrode. With the two half-reactions written according to the IUPAC convention, the overall equation is obtained by subtracting the more negative (zinc) half-equation from the less negative (copper) one:

$$Cu^{2+}(aq) + 2e^- \rightleftharpoons Cu(s)$$
$$- (Zn^{2+}(aq) + 2e^- \rightleftharpoons Zn(s))$$
$$\overline{Cu^{2+}(aq) + 2e^- - Zn^{2+}(aq) - 2e^- \rightleftharpoons Cu(s) - Zn(s)}$$

Rearranging, this gives:

$$Zn(s) + Cu^{2+}(aq) \rightleftharpoons Cu(s) + Zn^{2+}(aq)$$

This is the same reaction as would be predicted from the electrochemical series (see

the end of section 14.3), so that, when zinc metal is put in copper sulfate solution, we can write:

$$Zn(s) + CuSO_4(aq) \rightarrow ZnSO_4(aq) + Cu(s)$$

Thus, zinc forms zinc ions, and copper ions form metallic copper. Conventionally, the zinc electrode is referred to as 'negative' and the copper electrode as 'positive'.

Notice in Fig. 2 that there is a **salt bridge** to complete the circuit. The two half-reactions need to be kept separate, yet they still need to be connected by a **conductor**. The salt bridge provides an ionic connection between the two ionic solutions. The ions are free to move in the bridge, so the charge is transferred through the bridge solution and keeps each compartment of the cell electrically neutral. The salt bridge in Fig. 2 allows electrons to flow from the negative zinc electrode to the positive copper electrode.

Typically, a salt bridge contains a solution of a salt such as potassium chloride or potassium nitrate. A salt bridge solution can be set in agar jelly and held in a glass tube with a porous plug at each end. In commercial batteries, the bridge jelly is held in an absorbent material.

2 Write out half-reactions for the following, so that they obey the IUPAC convention:

a magnesium metal (Mg) in equilibrium with magnesium ions (Mg^{2+})

b iron(II) ions in equilibrium with iron(III) ions

c chlorine gas (Cl_2) in equilibrium with chloride (Cl^-) ions.

key facts

- When a metal is placed in a solution of its ions, some of the metal atoms form ions and go into solution, resulting in a slight build-up of electrons on the metal.

- The build-up of charge on the metal electrode produces an electrode potential between the metal and its solution.

- The equilibrium between the metal and its ions is called a half-reaction. Half-reactions are examples of redox reactions.

- Half-reactions are written as reductions according to the IUPAC convention, e.g. $M^{n+} + ne^- \rightarrow M(s)$.

- Two different half-reactions can be connected using a salt bridge to form an electrochemical cell. There is a potential difference (or e.m.f.) between the two electrodes of the cell.

14.3 Electrode potentials

Measuring electrode potentials

The position of an equilibrium is affected by factors such as temperature and concentration of solution. Because the two half-reactions that make up a cell are both in equilibrium, cell potentials can only be compared if they are measured under standard conditions, and against a standard half-reaction. Factors affecting cell potential are:

- concentration of ions in each half-reaction
- temperature
- pressure if gases form part of the cell
- cell current.

Measuring electrode potentials in the laboratory.

To produce standardised values, cell potentials are measured under standard conditions using a high-resistance voltmeter. The conditions for measuring are identified in Fig. 3, and the values measured in volts are called **standard cell (electrode) potentials**, symbol $E^{\ominus}$.

It is not possible to measure the potential of a single electrode. Only potential *differences* can be measured, so it is necessary to define a standard against which potential differences can be measured.

Standard hydrogen electrode (SHE)

All potentials are measured relative to the **standard hydrogen electrode** (SHE) operating under standard conditions (Fig. 3). This is assigned an electrode potential, $E^{\ominus} = 0$.

The cell consists of a platinum electrode with hydrogen gas bubbling over its surface. The electrode is dipped in a solution containing

Fig. 3   Standard hydrogen electrode

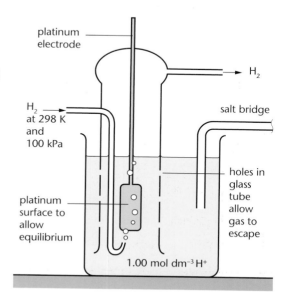

hydrogen ions at a concentration of 1 mol dm^{-3}. The purposes of the platinum electrode are to provide a non-reacting (inert) metal contact, and to act as a sink or source for electrons, thereby allowing hydrogen molecules to reach equilibrium with hydrogen ions. The half-reaction for this cell is:

$$2H^+(aq) + 2e^- \rightleftharpoons H_2(g)$$

Fig. 4 shows the conditions for measuring standard cell potentials, while Table 2 lists some combinations of different metal/metal-ion half-reactions and the e.m.f. each produces.

Convention for writing cells

Electrodes are written below in the conventional form, where the single vertical bar | represents the boundary between two different phases. Two electrodes in a cell can be represented by putting the notation for the two electrodes together, and joining them with a salt bridge, denoted by a double vertical bar ||. The oxidation reaction (more reactive metal) is on the left and the reduction reaction (less reactive metal) is on the right:

$$Zn(s) \mid Zn^{2+}(aq) \parallel Cu^{2+}(aq) \mid Cu(s)$$

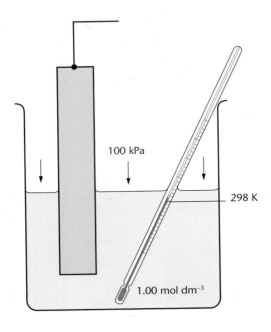

Fig. 4   Conditions for measuring standard cell potentials

100 kPa

298 K

1.00 mol dm⁻³

If a gas is present, as in the standard hydrogen electrode (SHE), the platinum is included in the notation:

$$Pt(s) \mid H_2(g) \mid H^+(aq)$$

Standard electrode potentials

Following on from above, these are defined as follows:

The standard electrode potential, $E^\ominus$, is the potential difference between the electrode under standard conditions and the standard hydrogen electrode.

Some values for standard electrode potentials are given in Table 2. The series of standard electrode potentials in Table 2 forms part of the **electrochemical series**. Electrodes that have more negative potentials have a greater tendency to form positive ions.

Table 2   Standard electrode potentials

Reduction half-equation	$E^\ominus$ (V)
$MnO_4^-(aq) + 8H^+(aq) + 5e^- \rightleftharpoons Mn^{2+}(aq) + 4H_2O(l)$	+1.51
$Cr_2O_7^{2-}(aq) + 14H^+(aq) + 6e^- \rightleftharpoons 2Cr^{3+}(aq) + 7H_2O(l)$	+1.33
$O_2(g) + 4H^+(aq) + 4e^- \rightleftharpoons 2H_2O(l)$	+1.23
$Ag^+(aq) + e^- \rightleftharpoons Ag(s)$	+0.80
$Cu^{2+}(aq) + 2e^- \rightleftharpoons Cu(s)$	+0.34
$2H^+(aq) + 2e^- \rightleftharpoons H_2(g)$	0.00
$Pb^{2+}(aq) + 2e^- \rightleftharpoons Pb(s)$	−0.13
$Fe^{2+}(aq) + 2e^- \rightleftharpoons Fe(s)$	−0.44
$Zn^{2+}(aq) + 2e^- \rightleftharpoons Zn(s)$	−0.76
$Mg^{2+}(aq) + 2e^- \rightleftharpoons Mg(s)$	−2.37
$Na^+(aq) + e^- \rightleftharpoons Na(s)$	−2.71
$Ca^{2+}(aq) + 2e^- \rightleftharpoons Ca(s)$	−2.87
$K^+(aq) + e^- \rightleftharpoons K(s)$	−2.92
$Li^+(aq) + e^- \rightleftharpoons Li(s)$	−3.04

3 Using the data from Table 2, write the correct notation for the following cells:

a a zinc electrode in zinc sulfate solution connected to a lead electrode in lead nitrate solution

b a zinc electrode in zinc sulfate solution connected to the SHE

c a copper electrode in copper(II) sulfate solution connected to a platinum electrode in a solution of iron(II) and iron(III) ions.

Summary
- The strongest reducing agents lose electrons easily and have more negative potentials.
- The strongest oxidising agents accept electrons easily and have more positive potentials.
- Half-reactions with more negative potentials correspond to electron loss (oxidation) reactions and go readily from right to left.
- Half-reactions with more positive potentials correspond to electron gain (reduction) reactions and go readily from left to right.

● Standard conditions for measuring electrode (cell) potentials are:
  – concentration, 1.00 mol dm⁻³
  – temperature, 298 K
  – pressure, 100 kPa (where gases are involved)
  – zero current.

● Electrode potentials are measured relative to an arbitrary standard.

● The standard reference cell is the standard hydrogen electrode (SHE), for which $E^{\ominus} = 0.0$ V.

● A list of reduction electrode potentials forms part of the electrochemical series.

14.4 Calculating cell potentials

Standard electrode potentials can be used to calculate standard cell potentials (or the e.m.f.) across electrochemical cells. We can determine standard cell potentials using the overall equation for the cell reaction written as a spontaneous change. For example, in the zinc/copper cell, the zinc is a more reactive metal than the copper. Its electrode potential is therefore more negative. The cell is written:

$$Zn(s) \mid Zn^{2+}(aq) \parallel Cu^{2+}(aq) \mid Cu(s)$$

more reactive   less reactive

more negative   less negative/more positive

The cell potential is calculated by subtracting the *left-hand* electrode potential from the *right-hand* one, so that:

$$E^{\ominus}_{cell} = E^{\ominus}_{right} - E^{\ominus}_{left}$$

For the cell reaction to be *spontaneous*, $E^{\ominus}_{cell}$ must be positive. For the zinc/copper cell, $E^{\ominus}_{cell}$ will be positive if the standard electrode potential for the $Zn^{2+} \mid Zn$ electrode is subtracted from the standard electrode potential of the $Cu^{2+} \mid Cu$ electrode (using figures from Table 2):

$$E^{\ominus}_{cell} = +0.34 \text{ V} - (-0.76 \text{ V})$$
$$E^{\ominus}_{cell} = +1.10 \text{ V}$$

Fig. 5   Calculating standard cell potentials

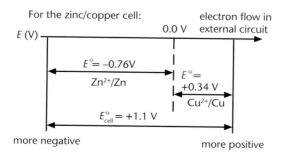

Fig. 5 gives a diagrammatic treatment of this calculation, which is for a positive value with a negative value. Figs 6(a) and (b) show calculations of cell potentials for two negative values and two positive values.

Fig. 6   Calculating standard cell potentials for (a) Fe/Pb and (b) Ag/Cu

(a) For the iron/lead cell

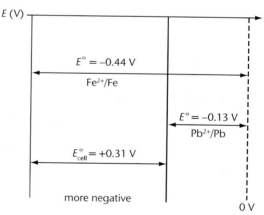

(b) For the copper/silver cell

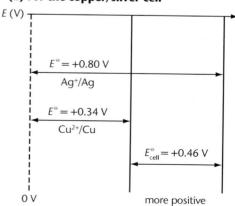

4   If you were choosing two metal electrodes for a cell to give a high voltage, which ones would you select from Table 2, based on potential difference? Why?

5   What will happen to the equilibrium in the zinc/zinc-ion system if the concentration of ions in the solution is increased?

6

a   Draw a diagram like Fig. 5 for the zinc/silver cell.

b   Calculate the standard cell potential for this cell.

c   Use Table 2 to calculate the cell e.m.f. using different combinations of the electrodes Mg^{2+}/Mg, Zn^{2+}/Zn and Ag^+/Ag.

key facts

- Standard electrode potentials of half-reactions can be used to calculate standard cell potentials (the e.m.f.) across electrochemical cells.

- We can determine standard cell potentials by subtracting the *left-hand* electrode potential from the *right-hand* one:

$$E^{\ominus}_{cell} = E^{\ominus}_{right} - E^{\ominus}_{left}$$

- Cell reactions are spontaneous if $E^{\ominus}_{cell}$ is positive. For this to happen, the more negative electrode potential is written on the left.

- We can determine standard cell potentials by using a diagrammatic representation of the cell.

- The electrochemical series applies to half-reactions involving non-metals as well as metal/metal-ion systems.

14.5 Predicting reaction direction

The direction of redox reactions can be predicted by using standard electrode potentials. In Table 2, the standard electrode potential is a measure of how readily electrons will be accepted for the half-reaction. The oxidised species in a half-reaction with a more positive potential will accept electrons more readily than will the oxidised species in a half-reaction with a more negative potential.

When two half-reactions are put together:

- the more positive system will gain electrons (be reduced), and

- the more negative system will lose electrons (be oxidised).

This is an important rule to remember. For example, the half-reaction:

$$Cl_2(g) + 2e^- \rightleftharpoons 2Cl^-(aq) \qquad E^{\ominus} = +1.36 \text{ V}$$

has a more positive electrode potential than the half-reaction:

$$Br_2(l) + 2e^- \rightleftharpoons 2Br^-(aq) \qquad E^{\ominus} = +1.07 \text{ V}$$

so Cl_2 will accept electrons from Br^- (Fig. 7), and the Cl_2 will oxidise Br^- ions to Br_2 and will itself form Cl^- ions when reduced.

Fig. 7 shows how the direction of redox reactions can be predicted using the potentials of half-reactions from the electrochemical series. Table 3 shows standard potentials for non-metals, and Fig. 8 shows how to write redox equations for cells.

Fig. 7 Predicting direction of reaction between chlorine and bromine ions

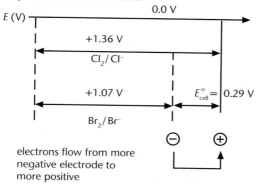

the half-reaction with the more positive potential oxidises the other

electrons flow from more negative electrode to more positive

Table 3 Standard electrode potentials for non-metals

Reduction half-equation	$E^{\ominus}$ (V)
$F_2(g) + 2e^- \rightleftharpoons 2F^-(aq)$	+2.87
$H_2O_2(aq) + 2H^+(aq) + 2e^- \rightleftharpoons 2H_2O(l)$	+1.78
$Cl_2(g) + 2e^- \rightleftharpoons 2Cl^-(aq)$	+1.36
$Br_2(l) + 2e^- \rightleftharpoons 2Br^-(aq)$	+1.07
$I_2(s) + 2e^- \rightleftharpoons 2I^-(aq)$	+0.54
$2SO_2(aq) + 2e^- \rightleftharpoons S_2O_4^{2-}(aq)$	+0.40
$O_2(g) + 2H_2O(l) + 4e^- \rightleftharpoons 4OH^-(aq)$	+0.40
$2H^+(aq) + 2e^- \rightleftharpoons H_2(g)$	0.00

Fig. 8 Writing redox equations using standard potentials

To write an overall equation for a reaction, we can use the following steps:

Step 1 Write the more negative (less positive) half-reaction as an oxidation:

$$2Br^-(aq) \rightleftharpoons Br_2(l) + 2e^-$$

Step 2 Write the more positive half-reaction as a reduction:

$$Cl_2(g) + 2e^- \rightleftharpoons 2Cl^-(aq)$$

Step 3 Balance the number of electrons being transferred in each equation if necessary.

Step 4 Combine ('add together') the two half-reactions:

$$2Br^-(aq) \rightleftharpoons Br_2(l) + 2e^-$$
$$Cl_2(g) + 2e^- \rightleftharpoons 2Cl^-(aq)$$

$$2Br^-(aq) + Cl_2(g) + 2e^- \rightleftharpoons Br_2(l) + 2e^- + 2Cl^-(aq)$$

The two electrons on each side of the new equation balance out, so they can be struck from the equation (if this is not the case you may need to go back to Step **3**):

$$2Br^-(aq) + Cl_2(g) + 2e^- \rightleftharpoons Br_2(l) + 2e^- + 2Cl^-(aq)$$

The redox equation for the combination of chlorine gas and bromine ions is therefore:

$$2Br^-(aq) + Cl_2(g) \rightleftharpoons Br_2(l) + 2Cl^-(aq)$$

(This is borne out in the laboratory.)

Predicting made easy

The electrochemical series and the standard electrode potentials of the corresponding half-reactions can be used to predict the direction of chemical reactions. The series forms into an 'electrode potential chart' and, by following simple rules (Fig. 9), the direction of reactions and cell potential can be determined. Cell potential is given by the difference in $E^{\ominus}$ between the two half-equations.

Fig. 9 Predicting reaction direction

Electrode half-equation	$E^{\ominus}$ (V)
$MnO_4^-(aq) + 8H^+(aq) + 5e^- \rightleftharpoons Mn^{2+}(aq) + 4H_2O(l)$	+1.51
$Cl_2(g) + 2e^- \rightleftharpoons 2Cl^-(aq)$	+1.36
$Cr_2O_7^{2-} + 14H^+(aq) + 6e^- \rightleftharpoons 2Cr^{3+}(aq) + 7H_2O(l)$	+1.33
$Br_2(l) + 2e^- \rightleftharpoons 2Br^-(aq)$	+1.07
$Ag^+(aq) + e^- \rightleftharpoons Ag(s)$	+0.80
$Fe^{3+}(aq) + e^- \rightleftharpoons Fe^{2+}(aq)$	+0.77
$I_2(s) + 2e^- \rightleftharpoons 2I^-(aq)$	+0.54
$Cu^{2+}(aq) + 2e^- \rightleftharpoons Cu(s)$	+0.34
$2H^+(aq) + 2e^- \rightleftharpoons H_2(g)$	0.00
$Pb^{2+}(aq) + 2e^- \rightleftharpoons Pb(s)$	−0.13
$Fe^{2+}(aq) + 2e^- \rightleftharpoons Fe(s)$	−0.44
$Zn^{2+}(aq) + 2e^- \rightleftharpoons Zn(s)$	−0.76
$Mg^{2+}(aq) + 2e^- \rightleftharpoons Mg(s)$	−2.37
$Na^+(aq) + e^- \rightleftharpoons Na(s)$	−2.71
$Ca^{2+}(aq) + 2e^- \rightleftharpoons Ca(s)$	−2.87
$K^+(aq) + e^- \rightleftharpoons K(s)$	−2.92

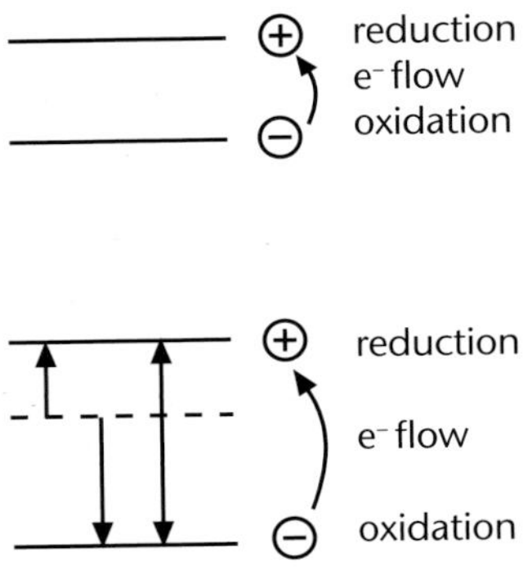

reduction
e⁻ flow
oxidation

reduction
e⁻ flow
oxidation

Steps

1 Draw horizontal lines against the two half-equations you are interested in.
2 Mark with a minus sign the one that is more negative.
3 Mark with a plus sign the one that is more positive.
4 Mark the direction of 'electron flow' (from the minus sign to the plus sign).
5 The 'electron flow' will produce a reduction reaction in the half-reaction marked with the plus sign, and an oxidation reaction in the half-reaction marked with the minus sign.

7 Use electrode potentials to explain why iodine will not displace bromine from a solution containing bromide ions. Use Fig. 7 to help you.

8

a Use the electrode potentials in Table 2 to determine the e.m.f. for the lithium cell (Li | MnO₂).

b Predict the reaction for the Li | MnO₂ cell.

9 Use electrode potentials in Tables 2 and 3 to answer the following, and explain each of your answers.

a Which metal will displace hydrogen from acid: zinc or copper?

b Will bromine oxidise iron(II) to iron(III)?

c Will iodine oxidise iron(II) to iron(III)?

d A common redox titration is acidified potassium manganate(VII) with iron(II) solution. Will acidified manganate(VII) oxidise iron(II)?

14.6 Fuel cells

A **fuel cell** produces electricity by using fuel (on the anode side) and an oxidant (on the cathode side), which react in the presence of an electrolyte. Generally, the reactants flow in and the products flow out, while the electrolyte remains in the cell. So fuel cells can operate virtually continuously as long as the necessary flows are maintained. There are no moving parts, so they are very reliable. Although fuel cells cannot store energy like a battery, they are sometimes combined with storage systems, which will in turn electrolyse the products, for

A typical fuel cell in a car.

Fig. 10   How a standard fuel cell works

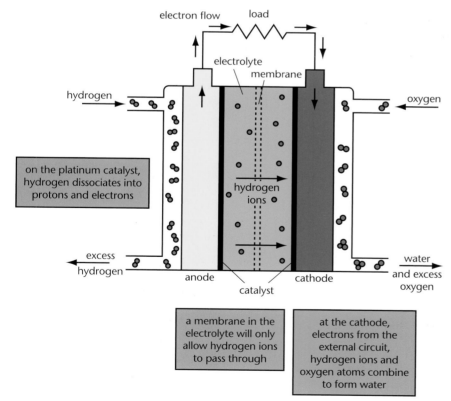

hydrogen (the fuel) is fed into the anode compartment and oxygen (the oxidant) into the cathode; unused gases are recycled

electron flow   load

electrolyte
membrane

hydrogen

oxygen

on the platinum catalyst, hydrogen dissociates into protons and electrons

hydrogen ions

excess hydrogen

water and excess oxygen

anode   cathode

catalyst

a membrane in the electrolyte will only allow hydrogen ions to pass through

at the cathode, electrons from the external circuit, hydrogen ions and oxygen atoms combine to form water

example, water, during a charging time. Fuel cells are different from batteries in that they consume reactants, which must be replenished, whereas batteries store and release energy in a closed system.

A hydrogen fuel cell uses hydrogen as fuel and oxygen as oxidant, although there are other combinations of fuel (such as hydrocarbons and alcohols) and oxidant (such as chlorine and chlorine dioxide). The catalyst is typically made of a platinum-group metal or alloy. A standard fuel cell and how it works is shown in the diagram in Fig. 10.

The e.m.f. produced by a standard fuel cell is only 0.40 V, so the efficiency needs to be as high as possible to match the output from silver | zinc or Li | SO_2 batteries. Increasing the cell surface area leads to increased current from each cell. One of the major advantages of fuel cells is the lightness of the components. Even with a smaller e.m.f., the fuel cell could match the energy density of other systems.

The electrochemical reactions in a fuel cell

On the anode side of a fuel cell, hydrogen diffuses to the anode catalyst, where it later dissociates into protons and electrons (Fig. 10).

These protons often react with oxidants. The protons are conducted through the membrane to the cathode, but the electrons travel in an external circuit. On the cathode catalyst, oxygen molecules react with the electrons (which have travelled through the external circuit) and protons to form water. Any excess gases are recycled, so water is the only waste product.

In a fuel cell, the typical reactions at the anode and cathode, respectively, are as follows:

$$H_2(g) \rightarrow 2H^+(aq) + 2e^- \qquad E^{\ominus} = 0.00 \text{ V}$$
$$O_2(aq) + 2H_2O + 4e^- \rightarrow$$
$$4OH^-(aq) \qquad E^{\ominus} = +0.40 \text{ V}$$

To maintain the balance of electrons in the reduction and oxidation processes, the reactions use up twice as much hydrogen as oxygen.

In a combined system, e.g. when solar cells are providing electricity, this can be used to electrolyse water for re-use as a fuel:

$$2H_2O \rightarrow 2H_2 + O_2$$
$$H_2O \rightleftharpoons H^+ + OH^-$$

So overall we can write this as follows:

$2H^+ + 2e^- \rightarrow H_2$	$2OH^- \rightarrow 2OH^{\bullet} + 2e^-$
$2H^+ + 2e^- \rightarrow H_2$	$2OH^{\bullet} \rightarrow H_2O + O^{\bullet}$
	$O^{\bullet} + O^{\bullet} \rightarrow O_2$
$4e^-$ used by forming $2H_2$	$4e^-$ released by forming O_2

10 Why does increasing the surface area not increase the voltage obtained from the cell?

11 Use the reduction potentials to calculate the minimum voltage needed to electrolyse the water to form hydrogen and oxygen.

12 Which gas is evolved at the cathode (negative electrode which supplies the electrons) in the electrolysis of water?

13 For the electrolysis of water balance both sets of equations in terms of electrons to show that twice as much hydrogen as oxygen is produced.

how science works

Fuel cells in transportation

The principle of the fuel cell was discovered by the German scientist Christian Friedrich Schönbein in 1838. Based on this work, the first fuel cell was developed by Welsh scientist Sir William Robert Grove in 1845. The 1966 General Motors *Electrovan* was the first attempt at an automobile powered by a hydrogen fuel cell. It could travel at up to 70 mph for 30 seconds. Today, 100 mph and a range of 300–500 miles is possible. Fuel cells are being developed for cars and for public transport.

Hydrogen fuel cells emit only water as a waste product during use. However, carbon dioxide is produced as a by-product during the majority of hydrogen production. This is because, commercially, the most common method for producing bulk quantities of hydrogen is from natural gas by steam reforming. In this reaction, steam reacts with methane to yield carbon monoxide and hydrogen:

$$CH_4 + H_2O \rightarrow CO + 3H_2$$

Then the carbon monoxide is converted to carbon dioxide and more hydrogen:

$$CO + H_2O \rightarrow CO_2 + H_2$$

But, because the hydrogen fuel cell operates at quite a low temperature, below 100 °C, there are no emissions of the oxides of nitrogen (NO_x) that happen at the high temperatures associated with internal combustion engines.

An important feature of fuel cells is that they are non-polluting, and research scientists believe that there are dozens of uses no-one has thought of yet. Scientists in the future will try to find uses for these and other types of fuel cells.

A London Fuel Cell Bus.

A modern car powered by a fuel cell.

14 How does the previous paragraph illustrate the difference between scientific principles and technological advancement?

15 What would be the advantages of a fuel cell for a bus?

16 Why do high temperatures produce the pollutants NO_x?

17 What are the benefits and risks associated with fuel cells?

1 The table below shows some standard electrode potentials.

	$E^{\ominus}(V)$
$Fe^{3+}(aq) + e^- \rightarrow Fe^{2+}(aq)$	+0.77
$Cr^{3+}(aq) + e^- \rightarrow Cr^{2+}(aq)$	−0.41
$Fe^{2+}(aq) + 2e^- \rightarrow Fe(s)$	−0.44
$Zn^{2+}(aq) + 2e^- \rightarrow Zn(s)$	−0.76
$Cr^{2+}(aq) + 2e^- \rightarrow Cr(s)$	−0.91

a Predict the products, if any, when the following substances are mixed. In each case use $E^{\ominus}$ values from the table to explain your answer.
 i iron metal with aqueous zinc(II) ions
 ii aqueous iron(III) ions with aqueous chromium(II) ions   (5)
b Calculate the e.m.f. of the following standard cell and deduce an equation for the overall cell reaction.

$Zn(s)|Zn^{2+}(aq)||Cr^{3+}(aq),Cr^{2+}(aq)|Pt$ (2)

Total 7

AQA, June 2007, Unit 5, Question 3 (a–b)

2 Use the data in the table below, where appropriate, to answer the questions which follow.

Standard electrode potentials	$E^{\ominus}(V)$
$Fe^{3+}(aq) + e^- \rightarrow Fe^{2+}(aq)$	+0.77
$Cl_2(g) + 2e^- \rightarrow 2Cl^-(aq)$	+1.36
$2BrO_3^-(aq) + 12H^+(aq) + 10e^- \rightarrow Br_2(aq) + 6H_2O(l)$	+1.52
$O_3(g) + 2H^+(aq) + 2e^- \rightarrow O_2(g) + H_2O(l)$	+2.08
$F_2O(g) + 2H^+(aq) + 4e^- \rightarrow 2F^-(aq) + H_2O(l)$	+2.15

Each of the above can be reversed under suitable conditions.

a i Identify the most powerful reducing agent in the table.

ii Identify the most powerful oxidising agent in the table.
iii Identify **all** the species in the table which can be oxidised in acidic solution by BrO_3^- (aq).   (4)
b The cell represented below was set up.

$Pt | Fe^{2+}(aq), Fe^{3+}(aq) || BrO_3^- (aq), Br_2(aq) | Pt$

 i Deduce the e.m.f. of this cell.
 ii Write a half-equation for the reaction occurring at the negative electrode when current is taken from this cell.
 iii Deduce what change in the concentration of $Fe^{3+}(aq)$ would cause an increase in the e.m.f. of the cell. Explain your answer.   (6)

Total 10

AQA, June 2006, Unit 5, Question 5

3 Where appropriate, use the standard electrode potential data in the table below to answer the questions which follow.

	$E^{\ominus}(V)$
$Zn^{2+}(aq) + 2e^- \rightarrow Zn(s)$	−0.76
$V^{3+}(aq) + e^- \rightarrow V^{2+}(aq)$	−0.26
$SO_4^{2-}(aq) + 2H^+(aq) + 2e^- \rightarrow SO_3^{2-}(aq) + H_2O(l)$	+0.17
$VO^{2+}(aq) + 2H^+(aq) + e^- \rightarrow V^{3+}(aq) + H_2O(l)$	+0.34
$Fe^{3+}(aq) + e^- \rightarrow Fe^{2+}(aq)$	+0.77
$VO_2^+(aq) + 2H^+(aq) + e^- \rightarrow VO^{2+}(aq) + H_2O(l)$	+1.00
$Cl_2(aq) + 2e^- \rightarrow 2Cl^-(aq)$	+1.36

a From the table above select the species which is the most powerful reducing agent.   (1)
b From the table above select
 i a species which, in acidic solution, will reduce $VO_2^+(aq)$ to $VO^{2+}(aq)$ but will **not** reduce $VO^{2+}(aq)$ to $V^{3+}(aq)$,

ii a species which, in acidic solution, will oxidise $VO^{2+}(aq)$ to $VO_2^+(aq)$. (2)

c The cell represented below was set up under standard conditions.

$Pt|Fe^{2+}(aq), Fe^{3+}(aq)||Tl^{3+}(aq),Tl^+(aq)|Pt$
Cell e.m.f. = + 0.48 V

i Deduce the standard electrode potential for the following half-reaction.
$Tl^{3+}(aq) + 2e^- \rightarrow Tl^+(aq)$

ii Write an equation for the spontaneous cell reaction. (3)

Total 6

AQA, June 2005, Unit 5, Question 4 (a–c)

4 Use the standard electrode potential data given in the table below, where appropriate, to answer the questions which follow.

	$E^\ominus$ (V)
$V^{3+}(aq) + e^- \rightarrow V^{2+}(aq)$	−0.26
$SO_4^{2-}(aq) + 4H^+(aq) + 2e^- \rightarrow H_2SO_3(aq) + H_2O$	+0.17
$VO^{2+}(aq) + 2H^+(aq) + e^- \rightarrow V^{3+}(aq) + H_2O(l)$	+0.34
$O_2(g) + 2H^+(aq) + 2e^- \rightarrow H_2O_2(aq)$	+0.68
$Fe^{3+}(aq) + e^- \rightarrow Fe^{2+}(aq)$	+0.77
$VO_2^+(aq) + 2H^+(aq) + e^- \rightarrow VO^{2+}(aq) + H_2O(l)$	+1.00
$2IO_3^-(aq) + 12H^+(aq) + 10e^- \rightarrow I_2(aq) + 6H_2O(l)$	+1.19
$MnO_4^-(aq) + 8H^+(aq) + 5e^- \rightarrow Mn^{2+}(aq) + 4H_2O(l)$	+1.52

Each of the above can be reversed under suitable conditions.

a The cell represented below was set up under standard conditions.

$Pt | H_2SO_3(aq),SO_4^{2-}(aq) || Fe^{3+}(aq),Fe^{2+}(aq) | Pt$

i Calculate the e.m.f. of this cell.
ii Write a half-equation for the oxidation process occurring at the negative electrode of this cell. (2)

b The cell represented below was set up under standard conditions.

$Pt | H_2O_2(aq),O_2(g) || IO_3^-(aq), I_2(aq) | Pt$

i Write an equation for the spontaneous cell reaction.
ii Give **one** reason why the e.m.f. of this cell changes when the electrodes are connected and a current flows.
iii State how, if at all, the e.m.f. of this standard cell will change if the surface area of each platinum electrode is doubled.
iv State how, if at all, the e.m.f. of this cell will change if the concentration of IO_3^- ions is increased. Explain your answer. (7)

Total 9

AQA, January 2005, Unit 5, Question 3 a,b

A solar rechargeable aircraft

AeroVironment, an American company based in California, has been developing prototypes for solar rechargeable aircraft (SRAs) since the early 1980s. *Pathfinder* is a recent addition to a line of prototypes for use in monitoring weather and relaying data transmitted through the atmosphere (in mobile communications). *Pathfinder* can also act like a **geostationary satellite**, but much closer to Earth.

The aircraft is solar powered during the day, but at night, until a technological solution is found, an SRA is still dependent to some extent on electrochemical cells, for its navigational lights, for example. Electrochemical cells were used during aircraft tests, to save on building expensive solar cell arrays.

According to an engineer working on the research: 'When we started work on *Pathfinder*, we did some calculations with $E^{\ominus}$ values to get an idea of the cells that

would give us a large voltage. But potential isn't everything. We needed to consider how much energy could be stored per kilogram of cell (energy density), how quickly it could be released safely (power density), and the cell had to be rechargeable.'

During the developmental stages, engineers investigated electrode potentials (Tables 2 and 3) for a variety of cells, including Ag | Zn, Li | MnO_2 and Li | SO_2 cells. Now they have settled on a combined fuel cell with electrochemical cells that are charged by the solar panels during daytime.

The eternal aeroplane is now a reality. The cost is only one-tenth of that to put a conventional satellite in position, because it does not need an expensive rocket launch. As well as studying weather systems, there is great interest in monitoring crops and potential drought areas. Ocean currents can be mapped, marine traffic can be monitored and oil spills can be tracked.

The *Pathfinder* prototype in flight. The craft has a take-off distance of just 24 metres; less than its own wing span! The 'flying wing' has reached an altitude of 15 385 m, and can travel at 24 kilometres per hour.

A1 Researchers worldwide need to use a standard notation system. Write out half-reactions that obey the IUPAC convention for the following:

a zinc metal (Zn) in equilibrium with zinc ions (Zn^{2+})

b manganese(II) ions in equilibrium with manganese(IV) ions in acidic solution

c oxygen gas (O_2) in equilibrium with oxide (OH^-) ions in aqueous solution.

d Explain what would happen to the electrode potential of the Zn^{2+} | Zn electrode if the Zn^{2+} concentration $[Zn^{2+}]$ was increased.

A2

a Write the correct notation for electrodes that have the following half-reactions:

i $Zn^{2+}(aq) + 2e^- \rightleftharpoons Zn(s)$

ii $Li^+(aq) + e^- \rightleftharpoons Li(s)$

iii $H^+(aq) + e^- \rightleftharpoons \frac{1}{2}H_2(g)$.

b What special purpose does the reaction in **a iii** have?

c What conditions are used for standard electrode potentials?

A3 Write the correct notation for the following cells:

a a zinc electrode in zinc sulfate solution connected to a silver electrode in silver sulfate solution

b a zinc electrode in zinc sulfate solution connected to the SHE, which is represented by: $Pt(s) | H_2(g) | H^+(aq)$.

A4

a The cell used in the *Pathfinder* prototype for test flights was a zinc | silver cell. Give one reason why this cell was chosen in preference to the zinc | copper cell. (Use Table 2 to help you.)

b Draw a diagram like Fig. 5 for the zinc | silver cell.

c Calculate the standard cell potential for this cell.

d The potential for the Li | SO_2 cell is +3.43 V. Give two advantages of this cell over the Zn | Ag cell.

A5 Predict what would happen (if anything) in the following:

a Zn(s) with $Ag_2SO_4(aq)$

b Ag(s) with $ZnSO_4(aq)$

c $I_2(g)$ with $Br^-(aq)$

d $Br_2(g)$ with $I^-(aq)$.

Explain your reasoning in each case.

15 Transition metals and their compounds

The simplest glazes that potters use are colourless, and include the oxides of silicon, sodium, calcium, aluminium and boron. To apply them to pottery, these compounds are finely powdered and suspended in water. Potters also want to create colourful designs in intricate patterns. So they need a range of colours that can be painted on and yet will withstand the heat of the kiln. Simple dyestuffs cannot be used, because they are organic compounds and will decompose at extreme temperatures. Instead, compounds of **transition metals** are used, because they are stable at high temperatures. Some produce the required colour only after firing.

The colour of glazes is produced because of the way the glaze compound (pigment) affects light. The pigment absorbs radiation from part of the visible spectrum, and we see as a colour the part of the visible spectrum that it reflects. In this chapter we learn about the arrangement of electrons within the transition metal atoms and how this gives rise to colour. The Chinese used iron oxides in glazes as long ago as 200 BC and could produce a whole range of shades for their pottery. Iron(II) oxide, FeO, has the outer electron configuration $4s^03d^6$ formed by the loss of the two 4s electrons. Iron can also lose a d electron and become iron(III), as in iron(III) oxide, Fe_2O_3, where the iron has electron configuration $4s^03d^5$. FeO is black and Fe_2O_3 is reddish-brown, so the change in oxidation state has produced a change in colour. By changing the firing conditions,

the final oxidation state of the glaze can be controlled. In oxidising conditions it forms Fe(III), while in reducing conditions it forms Fe(II).

A common compound for producing a rich blue glaze is cobalt(II) oxide, CoO. Like iron, cobalt is one of the d block elements of the Periodic Table.

The acidity or alkalinity of the glaze also affects the colour. This is because transition metal ions have other molecules or ions attached to them, called **ligands**, which alter when conditions change from acidic to alkaline, or vice versa. The potters of the ancient world did not understand the theory of ligand or redox chemistry, nor did they understand how colour is produced by absorbing various parts of the visible spectrum. Yet they used these properties to make some of the greatest artistic treasures of the world.

In modern industries, chemists and engineers are trying to produce maximum yield of product at the minimum cost, so **catalysts** are vital in their work. Certain transition metals, e.g. nickel and platinum, can catalyse a range of reactions. Transition metal ions can act as catalysts by changing from one oxidation state to another. When they do this, there is a transfer of electrons, producing a redox reaction.

The most important single use of catalysts nowadays is in pollution control for the protection of the environment. The use of fossil fuels for transport means that chemists are continually engaged in the work of solving the problem of exhaust emissions (Fig. 1). The combustion temperature inside an engine produces a mixture of various oxides of nitrogen, e.g. NO_2, NO, etc., that are often referred to as NO_x. These can oxidise O_2 to O_3, giving *ground-level* ozone, which can lead to eye irritation, as well as to a variety of respiratory problems such as bronchitis and emphysema. The catalytic converter removes gases such as unburnt hydrocarbons and nitrogen oxides by changing them to nitrogen, water and carbon dioxide.

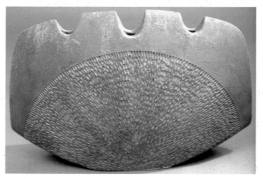

Various transition metals were used to produce the glaze on each pottery item above.

Fig. 1   A cut-away view of the type of catalytic converter used in car exhausts

Chemists need and use a vast array of catalysts. But it is not only the oxidation number of the transition element that is important. The way the surface is designed and the shape of the catalytic material can be just as important.

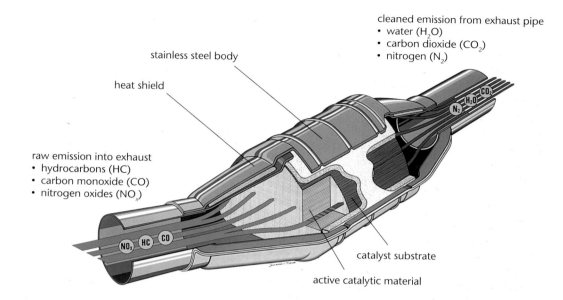

cleaned emission from exhaust pipe
• water (H_2O)
• carbon dioxide (CO_2)
• nitrogen (N_2)

stainless steel body

heat shield

raw emission into exhaust
• hydrocarbons (HC)
• carbon monoxide (CO)
• nitrogen oxides (NO_x)

catalyst substrate

active catalytic material

15.1 Transition metals

The **transition metal** elements are found in the central d block of the Periodic Table (see Fig. 2). The first transition series, in Period 4 of

Transition metals are used in a variety of alloys to add strength, hardness and resistance to corrosion. Centre: copper. Clockwise from upper left: nickel–chrome ore, nickel bars, titanium bars, iron–nickel ore, niobium bars, chromium granules.

the Periodic Table, contains the elements from scandium to copper. The Period 4 elements have common properties:

• They are generally hard metals.
• They form complex ions.
• Their ions are coloured.
• They show catalytic activity.
• Their oxidation states are variable.

A transition element is an element having an incomplete d (or f) shell either in the element or in one of its ions.

The properties of transition elements are directly related to the electronic structures of the atoms. A selection of properties of the Period 4 (3d block) transition elements is listed in Table 1.

The order of filling the sub-shells follows the pattern shown in the third row of Table 1. The pattern is not completely regular because the

Fig. 2   The Periodic Table (Periods 1 to 6) with the transition metals of d block highlighted

s block   p block

H 1																	He 2
Li 3	Be 4											B 5	C 6	N 7	O 8	F 9	Ne 10
Na 11	Mg 12				d block transition elements							Al 13	Si 14	P 15	S 16	Cl 17	Ar 18
K 19	Ca 20	**Sc** 21	**Ti** 22	**V** 23	**Cr** 24	**Mn** 25	**Fe** 26	**Co** 27	**Ni** 28	**Cu** 29	Zn 30	Ga 31	Ge 32	As 33	Se 34	Br 35	Kr 36
Rb 37	Sr 38	**Y** 39	**Zr** 40	**Nb** 41	**Mo** 42	**Tc** 43	**Ru** 44	**Rh** 45	**Pd** 46	**Ag** 47	**Cd** 48	In 49	Sn 50	Sb 51	Te 52	I 53	Xe 54
Cs 55	Ba 56	**La** 57	**Hf** 72	**Ta** 73	**W** 74	**Re** 75	**Os** 76	**Ir** 77	**Pt** 78	**Au** 79	**Hg** 80	Tl 81	Pb 82	Bi 83	Po 84	At 85	Rn 86

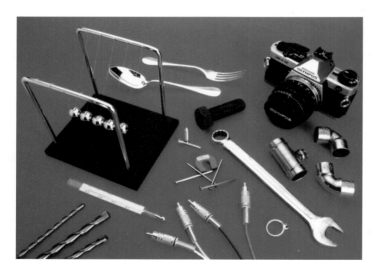

Many familiar objects such as those shown above are made from transition metal elements or alloys of them.

values of the energies of the sub-shells are similar to one another. The orbitals for Period 3 (Na to Ar) are filled according to a regular pattern of s followed by p, but the way the d orbitals in transition metals are filled is different and a little more complex, as Table 1 shows. (Note that the table shows the order of filling, but not the order in which a first electron is removed on ionisation.)

The energies of the 4s and 3d levels are similar (see *AS Chemistry*, page 19), and the energy levels change as new electrons are added. As the nuclear charge increases, so does its attraction for electrons. The sub-shells move closer to the nucleus, and so their energies are lowered. Each type of sub-shell is affected differently by the attraction of the nucleus and by repulsion between electrons in the occupied orbitals.

Table 1   Some properties of Period 4 elements

	Sc	Ti	V	Cr	Mn	Fe	Co	Ni	Cu	Zn
Melting point (°C)	1539	1675	1900	1890	1244	1535	1495	1453	1083	420
First ionisation energy (kJ mol⁻¹)	633	659	650	653	717	762	759	736	745	906
Outer electron configuration	$3d^14s^2$	$3d^24s^2$	$3d^34s^2$	$3d^54s^1$	$3d^54s^2$	$3d^64s^2$	$3d^74s^2$	$3d^84s^2$	$3d^{10}4s^1$	$3d^{10}4s^2$
Atomic radius (nm)	0.164	0.147	0.135	0.129	0.137	0.126	0.125	0.125	0.128	0.137

When the d sub-shells in Period 4 are empty, the 4s sub-shell is at a lower energy than 3d, but when the electrons occupy the d sub-shells, the 4s sub-shell is at a higher energy level than the 3d sub-shell. This means that, when transition metal atoms react, they lose the higher-energy 4s electrons first, acquiring a +2 oxidation state. This is one of the reasons why the transition metals have very similar chemical properties to each other and why +2 is the common oxidation state for metals.

As an atom, copper has the electron configuration $[Ar]3d^{10}4s^1$. When it reacts, it can lose the $4s^1$ electron to form Cu(I) compounds, which have a full 3d shell. In addition, however, it can lose the 4s electron plus one of its d electrons when it forms Cu(II).

Compare this with zinc. The d orbitals in zinc are so low in energy that they are not involved in bonding at all. For this reason, and since transition metals are defined as those elements that have an unfilled d orbital in their atoms or ions, zinc is not normally regarded as a transition metal.

Now consider scandium. The normal ion formed in scandium compounds is Sc(III). It has no electrons in the d orbital – its electron configuration is $[Ar]3d^04s^0$. So scandium compounds do not show the typical properties of transition metal compounds, and neither scandium nor zinc will be considered further in this chapter. But, as the element has the electron configuration $[Ar]3d^14s^2$, scandium is still classed as a transition element.

---

1 Write out the electron configurations for:

a Fe^0

b Fe^{2+}

c Fe^{3+}.

- Transition metals have several properties in common.

- Transition metal compounds have partially filled 3d sub-shells.

- When transition metals react, the 4s electrons are lost first.

15.2 Complex ions

Transition metal *ions* form links with specific numbers of molecules or ions that surround the central metal ion. Likewise, many transition metal *compounds* have a central transition metal ion bonded by **co-ordinate bonds** (covalent bonds) to atoms, groups of atoms or ions called **ligands**. Ligands can donate a pair of electrons to the metal ion. The bond is called co-ordinate because both the electrons in the bond are donated by the same atom. These bonds are often represented by arrows (see Fig. 3). When ions such as the one shown in Fig. 3 are dissolved in water,

they will become hydrated and be aqueous ions.

These transition metal ions with ligands attached are the species involved in transition metal chemistry, and they are called **complex ions**. The whole complex is an ion because it carries a charge, but the bonds within the complex are co-ordinate covalent bonds. The number of ligands associated with the central metal ion is called its **co-ordination number**. For example, $[Ag(H_2O)_2]^+$ has a co-ordination number of 2 (two water ligands attached), and $[Cu(H_2O)_6]^{2+}$ has a co-ordination number of 6.

Fig. 3   Co-ordinate bonds from H₂O to Mⁿ⁺

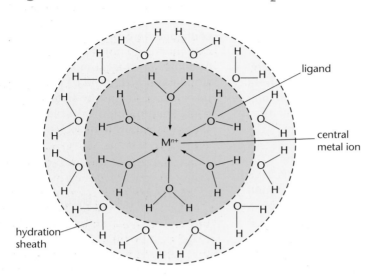

Shapes of complex ions

Complexes can be octahedral if the co-ordination number is 6, tetrahedral or square planar if the co-ordination number is 4, or linear if the co-ordination number is 2 (Fig. 5).

Fig. 5   General structure of some transition metal complexes

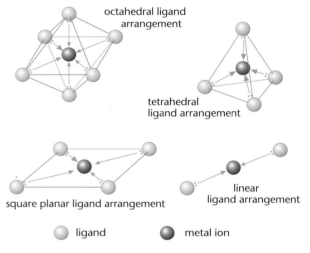

2 What are the co-ordination numbers of the copper and platinum ions in Fig. 4?

Fig. 4   Complex ions: (a) hydrated complex of copper(II) and (b) cisplatin

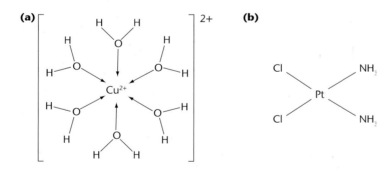

The size of the ligand has an effect on the shape of the complex ion. Water, ammonia and cyanide are small, and six ligands can fit around the central metal ion, forming an octahedral complex. With larger ions such as chloride, only four ligands can fit around the central metal ion, giving a tetrahedral ion. Some complexes with co-ordination number 4 are square planar, e.g. cisplatin (see Figs 4(b), 5 and 27), which has two Cl^- ligands and two NH_3 ligands. The complex ion

Ligands

Ligands may be molecules or ions, but they all donate a pair of electrons into vacant orbitals on the central metal ion. Water – called 'aqua' when it is part of a complex – is the most common ligand. Many others exist: ammonia (ammine), the hydroxide ion (hydroxo), the chloride ion (chloro) and the cyanide ion (cyano) all take part in complex formation.

3 Write down the formula for the copper complex in Fig. 6.

4 Give the bond angles in:

a octahedrally shaped complexes

b tetrahedrally shaped complexes.

Fig. 6 Copper(II) complex ion

$[Cu(NH_3)_4(H_2O)_2]^{2+}$ is often described as square planar, but it also has two water ligands at a greater distance than the ammine ligands, forming a distorted octahedral structure.

Some transition elements form complexes with a co-ordination number of 2. These are linear complexes. Examples include Ag(I) complexes and Cu(I) complexes. An example is $[Ag(NH_3)_2]^+$, the complex formed in Tollens' reagent, used in the test to distinguish between aldehydes and ketones.

Types of ligands

Each water molecule in diaquasilver(I) ions, $[Ag(H_2O)_2]^+$, forms *one* co-ordinate bond with the central silver ion, because there is only *one* atom (oxygen) in the water molecule with a pair of electrons available for co-ordinate bonding. Such a ligand is said to be a **unidentate ligand**, as it is only able to donate *one* lone pair of electrons (Fig. 7).

A **bidentate ligand** can form two bonds. An example is the ethanedioate ion (see Fig. 7). A lone pair of electrons on each of the two oxygen atoms can form co-ordinate bonds. A **multidentate ligand** can form several bonds with the central metal ion because it has a number of atoms with lone pairs of electrons available for bonding (see Fig. 7 and Table 2). A **hexadentate ligand** has six donor atoms with lone electron pairs. EDTA^{4-} is a hexadentate ligand.

The lone pairs in EDTA are on the two nitrogen atoms and on four of the oxygen atoms. EDTA forms one-to-one complexes with metal(II) atoms, such as $[Cu(EDTA)]^{2-}$ (Fig. 8). The complexes formed by multidentate ligands

Fig. 7 Types of ligands

Unidentate ligand

H_2O donates one pair of electrons per molecule.

Bidentate ligands

ethanedioate   ethane-1,2-diamine

These donate two pairs of electrons per molecule.

Hexadentate ligand

ethylenediaminetetraacetate ion EDTA^{4-}

This can donate six pairs of electrons per molecule.

Fig. 8 Chelating ligand structures

$[CuEDTA]^{2-}$

$[Cu(en)_3]^{2+}$

Table 2   Names of common ligands

Ion (molecule)	Formula	Ligand name	Type of ligand
chloride	Cl^-	chloro	unidentate
hydroxide	OH^-	hydroxo	unidentate
water	H_2O	aqua	unidentate
ammonia	NH_3	ammine	unidentate
cyanide	CN^-	cyano	unidentate
ethane-1,2-diamine	$H_2NCH_2CH_2NH_2$ or (en)	ethane-1,2-diamine or (en)	bidentate
ethanedioate	$(COO)_2^{2-}$	ethanedioate	bidentate
ethylenediaminetetraacetic acid	H_4EDTA	$EDTA^{4-}$	hexadentate
ethylenediaminetetraacetate ion	$EDTA^{4-}$	$EDTA^{4-}$	hexadentate

are very stable, because the central cation is firmly held by many co-ordinate bonds. They are sometimes called **chelating ligands** (the word 'chelate' is derived from the Greek *khele* = claw). Sometimes, bidentate ligands can form similar structures, e.g. $[Cu(en)_3]^{2+}$ (see Fig. 8).

The charge on complex ions

In the complex ion $[Cr(H_2O)_6]^{3+}$, the water ligands are neutral molecules, so the overall charge on the complex is the charge on the transition metal ion. In complexes such as $[CoCl_4]^{2-}$, the ligands are ions, so the overall charge on the complex is the sum of the charges on the central metal ion and the ligands. Some examples of complexes and ligands with their charges are shown in Table 3.

Haemoglobin

One of the most important compounds in the body is **haemoglobin**. Haemoglobin is the oxygen-carrying protein in the blood. It transports oxygen from the lungs to every other part of the body. Haemoglobin consists of a haem molecule (Fig. 9) bonded to a molecule of a protein called globin.

At the centre of the haem molecule is an iron(II) ion, surrounded by a **porphyrin** structure. The iron(II) complex is octahedrally co-ordinated. The porphyrin ligand provides four nitrogen atoms, each with a lone pair of electrons. All four are bonded to the iron(II) ion, so that porphyrin is a **tetradentate ligand**. The bonds form the square planar part of the octahedral structure. The haem is embedded in a globin protein, which has a nitrogen atom occupying the fifth position, and an oxygen forming the sixth bond (Fig. 10). When oxygen is released another ligand will take its place.

Table 3   Charges for some complex ions and ligands

Complex	Ligand	Charge due to ligands	Overall charge	Charge on metal
$[CoCl_4]^{2-}$	Cl^-	4^-	2^-	2^+
$[CoEDTA]^{2-}$	$EDTA^{4-}$	4^-	2^-	2^+
$[Cu(H_2O)_6]^{2+}$	H_2O	0	2^+	2^+
$[Ag(NH_3)_2]^+$	NH_3	0	1^+	1^+

Fig. 9   Haem structure

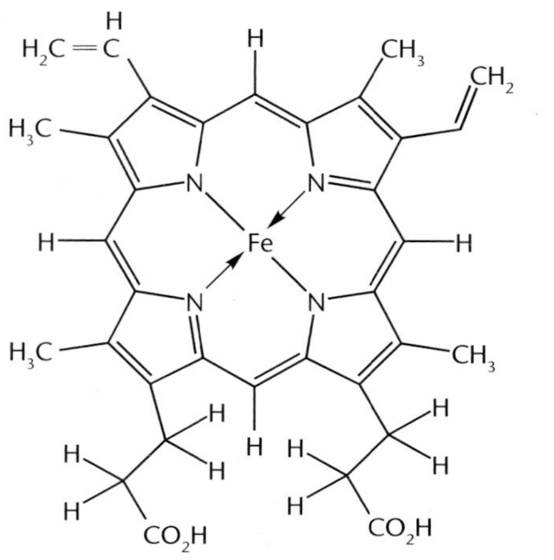

Fig. 10   The haemoglobin molecule

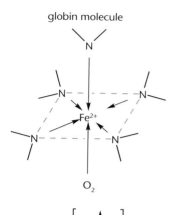

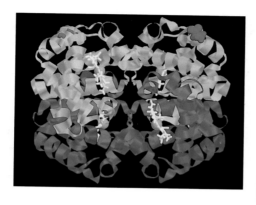

Computer graphic of haemoglobin. It has four globin groups (shown as yellow and blue) with a haem group (white) in each.

5 Read the text and look at the diagrams relating to haemoglobin and answer the following questions.

a What is the overall co-ordination number of the iron ion?

b What is the oxidation number of the iron?

c Is the porphyrin a neutral or negative ligand?

d Why is porphyrin called a tetradentate ligand?

e Draw the arrangement of the nitrogens linking to the iron in a square planar pattern.

key facts

- Co-ordination number is the number of ligands surrounding the central metal ion.

- Shapes of complex ions can be linear, square planar, tetrahedral and octahedral.

- Types of ligands are unidentate, bidentate and hexadentate (multidentate).

- The overall charge on the complex ion is the sum of the overall charges on the ligands and the central metal ion.

 A task sheet and practice questions on the Practical Skills Assessment 'Investigate the chemistry of transition metal compounds in a series of experiments' can be found at www.collinseducation.co.uk/advancedscienceaqa

15.3 Colour

A typical property of transition metal compounds is that they are coloured. Colour is produced when some parts of the visible spectrum are absorbed and others are reflected. The haem complex in haemoglobin is red and is responsible for the red colour of blood. The colour of these complexes is related to the 3d electron configuration of the transition metal and to the nature and number of the ligands. If the oxygen attached to the haemoglobin (making oxyhaemoglobin) is replaced by carbon monoxide, carboxyhaemoglobin is formed, which has a darker red colour, a sign of carbon monoxide poisoning.

The electron configuration for any element can be worked out using the Periodic Table. So, from the Periodic Table, the s,p,d notation for chromium is:

$1s^2 2s^2 2p^6 3s^2 3p^6 3d^5 4s^1$ (and $4p^0$)
This can also be written as $[Ar]3d^5 4s^1$.

6 What is the electron configuration of iron (atomic number 26)?

Paint pigments made from transition metal compounds are coloured because they each absorb a particular range of the frequencies of light in the visible spectrum, and reflect others.

How does absorption produce colour?

The chemical compounds we call 'pigments' exhibit an enormously wide range of colours. Light is electromagnetic radiation in the visible spectrum, and when it falls on pigments, they absorb and reflect different wavelengths of its energy. The wavelengths of visible (white) light range from 400 nm to 700 nm, made up of all the colours of the rainbow. Violet has the shortest wavelength (highest energy) and red the longest wavelength (lowest energy) of light.

If an electron absorbs wavelengths within that range, it will reflect a colour (which we see) made up of all the other visible wavelengths minus the wavelengths it absorbs. Only electrons in d energy levels do this. So if an ion or compound has atoms with no d electrons, or if they have a full (d^{10}) configuration, the ion or compound will absorb outside the visible region and appear colourless or white.

In 1900, Max Planck, working on his quantum theory, proposed that energy can only be absorbed (or emitted) in definite amounts (called **quanta**) and that each of these amounts of energy corresponds to a particular **frequency** of radiation (symbol v, pronounced nu). Frequency is the number of wavelengths of light passing a particular point in a second. Planck summed up his findings in his equation:

$$\Delta E = hv$$

where ΔE is an energy difference and h is Planck's constant.

If an outer electron of atom X absorbs the right amount of energy, it can move from a lower to a higher energy level: it makes a **transition**. When the electron moves to the higher energy level, it absorbs an amount of energy exactly equal to the energy difference (ΔE) between the two allowed energy levels for that electron in atom X. The energy absorbed can cover a range of frequencies. If the frequencies are in the visible spectrum, colour will be observed.

If the transition energy is larger, the radiation may fall in the ultraviolet region (sunscreens absorb harmful ultraviolet radiation). If the transition energy is smaller, the radiation may be in the infrared region.

Van Gogh used a chromium compound to provide his yellow colours (*chroma* means colour).

In a transition metal *atom*, all the electrons in the d orbitals are at the same energy level. When the atom forms part of a complex ion, however, the ligand 'splits' the d orbitals into two groups (Fig. 11).

Identifying transition metals

Each of the transition elements is different, so the electrons of each element have their own sets of values for allowed energy levels and their own absorption frequencies and so reflect particular colours. Different transition elements

Fig. 11   Splitting of d orbitals due to a ligand

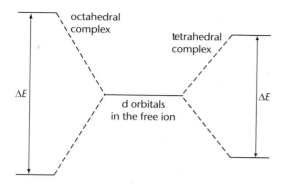

will have different nuclear charges and therefore different attractive forces for the electrons in their orbitals. A larger nuclear charge will have a stronger force of attraction, so more energy will be needed to move the electron from one d energy level to another. The absorption is therefore at a different frequency, and a different colour is produced. This property can be used to identify different transition metal compounds.

When white light passes through a solution and some of the frequencies are absorbed, the light that emerges will be different. If the red part of the spectrum is absorbed, the emerging light will have lost this part of the spectrum and will be bluer. An example of this is $[Cu(H_2O)_6]^{2+}$, which absorbs red light and so appears blue (Fig. 12).

Fig. 12   Light absorption by solutions

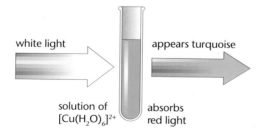

If the blue part of the spectrum (different energy) is absorbed, the emerging light will have a colour that is more yellow or red. The blue end of the visible spectrum is of higher energy, so ions that absorb blue light have a larger ΔE

value (Fig. 13). The factors that affect the value of ΔE are:

- the ligand
- the size of the ligand
- the strength of the ligand–metal bond in the complex
- the shape of the complex
- the co-ordination number
- the oxidation state.

Fig. 13   Splitting of d orbital and colour

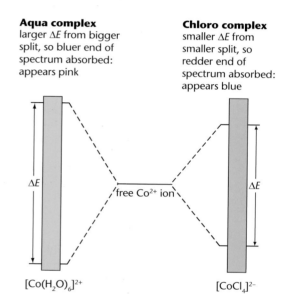

Aqua complex
larger ΔE from bigger split, so bluer end of spectrum absorbed: appears pink

Chloro complex
smaller ΔE from smaller split, so redder end of spectrum absorbed: appears blue

$[Co(H_2O)_6]^{2+}$ $[CoCl_4]^{2-}$

Changing the ligands
If a transition metal ion is dissolved in water, the lone pairs on the water molecules are attracted to the positive metal ion. The best way for these ligands to fit around the ion is in an octahedral arrangement (Fig. 14). If the ligand is changed, the value of ΔE is also changed.

Changing the oxidation state
Changing the oxidation state of a given element changes the number of electrons in the d levels. This will alter the value of ΔE. Table 4 summarises some examples.

> **7** Which end of the spectrum is more likely to be absorbed by an ion with a large energy split?

Table 4   Examples of factors affecting colour

Changing the ligand		Changing the co-ordination number	Changing the oxidation state	
$[Cr(H_2O)_6]^{3+}$ red-violet octahedral	$[Cr(NH_3)_6]^{3+}$ purple octahedral	$[Cu(H_2O)_6]^{2+}$ blue octahedral	$[Fe(H_2O)_6]^{2+}$ green octahedral	$[Fe(H_2O)_6]^{3+}$ pale violet octahedral
$[Cu(H_2O)_6]^{2+}$ blue octahedral	$[Cu(NH_3)_4(H_2O)_2]^{2+}$ blue-violet octahedral	$[CuCl_4]^{2-}$ yellow tetrahedral	$[Cr(H_2O)_6]^{3+}$ red-violet octahedral	$[Cr(NH_3)_6]^{2+}$ blue octahedral

Fig. 14 $[Co(H_2O)_6]^{2+}$ (octahedral) changing to $[CoCl_4]^{2-}$ (tetrahedral)

Water and chloride ions cause ligand and co-ordination number to change, but with Co^{2+} ions there is no change in oxidation state. With cobalt chloride paper, this colour change is used to detect the presence of water:

water present	water absent
$[Co(H_2O)_6]^{2+}$	$[CoCl_4]^{2-}$
pink	blue

The aqua complex absorbs blue, green and yellow, so it is pink. The chloro complex absorbs orange, red and pink, so it is blue.

Cobalt chloride paper before and after the addition of water.

8 Which ligand, Cl^- or H_2O, produces a larger d orbital split?

9 Why does the colour change if the ligand is changed?

10 If $[Cu(H_2O)_6]^{2+}$ is treated with excess CN^- ions, it will go through a series of reactions and eventually form the complex ion $[Cu(CN)_4]^{3-}$.

a Give the oxidation state for the copper in the two complexes above.

b Write the electronic configuration for the copper in each of these complexes.

c The aqua complex is blue and the cyano complex is colourless. Explain this change in terms of electronic configuration.

Analysing for colour

Absorption of light

The amount of light absorbed by a solution depends on the number of ions it interacts with, so it will be affected by:

- the nature of the ion (relates to ΔE)
- the concentration of the solution
- the distance the light has to travel through the solution (path length).

The more light that is absorbed, the less is transmitted (Fig. 15).

If a solution is more concentrated, more ions are present in a given volume, more will interact, so the colour will be more intense. If the light has to travel a greater distance, there will again be more ions to interact with the light.

Fig. 15 The effect of path length and concentration on light absorption

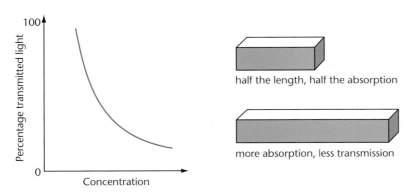

half the length, half the absorption

more absorption, less transmission

A more concentrated solution will allow less light to be transmitted.

A typical spectrophotometer has two radiation sources, to provide frequencies in both the ultraviolet and visible regions. The various frequencies are separated by using a prism (or more commonly a diffraction grating), which rotates very slowly. As the prism rotates, the different wavelengths pass, in turn, through a very narrow slit, producing a series of very precise wavelengths of light, each referred to as **monochromatic radiation**. As the radiation passes through the sample, particular frequencies are absorbed, giving a broad band of absorption characteristic of the ion. This absorption pattern is displayed as a spectrum drawn on a paper chart, as a spectrum on a visual display unit (VDU) or as a printout of absorbance at particular wavelengths. The height of the peak relates to the concentration of the solution (Fig. 17).

Ultraviolet/visible spectrophotometry

The instrument used to find the concentration of metal ions in solution is called a **spectrophotometer** (Fig. 16). It uses visible or ultraviolet (UV) radiation to shine through the sample. Some radiation is absorbed and the remainder passes through to the detector. The amount absorbed is displayed as a meter reading or as a graph. If the nature of the ion and the path length are fixed, we can find the concentration in a sample by comparing it with standard solutions.

Procedure. Because aqueous complexes have only very weak absorptions, a suitable ligand is first added to the ion to give an intense colour. The visible range is scanned to find the most intense absorption frequency, and then a suitable range of frequencies is passed through a solution of fixed path length.

SCN⁻ gives an intense red colour with Fe^{3+}, so it is used frequently for analysing Fe^{3+} compounds.

Fig. 16 Scheme for an ultraviolet/visible spectrophotometer

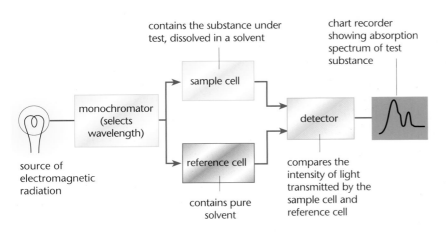

contains the substance under test, dissolved in a solvent

chart recorder showing absorption spectrum of test substance

sample cell

source of electromagnetic radiation

monochromator (selects wavelength)

detector

reference cell

contains pure solvent

compares the intensity of light transmitted by the sample cell and reference cell

11 Why does the colour of a solution become pale if water is added?

12 What is the wavelength of the peak absorption in Fig. 17?

Fig. 17   An absorption spectrum for a blue dye

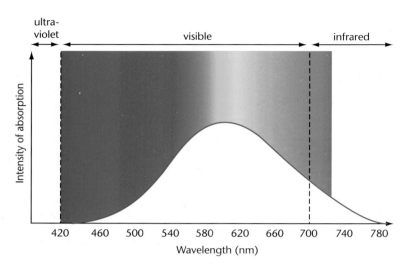

Colorimeter

A simpler instrument that can be used to measure the absorption of radiation is the **colorimeter**. This uses a lamp as a source of white light, which passes through a filter to produce light of one colour. This colour will be the one that the sample will absorb the most and is called its **complementary colour**. For example, a blue solution will absorb red, and therefore a red filter is used, so that only red light passes through the solution and maximum absorption occurs.

Usually, a set of standard solutions is prepared to give a calibration graph for the instrument, and then the unknown concentration can be determined from the calibration graph, using the colorimeter reading for the unknown.

key facts

● The colour of ions depends on which part of the visible spectrum is being absorbed.

● The energy of the radiation absorbed will depend on the energy split within the d orbitals.

● The frequency of the radiation absorbed is given by the relationship: $\Delta E = h\nu$.

● A ligand produces the splitting of the energy levels within the d orbitals.

● The energy split in the d orbitals depends on the element and its oxidation state.

● The extent of the ligand splitting will depend on the ligand and the shape of the complex ion formed.

● Concentration of ions can be determined using UV/visible spectrophotometry.

15.4 Changing oxidation states

One of the properties of transition metals is that of variable **oxidation state**. When metals react, they lose electrons, and the higher-energy electrons will be lost first. For transition metals these are the 4s electrons. This gives a commonly occurring oxidation state for metals of +2. However, transition metals can form compounds in which the transition metal has other oxidation states, e.g. iron can form Fe^{2+} or Fe^{3+} compounds.

When a transition metal or its ion is oxidised (loses electrons), it forms an ion with a higher oxidation state. The reacting species must be reduced (gains electrons) and forms a lower oxidation state. These are redox reactions. Metallic zinc is a good reducing agent. It reacts with dilute acid to form Zn^{2+} ions and releases electrons for the reduction:

$$Zn \rightarrow Zn^{2+} + 2e^-$$

We can see this process in the reactions of many transition elements. If you take the highest oxidation state of chromium, Cr(VI), you can form lower oxidation states using zinc and hydrochloric acid as a reducing agent. Air must be excluded from the Cr^{2+} species otherwise oxidation will occur, giving Cr^{3+} (see Table 5). Changing the oxidation state changes ΔE, the energy of the d orbital splitting, and therefore the colour of the complex. The oxidation states of chromium change in the presence of HCl as acid. Therefore, in Table 5, $[CrCl_2(H_2O)_4]^+$ (green) is the complex, not $[Cr(H_2O)_6]^{3+}$ (blue).

When hydrochloric acid is used for the reduction, the Cl^- ion will act as a ligand, donating to the Cr^{3+} ion. With sulfuric acid, the

If granulated zinc and sulfuric acid (1 mol dm^{-3}) are added to a solution of potassium dichromate (in the absence of air) the chromium is reduced and the solution changes colour from orange to blue.

Table 5   Oxidation states of chromium

The $Cr_2O_7^{2-}$ ion can be reduced using zinc and hydrochloric acid

Oxidation state	+6	+3	+2
Chromium ion	$Cr_2O_7^{2-}$	$[CrCl_2(H_2O)_4]^+$	$[Cr(H_2O)_6]^{2+}$
Colour in aqueous solution	orange	green	blue

complex ion is still green because both SO_4^{2-} and the water act as ligands. $[Cr(H_2O)_6]^{3+}$, which is red-violet, is not formed. Isomers of $CrCl_3(H_2O)_6$ are shown in Table 6.

The equation for the overall redox reaction can be shown as follows. Writing the half-equations for:

$$Cr_2O_7^{2-}(aq) + 8e^- \rightarrow 2Cr^{2+}(aq)$$

and

$$Zn(s) \rightarrow Zn^{2+}(aq) + 2e^-$$

gives:

$$Cr_2O_7^{2-}(aq) + 8e^- + 14H^+ \rightarrow 2Cr^{2+}(aq) + 7H_2O(l)$$

$$Zn(s) \rightarrow Zn^{2+}(aq) + 2e^-$$

Balancing the electron transfer gives:

$$Cr_2O_7^{2-}(aq) + 8e^- + 14H^+ \rightarrow 2Cr^{2+}(aq) + 7H_2O(l)$$

$$4Zn(s) \rightarrow 4Zn^{2+}(aq) + 8e^-$$

Adding these two half-equations gives:

$$Cr_2O_7^{2-}(aq) + \cancel{8e^-} + 14H^+ \rightarrow 2Cr^{2+}(aq) + 7H_2O(l)$$
$$4Zn(s) \rightarrow 4Zn^{2+}(aq) + \cancel{8e^-}$$

$$Cr_2O_7^{2-}(aq) + 14H^+ + 4Zn(s) \rightarrow 2Cr^{2+}(aq) + 7H_2O(l) + 4Zn^{2+}(aq)$$

13

a   Write a balanced redox equation for Zn reducing Cr(VI) to Cr(III).

b   Write a balanced redox equation for Zn reducing Cr(III) to Cr(II).

c   Write a balanced redox equation for O_2(g) oxidising Cr(II) to Cr(III).

Table 6   Isomers of $CrCl_3(H_2O)_6$

Molecular formula	Structural formula	Colour
$CrCl_3(H_2O)_6$	$[Cr(H_2O)_6]^{3+}$ $3Cl^-$	violet
$CrCl_3(H_2O)_6$	$[Cr(H_2O)_5 Cl]^{2+}$ $2Cl^-$ H_2O	light green
$CrCl_3(H_2O)_6$	$[Cr(H_2O)_4 Cl_2]^+$ Cl^- $2H_2O$	dark green

15.5 Changing redox properties

The effect of the ligands on the ease of oxidation can be shown with cobalt. In aqueous solution, the oxidation of $[Co(H_2O)_6]^{2+}$ to $[Co(H_2O)_6]^{3+}$ is not normally possible. However, in alkaline solution the precipitate $Co(OH)_2(aq)$ is formed initially, and this is readily oxidised to $Co(OH)_3$ by any air present (at the surface or dissolved in the solution). An oxidising agent such as H_2O_2 will also do this. Similarly, if an excess of concentrated ammonia solution is added to the initial precipitate of $Co(OH)_2(aq)$, it dissolves to form the pale-brown complex of $[Co(NH_3)_6]^{2+}$, which is again readily oxidised by air or by H_2O_2. This reaction produces the yellow complex hexaammine cobalt(III).

Another ion that can be oxidised by this method is Cr(III). First, the chromium(III) ions are reacted with sodium hydroxide to give $Cr(OH)_3(aq)$:

$$[Cr(H_2O)_6]^{3+} + 3OH^- \rightarrow [Cr(H_2O)_3(OH)_3]$$
$$\text{green}$$

This precipitate will dissolve in an excess of sodium hydroxide solution, giving a deep green solution of $[Cr(OH)_6]^{3-}$:

$$[Cr(H_2O)_3(OH)_3] + 3OH^- \rightarrow [Cr(OH)_6]^{3-}$$

When H_2O_2 is added, $[Cr(OH)_6]^{3-}$ is oxidised to CrO_4^{2-}:

$$2[Cr(OH)_6]^{3-} + 3H_2O_2 \rightarrow 2CrO_4^{2-} + 2OH^- + 8H_2O$$
$$\text{yellow}$$

The yellow tetraoxochromate(VI) ion forms. The tetraoxochromate(VI) can be converted to dichromate(VI) by simply adding acid:

$$2CrO_4^{2-}(aq) + 2H^+(aq) \rightleftharpoons Cr_2O_7^{2-}(aq) + H_2O(l)$$

Chromium has its highest oxidation state of +6, Cr(VI), in both the complexes CrO_4^{2-} and $Cr_2O_7^{2-}$. The position of the equilibrium:

$$2CrO_4^{2-} + 2H^+ \rightleftharpoons Cr_2O_7^{2-} + H_2O$$

depends on the pH of the solution. In acidic solution, the equilibrium lies to the right, so if H^+ is added, the equilibrium as written will shift from left to right. In high pH, e.g. if OH^- is added to $Cr_2O_7^{2-}$, the equilibrium as written below shifts to the right:

$$2Cr_2O_7^{2-} + 2OH^- \rightleftharpoons 2CrO_4^{2-} + H_2O$$

Another example of where a transition metal ion in a low oxidation state, in an alkaline solution, is readily oxidised to a higher oxidation state is iron(II) being oxidised to iron(III). Aqueous iron(II) ions must be stored as an acidified solution, because any air present will oxidise the solution to iron(III). This process is very rapid if alkali is added to the solution. If all air is excluded from the solution (including dissolved oxygen in the solution), a white precipitate is formed.

Normally, when OH^- is added to Fe^{2+} ions, a 'dirty' green solution is formed, because

General rules

$[M(H_2O)_6]^{2+}$ acid solution harder to oxidise	$[M(H_2O)_4(OH)_2]$ neutral	$[M(OH)_4]^{2-}$ alkaline solution easier to oxidise
High oxidation state $\rightarrow$ e.g. MnO_4^-	low oxidation state $[Mn(H_2O)_6]^{2+}$	use acid + reducing agent
Need to change O^{2-} to H_2O Need to change Mn(VII) to Mn(II)		
Low oxidation state $\rightarrow$ e.g. $[Mn(H_2O)_6]^{2+}$	high oxidation state MnO_4^-	use alkali + oxidising agent
Need to change H_2O to O^{2-} Need to change Mn(II) to Mn(VII)		

oxidation is taking place, giving a complex mixture of compounds. If the solution is left standing, the precipitate will go darker and a brown precipitate of hydrated Fe_2O_3 is formed, especially at the surface of the solution, where it is in contact with the atmosphere.

> **14** Use a calculation to show that there is no change in oxidation states in converting $CrO_4^{2-}(aq)$ to $Cr_2O_7^{2-}(aq)$.

15.6 Redox titrations

Potassium manganate(VII) is a strong oxidising agent and it can be used in titrations to estimate the amount of iron(II) ions in solution.

In the titration, the potassium manganate(VII) is the oxidising agent and it is reduced to $Mn^{2+}(aq)$. The iron is the reducing agent and it is oxidised to $Fe^{3+}(aq)$. The reaction must be acidified, and excess acid is added to the iron(II) ions before the reaction begins. If insufficient acid is present, the brown solid MnO_2 will be formed, and MnO_4^- to Mn^{4+} is only a 3e⁻ change, and has different stoichiometry. The acid used must not react

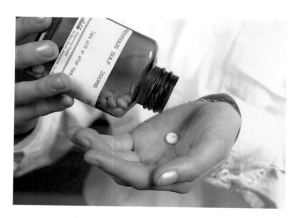

An iron supplement.

with the manganate(VII) ions, so the acid normally used is dilute sulfuric acid. Acids such as hydrochloric acid are not used because the chloride ions in the solution can be oxidised to chlorine.

The acid must:

- be a strong acid, because a high concentration of hydrogen ions is needed
- not be an oxidising agent, because it may react with the reductant and affect the titration results
- not be a reducing agent, because it may be oxidised by the manganate(VII) ions and affect the titration results.

We choose dilute sulfuric acid because it is a strong acid and the dilute acid does not oxidise under these conditions.

Titration of iron(II) with manganate(VII) ions.

We don't choose:

- hydrochloric acid, because it can be oxidised to chlorine by the manganate(VII) ions
- nitric acid, because it is an oxidising agent and may react with the reductant
- concentrated sulfuric acid, because it is an oxidising agent
- ethanoic acid, because it is a weak acid, so the concentration of hydrogen ions will be insufficient.

To find the stoichiometry for the reaction, we follow the usual steps:

Complete the two half-equations:
$$MnO_4^-(aq) + 5e^- + 8H^+(aq) \rightarrow Mn^{2+}(aq) + 4H_2O(l)$$
$$Fe^{2+}(aq) \rightarrow Fe^{3+}(aq) + e^-$$

Balance the electrons:
$$MnO_4^-(aq) + 5e^- + 8H^+(aq) \rightarrow Mn^{2+}(aq) + 4H_2O(l)$$
$$5Fe^{2+}(aq) \rightarrow 5Fe^{3+}(aq) + 5e^-$$

Add the two half-equations:
$$MnO_4^-(aq) + \cancel{5e^-} + 8H^+(aq) \rightarrow Mn^{2+}(aq) + 4H_2O(l)$$
$$5Fe^{2+}(aq) \rightarrow 5Fe^{3+}(aq) + \cancel{5e^-}$$

$$MnO_4^-(aq) + 8H^+(aq) + 5Fe^{2+}(aq) \rightarrow Mn^{2+}(aq) + 4H_2O(l) + 5Fe^{3+}(aq)$$

Check that the charges balance: 17+ on the left-hand side and 17+ on the right-hand side of the equation.

Potassium manganate(VII) acts as its own indicator. As the purple potassium manganate(VII) solution is added to the titration flask from a burette, it reacts rapidly with the $Fe^{2+}(aq)$. The manganese(II) ions have a very pale pink colour, but they are present in such low concentrations that the solution looks colourless. As soon as all the iron(II) ions have reacted with the added manganate(VII) ions, a pink tinge appears in the flask due to an excess of manganate(VII).

Calculating the amount of iron(II) in an iron tablet

An iron tablet weighing 0.850 g is dissolved in dilute sulfuric acid and the whole of this solution is titrated with 0.02 mol dm^{-3} potassium manganate(VII) solution. A titre of 17.4 cm^3 potassium manganate(VII) solution is needed to reach the endpoint. The equation (as above) for the reaction is:

$$MnO_4^-(aq) + 8H^+(aq) + 5Fe^{2+}(aq) \rightarrow$$
$$Mn^{2+}(aq) + 4H_2O(l) + 5Fe^{3+}(aq)$$

The number of moles in a solution is given by the equation:

$$\text{number of moles} = \frac{\text{volume} \times \text{molar concentration}}{1\,000}$$

We can work out the number of moles of manganate(VII) used in the titration:

$$\text{moles of } MnO_4^- \text{ used } = \frac{17.4 \times 0.02}{1\,000}$$
$$= 3.48 \times 10^{-4} \text{ moles}$$

Since five moles of iron(II) are required for every mole of manganate(VII) ion, we get:

$$\text{moles of iron(II)} = 5 \times 3.48 \times 10^{-4} \text{ moles}$$
$$= 1.74 \times 10^{-3} \text{ moles}$$

But:

$$\text{number of moles} = \frac{\text{mass}}{\text{relative atomic mass}}$$

So:

$$\text{mass} = \text{number of moles} \times \text{relative atomic mass}$$

and

$$\text{mass of iron(II)} = 1.74 \times 10^{-3} \times 56 \text{ g}$$
$$= 0.097\,4 \text{ g}$$

The percentage by mass of iron in the tablet is given by the expression:

$$\text{percentage by mass} = \frac{0.097\,4 \times 100}{0.850}$$
$$= 11.5\%$$

Manganate(VII) is in the burette and iron(II) is being pipetted from the volumetric flask into the conical flask.

In many titrations, 250 cm³ of the iron(II) solution will be made up in a volumetric flask. Usually, 25.0 cm³ of iron(II) solution is pipetted into a titration flask and manganate(VII) solution is titrated with this aliquot. When doing the calculations, you must remember to put this dilution factor into your calculation.

Titrating with potassium dichromate(VI) solution

Like the manganate(VII) ion, the dichromate(VI) ion can be used to find the amount of iron in iron tablets. Dichromate(VI) is a powerful

At the endpoint, the contents of the flask start to turn pink.

oxidising agent when it changes from the +6 oxidation state in the dichromate ion, $Cr_2O_7^{2-}$, to the +3 oxidation state in Cr^{3+}:

$$Cr_2O_7^{2-}(aq) + 14H^+(aq) + 6e^- \rightarrow 2Cr^{3+}(aq) + 7H_2O(l)$$

This reacts with iron(II) ions:

$$6Fe^{2+}(aq) \rightarrow 6Fe^{3+}(aq) + 6e^-$$

The colour change for this titration is orange to bluish-green. To give a more visible endpoint, the indicator sodium diphenylaminesulfonate is

used. This turns from colourless to purple at the endpoint.

A different brand of iron tablet, weighing 0.960 g, was dissolved in dilute sulfuric acid. A titre of 28.5 cm³ of 0.0180 mol dm⁻³ potassium dichromate(VI) solution was needed to reach the endpoint. What is the percentage by mass of iron in the tablet? Again, using the correct equation for the redox reaction and the relevant formulae, this can be calculated.

One mole of dichromate ions oxidises six moles of iron(II) ions and the overall equation is:

$$6Fe^{2+}(aq) + Cr_2O_7^{2-}(aq) + 14H^+ \rightarrow$$
$$6Fe^{3+}(aq) + 2Cr^{3+}(aq) + 7H_2O(l)$$

The number of moles of $Cr_2O_7^{2-}$ used in the titration to reach the endpoint is given by:

$$\text{number of moles} = \frac{28.5 \times 0.0180}{1\,000}$$
$$= 5.13 \times 10^{-4} \text{ moles}$$

$$\text{Moles of iron(II)} = 6 \times 5.13 \times 10^{-4} \text{ moles}$$
$$= 3.078 \times 10^{-3} \text{ moles}$$

$$\text{Mass of iron(II)} = 56 \times 3.078 \times 10^{-3}$$
$$= 0.172\,4 \text{ g}$$

The percentage by mass of iron in the tablet is given by:

$$\text{percentage by mass} = \frac{0.172\,4 \times 100}{0.960}$$
$$= 18.0\%$$

15 An iron tablet weighing 0.780 g was dissolved in dilute sulfuric acid and titrated with 0.018 mol dm⁻³ potassium manganate(VII). A titre of 21.5 cm³ of this solution was needed to reach the endpoint. What is the percentage by mass of iron in the tablet?

A task sheet and practice questions on the Practical Skills Assessment 'Carry out a redox titration' can be found at www.collinseducation.co.uk/advancedscienceaqa

16 The balanced redox equation for the reaction of $Cr_2O_7^{2-}(aq)$ with $Fe^{2+}(aq)$ is:

$$Cr_2O_7^{2-}(aq) + 14H^+(aq) + 6Fe^{2+}(aq) \rightarrow$$
$$2Cr^{3+}(aq) + 6Fe^{3+}(aq) + 7H_2O(l)$$

Use your knowledge of oxidation states to show that this is correct.

17 A sample of iron wire of mass 2.225 g was dissolved in dilute sulfuric acid to give a solution containing Fe(II) ions and was made up to 250 cm³ in a volumetric flask. Then 25.0 cm³ of this solution were acidified and titrated against a 0.018 5 mol dm⁻³ solution of potassium dichromate(VI). The iron solution needed 31.00 cm³ of dichromate(VI). Use the following steps to calculate the percentage of iron metal in the iron wire.

a Calculate the number of moles of dichromate(VI) in 31.0 cm³ of a 0.018 5 mol dm⁻³ solution.

b From the redox equation, write down the ratio of moles of iron(II) reacting with one mole of dichromate(VI).

c Calculate the number of moles of iron(II) in the 25.0 cm³ sample.

d Calculate the number of moles of iron(II) in the flask.

e Calculate the mass of iron(II) in the flask (made from 2.225 g of iron wire). [A_r(Fe) = 56.]

f Calculate the percentage of iron in the iron wire.

The following sequence can be used for all redox titrations when the reductant and its oxidation product are known:

Step 1 Write the half-equations for oxidant and reductant.

Step 2 Deduce the equation for the overall reaction.

Step 3 Calculate the number of moles of manganate(VII) or dichromate(VI) used.

Step 4 Calculate the ratio of moles of oxidant to moles of reductant from the redox equation.

Step 5 Calculate the number of moles in the sample solution of reductant.

Step 6 Calculate the number of moles in the original solution of reductant.

Step 7 Determine either the concentration of the original solution or the percentage of reductant in a known quantity of sample.

18 In a titration, 25.0 cm³ of a sodium sulfite solution needs 45.0 cm³ of 0.020 0 mol dm⁻³ potassium manganate(VII) solution to reach the endpoint. What is the concentration of the sodium sulfite solution?

19 Some ethanedioic acid-2-water (mass 2.145 g) was dissolved in water and diluted to 250 cm³ in a volumetric flask. Then 25.0 cm³ of this solution was titrated with potassium manganate(VII) solution and needed 35.0 cm³ to oxidise the acid solution. Calculate the concentration of the potassium manganate(VII) solution.

key facts

● For calculations in redox titrations: (a) write half-equations; (b) balance electron transfer; and (c) add these balanced half-equations.

● The commonly used oxidants, MnO_4^- and $Cr_2O_7^{2-}$, must be acidified.

● For solutions (for molar concentration in mol dm⁻³ and volume in dm³):

$$\text{number of moles} = \frac{\text{volume} \times \text{molar concentration}}{1000}$$

● For masses:

$$\text{number of moles} = \frac{\text{mass}}{M_r}$$

or

$$\text{number of moles} = \frac{\text{mass}}{A_r}$$

15.7 Catalysts

Transition metals and their compounds are widely used as catalysts. A **catalyst** alters the rate of a chemical reaction by providing an alternative reaction pathway that has a lower activation energy (Fig. 18). But a catalyst does not alter the equilibrium position, because at equilibrium both the forward and reverse reactions are speeded up equally. In most cases, a catalyst will be used to speed up a chemical reaction. However, some catalysts, called inhibitors or negative catalysts, slow down chemical reactions.

Fig. 18   Energy profile for catalysed and uncatalysed reactions

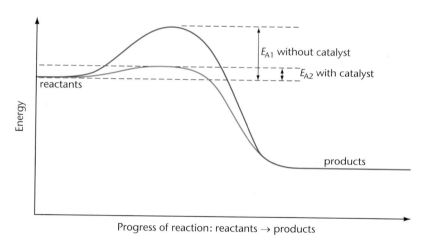

Heterogeneous catalysis

Metals used in catalysis are **heterogeneous** catalysts, because they are solids and in a different phase from the reactants, which will be liquids or gases. Heterogeneous catalysis occurs at the surface of the metal.

In heterogeneous catalysis, at least one of the reactants binds onto the metal's surface using available orbitals by a mechanism similar to ligand donation. This process is called **adsorption**. It is in this new 'state' that the reactant is more likely to undergo reaction. Adsorption of a reactant onto a metal surface can speed up a reaction for the following reasons:

- It can weaken bonds within the reactant molecule, reducing the activation energy.
- It can cause a reactant molecule to break up into more reactive fragments, reducing the activation energy.
- It can hold a reactant in a position, increasing the chance of a favourable collision.
- It can give a higher concentration of one reactant on the catalyst surface, increasing the chance of a favourable collision with the other reactant.

The strength of the bonding between the metal and the reactant is important in determining the suitability of a catalyst for a particular reaction. Metal atoms on the surface of the catalyst need to form bonds with the reactant gas molecules that are strong enough to hold the reactant in position while it reacts with other molecules (Figs 19 and 20). However, if the bond is too strong, the product molecule will not be released by the metal catalyst and the reaction will not proceed. (The opposite of adsorption is **desorption**.) Tungsten forms very strong bonds with some molecules, so it is not often used as a catalyst.

Weak adsorption also results in poor catalysis. Silver forms very weak bonds with molecules, so it is unable to hold onto the gas long enough for a reaction to take place, although it is used in the manufacture of epoxyethane. Good catalysts include palladium, rhodium and platinum, but unfortunately they can be expensive.

Fig. 19   Adsorption of gases on the surface of a catalytic converter

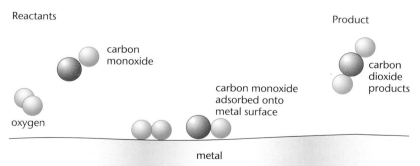

When gas particles react at a solid catalyst, they are adsorbed onto the surface where reaction occurs. The products are released in a process called desorption.

Fig. 20 Hydrogenation at nickel catalyst surface

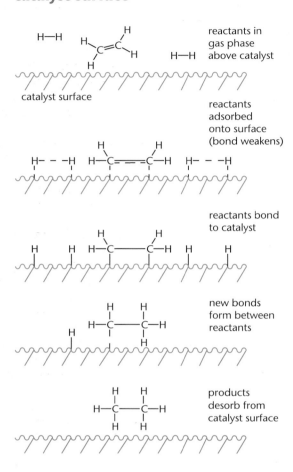

reactants in gas phase above catalyst

reactants adsorbed onto surface (bond weakens)

reactants bond to catalyst

new bonds form between reactants

products desorb from catalyst surface

To minimise costs, every last microgram of precious metal should be available for catalysis. To this end, it is more cost-effective to include a cheap support medium for the catalyst and to coat the support with the catalytic material. (Remember: the reactions to be catalysed take place only on the surface of the catalyst.) There is often a ceramic **support** mat that holds the catalyst in place and, as the temperature rises, the mat expands with the catalyst unit, holding it firmly. On this is a **substrate** that holds the catalyst. This too is a ceramic material and, to increase the surface area, it is made with tiny holes or **cells** about 2 mm^2 in size.

In a typical catalytic converter (Fig. 21) there will be 10 000 or more of these cells. The cells are lined with a **washcoat**, a mixture of aluminium oxide and cerium oxide. These oxides hold on to the precious metal catalysts,

Fig. 21 Catalytic converter unit

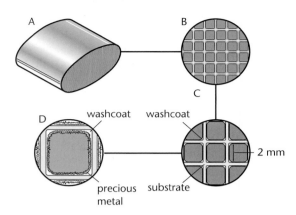

which are compounds of platinum, palladium and rhodium. The intricate structure of the washcoat increases the surface area by a factor of approximately 6 000, giving a surface 60 000 000 times the size of the converter housing. Also if the active material is only on the surface of the washcoat, the amount of metal catalyst used (the expensive part of the unit) is kept to a minimum, and therefore the cost is kept to a minimum. Research is being carried out into using nanoparticles of the precious metals instead of larger particles, so that less metal is needed to produce the same surface area over the ceramic base of the catalyst. This means at least a 50% reduction in the amount of metal used.

The metal catalyst provides a series of active sites. These are places on the surface of the catalyst where the reactions take place. The catalyst coating is not a smooth surface – it is applied in such a way that it has an irregular surface (Fig. 22).

Fig. 22 Catalyst surface

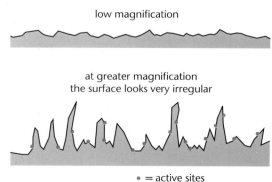

low magnification

at greater magnification the surface looks very irregular

● = active sites

Another way of maximising the surface area of the catalyst in contact with the reactants is to use a fluidised bed (Fig. 23). When gases are blown through a very fine powder, the powder 'floats' on the gas separating the catalyst particles, so that all the surface of the catalyst is available for reactions.

Fig. 23   A fluidised catalytic bed

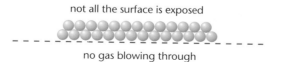

not all the surface is exposed

no gas blowing through

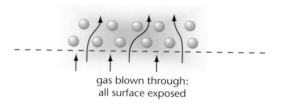

gas blown through:
all surface exposed

20 Why do you think the coating is deliberately applied so that its surface is not smooth?

Catalyst poisoning

Sometimes unwanted gases adsorb very strongly onto the catalyst. These 'block' the active sites on the catalyst, reducing the catalyst's effectiveness. This is called poisoning. During the Haber process (see further on in text), it is vital that traces of sulfur and carbon monoxide are removed, because these will poison the iron catalyst. Catalytic converters on cars (Fig. 21) contain a mixture of palladium, platinum and rhodium metals, coated onto cerium oxide. These will remove the unwanted products of combustion. If the exhaust emissions contain sulfur dioxide, this gas will also adsorb onto the catalyst. The sulfur dioxide is adsorbed very strongly and it 'blocks' the active sites on the catalyst, reducing its effectiveness. All petrol contains some sulfur, but the lower the sulfur content achieved during the refining process, the better.

To help overcome sulfur dioxide poisoning, manufacturers of catalytic converters mix in aluminium oxide with the catalyst. The aluminium oxide 'stores' the sulfur oxides under oxidising (normal running) conditions, and converts them to hydrogen sulfide under reducing (accelerating) conditions. This removes the sulfur periodically, so that it does not permanently poison the catalyst. This is why the emissions from catalytic converters occasionally smell of hydrogen sulfide.

Other metals are also capable of bonding permanently to the active sites of catalysts. Lead is a particular problem, and this is why it is absolutely vital that only unleaded fuel is used in cars that are fitted with a catalytic converter. The use of leaded fuel would completely poison the catalyst, and catalytic converters are very expensive to replace.

Industrial processes

Many industrial processes involve the use of catalysts under a variety of conditions. When a mixture of hydrogen and carbon monoxide in the ratio 2:1 is passed over the catalyst chromium(III)oxide, Cr_2O_3, under high pressure and at high temperature, methanol is formed. Two of the most important industrial processes in the economy of any industrialised nation are the manufacture of ammonia and the manufacture of sulfuric acid. Both of these processes involve equilibria, and for each process it is vital to obtain the maximum possible output, in the shortest possible time, at the lowest possible cost. A catalyst is used to increase the rate of reaction, allowing a much lower temperature to be used, yet maintaining sufficient output for the process to be cost-effective.

Haber process

The **Haber process** is an industrial method for the manufacture of ammonia (NH_3). In the Haber process an iron catalyst is used:

$$N_2(g) + 3H_2(g) \overset{Fe}{\rightleftharpoons} 2NH_3(g)$$

The iron is mixed with aluminium oxide and potassium oxide, which act as promoters. The promoter is present in smaller amounts than the iron, and improves the efficiency of the catalyst. The hydrogen for this reaction is obtained from methane, so trace amounts of steam and carbon monoxide are found as impurities in the products. If the carbon monoxide was allowed to remain in the gas mixture, it would poison the catalyst by forming an iron carbonyl compound, so it must be removed. The carbon monoxide is heated with an excess of steam in a two-stage process, first with an iron oxide catalyst and then with a zinc/copper catalyst. The products are carbon dioxide, which is easier to remove from the mixture, and hydrogen, which is used in the process.

Contact process

The **contact process** is an industrial method for the manufacture of sulfuric acid (H_2SO_4). The main step in the manufacture of sulfuric acid is the oxidation of sulfur dioxide gas to sulfur trioxide:

$$2SO_2(g) + O_2(g) \rightleftharpoons SO_3(g)$$

The reactant mixture is passed over a catalyst of vanadium(V) oxide, V_2O_5. This catalyst has replaced platinum, despite the fact that platinum produces a faster reaction rate, reducing the time needed to reach equilibrium, because V_2O_5 is cheaper and less prone to poisoning by impurities, e.g. any traces of compounds produced from the roasting of metal ores. When it behaves as a catalyst, it shows variable oxidation states. The catalyst, V_2O_5, has an oxidation state of +5. This reacts with the SO_2 and is reduced to the +4 oxidation state and the sulfur is oxidised to +6. The oxygen present then oxidises the +4 vanadium back to +5, so that it can now oxidise another molecule of SO_2. The vanadium(V) oxide catalyst takes part in the reaction, but is unchanged at the end:

$$V_2O_5(s) + SO_2(g) \rightarrow V_2O_4(g) + SO_3(g)$$
$$\quad +5 \qquad\qquad\qquad +4$$

$$2V_2O_4(s) + O_2(g) \rightarrow 2V_2O_5(g)$$
$$\quad +4 \qquad\qquad\qquad +5$$

Homogeneous catalysts

These are in the same phase as the reactants. The ability of transition metal ions to act as catalysts is often linked to a transition metal's ability to form ions in different oxidation states. Because these are ions in solution with the reactants, they are in the same phase, and hence they are **homogeneous** catalysts. An ion that behaves as a homogeneous catalyst is the hexaaquacobalt(II) ion $[Co(H_2O)_6]^{2+}(aq)$. Under suitable reaction conditions the Co^{2+} ion is easily oxidised to Co^{3+}, and this transition can be used to form temporary intermediates in the reaction between hydrogen peroxide and sodium potassium tartrate:

$$Na^+ \ ^-OOCCH(OH)CH(OH)COO^- \ ^+K$$

Cobalt(II) ions form a pink complex with water molecules. Fig. 24 plots the reduction potentials for $M^{3+}(aq)/M^{2+}(aq)$ systems for transition metals in aqueous solution and shows that the reduction Co(III) to Co(II) is favoured. With H_2O as ligands, reduction from Co(III) to Co(II) can occur spontaneously, but not the oxidation Co(II) to Co(III). A powerful oxidising agent would be needed to overcome this reduction potential. However, some ligands can lower the reduction potential sufficiently for a mild oxidising agent to produce the change Co(II) to Co(III). Here is an example.

If cobalt(II) ions are added to a solution of sodium potassium tartrate and hydrogen peroxide, the cobalt ions form an intermediate complex with the tartrate. In this intermediate the cobalt(II) ions are more easily oxidised to cobalt(III) by the hydrogen peroxide. (Changing

---

key facts

● A heterogeneous catalyst is in a different phase from the reactants, e.g. a *metal* catalyst and *gaseous* reactants.

● In heterogeneous catalysis, reaction occurs at the surface of the catalyst.

● Many transition metals are good catalysts.

● The strength of the bond formed between reactant and catalyst must allow both adsorption of reactant molecules and desorption of product molecules to occur, if the catalyst is to be effective.

● Different metal atoms form bonds of different strengths with reactants.

● Catalysts are poisoned if active sites are blocked.

● Catalysts are unchanged in their chemical composition at the end of the reaction.

Fig. 24   Reduction potentials of M^{3+}/M^{2+} systems for transition metals Ti to Co in aqueous solution

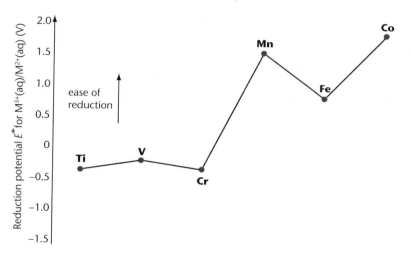

The reaction is quite slow even though it is energetically favourable. Both ions are negatively charged, so they are unlikely to make fruitful collisions with each other. However, if iron(II) ions are added to the reaction, the rate is much quicker. The positive Fe^{2+} ions will make effective collisions with the negative peroxodisulfate ions; and the iron(II) is oxidised to iron(III), which will rapidly oxidise the iodide ions to iodine. In this redox reaction, the iron(III) is reduced to iron(II). This will then continue the catalysis.

$$2Fe^{2+} + S_2O_8^{2-} \rightarrow 2Fe^{3+} + 2SO_4^{2-}$$
$$\underline{2Fe^{3+} + 2I^- \rightarrow 2Fe^{2+} + I_2}$$
$$S_2O_8^{2-} + 2I^- \rightarrow I_2 + 2SO_4^{2-}$$

The Fe^{2+} ions do not appear in the final equation because they are catalysts.

Autocatalysis

When manganate(VII) is titrated with a warmed acidified solution of ethanedioate ions, $C_2O_4^{2-}$, it is quite slow initially and, for the first addition of manganate(VII), the purple colour is slow to decolourise. When more manganate(VII) is added, the solution immediately turns colourless until the endpoint is reached. The reaction is catalysed by the Mn^{2+} ion, which is formed during the reaction.

To balance the electrons, $2MnO_4^-$(aq) will react with $5C_2O_4^{2-}$(aq). Then adding the two half-equations and cancelling gives:

$$2MnO_4^-(aq) + 8H^+(aq) + 5C_2O_4^{2-}(aq) \rightarrow$$
$$2Mn^{2+}(aq) + 10CO_2(g) + 4H_2O(l)$$

the ligands changes the electrode potential for oxidation of Co(II) to Co(III).) This means that a green cobalt(III) tartrate complex forms. The cobalt(III) ions in the complex are then able to oxidise the tartrate, to produce carbon dioxide gas and a carbonyl compound (Fig. 25), and the Co(III) is reduced back to the pink Co(II) complex $[Co(H_2O)_6]^{2+}$. Colour changes often accompany a change in oxidation state in transition metals, and the colour change reveals the catalytic ability of cobalt in this reaction.

Fig. 25   Catalysis by cobalt ions

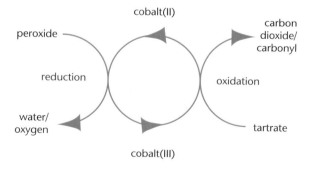

Another reaction that involves homogeneous catalysis is the oxidation of iodide ions by peroxodisulfate(VI) ions:

$$S_2O_8^{2-} + 2I^- \rightarrow I_2 + 2SO_4^{2-}$$

21

a   Write the half-equation for the reaction Mn(VII) to Mn(II).

b   Write the half-equation for the reaction $C_2O_4^{2-}$ to $2CO_2$.

c   Why is the manganate(VII)/ ethanedioate reaction an example of homogeneous catalysis?

The reaction does not speed up until some Mn^{2+} ions have been formed. The catalysis of a reaction by one of its products is called **autocatalysis**.

This reaction is slow initially because both the oxidant and reductant are negatively charged, so they are unlikely to make fruitful collisions. However, the positive Mn^{2+} ions can react with the MnO_4^- ions to form Mn^{3+} ions:

$$4Mn^{2+} + MnO_4^- + 8H^+ \rightarrow 5Mn^{3+} + 4H_2O$$

The Mn^{3+} ions can then react with $C_2O_4^{2-}$ ions to liberate CO_2 and re-form Mn^{2+} ions, which can then continue the autocatalysis:

$$2Mn^{3+} + C_2O_4^{2-} \rightarrow 2Mn^{2+} + 2CO_2$$

key facts

- Homogeneous catalysis proceeds via an intermediate (or intermediates).

- Transition metal ions taking part in homogeneous catalysis usually go through a temporary change in oxidation state.

- Autocatalysis occurs when one of the products catalyses the reaction.

15.8 Other important transition metal complexes

Haemoglobin

As mentioned in Section 15.2, haemoglobin carries oxygen around the body. At the centre of this molecule is the haem complex, which contains the Fe(II) ion. This ion will accept a pair of electrons from oxygen, which is behaving as a ligand. The oxygen is released in the cells for respiration and exchanged for carbon dioxide, which is carried back to the lungs for exhalation. Carbon monoxide is another ligand that will react with the haem molecule. The carbon monoxide molecule has a lone pair on the carbon atom, which can donate into the orbitals to the iron. Carbon monoxide forms a very strong link with the haem, stronger than the bond to oxygen. Any carbon monoxide in the blood, e.g. from smoking, will form the carboxyhaemoglobin complex and will prevent oxygen from linking with the Fe(II). This interferes with the transport of oxygen around the body and this is why carbon monoxide is toxic (Fig. 26).

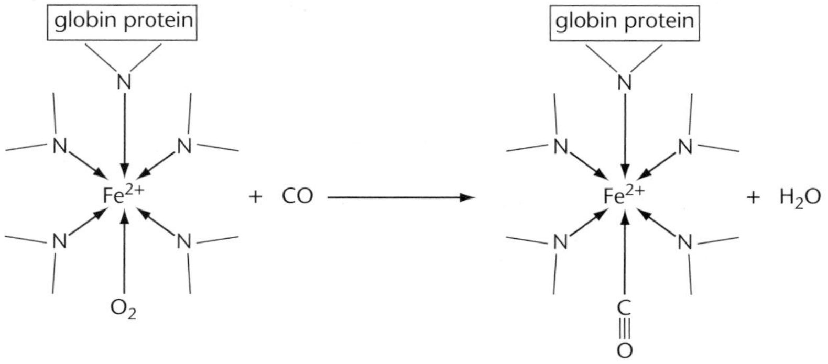

Most of the examples of complexes discussed so far have been with elements from the first transition series, Period 4, but there are some important complexes in Periods 5 and 6, especially those of silver and platinum. Platinum metal is used as a catalyst in the oxidation of ammonia by oxygen, which is a step in the manufacture of nitric acid.

Cancer treatment

One platinum complex ion has been at the forefront of cancer treatment. It was discovered accidentally, but is an example of how scientists need to be alert to unusual results. Barnett Rosenberg, a biophysicist, was studying the effect of alternating current on cell division and was testing his equipment on some bacterial cells. To his amazement, the cells stopped dividing and, after some further research, he found the platinum electrodes he was using in the electrolysis (which he thought would not react) reacted with the solution, forming a complex ion. Eventually, with the help of a

Fig. 26   Formation of carboxyhaemoglobin

chemist, Andy Thompson, he found that the ion producing this effect was the square planar complex, *cis*[Pt(NH$_3$)$_2$Cl$_2$], *cis*-diamminedichloroplatinum(II), more commonly called cisplatin (Fig. 27).

Fig. 27 Cisplatin

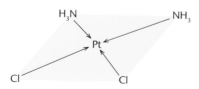

They then had the idea that this compound might be effective in the treatment of cancer cells, because cancer cells divide in an uncontrolled way. The complex ion exchanges its chloro ligands for the nitrogen atoms on the DNA. This distorts its structure, inhibits its function and eventually kills the cell. Cisplatin and some of its derivatives are now major drugs in cancer treatment. Although cisplatin is used as part of combined chemotherapy for a range of cancers, it has been found to be particularly effective in treating testicular and breast cancers. These are hormone-related cancers but, as yet, scientists do not understand why there should be this link. As with any medication, there may be side effects. Since cisplatin affects cell reproduction, it may also affect healthy cells; so the immune system will probably be weakened by this treatment.

Test for aldehydes and ketones

The diammine complex of silver is diamminesilver(I), [Ag(NH$_3$)$_2$]$^+$. This will react with compounds that are easily oxidised, to form metallic silver. Changing the ligand has altered the redox properties of the central metal ion. This property is used in the silver mirror test to distinguish between ketones and aldehydes. Dilute ammonia is added to silver nitrate solution until the precipitate of Ag$_2$O,

which is formed initially, just re-dissolves. The solution formed, called Tollens' reagent, contains the soluble [Ag(NH$_3$)$_2$]$^+$ ion. When Tollens' reagent is warmed with an aldehyde, the aldehyde is oxidised to an acid and the silver(I) ion is reduced to silver, which forms a silver mirror on the surface of the container:

$$CH_3CHO + H_2O + 2Ag^+ \rightarrow CH_3COOH + 2H^+ + Ag$$

Ketones are not so easily oxidised; they do not form a silver mirror on the surface of the container, and so can be readily distinguished from aldehydes.

In the presence of aldehydes, Tollens' reagent is reduced to metallic silver.

Test for silver halides

This diamminesilver(I) complex [Ag(NH$_3$)$_2$]$^+$ is also responsible for the observation that a precipitate of AgCl and AgBr will dissolve in aqueous ammonia.

- AgCl will dissolve in dilute ammonia solution.
- AgBr will dissolve in concentrated ammonia solution.
- AgI will not dissolve in any ammonia solution.

This property can be used to confirm the presence of and/or to distinguish between these halides.

key facts

- Iron in the haem complex is important for oxygen transport in the body.

- Cisplatin is a square planar platinum complex, important for cancer treatment.

- The diamminesilver(I) complex is used to distinguish aldehydes from ketones, and for identifying different silver halides.

1 One characteristic property of transition metals is variable oxidation state.

a For each of the following processes, write two equations to show how the transition metal catalyst reacts and is reformed. Identify the different oxidation states shown by the transition metal catalyst in each process.

   i the Contact Process catalysed by vanadium(V) oxide

   ii the oxidation of ethanedioate ions by acidified potassium manganate(VII), autocatalysed by $Mn^{2+}(aq)$ ions. (6)

b Cobalt(II) ions cannot easily be oxidised to cobalt(III) ions in water. Suggest why this oxidation can be carried out in aqueous ammonia and identify a suitable oxidising agent. (3)

c Metal ions $\mathbf{Q}^{2+}$ in acidified aqueous solution can be oxidised by aqueous potassium dichromate(VI). In a titration, an acidified 25.0 cm³ sample of a 0.140 mol dm⁻³ solution of $\mathbf{Q}^{2+}(aq)$ required 29.2 cm³ of a 0.040 mol dm⁻³ solution of potassium dichromate(VI) for complete reaction. Determine the oxidation state of the metal $\mathbf{Q}$ after reaction with the potassium dichromate(VI). (6)

Total 15

AQA, June 2007, Unit 5, Question 6

2 A 0.263 g sample of impure iron, containing an unreactive impurity, was reacted with an excess of hydrochloric acid. All of the iron in the sample reacted, evolving hydrogen gas and forming a solution of iron(II) chloride. The volume of hydrogen evolved was 102 cm³, measured at 298 K and 110 kPa. The percentage, by mass, of iron in the sample can be determined using either the volume of hydrogen produced or by titrating the solution of iron(II) chloride formed against a standard solution of potassium dichromate(VI).

a **i** Write an equation for the reaction between iron and hydrochloric acid.

   ii Calculate the number of moles of hydrogen produced in the reaction.

   iii Use your answers to parts **a i** and **ii** to determine the number of moles of iron and the mass of iron in the original sample.
(If you have been unable to complete part **a ii** you should assume the answer to be 4.25×10^{-3} mol. This is not the correct answer.)

   iv Calculate the percentage of iron in the original sample. (7)

b **i** Write half-equations for the oxidation of Fe^{2+} and for the reduction of $Cr_2O_7^{2-}$ in acidic solution, and use these to construct an overall equation for the reaction between these two ions.

   ii The number of moles of iron in the sample was determined in part **a iii**. Use this answer to calculate the volume of a 0.0200 mol dm⁻³ solution of potassium dichromate(VI) which would react exactly with the solution of iron(II) chloride formed in the reaction.
(If you have been unable to complete part **a iii** you should assume the answer to be 3.63×10^{-3} mol. This is not the correct answer.)

   iii Explain why an incorrect value for the number of moles of iron(II) chloride formed would have been obtained if the original solution had been titrated with potassium manganate(VII). (7)

Total 14

AQA, June 2006, Unit 5, Question 1

3

a Explain why the reaction between sodium ethanedioate, $Na_2C_2O_4$, and potassium manganate(VII) in acidified aqueous solution is initially slow but gradually increases in rate. Write equations to illustrate your answer. (6)

b State what is meant by the term *active site* as applied to a heterogeneous catalyst.
Explain how the number of active sites can be increased for a given mass of catalyst. The efficiency of a heterogeneous catalyst often decreases during use. Explain, using a specific example, why this happens. (4)

Total 10

AQA, June 2006, Unit 5, Question 9

4

a State and explain the effect of a catalyst on the rate and on the equilibrium yield in a reversible reaction. (5)

b Explain the terms *heterogeneous* and *active sites* as applied to a catalyst. Give **two** reasons why a ceramic support is used for the catalyst in catalytic converters in cars.
Explain how lead poisons this catalyst. (7)

c In aqueous solution, Fe^{2+} ions act as a homogeneous catalyst in the reaction between I^- and $S_2O_8^{2-}$ ions. Give one reason why the reaction is slow in the absence of a catalyst.
Write equations to show how Fe^{2+} ions act as a catalyst for this reaction. (5)

Total 17

AQA, June 2005, Unit 5, Question 5

5

a Complete the electronic arrangement of the Co^{2+} ion. (1)

b Give the formula of the cobalt complex present in an aqueous solution of cobalt(II) sulfate and state its colour. (2)

c i When a large excess of concentrated aqueous ammonia is added to an aqueous solution of cobalt(II) sulfate, a new cobalt(II) complex is formed. Give the formula of the new cobalt(II) complex and state its colour.

ii Write an equation for the formation of this new complex. (3)

d When hydrogen peroxide is added to the mixture formed in part **c**, the colour of the solution darkens due to the formation of a different cobalt complex. Identify this different cobalt complex and state the role of hydrogen peroxide in its formation. (2)

Total 8

AQA, January 2005, Unit 5, Question 6

6

a In the Haber Process for the manufacture of ammonia, the following equilibrium is established in the presence of a heterogeneous catalyst.

$$N_2(g) + 3H_2(g) \rightleftharpoons 2NH_3(g)$$

Identify the heterogeneous catalyst used in this process.
A heterogeneous catalyst can become poisoned by impurities in the reactants. Give one substance which poisons the heterogeneous catalyst used in the Haber Process and explain how this substance poisons the catalyst. (5)

b State what is observed when an excess of aqueous ammonia reacts with an aqueous iron(II) salt. Write an equation for this reaction. (4)

Total 9

AQA, January 2005, Unit 5, Question 9

Catalysts at work

Fig. 28 A catalytic cracker as used in oil refining

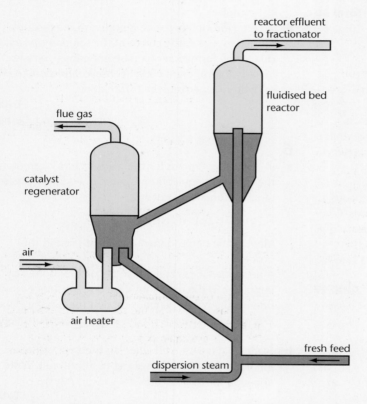

Oil refining

The catalytic cracker (Fig. 28) takes a number of feedstocks, including heavy gas oil, treated fuel oil and residue from the lubricant treatment plant. The feedstock is mixed with a hot zeolite catalyst and passes up through the reaction vessel. The long-chain hydrocarbons are split into shorter chains using the catalyst and moderately high temperatures (400 °C–500 °C). The main product is ethane, C_2H_6; the C_5 to C_8 hydrocarbons go into the petrol blend. The catalyst flows back into the regenerator on the left, where it is reheated to burn off the carbon ready for another round of catalysing. Each individual zeolite crystal is barely visible to the naked eye, but it has a large surface area due to its shape (see *AS Chemistry*, page 114). It flows around the cracker and regenerator along with billions of other crystals. They are supported on a bed of air and behave like a fluid.

A1 Why are feedstocks recycled and cracked?

A2 Why does the carbon that builds up on the surface of the zeolite have to be burnt off?

A3 Why is the catalyst fluidised?

Catalytic converters

Catalytic converters have proven to be reliable devices and have been successful in reducing noxious emissions from exhaust pipes. However, they may have some adverse environmental impacts in use. There is a requirement for the engine to run 'richer', so there is balance between reduction and oxidation. The manufacturing of catalytic converters requires palladium and/or platinum. A portion of the world's supply of these precious metals is produced near the Russian city of Norilsk, with significant negative environmental effects.

A4 Give an environmental advantage related to air quality of using a catalytic converter. What environmental problem associated with vehicle emissions do these devices not solve?

A5 What might the negative environmental effects of platinum and palladium production include?

Palladium and platinum deposits at Norilsk, Russia, lie at a depth of between 500 m and 1 500 m. The high-grade sulfide ores can be high in nickel and/or copper, and may contain up to 32% copper. Annual production currently includes about three million kg of palladium and 21 300 kg of platinum.

Catalysts for taste

Catalysts for pollution control form a very important part of the industry, but some catalytic materials have very different uses. The food industry makes significant use of catalysts, especially nickel. This is particularly used for hydrogenating oils to make fats. Often, these catalysts catalyse reactions that stop at a very precise stage of hydrogenation, before taste or texture, or both, are ruined.

Many foods are now manufactured from vegetable oils. Butter, chocolate and ice cream used to be all-dairy products, so contained animal fat. Oils and fats are very similar chemically. Vegetable oils contain long chains of carbon–carbon double bonds (unsaturated groups); oils contain a higher proportion than fats, and are healthier. Vegetable products are generally healthier than animal fats. Oils can be hydrogenated to make them solids for use in foods such as chocolate by converting the double bonds to single bonds. The catalyst is very finely divided nickel, deposited on small particles of an inert carrier material, which can be filtered out. Some chocolate is made from hydrogenated vegetable oils. The catalyst is nickel and it is mixed with the oil in the reactor.

The temperature for the hydrogenation reaction of oils is critical and must be controlled to within 1 °C, or the number of double bonds converted will not be correct. If the melting point is incorrect in chocolate, the fat will not release its flavour quickly enough, and there will be no flavour burst. This is why the extent of hydrogenation must be controlled very carefully.

Contact process

In the contact process, the sulfur dioxide is oxidised to sulfur trioxide:

$$SO_2 + V_2O_5 \rightarrow SO_3 + V_2O_4$$

To really enjoy eating a chocolate bar, the melting point has to be just right so you get that cooling, luxurious texture from the melting chocolate that makes it so enjoyable.

A6 Why is nickel called a heterogeneous catalyst?

A7 Why is it important that the nickel is finely divided?

A8 Why would increasing the proportion of double bonds in a molecule reduce the melting point?

A9 Why are vegetable oils considered healthier than animal fats?

Then the following reaction occurs:

$$V_2O_4 + \tfrac{1}{2}O_2 \rightarrow V_2O_5$$

Although the catalyst has been temporarily changed during the reaction, at the end it is chemically the same as it started.

The stream of gas containing SO_2, after necessary cooling, is passed through the catalytic converter bed column again, achieving up to 99.8% conversion of SO_2 to SO_3. The gases are again passed through the final absorption column beds to achieve high conversion.

A10 In the reaction:

$$SO_2 + V_2O_5 \rightarrow SO_3 + V_2O_4$$

what are the oxidation numbers of the two vanadium oxides?

A11 What will be the outer electronic configuration of the two vanadium oxides?

A12 How does this two-reaction sequence comply with the definition of a catalyst?

A13 Regulations now exist that require that virtually all the sulfur dioxide is converted and none is released. Why might this be so?

16 Inorganic compounds in aqueous solution

All living things need an energy source for all their life processes, and to build molecules such as proteins in order to grow healthily. The main elements required are carbon, nitrogen, hydrogen and oxygen. Both humans and plants need these for energy, growth and repair. The plants get carbon and oxygen from the air and water from the soil. But all living things need trace metal elements as well.

Plants need magnesium, which is the atom at the centre of the chlorophyll molecule, vital for photosynthesis. Chlorophyll (see the diagram and the computer graphic below) has many similarities to the haemoglobin molecule (Chapter 15, Fig. 10), which we need for transporting oxygen around the body. As a complex molecule, chlorophyll illustrates how atoms (in this case,

nitrogen) with lone pairs of electrons can donate into the empty sub-shells available on the central atom, forming co-ordinate bonds. Two of the nitrogen atoms around the magnesium do this. The bonds are represented by arrows and the two nitrogen atoms are called ligands.

As well as magnesium, plants need iron. This element transfers an electron as part of the energy exchange from light to chemical processes. Iron does this by changing its oxidation state. To carry out all the cellular processes, plants need other elements such as cobalt and manganese. All these elements are available if the soil (or growing medium) is fertilised properly. Plants need to extract the nutrients from the soil, so equilibria are set up between the aqueous solutions in the plant and the aqueous solutions in the soil. The positions of these equilibria will depend on the ligands attached to the central metal ions and, very importantly, on the pH of the soil.

Changing the soil pH will affect any water ligands attached to the metal ions, and this will affect how well the plant can take up the nutrients. An acid soil makes the complex ions more soluble, and they will be washed away by rainwater. Growers often **sequester** the nutrients in fertiliser, which means that the complex ion formed is very stable. This slows down the release of the nutrients to the plant, but the advantage is that it is not very soluble so that it is not washed away.

In this chapter you will see how transition metal ions behave in different aqueous solutions, and how they interact in solution with different ligands.

$$[phytyl = C_{29}H_{39}]$$

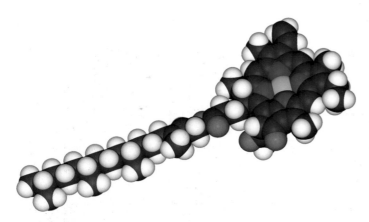

Computer graphic of a chlorophyll molecule. The magnesium atom is at the centre of a porphyrin ring structure and is bonded to it via four nitrogen atoms (see diagram above computer graphic).

Some of the reactions of photosynthesis rely on molecules that contain a central atom of either magnesium or iron. Other biochemical reactions require cobalt, manganese and other transition metal ions in trace quantities. Ligands bond with all these elements.

16.1 Aqueous reactions of inorganic compounds

The important properties of transition metal and other metal compounds are affected by the ligands that attach themselves to the central metal ion when a complex ion forms. A complex ion is formed when a ligand donates a pair of electrons. This leads to complexes being described in terms of acids and bases (see Chapter 3).

In 1938, G. N. Lewis defined acids and bases as follows:

- A **Lewis acid** is an electron pair acceptor (see Fig. 1).
- A **Lewis base** is an electron pair donor.

When a Lewis acid reacts with a Lewis base, a co-ordinate bond is formed between the two species, and this is represented by an arrow. The arrow goes from the donor to the acceptor. The donation of lone pairs means that a Lewis base is a ligand and a nucleophile.

In the diamminesilver(I) ion, $[H_3N{\rightarrow}Ag{\leftarrow}NH_3]^+$, the silver ion is accepting two electron pairs (one pair from each ammonia ligand) and is acting as a Lewis acid. Each ammonia ligand is thus acting as a Lewis base. In all metal complexes, the central metal atom is a Lewis acid and all the ligands are Lewis bases.

Fig. 1   Donation of a lone pair from H_2O to HCl

1 Which are the Lewis acids and the Lewis bases in the following reactions?

a $H_2O + H^+ \rightarrow H_3O^+$

b $BF_3 + NH_3 \rightarrow F_3B{\leftarrow}NH_3$

2 Which of the following are Lewis acids?

a SO_3

b HCl

c H_2SO_4

d Ag^+

e C_2H_5COOH

f Fe^{2+}

16.2 Acidity reactions of metal ions in water

The acid–base definitions given above can be used to describe metal ions in water.

Oxidation state +2

When a transition metal ion is in water, the lone electron pairs on the water molecules (Lewis base) form co-ordinate bonds with the metal ions (Lewis acid). Complex ions are produced. Often, there is a striking colour change if the ligand is changed (see photograph, right). Anhydrous cobalt chloride is blue, but the hexaaquacobalt(II) ion is pink:

$$CoCl_2 + 6H_2O \rightarrow [Co(H_2O)_6]^{2+} + 2Cl^-$$
blue   pink

As also shown on page 260, blue cobalt chloride paper before and after the addition of water.

Copper(II) and iron(II) form similar aqua ions. Anhydrous copper(II) sulfate is white, but $[Cu(H_2O)_6]^{2+}$ is blue. Anhydrous iron(II) sulfate is almost white, but $[Fe(H_2O)_6]^{2+}$ is green.

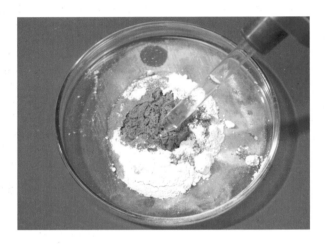

When water is added to white anhydrous $CuSO_4$, blue $[Cu(H_2O)_6]^{2+}$ is formed.

The reaction in which aqua ions are formed is called **hydration**. The hydration enthalpy of the ions present in the solid usually provides enough energy to break down the crystal lattice (to overcome the lattice energy), so the solid is water soluble. The mixture gets very hot.

The co-ordinate bond between the metal ion and the water can be strong enough to survive evaporation. For example, $FeSO_4 \cdot 7H_2O$ is green and contains the complex $[Fe(H_2O)_6]^{2+}$ formed when a warm, saturated solution of iron(II) sulfate is cooled. Many metal ion complexes are surrounded by six ligands, i.e. they have a co-ordination number of 6. These ions will have an octahedral shape. Two other hydrated salts of transition metals are:

- $CoCl_2 \cdot 6H_2O$, which is pink and contains the complex $[Co(H_2O)_6]^{2+}$;
- $Fe(NO_3)_3 \cdot 9H_2O$, which is pale violet and contains the complex $[Fe(H_2O)_6]^{3+}$.

Oxidation state +3

Metal(III) ions form similar aqua complexes. Anhydrous aluminium chloride, for example, dissolves in water to produce hexaaquaaluminium(III) ions:

$$AlCl_3 + 6H_2O \rightarrow [Al(H_2O)_6]^{3+} + 3Cl^-$$

When the oxidation state of the metal forming the complex is +3, the reaction is often very exothermic. Anhydrous aluminium chloride reacts quite violently with water, giving out heat and fuming strongly.

3 State the shapes and write the formulae for the metal–aqua complex ions formed with:

a vanadium(II)

b chromium(III)

c iron(III).

key facts

- Metal ions often form hexaaqua, octahedral complexes with water.
- The formation of aqua complexes often causes a colour change with transition metal ions.
- Many solid, hydrated salts contain hexaaquametal complex ions.

16.3 Reactions involving complex ions

We have seen in Chapter 15 that transition metals can take part in redox reactions by gain or loss of electrons, and that this can cause a colour change. The electron transfer can take place *without a ligand change*:

$$[M(H_2O)_6]^{2+} \rightarrow [M(H_2O)_6]^{3+} + e^-$$

If the co-ordinate bond between the metal ion and the water molecule is broken and replaced by another ligand, this is a **ligand substitution reaction**.

> **4** Why do these reactions result in a colour change?

If the O–H bond in a co-ordinated water molecule is broken, the reaction is called a **hydrolysis reaction** or **acidity reaction**. All metal–aqua complex ions formed by metal ions in an oxidation state of +3 can take part in hydrolysis (acidity) reactions, and change the pH of the water. In water, the following equilibria are established:

$$[M(H_2O)_6]^{2+} + H_2O \rightleftharpoons [M(H_2O)_5(OH)]^+ + H_3O^+$$

or

$$[M(H_2O)_6]^{3+} + H_2O \rightleftharpoons [M(H_2O)_5(OH)]^{2+} + H_3O^+$$

Fig. 2   The pK_a values for metal ions

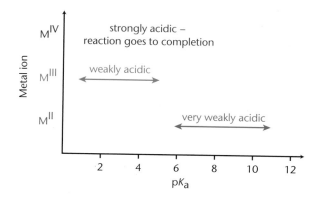

This is called a hydrolysis reaction because the ligand water molecule has split into H^+ and OH^- ions, and it is an acidity reaction because H_3O^+ ions are formed as a result.

The degree of acidity of the solution depends on how many H_3O^+ ions are formed. This equilibrium can be quantified by an equilibrium constant K_a, the **dissociation constant** or **acidity constant** (Chapter 3). For the first of these equilibria (see Chapter 3):

$$K_a = \frac{[[M(H_2O)_5(OH)]^+][H_3O^+]}{[[M(H_2O)_6]^{2+}][H_2O]}$$

The expression can be simplified to:

$$K_a \approx \frac{[H^+]^2}{[[M(H_2O)_6]^{2+}]}$$

Usually, it is easier to work with pK_a than with K_a itself, where pK_a is given by the expression:

$$pK_a = -\log_{10} K_a$$

The pH of a weakly acidic solution can be calculated using the equations for K_a and pH:

$$[H^+]^2 = [[M(H_2O)_6]^{2+}] \times K_a$$
and
$$-\log_{10}[H^+] = pH$$

See Chapter 3 for more details.

For metal(II) ions, K_a varies between 10^{-6} and 10^{-11}, so pK_a varies between 6 and 11. For metal(III) ions, the equilibrium:

$$[M(H_2O)_6]^{3+} + H_2O \rightleftharpoons [M(H_2O)_5(OH)]^{2+} + H_3O^+$$

lies much further to the right, and K_a varies between 10^{-2} and 10^{-5} (pK_a = 2 to 5).

For metal(IV) ions, the hydrolysis equilibrium lies so much further to the right that the reaction goes virtually to completion, the value being pK_a < 1. The pK_a values for metal ions are shown in Fig. 2.

These equations represent the acidity produced by the exchange of one aqua ligand. You should be aware that, if the complex ion has six ligands, there will be an equilibrium for each aqua ligand being replaced. There is an overall equilibrium constant, which will be the sum of all these successive, individual equilibria, and this dictates the overall acidity of the solution. The equilibrium constant for each successive removal is lower than for the previous step, and, since the K_a for subsequent

equilibria will be so small, the steps may be insignificant.

Generally, the pH of a metal ion solution may be written as:

$$[M(H_2O)_6]^{2+} \qquad\qquad [M(H_2O)_6]^{3+}$$

very weak acids   weak acids

pH ≈ 6   pH ≈ 3

16.4 Effect of charge/size ratio on K_a values

The features of metal ions that affect the degree of acidity in solution are:

- the charge on the metal ion
- the size of the metal ion.

Aluminium ions, Al^{3+}, are small. The combination of a high charge and a small radius means that Al^{3+} ions have a high charge/size ratio (see Fig. 4). In the $[Al(H_2O)_6]^{3+}$ complex, the Al^{3+} ions attract the oxygen electrons very strongly:

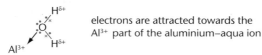

electrons are attracted towards the Al^{3+} part of the aluminium–aqua ion

The attraction of the metal ion particle for the electrons in a co-ordinated water molecule is often referred to as its polarising power. The ion distorts or polarises the water ligand's electron cloud. This attraction of 2+ and 3+ ions weakens the O–H bonds so that H⁺ ions can break away to form H_3O^+ (Fig. 3). When we compare a 2+ ion with a 3+ ion, we can see that the 3+ ion has a greater charge/size ratio and therefore a greater polarising power. The greater attraction for

oxygen weakens the O–H bond more, so more OH bonds break and more H⁺ ions are released. This results in a greater hydrogen-ion concentration [H⁺(aq)] and so a lower pH.

The presence of aluminium ions in solution gives a pH usually between 3 and 6 (slightly acidic depending on the concentration of Al^{3+}(aq) ions).

The 3+ charge on the ion is the difference between the number of protons and the number of electrons. For the ions Na^+, Mg^{2+} and Al^{3+}, the nuclear charge is increasing, the number of electrons is constant and the size of the ions is decreasing (Fig. 4). For simplicity, we just refer to the charge difference, so we talk about a 3+ ion for aluminium. When combined with size, this gives us the idea of charge/size ratio (Table 1), sometimes called charge density or charge/ionic radius ratio. The ionic charge is more significant than the size.

Fig. 4   Ionic charge/size ratio

Na⁺	Mg²⁺	Al³⁺
0.95 nm	0.65 nm	0.5 nm

Fig. 3   Schematic diagram of hydrolysis

highly charged cation attracts electrons from water molecule, weakening an O–H bond; H⁺ is released and becomes H_3O^+ with water, increasing acidity

Table 1   Charge/size ratios

Element	Charge	Ionic radius	Charge/ size ratio
Na	1+	0.95	1.1
Mg	2+	0.65	4.7
Al	3+	0.50	6.0

5 A solution contains chromium(III) ions.

a Write an equation to show the first equilibrium of Cr^{3+} in water.

b What pH value would you expect for this system?

c Explain your reasons for the pH you have chosen.

Even for 3+ ions, the first equilibrium lies well over to the left:

$$[M(H_2O)_6]^{3+} + H_2O \rightleftharpoons [M(H_2O)_5(OH)]^{2+} + H_3O^+$$

If the pH of this solution is 3, then $[H_3O^+]$ is 10^{-3}, so the ratio of 3+ to 2+ ions is:

$$[[M(H_2O)_6]^{3+}] : [[M(H_2O)_5(OH)]^{2+}] = 1\,000 : 1$$

For 2+ ions, the ratio is about 100 000 : 1.

If these salts are added to water, they will dissolve, but precipitates will not normally form. To produce a precipitate, an alkali such as sodium hydroxide must be added.

If an alkali, such as aqueous sodium hydroxide, is added to a solution of hexaaqua ions, H_3O^+ ions are removed from the solution and the equilibrium moves to the right, to replace the H_3O^+ ions removed. If an acid is added, the equilibrium will move to the left, to remove H_3O^+ ions from the system, and more metal–hexaaqua ions are produced.

Crystals of $Fe(NO_3)_3 \cdot 9H_2O$ are pale violet in colour. When they are added to water, the $[Fe(H_2O)_6]^{3+}$ ions present in the violet crystals react with the water to give hydrolysis products:

$$[Fe(H_2O)_6]^{3+} + H_2O \rightleftharpoons [Fe(H_2O)_5(OH)]^{2+} + H_3O^+$$
$$\text{pale violet} \qquad\qquad\qquad \text{brown}$$

Although the concentration of $[Fe(H_2O)_5(OH)]^{2+}$ ions is very low and $[Fe(H_2O)_6]^{3+}$ is still the main species, the intensity of the brown colour is so great compared with the pale violet of $[Fe(H_2O)_6]^{3+}$ that the solution appears brown.

If nitric acid is added to the brown solution, the equilibrium will shift to the left and the brown colour will disappear. If an alkali is added, the equilibrium shifts to the right and the brown colour is intensified.

key facts

● 2+ and 3+ metal–aqua ions take part in acidity or hydrolysis reactions.

● The pH of a solution of M(III) aqua ions is lower than the pH of a solution of M(II) aqua ions of the same concentration.

● The acidity of solutions of metal ions is decided by the charge and size of the metal ion.

16.5 Reactions of alkalis with aqua ions

Sodium hydroxide (strong base)

If a stronger base than water is added to a solution of the transition metal salt, the equilibrium will move even further to the right and an insoluble, neutral metal hydroxide can be formed. All transition metal salts form a metal hydroxide precipitate when aqueous sodium hydroxide is added to a solution

containing the transition metal ion mixed with an alkali. The precipitate can be removed by filtration. Alkalis can be used to precipitate metal hydroxides. When sodium hydroxide is added to water containing copper(II) ions, the following reaction takes place:

$$[Cu(H_2O)_6]^{2+} + H_2O \rightleftharpoons [Cu(H_2O)_5(OH)]^+ + H_3O^+$$

In water, this equilibrium lies well over to the left, but on addition of alkali the equilibrium is displaced. The hydroxide ions react with H_3O^+ ions:

$$OH^- + H_3O^+ \rightarrow 2H_2O$$

This removes H_3O^+ ions and moves the equilibrium completely to the right. If more OH^- is added, the second equilibrium:

$$[Cu(H_2O)_5(OH)]^+ + H_2O \rightleftharpoons$$
$$[Cu(H_2O)_4(OH)_2] + H_3O^+$$

is also displaced to the right by OH^- ions reacting with the H_3O^+ formed and $[Cu(H_2O)_4(OH)_2]$, blue copper(II) hydroxide, is precipitated. We can write the overall equation as:

$$[Cu(H_2O)_6]^{2+} + 2OH^- \rightleftharpoons$$
$$[Cu(H_2O)_4(OH)_2] + 2H_2O$$

Ca²⁺ Mg²⁺ Cu²⁺ Fe²⁺ Fe³⁺ Co²⁺ Ni²⁺ Mn²⁺ Cr³⁺ Ag⁺ Zn²⁺ Pb²⁺ Al³⁺

Aqueous sodium hydroxide can be used in qualitative analysis, because it gives characteristic coloured solutions (upper tubes) and precipitates (lower tubes) with aqueous metal ions.

This equilibrium can be reversed by adding a strong acid, such as nitric acid, to the metal hydroxide, so that metal–aqua ions are formed again.

Most metal hydroxides also react with excess hydroxide, OH^-, to form anionic complexes, i.e. negatively charged. Some, however, require a solution of sodium hydroxide that is more concentrated than is normally used as a laboratory solution. When sodium hydroxide solution is added to an aqueous solution of an aluminium salt, for instance, a white precipitate of aluminium hydroxide, $[Al(H_2O)_3(OH)_3]$, is formed initially. As more sodium hydroxide is added, the precipitate dissolves to give a colourless solution containing tetrahydroxoaluminate(III) ions $[Al(OH)_4]^-$, as follows:

$$[Al(H_2O)_6]^{3+} + 3OH^- \rightleftharpoons [Al(H_2O)_3(OH)_3] + 3H_2O$$
white precipitate

$$[Al(H_2O)_3(OH)_3] + OH^- \rightleftharpoons [Al(OH)_4]^- + 3H_2O$$
colourless solution

When dilute acid is added to $[Al(OH)_4]^-$, first there is a white precipitate of $[Al(H_2O)_3(OH)_3]$, and then this re-dissolves to give a colourless solution of $[Al(H_2O)_6]^{3+}$.

Metal hydroxides that can react with both acids and alkalis are called **amphoteric**. The overall system is like this:

$$[Al(H_2O_6)]^{3+} \rightleftharpoons [Al(H_2O)_3(OH)_3] \rightleftharpoons [Al(OH)_4]^-$$
acidic   neutral   alkaline

Chromium(III) gives a similar set of reactions. When sodium hydroxide solution is added to an aqueous solution of a chromium salt, a light green precipitate of chromium(III) hydroxide $[Cr(H_2O)_3(OH)_3]$ is formed initially. As more sodium hydroxide is added, the precipitate dissolves to give a green solution of chromate(III) ions. In excess alkali, the species is hexahydroxochromate(III) ions, $[Cr(OH)_6]^{3-}$, as follows:

$$[Cr(H_2O)_6]^{3+} + 3OH^- \rightleftharpoons [Cr(H_2O)_3(OH)_3] + 3H_2O$$
light-green precipitate

$$[Cr(H_2O)_3(OH)_3] + 3OH^- \rightleftharpoons [Cr(OH)_6]^{3-} + 3H_2O$$
green solution

If dilute hydrochloric acid is added to $[Cr(OH)_6]^{3-}$, first there is a light green precipitate of $[Cr(H_2O)_3(OH)_3]$ and then this re-dissolves to give a dark-green solution of $[Cr(H_2O)_4Cl_2]^-$.

Chromate(VI)/dichromate(VI) is another example of an equilibrium affected by the addition of acid or alkali:

$$2CrO_4^-(aq) + 2H^+(aq) \rightleftharpoons Cr_2O_7^{2-}(aq) + H_2O(l)$$

yellow   orange

Ammonia solution (weak base)

Similar reactions occur if aqueous ammonia is added to metal–aqua ions. This is because ammonia solution is alkaline on account of the equilibrium:

$$NH_3(aq) + H_2O(l) \rightleftharpoons NH_4^+(aq) + OH^-(aq)$$

The hydroxide ions that are formed in the equilibrium precipitate the metal as a hydroxide. If ammonia is in excess, most transition metal hydroxides react to form soluble ammine complexes. However, aluminium does not form an ammine complex, so it is considered insoluble in aqueous ammonia (although it is very slightly soluble in a large excess of ammonia). The substitution of the water ligand by ammonia in transition metal complex ions also leads to a colour change (see Section 15.3).

---

6 Consider the equilibrium:

$$[Fe(H_2O)_6]^{3+} + H_2O \rightleftharpoons$$
$$[Fe(H_2O)_5(OH)]^{2+} + H_3O^+$$

pale violet   brown

A series of changes take place on addition of different solutions to this equilibrium. Explain the changes that take place in each of the following, using equations in each case.

a Adding dilute hydrochloric acid changes the colour of the above solution from brown to pale violet.

b Adding dilute sodium hydroxide solution changes the colour of the solution from pale violet to brown.

c Adding excess sodium hydroxide solution gives a brown precipitate, which is insoluble in 2 mol dm^{-3} sodium hydroxide solution.

16.6 Reactions of carbonates with aqua ions

Carbonates, such as sodium carbonate, can also be used to precipitate metal hydroxides from solution. Different reactions are possible, depending on the oxidation state of the metal.

Oxidation state +2

Metal(II)–aqua ions hydrolyse as follows:

$$[M(H_2O)_6]^{2+} + H_2O \rightleftharpoons [M(H_2O)_5(OH)]^+ + H_3O^+$$

If carbonate ions are present and the concentration of H$^+$ is sufficient, the following equilibria move to the right and the carbonate ions form carbon dioxide, which is evolved as a gas:

$$CO_3^{2-} + H_3O^+ \rightleftharpoons HCO_3^- + H_2O$$
$$HCO_3^- + H_3O^+ \rightleftharpoons CO_2 + 2H_2O$$

However, metal(II) ions produce only a very weakly acidic solution, so there are very few H$_3$O$^+$ ions in the solution. In the presence of the carbonate ions added, there will not be sufficient concentration of H$_3$O$^+$ to release carbon dioxide gas. Since metal(II) carbonates are not very soluble in water, they form precipitates. Some important examples are:

$$[Fe(H_2O)_6]^{2+} + CO_3^{2-} \rightleftharpoons FeCO_3 + 6H_2O$$

pale-green solution   green precipitate

$$[Co(H_2O)_6]^{2+} + CO_3^{2-} \rightleftharpoons CoCO_3 + 6H_2O$$

pink solution   pink precipitate

$$[Cu(H_2O)_6]^{2+} + CO_3^{2-} \rightleftharpoons CuCO_3 + 6H_2O$$

blue solution   green-blue precipitate

Oxidation state +3

The metal(III) ions hydrolyse in much the same way as the metal(II) ions, but to a much greater extent. An ion of charge 3+ is much more polarising than one of charge 2+, so has a greater attraction for the metal oxygen electrons in the co-ordinate bond. This weakens the O–H bond in the water ligand, so more H_3O^+ ions are formed (Fig. 5). Now there are sufficient H_3O^+ ions to react with the carbonate ions and form carbon dioxide:

$$2H_3O^+ + CO_3^{2-} \rightarrow CO_2 + 3H_2O$$

This removes the H_3O^+ ions and the equilibrium moves to the right. Eventually, the following net equilibrium is set up:

$$[M(H_2O)_6]^{3+} + H_2O \rightleftharpoons [M(H_2O)_5(OH)]^{2+} + H_3O^+$$

then:

$$[M(H_2O)_5(OH)]^{2+} + H_2O \rightleftharpoons [M(H_2O)_4(OH)_2]^+ + H_3O^+$$

and then:

$$[M(H_2O)_4(OH)_2]^+ + H_2O \rightleftharpoons [M(H_2O)_3(OH)_3] + H_3O^+$$

The metal hydroxide rather than the metal carbonate forms as a precipitate. The overall equation is therefore:

$$2[M(H_2O)_6]^{3+} + 3CO_3^{2-} \rightarrow 2[M(H_2O)_3(OH_3)] + 3CO_2 + 3H_2O$$

For chromium(III), the following reactions illustrate the above:

$$[Cr(H_2O)_6]^{3+} + H_2O \rightleftharpoons [Cr(H_2O)_5(OH)]^{2+} + H_3O^+$$

then:

$$[Cr(H_2O)_5(OH)]^{2+} + H_2O \rightleftharpoons [Cr(H_2O)_4(OH)_2]^+ + H_3O^+$$

and then:

$$[Cr(H_2O)_4(OH)_2]^+ + H_2O \rightleftharpoons [Cr(H_2O)_3(OH)_3] + H_3O^+$$

and as before:

$$2H_3O^+ + CO_3^{2-} \rightarrow CO_2 + 3H_2O$$

The metal hydroxide precipitates, carbon dioxide is evolved and the overall equation is as follows:

$$2[Cr(H_2O)_6]^{3+} + 3CO_3^{2-} \rightarrow 2[Cr(H_2O)_3(OH)_3] + 3CO_2 + 3H_2O$$

green precipitate

No-one has ever made a metal(III) carbonate from an aqueous solution. Compounds such as $Cr_2(CO_3)_3$ do not exist. This relative instability

Fig. 5 Fe^{3+} has a high charge/size ratio: it weakens the O–H bond, releasing H^+ to form H_3O^+

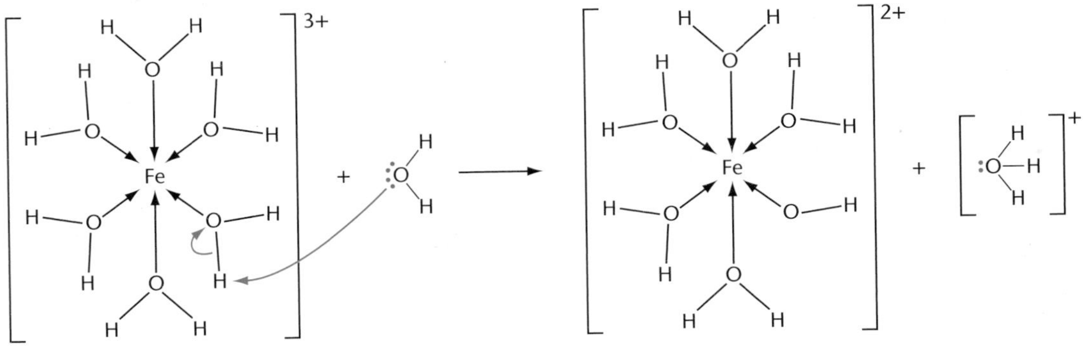

can again be explained in terms of charge/size ratio. The 3+ ion is so strongly polarising that it would distort the charge cloud on the carbonate ion, and so it forms a metal hydroxide in solution and carbon dioxide. These products have a greater overall stability than the theoretical metal(III) carbonate. The same argument would apply to the relative stabilities of the metal(III) oxide and carbon dioxide compared with the metal(III) carbonate. The carbonate ion is readily distorted but the smaller oxide ion is more difficult to distort (Tables 2 and 3).

7 Write down what you would expect to see, and give the equations for the reactions, when a solution of sodium carbonate is added to:

a a green aqueous solution of nickel(II) chloride

b a yellow aqueous solution of iron(III) chloride.

Table 2 Reactions of metal(II) ions with bases

Aqueous M(II) ion solution	Base added				
	OH^- little	OH^- excess (2M)	NH_3 little	NH_3 excess	CO_3^{2-}
Mg(II) colourless	White precipitate, $Mg(OH)_2$	Does not dissolve	White precipitate, $Mg(OH)_2$	Does not dissolve	White precipitate, $MgCO_3$
Fe(II) green, $[Fe(H_2O)_6]^{2+}$	Green precipitate, $Fe(OH)_2$	Does not dissolve	Green precipitate; easily oxidised by air – turns brown $Fe(OH)_2$	Green precipitate; dissolves to give pale-brown solution – turns brown in air	Green precipitate, $FeCO_3$
Co(II) pink, $[Co(H_2O)_6]^{2+}$	Blue precipitate, $Co(OH)_2$; easily oxidised by air – turns brown	Does not dissolve	Blue precipitate; easily oxidised by air – turns brown	Pale, straw-coloured solution	Pink precipitate, $CoCO_3$
Cu(II) blue, $[Cu(H_2O)_6]^{2+}$	Pale blue precipitate, $Cu(OH)_2$	Does not dissolve	Pale blue precipitate, $Cu(OH)_2$	Deep-blue solution, $[Cu(NH_3)_4(H_2O)_2]^{2+}$	Green-blue precipitate, $CuCO_3$
Zn(II) colourless, $[Zn(H_2O)_6]^{2+}$	White precipitate, $Zn(OH)_2$	Dissolves to form colourless solution, $[Zn(H_2O)_2(OH)_4]^{2-}$	White precipitate, $Zn(OH)_2$	Does not dissolve	White precipitate, $ZnCO_3$

A task sheet and practice questions on the Practical Skills Assessment 'Investigate the chemistry of transition metal compounds in a series of experiments' can be found at www.collinseducation.co.uk/advancedscienceaqa

Table 3   Reactions of metal(III) ions with bases

Aqueous M(III) ion solution	Base added				
	OH⁻ little	**OH⁻ excess (2M)**	**NH₃ little**	**NH₃ excess**	**CO₃²⁻**
Fe(III) violet, $[Fe(H_2O)_6]^{3+}$ (appears brown due to hydrolysis)	Brown precipitate, $[Fe(H_2O)_3(OH)_3]$	Does not dissolve	Brown precipitate, $[Fe(H_2O)_3(OH)_3]$	Does not dissolve	Brown precipitate of hydroxide, $[Fe(H_2O)_3(OH)_3]$, and CO_2 evolved
Cr(III) ruby, $[Cr(H_2O)_6]^{3+}$	Green precipitate, $[Cr(H_2O)_3(OH)_3]$	Dissolves to give green solution, $[Cr(OH)_6]^{3-}$	Green precipitate, $[Cr(H_2O)_3(OH)_3]$	Dissolves to give purple solution, $[Cr(NH_3)_6]^{3+}$	Green precipitate of hydroxide, $[Cr(H_2O)_3(OH)_3]$, and CO_2 evolved
Al(III) colourless	White precipitate, $Al(OH)_3$	Dissolves to form colourless solution, $[Al(OH)_4]^-$	White precipitate, $Al(H_2O)_3(OH)_3$	Does not dissolve	White precipitate of hydroxide of $Al(OH)_3$ and CO_2 evolved

key facts

- Metal(III) ions produce greater acidity than metal(II) ions and this determines the products of the reaction.
- Metal(II) aqua ions give precipitates of carbonates on addition of sodium carbonate solution.
- Metal(III) aqua ions give precipitates of hydroxides and carbon dioxide gas on addition of sodium carbonate solution.
- A colour change occurs during the reaction.

16.7 Substitution of ligands in transition metal compounds

As with the acid–base reactions in Section 16.5, ammonia molecules can affect the hydrolysis equilibrium in an aqua complex. Ammonia can behave as a base, with the equilibrium:

$$NH_3(aq) + H_2O(l) \rightleftharpoons NH_4^+(aq) + OH^-(aq)$$

The equilibrium for the metal(II) ions exists as before (Section 16.4):

$$[M(H_2O)_6]^{2+} + H_2O \rightleftharpoons [M(H_2O)_5(OH)]^+ + H_3O^+$$

In water, the equilibrium between the hydroxide ions and H_3O^+ ions is established:

$$OH^- + H_3O^+ \rightleftharpoons 2H_2O$$

This removes H_3O^+ ions and moves the equilibrium completely to the right. If more OH⁻ is added, the second equilibrium:

$$[M(H_2O)_5(OH)]^+ + H_2O \rightleftharpoons [M(OH)_2(H_2O)_4] + H_3O^+$$

is also displaced to the right by OH⁻ ions reacting with the H_3O^+ formed and $[M(H_2O)_4(OH)_2]$, metal(II) hydroxide, is precipitated. Even though ammonia is a weak base, the concentration of OH⁻ is sufficient to shift the equilibrium to the right to allow the precipitate to form. We can write the overall equation as follows:

$$[M(H_2O)_6]^{2+} + 2OH^- \rightleftharpoons [M(H_2O)_4(OH)_2] + 2H_2O$$

The addition of OH⁻ shifts the equilibrium to the right and eventually the precipitate forms.

As well as the acid–base reactions giving the precipitate, most transition metal ions give a further sequence of reactions in which the aqua ligands are substituted by ammine ligands. When a water molecule is replaced by any other ligand, it is a **substitution reaction** and, because a lone pair of electrons is being donated, it is an example of **nucleophilic substitution**. Ligand replacement in a complex ion is taking place continually, and the picture we represent is the 'average'.

There are two types of ligands:

- neutral ligands – molecules that have no overall charge, e.g. H_2O and NH_3
- anionic ligands – ligands that carry a negative charge, e.g. Cl^- and OH^-.

These complex ions formed by ligand replacement are soluble, so a precipitate formed by the acid–base reaction will re-dissolve when it forms the complex ion. A series of equilibria is set up and the overall equation for the substitution reaction is:

$$[M(H_2O)_6]^{2+} + 6NH_3 \rightleftharpoons [M(NH_3)_6]^{2+} + 6H_2O$$

This reaction can be written as occurring in six steps, as shown in Fig. 6.

Fig. 6   Steps in ammonia ligand substitution for metal(II) complexes

$$[M(H_2O)_6]^{2+} + NH_3 \rightleftharpoons [M(NH_3)(H_2O)_5]^{2+} + H_2O$$

$$[M(NH_3)(H_2O)_5]^{2+} + NH_3 \rightleftharpoons [M(NH_3)_2(H_2O)_4]^{2+} + H_2O$$

$$[M(NH_3)_2(H_2O)_4]^{2+} + NH_3 \rightleftharpoons [M(NH_3)_3(H_2O)_3]^{2+} + H_2O$$

$$[M(NH_3)_3(H_2O)_3]^{2+} + NH_3 \rightleftharpoons [M(NH_3)_4(H_2O)_2]^{2+} + H_2O$$

$$[M(NH_3)_4(H_2O)_2]^{2+} + NH_3 \rightleftharpoons [M(NH_3)_5(H_2O)]^{2+} + H_2O$$

$$[M(NH_3)_5(H_2O)]^{2+} + NH_3 \rightleftharpoons [M(NH_3)_6]^{2+} + H_2O$$

8 What is the general pattern in the reactions in Fig. 6?

In these reactions, the ammonia is being written as donating a lone pair of electrons to the central metal ion, so it is a **Lewis base**. In the hydrolysis equilibria, ammonia was being considered as donating a lone pair to a proton, so it is also a Lewis base.

Different complexes in the sequence in Fig. 6 will have different stabilities. For the first substitution:

$$K_c = \frac{[[M(H_2O)_5(NH_3)]^{2+}][H_2O]}{[[M(H_2O)_6]^{2+}][NH_3]}$$

but the overall equilibrium can be defined by the equilibrium constant:

$$K_c = \frac{[[M(NH_3)_6]^{2+}][H_2O]^6}{[[M(H_2O)_6]^{2+}][NH_3]^6}$$

Effects of changing ligands

Since the presence of a ligand affects the split between the energy levels in the d orbitals, and hence the frequency of light absorbed, changing the ligands often changes the colour of the complex. The size and charge of the ligand and the strength of the bond formed by donating the lone pairs of electrons into the central metal ion are the most significant factors in changing properties.

The ammonia and water ligands are similar in size, and both form octahedral complexes with transition metal ions. There is no change in shape. Cobalt(II) ions in ammonia solution and copper(II) ions in ammonia solution are examples of this system. Ligand substitution also causes a colour change in the cobalt and copper systems, but no change in co-ordination number.

When concentrated aqueous ammonia is added to a solution containing pink cobalt(II) ions, a green-blue precipitate of cobalt(II) hydroxide forms at first. This is the result of the acidity reaction of the cobalt(II) ions:

$$[Co(H_2O)_6]^{2+}(aq) + 2NH_3(aq) \rightarrow$$
$$[Co(H_2O)_4(OH)_2](aq) + 2NH_4^+(aq)$$

pink   blue-green precipitate

If excess aqueous ammonia is added, the precipitate dissolves. A pale-brown (straw-coloured) solution forms:

$$[Co(H_2O)_4(OH)_2](aq) + 6NH_3 \rightarrow$$
$$[Co(NH_3)_6]^{2+} + 4H_2O + 2OH^-$$

blue/green   pale brown

We can write the overall reaction as:

$$[Co(H_2O)_6]^{2+}(aq) + 6NH_3(aq) \rightarrow$$
$$[Co(NH_3)_6]^{2+} + 6H_2O$$

pink   pale brown

When preparing compounds containing the $[Co(NH_3)_6]^{2+}$ ion, it is important to keep the solution of the hexaamminecobalt(II) ion away from air because the hexaamminecobalt(II) ion is easily oxidised in air to form the hexaamminecobalt(III) ion:

$$[Co(NH_3)_6]^{2+} \xrightarrow{O_2} [Co(NH_3)_6]^{3+}$$

pale yellow   brown/yellow
octahedral   octahedral

Sometimes, when ligands are replaced, not all of them are exchanged. The ligands are exchanged in a stepwise manner (see Fig. 6) and there is an equilibrium constant for each step. The most common example of partial exchange is the formation of the tetraamminebisaquacopper(II) complex. This complex is formed by simply adding dilute ammonia solution to copper sulfate solution until the precipitate of copper hydroxide re-dissolves, giving a deep-blue solution:

$$[Cu(H_2O)_6]^{2+} + 2NH_3 \rightleftharpoons$$
$$[Cu(NH_3)_4(OH)_2] + 2NH_4^+$$

blue solution   pale-blue precipitate

$$[Cu(H_2O)_6]^{2+} + 4NH_3 \rightleftharpoons$$
$$[Cu(NH_3)_4(H_2O)_2]^{2+} + 4H_2O$$

blue solution   deep-blue solution

M(III) complexes undergo a similar sequence of liquid substitutions.

However, under these conditions the equilibrium does not go any further. We can gain an idea of why this happens if we look at the structure of the complexes. In both complexes, two of the ligands are further away from the copper(II) ion than the other four (see Fig. 7). You can see from Fig. 7 that the four ligands in the square planar arrangement are replaced by the ammonia molecules. The long bonds are weaker and break most easily, so in solution they are most likely to be replaced by the surrounding ligands. In aqueous solution, these are most likely to be aqua ligands.

Fig. 7   Copper(II) ions in concentrated aqueous ammonia

When concentrated aqueous ammonia is added to copper(II) ions, a blue precipitate of copper(II) hydroxide forms:

$$[Cu(H_2O)_6]^{2+} + 2NH_3 \rightleftharpoons [Cu(OH_2)(H_2O)_4] + 2NH_4^+$$
blue   pale blue

When excess aqueous ammonia is added, the precipitate dissolves to give a deep-blue solution of tetraamminebisaquacopper(II) ions:

$$[Cu(H_2O)_6]^{2+} + 4NH_3 \rightleftharpoons [Cu(NH_3)_4(H_2O)_2] + 4H_2O$$
blue   blue-violet
               tetraamminebisaquacopper(II) ion

Note: when naming a complex with two or more different types of ligands, you must list the ligands in alphabetical order (disregarding prefixes like di-, tri- and so on).

Only four of the six aqua ligands are substituted by ammonia. The structure is:

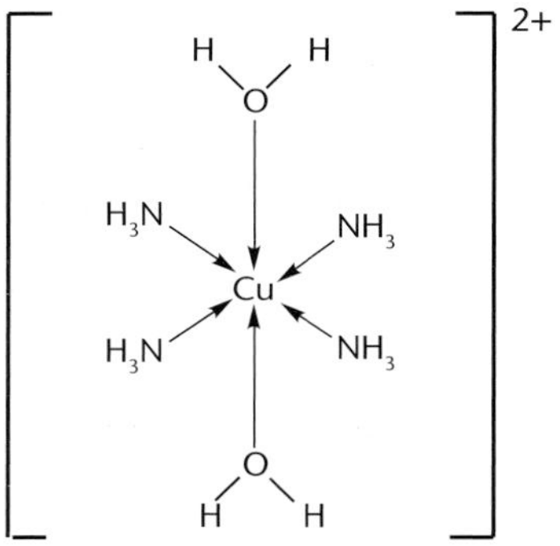

9 How should increasing the ammonia concentration affect the equilibrium?

To substitute all the aqua ligands, the concentration of the ammonia must be increased. One way to achieve this is to use liquid ammonia instead of aqueous ammonia solution.

A task sheet and practice questions on the Practical Skills Assessment 'Prepare an inorganic complex' can be found at www.collinseducation.co.uk/advancedscienceaqa

16.8 Substitution of H$_2$O ligands by Cl$^-$ ligands

The octahedral structure is clearer in other complex ions. The hydrated cobalt(II) ion $[Co(H_2O)_6]^{2+}$ is pink and is octahedral in shape (Fig. 8). The co-ordination number of cobalt in this complex ion is 6. The cobalt ion is bonded to six ligands. When the chloride ion concentration is high, the blue tetrachlorocobaltate(II) ion $[CoCl_4]^{2-}$ forms. This is tetrahedral (Fig. 8).

The chloride anion is much larger than the chlorine atom from which it is formed (Fig. 9).

The chloride ion has the electronic configuration of a noble gas, with four lone pairs of electrons. When the chloride ion acts as a ligand, one of these four pairs is donated to the metal ion.

Concentrated hydrochloric acid, with a higher solubility, has a higher concentration of chloride ions than sodium chloride. Adding concentrated hydrochloric acid to a solution containing a metal–aqua ion gives a high enough concentration of Cl$^-$ ions to displace the equilibrium:

$$[M(H_2O)_6]^{2+} + 4Cl^- \rightleftharpoons [MCl_4]^{2-} + 6H_2O$$

$$[Co(H_2O)_6]^{2+} + 4Cl^- \rightleftharpoons [CoCl_4]^{2-} + 6H_2O$$

pink   deep-blue
octahedral   tetrahedral

A deep-blue solution of ions is formed. If water is added, the solution turns pink again, as the equilibrium is pushed to the left. Adding more concentrated hydrochloric acid turns it deep blue again, pushing the equilibrium to the right. This time, the colour change is due not only to the change in ligand, but also to the change in co-ordination number.

You can use the different colours of these cobalt complexes to test for the presence of

Fig. 8 Equilibrium between hexaaquacobalt(II) and tetrachlorocobaltate(II)

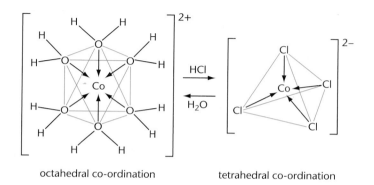

octahedral co-ordination   tetrahedral co-ordination

Fig. 9 Comparative sizes of some atoms and ions

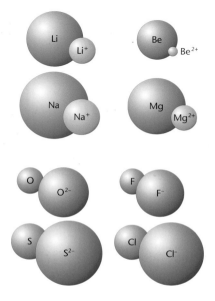

Adding concentrated HCl changes pink $[Co(H_2O)_6]^{2+}$ ions to blue $[CoCl_4]^{2-}$ ions.

water. Cobalt chloride paper contains high levels of chloride ions, and so the blue $[CoCl_4]^{2-}$ ion is present. If you moisten cobalt chloride paper, it turns pink. Water molecules replace the chloride ligands and the hydrated cobalt(II) ion forms.

The co-ordination number changes because the large chloride ion is negatively charged. The ligands around the central metal ion of the

---

10

a   For the complex $[CoCl_4]^{2-}$, what is the co-ordination number and oxidation state of cobalt?

b   Write an equation for the reaction when concentrated hydrochloric acid is added to aquacobalt(II) ions. What is the change in co-ordination number?

Fig. 10   The tetrachlorocuprate(II) ion

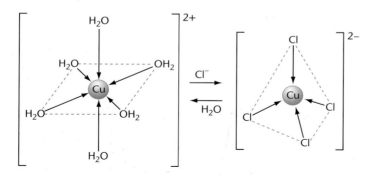

complex repel each other. With larger ligands, there comes a point at which a tetrahedral structure is more stable than an octahedral structure, so the co-ordination number changes. For $M^{2+}(aq)$ ions the general equation for ligand substitution by chloride ions is:

$$[M(H_2O)_6]^{2+} + 4Cl^- \rightleftharpoons [MCl_4]^{2-} + 6H_2O$$

When concentrated hydrochloric acid is added to aqueous copper(II) ions, the colour changes from blue to yellow-green. Each solution contains complex copper(II) ions.

Under completely anhydrous conditions, the tetrachlorocuprate(II) complex ion $[CuCl_4]^{2-}$ is yellow. But even with concentrated hydrochloric acid there is a significant concentration of aqua ligands and a yellow-green complex ion forms. Although $[CuCl_4]^{2-}$ is yellow, there will always be some replacement by aqua ligands from any water present. Colour absorption by the ligands splitting the energy levels will give a mixture of yellow and blue, so the solution appears green. It is acceptable to consider the yellow-green complex as tetrachlorocuprate(II), $[CuCl_4]^{2-}$.

When this solution is diluted, an equilibrium is set up between the $[CuCl_4]^{2-}$ ion and the hydrated copper(II) ion (Fig. 10):

$$[CuCl_4]^{2-}(aq) + 6H_2O(l) \rightarrow$$
$$[Cu(H_2O)_6]^{2+}(aq) + 4Cl^-(aq)$$

yellow   blue

The tetrachlorocuprate(II) ion is an anionic (negative) complex ion. The central copper(II) ion is bonded with four chloride ions, using the lone pairs on the chloride ions. The co-ordination number of the copper is 4 and the ion is tetrahedral in shape.

16.9 Types of ligands

A further factor that affects the stability of complexes is the number of links a single ligand can form with the central metal ion. The ligands discussed so far (Section 15.2) have been **unidentate**, i.e. one pair of electrons is donated from each ion or molecule. A **bidentate** ligand, e.g. ethanedioate $C_2O_4^{2-}$, will donate two electron pairs into the available orbitals on the central metal ion. A **hexadentate** ligand has six donor atoms with lone electron pairs. EDTA^{4-} is a hexadentate

ligand, and this is an example of a **chelating ligand** (Section 15.2).

Again, equilibria exist for these ligand replacements; ethane-1,2-diamine, $H_2NCH_2CH_2NH_2$, often written as (en) for simplicity, will replace aqua ligands in a metal(II)–aqua complex according to the equation:

$$[M(H_2O)_6]^{2+} + H_2NCH_2CH_2NH_2 \rightleftharpoons$$
$$[M(H_2O)_4(H_2NCH_2CH_2NH_2)]^{2+} + 2H_2O$$

Further substitution can occur until all the aqua ligands are replaced:

$$[M(H_2O)_4(H_2NCH_2CH_2NH_2)]^{2+} + H_2NCH_2CH_2NH_2 \rightleftharpoons$$
$$[M(H_2O)_2(H_2NCH_2CH_2NH_2)_2]^{2+} + 2H_2O$$

and then:

$$[M(H_2O)_2(H_2NCH_2CH_2NH_2)]^{2+} + H_2NCH_2CH_2NH_2 \rightleftharpoons$$
$$[M(H_2NCH_2CH_2NH_2)_3]^{2+} + 2H_2O$$

metal(III) trisethane-1,2-diamine
complex (tris means 'three')

The position of equilibrium for these complexes lies well over to the right, and the equilibrium constant for the formation of trisethane-1,2-diamine complexes is approximately 10^{20}. This much higher equilibrium constant means that these complexes are very stable when compared with the aqua complexes. Metal(III) trisethane-1,2-diamine complexes can also be formed:

$$[M(H_2O)_6]^{3+} + 3H_2NCH_2CH_2NH_2 \rightleftharpoons$$
$$[M(H_2NCH_2CH_2NH_2)_3]^{3+} + 6H_2O$$

These have equilibrium constants of the order of 10^{30}, so are even more stable compared with the metal(II) complexes.

EDTA^{4-} has the structure shown in Fig. 11. The lone pairs in EDTA are on the two nitrogen atoms and on four of the oxygen atoms. EDTA^{4-} forms one-to-one complexes with metal(II) atoms, such as [Cu(EDTA)]$^{2-}$ (Fig. 12). The complexes formed by multidentate ligands are very stable, because the central cation is firmly held by many co-ordinate bonds.

The bidentate ligands can form similar structures, e.g. [Cu(en)$_3$]$^{2+}$ (Fig. 13). There are mixed complexes containing bidentate and unidentate ligands, e.g. [CuCl$_2$(en)$_2$]$^{2+}$ (Fig. 14). These complexes involving multidentate or chelating ligands such as EDTA^{4-} will be more stable and have higher K_c values than those with unidentate ligands, such as NH_3.

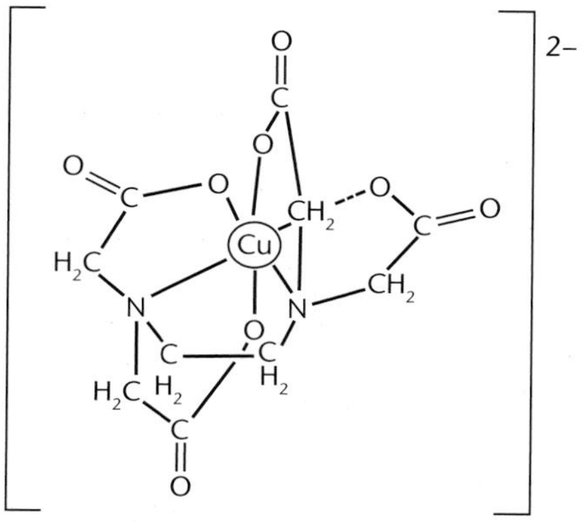

Fig. 13 Chelating effect of ethylenediamine

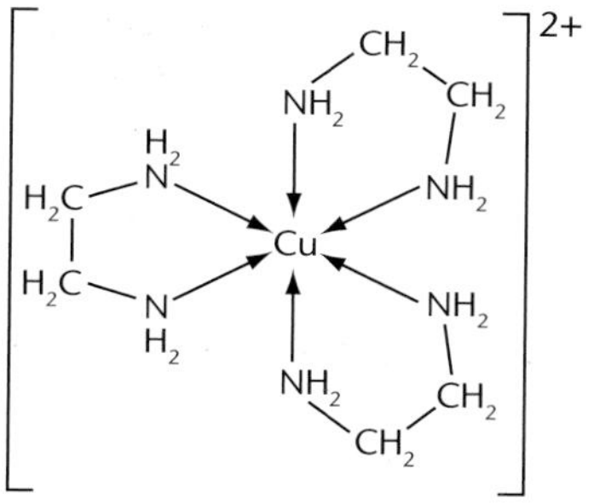

Fig. 11 Displayed formula of EDTA^{4-}

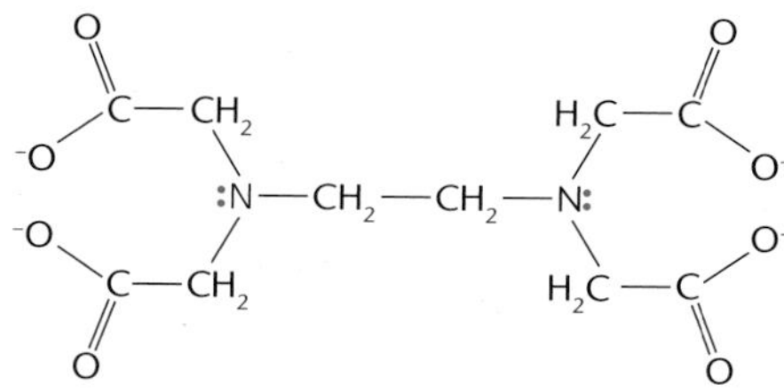

Fig. 14 Mixed complex of ethane-1,2-diamine and chloro ligands

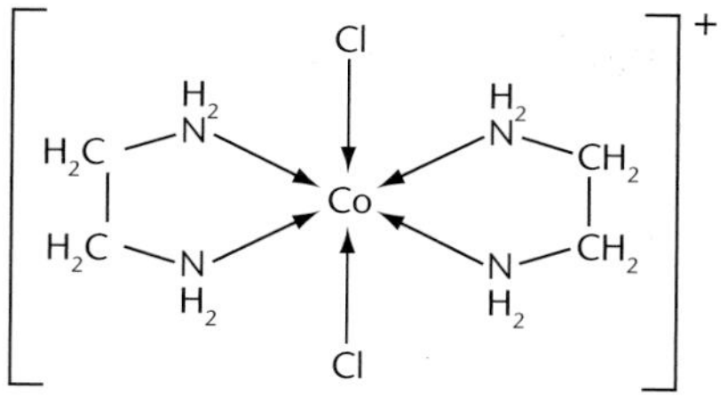

Fig. 12 Displayed formula of EDTA/Cu

11 Write equations for the exchanges that will take place if the following pairs of chemicals are mixed:

a aqueous [Co(H$_2$O)$_6$]$^{2+}$ with EDTA^{4-}

b [Fe(H$_2$O)$_6$]$^{3+}$ and ethanedioate (C$_2$O$_4{}^{2-}$) ions.

c Draw the structure of the product in part **b**.

Ultimately, the value of K_c will depend on:

- the charge on the ion
- the size and charge of the ligands
- the co-ordination number of the central metal ion
- the number of bonds per ligand
- the chelate effect.

Entropy and stability of complexes

The stabilities of complexes with chelating ligands can be explained in terms of the increase in entropy of the system. The overall feasibility of a reaction is determined by the change in free energy (see Chapter 12) calculated using:

$$\Delta G^{\ominus} = \Delta H^{\ominus} - T\Delta S^{\ominus}$$

If $\Delta G^{\ominus}$ has a negative value, the reaction is feasible. $\Delta H^{\ominus}$ is the enthalpy term and if $\Delta H^{\ominus}$ becomes more negative, energy is released and the system moves to a lower energy, so the reaction is more favoured. $\Delta S^{\ominus}$ is the entropy term and this can be thought of as the degree of disorder in the system (Chapter 12). When entropy increases in a reaction, $\Delta S^{\ominus}$ is positive, and $-T\Delta S^{\ominus}$ will have a more negative value. Then, $\Delta G^{\ominus}$ will be more negative and the reaction will be more favoured.

The effect can be illustrated using the ligands H_2O, NH_3 and $EDTA^{4-}$ as examples. If a transition metal ion is dissolved in water, it is surrounded by aqua ligands. When another unidentate ligand replaces a water molecule, it may donate more strongly and this will give a negative $\Delta H^{\ominus}$ value and the exchange is likely to be favoured.

If ammonia solution is added to $[Cu(H_2O)_6]^{2+}$, then some ligands are replaced:

$$[Cu(H_2O)_6]^{2+} + 4NH_3 \rightleftharpoons [Cu(NH_3)_4(H_2O)_2]^{2+} + 4H_2O$$
five particles   five particles

In this example, although the $\Delta H^{\ominus}$ value has changed, the entropy of the system will be very similar, $\Delta S^{\ominus}$ will be small and $T\Delta S^{\ominus}$ insignificant. This is because one particle moving randomly in the aqueous solution has been replaced by one water molecule, which will also move about randomly in the solution. So the total number of particles remains constant and there is minimal change in the disorder.

If a multidentate ligand such as $EDTA^{4-}$ replaces the unidentate ligands, one $EDTA^{4-}$, which is a hexadentate ligand, replaces six water molecules. This means that previously there was one particle ($EDTA^{4-}$) moving randomly and now there are six particles (water molecules) moving randomly. The system now has a much higher entropy value, so the $-T\Delta S^{\ominus}$ term for the reaction is large:

$$[Cu(H_2O)_6]^{2+} + EDTA^{4-} \rightarrow [Cu(EDTA)]^{2-} + 6H_2O$$
two particles   seven particles

More particles gives a greater number of possible arrangements, which in turn gives a greater disorder, and this increases the entropy.

The enthalpy change in ligand substitution reactions is usually small, so the large value of $-T\Delta S^{\ominus}$ means that $\Delta G^{\ominus}$ is negative and the reaction is feasible. Ligand substitution occurs and the reaction proceeds, essentially to completion (Fig. 15).

12 Why does a more negative $\Delta H^{\ominus}$ value mean a more stable complex ion?

key facts

- Ammonia and water molecules can act as neutral ligands.
- Ammonia will replace water in aqua complexes, with no change of co-ordination number.
- The reactions of transition metal complexes often result in a colour change, because of a change of ligand, and/or a change of co-ordination number, and/or a change of oxidation state.

- Ligand substitution reactions of ammonia or water by chloride ions involve a change of co-ordination number from 6 to 4.
- Ligands are commonly unidentate, bidentate or hexadentate.
- Chelating ligands form very stable complexes.
- Forming complexes with chelating ligands increases the entropy of the system.

Fig. 15   Increasing entropy effect of chelating ligands

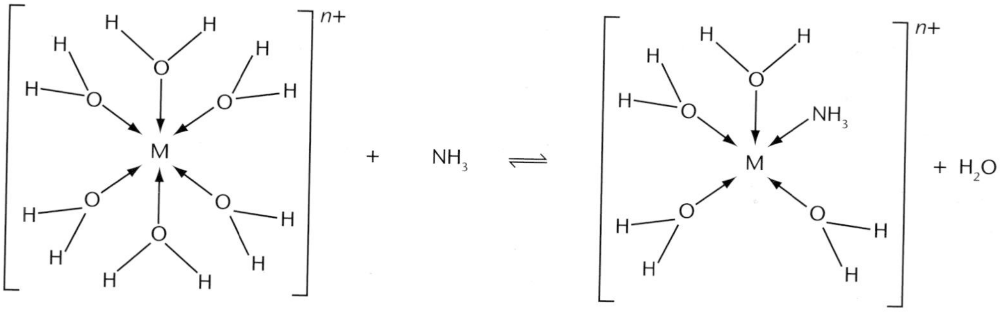

two particles $\longrightarrow$ two particles

one ammine ligand replaces one aqua ligand: minimal entropy change

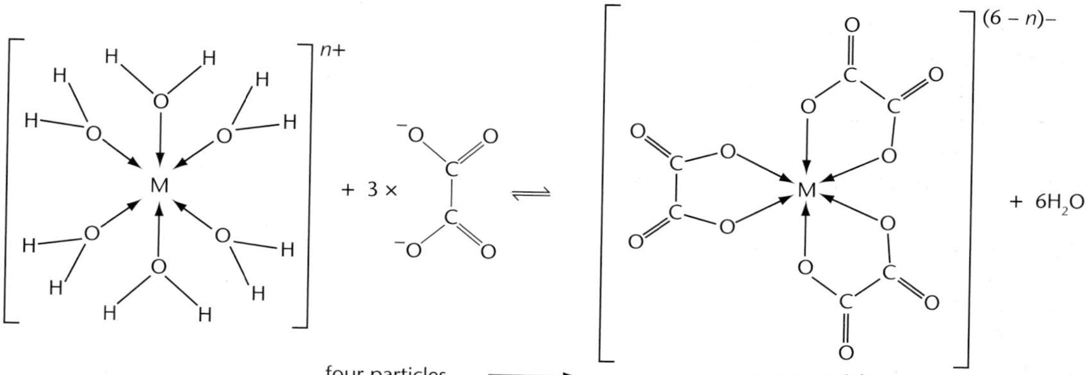

four particles $\longrightarrow$ seven particles

three ethanedioate ligands replace six aqua ligands: entropy increases

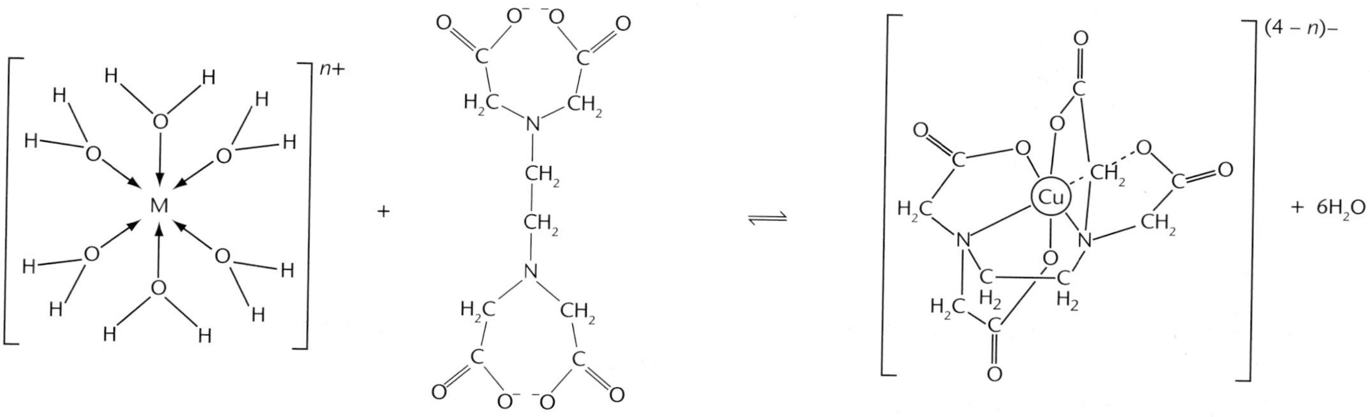

two particles $\longrightarrow$ seven particles

one EDTA^{4-} ligand replaces six aqua ligands: larger entropy increase

1

a Chromium(III) ions are weakly acidic in aqueous solution as shown by the following equation.

$$[Cr(H_2O)_6]^{3+}(aq) \rightleftharpoons [Cr(H_2O)_5(OH)]^{2+}(aq) + H^+(aq)$$

The value of K_a for this reaction is 1.15×10^{-4} mol dm^{-3}. Calculate the pH of a 0.500 mol dm^{-3} solution of $[Cr(H_2O)_6]^{3+}(aq)$. (5)

b State what you would observe after addition of the following reagents to separate aqueous solutions containing $[Cr(H_2O)_6]^{3+}$ ions. In each case give the formula of the chromium-containing product.

 i an excess of NaOH(aq)

 ii Na$_2$CO$_3$(aq) (5)

Total 10

AQA, June 2007, Unit 5, Question 3 (c–d)

2 The following scheme shows some reactions of chromium compounds in aqueous solution.

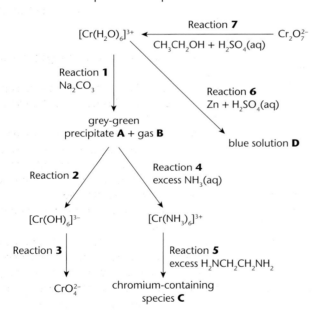

a Identify the grey-green precipitate **A** and the gas **B** formed in Reaction **1**. Write an equation for this reaction. (3)

b **i** Identify a reagent for Reaction **2**.

 ii Deduce the oxidation state of chromium in CrO_4^{2-}

 iii Identify a reagent needed for Reaction **3**. Write a half-equation for the conversion of $[Cr(OH)_6]^{3-}$ into CrO_4^{2-} (4)

c Draw the structure of the chromium-containing species **C** formed in Reaction **5**. Indicate the charge on species **C**. (2)

d Identify the chromium-containing species present in the blue solution **D** formed in Reaction **6** and state the role of zinc in its formation. (2)

e Two organic compounds are formed in Reaction **7**. One of these compounds has a low boiling point and can be distilled readily from the reaction mixture. The other compound has a higher boiling point and is the main organic product formed when the reaction mixture is refluxed.

 i Identify the organic product which has a low boiling point.

 ii Identify the main organic product formed when the mixture is refluxed. (2)

Total 13

AQA, June 2006, Unit 5, Question 3

3 Consider the reaction scheme below and answer the questions which follow.

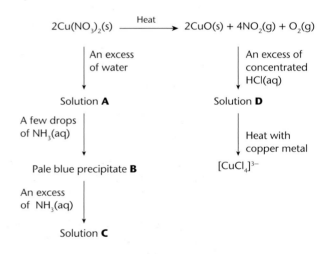

a A redox reaction occurs when Cu(NO$_3$)$_2$ is decomposed by heat. Deduce the oxidation state of nitrogen in Cu(NO$_3$)$_2$ and in NO$_2$ and identify the product formed by oxidation in this decomposition. (3)

b Identify and state the shape of the copper-containing species present in solution **A**. (2)

c **i** Identify the pale blue precipitate **B** and write an equation, or equations, to show how **B** is formed from the copper-containing species in solution **A**.

 ii In what way does the NH$_3$ behave as a Brønsted–Lowry base? (3)

d **i** Identify the copper-containing species present in solution **C**. State the colour of this copper-containing species and write an equation for its formation from precipitate **B**.

ii In what way does the NH_3 behave as a Lewis base? (4)

e Identify the copper-containing species present in solution **D**. State the colour and shape of this copper-containing species. (3)

f The oxidation state of copper in $[CuCl_4]^{3-}$ is +1.

i Give the electron arrangement of a Cu^+ ion.

ii Deduce the role of copper metal in the formation of $[CuCl_4]^{3-}$ from the copper-containing species in solution **D**. (2)

Total 17

AQA, June 2005, Unit 5, Question 1

4

a **i** The addition of aqueous silver nitrate, followed by concentrated aqueous ammonia, can be used to distinguish between separate aqueous solutions of sodium bromide and sodium iodide.
Record what is observed in the table below.

	The addition of $AgNO_3$	followed by the addition of concentrated $NH_3(aq)$
Observation with NaBr(aq)		
Observation with NaI(aq)		

ii Explain why it is not possible to distinguish between separate solutions of sodium nitrate and sodium fluoride by the addition of silver nitrate solution. (5)

b When aqueous sodium thiosulphate is added to solid silver bromide a reaction occurs and a colourless solution is formed.

i Identify the silver-containing species present in the colourless solution.

ii Write an equation for this reaction.

iii Give **one** use of this reaction. (3)

c Aqueous silver nitrate can be used to distinguish between chloroethanoic acid and ethanoyl chloride.

i Draw the structure of ethanoyl chloride. Predict what, if anything, you would observe when ethanoyl chloride is added to aqueous silver nitrate.

ii Draw the structure of chloroethanoic acid. Predict what, if anything, you would observe when chloroethanoic acid is added to aqueous silver nitrate. (4)

d **i** Tollens' reagent is formed by the addition of aqueous ammonia to aqueous silver nitrate. Identify the silver-containing complex present in Tollens' reagent and state its shape.

ii Draw the structure of methanoic acid. By reference to this structure, suggest why a silver mirror is formed when this acid reacts with Tollens' reagent.

iii Deduce the identity of a carbon-containing species formed when methanoic acid reacts with Tollens' reagent. (5)

Total 17

AQA, June 2005, Unit 5, Question 3

5

a Complete the electronic arrangement of the Co^{2+} ion. (1)

b Give the formula of the cobalt complex present in an aqueous solution of cobalt(II) sulfate and state its colour. (2)

c **i** When a large excess of concentrated aqueous ammonia is added to an aqueous solution of cobalt(II) sulfate, a new cobalt(II) complex is formed. Give the formula of the new cobalt(II) complex and state its colour.

ii Write an equation for the formation of this new complex. (3)

d When hydrogen peroxide is added to the mixture formed in part **c**, the colour of the solution darkens due to the formation of a different cobalt complex. Identify this different cobalt complex and state the role of hydrogen peroxide in its formation (2)

Total 8

AQA, January 2005, Unit 5, Question 5

Soil contamination

Society is now much more environmentally aware than in the past. But environmental awareness has not always been the case, and 150 years ago (and even much more recently) it was quite common for highly toxic waste from mines to be dumped on land or emptied into rivers. In the past decade or so, the UK agency called the 'Environment Agency' has set out legislation to control soil and land contamination. It has been estimated that there could be up to 100 000 seriously contaminated sites in the UK.

Water was an essential resource for mining and other metal manufacturing processes, so watercourses have been contaminated with heavy metals such as copper, silver and lead by leaching. If a metal ion is present in water, a hydrolysis reaction can occur.

A1 Write equations for $Cu^{2+}(aq)$ hydrolysis and $Cr^{3+}(aq)$ hydrolysis in water.

A2 Why are they called hydrolysis reactions?

A3 Explain why hydrolysis is more significant with Cr^{3+} than with Cu^{2+}.

A4 State how hydrolysis will affect the pH of the water.

A5 Explain why there are higher amounts of dissolved copper in soft water than in hard water.

A6 If 100 cm³ of a water sample was titrated with $EDTA^{4-}$ and 4.80 cm³ of 0.05 mol dm⁻³ $EDTA^{4-}$ were needed to reach the endpoint:

a Calculate the number of moles of $EDTA^{4-}$ used in the titration.

b Calculate the number of moles of copper complexed.

c Calculate the concentration of copper as mg dm⁻³ in the original sample.

At low pH, nearly all metals are more soluble than in neutral water. Oxides and hydroxides have high lattice energies, so many of them are insoluble. If a complex ion can be formed, more hydration can take place, releasing more energy to break down the lattice. Generally, soft water contains more aluminium ions (dissolved from soil and rocks) than hard water.

Copper, often found in high concentrations in mining areas, is toxic to plants and micro-organisms, especially at low pH. As already mentioned, this copper can leach into watercourses. 'Environmental forensics' is a developing area

There may be contamination of this site by heavy metals. It is easy to see if there is discoloured water, or the site may need further testing to determine the extent of the contamination.

of science that involves analytical studies and both data interpretation and data modelling connected with the attribution of pollution events to their causes. Often the scientists involved will use spectroscopic techniques, but the formation of the $[Cu(EDTA)]_2$ complex can be used to determine the amounts of copper in water because the complex is so stable.

The Environment Agency will use its environmental scientists to determine liability for site pollution and hence decontamination. Where they can attribute liability, the 'polluter pays'. An old copper mine on Parys Mountain in Anglesey used to be one of the world's biggest copper-producing sites, but it was abandoned in the late 18th century. The mine contained pipes that were used

periodically to release water that was building up inside the mine. This water was highly acidic, and contaminated with copper and iron. In 2003, the Environment Agency allowed the local council to pump 200 000 cubic metres of untreated water out of the mine into the Irish Sea.

Now a science team is studying mussels, which are filter feeders, and seaweed in the Irish Sea. The long-term plan is to decontaminate the site, but any links to the original owners of the mine are long gone.

The uptake of heavy metals by flora and fauna can be used for long-term studies of water pollution.

A7 Give arguments for and against the permission to release the water from the mine by the Environment Agency.

A8 The water in pools around a copper mine is clear and blue. Give a chemical explanation for the water's appearance.

A9 How will these studies help the Environment Agency in their monitoring role?

A10 How will the scientists use analytical studies, data interpretation and modelling to study the impact?

A11 Who should pay for this work to be done? Justify your answer.

A12 Old industrial sites are often referred to as 'brownfield' sites. Why might companies be wary of developing on these sites?

Data section

The Periodic Table

The Periodic Table of the Elements

Key

| relative atomic mass |
| **atomic symbol** |
| name |
| atomic (proton) number |

| 1.0
H
hydrogen
1 |

(1)	(2)		(3)	(4)	(5)	(6)	(7)	(8)	(9)	(10)	(11)	(12)	(13)	(14)	(15)	(16)	(17)	0 (18)
		1																4.0 **He** helium 2
6.9 **Li** lithium 3	9.0 **Be** beryllium 4	2											10.8 **B** boron 5	12.0 **C** carbon 6	14.0 **N** nitrogen 7	16.0 **O** oxygen 8	19.0 **F** fluorine 9	20.2 **Ne** neon 10
23.0 **Na** sodium 11	24.3 **Mg** magnesium 12	3											27.0 **Al** aluminium 13	28.1 **Si** silicon 14	31.0 **P** phosphorus 15	32.1 **S** sulfur 16	35.5 **Cl** chlorine 17	39.9 **Ar** argon 18
39.1 **K** potassium 19	40.1 **Ca** calcium 20	4	45.0 **Sc** scandium 21	47.9 **Ti** titanium 22	50.9 **V** vanadium 23	52.0 **Cr** chromium 24	54.9 **Mn** manganese 25	55.8 **Fe** iron 26	58.9 **Co** cobalt 27	58.7 **Ni** nickel 28	63.5 **Cu** copper 29	65.4 **Zn** zinc 30	69.7 **Ga** gallium 31	72.6 **Ge** germanium 32	74.9 **As** arsenic 33	79.0 **Se** selenium 34	79.9 **Br** bromine 35	83.8 **Kr** krypton 36
85.5 **Rb** rubidium 37	87.6 **Sr** strontium 38	5	88.9 **Y** yttrium 39	91.2 **Zr** zirconium 40	92.9 **Nb** niobium 41	95.9 **Mo** molybdenum 42	[98] **Tc** technetium 43	101.1 **Ru** ruthenium 44	102.9 **Rh** rhodium 45	106.4 **Pd** palladium 46	107.9 **Ag** silver 47	112.4 **Cd** cadmium 48	114.8 **In** indium 49	118.7 **Sn** tin 50	121.8 **Sb** antimony 51	127.6 **Te** tellurium 52	126.9 **I** iodine 53	131.3 **Xe** xenon 54
132.9 **Cs** caesium 55	137.3 **Ba** barium 56	6	138.9 **La*** lanthanum 57	178.5 **Hf** hafnium 72	180.9 **Ta** tantalum 73	183.8 **W** tungsten 74	186.2 **Re** rhenium 75	190.2 **Os** osmium 76	192.2 **Ir** iridium 77	195.1 **Pt** platinum 78	197.0 **Au** gold 79	200.6 **Hg** mercury 80	204.4 **Tl** thallium 81	207.2 **Pb** lead 82	209.0 **Bi** bismuth 83	[209] **Po** polonium 84	[210] **At** astatine 85	[222] **Rn** radon 86
[223] **Fr** francium 87	[226] **Ra** radium 88	7	[227] **Ac†** actinium 89	[261] **Rf** rutherfordium 104	[262] **Db** dubnium 105	[266] **Sg** seaborgium 106	[264] **Bh** bohrium 107	[277] **Hs** hassium 108	[268] **Mt** meitnerium 109	[271] **Ds** darmstadtium 110	[272] **Rg** roentgenium 111	[285] **Uub** Ununbium 112	[284] **Uut** Ununtrium 113	[289] **Uuq** Ununquadium 114	[288] **Uup** Ununpentium 115	[293] **Uuh** Ununhexium 116	[294] **Uuo** Ununoctium 118	

* 58 – 71 Lanthanides

140.1 **Ce** cerium 58	140.9 **Pr** praseodymium 59	144.2 **Nd** neodymium 60	144.9 **Pm** promethium 61	150.4 **Sm** samarium 62	152.0 **Eu** europium 63	157.3 **Gd** gadolinium 64	158.9 **Tb** terbium 65	162.5 **Dy** dysprosium 66	164.9 **Ho** holmium 67	167.3 **Er** erbium 68	168.9 **Tm** thulium 69	173.0 **Yb** ytterbium 70	175.0 **Lu** lutetium 71

† 90 – 103 Actinides

232.0 **Th** thorium 90	231.0 **Pa** protactinium 91	238.0 **U** uranium 92	237.0 **Np** neptunium 93	239.1 **Pu** plutonium 94	243.1 **Am** americium 95	247.1 **Cm** curium 96	247.1 **Bk** berkelium 97	252.1 **Cf** californium 98	[252] **Es** einsteinium 99	[257] **Fm** fermium 100	[258] **Md** mendelevium 101	[259] **No** nobelium 102	[260] **Lr** lawrencium 103

Units

Chemists usually use the International System of Units (Système International, or SI). The base SI units that are most often used in chemistry are shown below.

Base SI units

Quantity	Unit name	Symbol
length	metre	m
mass	kilogram	kg
time	second	s
electric current	ampere	A
temperature	kelvin	K
amount of substance	mole	mol

For convenience, any of the prefixes below may be used with any unit: for example, the kilometre (1 km = 10^3 m) and the milliampere (1 mA = 10^{-3} A) are often useful.

Prefixes for units

Prefix	Symbol	Meaning
tera	T	10^{12}
giga	G	10^9
mega	m	10^6
kilo	k	10^3
deci	d	10^{-1}
centi	c	10^{-2}
milli	m	10^{-3}
micro	p	10^{-6}
nano	n	10^{-9}
pico	p	10^{-12}

Other units can be derived from the base units. For example, energy is normally measured in joules (symbol J), or multiples of joules (kj, MJ), defined in terms of base units as kg m^2 s^{-2}. Some non-SI units can be converted to SI units as shown below.

Units conversions

Unit	Symbol	SI equivalent
length	metre	m
atomic mass unit	U	1.661×10^{-27} kg
atmosphere	atm	101 325 Pa
degree Celsius	°C	1 K
litre	dm^3	10^{-3} m^3
tonne	t	10^3 kg

Formulae

Ideal gas equation

$pV = nRT$

Amount of substance

$$\text{number of moles} = \frac{\text{mass}}{\text{r.m.m.}}$$

Equilibrium law

For the reaction
$mA + nB \rightleftharpoons pC + qD$ the equilibrium constant K_c is given by

$$K_c = \frac{[C]^p[D]^q}{[A]^m[B]^n}$$

where values in square brackets are equilibrium concentrations.

pH

$pH = -\log_{10} [H^+]$

Ionic product of water

$K_w = [H^+] [OH^-]$
$\quad = 1 \times 10^{-14}$ mol^2 dm^{-6} at s.t.p.

Order of reaction

For a zero-order reaction: $\dfrac{-d[A]}{dt} = k_0$

For a first-order reaction: $\dfrac{-d[A]}{dt} = k_1[A]^1$

For a second-order reaction: $\dfrac{-d[A]}{dt} = k_2[A]^2$

Important values, constants and standards

Constant	Symbol	Value
molar gas constant	R	8.31 J K^{-1} mol^{-1}
Faraday constant	F	9.65×10^4 $Cmol^{-1}$
Avogadro constant	L	6.02×10^{23} mol^{-1}
Planck constant	h	6.63×10^{-34} J Hz^{-1}
speed of light in a vacuum	c	3.00×10^{-8} m s^{-1}
mass of proton	m_p	1.67×10^{-27} kg
mass of neutron	m_n	1.67×10^{-27} kg
mass of electron	m_e	9.11×10^{-31} kg
electronic charge	e	1.60×10^{-19} C
molar volume of gas	V_m	22.4 dm^3 mol^{-1} (at s.t.p.)
specific heat capacity of water		4.18 kJ kg^{-1} K^{-1}

s.t.p. is approximately 101 kPa and 273 K (0 °C)

Bond angles

Compound	Sequence	Angle	Bond	Bond length (nm)
CCl_4	Cl–C–Cl	109.5	Cl–C	0.1770
CH_4	H–C–H	109.5	H–C	0.1090
C_2H_4	H–C–H	117.3	H–C	0.1090
C_6H_6 (benzene)	C–C–C	120.0	C–C	0.1397
H_2O	H–O–H	104.5	H–O	0.0960
NH_3	H–N–H	107.0	H–N	0.1010
PCl_5	Cl–P–Cl	120.0	Cl–P	0.2040
SF_6	F–S–F	90.0	F–S	0.1560

Bond lengths and bond energies

Bond	in	Bond length (nm)	Bond energy (kJ mol^{-1})	Bond	in	Bond length (nm)	Bond energy (kJ mol^{-1})
Br–Br	Br_2	0.228	193	O–Si	$SiO_2(s)$	0.161	466
Br–H	HBr	0.141	366	O=Si	$SiO_2(g)$	–	638
Cl–Cl	Cl	0.199	243	O=Si	SiO	–	805
Cl–H	HCl	0.127	432	P–P	P_4	0.221	198
F–F	F_2	0.142	158	P=P	P_2	0.189	485
F–H	HF	0.092	568	C–C	average	0.154	347
I–I	I_2	0.267	151	C=C	average	0.134	612
H–I	HI	0.161	298	C≡C	average	0.120	838
H–H	H_2	0.074	435	C–H	average	0.108	413
H–Si	SiH_4	0.148	318	C–H	CH_4	0.109	435
H–Ge	GeH_4	0.153	285	C–F	average	0.138	467
H–N	NH_3	0.101	391	C–F	CH_3F	0.139	452
H–P	PH_3	0.144	321	C–F	CF_4	0.132	485
H–As	AsH_3	0.152	297	C–Cl	average	0.177	346
H–O	H_2O	0.096	464	C–Cl	CCl_4	0.177	327
H–S	H_2S	0.134	364	C–Cl	C_6H_5Cl	0.170	–
H–Se	H_2Se	0.146	313	C–Br	average	0.194	290
Na–Na	Na_2	0.308	72	C–Br	CBr_4	0.194	285
K–K	K_2	0.392	49	C–I	average	0.214	228
N–N	N_2H_4	0.145	158	C–I	CH_3I	0.214	234
N=N	$C_6H_{14}N_2$	0.120	410	C–N	average	0.147	286
N≡N	N_2	0.110	945	C=N	average	0.130	615
N–O	HNO_2	0.120	214	C≡N	average	0.116	887
N=O	NOF, NOCl	0.114	587	C–N	phenylamine	0.135	–
N=P	PN	0.149	582	C–O	average	0.143	358
O–O	H_2O_2	0.148	144	C–O	CH_3OH	0.143	336
O–O	O_3	0.128	302	C=O	CO_2	0.116	805
O=O	O_2	0.121	498	C=O	HCHO	0.121	695
S–S	S_8	0.205	266	C=O	aldehydes	0.122	736
S=S	S_2	0.189	429	C=O	ketones	0.122	749
O–S	SO_3	0.143	469	C=O	CO	0.113	1077
Si–Si	Si(s), SiH_4	0.235	226	C–Si	$(CH_3)_4Si$, SiC(s)	0.187	307

Infrared spectroscopy: characteristic absorption bands

Compound	Wavelength(nm)
C—H stretching vibrations	
alkane	3376–3505
alkene	3231–3322
arene	3300
aldehyde	3448–3546
	3603–3703
C—H bending vibrations	
alkane	6734–7326
arene	11 364–14 300
O—H stretching vibrations	
alcohols	
(not hydrogen-bonded)	2740–2786
(hydrogen-bonded)	2667–3125
carboxylic acids	
(hydrogen-bonded)	3030–4000
Carbon–halogen stretching vibrations	
C—F	7142–10 000
C—Cl	12 500–16 667
C—Br	16 667–20 000
C—I	about 20 000
C=C stretching vibrations	
alkene	5991–6079
arene	6250–6897
C=O stretching vibrations	
aldehydes, saturated alkyl group	5747–5814
ketones	5882–5952
carboxylic acids	
saturated alkyl	5797–5882
aryl (from arene)	5882–5952
esters (saturated)	5714–5763

Infrared wavenumber data

Bond	Wavenumber (cm⁻¹)
C—H	2850–3300
C—C	750–1100
C=C	1620–1680
C=O	1680–1750
C—O	1000–1300
O—H (alcohols)	3230–3550
O—H (acids)	2500–3000

Proton n.m.r. chemical shift data

Type of proton	δ/ppm
RCH_3	0.7–1.2
R_2CH_2	1.2–1.4
R_3CH	1.4–1.6
$RCOCH_3$	2.1–2.6
$ROCH_3$	3.1–3.9
$RCOOCH_3$	3.7–4.1
ROH	0.5–5.0

Selected data for some elements

Element	Symbol	Atomic number	Stable mass number (% abundance)	Molar mass (g mol⁻¹)	Melting point (°C)	Boiling point (°C)	Electro-negativity[1]	Atomic radius[2] (nm)	Ionic radius[3] (nm)	Ionisation energies (kJ mol⁻¹) 1st	2nd	3rd	4th
Aluminium	Al	13	27(100)	27.0	660	2467	1.5	m0.143	$^{+3}$0.053	578	1817	2745	11578
Argon	Ar	18	40(99.6), 36(0.34), 38(0.063)	39.9	–189	–186	–	v0.190	–	1521	2666	3931	5771
Barium	Ba	56	138(71.7), 137(11.32), 136(7.81), 135(6.59)	137.3	725	1640	0.9	m0.224	$^{+2}$0.136	503	965	–	–
Beryllium	Be	4	9(100)	9.01	1278	2970	1.5	m0.112	$^{+2}$0.027	900	1757	14849	21007
Boron	B	5	11(80.3), 10(19.7)	10.8	2300	2550	2.0	m0.098	$^{+3}$0.012	801	2427	3660	25026
Bromine	Br	35	79(50.5), 81(49.5)	79.9	–7	59	2.8	c0.114	$^{-1}$0.195	1140	2100	3500	4560
Caesium	Cs	55	133(100)	132.9	29	669	0.7	m0.272	$^{+1}$0.170	376	2420	3300	–
Calcium	Ca	20	40(96.97), 44(2.06), 42(0.64)	40.1	839	1484	1.0	m0.197	$^{+2}$0.100	590	1145	4912	6474
Carbon	C	6	12(98.9), 13(1.1)	12.0	3652	4827	2.5	c0.077	–	1086	2353	4621	6223
Chlorine	Cl	17	35(75.5), 37(24.5)	35.5	–101	–35	3.0	c0.099	$^{-1}$0.180	1251	2297	3822	5158
Chromium	Cr	24	52(83.8), 53(9.55), 50(4.31)	52.0	1857	2670	1.6	m0.129	$^{+3}$0.062	653	1592	2987	4740

Element	Symbol	Atomic number	Stable mass number (% abundance)	Molar mass (g mol⁻¹)	Melting point (°C)	Boiling point (°C)	Electronegativity[1]	Atomic radius[2] (nm)	Ionic radius[3] (nm)	Ionisation energies (kJ mol⁻¹) 1st	2nd	3rd	4th
Cobalt	Co	27	59(100)	58.9	1495	2870	1.8	m0.125	$^{+2}$0.065	758	1646	3232	4950 Co
Copper	Cu	29	63(69.1), 65(30.9)	63.5	1083	2567	1.9	m0.128	$^{+2}$0.073	746	1958	3554	5330 Cu
Fluorine	F	9	19(100)	19.0	−220	−188	4.0	c0.071	$^{-}$0.133	1681	3374	6051	8408 F
Helium	He	2	4(100)	4.0	−263	−269	–	v0.180	–	2372	5251	–	– He
Hydrogen	H	1	1(99.98), 2(0.015)	1.0	−259	−253	2.1	c0.037	$^{-}$0.208	1312	–	–	– H
Iodine	I	53	127(100)	126.9	114	184	2.5	c0.133	$^{-}$0.215	1008	1846	3200	– I
Iron	Fe	26	56(91.7), 54(5.8), 57(2.2)	55.8	1535	2750	1.8	m0.126	$^{+3}$0.055	759	1561	2958	5290 Fe
Krypton	Kr	36	84(56.9), 86(17.4), 82(11.5), 83(11.5)	83.8	−157	−152	–	v0.200	–	1351	2368	3565	5070 Kr
Lithium	Li	3	7(92.6), 6(7.4)	6.9	171	1342	1.0	m0.157	$^{+}$0.074	520	7298	11815	– Li
Magnesium	Mg	12	24(78.6), 25(10.1), 26(11.3)	24.3	649	1107	1.2	m0.160	$^{+2}$0.072	738	1451	7733	10541 Mg
Manganese	Mn	25	55(100)	54.9	1244	1962	1.5	m0.137	$^{+2}$0.067	717	1509	3249	4940 Mn
Neon	Ne	10	20(90.9), 22(8.8)	20.2	−248	−246	–	v0.160	–	2081	3952	6122	9370 Ne
Nickel	Ni	28	58(67.8), 60(26.2), 62(3.7)	58.7	1455	2730	1.8	m0.125	$^{+2}$0.070	737	1753	3394	5300 Ni
Nitrogen	N	7	14(99.6), 15(0.4)	14.0	−210	−196	3.0	c0.075	$^{-}$0.171	1402	2856	4578	7475 N
Oxygen	O	8	16(99.8), 18(0.2)	16.0	−218	−183	3.5	c0.073	$^{-}$0.140	1314	3388	5301	7469 O
Phosphorus	P	15	31(100)	31.0	44 (white)	280 (white)	2.1	c0.110	$^{-}$0.190	1012	1903	2912	4957 P
Potassium	K	19	39(93.2), 41(6.8)	39.1	63	760	0.8	m0.235	$^{+}$0.138	419	3051	4412	5877 K
Rubidium	Rb	37	85(72.15), 87(27.85)	85.5	39	686	0.8	m0.250	$^{+}$0.149	403	2632	3900	5080 Rb
Scandium	Sc	21	45(100)	45.0	1541	2831	1.3	m0.164	$^{+3}$0.075	631	1235	2389	7089 Sc
Silicon	Si	14	28(92.2), 29(4.7), 30(3.1)	28.1	1410	2355	1.8	c0.118	$^{+4}$0.04	789	1577	3232	4356 Si
Sodium	Na	11	23(100)	23.0	98	883	0.9	m0.191	$^{+}$0.102	496	4563	6913	9544 Na
Strontium	Sr	38	88(82.6), 86(9.9), 87(7.0)	87.6	769	1384	1.0	m0.215	$^{+2}$0.113	550	1064	4210	5500 Sr
Sulphur	S	16	32(95), 34(4.2), 33(0.8)	32.1	119	445	2.5	c0.102	$^{-2}$0.185	1000	2251	3361	4564 S
Titanium	Ti	22	48(74), 46(8.0), 47(7.3), 49(5.5)	47.9	1660	3287	1.5	m0.147	$^{+4}$0.061	658	1310	2653	4175 Ti
Vanadium	V	23	51 (99.7), 50 (0.3)	50.9	1890	3380	1.6	m0.135	$^{+3}$0.064	650	1414	2828	4507 V
Xenon	Xe	54	Many	131.3	−112	−107	–	v0.220	–	1170	2047	3100	– Xe
Zinc	Zn	30	Several	65.4	420	907	1.6	m0.137	$^{+2}$0.075	906	1733	3833	5730 Zn

[1] Pauling electronegativity index   [2] m = metallic radius; v = van der Waals radius; c = covalent radius   [3] Superscript shows the charge on the ion

Selected data for some inorganic compounds

Compound	Formula	State	Molar mass (g mol^{-1})	T_m (K)	T_b (K)	ΔH (kJ mol^{-1})
Aluminium fluoride	AlF_3	s	84.0	1564 (sub)	–	−1504.0
Aluminium chloride	$AlCl_3$	s	133.3	463	451 (sub)	−704.0
Aluminium oxide	Al_2O_3	s	102.0	2345	3253	−1676.0
Caesium fluoride	CsF	s	151.9	955	1524	−553.0
Caesium chloride	CsCl	s	168.4	918	1563	−443.0
Caesium oxide	Cs_2O	s	281.8	763 (in N_2)	673 (dec)	−346.0
Carbon monoxide	CO	g	28.0	74	82	−110.0
Carbon dioxide	CO_2	g	44.0	217 (at 5.2 atm)	195	−393.0
Hydrogen fluoride	HF	g	20.0	190	293	−271.0
Hydrogen chloride	HCl	g	36.5	158	188	−92.3
Hydrogen bromide	HBr	g	80.9	185	206	−36.4
Hydrogen iodide	HI	g	127.9	222	238	26.5
Water	H_2O	l	18.0	273	373	−286.0
Hydrogen sulphide	H_2S	g	34.1	188	212	−20.6
Lithium fluoride	LiF	s	25.9	1118	1949	−616.0
Lithium chloride	LiCl	s	42.4	878	1613	−408.6
Lithium oxide	Li_2O	s	29.9	>1973	–	−598.0
Magnesium chloride	$MgCl_2$	s	95.2	987	1685	−641.0
Magnesium oxide	MgO	s	40.3	3125	3873	−602.0
Hydrazine	N_2H_4	l	32.0	275	387	50.6
Ammonia	NH_3	g	17.0	195	240	−46.1
Nitrogen chloride	NCl_3	l	120.4	<233	<344	230.1
Phosphorus(III) choride	PCl_3	l	137.3	161	349	−320.0
Phosphorus(V) choride	PCl_5	s	208.2	435 (sub)	440 (dec)	−443.0
Silicon(IV) chloride	$SiCl_4$	l	169.9	203	331	−687.0
Silicon dioxide	SiO_2	s	60.1	1883	2503	−911.0
Sodium fluoride	NaF	s	42.0	1266	1968	−574.0
Sodium chloride	NaCl	s	58.4	1074	1686	−411.0
Sodium bromide	NaBr	s	102.9	1020	1663	−361.0
Sodium oxide	Na_2O	s	62.0	1548 (sub)	–	−414.0
Sulphur(II) chloride	SCl_2	g	103.0	195	332 (dec)	−20.0
Sulphur(IV) chloride	SCl_4	l	173.9	243	258 (dec)	−56.0
Sulphur(IV) oxide	SO_2	g	64.1	200	263	−297.0
Sulphur(VI) oxide	SO_3	l	80.1	290	318	−441.0

s = solid, l = liquid, g = gas

T_m melting point; sub = sublimes; dec = decomposes

T_b boiling point at 1 atmosphere

ΔH_f Standard molar enthalpy change of formation (i.e. at 298 K and 1 atmosphere)

Selected data for some organic compounds

Compound	Formula	State	Molar mass (g mol^{-1})	T_m (K)	T_b (K)	ΔH_c (kJ mol^{-1})	ΔH_f (kJ mol^{-1})
Alkanes							
Methane	CH_4	g	16.0	91.1	109.1	−890	−75
Ethane	CH_3CH_3	g	30.1	89.8	184.5	−1560	−85
Propane	$CH_3CH_2CH_3$	g	44.1	83.4	231.0	−2219	−104
Butane	$CH_3(CH_2)_2CH_3$	g	58.1	134.7	272.6	−2876	−126
Pentane	$CH_3(CH_2)_3CH_3$	l	72.2	143.1	309.2	−3509	−173
Hexane	$CH_3(CH_2)_4CH_3$	l	86.2	178.1	342.1	−4163	−199
Alkenes							
Ethene	$CH_2{=}CH_2$	g	28.1	104.1	169.4	−1411	+52
Propene	$CH_2{=}CHCH_3$	g	56.1	87.8	266.8	−2717	−0.4
trans-But-2-ene	$CH_3CH{=}CHCH_3$	g	56.1	167.6	274.0	−2705	−12
cis-But-2-ene	$CH_3CH{=}CHCH_3$	g	56.1	134.2	276.8	−2709	−8
Arenes							
Benzene	C_6H_6	l	78.1	278.6	353.2	−3267	+49
Haloalkanes							
Fluoromethane	CH_3F	g	34.0	131.3	194.7	–	−247
Chloromethane	CH_3Cl	g	50.5	176.0	248.9	−764	−82
Bromomethane	CH_3Br	g	94.9	179.5	276.7	−770	−37
Iodomethane	CH_3I	l	141.9	206.7	315.5	−815	−15
Dichloromethane	CH_2Cl_2	l	84.9	178.0	313.1	−606	−124
Trichloromethane	$CHCl_3$	l	119.4	209.6	334.8	−474	−135
Tetrachloromethane	CCl_4	l	153.8	250.1	349.6	−360	−130
Alcohols							
Methanol	CH_3OH	l	32.0	179.2	338.1	−726	−239
Ethanol	CH_3CH_2OH	l	46.1	155.8	351.6	−1367	−277
Propan-1-ol	$CH_3CH_2CH_2OH$	l	60.1	146.6	370.5	−2021	−303
Propan-2-ol	$CH_3CHOHCH_3$	l	60.1	183.6	355.5	−2006	−318
Butan-1-ol	$CH_3(CH_2)CH_2OH$	l	74.1	183.6	390.3	−2676	−327
Pentan-1-ol	$CH_3(CH_2)CH_2OH$	l	88.2	194.1	411.1	−3329	−354
Hexan-1-ol	$CH_3(CH_2)_4CH_2OH$	l	102.2	226.4	431.1	−3984	−379
Aldehydes							
Methanal	$HCHO$	g	30.0	181.1	252.1	−571	−109
Ethanal	CH_3CHO	g	44.1	152.1	293.9	−1167	−191
Propanal	CH_3CH_2CHO	l	58.1	192.1	321.9	−1821	−217
Ketones							
Propanone	CH_3COCH_3	l	58.1	177.8	329.3	−1816	−248
Butanone	$CH_3CH_2COCH_3$	l	72.1	186.8	352.7	−2441	−276
Carboxylic acids							
Methanoic	$HCOOH$	l	46.0	281.5	373.7	−254	−425
Ethanoic	CH_3COOH	l	60.1	289.7	391.0	−874	−484
Propanoic	CH_3CH_2COOH	l	74.1	252.3	414.1	−1527	−511
Butanoic	$CH_3CH_2CH_2COOH$	l	88.1	268.6	438.6	−2183	−534

s = solid, l = liquid, g = gas
T_m melting point
T_b boiling point at 1 atmosphere
ΔH_c Standard molar enthalpy change of combustion
ΔH_f Standard molar enthalpy change of formation (i.e. at 298 K and 1 atmosphere)

Answers to in-text questions

Chapter 1

1a The curve shows the number of particles with particular energies, and the peak shows that more particles have this energy value than any other energy value.

1b The value for both axes is zero at the origin, so no particles in the gas have zero energy.

1c The curve will not touch the axis after zero energy because there is not a limit to the energy that a particular particle may receive.

2a Reactions occur at the surface of a solid, so the greater the surface area, the faster the rate. A 2 cm cube has a surface area of $6 \times 4 = 24$ cm^2. Eight 1 cm cubes have a total area of $8 \times 6 = 48$ cm^2, so the rate increases by a factor of 2.

2b Only those particles with an energy greater than or equal to the activation energy can produce collisions that result in a reaction. Increasing the temperature increases the number of particles with the activation energy, so more particles can react. A 10° rise in temperature will approximately double the number of particles having energy greater than or equal to the activation energy so will approximately double the rate of reaction.

3a The reactant is used up fastest at the start of the reaction when its concentration is greatest. At this point the slope of the curve is at its steepest.

3b For the same reasons, the rate at which the product is formed is fastest at the start: product formation rate decreases as the reaction proceeds.

4a Order = the power to which the concentration terms are raised. In the rate equation, the power of NO is 2, so the reaction is second order with respect to NO.

4b Cl_2 is to the power 1, so the reaction is first order w.r.t. Cl_2

4c Overall order = the sum of the powers to which the reactant concentration terms are raised. In the rate equation, the powers are $2 + 1 = 3$, so the reaction is third order.

4d Units for k = (units of rate) / (units of concentration) to their respective powers: (mol dm^{-3} s^{-1}) / [(mol dm^{-3})^2 × mol dm^{-3}] = mol^{-2} dm^6 s^{-1}.

5a Graph A

5b Graph B

5c As the temperature is increased the value of the rate constant increases: k = rate/concentration terms; the rate increases with temperature and the concentrations have not changed.

A1 They may have assumed any data outside the restrictions was likely to be flawed; also, they may want to save data processing time by eliminating certain ranges.

A2 They might have business interests, profits might be affected, they may have a particular standpoint.

A3 One nation on its own cannot solve the problem of ozone depletion. Countries need to agree and this may be against a particular country's interests in the short term.

A4 Yes. The data 1980–2000 shows a levelling off and after 2000 a drop but 2003 to 2006 shows an increase. All the data might be affected by weather / climate changes.

A5 More evidence could show that the downward trend is maintained. Data showing a sustained decrease in the size of the ozone hole would confirm the protocol's success.

A6 Peer review is where other scientists will examine critically particular data or an idea to test validity. It is important because ozone depletion is a global issue and the evidence and possible actions will have to be agreed by the vast majority of the scientific community.

A7 CFCs form free radicals which act as catalysts in the breakdown of ozone, so a little CFC goes a very long way. Ozone depletion reactions in the upper atmosphere are very complex and this is one possible sequence.

E.g. $CCl_2F_2 \xrightarrow{h\nu} CClF_2 + Cl\bullet$
$Cl\bullet + O_3 \rightarrow OCl\bullet + O_2$
$OCl\bullet + O \rightarrow Cl\bullet O_2$ etc
Other reactions are possible and the sequence of reactions will vary depending on the ozone concentration, the free radicals present and the intensity of the sunlight.

A8 **Box model**, advantages – cheap. Little computing power, can consider complex reactions. Disadvantages – only considering what is happening at a single point. **Trajectory model**, advantages – more data given along a line. Disadvantages – more computing power needed, approximations about chemistry will have to be made. **Three dimensional model**, advantages – a much more complete picture considering a range of factors. Disadvantages – needs powerful supercomputers, limits the complexity of the chemical reactions being considered.

Chapter 2

1a Assuming that H_2 and I_2 are mixed at the start of the reaction, curve A represents their concentration and curve B represents the concentration of HI. At the start, the concentration of the reactants is high and decreases as they react. Conversely, HI is not present at the start of the reaction and its concentration increases as it is formed.

1b Increasing the temperature will increase the rate of the forward and the reverse reactions (but not equally).

2a $K_c = [CO] [NO_2] / [CO_2][NO]$.
K_c has no units.

2b $K_c = [C_2H_4][H_2] / [C_2H_6]$. Units of $K_c = mol\ dm^{-3}$

2c $K_c = [NO_2]^2 / [NO]^2[O_2]$. Units of $K_c = mol^{-1}\ dm^3$

3a $K_c = [CuA] [H^+]^2/ [Cu^{2+}][H_2A]$

3b The equilibrium lies well over to the right, so the value of K_c will be quite large.

3c At equilibrium, in mol dm^{-3},
$[Cu^{2+}] = 0.0001$,
$[H^+] = 0.0049 \times 2 = 0.0098$

3d $K_c = 47.06\ mol\ dm^{-3}$

3e It shifts the equilibrium from the right to the left (Le Chatelier)

3f The value of K_c is unchanged by changes in concentration.

4 The price of copper is increasing and natural resources are dwindling, so it is becoming more economically viable to recover copper from lower grade ores. Pollution regulations are becoming stricter so water has to have ever-diminishing levels of copper present.

5a At 100°C increasing the pressure has a slight increase in yield of ammonia up to 200 atm but then yield is 100% so no further benefit. At 500°C, there is a steady increase in yield through the whole of the pressure range.

5b The catalyst provides an alternative route for the reaction with a lower activation energy; more reactants have this (lower) energy, so more are able to react. The catalyst often does this by providing a site on its surface where reactant molecules can align; there is a tendency to bond with the catalyst and this weakens the bonding between atoms on the reactant making them easier to separate.

5c Energy costs to heat the reactants to 450°C; a plant that can withstand high temperature and pressure; the cost of the catalyst; whether the catalyst will have to be replenished; poisoning of the catalyst; safety considerations; and workforce needed.

6 Only a small amount of product is formed because K_c is very small, so the reaction can be considered as unlikely to occur.

7 At the higher temperature the value of K_c will be higher and the yield of NO will increase.

8 Endothermic because K_c has increased with increase in temperature, $K_c = [NO]^2/[N_2][O_2]$ so the yield of NO (right-hand side of equation) increases. Le Chatelier's principle predicts that if temperature is increased a reaction will shift in the endothermic direction.

9 At midnight (the start of graph) the concentration of NO is quite low. As traffic starts to build up the concentration of NO increases. Following the production of NO then it is converted to NO$_2$ by oxidation from the oxygen in the atmosphere. The NO is being removed as it is formed so this reaches a maximum value. Also, as the light intensity increases the concentration of NO$_2$ decreases as it undergoes a series of photochemical reactions; (one of the products is 'ground-level ozone'.) As the level of traffic decreases later in the morning, the concentration of NO$_2$ decreases. There is then a slight increase in the level of NO from increased traffic in the afternoon (but this is removed as it is formed by the ground-level ozone present in the atmosphere from the previous reactions). From then the levels of NO and NO$_2$ will decrease.

10 Arguments supporting opinion in favour of LEZs: Fossil fuel driven vehicles produce pollution. The photograph shows a brown haze of nitrogen dioxide (which in turn produces low-level ozone;) this can cause many breathing problems. Arguments against LEZs: People may have to drive around cities to carry out their legitimate work e.g. taxi drivers, delivery drivers.

11a The reaction to produce ethanol is exothermic so the equilibrium yield of ethanol will be decreased by an increase in temperature.

11b The increase in temperature will decrease the equilibrium yield but the rate of reaction will increase so ethanol is produced faster. So over a given time more ethanol is obtained.

A1 Galen based his ideas on some evidence, but there were limitations in his evidence and he made some assumptions. Harvey did systematic research based on many dissections and calculations so his model was superior to that of Galen. Landsteiner examined the structure of proteins and other compounds in blood attached to the red blood cells and noticed there were different types. It was this evidence that led to the ABO blood typing.

A2 Harvey had to consider some of the ideas previous ideas. Galen had proposed that blood was continuously produced and used up, but Harvey's calculations showed this to be impossible and he demonstrated that blood was re-used. Transfusions were successful sometimes but fatal on others and Landsteiner's ideas about blood typing solved this problem.

A3 Benefits: Supplies free from disease; easy storage and longer shelf life. Objections: the process involves genetic engineering to produce the blood; and some people have ethical objections to genetic modification.

A4 A randomised controlled trial uses random choice of subjects and the results are compared to a 'control group'. A blind trial is where the subject does not know whether he or she is receiving the treatment or a placebo. In a double blind trial neither the researcher nor the subject knows.

A5 The blood could be modified by genetic engineering, affecting the oxygen equilibrium in haemoglobin. This could lead to greater use of oxygen from the red blood cells before signs of stress are demonstrated. The recipient may exhibit greater endurance under low oxygen levels.

A6 Arguments for genetic modification: the athlete may be born with a slightly different haemoglobin molecule which is more efficient, and a different athlete may achieve this type of haemoglobin by genetic engineering so they both have the same haemoglobin.
Against: athletes should only achieve performance by training.

Chapter 3

1a $HCl(aq) + KOH(aq) \rightarrow$
$$KCl(aq) + H_2O(l)$$
$$H^+(aq) + OH^-(aq) \rightarrow H_2O(l)$$

1b $H_2SO_4(aq) + 2NaOH(aq) \rightarrow$
$$2NaCl(aq) + 2H_2O(l)$$
$$2H^+(aq) + 2OH^-(aq) \rightarrow 2H_2O(l)$$

2a The hydrogens in methane are held by covalent bonds between elements with similar electronegativities, so there is no polarisation of the C–H bond. In CH_3COOH one of the hydrogens is attached to an oxygen atom, an element with a high electronegativity. The difference in electronegativity means there is a polarisation of the O–H bond and it dissociates more easily, releasing H^+ (H_3O^+) ions.

2b $HCOOH(aq) + H_2O(l) \rightleftharpoons$
$$HCOO^- + H_3O^+(aq)$$

3a $CuO(s) + H_2SO_4(aq) \rightleftharpoons$
Base$$Acid
$$CuSO_4(aq) + H_2O(l)$$

3b $NH_4^+(aq) + OH^-(aq) \rightleftharpoons$
Acid$$Base
$$NH_3(aq) + H_2O(l)$$

3c $CH_3COO^-(aq) + H_3O^+(aq) \rightleftharpoons$
Base$$Acid
$$CH_3COOH(aq) + H_2O(l)$$

4 $K_a = \dfrac{[H^+] \times [CH_3(CH_2)_2COO^-]}{[CH_3(CH_2)_2COOH]}$

5 The strength of the acid depends upon the value of K_a, stronger acids have higher K_a values. K_a for reaction 1: sulfuric(IV) acid →

hydrogensulfate is 1.5×10^{-2} mol dm^{-3} which is higher than 6.2×10^{-8} mol dm^{-3} for reaction 2: hydrogensulfate → sulfate. Therefore reaction 1 is the stronger acid.

6 $pH = -\log_{10}[H^+]$,
6a $-\log_{10} 0.2 = 0.70$
6b $-\log_{10} 1.2 \times 10^{-2} = 1.92$
6c $-\log_{10} 6.7 \times 10^{-7} = 6.17$

7 $pH = -\log_{10}[H^+]$,
$$= -\log_{10} 2.0 = -0.30$$

8a $[H^+] = 10^{-pH} = 10^{-5.49}$
$$= 3.24 \times 10^{-6} \text{ mol dm}^{-3}$$
8b $[H^+] = 10^{-2.75} = 1.78 \times 10^{-3}$ mol dm^{-3}
8c $[H^+] = 10^{+0.5} = 3.16$ mol dm^{-3}

9 $[H^+] = \sqrt{\text{acid concentration} \times K_a}$
$$= \sqrt{0.01 \times 1.34 \times 10^{-5}}$$
$$= 3.66 \times 10^{-4}$$

10 $K_w = 10^{-14} = [H^+][OH^-]$, $[OH^-]$
$$= 10^{-7} \text{ mol dm}^{-3}$$

11a $[H^+] = K_w/[OH^-] = 10^{-14}/0.01 = 10^{-12}$,
$pH = -\log_{10}[H^+] = -\log_{10}10^{-12} = 12$
11b $[H^+] = K_w/[OH^-] = 10^{-14}/0.3$
$$= 3.33 \times 10^{-14}, pH = -\log_{10}[H^+]$$
$$= -\log_{10}3.33 \times 10^{-14} = 13.5$$

12a $K_a = [H^+]^2/[HA] = (7.94 \times 10^{-4})^2/0.01$
$$= 6.30 \times 10^{-5}$$
12b This value for K_a is a small value, so benzoic acid is a weak acid.
12c $pK_a = -\log_{10} 6.30 \times 10^{-5} = 4.2$

13a $K_a = 10^{-pK_a} = 10^{-3.075} = 8.41 \times 10^{-4}$.

13b $[H^+] = \sqrt{Ka \times [HA]}$
$$= \sqrt{8.41 \times 10^{-4} \times 0.01}$$
$$= \sqrt{8.41 \times 10^{-6}} = 2.90 \times 10^{-3}$$
13c $pH = -\log_{10}2.90 \times 10^{-3} = 2.54$

14 A weak acid

15a
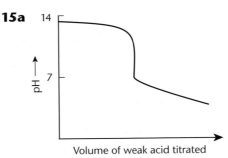

15b Equivalence point pH 8.5 but a suitable answer between 8 and 10 is acceptable.

16a i methyl orange
**ii** phenolphthalein
**iii** none suitable

16b
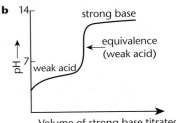
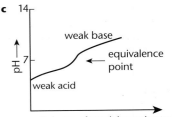

17a NH_3 is a weak base:
$NH_3(aq) + H_2O(l) \rightleftharpoons$
$$NH_4^+(aq) + OH^-(aq)$$
The salt NH_4Cl provides a supply of NH_4^+ ions. If H^+ ions are added to the buffer solution the ions will react with NH_3 to produce NH_4^+ ions, thereby removing H^+ ions from the solution:
$NH_3(aq) + H^+(aq) \rightleftharpoons NH_4^+(aq)$
If OH^- ions are added to the buffer they will react with NH_4^+ ions to produce NH_3 thereby removing OH^- ions from solution:
$NH_4^+(aq) + OH^-(aq) \rightleftharpoons$
$$NH_3(aq) + H_2O(l)$$
17b $[H^+] = \dfrac{K_a \times [CH_3CH_2COOH]}{[CH_3CH_2COO^-]}$
$$= 1.3 \times 10^{-5} \times 0.05/0.02$$
$$= 3.25 \times 10^{-5}$$
$pH = -\log_{10}3.25 \times 10^{-5} = 4.49$

18 $[H^+] = \dfrac{K_a \times [CH_3CH_2COOH]}{[CH_3CH_2COO^-]}$

No of moles of CH_3CH_2COOH
$= 25.0 \times 2/1000 = 5 \times 10^{-2}$
No of moles of $CH_3CH_2COO^-$
$= 20.0 \times 1.5/1000 = 3 \times 10^{-2}$
$[H^+] = 1.34 \times 10^{-5} \times (5 \times 10^{-2})/$
$(3 \times 10^{-2}) = 2.23 \times 10^{-5}$ pH
$= -\log_{10} [H^+] = 4.65$

A1 Ideas that may be included:
CO_2 causes a warming by absorbing infrared.
CO_2 is released into the atmosphere from burning, respiration and decomposition.
Amount of CO_2 released has increased rapidly in last 200 years.
CO_2 dissolves in the oceans and sets up an equilibrium and lowers pH,
CO_2 reacts and forms HCO_3^- and CO_3^{2-} which react to form shells of sea creatures and eventually rocks.
Carbonates act as a buffer.
Change in pH and ability of oceans to buffer this must be fully understood.
Impact of climate change on weather and marine life is not fully understood.

Chapter 4

1 heptane, octane and decane

2 **a**

H H H H H
H—C—C—C—C—C—H
H H H H H

b

H H H H H H
H—C—C—C—C—C—C—H
H H H H H H

3 2-methylpropane

4

H CH₃ H CH₃ H
H—C—C—C—C—C—H
H H H H H

5 hexane

6 $CH_3CH(CH_3)CH_2CH_2CH_3$
2-methylpentane

$CH_3CH(CH_3)CH(CH_3)CH_3$ or
$CH_3C(CH_3)_2CH_2CH_3$
2,3-dimethylbutane or
2,2-dimethylbutane.

7

8

9 **i** bromoethane CH_3CH_2Br

ii propanoic acid $CH_3CH_2—C{\small\substack{O\\OH}}$

iii propanal $CH_3CH_2—C{\small\substack{O\\H}}$

iv butan-2-one $CH_3—C—CH_2CH_3$ (C=O)

v methylethanoate $CH_3—C—O—CH_3$ (C=O)

vi 2-chloropropane
$CH_3—\underset{Cl}{\overset{H}{C}}—CH_3$

vii 4-methyl-1-nitrobenzene

viii pent-2-ene
$CH_3—CH=CH—CH_2CH_3$

ix methanoic acid $H—C{\small\substack{O\\OH}}$

x methylpropene $CH_3—\underset{CH_3}{C}=CH_2$

xi butan-1-ol $CH_3CH_2CH_2CH_2OH$

xii 2-methylpropan-2-ol
$CH_3—\underset{OH}{\overset{CH_3}{C}}—CH_3$

xiii but-1,3-diene $CH_2=CH=CH=CH_2$

xiv 2-amino-2-phenylethanoic acid

xv N-methylamino methane $CH_3—\underset{H}{N}—CH_3$

xvi methanoic ethanoic anhydride

$H—C—O—C—CH_3$ (both C=O)

xvii butanoyl chloride $CH_3CH_2CH_2—C{\small\substack{O\\Cl}}$

xviii ethyl methanoate $H—C—O—CH_2CH_3$ (C=O)

10a bromomethane,
10b chlorobenzene,
10c butan-2-ol,
10d ethanoic acid,
10e hexanal,
10f aminoethane,
10g propanone,
10h 1, 2-dibromoethane,
10i 1, 1-dibromoethane,
10j but-1-ene,
10k phenylmethanoic (benzoic) acid,
10l ethylpropanoate,
10m butanoyl chloride,
10n butanoic anhydride,
10o butyl ethanoate,
10p hexan-3-one,
10q 2-methylhex-3-ene,
10r propanenitrile,
10s 2-hydroxybutanenitrile

11 CH_3COCH_3

12 CH_3CH_2CHO propanal

13 CH_3CH_2COOH propanoic acid,
$CH_3CH_2CH_2OH$ propan-1-ol

14 $CH_3CH_2COOCH_2CH_3$ ethyl propanoate
$CH_3COOCH_2CH_2CH_3$ propyl ethanoate. Positional isomers.

15 (from top and left): propan-2-ol; 2-bromopropane; 2-aminopropane; 2-methylpropanenitrile; 1-amino-2-methylpropane

16 It is a system used by all chemists to uniquely identify a chemical compound.

17 $CH_3CH(CH_3)CH_2CH_2CH_3$
2-methylpentane
$CH_3CH_2CH(CH_3)CH_2CH_3$
3-methylpentane
$CH_3C(CH_3)_2CH_2CH_3$
2,2-dimethylbutane
$CH_3CH(CH_3)CH(CH_3)CH_3$
2,3-dimethylbutane

18a $CH_3CH_2CH_2CHO$ butanal
$CH_3CH(CH_3)CHO$ 2-methylpropanal
$CH_3COCH_2CH_3$ butan-2-one
18b $CH_3CH_2CH_2CH_2OH$ propan-1-ol
$CH_3CH(OH)CH_3$ propan-2-ol
$CH_3OCH_2CH_3$ methoxyethane
18c $CH_3CH_2CH_2COOH$ butanoic acid
$CH_3CH(CH_3)COOH$
2-methylpropanoic acid
$CH_3CH_2COOCH_3$ methyl propanoate
$CH_3COOCH_2CH_3$ ethyl ethanoate
$HCOOCH_2CH_2CH_3$ 1-propyl methanoate
$HCOOCH(CH_3)CH_3$ 2-propyl methanoate

19

b Z-pent-2-ene

E-pent-2-ene

Z-cyclohexan-1,4-diol   E-cyclohexan-1,4-diol

20 $CH_3CH_2CH_2CH_2CH_2CH_2CH_3$ and
$CH_3C(CH_3)_2CH_2CH(CH_3)CH_3$

21 No, they have different total numbers of carbon atoms.

22
1 2-methylhexane
$CH_3CH(CH_3)CH_2CH_2CH_2CH_3$
2 3-methylhexane
$CH_3CH_2CH(CH_3)CH_2CH_2CH_3$
3 2,3-dimethylpentane
$CH_3CH(CH_3)CH(CH_3)CH_2CH_3$

4 2,4-dimethylpentane
$CH_3CH(CH_3)CH_2CH(CH_3)CH_3$
5 2,2-dimethylpentane
$CH_3C(CH_3)_2CH_2CH_2CH_3$
6 3,3-dimethylpentane
$CH_3CH_2C(CH_3)_2CH_2CH_3$
7 2,2,3-trimethylbutane
$CH_3C(CH_3)_2CH(CH_3)CH_3$

23 1-bromoheptane
$CH_3CH_2CH_2CH_2CH_2CH_2CH_2Br$
2-bromoheptane
$CH_3CH_2CH_2CH_2CH_2CHBrCH_3$
3-bromoheptane
$CH_3CH_2CH_2CH_2CHBrCH_2CH_3$
4-bromoheptane
$CH_3CH_2CH_2CHBrCH_2CH_2CH_3$

24 hept-1-ene
$CH_3CH_2CH_2CH_2CH_2CH=CH_2$
hept-2-ene
$CH_3CH_2CH_2CH_2CH=CHCH_3$

25 Hept-1-ene has no E/Z isomers

Z-hept-2-ene   E-hept-2-ene

26

b

c

d

27a cis is the Z isomer, trans is the E isomer
27b Cisplatin forms links on the same DNA strand (intrastrand), interfering with cell division. Trans links across both strands, so does not interfere with cell division.

28a Advantage: Bupivacaine is a local anaesthetic, so gives pain relief in a particular part of the body. Disadvantage: there is a possibility of cardiac arrest with some patients.
28b Ropivacaine can be produced as only the laevorotatory isomer eliminating the need for separation from the more harmful dextrorotatory isomer.

A1a A randomised controlled trial
A1b Most trials at a later stage in drug development are randomised double blind placebo-controlled trials where a placebo is administered to a randomised sample of patients and neither the researcher nor the subject know which treatment is being administered. This reduces the possibility of bias in the trial.
A1c Pregnant women since thalidomide interferes with foetal development.

A2a To give an order and system to the naming of the ever increasing number of new compounds.
A2b To enable scientists to communicate with each other without ambiguity.
A2c Because molecules in living systems often have a complex shape and the drug will only interact with certain sites, so it has an arrangement of atoms that fits with that shape.

A3a This is where other scientists review another scientist's work.
A3b To check its validity.
A3c Possibly because it had an effect on such a limited range of the population, that stage of pregnancy when the limbs were developing.
A3d After sufficient evidence is available from the trials and before the drug is licensed for use.

A4 A charity will attract funding from non-industrial sources and can use or donate these to fund its particular interests. This may be a field of research that cannot attract sufficient funding from the drug companies.

Chapter 5

1 **a** methanal   methanoic acid

$$H - C\overset{O}{\underset{H}{\big\langle}} \qquad H - C\overset{O}{\underset{OH}{\big\langle}}$$

b propanal   propanoic acid

$$CH_3CH_2 - C\overset{O}{\underset{H}{\big\langle}} \qquad CH_3CH_2 - C\overset{O}{\underset{OH}{\big\langle}}$$

2 Cr(+6) to (+3)

3 $CH_3CH_2CH_2CH_2OH + [O] \longrightarrow$

$$CH_3CH_2CH_2 - C\overset{O}{\underset{H}{\big\langle}} + H_2O$$
butanal

then:

$$CH_3CH_2CH_2 - C\overset{O}{\underset{H}{\big\langle}} + [O] \longrightarrow$$

$$CH_3CH_2CH_2 - C\overset{O}{\underset{H}{\big\langle}}$$
butanoic acid

4 **a** $CH_3CH_2CH_2CH(OH)CH_3$ pentan-2-ol

b ⬡—CH(OH)CH₃
1-Phenyl ethanol

5

⬡ with H, OH + [O] ⟶ ⬡ with =O + H₂O
cyclohexanone

6 CH_3CH_2OH

7 Primary. OH group is positioned at the end of a carbon chain.

8 $CH_3CH_2OH + [O] \rightarrow$
    $CH_3CHO + H_2O$; ethanal
$CH_3CHO + [O] \rightarrow CH_3COOH$;
      ethanoic acid

8a $Cr_2O_7^{2-}$ and Cr^{3+}
8b Reduction

9a $CH_3CH_2CH_2CH_2OH$;
$CH_3CH(OH)CH_2CH_3$;
$CH_3C(CH_3)(OH)CH_3$;
$CH_3CH_2CH_2COOH$
9b 1-butylbutanoate;
$CH_3CH_2CH_2CO\cdot OCH_2CH_2CH_2CH_3$

10 $CH_3CH_2CH_2CO\cdot OCH_2CH_2CH_2CH_3$ +
            H_2O
$CH_3CH_2CH_2COOH$ +
           $CH_3CH_2CH_2CH_2OH$

11 The colour change with the breathalyser is not always easy to see so it is less precise; the intoximeter gives a display of lights so is more precise. The accuracy of the breathalyser is not as great because the chemical reaction can vary more than the absorption of IR.

12 **a** $CH_3CH_2 - C\overset{O}{\underset{H}{\big\langle}} + HCN$

↓

$$CH_3CH_2 - \underset{CN}{\overset{OH}{\underset{|}{\overset{|}{C}}}} - H$$
2-hydroxybutanenitrile

b $CH_3 - \underset{O}{\overset{||}{C}} - CH_2CH_3 + HCN$

↓

$$CH_3 - \underset{CN}{\overset{OH}{\underset{|}{\overset{|}{C}}}} - CH_2CH_3$$
2-hydroxy-2-methyl butanenitrile

13 **a**

$$\underset{H}{\overset{OH}{\underset{CH_2CH_3}{\overset{|}{C}}}}\cdots CN \qquad NC\cdots\underset{CH_3CH_2}{\overset{HO}{\underset{|}{\overset{|}{C}}}}-H$$

b

$$\underset{CH_3}{\overset{OH}{\underset{CH_2CH_3}{\overset{|}{C}}}}\cdots CN \qquad NC\cdots\underset{CH_3CH_2}{\overset{HO}{\underset{|}{\overset{|}{C}}}}-CH_3$$

14 Stage 1: Warm separate samples with dilute, acidified dichromate solution. Tertiary alcohol will remain orange; others will change from orange to green. Stage 2: Distil the organic product from the other

samples from Stage 1. Warm each with Fehling's solution. Primary alcohol product (aldehyde) will cause a change from blue to red-brown ppt; secondary alcohol will remain blue.

15

a $CH_3CH_2 - C\overset{O}{\underset{H}{\big\langle}} + 2[H] \longrightarrow CH_3CH_2CH_2CH$
                           propan-1-ol

b $CH_3CH_2CH_2 - \underset{O}{\overset{||}{C}} - CH_3 + 2[H]$

↓

$$CH_3CH_2CH_2 - \underset{OH}{\overset{H}{\underset{|}{\overset{|}{C}}}} - CH_3$$
pentan-2-ol

c $CH_3CH_2CH_2 - C\overset{O}{\underset{OH}{\big\langle}} + 2[H]$

↓

$$CH_3CH_2CH_2 - C\overset{O}{\underset{H}{\big\langle}} + H_2O$$
butanal

then $CH_3CH_2CH_2 - C\overset{O}{\underset{OH}{\big\langle}} + 2[H]$

↓

$$CH_3CH_2CH_2CH_2OH$$
butan-1-ol

16 methanoic acid < ethanoic acid < benzoic acid

17

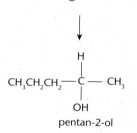

$$CH_3CH_2CH_2 - C\overset{O}{\underset{OH}{\big\langle}} + CH_3CH_2CH_2OH$$

↓

$$CH_3CH_2CH_2 - C\overset{O}{\underset{O-CH_2CH_2CH_3}{\big\langle}} + H_2O$$
propyl butanoate

18

a

$$CH_3CH_2CH_2CH_2 - \overset{\displaystyle CH_2CH_3}{\underset{\displaystyle H}{\overset{|}{\underset{|}{C}}}} - CH_2OH$$

b

$$HO - \overset{\|}{\underset{O}{C}} - CH_2CH_2CH_2CH_2 - \overset{\|}{\underset{O}{C}} - OH$$

c

$$2CH_3CH_2CH_2CH_2 - \overset{\displaystyle CH_2}{\underset{\displaystyle H}{\overset{\|}{\underset{|}{C}}}} - CH_2OH \; +$$

$$HO - \overset{\|}{\underset{O}{C}} - (CH_2)_4 - \overset{\|}{\underset{O}{C}} - OH$$

$$\downarrow$$

$$CH_3(CH_2)_3 - \overset{\displaystyle CH_2CH_3}{\underset{\displaystyle H}{\overset{|}{\underset{|}{C}}}} - CH_2 - O - C - (CH_2)_4$$

$$C - O - CH_2 - \overset{\displaystyle CH_2CH_3}{\underset{\displaystyle H}{\overset{|}{\underset{|}{C}}}} - (CH_2)_3CH_3 + 2H_2O$$
$$\overset{\|}{\underset{O}{}}$$

19

a $CH_3 - \overset{\|}{\underset{O}{C}} - OCH_2CH_3 + H_2O$

$$\downarrow$$

$$CH_3 - \overset{\|}{\underset{O}{C}} - OH + CH_3CH_2OH$$

     ethanoic acid   ethanol

b $CH_3CH_2 - \overset{\|}{\underset{O}{C}} - OCH_3 + NaOH$

$$\downarrow$$

$$CH_3CH_2 - \overset{\|}{\underset{O}{C}} - \overset{-}{O}\overset{+}{Na} + CH_3OH$$

  sodium propanoate   methanol

20 $C_6H_{12}O_6$ for both. They are isomers.

21

$$\overset{\displaystyle H \quad H \quad H}{\underset{\displaystyle OH \quad OH}{O = \overset{|}{C} - \overset{|}{C} - \overset{|}{C} - H}}$$

1,2-dihydroxypropanal

22 Glucose – circles around C1; squares around C2, C3, C4 and C5 Fructose – circles around C1 and C6; squares around C2, C3 and C4 There are no tertiary alcohol groups.

   glucose   +   fructose

$$\begin{array}{cc}
H\diagdown C \diagup^{O} & OH \\
H - \boxed{C} - OH & H - \overset{}{\underset{}{\textcircled{C}}} - H \\
HO - \boxed{C} - H & C = O \\
H - \boxed{C} - OH & HO - \boxed{C} - H \\
H - \boxed{C} - OH & H - \boxed{C} - OH \\
H - \textcircled{C} - H & H - \boxed{C} - OH \\
OH & H - \textcircled{C} - H \\
& OH
\end{array}$$

23 Glucose is an aldehyde; fructose is a ketone.

24 When heated with Fehlings's solutions, only glucose should produce a brick red precipitate because only the glucose structure contains a reducing aldehyde group.

25 By transfer of [H], the ketone group is reduced to a secondary alcohol group and the primary group is oxidised to an aldehyde group.

26 Aldehyde group, –CHO, changed to carboxylic acid group, –COOH.

$$HO - \overset{H}{\underset{H}{\overset{|}{\underset{|}{C}}}} - \overset{H}{\underset{OH}{\overset{|}{\underset{|}{C}}}} - \overset{H}{\underset{OH}{\overset{|}{\underset{|}{C}}}} - \overset{OH}{\underset{H}{\overset{|}{\underset{|}{C}}}} - \overset{H}{\underset{OH}{\overset{|}{\underset{|}{C}}}} - C\diagup^{O-H}_{\diagdown O}$$

27 Ketone group, C=O, changed to HO—C—CN.

$$HO - \overset{H}{\underset{H}{\overset{|}{\underset{|}{C}}}} - \overset{H}{\underset{OH}{\overset{|}{\underset{|}{C}}}} - \overset{H}{\underset{OH}{\overset{|}{\underset{|}{C}}}} - \overset{OH}{\underset{H}{\overset{|}{\underset{|}{C}}}} - \overset{CN}{\underset{OH}{\overset{|}{\underset{|}{C}}}} - C - OH$$

28 Nucleophilic addition

29 Nucleophilic addition: $-C_5OH$ adds across C=O at C_1

30 Aldehyde group, –CHO, changed to carboxylic acid group, –COOH. CH_3CH_2OH

31 Change any one (or more) of the –OH groups in fructose to $-O-COCH_3$. Purpose: to act as a catalyst.

$$HO - \overset{H}{\underset{H}{\overset{|}{\underset{|}{C}}}} - \overset{H}{\underset{OH}{\overset{|}{\underset{|}{C}}}} - \overset{OH}{\underset{O}{\overset{|}{\underset{|}{C}}}} - \overset{H}{\underset{H}{\overset{|}{\underset{|}{C}}}} - \overset{}{\underset{O}{\overset{\|}{C}}} - \overset{H}{\underset{H}{\overset{|}{\underset{|}{C}}}} - OH$$

$$\overset{}{\underset{O \diagdown C \diagup CH_3}{}}$$

$$CH_3 - \overset{\|}{\underset{O}{C}} - \overset{Cl}{\underset{Cl}{\overset{|}{\underset{|}{Cl: \frown Al}}}} - Cl \rightarrow CH_3 - \overset{+}{\underset{O}{\overset{\|}{C}}} + AlCl_4^-$$

A1 It is a resource which can be replenished.

A2 The amount of carbon (usually carbon dioxide) released is equal to the amount of carbon dioxide captured.

A3 Particulates can cause asthma. Carbon monoxide is a poisonous gas which interferes with oxygen transport in the blood. Nitrogen oxides can convert oxygen to ground-level ozone which can affect breathing and the growth of plants. Greenhouse gases result in warming of the atmosphere and cause climate change. Sulfur oxides are acidic and can damage buildings and living organisms.

A4 Land that was used for growing food could be taken for biodiesel production, thus increasing world hunger.

A5 The ester.

A6 Hydrolysis/alcoholysis.

A7 Sugar cane and corn are first generation, straw and wood chip would be second generation.

A8 Second generation biofuels are not using food crops as their source and second generation sources can be grown on land not fertile enough for food crops.

Chapter 6

1 The 1,2-isomer has a double bond between the carbons that have the bromine atoms attached; the 1,6-isomer has a single bond in that position.

2 Decolourise orange bromine solution or decolourise purple potassium permanganate solution. Also consider any electrophilic addition reaction.

3 The bond energy for hydrogenation of one double bond is -119 kJ mol^{-1} so 3 times this would be -357 kJ mol^{-1} but the enthalpy of hydrogenation of benzene is only -208 kJ mol^{-1} which means that benzene is more stable than if it had three separate double bonds.

4 Carbon-carbon bond lengths were shown by X-ray crystallography to be all the same, whereas double bonds would be shorter than single bonds.

5 Pauling had applied quantum theory to provide an explanation for the bonding in benzene but he needed Lonsdale's X-ray data to confirm equal bond lengths.

6 Empirical formula can be determined by burning the benzene in oxygen – the products will be carbon dioxide and water. The water can be absorbed by a material such as anhydrous calcium chloride and the carbon dioxide can be absorbed

using sodium hydroxide. From the gain in mass, the mass of hydrogen, and the mass of carbon can be calculated. This gives the ratio of carbon to hydrogen – hence we can use atomic mass to calculate the empirical formula. Since benzene is volatile it is possible to determine its molecular mass from the volume of vapour and from this the molecular formula.

Bond energies can be determined using a calorimeter. Some calorimeters can be used to calculate a heat of reaction for hydrogenation, or they can be used to determine heats of combustion for cyclohexene and benzene and from these the enthalpy of hydrogenation.

7

2-nitromethylbenzene

3-nitromethylbenzene

4-nitromethylbenzene

8 Electrophilic substitution by nitronium ion (NO_2^+).

9

10 Increase.

11 Decrease.

12

4-aminoethylbenzene

13 An azo dye.

14

15 A lone pair acceptor.

16

(or other positional isomers)

17 React benzene with ethanoyl chloride CH_3COCl or ethanoic anhydride $(CH_3CO)_2O$ in the presence of AlCl3 Friedel-Crafts catalyst.

18

reduction

19a

19b Poly(phenylethene), popularly known as polystyrene.

19c

19d Packing and thermal insulation.

Chapter 7

1a   i

$$CH_3CH_2 - N - CH_2CH_2CH_2CH_3$$

1a   ii

$$CH_3CH_2 - N - CH_2CH_2CH_3$$

317

1b Secondary; tertiary.

2a Bromoethane.
2b 2-bromopropane.
2c 1,6-dibromohexane.

3 Diethylamine, triethylamine and tetramethylammonium ion.

4a 2-bromobutane + KCN →
2-methylbutanenitrile
2-methylbutanenitrile + LiAlH$_4$ →
2-methylbutylamine.
4b No, because the required amine has the NH$_2$ group bonded midway along the carbon chain, whereas the nitrile reduction introduces the group at the end of the chain.

5

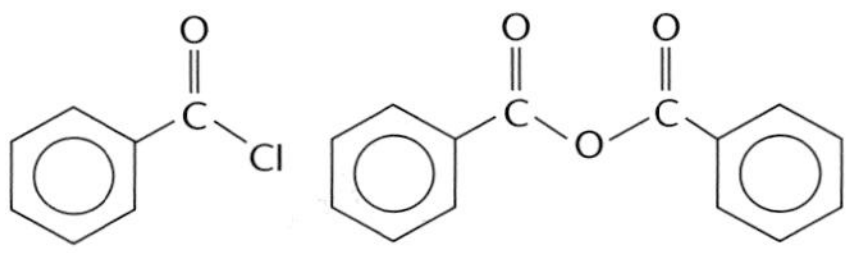

6

a

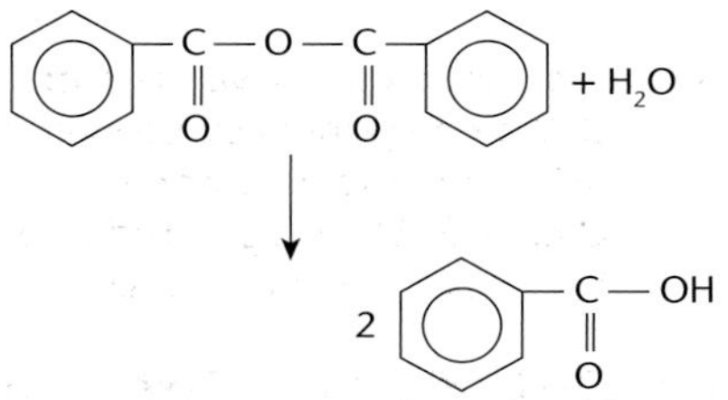

benzoic acid

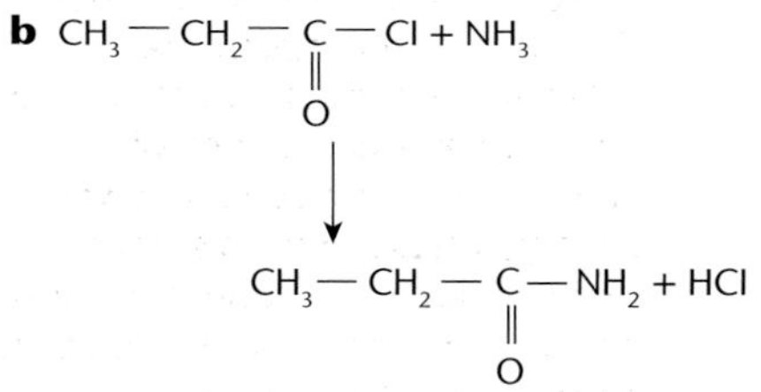

b CH$_3$ — CH$_2$ — C — Cl + NH$_3$

CH$_3$ — CH$_2$ — C — NH$_2$ + HCl
propanamide

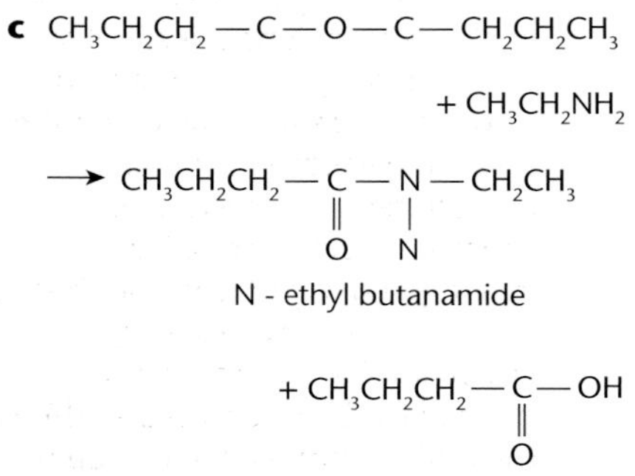

c CH$_3$CH$_2$CH$_2$ — C — O — C — CH$_2$CH$_2$CH$_3$
+ CH$_3$CH$_2$NH$_2$

→ CH$_3$CH$_2$CH$_2$ — C — N — CH$_2$CH$_3$
N - ethyl butanamide

+ CH$_3$CH$_2$CH$_2$ — C — OH
butanoic acid

7 Ethanoic anhydride is used because: it is cheaper; it reacts slowly; and it does not evolve HCl.

8

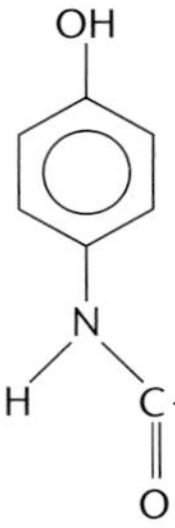

paracetamol

9

a + HNO$_3$ (conc.) $\xrightarrow[50°C]{conc.\ H_2SO_4}$ NO$_2$ + H$_2$O

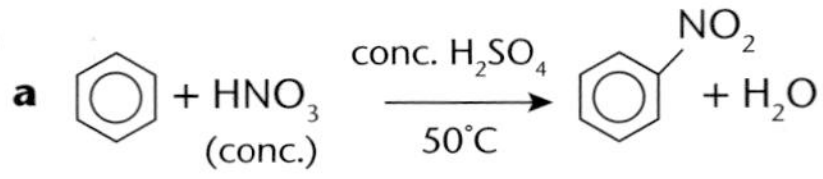

b NO$_2$ + 6[H] $\xrightarrow{Sn/HCl}$ NH$_2$ + 2H$_2$O

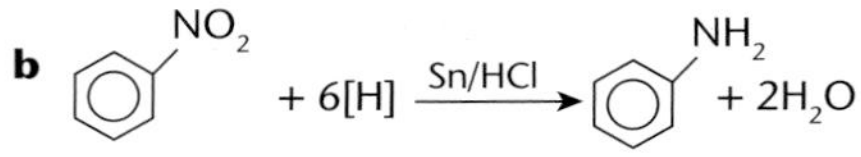

10

HNO$_3$ + 2H$_2$SO$_4$ ⟶ NO$_2^+$ + 2HSO$_4^-$ + H$_3$O$^+$

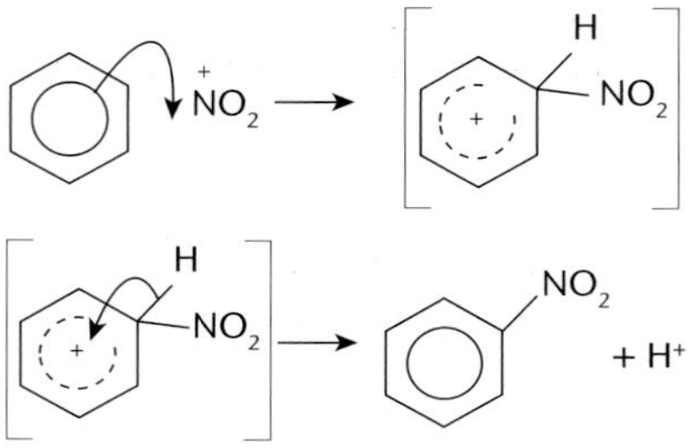

H$^+$ + HSO$_4^-$ ⟶ H$_2$SO$_4$

11a

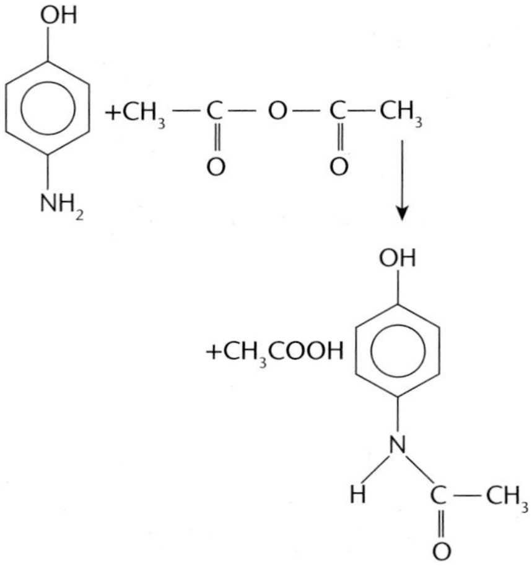

11b

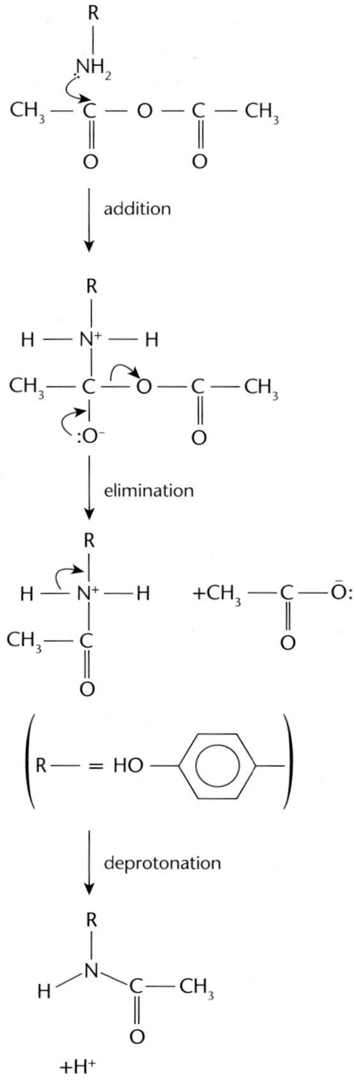

addition

elimination

(R — = HO —)

deprotonation

+H$^+$

11c No HCl is produced; it is cheaper.

12 The cost of drugs is related to the enormous expense of research and drug trialling which may not even lead to a saleable product. In favour of large profits: these have to fund further research, and profitable companies are more likely to attract financial backing. Against: some of the large profits could be used to reduce the price of drugs, saving health services a lot of money. Some of the profits could be used to subsidise drugs in developing countries.

13 Rainforests are a potential source of new drugs and these are being reduced by logging, so plants and unknown compounds may be lost forever.

Chapter 8

1a i

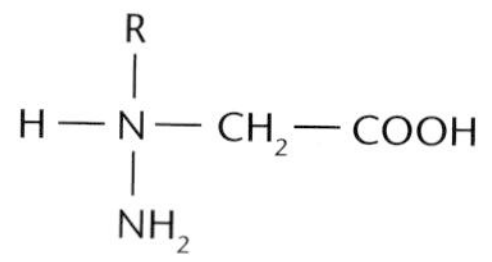

$$H - N - CH_2 - COOH$$
with R above N and NH_2 below N

1a ii

$$H - N - CH_2 - CH_2 - CH_2 - COOH$$
with R above N and NH_2 below N

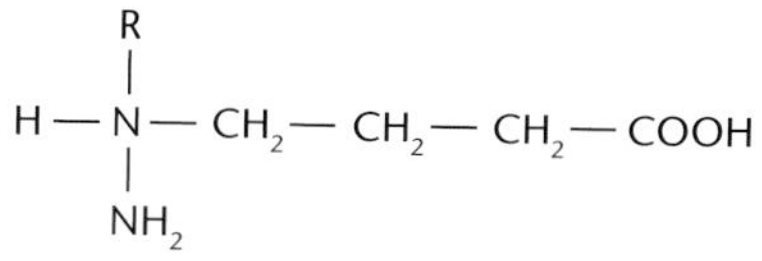

1b 4-aminobutanoic acid

2 No carbon atom with four different groups bonded to it.

3a Negative electrode.
3b Positive electrode.

4 No movement

5

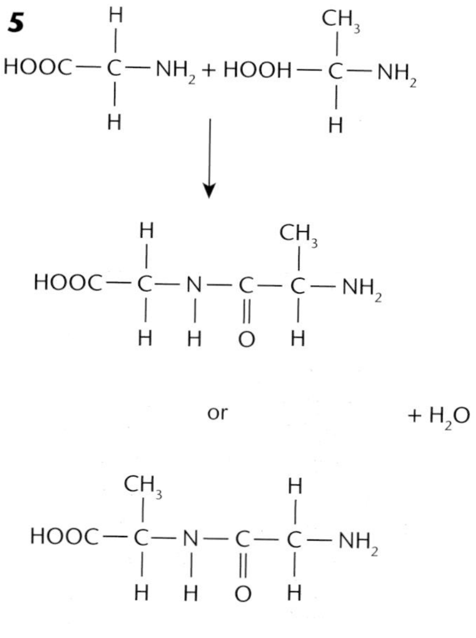

$$HOOC - C - NH_2 + HOOH - C - NH_2$$

with H below and H on left C, CH_3 above and H below right C

↓

$$HOOC - C - N - C - C - NH_2$$
with H, H, O, H below and CH_3 above

or   + H_2O

$$HOOC - C - N - C - C - NH_2$$
with CH_3, H, H, O, H

6 Catalyst, providing H^+ ions.

7 Number of amino acid residues shows that A and B = dipeptides, C = tripeptide.

8

a

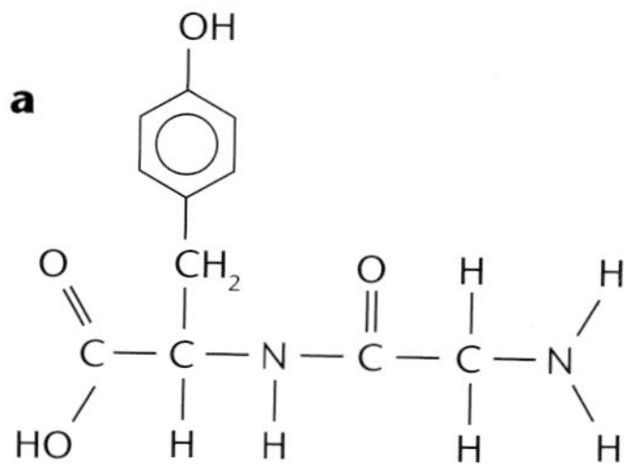

$$C - C - N - C - C - N$$
with OH, CH_2, O, H, H, H, H, HO groups

b

$$C - C - N - C - C - N - C - C - N$$
with O, H, O, H, O, CH_2, H groups and phenyl ring

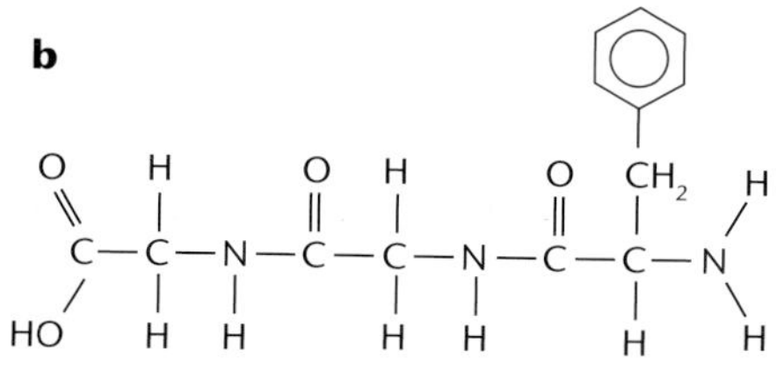

9 HOOC–Tyr–Gly–Gly–Phe–Leu–NH_2
        ↑   ↑   ↑   ↑   ↑
       (3)   (1) (2)   (3)
Hydrolysis at link (1) forms A.
Hydrolysis at link (2) forms B.
Hydrolysis at link (3) forms C.

10 Glycine – no carbon atom is bonded to four different groups.

11

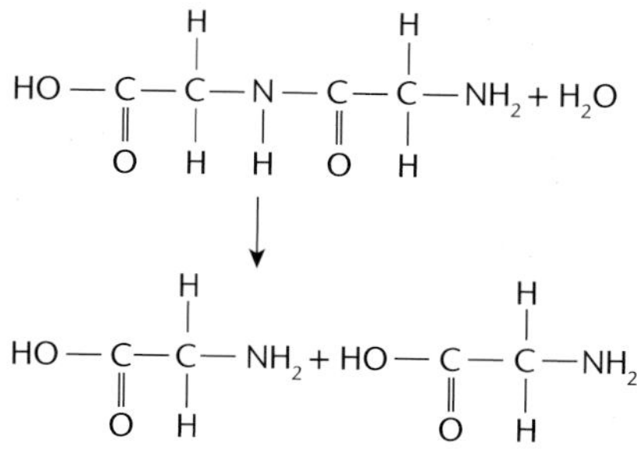

$$HO - C - C - N - C - C - NH_2 + H_2O$$
with H, O, H, H, O, H groups

↓

$$HO - C - C - NH_2 + HO - C - C - NH_2$$
with H, O, H and H, O, H groups

12 Structures for:
Alanine $HOOCCH(CH_3)NH_2$
aspartic acid
$HOOCCH(CH_2COOH)NH_2$
lysine
$HOOCCH(CH_2CH_2CH_2CH_2NH_2)NH_2$

13

lysine

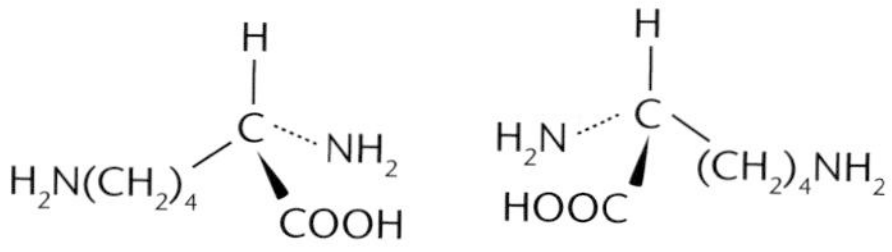

$$H_2N(CH_2)_4 - C - NH_2 \text{ with } COOH$$
$$H_2N - C - (CH_2)_4NH_2 \text{ with } HOOC$$

They are chemically and physically the same except they cause plane polarised light to rotate in opposite directions.

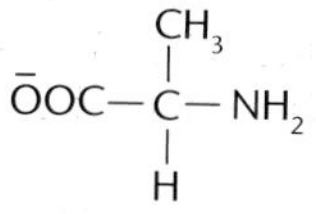

14 Lysine has an extra basic NH_2 group, causing it to be most alkaline. Aspartic acid has an extra acid COOH group causing it to be most acidic.

15 a

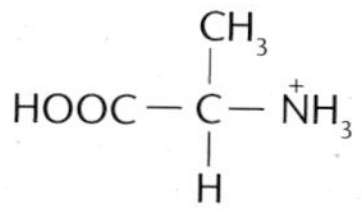

$$HOOC - C - \overset{+}{N}H_3$$
with CH_3 above and H below

b

$$\overline{O}OC - C - NH_2$$
with CH_3 above and H below

c

$$\overline{O}OC - C - \overset{+}{N}H_3$$
with CH_3 above and H below

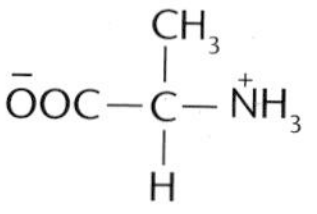

A1 Yes, they would have the same DNA fingerprint because identical twins are produced when an already fertilised egg divides so both cells have identical DNA.

A2 The bands from the DNA sample of the victim's blood match closely the blood found on the defendant's shirt and do not match the defendant's own blood. There is a match on the position of all 8 bands shown so you can be very strongly certain that this is the victim's blood. This does not show how or when the victim's blood got on the defendant's shirt.

A3 With such a high probability, the evidence is so conclusive that you don't need a jury to confirm this. However there may still be doubts about the validity of the test procedures. Also the issue of consent would need to be investigated as just because there is semen doesn't make it a rape case. The DNA science cannot provide evidence on that, so this is the main reason why you would still need a jury.

A4 Students can give an opinion here and possibly a probability, but currently DNA fingerprinting techniques are accurate enough to be admitted as part of the evidence.

A5 Points to discuss might be:
Deterrent to potential criminals
Help in solving paternity issues
Identifying 'at risk' individuals
What other information will be on the database?
Who will have access to the database and how secure is it?
Personal privacy

A6 Personal opinion with justification.

A7 Points to discuss might be: knowing the risks might lead to better preparation, improved lifestyle. Risk of some people with genetic disorders being uninsurable. Parents' dilemmas concerning PGD, will parents or doctors select the embryo(s) to be implanted or will they choose randomly, in which case a disease may be present in the embryo.

Chapter 9

1 Both involve Van der Waals intermolecular forces, but LDPE molecules are branched, which does not allow them to get close together, so the intermolecular forces are less effective.

2 If you increase the number of OH groups this will increase the solubility because the OH groups can hydrogen bond to the water. But too many OH groups will lead to intramolecular hydrogen bonding so decreased solubility in water.

3 All bonds in (poly)ethane are single bonds; the molecules are saturated hydrocarbons.

4 $HOOC(CH_2)_8COOH$ and $HO[CO(CH_2)_8-NH-(CH_2)_6-NH]_nH$

5a

a $CH_3-C(=O)-O-CH_2CH_3 + H_2O$

↓

$CH_3-C(=O)-OH + CH_3CH_2OH$

$CH_3-C(=O)-N(H)-CH_2CH_3 + H_2O$

↓

$CH_3-C(=O)-OH + CH_3CH_2NH_2$

5b Hydrolysis.

5c Long-chain polyester and polyamide plastics will be broken down by repeated hydrolysis reactions at the ester or amide links.

6a

6b

7a

7b

8 Hydrogen bonds.

9
Chain 1 ⁓⁓⁓ C
$\parallel$
O
hydrogen bond ⋯
H
$\mid$
Chain 2 ⁓⁓⁓ N

10 Kevlar® because the 1,4 monomers cause the polymer chain to be less zig-zag shaped, so the molecules lie close together and the intermolecular forces can be most effective.

A1 Re-use plastic bags.
Buy products manufactured using natural materials.
Buy clothing products made using natural materials.
Re-use some drinks bottles.
Recycle used plastics.

A2 Economic benefits to developed countries.
Economic benefits to China.
Transportation uses fossil fuels, which we should be conserving for future generations so issues of sustainability are raised.

A3 Recycling conserves diminishing resources of oil.
Recycling reduces emissions compared to landfill and incineration.
Suitable landfill sites are rapidly being used.
Plastics take a long time to biodegrade.
Landfill sites can be unstable in terms of emissions Incineration can produce toxic emissions and contribute to global warming.

Chapter 10

1 Less oxygen/air is needed to sustain combustion.

2 Br^+

3 1,2-dibromobutane

4 $RX + OH^- \rightarrow ROH + X^-$

5 It is partially ionised in solution.

6 –OH

7 Water contains OH groups and would cause interference.

8 $Cr^{3+}(aq)$

9 Cu_2O

10 Ag

11 Apply a test to distinguish an aldehyde from a ketone.

12 Addition–elimination; condensation.

13 Lone pair on N atom of NH_2.

14 Amino acids are buffers allowing a slower rise in pH.

15a pH (<7).
15b Dichromate oxidation (green) and Fehling's test (negative).
15c Boil with NaOH(aq); acidify (HNO_3); add silver nitrate (cream precipitate).
15d As (b) but Fehling's test positive.
15e As (a) and (b).
15f Add water; add $AgNO_3$(aq) (white precipitate).
15g Add bromine solution (turns colourless).
15h Sodium test (H_2 evolved) and pH (7) and dichromate oxidation (negative).
15i pH (>7) in water.

16a Heat with acidified dichromate.
16b Heat with NaOH(aq); acidify (HNO_3); add $AgNO_3$(aq).
16c Add aqueous bromine solution.
16d Fehling's test or silver mirror test.
16e Add sodium metal.

17 $100 \times (0.5 \times 0.4 \times 0.75) = 15\%$

18a Excess hot acidified dichromate solution.

$$CH_3CH_2CH(OH)CH_3 + [O]$$

$$\downarrow$$

$$CH_3CH_2-\underset{\underset{O}{\|}}{C}-CH_3 + H_2O$$

18b CH_3COOH and concentrated sulfuric acid; catalyst warm.

$$CH_3CH_2CH_2OH + CH_3COOH \longrightarrow$$

$$CH_3CH_2CH_2-O-\underset{\underset{O}{\|}}{C}-CH_3 + H_2O$$

18c Concentrated sulfuric acid; 170 °C
$$CH_3CH_2CH_2CH_2OH \rightarrow$$
$$CH_3CH_2CH=CH_2 + H_2O$$
18d $LiAlH_4$ in ethoxyethane.
$$CH_3CH_2CH_2COOH + 4[H] \rightarrow$$
$$CH_3CH_2CH_2CH_2OH + H_2O$$
18e Excess ammonia in ethanol; heat and pressure.
$$CH_3CH_2Br + 2NH_3 \rightarrow$$
$$CH_3CH_2NH_2 + NH_4Br$$

19a $CH_3CH_2Cl + NaOH(aq) \xrightarrow{reflux}$
$CH_3CH_2OH + NaCl$

$$CH_3CH_2OH + 2[O] \xrightarrow[\text{excess. Reflux}]{Cr_2O_7^{2-}/H^+ \text{ in}} CH_3COOH + H_2O$$

19b

$$CH_2=CH_2 + HBr \longrightarrow CH_3CH_2Br$$

$$CH_3CH_2Br + KCN \xrightarrow[\text{ethanol soln.}]{\text{Reflux in}} CH_3CH_2CN$$

$$CH_3CH_2CN + 2H_2O \xrightarrow[H_2SO_4]{\text{Reflux in}} CH_3CH_2COOH + NH_3$$

19c

$$CH_3-CH=CH_2 \xrightarrow[H_3PO_4]{H_2O} CH_3-\underset{\underset{OH}{|}}{CH}-CH_3$$

$$\xrightarrow[H^+]{K_2Cr_2O_7} CH_3-\underset{\underset{O}{\|}}{C}-CH_3$$

19d

$$CH_3CH_2OH + 2[O] \xrightarrow[\text{excess. Reflux}]{Cr_2O_7^{2-}/H^+ \text{ in}} CH_3CH_2COOH + H_2O$$

$$CH_3COOH + CH_3CH_2OH \xrightarrow[H_2SO_4 \text{ catalyst}]{\text{Reflux. conc.}}$$
$$CH_3CO.OCH_2CH_3 + H_2O$$

19e

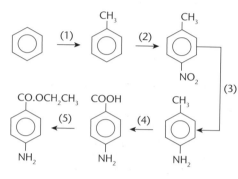

A1

A2 CH_3 group must be introduced before NO_2 group to ensure 1,4-isomer can be made. Reduction of NO_2 to NH_2 must occur before oxidation of CH_3 to COOH because COOH can also be reduced.

Step

(1) benzene $+ CH_3Cl \xrightarrow{AlCl_3}$ toluene $+ HCl$

(2) toluene $+ HNO_3 \xrightarrow{H_2SO_4}$ 4-nitrotoluene $+ H_2O$

(3) 4-nitrotoluene $+ 4[H] \xrightarrow{Sn/HCl}$ 4-methylaniline $+ 2H_2O$

(4) 4-methylaniline $+ 3[O] \xrightarrow[\text{in OH}^-]{KMnO_4}$ 4-aminobenzoic acid $+ H_2O$

(5) 4-aminobenzoic acid $+ CH_3CH_2OH \xrightarrow[H_2SO_4]{\text{conc.}}$ ethyl 4-aminobenzoate $+ H_2O$

A3 A continuous process can run without interruption; in a batch process, products have to be removed, plant cleaned and re-charged.

A4 By-products represent a loss in revenue and they may have to be disposed of – at a cost.

A5 These can often be automated thus saving on employment costs. Running continuously can allow for energy saving e.g. by heat exchange.

A6 The main products and by-products have to be removed completely to avoid contamination of the next batch.

A7 Recycling conserves diminishing resources and reduces costs of having to buy more reactant. Recycling reduces emissions.

A8 Crude oil does not contain the proportions of different fractions which match the demand. Extra amounts of these 'in demand' products are made by cracking and reforming.

A9 They would be by-products, because they are not saleable.

A10 Heavy metal waste which is toxic, the heavy metals are recovered and reprocessed.
Sulfur in petrol produces sulfur dioxide which leads to acid rain. The sulfur is removed in the oil refineries.
Slag heaps or other mining spoil affect the local environment and are an eyesore to local residents. Often when mining has finished these are converted to wildlife habitats or other public amenities.

A11 Often industrial processes involve flammable materials and an industrial plant is on a much larger scale, so a serious fire could result; their emergency procedures would be appropriate to the risk.
Because routine maintenance will have to be carried out while the plant is operating, Health and Safety regulations will be stricter. Air monitoring and breathing apparatus for maintenance may be required for some equipment in some industrial processes.

Chapter 11

1 C_2H_4O
($0.88 \times 12/44 = 0.24$ g C, $0.36 \times 2/18 = 0.04$ g H, $= 0.44 - 0.24 - 0.04 = 0.16$ g O
No of moles of each $= 0.24/12 = 0.02$ moles C, $0.04/1 = 0.04$ moles H, $0.16/16 = 0.01$ moles O,
ratio $= 2:4:1$)

2 $C_4H_8O_2$

3 Acid (–COOH), not ester, ketol or aldol $CH_3CH_2CH_2COOH$, or $CH_3CH(CH_3)COOH$

4 1.67×10^{-5} to 2.5×10^{-6} m

5 1.8×10^{13} to 1.2×10^{14} s^{-1}

6 7.18 to 47.9 kJ mol^{-1}

7 The heavier Br atom causes a lower frequency vibration.

8 Absorptions caused by the solvent molecules need to be eliminated and such absorptions may obscure absorptions caused by the sample molecule.

9 $-$C$-$H at $\approx$ 2950 cm^{-1}, $=$C$-$H at 3084 cm^{-1}, $\equiv$C$-$H at 3312 cm^{-1}
Higher wavenumbers correspond to stronger bonds, so the C$-$H bonds must be influenced by the adjacent C$-$C, C$=$C or C$\equiv$C bond.

10 1-C$-$H
2-C$-$H
3-C$-$H
4-O$-$H
5-C$-$H
6-C$-$H
7-C$-$H
8-C$-$H
9-C$-$H
10-C$=$O
11-C$-$H

11a

hex-1-ene

ethanenitrile

hexane

3-methylbutanal

11b hex-1-ene: alkane C$-$H, alkene C$-$H, C$-$C, C$=$C
ethanenitrile: alkane C$-$H, C$-$C, C$\equiv$N
hexane: alkane C$-$H, C$-$C
3-methylbutanal: alkane C$-$H, aldehyde C$-$H, C$-$C, C$=$O
See Table 1 in data section for wavenumbers.

11c i hex-1-ene
ii 3-methylbutanal
iii hexane
iv ethanenitrile.

12 They will collide with the electrode, pick up electrons and revert to being neutral particles.

13a X
13b Z
13c Y

14 They contain different numbers of neutrons in their nuclei; ^{12}C has six neutrons, ^{13}C has seven.

15 A_r(Zn) = 65.45 (4 sf)

16 9:6:1

17 Pairs of peaks with a mass difference of 2 in a ratio of 3:1 (containing ^{35}C and ^{37}C).

18 29 and 43.

19 The presence of small numbers of molecules containing heavier isotopes (particularly ^{13}C).

20 The spectrum will be much simpler because of the symmetry of the methoxymethane molecule. It will contain significant signals at 46 ($CH_3OCH_3^+$), 31 (CH_3O^+) and 15 (CH_3^+) only.

21 $C_8H_6O_2$, $C_6H_{14}O_3$, $C_5H_{10}O_4$, $C_4H_6O_5$

22 Propan-1-ol would produce signals at 29 ($C_2H_5^+$) and 43 ($C_3H_7^+$) which propan-2-ol would not.

23 The 10^6 factor scales the chemical shift values so most fall between 1 and 10.

24 The electronegative oxygen atom near to the aldehyde hydrogen atom causes the hydrogen nucleus to resonate at a lower magnetic field.

25 Each hydrogen atom is bonded to the same C atom.

26a 1
26b 2
26c 3
26d 1
26e 2

27a 3:1
27b 3:1
27c 3:2:21

28 A quartet in a 1:3:3:1 ratio.

29 A quartet (from the CH_3 group) of doublets (from the OH group).

A1a Balance of: costs with number caught taking drugs, there is financial gain in being a leading sportsperson, the more effective testing techniques tend to be more expensive to carry out.
A1b It may depend on the type of work e.g. if there are safety issues. Taking recreational drugs can lead to reduced performance. This is balanced against civil liberties, also who does the testing, who has access to the information, how secure is the information.

A2 The gas chromatography will separate the metabolites and mass spectrometry can be used to identify key structures.

A3 Sensitivity is related to the concentration of the compound in the sample. The greater the sensitivity of the apparatus the lower the concentration of the compound that can be in the sample.

A4 A false positive is a result which indicates the presence of a drug or metabolite and no drug has been taken. This may depend on the sensitivity of the test; also, other 'allowed' substances may lead to identical metabolites, or a particular genetic make-up may lead to presence of metabolites.

A5 No, because the testing system has inaccuracies. The person carrying out the test may make a mistake in preparing the sample or analysing the results. There may be some contamination during the collection of the sample.

A6 There is ever-increasing strictness of the regulations concerning testing times; the analysis techniques are improving; and public opinion in the main is supporting drug testing.

A7

Chapter 12

1 Energy must be supplied to overcome the attractive forces between the positively charged nucleus and the negatively charged electrons.

2 For element **a** there is a large increase in ionisation enthalpy after the 3rd electron has been removed. This indicates that the atom is in Group 3. For similar reasons element **b** is in Group 4 and element **c** is in Group 6.

3 The energy has to be supplied to break the bonds between atoms.

4

clockwise = anticlockwise:
$\Delta H_1 + \Delta H_r = \Delta H_2$
$\Delta H_r = \Delta H_2 - \Delta H_1 = -1810.0$
$-(-1901.6) = +91.6$ kJ mol^{-1}.
The reaction is endothermic.

5 The enthalpy change for the formation of hydrogen chloride: breaking the bonds in $Cl_2(g)$ and $H_2(g)$ to form $Cl(g) + 3H(g)$

$\frac{1}{2} Cl_2(g) = \frac{1}{2} \times 234.4 = + 121.7$
$\frac{1}{2} H_2(g) = \frac{1}{2} \times 435.9 = \underline{+ 217.95}$
$= 339.65$

Forming the bonds in $HCl(g)$
$= -432.0$

Total enthalpy change for bond breaking and bond forming:
$= +339.65 + (-432)$
$= -92.35 kJ \, mol^{-1}$

Experimental value for ΔH_f
$= -92.3 \, kJ \, mol^{-1}$

The value is quite close to the experimental value, so mean bond enthalpy values are satisfactory here.

6 The steps you need to make to calculate are: **i** the standard enthalpy change; **ii** the standard entropy change; **iii** the Gibb's free energy change at 298 K. Above what temperature might the reaction proceed spontaneously?

i Enthalpy change for $NaHCO_3(s) \rightarrow$
$Na_2CO_3(s) + H_2O(g) + CO_2(g)$
$= -1131 + (-242) + (-394) -$
(2×-951)
$= -1767 - (-1902) = + 135 \, kJ \, mol^{-1}$

ii Remember the units for entropy include J (not kJ) i.e. $J \, K^{-1} \, mol^{-1}$
Entropy change for $NaHCO_3(s) \rightarrow$
$Na_2CO_3(s) + H_2O(g) + CO_2(g)$
$2 \times 102 \rightarrow 135 + 189 + 214$
Entropy increase $= 538 - 204$
$= 334 \, J \, mol^{-1}$

iii At 298 K the combined entropy term $-T\Delta S^\ominus = 298 \times 334/1000$
$= 99.5 kJ \, mol^{-1}$
At 298 K $\Delta G^\ominus = \Delta H^\ominus - T\Delta S^\ominus$
$= 135 - 99.5$
$= 35.5 \, kJ \, mol^{-1}$
$\Delta G = \Delta H - T\Delta S$ is positive; the reaction is not thermodynamically feasible at this temperature. The temperature at which feasibility occurs is when $\Delta G^\ominus = 0$.
$\Delta G^\ominus = \Delta H^\ominus - T\Delta S^\ominus$
So when $\Delta G^\ominus = 0$, $T\Delta S^\ominus = \Delta H^\ominus$
$T = \Delta H^\ominus / \Delta S^\ominus = 135/0.334 = 404 \, K$
This means that the $NaHCO_3$ must be heated to at least 404 K (131°C). Note this is only the temperature at which the reaction becomes feasible and it gives no indication of the rate.

A1 & A2

All values in $kJ \, mol^{-1}$

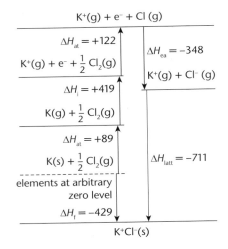

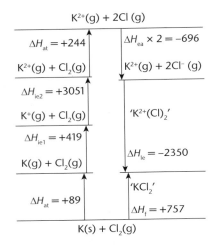

Generally an energy input is needed to overcome attractive forces, and energy is released when particles are attracted and move towards each other. Atomisation is endothermic. An energy input is needed. In metals the lattice of positive ions is held together by the sea of mobile, negative electrons. Covalent molecules – an energy output is needed to form the separate atoms by breaking covalent bonds. Ionisation enthalpy is endothermic. An energy input is needed. The negative electrons are attracted to the positive nucleus. Electron affinity is exothermic for the first electron and endothermic for any further electrons. Electrons are attracted towards the positive

nucleus so energy is released. If more electrons are introduced then the electron–electron repulsion means that an energy input is needed.
Lattice enthalpy is exothermic. There are attractive forces between the positive and negative ions, so energy is released.
ΔH_f for KCl is $-429 \, kJ \, mol^{-1}$, so there is a net release of energy. ΔH_f for KCl_2 is $+757 \, kJ \, mol^{-1}$, the process is endothermic , so KCl is the more favoured energetically.

A3

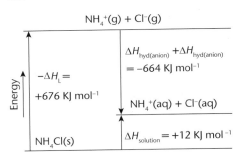

A4 For a reaction to be spontaneous Gibb's free energy must be zero or negative and $\Delta G = \Delta H - T\Delta S$. Process can proceed spontaneously because there is an increase in entropy as the ordered crystal arrangement is changing to a disordered system in solution. Even though ΔH is positive the increase in entropy and the combined $-T\Delta S$ is sufficiently negative to make ΔG negative.

A5 $\Delta H = mc \Delta T = 200 \, g \times 4.17 \, J \, g^{-1} \, K^{-1}$
$\times 16.5 \, K = 13760 \, J = 13.76 \, kJ$

A6 The molar enthalpy change for ammonium nitrate is $+26.5 \, kJ \, mol^{-1}$ so the number of moles needed is $13.76/26.5 = 0.519 \, mol$
number of moles $=$ mass $\times M_r$
$= 0.519 \times 80.0 = 41.5 \, g$

Chapter 13

1 Kekule thought about the structures proposed by others, but he proposed a novel ring structure. However his model had alternate double and single bonds which would be of differing lengths and bond energies. Later data which showed equal bond lengths, shown by X-ray photographs, and bond energies challenged this so a new explanation e.g. resonance was needed.

2 Pauling had data about bond lengths and energies and he applied quantum theory to this problem proposing the concept of hybridisation – an entirely new way of thinking about bonding.

3a Pauling was able to do the calculation from first principles because he was a great scientist and had a thorough understanding of the underlying theory. He did not have to rely on others telling him the answers.

3b Science moves forward by scientists questioning other scientists' work, sometimes as new data comes to light. Current theories are not necessarily 'correct'; they are simply the current 'accepted' explanation, based on the data available.

3c Research scientists think of many ideas as to why things are the way they are. An important consideration is: does the data support your hypothesis? So here the fit with the data is the selection principle.

3d There are limitations to scientific data, the answer is only correct within certain limits possibly determined by the instruments or technique. Hence the value of quoting error limits. Sometimes scientists have to make approximations to obtain any sort of answer at all.

4 Allred had access to more precise data so was able to re-calculate Pauling's original values. Now scientists can make better predictions and more reliable explanations about chemical bonding.

5 Cl atoms are identical so the attraction for the electrons in the bond between the atoms will be identical, so the bond will be

completely covalent. In an ionic bond there is always some attraction from the positive ion for the electrons on the negative ion, so there is always a polarising effect and distortion of the charge cloud (covalent character).

6 −1, +7

7a Nuclear charge is increasing across Period 3, which increases the attraction for the electrons, which decreases the atomic radius.

7b The metal lattice is held together by the forces of attraction between the positive nucleus and the negative outer (delocalised) electrons. The nuclear charge of magnesium is greater than that for sodium so the attraction for the delocalised electrons is greater, so more energy is needed to overcome these forces.

7c The nuclear charge for sodium is the least of all the Period 3 elements, so the attraction for the outer electrons is the lowest, so the energy to remove one electron is the least. Across Period 3 nuclear charge is increasing, the inner electron screening remains constant, so the first ionisation energy increases from left to right.

8 For sodium oxide there is the largest difference in electronegativity values for Period 3, so Na_2O will have the greatest ionic character. Mg has a greater nuclear charge, so a greater attraction for the electrons on the O^{2-} ion. This produces less ionic/more covalent character. At SiO_2 the electronegativity difference between the two atoms is small so the electrons are shared – this tendency will increase across the period.

9 The melting point is affected by the force of attraction between the positive and the negative ions. In the fluorides, magnesium 2+ has a greater ionic charge than sodium 1+, so there is a greater force of attraction between ions, so more energy is needed to separate them.

10 The melting point of silicon dioxide is relatively high for a covalent compound because the structure is macromolecular and is held together by covalent bonds. The oxides of sulfur have low melting points. Sulfur (VI) oxide is covalent and unimolecular, sulfur (VI) oxide is a trimer at room temperature and it melts or sublimes very easily.

11 O^{2-} ions cannot exist in water so they combine with H_2O molecules to form OH^- ions. If we look at the M–O–H system then the M–O bond will be weakest for Na–O–H and will increase in strength Na → Mg → Al. The weaker the M–O bond, the greater will be the number of OH^- ions produced, so the higher the pH. In addition, the solubility of the oxides decreases Na → Mg → Al, so fewer OH^- ions will be released in the water, so the lower will be the pH.

A1 They both have a density less than that of water.

A2 $2Na(s) + 2H_2O(l) \rightarrow 2NaOH(aq) + H_2(g)$,
$2K(s) + 2H_2O(l) \rightarrow 2KOH(aq) + H_2(g)$

A3 The first ionisation energy for potassium is lower than that for sodium. The value for the melting point for potassium is lower than for sodium.

A4 For a substance to dissolve, ΔH_{sol} needs to be negative or slightly positive. ΔH_{sol} is the difference between the lattice dissociation enthalpy and the hydration enthalpy. For sodium oxide, ΔH_{le} is much less negative than ΔH_{hyd} so ΔH_{sol} is negative and it dissolves. For both magnesium oxide and aluminium oxide ΔH_{le} is much more negative than ΔH_{hyd} so ΔH_{sol} is positive and it does not dissolve. The increase in entropy on dissolving will not compensate for the large positive ΔH_{sol}.

A5 $Na_2O(s) + H_2O(l) \rightarrow 2NaOH(aq)$

A6 $Al_2O_3(s) + 6HCl(aq) \rightarrow$
$\qquad 2AlCl_3(aq) + 3H_2O(l)$
or $Al_2O_3(s) + 6HCl(aq) + 3H_2O(l) \rightarrow$
$\qquad 2[Al(H_2O)_6]^{3+}(aq) + 6Cl^-(aq)$
$Al_2O_3(s) + 2NaOH(aq) + 3H_2O(l) \rightarrow$
$\qquad 2[Al(OH)_4]^-(aq) + 2Na^+(aq)$

A7 This behaviour is described as amphoteric. The aluminium ions have an overall charge of 3+ which means it has a strong attractive force for the lone pairs in the H_2O molecule, so in alkaline conditions the H_2O molecule will lose H^+ and form the aluminate ion, but in acidic conditions the H^+ ion will be retained and it forms the hexaaquaaluminium ion.

A8 $P_4O_{10}(s) + 6H_2O(l) \rightarrow 4H_3PO_4(aq)$,
$SO_2(g) + H_2O(l) \rightarrow H_2SO_3(aq)$.

A9 Both these compounds will then release H^+ ions forming an acidic solution. Phosphorous and sulfur both have high electronegativities so the bonds P–O and S–O are quite strong and the O–H bond is weakened, therefore H^+ ions are released. For sodium and magnesium the electronegativities are lower, so they stay as Na^+ and Mg^{2+} ions thus releasing OH^- ions, so the solutions are basic.

Chapter 14

1a $= +3$
1b $= +6$
1c $= +6$
1d $= +1$

2a $Mg^+(aq) + 2e^- \rightleftharpoons Mg(s)$
2b $Fe^{3+}(aq) + e^- \rightleftharpoons Fe^{2+}(aq)$
2c $\frac{1}{2}Cl_2(g) + e^- \rightleftharpoons Cl^-(aq)$

3a $Zn(s) \mid Zn^{2+}(aq) \parallel Pb^{2+}(aq) \mid Pb(s)$
3b $Zn(s) \mid Zn^{2+}(aq) \parallel H^+(aq) \mid H_2(g) \mid Pt(s)$
3c $Cu(s) \mid Cu^{2+}(aq) \parallel Fe^{3+}(aq), Fe^{2+}(aq) \mid Pt(s)$

4 You would choose two electrodes which gave you as large an e.m.f. as possible, e.g. $Ag^+(aq) \mid Ag(s)$ cell with $Li^+(aq) \mid Li(s)$ cell. In reality you would need to consider many other

factors as well, such as mass (lower mass is preferred), cost (the cheaper the materials and construction costs, the better) and chemical hazards (e.g. reactivity of electrode chemicals with air and water, their toxicity etc.).

5 The equilibrium will move from left to right towards zinc to reduce the number of zinc ions in solution.

6a
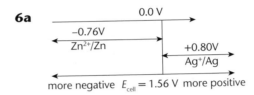
more negative $\quad E_{cell} = 1.56$ V more positive

6b $-0.76 + (+0.80)V = 1.56$ V. The zinc-silver cell gives a larger e.m.f. (1.56V) than the zinc-copper cell (1.10V).

6c A cell of electrodes Mg^{2+}/Mg and Zn^{2+}/Zn produces an e.m.f. of 1.61 V (difference between -2.37 and -0.76). A cell of electrodes Zn^{2+}/Zn and Ag^+/Ag produces an e.m.f. of 1.56 V (difference between -0.76 and $+0.80$). A cell of electrodes Mg^{2+}/Mg and Ag^+/Ag produces an e.m.f. of 3.17 V (difference between -2.37 and $+0.80$).

7 For iodine to displace bromine from solution the following two half-reactions must occur:
$I_2(s) + 2e^- \rightleftharpoons 2I^-$ (aq) $E^\ominus = +0.54$ V
$2Br^-$ (aq) $\rightleftharpoons Br_2(l) + 2e^-$ $E^\ominus = -1.07$ V
The sum of these two half-reactions is:
$I_2(s) + 2Br^-$ (aq) $\rightleftharpoons 2I^-(aq) + Br_2(l)$
$E^\ominus = -0.53$ V.
For this reaction to be spontaneous $E^\ominus$ must be positive. Therefore iodine does not displace bromine from solution.

8a For a spontaneous cell reaction to occur $E^\ominus$ must be positive, so for the Li/MnO_2 cell: $E^\ominus = +1.23 -(-3.03) = +4.26$ V.

8b To work out the reaction for the cell, write the more negative half-reaction as an oxidation, and the more positive half-reaction as a reduction. Then balance the

number of electrons in each half-reaction and add the two together:
$2Li \rightleftharpoons 2Li^+ + 2e^-$
$MnO_2 + 4H^+ + 2e^- \rightleftharpoons Mn^{2+} 2H_2O$
$\overline{2Li + MnO_2 + 4H^+ \rightleftharpoons 2Li^+ Mn^{2+} 2H_2O}$

9a Zinc because Zn^{2+}/Zn has a more negative electrode potential than H^+/H_2 so that electrons flow from the zinc half-reaction to the hydrogen ions in the acid, producing hydrogen gas molecules.

9b Yes. Fe^{3+}/Fe^{2+} has a more negative electrode potential than Br_2/Br^- so electrons flow towards Br_2/Br^-. This oxidises iron(II) ions to iron(III).

9c No. I_2/I^- has a more negative electrode potential than Fe^{2+}/Fe so electrons flow towards Fe^{2+}/Fe. This reduces iron(III) ions to iron(II).

9d Yes. Fe^{3+}/Fe^{2+} has a more negative electrode potential than $MnO_4^-, H^+/Mn^{2+}$.

10 The voltage depends on the reactants used (and their electrode potentials) not their amounts.

11 0.4 V

12 Hydrogen

13 $H_2O(l) \leftrightarrow H^+(aq) + OH^-(aq)$
$4H^+(aq) + 4e^- \rightarrow 2H_2(g)$
$4OH^-(aq) \rightarrow O_2(g) + 2H_2O(l) + 4e^-$

14 The first fuel cells powered a vehicle for only 30 seconds, but now with technological advances more than 300 miles is possible. The voltage of the fuel cell and the chemical reactions – which depend upon the scientific principles – are just the same.

15 No pollutants of carbon dioxide and nitrogen compounds produced while the bus is using its full cell. They are quiet.

16 Air is a mixture of nitrogen and oxygen, when the fuel burns at high temperatures these two combine to form nitrogen oxides.

17 Fuel cells are non polluting when they are used, with no moving parts so they are reliable. But there is a store of hydrogen, which is flammable and has to be pressurised.

A1a $Zn^{2+}(aq) + 2e^- \rightleftharpoons Zn(s)$
A1b $Mn^{4+}(aq) + 2e^- \rightleftharpoons Mn^{2+}(aq)$
A1c $\frac{1}{2}O_2(g) + H^+ + 2e^- \rightleftharpoons OH^-(aq)$
A1d Reduction is more likely because the equilibrium goes from left to right. Therefore, the cell potential will be less negative.

A2ai $Zn(s)|Zn^{2+}(aq)||$
A2aii $Li^+(aq)|Li(s)||$
A2aiii $Pt(s)|H_2(g)|H^+(aq)||$
A2b Under standard conditions it is the Standard Hydrogen Electrode. It is assigned a value zero and all other standard electrode potentials are measured relative to this.
A2c Hydrogen pressure = 1 bar, temperature = 298 K, $[H^+] = 1$ mol dm^{-3}.

A3a $Zn(s)|Zn^{2+}(aq)||Ag^+(aq)|Ag(s)$
A3b $Pt(s)|H_2(g)|H^+(aq)||Zn^{2+}(aq)|Zn(s)$

A4a The zinc/silver cell gives a larger e.m.f. (1.56 V) than the zinc/copper (1.10 V).

A4b
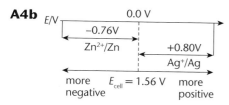

A4c $-0.76 + (+0.80)$ V = 1.56 V
A4d It has a higher cell potential. The cell reactants have a lower density.

A5a Silver will be displaced. For zinc to displace silver from aqueous silver solution the following two half-reactions must occur:
$Zn(s) \rightleftharpoons Zn^{2+}(aq) + 2e^-$
$E^\ominus = -(-0.76)$ V
$Ag^+(aq) + e^- \rightleftharpoons Ag(s)$
$E^\ominus = +0.80$ V
The sum of these two half-reactions is:
$Zn(s) + Ag^+(aq) \rightleftharpoons Zn^{2+}(aq) + Ag(s)$
$E^\ominus = +1.56$ V
For this reaction to be spontaneous, $E^\ominus$ must be positive. Therefore zinc does displace silver from solution.

A5b No reaction. This is the reverse of the reaction in part **i**. $E^\ominus$ is negative. For this reaction to be spontaneous $E^\ominus$ must be positive, so no reaction occurs.

A5c No reaction. For iodine to displace bromine from bromide solution the following two half-reactions must occur:
$I_2(s) + 2e^- \rightleftharpoons 2I^-(aq)$ $E^\ominus = +0.54$ V
$2Br^-(aq) \rightleftharpoons Br_2(l) + 2e^-$ $E^\ominus = -1.07$ V
The sum of these two half-reactions is:
$I_2(s) + 2Br^-(aq) \rightleftharpoons 2I^-(aq) + Br_2(l)$
For this reaction to be spontaneous $E^\ominus$ must be positive. But $(-1.07$ V$) + (+0.54$ V$) = -0.53$ V. Therefore, iodine does not displace bromine from solution.

A5d This is the reverse of the reaction in part **iii**. $E^\ominus$ is positive. +0.54 V $-(-1.07$ V$) = +0.53$ V. Therefore, bromine does displace iodine from iodide solution.

Chapter 15

1a Fe^0 = [Ar] $3d^6 4s^2$
1b Fe(II) = [Ar] $3d^6 4s^0$
1c Fe(III) = [Ar] $3d^5 4s^0$

2 Cu = 6 Pt = 4

3 $Cu[(NH_3)_4(H_2O)_2]^{2+}$

4a 90°
4b 109.5°

5a 6
5b 2+
5c neutral
5d the ligand forms four co-ordinate bonds with the central metal ion
5e as shown for the four N atoms in the square planar arrangement, Fig.10 page 257

6 [Ar] $3d^6 4s^2$

7 Blue is at the high-energy end of the spectrum, so blue is more likely to be absorbed.

8 H_2O because the solution appears pink, so the blue end of the spectrum is being absorbed.

9 If the ligand is changed in a complex, the 2:3 split of the d orbitals changes and the energy difference changes so the energy of the light absorbed changes and therefore the colour changes.

10a $[Cu(H_2O)_6]^{2+}$ = +2 $[Cu(CN)_4]^{3-}$ = +1
10b $[Cu(H_2O)_6]^{2+}$ = [Ar] $3d^9 4s^0$
$[Cu(CN)_4]^{3-}$ = [Ar] $3d^{10} 4s^0$
10c In $[Cu(H_2O)_6]^{2+}$ not all the d orbitals are occupied, so the photons in the visible region of the spectrum can be absorbed and colour is produced. $[Cu(CN)_4]^{3-}$ has all its d orbitals occupied, so absorption is not in the visible region so the substance is not coloured.

11 Absorption of colour is by photons interacting with the ions present in solution, so if the solution is diluted there is a lower concentration of ions, therefore fewer interactions as the light passes through it. This will result in a less intense (paler) appearance but the actual colour will be unchanged.

12 Between 610 and 620 nm.

13a $3Zn + Cr_2O_7^{2-} + 14H^+ \rightarrow$
$3Zn^{2+} + 2Cr^{3+} + 7H_2O$
13b $Zn + 2Cr^{3+} \rightarrow Zn^{2+} + 2Cr^{2+}$
13c $4Cr^{2+} + O_2 + 4H^+ \rightarrow 4Cr^{3+} + 2H_2O$

14 $Cr_2O_7^{2-}$: Cr 2 x +6 O 7 × 2–
overall charge –2
CrO_4^{2-}: Cr + 6 O 4 x 2–
overall charge –2

15 Moles of MnO_4^- used 21.5 x 0.018/1000 = 3.87×10^{-4} mol
The balanced half equations give this full equation:
$MnO_4^-(aq) + \cancel{5e} + 5Fe^{2+}(aq) + 8H^+(aq) \rightarrow Mn^{2+}(aq) + 5Fe^{3+}(aq) + \cancel{5e} + 4H_2O(l)$
1 mol of manganate(VII) reacts with 5 mol iron(II) ions so:
Moles of Fe(II) = $5 \times 3.87 \times 10^{-4}$
= 1.935×10^{-3} mol.
Mass of Fe^{2+} = $56 \times 1.935 \times 10^{-3}$
= 0.108 g
% mass of iron in the tablet
= 0.108 × 100/0.780
= 13.9% (to 3 s.f.)

16 Oxidation state:
$$Cr_2O_7^{2-} + 14H^+ + 6e^- \rightarrow 2Cr^{3+} + 7H_2O$$
$$+6 \qquad\qquad +3$$
Oxidation state:
$$6Fe^{2+} \rightarrow 6Fe^{3+} + 6e^-$$
$$+2 \qquad +3$$
There is a transfer of 6 electrons from the Fe^{2+} to the $Cr_2O_7^{2-}$.
Adding the two half reactions:
$$Cr_2O_7^{2-} + 14H^+ + 6Fe^{2+} + \cancel{6e^-} \rightarrow$$
$$2Cr^{3+} + 6Fe^{3+} + \cancel{6e^-} + 7H_2O$$
Cancelling electrons gives the equation.

17a Moles of $Cr_2O_7^{2-}$ used
$31.0 \times 0.0185/1000 = 5.74 \times 10^{-4}$ mol

17b The equations for the two half reactions are:
$$Cr_2O_7^{2-} + 14H^+ + 6e^- \rightarrow 2Cr^{3+} + 7H_2O$$
$$Fe^{2+} \rightarrow Fe^{3+} + e^-$$
Balancing the electron transfer gives $6Fe^{2+} \rightarrow 6Fe^{3+} + 6e^-$
And the overall equation is:
$$Cr_2O_7^{2-} + 14H^+ + 6Fe^{2+} \rightarrow 2Cr^{3+} + 6Fe^{3+} + 7H_2O$$
1 mol of dichromate(VI) reacts with 6 mol iron(II) ions.

17c Moles of Fe(II) $= 6 \times 5.74 \times 10^{-4}$
$= 3.45 \times 10^{-3}$ mol

17d Moles of Fe(II) in the whole solution
$= 3.45 \times 10^{-2}$ mol

17e Mass of $Fe^{2+} = 56 \times 3.45 \times 10^{-2}$
$= 1.93$ g

17f % mass of iron in the wire
$= 1.93 \times 100/2.225$
$= 86.7\%$ (to 3 s.f.)

18 Moles of MnO_4^- used
$45.0 \times 0.0200/1000 = 9.0 \times 10^{-4}$ mol
The balanced half equations give this full equation:
$$MnO_4^- (aq) + 5e^- + 8H^+(aq) \rightarrow Mn^{2+} (aq) + 4H_2O(l)$$
$$SO_3^{2-}(aq) + H_2O(l) \rightarrow SO_4^{2-} (aq) + 2e^- + 2H^+$$
$$2MnO_4^- (aq) + \cancel{10e^-} + 5SO_3^{2-}(aq) + 6H^+(aq)$$
$$\rightarrow 2Mn^{2+} (aq) + 5SO_4^{2-}(aq) + \cancel{10e^-} + 3H_2O(l)$$
1 mol of manganate(VII) reacts with 5/2 mol SO_3^{2-} ions so:
Moles of $SO_3^{2-} = 5/2 \times 9.0 \times 10^{-4}$
$= 2.25 \times 10^{-3}$ mol (in 25.0 cm^3)
Concentration of SO_3^{2-}
$= 1000 \times 2.25 \times 10^{-3}/25$

$= 9.00 \times 10^{-2}$ mol dm^{-3}

19 Ethanedioic acid is $(COOH)_2.2H_2O$ ($M_r = 126$) and in water it behaves as the ethanedioate ion $C_2O_4^{2-}(aq)$. The balanced half equations give this full equation:
$$MnO_4^- (aq) + 5e^- + 8H^+(aq) \rightarrow Mn^{2+} (aq) + 4H_2O (l)$$
$$C_2O_4^{2-}(aq) \rightarrow 2CO_2 (g) + 2e^-$$
$$2MnO_4^- (aq) + \cancel{10e^-} 5C_2O_4^{2-}(aq) + 16H^+(aq)$$
$$\rightarrow 2Mn^{2+}(aq) + 10CO_2(g) + \cancel{10e^-} + 8H_2O(l)$$
1 mol of $C_2O_4^{2-}$ (aq) reacts with 2/5 mol manganate(VII) so:
Moles of $(COOH)_2.2H_2O$ (to give $C_2O_4^{2-}(aq)$) = 2.145/126 = 1.702 $\times 10^{-2}$ mol (dissolved in 250 cm^3)
Moles of $(COOH)_2.2H_2O$ in 25.0 cm^3 = 1.702 x 10^{-3} mol
Moles of MnO_4^- used
$= 2 \times 1.702 \times 10^{-3}/5$
$= 6.81 \times 10^{-3}$ mol
Concentration of MnO_4^-
$= 1000 \times 6.81 \times 10^{-3}/35.0$
$= 0.0195$ mol dm^{-3}

20 A rough surfaced coating has more surface area and more active sites.

21a $MnO_4^- (aq) + 5e^- + 8H^+(aq) \rightarrow Mn^{2+} (aq) + 4H_2O (l)$

21b $C_2O_4^{2-}(aq) \rightarrow 2CO_2 (g) + 2e^-$

21c This is homogeneous catalysis because both reactants are in the same phase.

A1 The unused feedstock can be recycled to save costs and are cracked because the amounts in the feedstocks will not necessarily match the demand for the products.

A2 A build-up of carbon will reduce the surface area of the catalyst available for reaction. Burning off the carbon will regenerate the catalyst.

A3 To expose the maximum amount of catalyst to the reactants.

A4 The catalytic converter removes hydrocarbons, carbon monoxide, sulfur oxides and nitrogen oxides. They do not remove carbon dioxide, a greenhouse gas.

A5 The use of non-renewable resources, dust hazards, health risks to miners, spoliation of the landscape due to mining.

A6 A catalyst in a different phase to the reactants is considered heterogeneous.

A7 To provide a greater surface area to the reactants.

A8 The presence of double bonds increases the distance between adjacent molecules and this reduces van der Waals forces of attraction between the molecules, reducing the melting point.

A9 Animal fats contain a greater proportion of saturated fats which it is claimed contribute to heart disease.

A10 5+ in V_2O_5, 4+ in V_2O_4

A11 s^0d^0 in V_2O_5, s^0d^1 in V_2O_4

A12 The catalyst is regenerated in the same oxidation state at the end of the reaction so is the same chemically.

A13 SO_2 can form acid rain in the atmosphere, which damages living organisms and buildings.

Chapter 16

1a Lewis acid = H^+ , Lewis base = H_2O
1b Lewis acid = BF_3 , Lewis base = NH_3

2 d and f

3a octahedral $[V(H_2O)_6]^{2+}$
3b octahedral $[Cr(H_2O)_6]^{3+}$
3c octahedral $[Fe(H_2O)_6]^{2+}$

4 Transition metal ions have colour because there is an energy difference between groups of the d orbitals. Light is absorbed which corresponds to the visible region of the spectrum as electrons move between orbitals. The energy difference between the groups of orbitals is affected by the nuclear charge and the nature of the ligands. If the energy difference changes then the energy of the light absorbed will be different and the colour of the light not absorbed will not change.

5a $[Cr(H_2O)_6]^{3+} + H_2O \rightleftharpoons$
$[Cr(H_2O)_5(OH)]^{2+} + H_3O^+$
5b pH 3–6
5c The highly polarising 3+ ion attracts electrons from the metal–oxygen bond and therefore weakens the oxygen–hydrogen bond in the ligand. This releases some H^+ ions forming H_3O^+ ions, producing acidity and lowering the pH value below 7.

6a Adding H^+ ions drives the equilibrium to the left, from the brown $[Fe(H_2O)_5(OH)]^{2+}$ complex to the pale violet $[Fe(H_2O)_6]^{3+}$ complex.
6b Adding OH^- ions means they will react with the H^+ ions (forming H_2O) and removing H^+ ions from solution. The equilibrium will shift to replace these H^+ ions so the equilibrium will shift from left to right and produce a brown colour.
6c Adding excess OH^- ions will send the equilibrium as far right as is feasible and a brown precipitate of $Fe(H_2O)_3(OH)_3$ forms.

7a $[Ni(H_2O)_6]^{2+} + CO_3^{2-} \rightarrow$
$NiCO_3 + 6H_2O$
$NiCO_3$ is a green precipitate
7b $2[Fe(H_2O)_4(Cl)_2]^+ + H_2O + 3CO_3^{2-} \rightleftharpoons$
$2[Fe(H_2O)_3(OH)_3] + 3CO_2 + 4Cl^-$
A brown precipitate of $[Fe(H_2O)_3(OH)_3]$ and an effervescence of carbon dioxide gas would be seen.

8 One ammine ligand replaces one aqua ligand at each step.

9 The equilibrium should shift to the right, replacing all the aqua ligands with ammine ligands, but the two aqua ligands are not replaced because they are further away from the central metal ion.

10a The co-ordination number is 4 and the oxidation state is +2

10b $[Co(H_2O)_6]^{2+} + 4Cl^- \rightleftharpoons$
$[CoCl_4]^{2-} + 6H_2O$
The co-ordination number changes from 6 in the aqua complex to 4 in the chloro complex.

11a $[Co(H_2O)_6]^{2+} + EDTA^{4-} \rightleftharpoons$
$[CoEDTA]^{2-} + 6H_2O$
11b $[Fe(H_2O)_6]^{3+} + 3C_2O_4^{2-} \rightleftharpoons$
$[Fe(C_2O_4)_3]^{3-}$
11c $[Fe(C_2O_4)_3]^{3-}$

12 Energy is released in the process, so the products are at a lower energy level (more stable) than the reactants were.

A1 $[Cu(H_2O)_6]^{2+} \rightleftharpoons [Cu(H_2O)_5(OH)]^+ + H^+$; $[Cr(H_2O)_6]^{3+} \rightleftharpoons$
$[Cr(H_2O)_5(OH)]^{2+} + H^+$

A2 These are hydrolysis reactions because the ion reacts with water and releases hydrogen ions giving an acidic solution.

A3 The Cr^{3+} ion has a higher ionic charge than Cu^{2+} so the attraction for the lone pairs on the water molecule is greater and this weakens the O–H bond more.

A4 The equilibrium for Cr^{3+} lies further to the right, the solution is more acidic, and pH is lower for Cr^{3+} than Cu^{2+}.

A5 The hydrolysis of the aluminium aqua ion in soft water lowers the pH of the water. Copper is more soluble at low pH values, the equilibrium
$[Cu(H_2O)_6]^{2+} \rightleftharpoons$
$[Cu(H_2O)_5(OH)]^+ + H^+$
lies further to the left. In tap water, the copper comes from the copper pipes.

A6a Moles of EDTA = $4.80 \times 10^{-3} \times 0.05$
= 2.4×10^{-4} mol.
A6b Amount of Cu^{2+} in 100 cm^3 sample = 2.4×10^{-4} mol (because it forms a 1:1 complex with EDTA).
A6c Concentration of Cu^{2+}
= $2.4 \times 10^{-4}/100 \times 10^{-3}$
= 2.4×10^{-3} mol dm^{-3}
1 mol Cu^{2+} has a mass of 64g so
concentration = $64 \times 1000 \times 2.4 \times 10^{-3}$
= 153.6 mg dm^{-3}

A7 Water pressure was increasing so there might have been a non-planned release of contaminants. There would be unknown effects caused by pollution of the environment.

A8 The water is acidic and contains copper ions. In acid conditions the equilibrium favours $[Cu(H_2O)_6]^{2+}$ which is the blue ion, and does not favour the insoluble hydroxo complex which would make the water cloudy.

A9 The organisms studied are "bottom feeders" and slow growing, and they filter out and trap the heavy metal contaminants. The scientists can use these studies to monitor the amount of heavy metal in the water that the organisms grow in.

A10 From the living organisms they will determine the concentration of heavy metals in the water. They will have to determine the ratio of heavy metal in the organisms to the concentration of heavy metals in the water. They will use models to determine how the tidal and river flow and rainfall will affect future contamination levels in the water. Also it is known that certain organisms can "clean up" contaminated water so they can use modelling to make predictions as to how quickly this might happen.

A11 Student choice with a justification such as:
Industry because it is as a result of the extraction of copper for profit. Local taxes because it is a local problem and it is not possible now to allocate blame for the pollution National authorities because the costs of removing pollution is a national problem and should be shared among the total population.

A12 There may be hidden pollution problems and companies may be liable for compensation claims in the future.

Glossary

acid
A substance that donates protons in a reaction.

acid dissociation constant
See **dissociation constant**.

acidity constant
See **dissociation constant**.

acidity reaction
During the hydrolysis of a water molecule ligand, H^+ ions are lost and form H_3O^+ ions. The reaction is described as an acidity reaction.

activation energy
The minimum energy required by particles in collision to bring about a chemical reaction.

acylating agent
Groups which introduce acyl groups into molecules. They can be acyl chlorides or acid anhydrides.

acylation
A substitution reaction in which an acyl group (right) substitutes for another group.

addition–elimination reaction
A reaction which has an addition phase where a group such as an acyl group is added followed by an elimination phase where a chloride or ethanoate ion is removed.

addition polymer
Many molecules of a monomer form one large molecule of polymer. No other substances are formed. Ethene forms poly(ethene) by addition polymerisation.

addition reaction
A reaction in which two molecules react together to form one molecule.

adsorption
The process in which (usually) a gas bonds to the surface of a solid catalyst. The gas (or its products) is released after reaction occurs.

alcohols
Alcohols have the general formula R–OH, where R is an alkyl group. Their names end in -ol. Ethanol, C_2H_5OH, is an alcohol. A primary alcohol has the general formula RCH_2OH. A secondary alcohol has the general formula R^1R^2CHOH. A tertiary alcohol has the general formula $R^1R^2R^3COH$.

aldehyde
A carbonyl compound with the general formula RCHO. The names of aldehydes end in -al. Ethanal, CH_3CHO, is an aldehyde.

alkane
A hydrocarbon with the general formula C_nH_{2n+2}. The first three alkanes are CH_4, C_2H_6 and C_3H_8.

alkene
A hydrocarbon with the general formula C_nH_{2n}. Alkene molecules contain double bonds. The first two alkenes are C_2H_4 and C_3H_6.

amide
Molecules containing the group $CONH_2$.

amine
An organic compound containing the functional group $-NH_2$.

amino acids
A molecule containing both an acid group and an amine group.

amphoteric
Having both acidic and basic properties. For example, aluminium oxide is an amphoteric oxide. It forms salts both with acids and with alkalis.

analysis
The determination of the chemical composition, the structure and the chemical characteristics of a compound.

anionic detergent
Cleaning agents in which the long chain is an anion.

aramids
A family of nylons containing aromatic rings e.g. Kevlar ™. They have particular strength.

arene
An aromatic compound which is a hydrocarbon. All arenes contain one or more benzene rings. Benzene and naphthalene are arenes.

aromatic compound
Compound containing rings such as benzene where the molecule is delocalised.

asymmetric
A compound containing carbon atoms with four different groups attached also called chiral.

autocatalysis
The ability of one of the products of a reaction to catalyse the reaction producing it. In autocatalysis the initial reaction rate increases, as more catalyst is produced.

azo dye
A coloured compound formed from a reaction of benzene diazonium chloride with another group with significant delocalisation.

base
A substance that accepts protons in a reaction.

batch process
An industrial process which is started and stopped at intervals. In titanium production, the extraction apparatus is loaded, operated, cooled and emptied before the cycle is repeated. Each cycle produces a batch of titanium.

bidentate
A ligand that forms two coordinate bonds with the central cation in a metal complex is described as bidentate, e.g. the ethanedioate ion.

biodegradable
A substance which can be broken down into smaller units by the action of microorganisms.

bifunctional compound
A compound such as amino acids with two functional groups that can react with each other.

Born-Haber cycle
A diagram representing all the enthalpy changes involved in the formation of one mole of a solid ionic compound from its constituent elements in their standard states, under standard conditions. The sum of all the enthalpy changes in a Born-Haber cycle is zero (this follows from the first law of thermodynamics – conservation of energy). Any one enthalpy change in the cycle can be calculated, if the others are known, e.g. lattice enthalpies which are difficult to measure experimentally.

Brady's reagent
A solution used to identify carbonyl groups by forming an orange or red precipitate.

Bronsted–Lowry base
Defined as an acceptor of protons.

carbonyl compound
A compound containing the functional group C=O. Carbonyl compounds include aldehydes and ketones.

carboxylic acids
Organic acids having the general formula RCOOH. Their names end in -oic acid. Ethanoic acid has the formula CH_3COOH.

catalyst
A substance that usually speeds up the rate of a chemical reaction. It changes the nature of the intermediate compounds formed between reactants and products and so reduces the activation energy. A catalyst remains chemically unchanged at the end of the reaction.

cationic surfactant
A cation that will act at a surface reducing surface tension.

chain isomer
Chain isomers are types of structural isomers. They have the same molecular formula, but the carbon atoms are bonded in different orders.

charge/size ratio
The charge on an ion divided by its size.

chelating ligand
A group which will coordinate to a central ion at many points.

Chemical environment
neighbouring atoms surrounding a particular atom producing differing NMR absorptions.

chemical shift
The position, relative to the proton absorption of tetramethylsilane, where a nucleus absorbs in an NMR spectrum.

chiral
A molecule where a central carbon atom (the chiral atom) is attached to four different groups.

chlorofluorocarbons or **CFCs**
Hydrocarbons in which some or all the hydrogen atoms have been replaced by chlorine and fluorine atoms.

chlorophyll
Green pigment in leaves essential in photosynthesis.

chromophore
A functional group which causes an organic molecule to be coloured. Examples are the nitro ($-NO_2$) and azo (C–N=N–C) groups.

colorimeter
An instrument which measures the absorption of a range of radiation.

complementary colour
A colour that a sample will absorb the most.

complex ion
An ion that contains a central atom to which other atoms or ions are bonded. In a transition metal complex, the transition metal is the central atom. The atoms or ions bonded to the central atom are called ligands. An example is the tetra-amminecopper(II) ion, $Cu(NH_3)_4^{2+}$.

condensation polymer
A polymer formed in a reaction where a simple molecule such as water or ammonia is eliminated.

condensation reaction
A reaction in which two or more organic molecules (e.g. an alcohol and an acid) are linked to form a larger organic molecule (e.g. an ester) by elimination of a small molecule such as water, hydrogen chloride or methanol. Overall, it is an addition reaction followed by an elimination reaction.

conductor
A substance that will allow heat or electricity to pass through it easily.

conjugate acid
A molecule in a pair of compounds that releases a proton to the other molecule.

$HX + H_2O \ß> H_3O^+ + X^-$

Acid base   acid   base

$HCl + NH_3 \ß> NH_4^+ + Cl^-$

Acid base   conjugate acid   conjugate base

Donates protons   accepts proton

conjugate base
A molecule in a pair of compounds that accepts a proton from the other molecule.

$HX + H_2O \ß> H_3O^+ + X^-$

Acid base   acid   base

$HCl + NH_3 \ß> NH_4^+ +$ Cl^-

Acid base   conjugate acid   conjugate base

Donates protons   accepts proton

conjugation
A system of alternating single and double bonds. The electrons in the π bonds delocalise to spread throughout the system.

Contact process
The process used to make sulfuric acid from sulfur, oxygen and water.

continuous process
An industrial process in which a material is produced continuously. An example is iron, with the iron ore fed continuously into the apparatus and cast iron continuously removed.

co-ordinate bond
A covalent bond in which the shared electron pair originates from the same atom. It can be written as X→Y, showing that the shared electron pair originated from X.

co-ordination number
The number of ligands to which a central metal atom is bonded in a complex ion. For example, in the tetra-amminecopper(II) ion, $Cu(NH_3)_4^{2+}$, the coordination number of copper is 4.

coupled
Two atoms in a molecule are coupled when the magnetic field experienced by one is altered by the effect of the magnetic field created by the other.

coupling effect
The interaction between the nuclear spins of neighbouring atoms in a molecule.

coupling reaction
A reaction between benzene diazonium chloride and another group containing delocalisation.

covalent bond
A bond in which two atoms share one or more pairs of electrons. A hydrogen molecule, H–H, has a single covalent bond. In a double covalent bond there are two shared pairs of electrons, such as in the oxygen molecule, O=O.

cycloalkane
An alkane with a cyclic structure.

delocalisation energy
The extra stability in a compound produced by delocalisation of the electrons.

delocalised electrons
Electrons that are not located at one particular atom, but are free to move between all atoms in the structure. Examples of materials with delocalised electrons are metals, graphite and benzene.

deprotonation
Removing protons from an acid.

desorption
The process in which a substance (usually a gas) is released from the surface of a solid catalyst following reaction.

dextrorotatory
Rotates the plane of plane-polarised light to the right.

diazotisation
Reaction between an aromatic amine and nitrous acid to produce benzene diazonium chloride.

dipeptide
A compound formed when two amino acids react together eliminating a molecule of water.

dissociation constant, K_a
A measure of the degree to which an acid dissociates into ions. the larger the value of K_a the more the acid dissociates into ions, and the stronger it is. For the reaction: $HA + H_2O \rightleftharpoons H_3O^+ + A^-$

$$K_a = \frac{[H^3O^+][A^-]}{[HA][H_2O]}$$

dobson unit
1 Dobson Unit (DU) is defined to be 0.01 mm thickness of ozone from a column of air covering a 10 x 5 deg area of the earth's surface compressed down to stp.

doublet
A group of two signals in the ratio of 1:1 produced when a set of equivalent protons with only one neighbouring proton in the molecule undergoes NMR resonance.

dynamic equilibrium
A stage in a reaction where the forward reaction equals the backward reaction so that there is no net change in the concentration of the substances involved in the reaction.

electrochemical cell
The minimum requirement for an electrochemical cell consists of two electrodes immersed in an electrolyte. In practice the electrodes are immersed in separate electrolytes, in separate electrode compartments, and a salt bridge connects the two compartments.

electrochemical series
A list of half-reactions and their electrode potentials. The half-reactions are written as reductions. The series can contain half-reactions involving metals and non-metals.

electrode potential
See **standard electrode potential**

electron affinity
A measure of the attraction of an atom for an electron or electrons. It is measured as the amount of energy in kJ mol^{-1} required to remove an electron from a gaseous negative ion.

electronegativity
The tendency of an atom to gain or retain electrons. Elements whose atoms gain electrons easily are the most electronegative. Fluorine is the most electronegative element. Elements whose atoms lose outer electrons easily are described as being electropositive. Caesium is the most electropositive element.

electrophile
An electron-seeking group. Electrophiles are positively charged, e.g. the nitryl group NO_2^+.

electrophilic substitution
A reaction in which an electrophile is attracted to an area of high electron density. The electrophile replaces an atom or group in a substitution reaction.

elimination reaction
A reaction in which the products include a small molecule, often water. The small product molecule is said to be eliminated from the reacting molecule(s).

e.m.f. (electromotive force)
The emf for a cell is:

$E^{\ominus}_{cell} \quad E^{\ominus}_{RHS} \quad E^{\ominus}_{LHS}$

For an electrochemical cell or battery the emf is the output voltage. Stictly, emf is the cell potential measure when zero-current flows.

enantiomers
Isomers formed in a molecule with a chiral carbon atom. They rotate plane polarised light.

end-point
The point in a titration where exact reacting amounts of each reactant is present.

endothermic reaction
A chemical reaction in which energy is absorbed.

enthalpy change
An amount of energy that is transferred (absorbed or released) during a chemical reaction at a constant pressure.

enthalpy of hydration ($\Delta H^{\ominus}_{hyd}$)

The enthalpy change for the process:

$M^+(g) \xrightarrow{water} M^+(aq)$ (see infinite dilution)

It is only possible to measure the enthalpy change of hydration for pairs of co-ions, i.e. a cation and an anion.

enthalpy of solution ($\Delta H^{\ominus}_{sol}$)

The enthalpy change when one mole of an ionic solid is completely dissolved. The solution is usually water and the extent of dilution should be enough to separate the ions to the point where they do not interact with each other (the point of 'infinite dilution').

entropy (S)

Entropy is a measure of the amount of disorder in a system. Gases have higher entropy than solids because the particles in a gas are more randomly arranged (disordered) than in a solid. All chemical reactions and physical processes involve an overall increase in the entropy *for the universe* (system and surroundings). For an individual system there may be a *decrease* in entropy: e.g. the reaction $2Mg(s) + O_2(g) \rightleftharpoons 2MgO(s)$ involves a decrease in entropy. However, the overall entropy for a system and its surroundings will increase. The oxidation of magnesium by oxygen gas produces heat which increases the entropy of the surroundings, and for the overall universe.

equilibrium constant

A measure of the ratio of the amount of products formed from the readouts. The larger K_c the greater the amount of product formed. $K_c = [\text{products}]/[\text{reactants}]$

equilibrium position

The dynamic stage in a chemical reaction where the rate of the forward reaction equals the rate of the backward reaction, so that there is no net change in the concentrations of the substances involved in the reaction.

equilibrium

The state reached in a reversible reaction at which the rates of the two opposing reactions are equal, when the system has no further tendency to change. This is a dynamic equilibrium, as reactants and products are both still being formed, but at equal rates.

equivalence point

The exact neutralisation point of an acid–base titration.

ester

$$\overset{O}{\underset{\|}{}}$$

$-O-C-$ A compound containing the ester linkage connecting small molecules or monomers.

esterification

Formation of an ester from an acid and an alcohol.

exothermic reaction

A chemical reaction in which energy is released.

E z isomers

Geometrical isomers. The z isomer has the two attached groups on the same side of the double bond. The e isomers has the attached groups on opposite sides of the double bond.

E/Z isomers

Isomers resulting from different spatial arrangements of functional groups relative to a double bond. They are called *cis* when groups are on the same side of the double bond, and *trans* when groups are on different sides.

fatty acid

Consists of a carbon chain with a carboxylic acid group at one end. These are part of fat and oil molecules.

Fehling's solution

Reagent producing brick-red coppers (1) oxide in the presence of an aldehyde group.

first order reaction

A reaction whose rate is proportional to the concentration of a reactant. Rate $= k[A]^x$ where $x = 1$.

fragmentation

A breaking up of a molecule into identifiable parts in mass spectrometry.

free radical

A species that has an odd number of electrons, it tends to be extremely reactive.

frequency (of radiation)

Number of peaks passing a particular point in one second.

fuel cell

Cell producing electricity by using fuel reacting with an oxidant.

functional group

A reactive atom or group of atoms in an organic molecule that largely determines the properties of the molecule.

functional group isomer

Compounds with the same chemical formula but different functional groups

geostationary satellite

A satellite is geostationary if it moves in a geosynchronoous orbit, i.e. it moves in such a way that it remains in a fixed position relative to the earth. Most communications satellites are geostationary.

Gibbs free energy change ΔG

A measure of the capability of a reaction to do useful work. $\Delta G^{\ominus}$ is related to the standard enthalpy change and standard entropy change for a reaction by the equation:

$\Delta G^{\ominus} \rightleftharpoons \Delta H^{\ominus} - T\Delta S^{\ominus}$

$\Delta G^{\ominus}$ must be negative for the reaction to be spontaneous.

group

The elements in a column (vertical row) of the Periodic Table, e.g. Group 2 elements are the elements in the second column of the Periodic Table, from beryllium to radium.

Haber process

Manufacturing process for the production of ammonia from nitrogen and hydrogen.

haemoglobin

An oxygen-carrying protein found in red blood cells. Haemoglobin transports oxygen to body cells, and exchanges the gas for carbon dioxide produced by cell respiration.

half-equation

An equation representing the oxidation or reduction reaction in a chemical reaction.

haloalkane or halogenoalkane
An alkane molecule in which one or more of the hydrogen atoms are replaced by a halogen atom.

haloalkanes
A homologous series of compounds consisting of alkanes in which one or more hydrogen atoms has been replaced by halogen atoms.

halogenoalkanes
A homologous series of compounds consisting of alkanes in which one or more hydrogen atoms has been replaced by halogen atoms.

Hess's law
If a chemical change can occur by more than one route, then the overall enthalpy change for each route must be the same, provided that the starting and finishing conditions are the same.

heterogeneous catalysis
A reaction for which the catalyst and the reactants are in different states, e.g. a solid iron catalyst in the Haber process reaction: $3H_2(g) + N_2(g) \rightarrow 2NH_3(g)$

heterogeneous equilibrium
An equilibrium in which the reactants are in different states, e.g. the equilibrium mixture obtained by heating ammonium chloride in a sealed tube: $NH_4Cl(s) \rightarrow NH_3(g) + HCl(g)$

high-resolution mass spectrometry
A very accurate mass spectrometry which measures the mass of the molecular ion to (e.g.) seven significant figures.

homogeneous catalysis
A reaction for which the catalyst and the reactants are in the same state, e.g. the oxidation of sulfuric(IV) acid is catalysed by transition metal ions in solution.

homogeneous equilibrium
An equilibrium in which all the reactants are in the same state, e.g. the equilibrium mixture obtained by heating hydrogen and iodine in a sealed tube: $H_2(g) + I_2(g) = 2HI(g)$

hydration
The addition of water. In organic chemistry examples include the conversion of alkenes into alcohols, and in inorganic chemistry the formation of aqua ions by the addition of water ligands to metal ions, e.g. hydration of $CuSO_4$ to form $CuSO_4.nH_2O$.

hydration number
The number of water molecules surrounding a central ion at a particular dilution.

hydrolysis
The splitting up of a compound by reaction with water, e.g. ester hydrolysis: $CH_3COOCH_3 + H_2O = CH_3COOH + CH_3OH$

infinite dilution
The point at which a substance is dissolved in a sufficiently large amount of solvent such that there are no interactions between the solute particles.

infrared spectroscopy
Analysis of the structure of molecules using radiation in the infra red region. When bonds stretch and bend the infra red radiation is absorbed and this leads to the spectrum.

isomers
Compounds that have the same molecular formula but different structural formulae.

integrated spectrum
A series of peaks which represent the areas under NMR peaks. These are equivalent to the number of protons in various groups.

intermediate
A species that forms and reacts during a reaction sequence so that it is not present in the reactants or products.

ionic bond
An attraction between a positively charged ion and a negatively charged ion.

ionic equation
An equation showing only ions that change in a reaction.

ionic product of water
The expression for the equilibrium constant for water forming its ions. $K_w = [H+][OH-]$

isoelectric pH
The pH at which an amino acid exists as a zwitterion.

ketone
A carbonyl compound with the general formula: $RR^1C=O$. Propanone, CH_3COCH_3, is a ketone.

kinetics of reaction or rate of reaction
The study of factors that affect the way in which the concentrations of the reactants and products change with time during a chemical reaction.

laevorotatory
Rotates the plane of plane-polarised light to the left.

Le Chatelier's principle
When an equilibrium reaction mixture undergoes a change in conditions, the composition of the mixture adjusts to counteract the change. For example, if the concentration of one of the reactants in an equilibrium mixture is suddenly increased, the equilibrium will adjust so as to reduce the increase in concentration.

Lewis acid
An electron pair acceptor.

Lewis base
An electron pair donor.

ligand substitution reaction
Replacing ligand(s) by different ligand(s).

magnetic field
The region surrounding a magnetic north or south pole in which attractive and repulsive forces are felt.

magnetic moment
A property shown by nuclei with odd atomic numbers or mass numbers which is related to the strength of the interaction with a magnetic field.

mass spectrometer
A scientific instrument used to produce a mass spectrum.

mass spectrometry
A technique used to find the relative atomic mass of an element or the relative molecular mass of a molecule. It can identify the types and amounts of any isotopes present in an element or compound.

mass spectrum

A chart from a mass spectrometer showing the relative abundance of different ionised atoms and molecules.

Maxwell–Boltzmann distribution

For a sample of gas at a particular temperature, it represents the number of gas molecules at each energy over the whole range of energies present, and can be represented by a curved graph.

Mobile phase

The liquid in chromatography that moves through the solid medium and carries the sample.

mole

An amount of substance that contains 6.022×10^{23} particles. The particles may be atoms, ions, molecules or electrons.

molecular formula

A formula showing the number and types of atoms present in a molecule, e.g. the molecular formula for calcium carbonate is $CaCO_3$.

molecular ion

A molecule that has lost one or more electrons.

molecular ion peak

The peak on a mass spectrum which represents the molecular mass of the sample. It is the heaviest ion produced in the mass spectrometer.

monochromatic radiation

Radiation of one particular frequency, wavelength.

monomer

A molecule that can react with many other similar molecules to build up a large molecule, a polymer, e.g. the monomer ethene gives rise to the polymer poly(ethene).

multidentate

A ligand that forms more than one coordinate bond with a central cation is described as multidentate or polydentate

n + 1 rule

The NMR absorption of a proton which has n equivalent neighbouring protons will be split into n + 1 peaks.

neutralisation reaction

A reaction between an acid and a base or alkali to form a neutral solution.

nitration

Substitution of a nitro group into a benzene ring.

nitrile

Molecules containing the nitrile ($-C \equiv N$) functional group.

NMR spectroscopy

Analysis of organic molecules to show the position and number of protons, using the interaction of certain atoms (often protons) in the presence of a magnetic field.

NMR spectrum

The peaks produced by NMR spectroscopy.

non-biodegradable

A polymer which will last for many years and will not degrade in land fill sites.

nuclear magnetic resonance

See **NMR spectroscopy.**

nuclear spin

A property of nuclei with odd atomic numbers or mass numbers, behaving as if they were bar magnets.

nucleophile

An atom or group of atoms that is attracted to a positive charge, e.g. NH_3, $-OH$ and H_2O.

nucleophilic addition reaction

A reaction in which a nucleophile is attracted to a positively charged molecule or group and reacts with it, e.g. the reaction between the nucleophilic bromide ion and a carbocation: $Br^- + CH_3=CH_2+ \rightarrow CH_2BrCH_2Br$

nucleophilic substitution reaction

A chemical reaction in which one nucleophile replaces another in a molecule. For example, in the reaction of bromoethane with alkali, the nucleophilic hydroxide ion replaces the bromide ion in the bromoethane molecule: $C_2H_5Br + OH^- \rightarrow C_2H_5OH + Br^-$

nylon

A thermoplastic condensation polymer containing repeating units of combined amino acids. It is a polyamide.

nylon- 6,6

Nylon 6,6 is made from the condensation of hexamethylene diamine and adipic acid, which gives the molecule 6 carbon atoms in each unit.

optical activity

Physical properties of a chiral or asymmetric molecules, they rotate the direction of plane polarised light.

optical isomers

Compounds whose molecules, though alike in every other way, are mirror images of each other.

order of reaction

The proportionality of the rate to the concentration of reactants. Rate = k[A]x where x = the order.

oxidant

Another term for oxidising agent.

oxidation

A process in which a species loses one or more electrons; also defined as an increase in oxidation state of an element. Oxidation and reduction occur together in a redox reaction.

oxidation state

The charge that an element would have if it were totally ionically bonded. For an ion, it is the charge on the ion. In a covalent compound, it is the theoretical number assigned to each atom in a molecule if it were an ionic compound. For example, in water the oxidation state of hydrogen is +1 and that of oxygen is −2, even though water is covalently bonded. Oxidation state can change in a redox reaction. The oxidation state of elements is zero.

ozone hole

The thinning of the stratospheric ozone layer over Antarctica that develops during the Antarctic spring.

parent ion

This is the ion formed in mass spectrometry by removal of one electron. It is the largest ion produced because there is no fragmentation.

peptide bond

The C-N bond within a peptide link.

peptide link
The CONH group that links two amino acids.

period
The elements in a horizontal row in the Periodic Table, e.g. Period 2 elements are the elements in the second horizontal row of the Periodic Table, from lithium to neon.

Periodic table
A classification of the elements in order of their atomic numbers. Elements with similar properties appear in columns, known as groups. Metals lie on the left of the table and non-metals on the right, with a gradual change of properties across the rows, or periods.

periodicity
The repeating pattern of trend in properties of the elements across a period.

pH
A measure of the acidity or alkalinity of a solution. pH = −log10[H+].

pH curve
A graph which shows the change in pH values when an acid is mixed with the base.

plane-polarised
When light is passed through a polariser the light vibrates in one particular plane.

plastics
Polymers of high molecular mass, they can be thermoplastic or thermosetting.

plasticiser
A substance added to a plastic in order to increase its flexibility.

polarimeter
An instrument which measures the amount of rotation of plane polarised light.

polarisation
Distortion of charge clouds in ions. This small, relatively highly charged, positive ion, distorts the charge cloud on the negative ion, producing some covalent character in the bond.

polariser
A strip of material that will allow light to pass through vibrating in one plane only.

polyamide
a polymer formed from the condensation of many amino acids.

polyester
A polymer formed from the condensation of alcohol groups with acid groups.

polymer
A large molecule formed when many smaller monomer molecules react together, e.g. plastics like polythene, and synthetic fibres like nylon and terylene.

polypeptide
A polymer containing many peptide links as in a polyamide.

porphyrin
A ring-shaped molecule made from carbon, hydrogen and nitrogen atoms with a central space in which a metal ion (e.g. Fe in haem; Mg in chlorophyll) can be housed to form a complex ion. Haemoglobin and chlorophyll have porphyrin structures.

positional isomer
A molecule with the same functional groups in a different position on the longest chain.

potential difference
The difference between two electrode potentials in a cell.

primary structure
A continuous chain of repeated peptide links.

quanta
single packets of energy in light photons are quanta.

quartet
A group of four signals in the ratio 1:3:3:1 produced when a set of equivalent protons with three equivalent neighbouring protons in the molecule undergoes NMR resonance.

quaternary ammonium ion
A compound derived from the ammonium ion (NH_4^+) by substituting all four of the hydrogen atoms by hydrocarbon groups.

racemate
A 50:50 mixture of optical isomers, where the rotation effects on plane polarised light cancel each other out.

rate constant
The constant k in the rate equation.

rate equation
Rate = k[A]^x where x = the order.

rate-determining step
The slowest step in any sequence of intermediate stages. This will determine the rate of reaction.

rate of reaction
The change over time of the concentration of a reactant or a product of a reaction. Its units are mol dm^{-3} s^{-1}.

redox reaction
A reaction in which oxidation and reduction both occur. One species is oxidised, while another is reduced. The two processes can be shown as half-equations.

reduction
A process in which a species gains one or more electrons. It can also be defined as a decrease in oxidation state for an element. Reduction and oxidation occur together in a redox reaction.

relative atomic mass, symbol A_r
The mass of one atom of an element compared with one-twelfth of the mass of one atom of carbon-12.

relative molecular mass, symbol M_r
The mass of one molecule of an element or compound compared with one-twelfth of the mass of one atom of carbon-12.

repeat unit
The part of the monomer molecule that is repeated in the polymer.

resonance
The natural vibrational frequency of a bond when subjected to IR radiation or the protons when subjected to a radio frequency radiation.

retention time
The time taken to pass through a GLC column, depends upon the nature of and attraction between the solute and the stationary and mobile phases and the volatility of the solute.

reversible reaction
A chemical reaction which can take place in both directions and so does not go to completion. A mixture of reactants and products is obtained when the reaction reaches equilibrium. The composition of the equilibrium mixture is the same whether the reaction starts from the substances on the left or the right of the reaction equation.

salt bridge
An electrolyte solution (e.g. saturated potassium chloride or potassium nitrate in agar jelly) which allows movement of ions between two half-reactions of an electrochemical cell which are in separate electrode compartments. The salt bridge completes the electrical circuit within the cell.

saponification
The process of forming a soap by the hydrolysis of a fat or oil, usually with sodium or potassium hydroxide.

secondary structure
A helical shape produced when a polyamide chain forms hydrogen bonds between the C=O and N-H.

second-order reaction
A reaction whose rate is quadrupled when the concentration of a reactant is doubled. Rate = k[A]^x where x = 2

self-protonating
A species that can act as an acid or a base.

sequester
Forming a stable complex that will release the central ion slowly to a growing medium.

singlet
A signal produced when a set of equivalent protons with no neighbouring protons in the molecule undergoes NMR resonance.

soaps
A cleaning agent which is the salt of a long chain carboxylic (fatty) acid.

spectator ions
Ions present in a solution that do not take part in the reaction.

spectrophotometer
An instrument used to carry out spectroscopy –the analysis of a compound by detecting its response to electromagnetic radiation.

standard amount
An amount agreed by chemists (the mole) so that comparisons can be made between different measurements.

standard cell (electrode) potential
The potential of an electrode measured relative to the Standard Hydrogen electrode (SHE), under standard conditions.

standard conditions
A temperature of 298 K, or 25 °C, and a pressure of 1 atmosphere (101 kPa).

standard enthalpy change of a reaction ($\Delta H_{298}^{\ominus}$)
The amount of energy that is released (or taken in) by a reaction when its reactants react under standard conditions

standard enthalpy of formation, $H_{f,298}^{\ominus}$
The energy absorbed when one mole of a substance is formed from its elements in their standard states.

standard hydrogen electrode (SHE)
The standard reference electrode (or half-reaction) for measuring the electrode potentials of cells. The SHE is arbitrarily assigned an electrode potential of 0 V when operating under standard conditions. The cell consists of hydrogen gas at 1 bar bubbling over an electrode of finely divided platinum, dipped into a solution of 1 mol dm^{-3} hydrochloric acid.

standard state
The most stable physical state (solid, liquid or gas) of a substance at 1 atmosphere pressure and at a stated temperature, usually 298 K.

stationary phase
The solid used in GLC it is usually diatomaceous earth or keiselghur (the ground remains of very small plant skeletons).

stereoisomers
Isomers that have the same molecular formula and structural formula but different arrangements of their atoms in space. Optical and E-Z geometrical isomers are stereoisomers.

stoichiometric equation
A balanced equation, showing the amounts that combine with each other

structural formula
A formula that shows how the atoms are bonded together in a compound. It can either be written out in full, with each bond shown, or as groups of atoms in sequence.

structural isomers
Isomers having the same molecular formula, but different structural formulae. Butane and 2-methylpropane are structural isomers of C_4H_{10}.

substitution reaction
A reaction in which an atom or group forming part of a molecule is replaced by a different group or atom.

substrate (and catalytic converters)
A support medium designed to hold expensive, finely divided catalyst material, and to maximise the surface area of catalyst.

substrate (and enzymes)
The molecule which reacts with the enzyme in enzyme-catalysed reactions. The space of the substrate is very important because it must match the shape of the enzyme for reaction to occur.

synthesis
The joining of reactants together to form a compound.

tertiary structure
Produced by a helical secondary structure of a peptide-folds into a 3-dimensional structure.

tetradentate ligand
A ligand that forms four coordinate bonds with a central metal ion in a complex.

tetramethylsilane (TMS)
A silicon atom surrounded by four methyl groups used as a standard in NMR.

third-order reaction
A reaction whose rate is increased by a factor of 9 when the concentration of a reactant is trebled. Rate = k[A]x where x = 3.

Tollen's reagent
A reagent use to identify aldehydes by the formation of a silver mirror. It contains the diamminesilver(I) ion.

transition
The movement of an electron between energy levels.

transition metals
Elements whose atoms or ions have incomplete electron sub-shells within the outermost shell. First-row transition metals (scandium to copper) have an incomplete 3d sub-shell.

tri-esters
A compound formed when a carboxylic acid reacts with a trihydric alcohol e.g. glycerol.

triplet
A group of three signals in the ratio 1:2:1 produced when a set of equivalent protons with two equivalent neighbouring protons in the molecule undergoes NMR resonance.

ultraviolet
electromagnetic radiation which is higher energy than the violet part of the visible spectrum.

unidentate ligand
A ligand that forms one coordinate bond with the central cation in a metal complex is described as unidentate (or monodentate), e.g. water.

variable oxidation state
A characteristic of transition elements where they exhibit a variety of oxidation states by loss of electrons.

washcoat
A mixture of aluminium oxide and cerium oxides in the cells of a catalytic converter which support the precious metal catalysts.

zero-order reaction
A reaction whose rate does not change when the concentration of a reactant is changed. Rate = k[A]x where x = 0.

zwitterion
An amino acid existing as both an anion and a cation. This happens at a particular pH.

Index